Street by Street

MA...R

C000145810

3rd edition October 2007

© Automobile Association
Developments Limited 2007

Original edition printed
May 2001

Enabled by Ordnance Survey® This product includes map
data licensed from Ordnance
Survey® with the permission of
the Controller of Her Majesty's
Stationery Office.
© Crown copyright 2007.
All rights reserved.
Licence number: 100021153.

The copyright in all PAF is
owned by Royal Mail Group plc.

Published by AA Publishing
(a trading name of
Automobile Association
Developments Limited,
whose registered office is
Fanum House, Basing View,
Basingstoke RG21 4EA.
Registered number 1878835).

Produced by the Mapping Services Department of The Automobile Association. (A03490)

A CIP Catalogue record for this book is available from the British Library.

Printed by Oriental Press in Dubai

Ref: MN042y

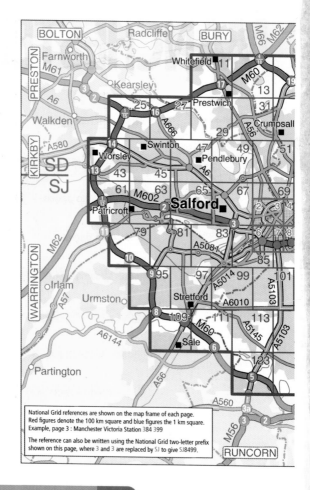

National Grid references are shown on the map frame of each page.
Red figures denote the 100 km square and blue figures the 1 km square.
Example, page 3 : Manchester Victoria Station 384 399

The reference can also be written using the National Grid two-letter prefix
shown on this page, where 3 and 3 are replaced by SJ to give SJ8499.

Enlarged scale pages 1:10,000   6.3 inches to 1 mile

0	miles	1/4
0	1/4 kilometres	1/2

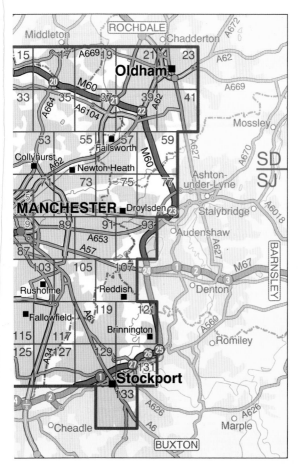

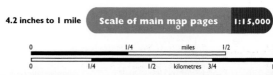

iv

Junction 9	Motorway & junction
Services	Motorway service area
	Primary road single/dual carriageway
Services	Primary road service area
	A road single/dual carriageway
	B road single/dual carriageway
	Other road single/dual
	Minor/private road, access may be restricted
← ←	One-way street
	Pedestrian area
	Track or footpath
	Road under construction
	Road tunnel
P	Parking
P+	Park & Ride
	Bus/coach station
	Railway & main railway station
	Railway & minor railway station
⊖	Underground station
⊖	Light railway & station
	Preserved private railway
LC	Level crossing
●—●—●	Tramway
– – – – –	Ferry route
....	Airport runway
– · – · –	County, administrative boundary
93	Page continuation 1:20,000
7	Page continuation to enlarged scale 1:10,000
	River/canal, lake, pier
	Aqueduct, lock, weir
	Beach
	Woodland
	Park
	Cemetery
	Built-up area

	Industrial/business building	⛪	Abbey, cathedral or priory
	Leisure building	♜	Castle
	Retail building		Historic house or building
	Other building	Wakehurst Place (NT)	National Trust property
⊓⊔⊓⊔	City wall	Ⓜ	Museum or art gallery
A&E	Hospital with 24-hour A&E department		Roman antiquity
PO	Post Office		Ancient site, battlefield or monument
📖	Public library		Industrial interest
𝒊	Tourist Information Centre	✽	Garden
🅿🅿	Petrol station, 24 hour Major suppliers only	◉	Garden Garden Centre Association Member
†	Church/chapel	❀	Garden Wyevale Garden Centre
🚺🚹	Public toilets	♣	Arboretum
♿	Toilet with disabled facilities		Farm or animal centre
PH	Public house AA recommended		Zoological or wildlife collection
🍴	Restaurant AA inspected		Bird collection
Madeira Hotel	Hotel AA inspected		Nature reserve
🎭	Theatre or performing arts centre		Aquarium
🎥	Cinema	V	Visitor or heritage centre
⚑	Golf course	Y	Country park
▲	Camping AA inspected	⌒	Cave
🚐	Caravan site AA inspected	🏚	Windmill
▲🚐	Camping & caravan site AA inspected	🛢	Distillery, brewery or vineyard
🎡	Theme park		

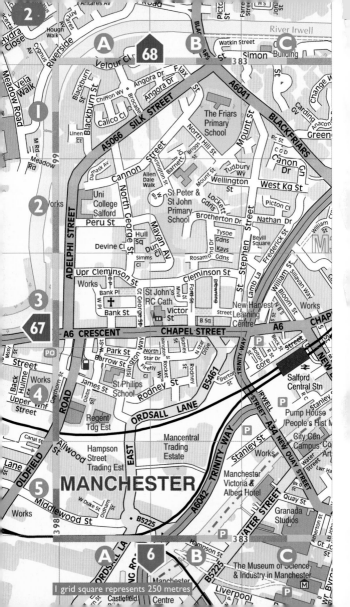

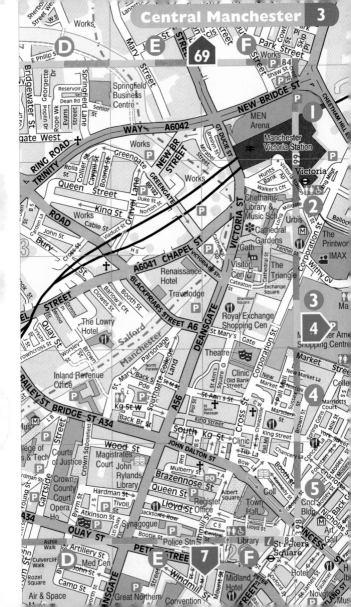

69

Sherbo Street We
Street W

Works

E Phillip St

Bridgewater St

Georgette
Poplin dr
Rope Wk
Evans St
Senior

Springfield Lane
Dean Rd

Reservoir
St

Springfield
Business
Centre

Park Street

Works

Shaw St

NEW BRIDGE ST

CHEETHAM HILL R

MEN
Arena

Manchester
Victoria Station

Victoria

Balloo

gate West

RING ROAD

WAY A6042

NEW BR STREET

GT DUCIE ST

Breezy St

Mirabel

Hunts
Bank

Walker's Crt

Victoria Station

Cheethams
Library &
Music Sch

Urbis

Millgate

Corporation St

The
Printwor

IMAX

TRINITY

Rolla
St

Collier St

Cawshill St

Boond St

Greengate

GREENGATE

Duke St

Norton St

BP182

Queen Street

King St

Cable St

Viaduct St

Works

Cathedral

St

VICTORIA ST

Gath
Cathedral
Gardens

M

Fennel St

Withy Gv

ROAD

Bury

Cross St

John St

St

CHAPEL ST A6041

BLACKFRIARS STREET A6

VICTORIA B'DGE ST

Visitor
Cen

Cateaton St

Cathedral St

The
Triangle

Renaissance
Hotel

Travelodge

Exchange
Square

Shambles
Square

Royal Exchange
Shopping Cen

St Mary's Gate

Corporation St

3

Ma

STREET

Wood

Dronma

Barrows Crt

Clowes St

Booth St

The Lowry
Hotel

Salford

Quay St

Crowncross St

Worsley

Brown

Manchester

Parsonage

Southgate College
Land

North Parade

St Mary's

Back St

St Ann's
Square

Theatre

Clinic
Old Bank
Street

New
Market

New Market La

Norfolk

4

Manchester Arn
Shopping Centre

Market
Street

Colle

Inland Revenue
Office

BAILEY ST

BRIDGE ST A34

M

Mus

College of
s & Tech

ardman st

Cartside

Crown
County
Court

Opera
Ho

A434

Courts
of Justice

Magistrates
Court

John
Rylands
Library

Wood St

Crown Sq

Coldfield

Hardman St

Brym St

Atkinson St

Tivoli

P

QUAY ST

Ashill
Walk

Culvercliff
Walk

Rozel
Square

Camp St

John St

DEANSGATE

A56

Back Br St

St G

Kg St

Pde

St M St

Pol St

South Kg St

JOHN DALTON ST

Mulberry St

Brazennose St

Queen St

Lloyd St

Jackson's Row

Synagogue

Bootle St

Police Stn

PETER STREE

Med Cen

D

CROSS ST

St Ann's
Passage

King Street

Clinic

New
Market

Tib La

Bow

PO

Albert
Square

Register
Office

Register

Town
Hall

Lloyd St

Central

Library

PETER

E

7

12

St Peters
Square

Marriotts
Court

Spring Gdns

York Street

Chancery La

Concel

York Street

Mosley St

Ch Foulston

Nicholas S

PRINCESS

Art
Gall

Pall Mall

Marsden

King Street

Booth St

Kennedy St

Chancery La

Coll

Cncl
Bldg

Back

4

5

St Peters
Square

F

Hotel

Oxford St

Novotel M

Mus

St James St

Faulkner

Windmill St

Midland
Hotel

Great Northern
Convention

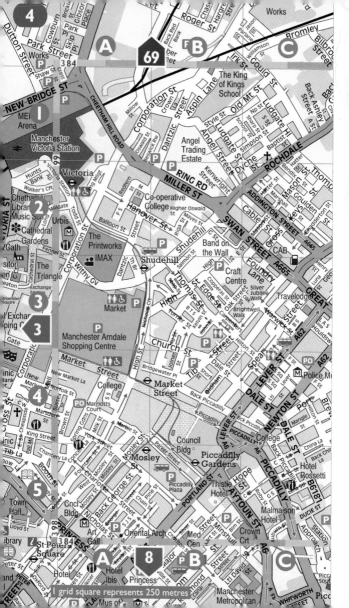

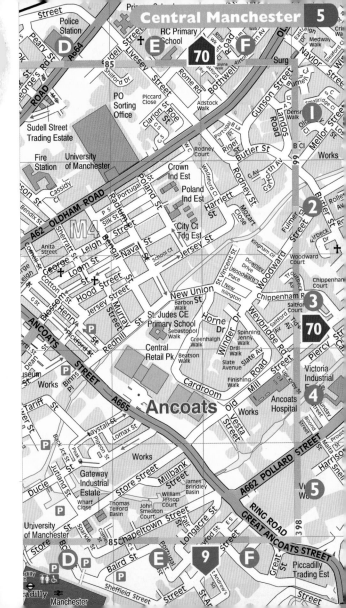

Street

Primrose

Police Station

D A664

Peary St

St George's Rd

ROAD

A664

Idell Street

Livesey Street

† RC Primary School

E

70

Walk

ack Road

Flinton

Av

F

East Leigh Walk

Medway Walk

Seaford Walk

Naylor Stree

Cri

Wa

PO Sorting Office

Piccard Close

Clarion St

Rome Rd

Roe Street

Adstock Walk

Bothwell Road

Surg

Gunson Street

Landos Road

Densmore Walk

Smallridge Cl

Mellor Stre

Works

I

Sudell Street Trading Estate

Fire Station

University of Manchester

Cassidy Cl

Bendix St

Anita Street

George St

Cotton

OLDHAM ROAD

A62

M4

Sherratt St

Portugal St

Silk St

Leigh St

Bengal St

Poland Street

Rodney Court

Crown Ind Est

Poland Ind Est

Harriett St

Mozart Close

Butler St

Rigel

C.S

Rodney St

North Av

G.AV

Wadford Cl

B CI

2

Butler St

Roller

Ro

Naval St

School Ct

City Ct Tdg Est

Jersey St

Kingham St

St Vincent St

Downley Drive

Woodward Place

Fulmer Dr

Woodward Court

Birbeck Dr

Chippenham Court

George

Cotton St

Loom St

Hood Street

Jersey Street

Murray Street

New Union St

Barbon Walk

St. Judes CE Primary School

New Islington

Horne Dr

Sebastopol Walk

Greenhalgh Walk

Chippenham R

Weybridge Road

Saltford Court

Saltford Av

3

70

Piercy Str

Blossom

Henry St

Pickford St

P

Redhill St

Central Retail Pk

Beatson Walk

Spinning Jenny Walk

Drill Walk

Slate Avenue

Slate Av

Finishing Walk

Victoria Industrial E

4

ANCOATS

North St

Dean St

useum

STREET

P

Binns Pl

A665

Cardroom

Winder Dr

Mill Road

Old

Vesta Street

Works

Ancoats Hospital

Kirby St

Lundry Street

Tariff St

wer St

P

Laystall St

Lomax St

Back Pigeon St

Peak St

Jutland St

Ducie St

P

Works

Gateway Industrial Estate

Store Street

Millbank Street

Wharf Close

Thomas Telford Basin

John Smeaton Court

James Brindley Basin

William Jessop Court

Ancoats

Old Works

A662 POLLARD STREET

Harrison

V

Wo

5

University of Manchester

P

Store St

85

Chapeltown Street

Sparke St

Cornell St

Longacre St

Portugal Street

St

GREAT ANCOATS STREET

RING ROAD

Great St

3 398

St Andrew's

Piccadilly Trading Est

Piccadilly

D P

Baird St

E

Sheffield Street

9

Street

F

Street

Manchester

grid square represents 250 metres

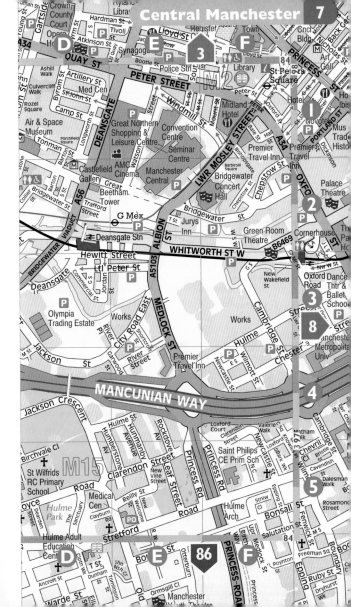

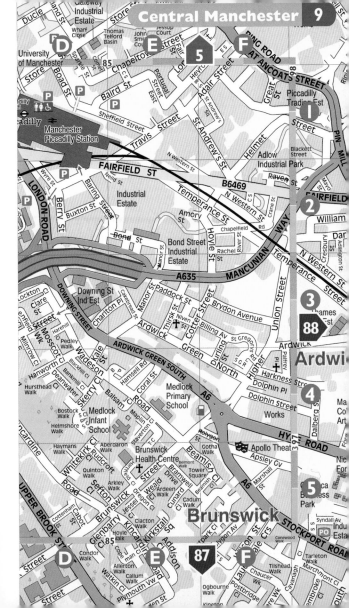

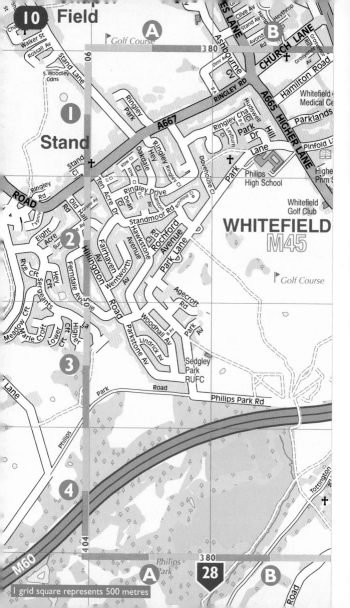

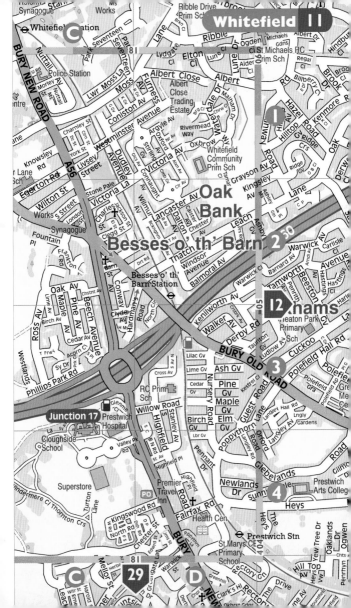

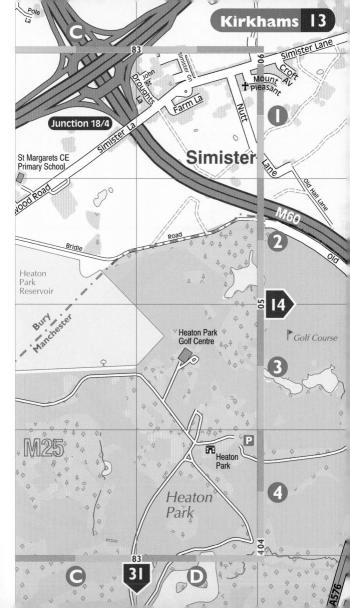

Pole La

C

83

Simister Lane

06

Croft Av

John St

Simister Gn

Mount Pleasant

Droughts La

Farm La

Nutt

I

Junction 18/4

Simister La

Simister

Lane

Old Hall Lane

St Margarets CE Primary School

wood Road

M60

Old

Bridle

Road

2

Heaton Park Reservoir

14

Bury
Manchester

Heaton Park Golf Centre

Golf Course

3

M25

P

Heaton Park

4

Heaton Park

404

C

83

31

D

A576

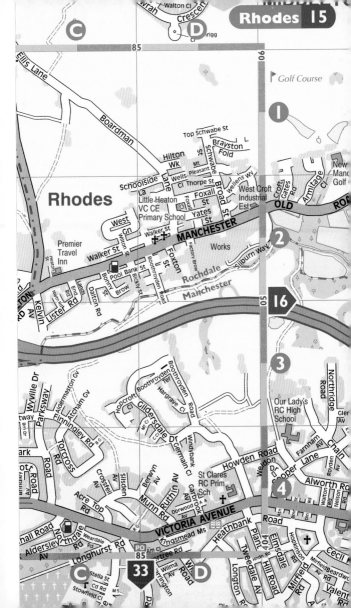

Walton Cl

Crescent

Brigg Cl

85

90

Ellis Lane

Boardman

Golf Course

1

Top Schwabe St

Brayston
Fold

L

Hilton
Wk

Schwabe St

Mt
Pleasant

Wells
Cl

Thorpe St

Schoolside

La

Rhodes

Little Heaton
VC CE
Primary School

Foxall
St

Foxall St

Broad St

Yates
St

Wellens Wy

West Croft
Industrial
Est

OLD

ROAD

New
Manc
Golf

Croft Gates Rd

Armitage

West
Gn

Wilton St

Walker St

MANCHESTER

2

Premier
Travel
Inn

Walker St

Heaton St

Pool Bank St

Foxton

Boothroyden Rd

Blakin St

Factory Brow

Works

Rochdale

Rochdale

Siburn Way

Manchester

16

05

Kelvin

Lister Rd

Lands
St

Bonny
Brow

Dalton Rd

Newton Rd

Endsl
Rd

TON
RD AV

3

Wyville Dr

Parksway

Aldermaston Gv

Atcham Gv

Finningley Rd

Hopcroft Cl

Boothroyden
Gv

Gildersdale
Dr

Hargrave Rd

Boothroyden
Ter

Boothroyden Road

Northridge
Road

Our Lady's
RC High
School

Glen
Av

ark

Torcross
Rd

ot
Road

Crossfell
Av

Silsden
Av

Berwyn
Av

Germain Cl

Windybank
Cl

Ruthin Av

St Clares
RC Prim
Sch

Carbrook
Av

Howden Road

Farnham
Av

Cooper Lane

Weldon
Dr

Royden Av

Chain
Lane

Alworth Rd

4

Watton St

Nelson
St

Acre Top
Rd

Munn Rd

Dorwood Av

VICTORIA AVENUE

Heathbank

Road

Plant

Hopkinson

Elmsdale
Av

Cecil

hall Road

Aldersley
Av

Weardale
Rd

Noyna Ave

Longhurst Rd

PO

Am Cl

Portree Rd

Kingsmead Ms

Wilma
Av

Warrington

85

33

Longton Rd

Tweedale Av

Hill Road

Mirfield Rd

Beardwood
Av

Valent
Rd

C

Stella St

Cd Rd

Stowfield Cl

M St

C

D

C

D

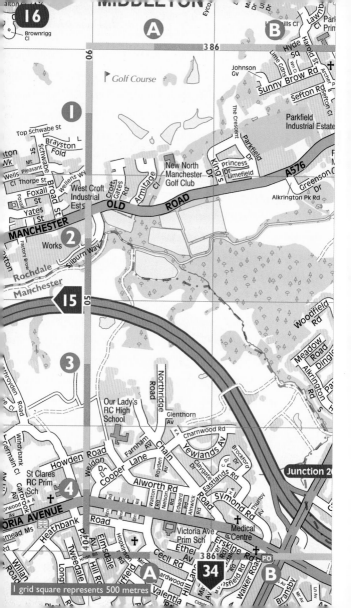

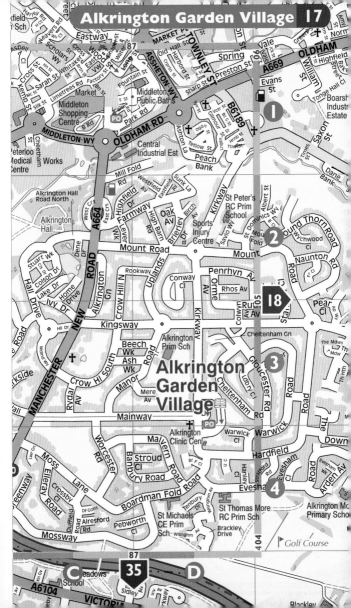

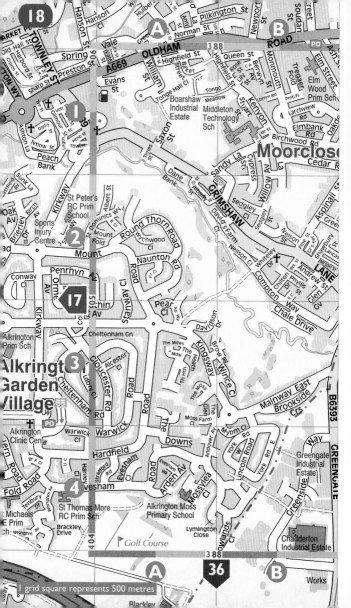

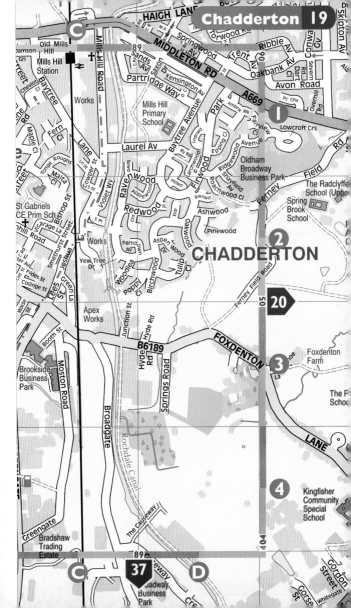

HAIGH LANE

Old Mills Hill

Damson

Mills Hill Station

MIDDLETON RD

Springwood
Torwood
Ribble
Skipton Av
Conway
Severn Av
Aldi

Mills Hill Road

Sands
Av
Saxon
Kensington Av
Partridge Way

Trent
Oakbank Av
Dart
Cl

A669

Avon Road

Works

Mills Hill Primary School

Baytree Avenue

Laurel Av

Firwood
Park

Undrew
Epping Cl
Ridgewood
Larchwood
Roachwood Cl

Ambry RN
Fairview
Avenue

Lowcroft Crs

Cheviot
Baytree
Maple Cl
Fern
Cl

Torge
Roughs
Malta
Cl

Violet Wy
Cowper
Lr St
S St
C St

Ravenwood

Alpine

Redwood
SL

Ashwood
Av
Sharfield
Av

Oldham Broadway Business Park

Ferney
Field
Rd

The Radclyffe School (Uppe

Spring Brook School

St Gabriels CE Prim Sch

Bishop St
Garage La
Slaithwaite St

S Pl

Works

Ferndl
Av

Elder

Poowood

Ashwood

Pinewood

CHADDERTON

Ferney Field Road

2

Yew Tree Dr

Woodley
Birchwood

Aspen
Wood
Tulip
Cl

Poppy
Cl

Exeter Av
Fildes St
Collinge St

Lees St
Green La

Wade St

Apex Works

Junction St

Hyde Rd

B6189

Hyde Rd

FOXDENTON

3

Joe
Foxdenton
Farm
La

20

05

Brookside Business Park

Moston Road

Booth St

Broadgate

Springs Road

Rochdale Canal

The F
Schoo

LANE

4

Kingfisher Community Special School

404

Greengate

Bradshaw Trading Estate

37

The Causeway

89

C

D

adway
Business Park

Gordon
Street
Gorse
St
Whitegate

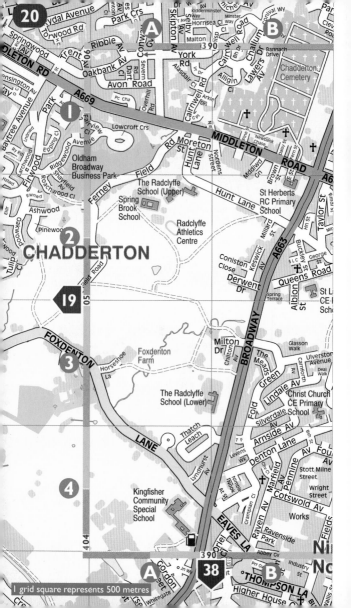

20

Rydal Avenue
Park Crs
A
Kidderminster Av
Hornsea Cl
B
Percival Wy
Skipton Cl
Selby
Malton
Minster Wy
Clev

Springwood
Torwood Rd
Ribble
Av
390
Crisp
Well
Rd
Chalum
Bannach Drive

DLETON RD
A669
Trent
90
Oakbank Av
Dart
Severn Rd
York Rd
Cairn
Well
Rd
Lawers Dr
Chalum Av
Chadderton Cemetery

ensington Av
Avon Road
Pc Cha
Ouvenhill
Alasdair Cl
Alligin Cl
Arkie Dr
Cairn Cl

eatree Avenue
Park
Epping Cl
Fairview Cl
Lowcroft Crs
Moreton St
Hunt Lane
Nordens Street
MIDDLETON ROAD
Newbank Chase
A6

Finwood
Ridgewood
Shayfield Av
Roachwood Cl
Avenue
Ferney
Field
Oldham Broadway Business Park
The Radclyffe School (Upper)
Hunt Lane
St Herberts RC Primary School
Middleton
Brown St
Taylor St

Ashwood
R.Wholf
Pinewood
Spring Brook School
Radclyffe Athletics Centre
Millard St
Buckley
A663
George
S L C

2 CHADDERTON
Field Road
Coniston Close
Keswick
Derwent Dr
Albion St
Queens Road
St L
CE
Scho

19
Foxdenton Farm
Spring Terrace

FOXDENTON
Horseshoe La
Milton Dr
Chilton
BROADWAY
The Meads
Glasson Walk
Ulverston Avenue
Deal Walk
Cranforth

3
The Radclyffe School (Lower)
Fold
Green
Lindale Av
Christ Church CE Primary School

LANE
Thatch Leach
Levens Wk
Silverdale Av
Arnside Av
Denton Lane
Pennine Av
Marfield Av
Fou Av

4
Lyndhurst
Nimble Nook
At St
Cotswold Av
Stott Milne Street
Wright Street
Works

Kingfisher Community Special School
Grampian Cl
Raven Av
EAVES LA
390
Cri
Ravenside Park
Abbey Gv
Fields
Industry
N
No

404
A
Gordon
Jn Wy
38
B
Prr
THOMPSON LA
Bi

Whitegate
Higher House

1 grid square represents 500 metres

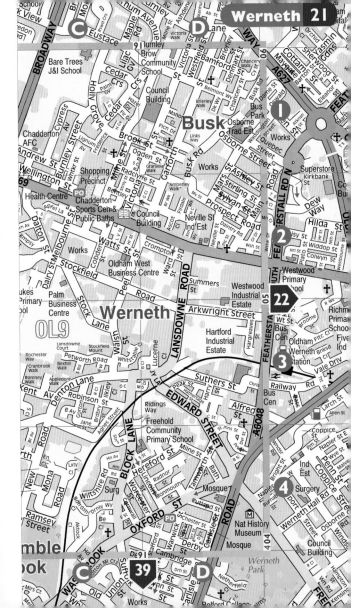

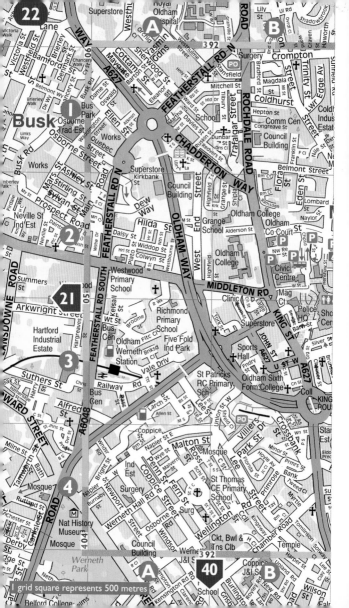

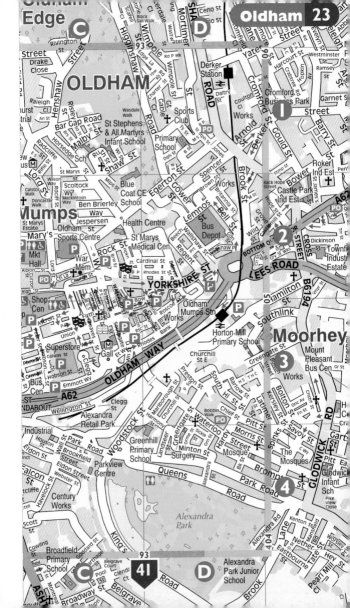

Oldham Edge

OLDHAM

Mumps

Moorhey

Alexandra Park

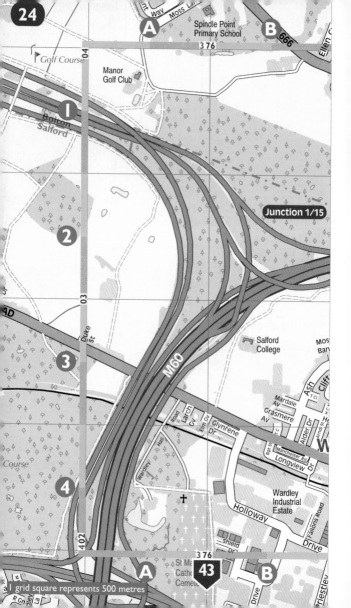

Way
Moss La

A

Spindle Point
Primary School

B
666

3 76

Ellen

Golf Course

Manor
Golf Club

1
Bolton
Salford

2

Junction 1/15

04

03

Duke St

AD

3

Salford
College

Mos
Ban

Ash

Clift

Mardale
Av

Grasmere
Av

Larch
Gv

Elm Gv

Glynrene
Dr

Alder Dr

H

Manchester Rd

Longview
Dr

W

4

Course

Wardley
Hall

Wardley
Industrial
Estate

Holloway

Fallons Road

Drive

shield

402

St Ma
Cath
Ceme

3 76

43

A

B

Drive

Priestle

al 1 grid square represents 500 metres

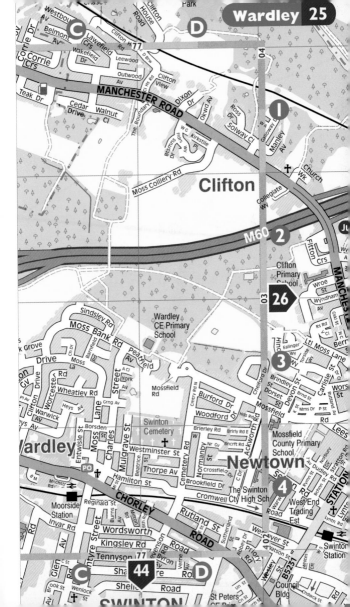

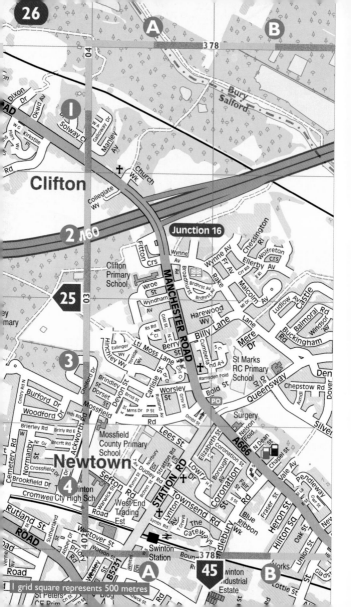

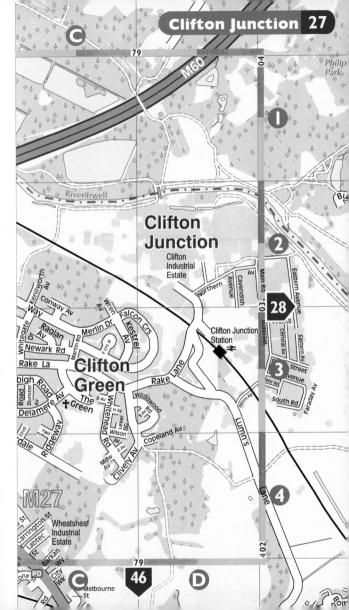

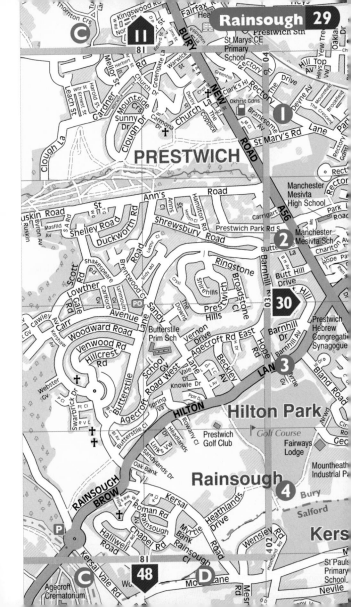

PRESTWICH

Hilton Park

Rainsough

Kers

Agecroft
Crematorium

Manchester
Mesivta
High School

Manchester
Mesivta Sch

Prestwich
Hebrew
Congregati
Synagogue

Prestwich Golf Club

Golf Course

Fairways
Lodge

Mountheath
Industrial Pa

St Pauls
Primary
School
Neville

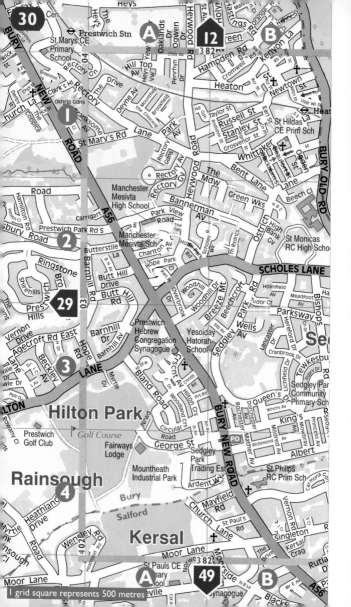

I grid square represents 500 metres

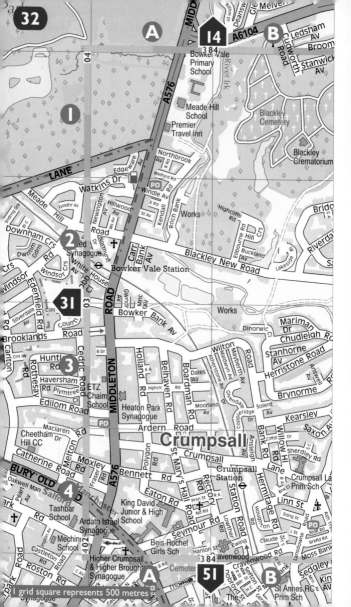

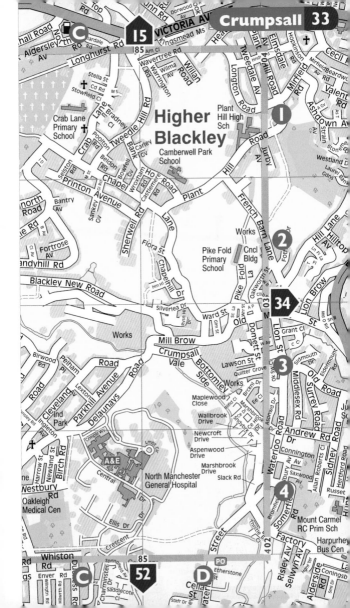

15
VICTORIA AV

Higher Blackley

Plant Hill High Sch

1

Crab Lane Primary School

Camberwell Park School

Printon Avenue

Pike Fold Primary School

Cncl Bldg

Works

French Barn Lane

2

Blackley New Road

Silverlea Dr

Ward St

Old

34

Lion Brow

Works

Mill Brow

Crumpsall Vale

Bottomley Side

Lawson St

Quilter Grove

Works

3

Middlesex Rd

Old Surrey Road

Cleveland Ind Park

Parkhill Avenue

Delaunays

Maplewood Close

Wallbrook Drive

Newcroft Drive

Aspenwood Drive

Marshbrook Drive

Slack Rd

Andrew Rd

Connington Av

Sidney Rd

Hertford Road

Waterloo Rd

A&E

Central

North Manchester General Hospital

Ellis Dr

4

Somerfield

Factory

Mount Carmel RC Prim Sch

Harpurhey Bus Cen

Oakleigh Medical Cen

Westbury Rd

Whiston Rd

C

52

Springvale

D

PO

Etherstone St

Cellar

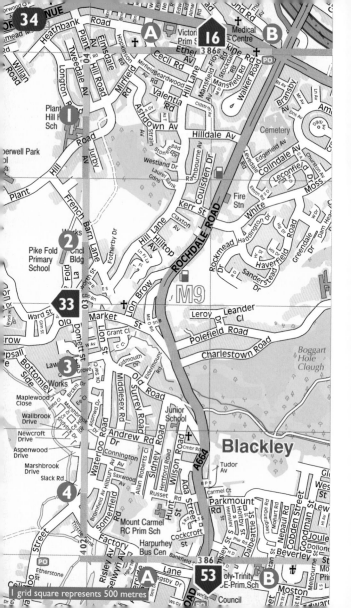

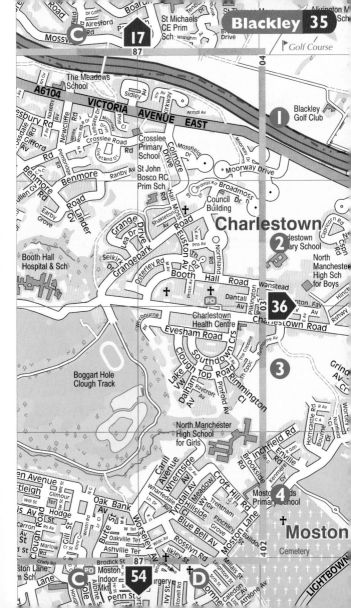

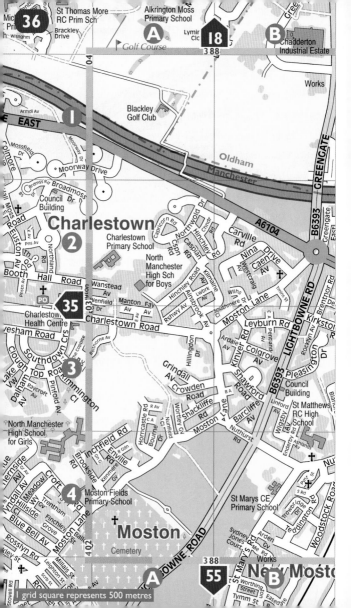

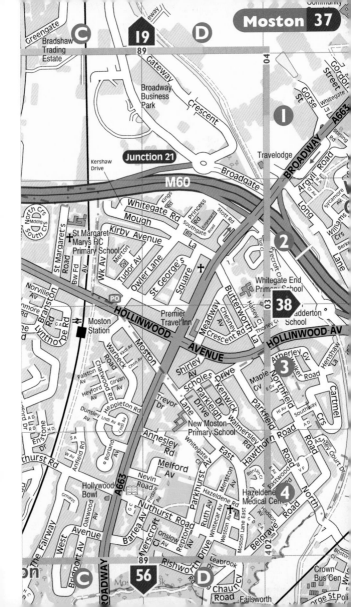

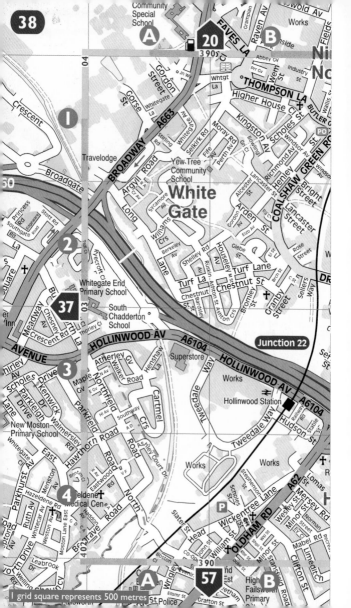

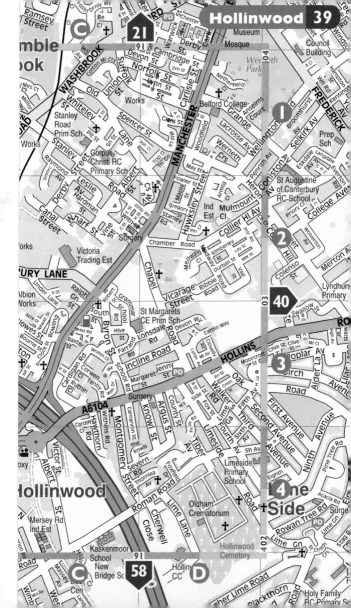

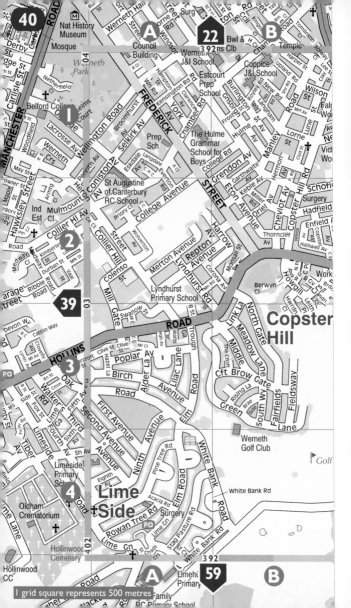

I grid square represents 500 metres

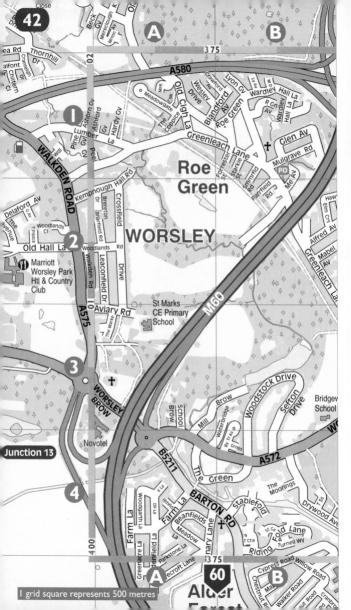

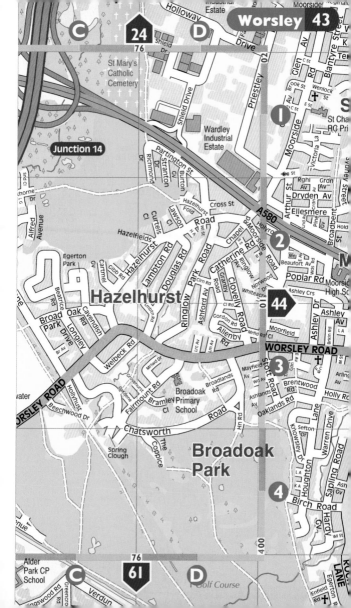

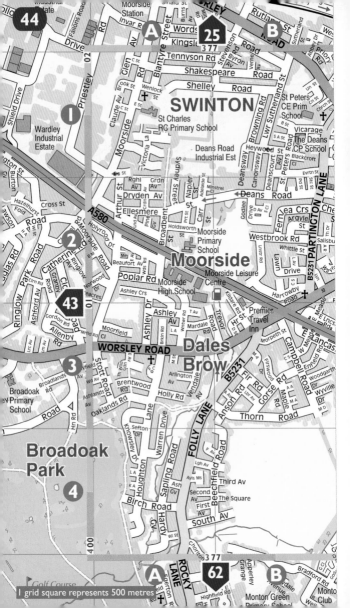

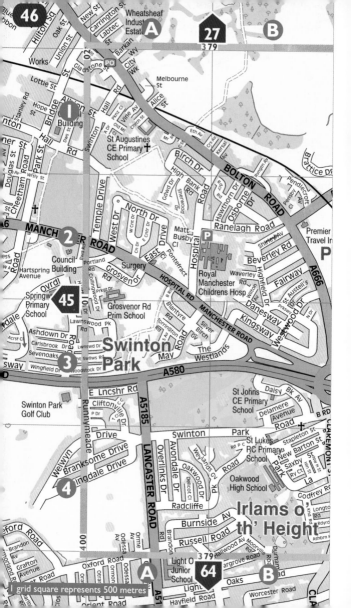

I grid square represents 500 metres

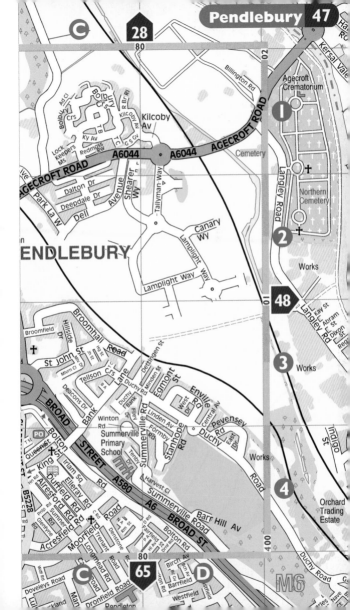

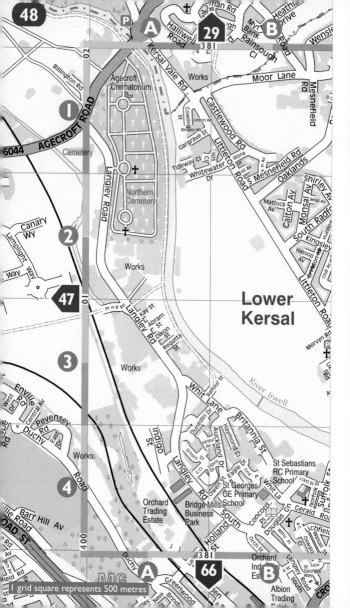

48

P

A

Halliwell Road

29
381

Othman Rd

MYT Bank
Rainsough Cl

Heath
Drive

B

Wensle

Billington Rd

Kersal Vale Rd

Works

Moor Lane

Mesnefield Rd

1

AGECROFT ROAD

Agecroft
Crematorium

Castlewood Rd

Littleton Road

Cowlishw St

Linton Wk

Bindley Wy

6044

Cemetery

Gargrave St

Tideway Cl

Isis

Illona
Dr

Mesnefield Rd

Oaklands

Shirley Av

Whitewater Dr

S Mesnefield Rd

Mnsl Av

Langley Road

Northern
Cemetery

Matlock
Av

Calton Av

Monsal Av

South Radfor

Kingsley

Hassop
AV

Chdl Rd

2

Canary
Wy

47

Lamplight Way

Way

Works

Pr H B Rd

Langley Rd

Kay St

Abram
St

Dixon
St

Regatta
St

Lower
Kersal

Mervyn Rd

P

3

Works

Whit Lane

Balfoot St

River Irwell

Enville
Rd

West
Rd

Central Av

Pevensey
Rd

East
Av

Indigo
St

Langley Rd

Dunedin Dr

Auckland Dr

Haymond Av

Winsford

Britannia St

St Sebastians
RC Primary
School

Lcktt St

Suffolk c

Rd

Duchy

Works

Orsmc Dr

Eagle St

St Georges
CE Primary
School

Cobion St

Whit La

Gerald

Norfolk St

RC

Road

Lichfield

Walsall

Oswald

4

Barr Hill Av

Orchard
Trading
Estate

Bridge Mills
Business Park

South Holland St

Concord
Pl

Douglas St

RC

Orch St

Langley Rd South

ROAD ST

MC

A

66
381

Duchy Road

Greenwood

Brindi

Nave

Orchard
Ind
Es

B

St
Georges
Way

A

Unn

Albion
Trading

CRO

I grid square represents 500 metres

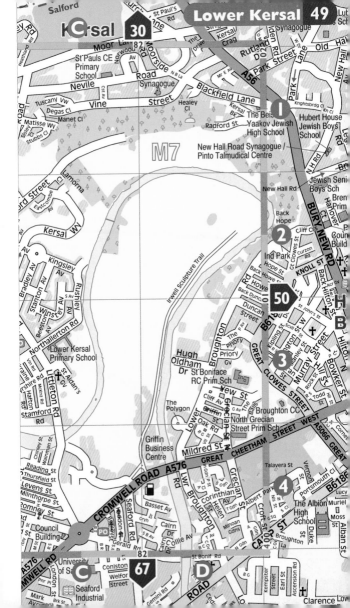

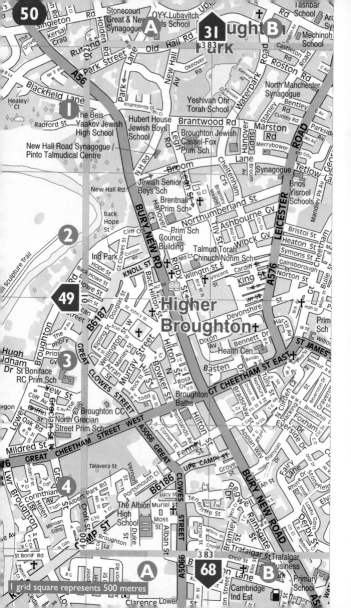

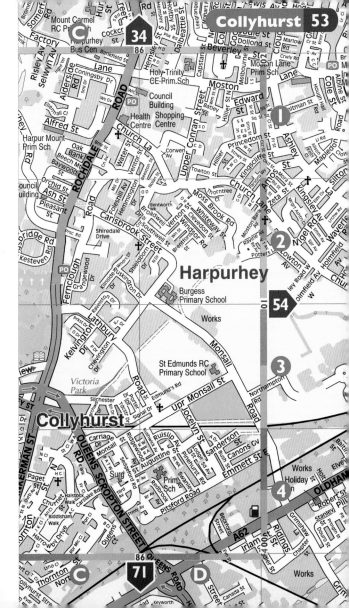

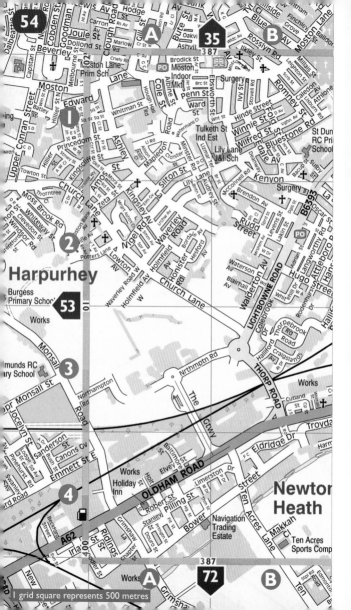

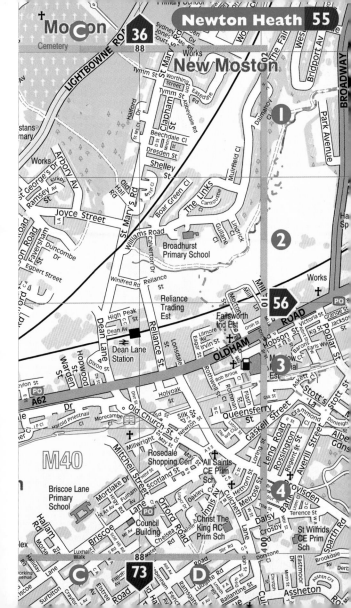

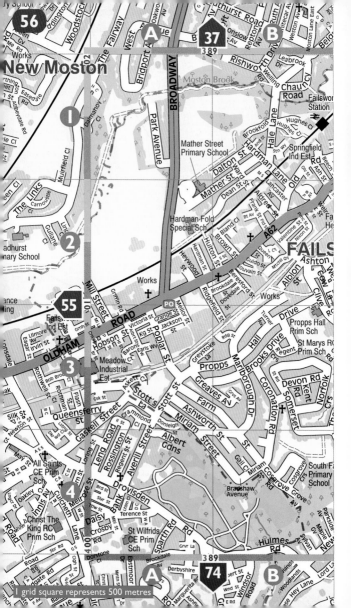

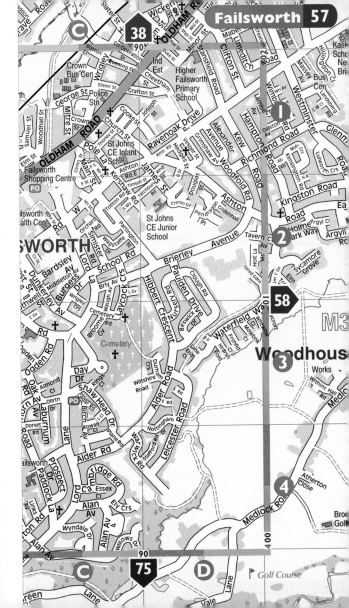

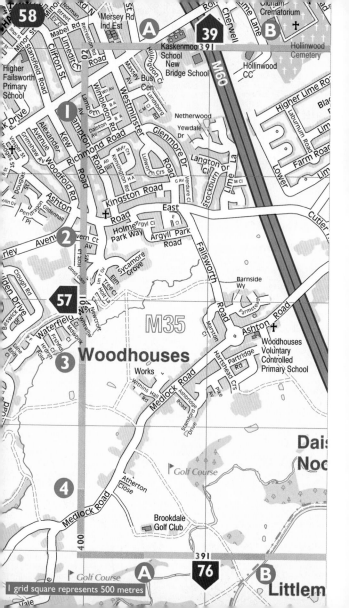

58

A

39 391

B

Oldham
Crematorium

Hollinwood
Cemetery

Mersey Rd
Ind Est

Kaskenmoor
School
New
Bridge School

Hollinwood
CC

Higher Lime Rd

Higher
Failsworth
Primary
School

Mabel St
Minor St

Mino (Norman)
St

Massey Rd

Recreation Rd
Clifton St
Limeditch

Netherwood

Yewdale
Dr

Langton
Cl
Dr

Stockbury Cl

Black

Lime

Laburnum Road
Farm Rd

Lower

Wimbledon
Westminster
Road

Hislington Dr

Landseer
Rd

Richmond Road

Lambeth
Av

Dalston
Av

Kensington
Rd

Glenmore Dr

Myr
Cl

Luwon
Crs

Verdure Cl

G AV

M Cl

I

Alexander
Avenue
Woodfold Rd

Kew

Lampton
Road

Crinshaw Av
Vesper St

Douglas

Ashton

Gildenhall
Pendragon
Pl

Kingston Road

Road

East

Holme
Park Way

Argyll Cl
AV

Argyll Park
Road

E

2

Avern Ct

Aven

Avenu

Circa Cres

H A

Sycamore
Grove

Elm
Tree Cl
Holt La

Lim Tow

Whitwhi

Faisworth Road

Marston
Cl

Barnside
Wy

Farmstead

Ashton

Woodhouses
Voluntary
Controlled
Primary School

57 101

Waterfield

Newcroft

Network

Freyhof
Hraem
Fold

3

Beswick Drive

Clough Rd
Golden Drive

Woodhouses

Works

Medlock Road

Witnins Hall
Rd

Ashbridge
Road

Stamford
Drive

Partridge
Rd

Hartshead Crs

Pixie

M35

**Dais
Noo**

4

Medlock Road

400

Atherton
Close

Golf Course

Brookdale
Golf Club

Golf Course

A

391

76

B

Littlem

I grid square represents 500 metres

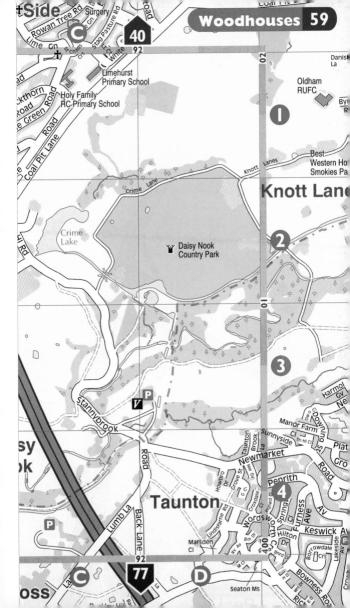

C
43
76

Alder Park CP School
Golf Course

Kingswood Rd
Greencroft
Westwood Rd
Grasmere
Verdun Crescent
Road
Rydal Av

Worsley Golf Club
I
Enfield Rd
Egerton Road
LANE
Brackley Road
MONTON GR
Oak
Dad
Pk

tstwood
ark

Westwood
Crescent
Road
Road
Westbourne Street
Anson Street
Lambton Rd
PARRIN LANE
Napier Road
Westwood Park Primary School
Trevor Road
Montonfields

Monton Medical Centre
Alfred Street
Grayville Street
Francis
Crawford St
Algernon Street
Kirtley Av
Stanley
PO
Sur

Taunton
Stroud Av
Bray
Dale
M602
CANAL BANK
Monton Mill
Shackleton St
Mitchell
Mnt

2
Monton
Lansdowne Rd
Carlton
Corb

Bulteel
Sutherland St
Weymouth Road
Gee Lane
Winton
Woodford Av
Dartford Av
Breck Road
Nwbry Dr

Lulworth Rd
B5231
Works

Nasmyth Business Centre
Patricroft Station
62
Patricroft
Lyntown Trading Estate

alford College
Colborne Avenue
Dover St
Blandford Rd
Gillingham Rd
Cambell Rd

Business & Technology Centre
WORSLEY
GREEN LANE

Watson St
Cromwell Rd
3
Hampden
Cromwell
Nelson St
Shakespeare C

St Patrick's Catholic High School
Guilford Road
New Lane
Bridgewater St
South
Millers
Barlow La
Hall Bank
Water St

Christchurch CE Prim Sch
Vine St
Cawdor
The Av
PO
Renshaw St
Ellesmere St
Mellor St
Keats Rd
Lewis

4
Lime St
Armitage

Clandon
Hatherop
Fint
Stock
Lily st
Arthur st
LIVERPOOL ROAD
Woodfield Gv
Eldon St
ROAD
Barton Business Park

Barrow
Adelaide St
Finty Grove
Trafford

M30
Redmans Cl
Barton Hall Works
Hardy Street
Green Street
Alexandra
Stanley
Edison Road
76
BARTON RO
Bell
Holy Cross & All Saints RC Primary School

C
78
D
CE Prim

A57

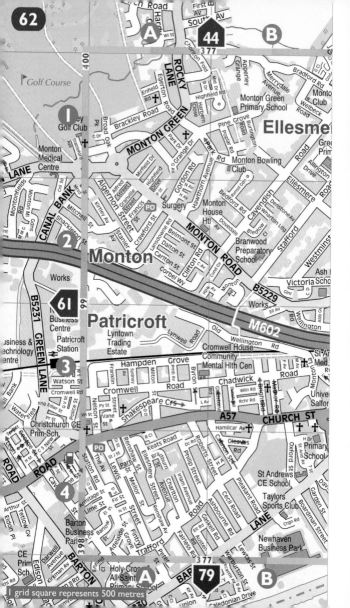

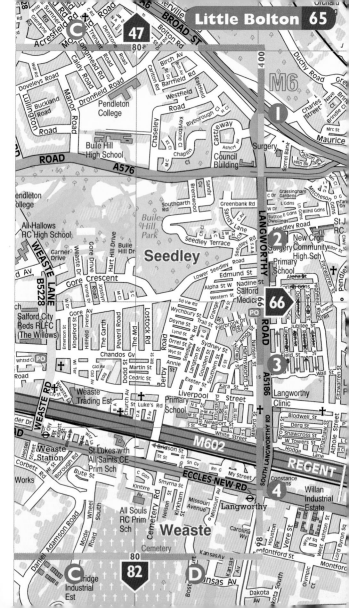

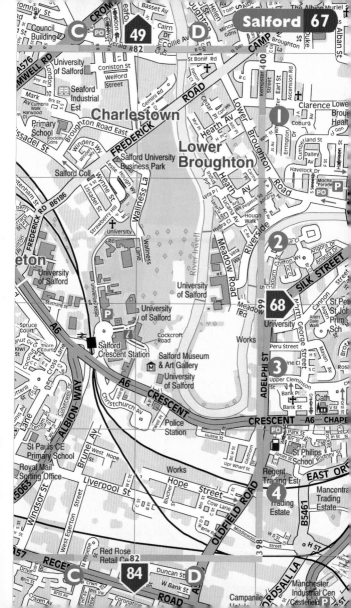

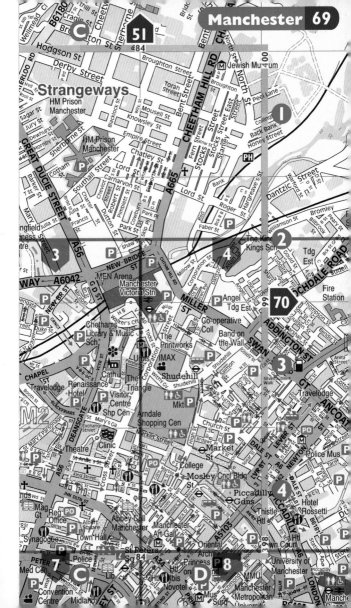

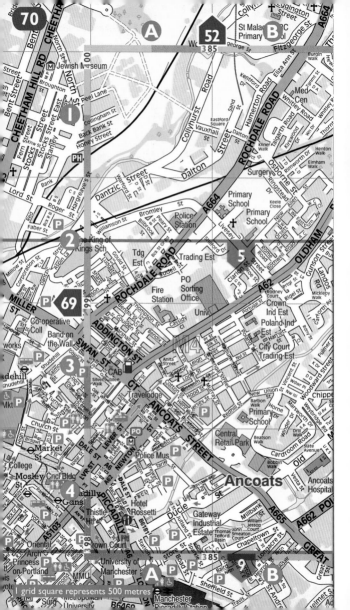

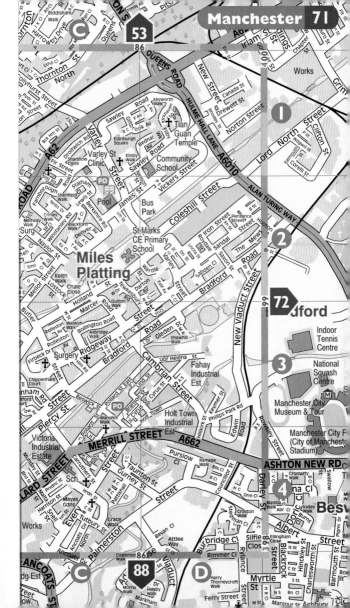

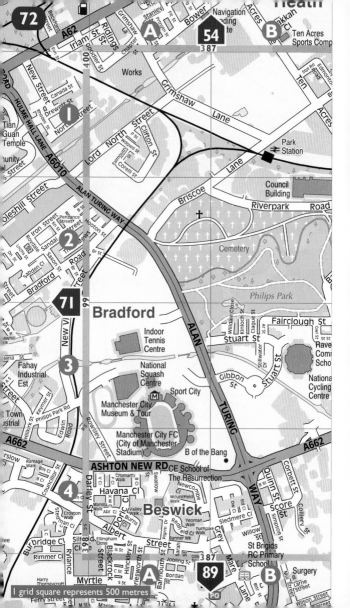

I grid square represents 500 metres

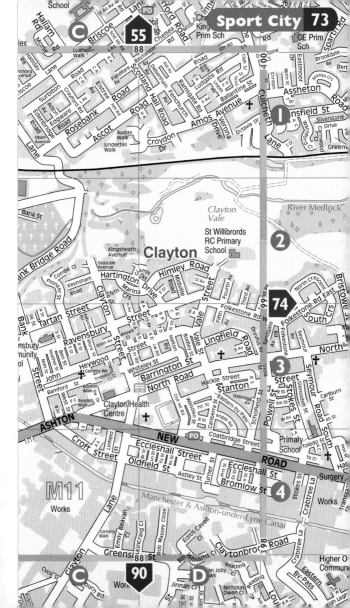

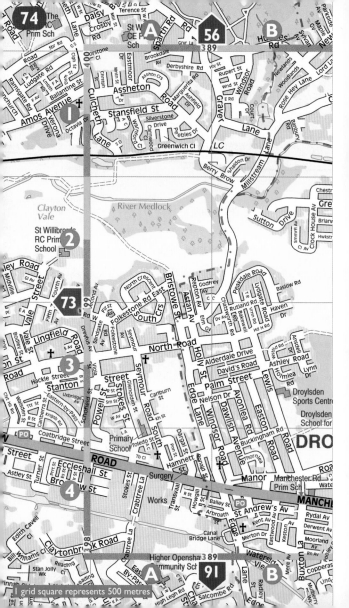

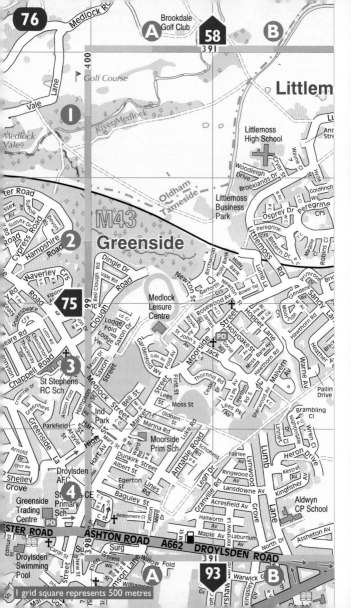

I grid square represents 500 metres

C

P

59
92

Lumb La

Marsden Cl

Av

Hilton Dr

Botherowdale Crs

Bowness Road

Lakeside

OSS

umb

Andrew Street

Cross La

Cross La

Back La

M60

Back La

Buckley Hill Farm

Seaton Ms

Richmond St

Kendal Av

OL I

Thi

PO

Crowthe

Larks Rd

Partridge

Rd

Starling Cl

Dove Cre

Saddle Cl

Benny La

The Shires

Drayfields

Rainer

Lane

Richmond Park Athletics Stadium

Robinson Lane

Lane

Rayn

ASHTON-UNDER

LORD SHELDON WAY

2

Kayley Industrial Estate

Martingale Way

Riding

Cl

Oaters

Cavenen Cl

Avenue

99

Curzon Ashton FC

Thornway Drive

3

Rayner Lane

LORD SHELDON WY

Moss

Lane

Prim Sch

Katherine St

Earle Street

William

Rayner

Lane

Alexandria Drive

Alexandria Drive

Junction 23

A6140

MANCHESTER

ROAD

Smith St

Holly St

Rawley St

Crofton

4

West E Medica

Brendon Dr

Thankerton Av

North Rd

Gainsborough Rd

Astbury

Milton Road

Boswell Av

Thrapston Av

Windsor Dr

A635

Snipe Wy

Guide Bridge

Rivercroft St

Park

Sharon

Birch

Gate La

Pelham St

Mansf

St

Kelvin

Howe

Pottinger

Trafalgar

Marlborough

AA Bennett St

Fitzroy

St

Marlborough

Lambert St

STOCKPORT ROAD

Surgery

St Wes

Pott

C

Snipe Retail Park

Assheton

Snipe

92

D

Gate La

Ambrook

A6140

SOUTH

Guide Br Tdg Est

398

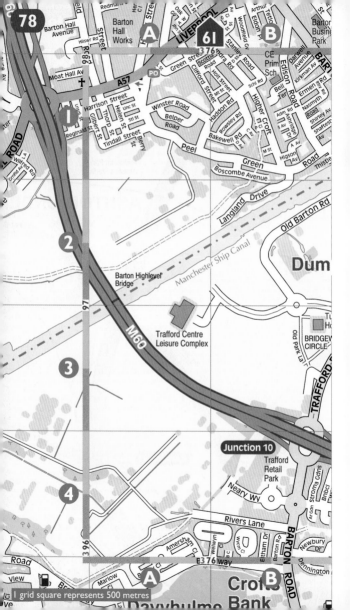

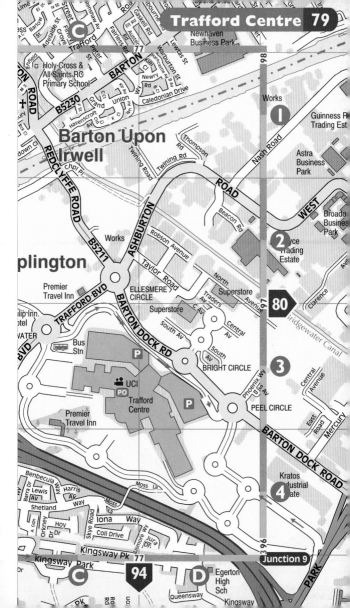

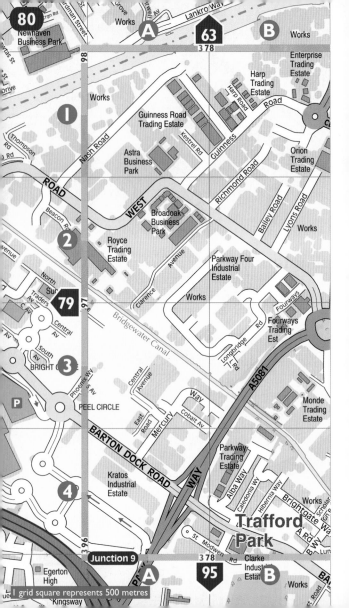

80
Newhaven
Business Park

Grove
Works

A

Lankro Way

63
3 78

B

Works

Enterprise
Trading
Estate

Works

Harp
Trading
Estate

Guinness Road
Trading Estate

Harp Road

Guinness Road

Orion
Trading
Estate

I

Nash Road

Astra
Business
Park

Kestrel Rd

Richmond Road

Bailey Road

Lyons Road

Thompson Rd

ROAD

Beacon Rd

WEST

Broadoak
Business
Park

Works

2

Royce
Trading
Estate

Clarence Avenue

Parkway Four
Industrial
Estate

North
Traders Av

79

Central Av

Bridgewater Canal

Works

Fourways

Fourways
Trading
Est

A5081

South Av

3

BRIGHT C

Phoenix Wy

Central Avenue

Longbridge Rd

P

PEEL CIRCLE

East Road

Mercury Way

Cobalt Av

Monde
Trading
Estate

BARTON DOCK ROAD

WAY

Parkway
Trading
Estate

Alba Way

Caledonia Wy

Hibernia Way

Brightgate

Works

4

Kratos
Industrial
Estate

**Trafford
Park**

St Modwen

A Rd

Scholar

Junction 9

A

PAR

378

95

Rd

Clarke
Industrial
Estate

B

BA

Egerton
High

Kingsway

Works

1 grid square represents 500 metres

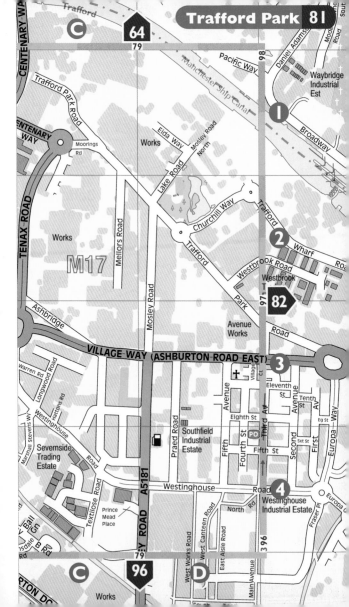

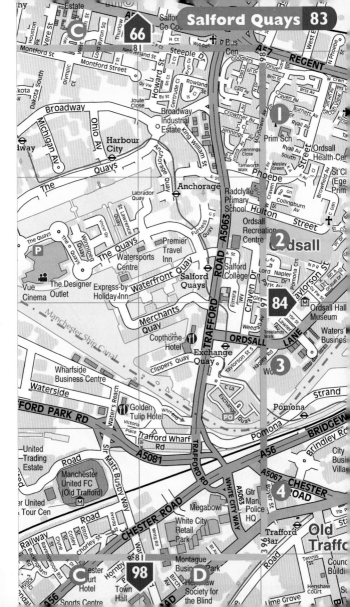

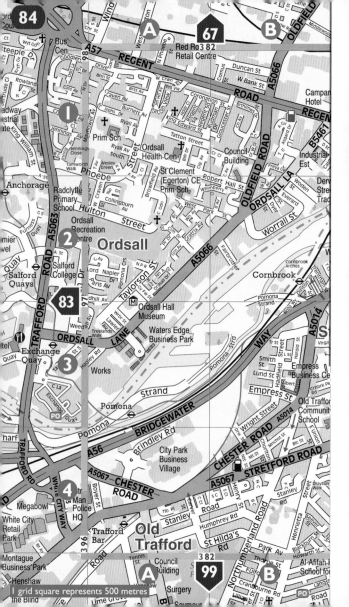

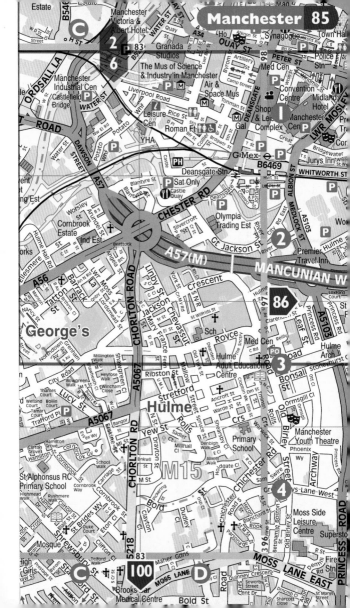

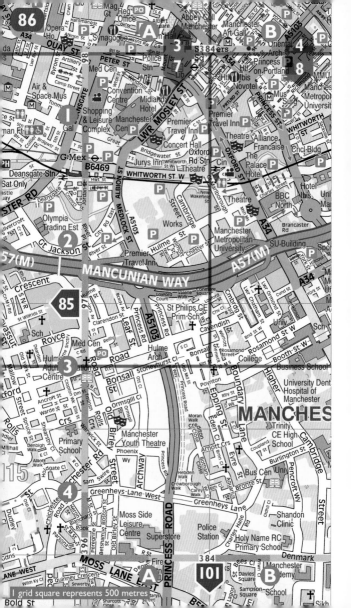

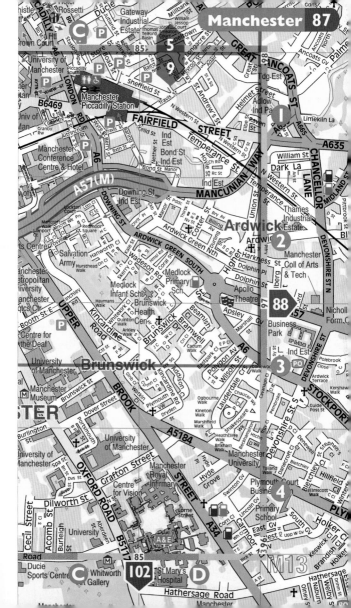

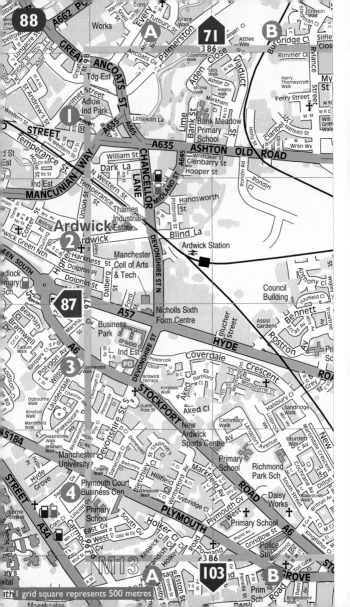

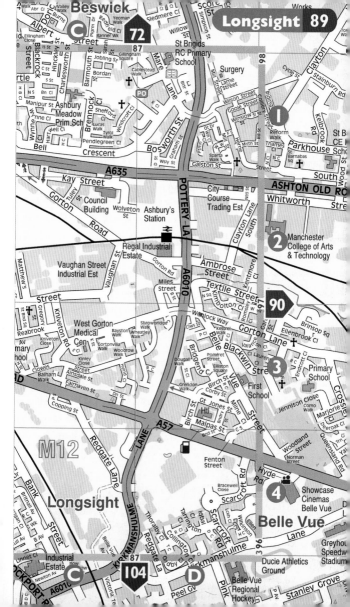

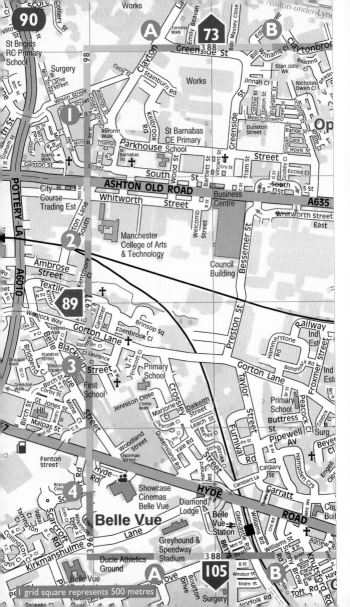

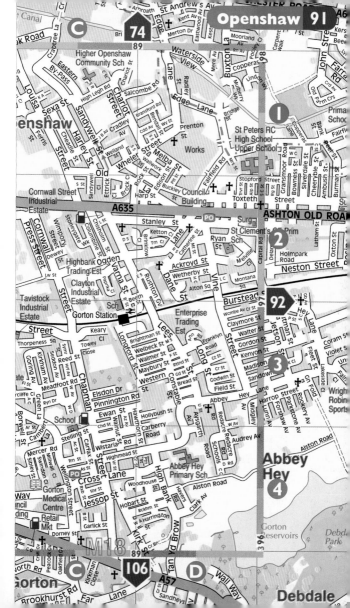

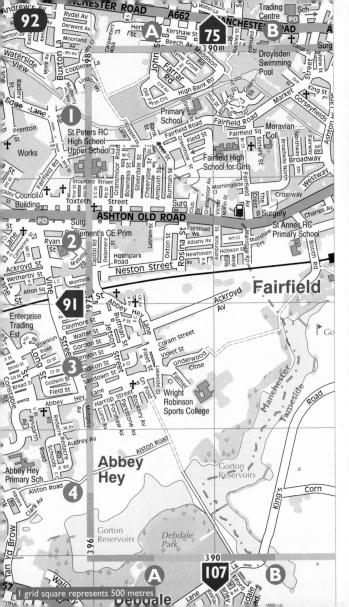

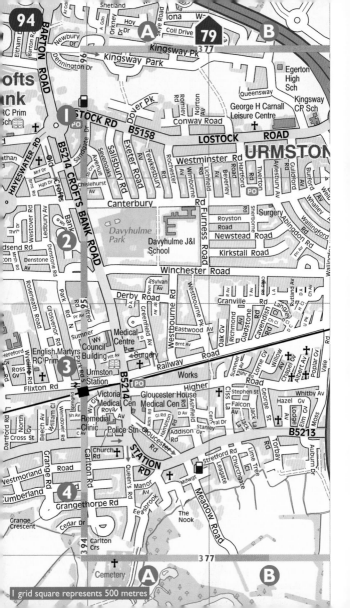

I grid square represents 500 metres

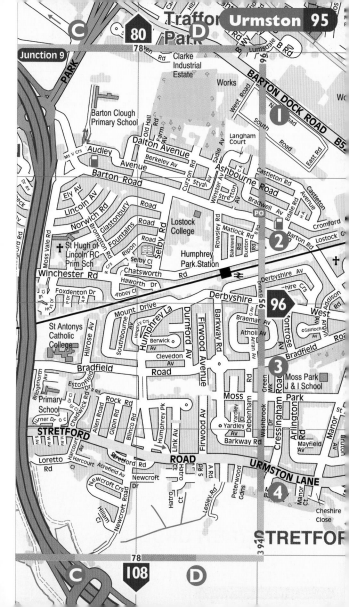

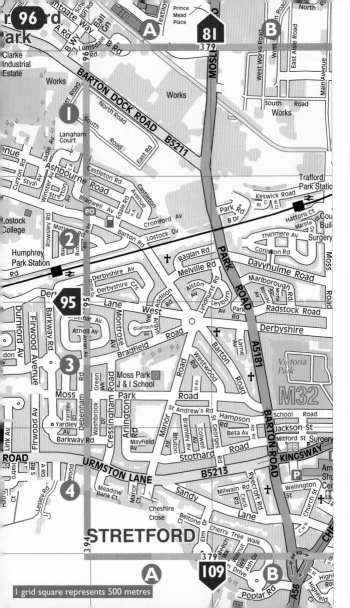

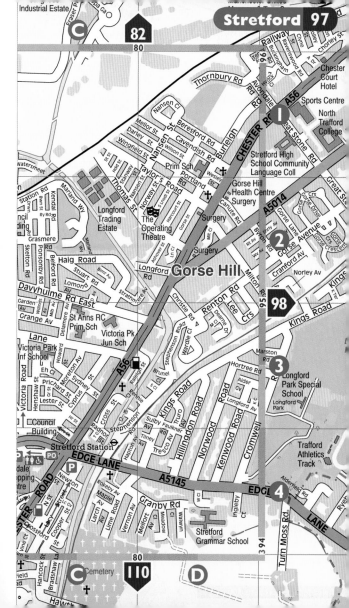

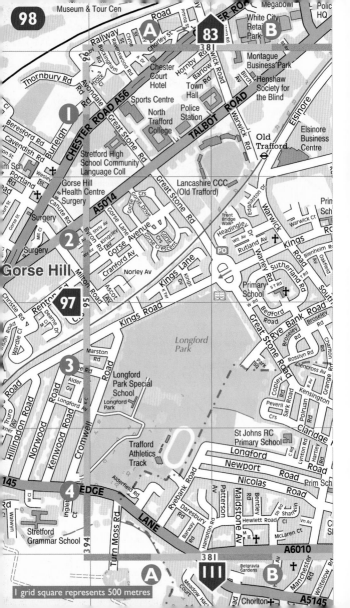

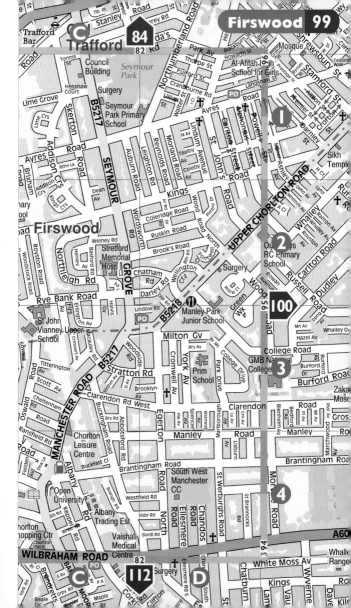

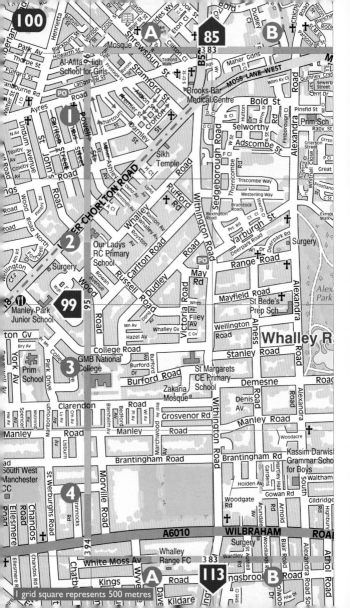

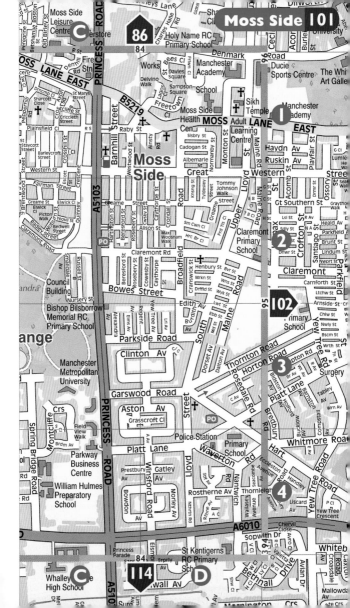

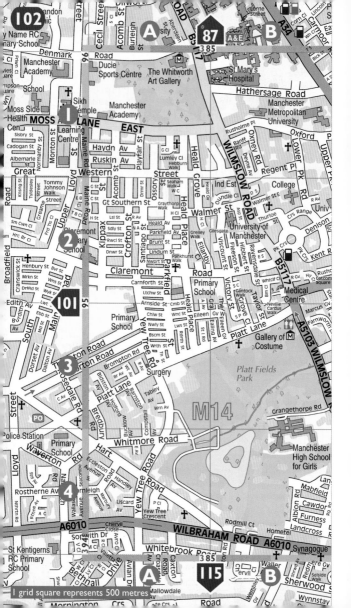

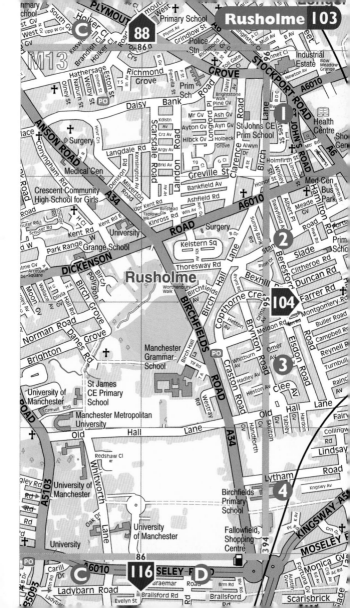

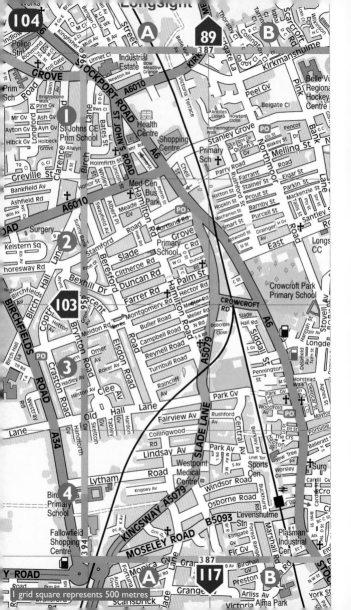

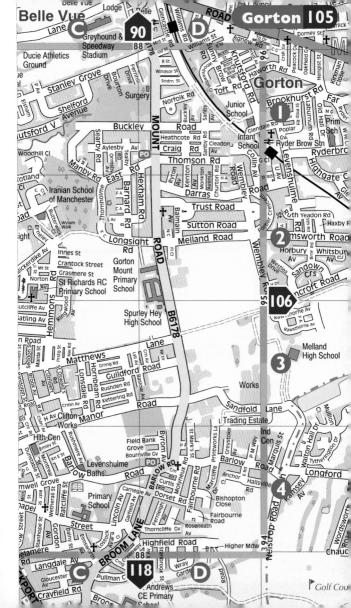

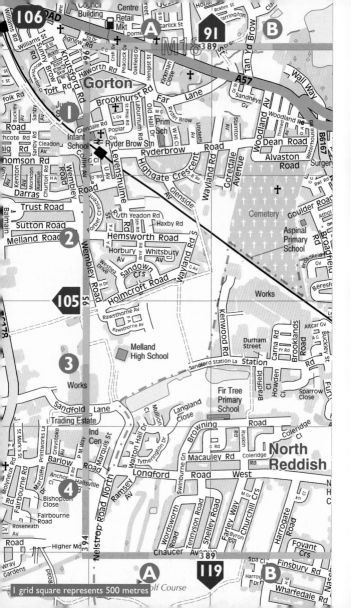

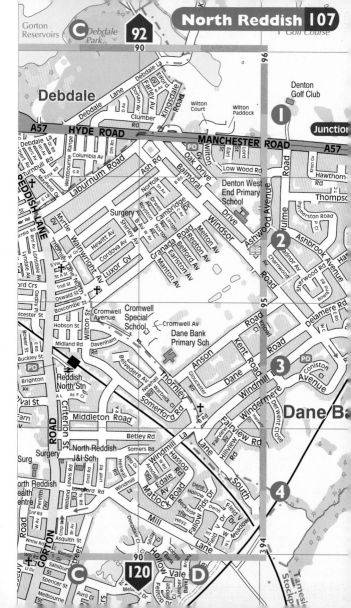

North Reddish 107

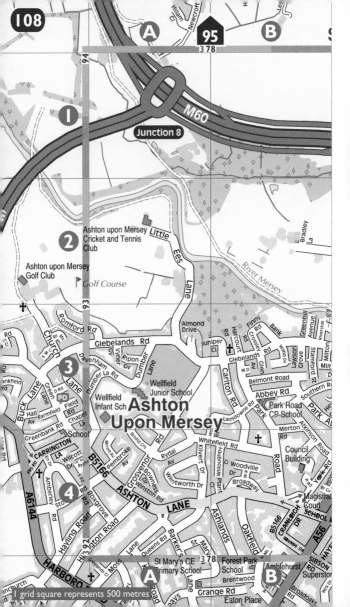

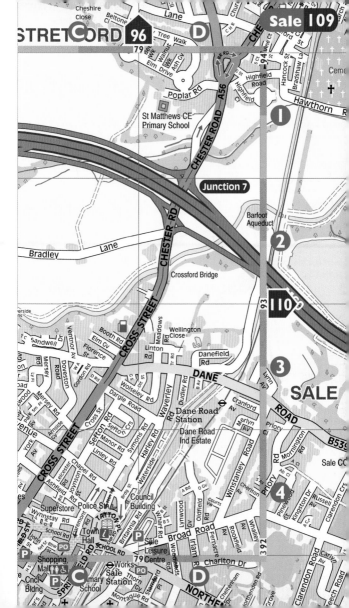

110

CHESTER
CHR
Church
Walk
B RD
Crossford
Cooper St
Larch Av
Lime Road
Meadow
Ranby Rd
Ingle Ct
A
97
380
B
tford
Grammar School
rammar School

Poplar Rd
CHESTER ROAD—A56
Highfield Road
Highfield Ct
Hancock St
Bradshaw La
Cemetery

1

Hawthorn   Road

Hawthorn   Road

Junction 7

Barfoot
Aqueduct

2

Crossford Bridge

109

M60

ellington
ose

Danefield
Rd

3

DANE

Dudley Rd
Danefield
Rd
Dane Road
Station
Dane Road
Ind Estate

Lynn Av
Cranford
Av
Merlyn
AV

ROAD
Priory
Ci
Mornington
Rd
Priory
Rd

SALE

Trafford Water
Sports Centre

Sale

Cow

Cow Lane

Arnesby Av

Ravenstone Dr
Oulton
Avenue
Caldbeck
Av
Stapleford
Ci
Vale Av

Winstanley   Road
elton

4

Pinewood
Dr
Kingston Dr
A Ci

Russell Crs
Claredon Crs

Sale CC

B5397

DANE   ROAD

High
Gates

B5397

OLD HALL—ROAD

Lynwood
Road
Oldfield
Av
Rookfield
AV
Fernacre
AV
Courts
W

Irlam
Road

3 9 2
Whalley
Rd

London Road
Charlton Dr

Carlyn
S

Beech Road
A
380
Yew Tree Dr
Broad
Rd
Evesham Gv
Thorold Gv
Leith
AV
B

Junior
School

Road

I grid square represents 500 metres

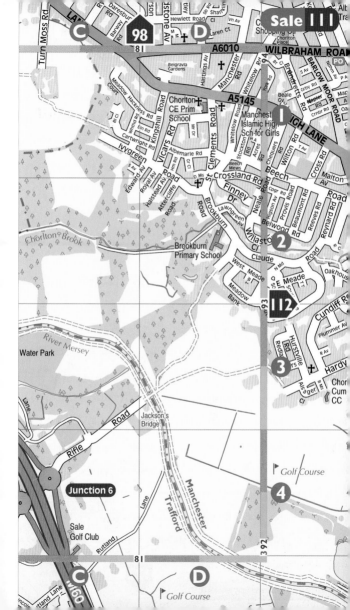

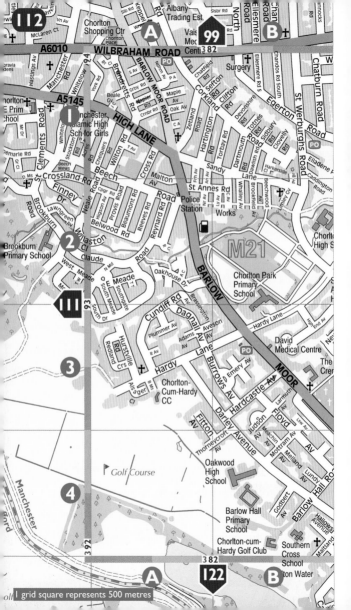

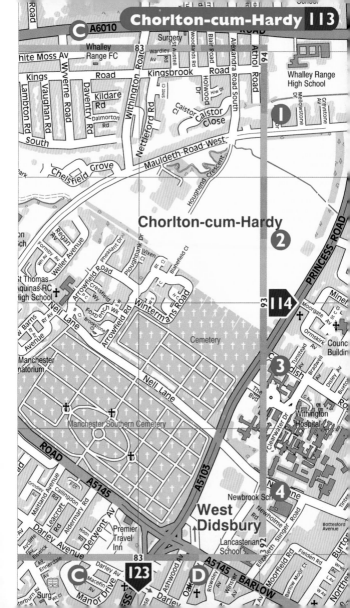

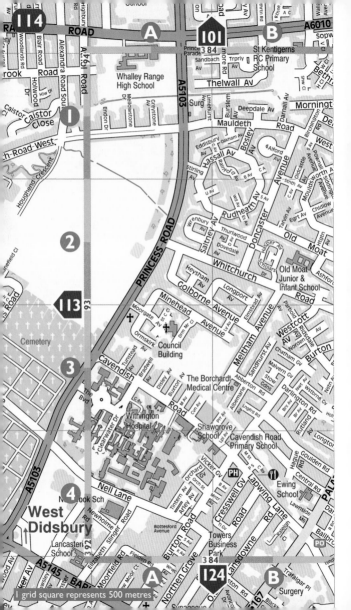

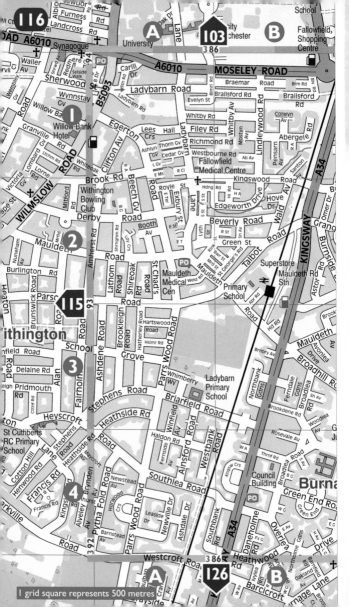

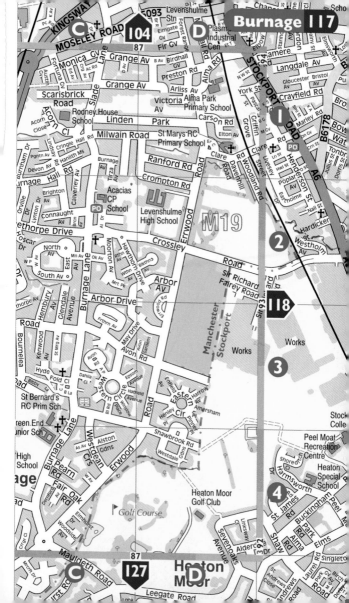

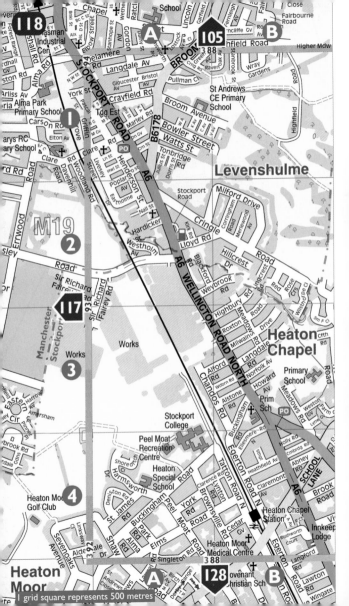

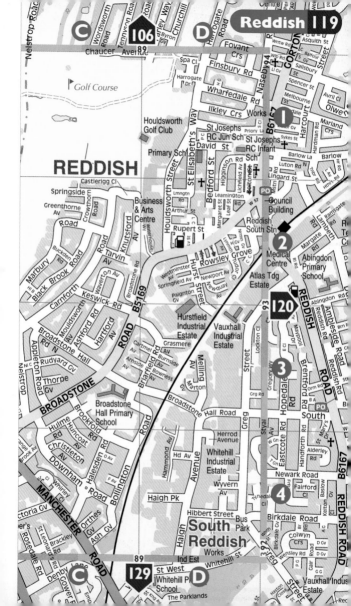

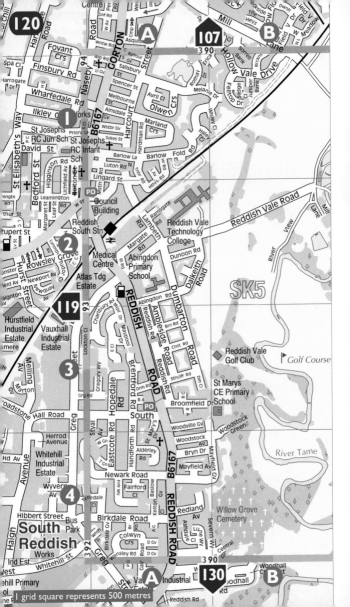

I grid square represents 500 metres

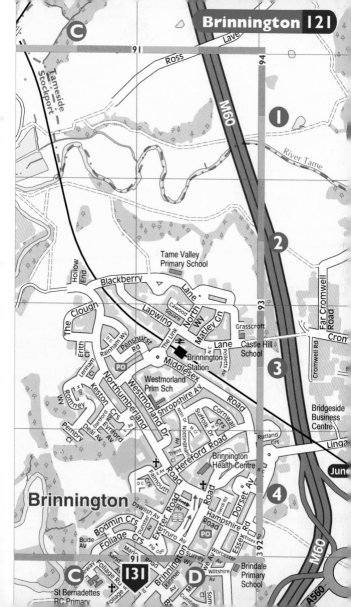

122

A

112
3 82

B

Barlow Hall
Primary
School

orlton-cum-
nardy Golf Club

Southern
Cross
School

Chorlton Water
Park

Ford

Col
AV

Barl

Hallows
Avenue

Maitland

Golf Course

Caldervale

Woodla

1

Fairy Lane

2

3
SALE

4

92

91

390

HAWKWICK

mby
Rd

AD

Southwick Road

Cleeve
Road

Brent
Rd

npark Rd

Stortford Dr

Tipton Dr

Piper
Hill Sch

Cherington
Rd

Pepler
Rd

Raymond
Rd

M AV

Barry Road

Willenhall Rd

Willenhall Rd

Moor
Lane

llend
Road

Surtees
Tr AV
Brows
Av

Road

WD GV

Council
Building

PO

Yewtree

Newhall Dr

ROAD

Pingot
Rd

Rackhouse Rd

Purley Av

Lane

Hollyhey Drive

V A

K A

Fairmead
Road

PRINCESS

PARKWAY

Heys
AV

Kerne
Gv

Orton

Nightingale Drive

Rack House
Prim Sch

Yarmouth Dr

Cartoon Road

Daine
Av

Millom Av

Moss Hey Dr

City College
Manchester

Homewood Rd

xton

Orton

Levcett Dr

Road

St Aidans Catholic
Primary School

D s cor

B5166

Callas Gv

A

B

HENSHAWE

ROAD

B5167

3 82

Wi   enshawe Hall
ntry Park

ARKWAY

Shav

Br AV

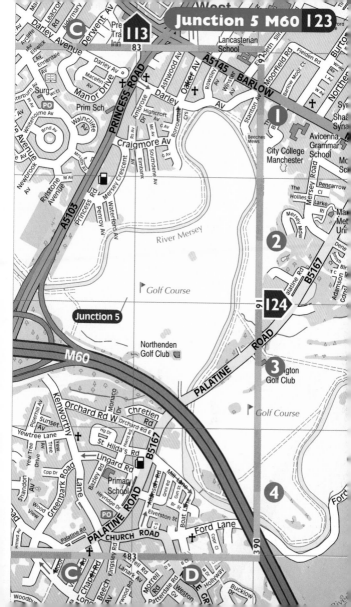

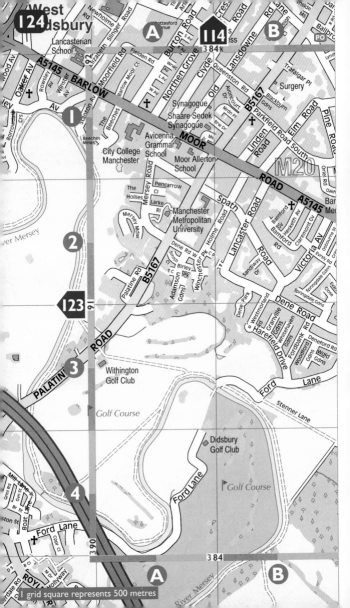

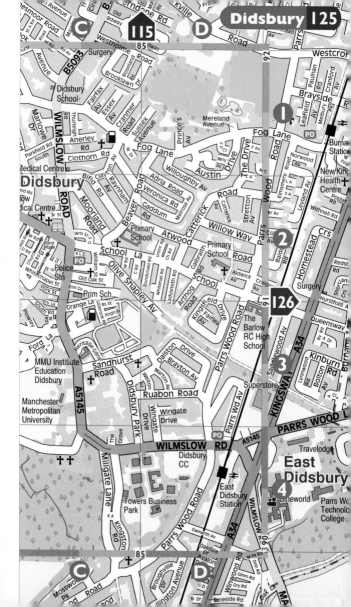

3 86

Leaside
Newville
Ashdale Dr

Parrs Wood Rd

Pytha F

Avelet
Alveleigh

Road

Barnstead

Parrs Wood Rd

Westcroft Road

KINGSWAY

Daneholme
54

Teen End

Heathwood
Rd

Northumbria Gdns

B

DRIVE

Brayside

Road

Leafield

Pauhan
Cranford Rd
Melbury Rd

Barcicroft

Oakland

Burnage Lane

Road

Mereland
Avenue

1

Fog Lane

The Drive

Austin

Road

Roughby Av

Wood

Norwood
Av

PO

Burnage
Station

Fog La

Milton

Cranwell
Cranwell Av
Ashby
Moorby
Dr
Av

Wilma

Grrecz Dr

Milton
Cr

Brassington
Rd upton

Rd

New Kingsway
Health
Centre

Lane End Road

Poplar

Works

Stretton Rd

Catterick

Elmsmere
Road
Leyland Av

Br Av

Craigwell

Br Av

Colemore
Av

Baldock

Aldwick

Withnell Rd

Burnage Lane

Lavister Av

Uppermill Dr

Denshaw

Darden Cl

Fenwick
Cl

Alwinton Av

Bluestone Drive

Willow

Primary
School
Galbraith

Road

Homestead
Crs

Kentstone Av

Ingram Cl

Chevington drive

Heaton
Mersey

School

Arthog
Road

Kingsf'd
Fairlea
eld Drive

125

Surgery

Craigwell

Lane

Redstone
Rd

Maidstone
Rd

Rosall

Hawth

St Johns
CE Primary
School

Drive

ton Av

Road
ate

Parrs Wood RD

Parrs Wd Av

The
Barlow
RC High
School

3

Superstore

Hurstfold Av

Queensway

Saddlewood Av

KINGSWAY A34

Lynnwood

Bolton
Rd

Kinburn
Rd

Burnage Lane

Ashdene Rd

Berwick Av

Lineham

Wells

Harwood
Crossgate

Cloister Rd

Woodlands Road

New Beech Road

Poplar
Lyme

School

St. Jhn

Br Cl

Grundy

Hawthorne

PO

WINSLOW RD
Didsbury
CC

A5145

PARRS WOOD LANE

A5145

Travelodge

East
Didsbury

WILMSLOW ROAD

East
Didsbury
Station

4

Cineworld

Parrs Wood
Technology
College

Chapel St

Green
Pastures

Meltham Rd
Meltham Close

Burnage
Rugby
Club

Statio

Bletch

Battersea

A34

Gsworth Av

Oakdale
Dr
Avalon
Dr

Crandon
Dr

Wood Rd

Glynn Rd

M 3 90

PER RD

3 86

Barton
Rd

Barton Rd

A

B

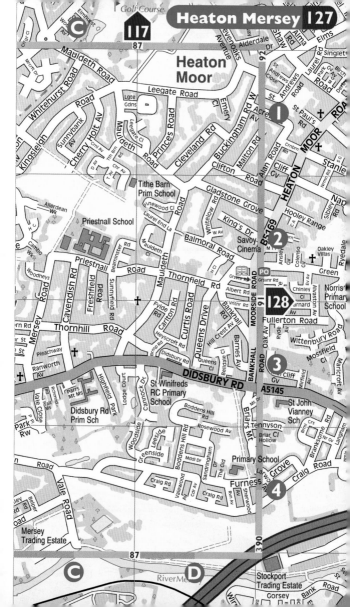

128

Heaton Moor

118 cal Centre

B Heaton Chapel Station

Innkeeper Lodge

SK4 Heaton Moor RUFC

Heaton Norris

STO

127

I

2

3

4

Didsbury Rd

A5145

DIDSBURY ROAD

A5145

Norris Bank Primary School

Green Lane Ind Est

M60

Junction 1

1 grid square represents 500 metres

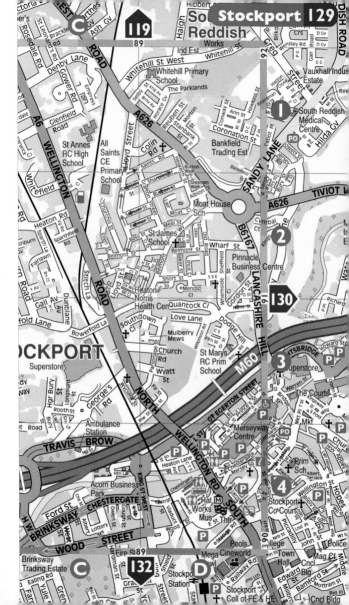

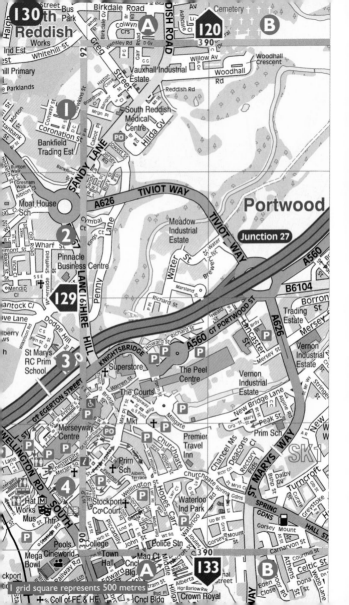

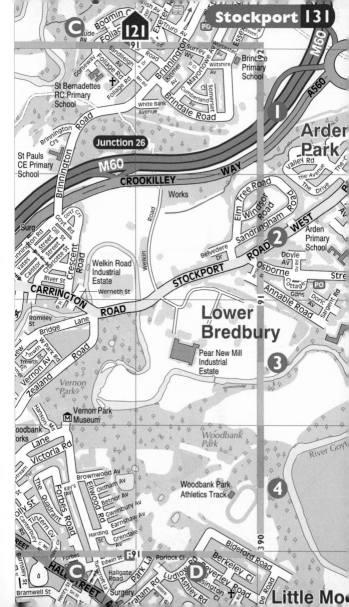

C

Bodmin Cl
Jude Av
Foliage
Cleish Av
Eyetou Rd
Truro St
Surrey
Worcester
Essex
PO

121
91
Corseway
Foliage Rd
Sandileigh Av
Foliage Av
Mayorlowe Av
Wiltshire Av
Somerset Av

St Bernadettes
RC Primary
School
White Bank
Avenue
Brinnington Road
Kinmel Av
Cumberland Av
Brindale Road

Brincliffe
Primary
School

**Arden
Park**

St Pauls
CE Primary
School

Brinnington Crs

Junction 26

M60

Valley Rd
The Avenue
The Drive

CROOKILLEY
WAY

Works

Elm Tree Road
Windsor Road
Sandringham Road

ROAD
WEST

Arden
Primary
School

Doyle Av
Dv Rd

Golf Crs
Golf Rd
W Street
Street
Charlotte St
Calstor St
Yates St
River St
Crescent Road

Welkin Road
Industrial
Estate

Welkin Road
Werneth St

Belvedere Dr

STOCKPORT

ROAD

Osborne
Octagon Gdns
PO
Doric St
Sargent Rd
Street

Annable Road

CARRINGTON

ROAD

Romiley St
Bridge Lane
W Park Rd
Tmwth Av
Tmwth Gn
Vernon Av
Zealand

**Lower
Bredbury**

Pear New Mill
Industrial
Estate

Vernon
Park

Hanson Ms
Vernon Park
M Museum

Woodbank
Park

River Goyt

Woodbank
Works
Lane

Victoria Rd
The Quadrant
Forbes Road
Brownwood Av
Oldham Av
Elwood Rd
Betnor Av
Gwenbury Av
Kay's Av
Harding St
Earnshaw Av
Grendale Av

Woodbank Park
Athletics Track

Bideford Road
Berkeley Cl
Beverley Road
Waverley Road

River Goyt

Holly St
Tintern Cv
Canterbury Cl
C Ms

Forbes
Edwin St
F91
Porlock Cl
Park La
Ludlow Rd
Ashley Rd
Lissington Cl

C

D

Barnsley St
Bramwell St
Henry St
Turfpit St
Hallgate
Road
Surgery
Graham Rd

Kensington Cl

Little Mo

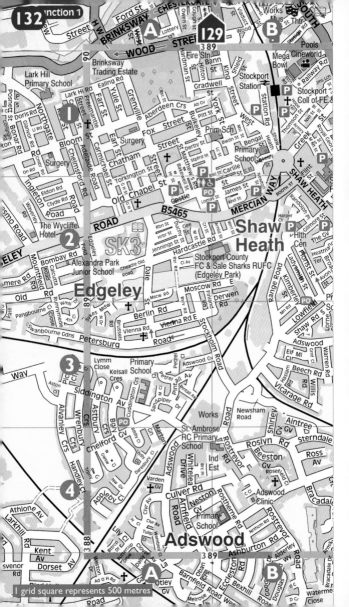

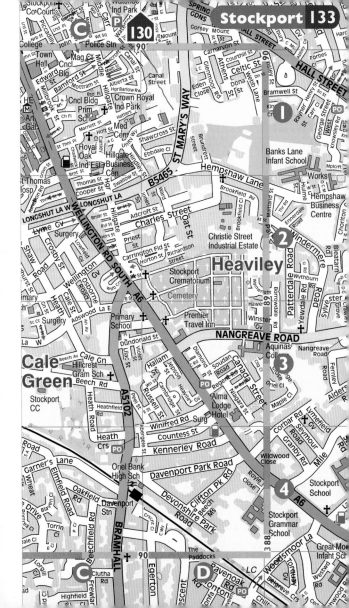

Abbey Hey	92	A4
Adswood	132	A4
Alder Forest	60	A1
Alkrington Garden Village	17	D3
Ancoats	5	E4
Ardwick	87	D2
Ashton-under-Lyne	77	D2
Ashton upon Mersey	108	A3
Bardsley	41	D4
Barton Upon Irwell	79	C1
Belle Vue	90	A4
Besses o' th' Barn	11	C2
Beswick	72	C1
Blackley	34	B4
Bradford	72	A3
Brinnington	121	C4
Broadoak Park	43	D4
Broughton Park	31	C4
Brunswick	9	E5
Burnage	116	B4
Busk	21	D1
Cale Green	133	C3
Castlefield	6	B2
Chadderton	19	D2
Charlestown	35	D2
Charlestown	67	C1
Cheetham Hill	52	A3
Chorlton-cum-Hardy	113	C2
Clayton	73	D2
Clifton	25	D2
Clifton Green	27	C3
Clifton Junction	27	D2
Collyhurst	53	C3
Copster Hill	40	B3
Crumpsall	32	A4
Daisy Nook	58	B4
Dales Brow	44	A3
Debdale	107	C1
Didsbury	125	C2
Droylsden	74	B4
Dumplington	78	B2
East Didsbury	126	A4
Eccles	63	D4
Ellesmere Park	62	B1
Failsworth	56	B2
Fairfield	92	B2
Fallowfield	115	C1
Firswood	99	C2
Fitton Hill	41	D3
Gorse Hill	97	D2
Gorton	105	D1
Greenside	76	A2
Guide Bridge	77	D4
Harpurhey	53	D2
Hathershaw	41	C2
Hazelhurst	43	C3
Heaton Chapel	118	B3
Heaton Mersey	126	B2
Heaton Moor	127	D1
Heaton Norris	128	B2
Heaviley	133	D2
Higher Blackley	33	D1
Higher Broughton	50	A3
Hilton Park	29	D3
Hollinwood	38	B4
Hulme	85	D3
Irlams o' th' Height	46	B4
Kersal	30	A4
Kirkhams	12	A3
Levenshulme	118	B1
Lime Side	40	A4
Little Bolton	64	A3
Littlemoss	76	B1
Longsight	89	C4
Lower Bredbury	131	D3
Lower Broughton	67	D1
Lower Kersal	48	B3
Manchester	2	A5
Miles Platting	71	C2
Monton	62	A2
Moorclose	18	B1
Moorside	44	A2
Moss Side	101	C1
Moston	36	A4
Mumps	22	B2
New Moston	55	D1
Newton Heath	54	B4
Newtown	25	D4
Nimble Nook	38	B1
North Reddish	106	B4
Oak Bank	11	D2
Oldham	23	C1
Old Trafford	84	A4
Openshaw	90	B1
Ordsall	84	A2
Patricroft	61	D3
Pendlebury	46	B2
Pendleton	66	B2
Portwood	130	B2
Prestwich	29	C1
Rainsough	29	D4
Reddish	119	C1
Rhodes	15	C2
Roe Green	42	A1
Rusholme	103	C2
St George's	6	A5
Sale	110	A3
Salford	66	A4
Salford Quays	82	B2
Sedgley Park	30	B3
Seedley	65	D2
Shaw Heath	132	B2
Simister	13	D1
South Reddish	119	D4
Stockport	128	B3
Strangeways	69	C1
Stretford	109	C1
Swinton	44	A1
Swinton Park	46	A3
Taunton	59	D4
Trafford Park	80	B4
Urmston	94	B1
Wardley	24	B4
Weaste	65	D4
Werneth	21	C3
West Didsbury	113	D4
Westwood Park	60	B1
Whalley Range	100	B3
Whitefield	10	B2
White Gate	38	A2
Winton	61	D2
Withington	115	D3
Woodhouses	57	D3
Worsley	42	A2

USING THE STREET INDEX

Street names are listed alphabetically. Each street name is followed by its postal town or area locality, the Postcode District, the page number, and the reference to the square in which the name is found.

Standard index entries are shown as follows:

Abberley Dr *NEWH/MOS* M40 ....**37** C3

Street names and selected addresses not shown on the map due to scale restrictions are shown in the index with an asterisk:

Abbeyfield Sq *OP/CLY* M11 * **90** A1

GENERAL ABBREVIATIONS

ACC	ACCESS	EMB	EMBANKMENT
ALY	ALLEY	EMBY	EMBASSY
AP	APPROACH	ESP	ESPLANADE
AR	ARCADE	EST	ESTATE
ASS	ASSOCIATION	EX	EXCHANGE
AV	AVENUE	EXPY	EXPRESSWAY
BCH	BEACH	EXT	EXTENSION
BLDS	BUILDINGS	F/O	FLYOVER
BND	BEND	FC	FOOTBALL CLUB
BNK	BANK	FK	FORK
BR	BRIDGE	FLD	FIELD
BRK	BROOK	FLDS	FIELDS
BTM	BOTTOM	FLS	FALLS
BUS	BUSINESS	FM	FARM
BVD	BOULEVARD	FT	FORT
BY	BYPASS	FTS	FLATS
CATH	CATHEDRAL	FWY	FREEWAY
CEM	CEMETERY	FY	FERRY
CEN	CENTRE	GA	GATE
CFT	CROFT	GAL	GALLERY
CH	CHURCH	GDN	GARDEN
CHA	CHASE	GDNS	GARDENS
CHYD	CHURCHYARD	GLD	GLADE
CIR	CIRCLE	GLN	GLEN
CIRC	CIRCUS	GN	GREEN
CL	CLOSE	GND	GROUND
CLFS	CLIFFS	GRA	GRANGE
CMP	CAMP	GRG	GARAGE
CNR	CORNER	GT	GREAT
CO	COUNTY	GTWY	GATEWAY
COLL	COLLEGE	GV	GROVE
COM	COMMON	HGR	HIGHER
COMM	COMMISSION	HL	HILL
CON	CONVENT	HLS	HILLS
COT	COTTAGE	HO	HOUSE
COTS	COTTAGES	HOL	HOLLOW
CP	CAPE	HOSP	HOSPITAL
CPS	COPSE	HRB	HARBOUR
CR	CREEK	HTH	HEATH
CREM	CREMATORIUM	HTS	HEIGHTS
CRS	CRESCENT	HVN	HAVEN
CSWY	CAUSEWAY	HWY	HIGHWAY
CT	COURT	IMP	IMPERIAL
CTRL	CENTRAL	IN	INLET
CTS	COURTS	IND EST	INDUSTRIAL ESTATE
CTYD	COURTYARD	INF	INFIRMARY
CUTT	CUTTINGS	INFO	INFORMATION
CV	COVE	INT	INTERCHANGE
CYN	CANYON	IS	ISLAND
DEPT	DEPARTMENT	JCT	JUNCTION
DL	DALE	JTY	JETTY
DM	DAM	KG	KING
DR	DRIVE	KNL	KNOLL
DRO	DROVE	L	LAKE
DRY	DRIVEWAY	LA	LANE
DWGS	DWELLINGS	LDG	LODGE
E	EAST	LGT	LIGHT

LK	LOCK	RBT	ROUNDABOUT
LKS	LAKES	RD	ROAD
LNDG	LANDING	RDG	RIDGE
LTL	LITTLE	REP	REPUBLIC
LWR	LOWER	RES	RESERVOIR
MAG	MAGISTRATE	RFC	RUGBY FOOTBALL CLUB
MAN	MANSIONS	RI	RISE
MD	MEAD	RP	RAMP
MDW	MEADOWS	RW	ROW
MEM	MEMORIAL	S	SOUTH
MI	MILL	SCH	SCHOOL
MKT	MARKET	SE	SOUTH EAST
MKTS	MARKETS	SER	SERVICE AREA
ML	MALL	SH	SHORE
MNR	MANOR	SHOP	SHOPPING
MS	MEWS	SKWY	SKYWAY
MSN	MISSION	SMT	SUMMIT
MT	MOUNT	SOC	SOCIETY
MTN	MOUNTAIN	SP	SPUR
MTS	MOUNTAINS	SPR	SPRING
MUS	MUSEUM	SQ	SQUARE
MWY	MOTORWAY	ST	STREET
N	NORTH	STN	STATION
NE	NORTH EAST	STR	STREAM
NW	NORTH WEST	STRD	STRAND
O/P	OVERPASS	SW	SOUTH WEST
OFF	OFFICE	TDG	TRADING
ORCH	ORCHARD	TER	TERRACE
OV	OVAL	THWY	THROUGHWAY
PAL	PALACE	TNL	TUNNEL
PAS	PASSAGE	TOLL	TOLLWAY
PAV	PAVILION	TPK	TURNPIKE
PDE	PARADE	TR	TRACK
PH	PUBLIC HOUSE	TRL	TRAIL
PK	PARK	TWR	TOWER
PKWY	PARKWAY	U/P	UNDERPASS
PL	PLACE	UNI	UNIVERSITY
PLN	PLAIN	UPR	UPPER
PLNS	PLAINS	V	VALE
PLZ	PLAZA	VA	VALLEY
POL	POLICE STATION	VIAD	VIADUCT
PR	PRINCE	VIL	VILLA
PREC	PRECINCT	VIS	VISTA
PREP	PREPARATORY	VLG	VILLAGE
PRIM	PRIMARY	VLS	VILLAS
PROM	PROMENADE	VW	VIEW
PRS	PRINCESS	W	WEST
PRT	PORT	WD	WOOD
PT	POINT	WHF	WHARF
PTH	PATH	WK	WALK
PZ	PIAZZA	WKS	WALKS
QD	QUADRANT	WLS	WELLS
QU	QUEEN	WY	WAY
QY	QUAY	YD	YARD
R	RIVER	YHA	YOUTH HOSTEL

POSTCODE TOWNS AND AREA ABBREVIATIONS

ANC	Ancoats	DID/WITH	Didsbury/Withington
AULW	Ashton-under-Lyne west	DROY	Droylsden
BKLY	Blackley	DTN/ASHW	Denton/Audenshaw
BNG/LEV	Burnage/Levenshulme	ECC	Eccles
BRO	Broughton	EDGY/DAV	Edgeley/Davenport
BRUN/LGST	Brunswick/Longsight	FAIL	Failsworth
CCHDY	Chorlton-cum-Hardy	FWTH	Farnworth
CHAD	Chadderton	GTN	Gorton
CHD/CHDH	Cheadle (Gtr. Man)/	HTNM	Heaton Moor
	Cheadle Hulme	HULME	Hulme
CHH	Cheetham Hill	MDTN	Middleton (Gtr. Man)
CMANE	Central Manchester east	MPL/ROM	Marple/Romiley
CMANW	Central Manchester west	NEWH/MOS	Newton Heath/Moston
CSLFD	Central Salford	NTHM/RTH	Northern Moor/Roundthorn

OFTN	Offerton
OLD	Oldham
OLDE	Oldham east
OLDS	Oldham south
OLDTF/WHR	Old Trafford/Whalley Range
OP/CLY	Openshaw/Clayton
ORD	Ordsall
PWCH	Prestwich
RAD	Radcliffe
RDSH	Reddish
RUSH/FAL	Rusholme/Fallowfield
SALE	Sale

SALQ	Salford Quays
SLFD	Salford
STKP	Stockport
STRET	Stretford
SWIN	Swinton
TRPK	Trafford Park
TRPK	Trafford Park
URM	Urmston
WALK	Walkden
WGTN/LGST	West Gorton/Longsight
WHTF	Whitefield
WYTH/NTH	Wythenshawe/Northenden

Index - streets

Abb - Agn

A

Abberley Dr NEWH/MOS M40	37	C3
Abberton Rd DID/WITH M20	114	B3
Abbey Cl STRET M32	95	C2
Abbeydale Rd NEWH/MOS M40	55	D1
Abbey Dr SWIN M27	44	B1
Abbeyfield Sq OP/CLY M11 *	90	A1
Abbey Gv CHAD OL9	38	B1
ECC M30	62	B3
Abbey Hey La GTN M18	91	D3
Abbey Lawn OLDTF/WHR M16	99	C4
Abbey Rd DROY M43	75	C2
FAIL M35	58	A1
SALE M33	108	B3
Abbeyville Wk HULME M15 *	85	D4
Abbeywood Av GTN M18 *	106	B1
Abbots Cl SALE M33	110	A4
Abbotsford Rd CCHDY M21	99	C4
CHAD OL9 *	19	D1
Abbotside Cl OLDTF/WHR M16	100	A2
Abercarn Cl CHH M8	51	D2
Abercrombie Ct SALE M33	110	A4
Aberdaron Wk BRUN/LGST M13	9	F1
Aberdeen Crs EDGY/DAV SK3	132	A1
Aberdeen Gv EDGY/DAV SK3	132	A1
Aberdeen St BRUN/LGST M13	87	C4
Abergele Rd RUSH/FAL M14	116	B1
Abergele St OFTN SK2	133	C3
Abernant Cl OP/CLY M11	72	A4
Abersoch Av RUSH/FAL M14	116	B1
Abingdon Cl CHAD OL9 *	39	C1
Abingdon Rd RDSH SK5	120	A1
URM M41	94	B2
Abingdon St CMANE M1	8	A1
Abney Rd HTNM SK4	118	B4
Abram Cl RUSH/FAL M14	101	C4
Abram St SLFD M6	48	A3
Absalom Dr CHH M8	51	C2
Acacia Av SWIN M27	44	B3
Acacia Dr SLFD M6	64	B1
Acacia Rd RDSH SK5	130	A1
Acacia Rd OLDS OL8	40	A1
The Acacias URM M41 *	94	B3
Academy Wk HULME M15 *	85	D4
Ace Ml CHAD OL9 *	38	A1
Acer Gv BRO M7	50	B4
Acheson St GTN M18	91	C4
Ackers St BRUN/LGST M13	87	C4
Ackroyd Av GTN M18	92	B3
Ackroyd St OP/CLY M11	91	D2
Ackworth Rd SWIN M27	25	D4
Acme Dr SWIN M27	46	A1
Acomb St HULME M15	87	C4
RUSH/FAL M14	102	A2

Acorn Cl BNG/LEV M19	117	C1
WHTF M45	11	C3
Acorn Wy OLD OL1 *	22	B2
Acrefield Av HTNM SK4	127	D1
URM M41	95	C1
Acresfield Av DTN/ASHW M34	76	A4
Acresfield Cl SWIN M27	45	D3
Acresfield Rd SLFD M6	47	C4
Acres Rd CCHDY M21	111	D1
Acre St CHAD OL9	39	C3
Acre Top Rd BKLY M9	15	C4
Acton Av NEWH/MOS M40	73	C1
Acton St OLD OL1	23	D1
Adair St CMANE M1	9	F1
Adams Av CCHDY M21	112	A3
Adamson Gdns DID/WITH M20	124	A2
Adamson Rd ECC M30	78	B1
Adamson Wk RUSH/FAL M14 *	102	A2
Adam St OLDS OL8	41	C3
Ada St BKLY M9	34	A4
Adbaston Rd STRET M32	80	B4
Adcroft St STKP SK1	133	C2
Addenbrook Rd CHH M8	50	B4
Addingham Cl BKLY M9	33	D1
Addington St ANC M4	4	C2
Addison Cl BRUN/LGST M13	87	D3
Addison Crs OLDTF/WHR M16	99	C4
Addison Rd STRET M32	96	A3
URM M41	94	A4
Adelaide St CHH M8	51	C4
ECC M30	62	A4
MDTN M24	17	C3
SWIN M27	44	A2
Adelphi St CSLFD M3	2	A3
Aden Cl WGTN/LGST M12	88	A1
Adlington Dr STRET M32	98	A1
Adlington St WGTN/LGST M12	88	A1
Adlington Wk STKP SK1 *	129	C4
Adrian St NEWH/MOS M40	54	B2
Adria Rd DID/WITH M20	125	D2
Adscombe Av OLDTF/WHR M16	100	B4
Adstock Wk NEWH/MOS M40	5	E1
Adstone Cl ANC M4	71	C4
Adswood Gv EDGY/DAV SK3	132	A3
Adswood La East OFTN SK2	133	C3
Adswood La West EDGY/DAV SK3	132	B3
Adswood Rd EDGY/DAV SK3	132	A4
Adswood St NEWH/MOS M40	71	D3
Adswood Ter EDGY/DAV SK3	132	B3
Aegean Cl BRO M7	49	D2
Agecroft Enterprise Pk SWIN M27	47	D2
Agecroft Rd SWIN M27	47	D1
WHTF M45	10	A3
Agecroft Rd East PWCH M25	29	D3
Agecroft Rd West PWCH M25	29	D3
Agnes Cl CHAD OL9	39	D1
Agnes St BNG/LEV M19	104	B3
BRO M7	51	C2

CHAD OL9 .... **21** C4
Agnew Pl *SLFD* M6 .... **66** B1
Agnew Rd *GTN* M18 .... **90** B4
Aigburth Gv *RDSH* SK5 .... **106** B3
Ailsa Cl *NEWH/MOS* M40 .... **53** C4
Ainsbrook Av *BKLY* M9 .... **36** A2
Ainsdale Av *BRO* M7 .... **31** C4
Ainsdale Cl *OLDS* OL8 .... **40** A1
Ainsdale Gv *RDSH* SK5 .... **120** A1
Ainsdale St *WGTN/LGST* M12 .... **89** C3
Ainsford Rd *DID/WITH* M20 .... **116** A4
Ainsty Rd *RUSH/FAL* M14 .... **101** D1
Aintree Gv *EDGY/DAV* SK3 .... **132** B4
Aintree St *OP/CLY* M11 .... **73** C4
Aintree Wk *CHAD* OL9 * **21** D2
Airton Cl *NEWH/MOS* M40 .... **70** B2
Aitken St *BNG/LEV* M19 * **105** D4
Aked Cl *WGTN/LGST* M12 .... **88** B3
Alan Av *FAIL* M35 .... **57** C4
Alanbrooke Wk *HULME* M15 * **85** D4
Alan Rd *DID/WITH* M20 .... **115** D3
  HTNM SK4 .... **128** A1
Alan Turing Wy *NEWH/MOS* M40 .... **71** D2
Alasdair Cl *CHAD* OL9 .... **20** A1
Alba Cl *ECC* M30 .... **62** A4
Alban St *BRO* M7 .... **50** A4
Albany Av *OP/CLY* M11 .... **92** A2
Albany Rd *CCHDY* M21 .... **99** C4
  ECC M30 .... **61** C2
Albany St *MDTN* M24 .... **18** A2
Albany Wy *SLFD* M6 .... **66** B2
Alba Wy *STRET* M32 .... **80** B3
Albemarle Av *DID/WITH* M20 .... **114** B3
Albemarle Rd *CCHDY* M21 .... **111** D1
Albemarle St *RUSH/FAL* M14 .... **101** D1
Albermarle Rd *SWIN* M27 .... **44** B2
Alberta St *STKP* SK1 .... **133** C1
Albert Av *GTN* M18 .... **106** B1
  PWCH M25 .... **30** B1
  URM M41 .... **94** B3
Albert Cl *WHTF* M45 .... **11** D1
Albert Gdns *NEWH/MOS* M40 .... **56** A4
Albert Gv *WGTN/LGST* M12 .... **104** B1
Albert Hill St *DID/WITH* M20 * **125** C2
Albert Park Rd *BRO* M7 .... **49** D4
Albert Pl *BRUN/LGST* M13 .... **104** A2
Albert Rd *ECC* M30 .... **63** C3
  HTNM SK4 .... **127** D2
  WHTF M45 .... **11** D1
Albert Sq *CMANW* M2 .... **3** F5
Albert St *CHAD* OL9 .... **39** C2
  DROY M43 .... **76** A4
  EDGY/DAV SK3 .... **129** A4
  MDTN M24 .... **18** A2
  OLDS OL8 .... **39** C4
  OLDTF/WHR M16 .... **84** B3
  OP/CLY M11 .... **72** A4
  PWCH M25 * **12** B4
Albert St West *FAIL* M35 .... **56** A3
Albert Ter *STKP* SK1 .... **130** A4
Albine St *NEWH/MOS* M40 .... **54** A1
Albion Cl *HTNM* SK4 .... **129** D2
Albion Dr *DROY* M43 .... **75** D3
Albion Fold *DROY* M43 .... **75** D3
Albion Pl *BRO* M7 * **49** D4
  ORD M5 .... **67** D3
  PWCH M25 .... **29** D1
Albion Rd *RUSH/FAL* M14 .... **102** B4
Albion St *CHAD* OL9 .... **20** B3
  CMANE M1 .... **7** E2
  FAIL M35 .... **56** B2
  OLD OL1 .... **23** C2
  OLDTF/WHR M16 .... **100** A1
  SWIN M27 .... **45** D1
Albion Wy *ORD* M5 .... **67** C4
Albury Dr *BNG/LEV* M19 .... **126** A3
Albyns Av *CHH* M8 .... **51** D2

Alcester Cl *MDTN* M24 .... **18** A3
Alcester St *CHAD* OL9 .... **38** B2
Aldborough Cl *DID/WITH* M20 .... **115** C3
Aldbourne Cl *NEWH/MOS* M40 .... **53** C4
Aldcroft St *GTN* M18 * **92** A3
Alden Cl *WHTF* M45 .... **11** D1
Alder Ct *CHH* M8 * **32** A4
Alderdale Dr *DROY* M43 .... **74** A3
  HTNM SK4 .... **117** D4
Alder Dr *SWIN* M27 .... **24** B4
Alderfield Rd *STRET* M32 .... **98** A4
Alder Forest Av *ECC* M30 .... **60** B1
Alderglen Rd *CHH* M8 .... **51** C3
Alder Gv *STRET* M32 .... **97** D3
Alder La *OLDS* OL8 .... **40** A3
Alderley Rd *RDSH* SK5 .... **120** A4
Alderman Sq *WGTN/LGST* M12 .... **88** B1
Aldermary Rd *CCHDY* M21 .... **113** C4
Aldermaston Gv *BKLY* M9 .... **15** C3
Aldermoor Cl *OP/CLY* M11 .... **90** B1
Alder Rd *FAIL* M35 .... **57** D3
Alderside Rd *BKLY* M9 .... **53** C1
Aldersley Av *BKLY* M9 .... **33** C1
Alderson St *CHAD* OL9 .... **22** B2
  SLFD M6 .... **66** B1
Alder St *ECC* M30 .... **60** B1
  SLFD M6 .... **66** A3
Aldford Cl *DID/WITH* M20 * **125** D2
Aldham Av *NEWH/MOS* M40 .... **73** D1
Aldred Cl *CHH* M8 .... **52** A3
Aldred St *ECC* M30 .... **61** D4
  FAIL M35 .... **56** B2
  ORD M5 .... **67** C3
Aldsworth Dr *NEWH/MOS* M40 .... **53** D4
Aldwick Av *DID/WITH* M20 .... **125** D2
Aldwych Av *RUSH/FAL* M14 .... **102** A3
Aldwyn Park Rd *DTN/ASHW* M34 ...... **93** D2
Alexander Av *FAIL* M35 .... **57** D1
Alexander Gdns *BRO* M7 .... **68** A1
Alexander St *SLFD* M6 * **65** D3
Alexandra Av *RUSH/FAL* M14 .... **101** C3
  WHTF M45 .... **11** D1
Alexandra Dr *BNG/LEV* M19 .... **117** C2
Alexandra Ms *OLDS* OL8 * **23** C4
Alexandra Rd *ECC* M30 .... **61** C4
  HTNM SK4 .... **128** A1
  OLDS OL8 .... **23** D4
  OLDTF/WHR M16 .... **100** B1
Alexandra Rd South *OLDTF/WHR* M16 ... **100** B2
Alexandra St *BRO* M7 * **68** A2
  OLDS OL8 .... **23** D4
Alexandra Ter *BNG/LEV* M19 .... **104** B4
Alexandria Dr *AULW* OL7 .... **77** D3
Alford Av *DID/WITH* M20 .... **114** B3
Alford Rd *HTNM* SK4 .... **118** A3
Alford St *CHAD* OL9 .... **39** C3
Alfred Av *WALK* M28 .... **43** C2
Alfred James Cl *NEWH/MOS* M40 * **5** D1
Alfred St *BKLY* M9 .... **53** C1
  CHAD OL9 .... **21** D3
  ECC M30 .... **62** A4
Algernon St *ECC* M30 .... **62** A2
  SWIN M27 .... **44** A1
Alice St *SWIN* M27 .... **46** A1
Alison Kelly Cl *BKLY* M9 .... **54** A1
Alison St *RUSH/FAL* M14 .... **101** C2
Alker Rd *NEWH/MOS* M40 * **71** C2
Alkrington Gn *MDTN* M24 .... **17** C3
Alkrington Hall Rd North *MDTN* M24 ... **17** C3
Alkrington Hall Rd South *MDTN* M24 ... **16** B3
Alkrington Park Rd *MDTN* M24 .... **16** B2
Allandale Rd *BNG/LEV* M19 * **104** B4
Allan Roberts Cl *BKLY* M9 .... **34** A4
Allanson Rd *WYTH/NTH* M22 .... **123** D4
Aldis Cl *WGTN/LGST* M12 .... **88** B4
Allenby Rd *SWIN* M27 .... **43** D3
Allen Dale Av *CSLFD* M3 .... **2** A2

Allen Rd URM M41	95	C4
Allen St OLDS OL8	22	A3
Allerdean Wk HTNM SK4	127	C2
Allerford St OLDTF/WHR M16	100	B1
Allerton Wk BRUN/LGST M13 *	87	C3
Allesley Dr BRO M7	51	C4
Alligin Cl CHAD OL9	20	B1
Allingham St BRUN/LGST M13	103	D1
Allington Dr ECC M30	62	B1
Alliott Wk HULME M15	85	D4
Allison Gv ECC M30	61	C4
Allison St CHH M8	51	C4
All Saints Ct STRET M32 *	96	A3
All Saints' Rd HTNM SK4	129	C2
All Saints' St NEWH/MOS M40	55	D4
Alma Rd BNG/LEV M19	117	D1
HTNM SK4	118	A4
Alma St ECC M30	63	C4
Alminstone Cl NEWH/MOS M40	74	A1
Almond Cl FAIL M35	57	C3
SLFD M6	66	B3
Almond Dr SALE M33	108	A3
Almond St NEWH/MOS M40 *	70	A1
Alms Hill Rd CHH M8	51	D2
Alnwick Rd BKLY M9	16	A4
Alpha Pl HULME M15 *	7	D3
Alpha Rd STRET M32	96	B3
Alpha St OP/CLY M11	91	D2
SLFD M6	66	A2
Alpha St West SLFD M6	65	D2
Alphonsus St OLDTF/WHR M16	99	D1
Alpine Rd STKP SK1	130	B4
Alpine St OP/CLY M11	73	C2
Alport Av OLDTF/WHR M16	99	D3
Airesford Rd MDTN M24	17	C4
SLFD M6	47	C4
Alsager Cl CCHDY M21	112	A3
Alsop Av BRO M7 *	49	C2
Alston Av STRET M32	96	A2
Alstone Rd HTNM SK4	118	B3
Alston Gdns BNG/LEV M19	117	C4
Alston Rd GTN M18	91	D4
Altair Pl BRO M7	67	D1
Aitcar Gv RDSH SK5	106	B3
Alton Sq OP/CLY M11	91	D2
Alton St OLDS OL8	41	C2
Altrincham St CMANE M1	8	C2
Alvan Sq OP/CLY M11 *	91	D2
Alvaston Av HTNM SK4	128	A2
Alvaston Rd GTN M18	106	B1
Aveley Av DID/WITH M20	115	D4
Alverstone Rd DID/WITH M20	115	D3
Alwinton Av HTNM SK4	126	B2
Alworth Rd BKLY M9	16	A4
Alwyn Dr BRUN/LGST M13	103	D1
Amberley Wk CHAD OL9	21	D2
Amberwood CHAD OL9	19	D3
Ambleside Rd RDSH SK5	120	A3
Ambrose Ct WYTH/NTH M22 *	123	C4
Ambrose Dr DID/WITH M20	123	D1
Ambrose St WGTN/LGST M12	89	D2
Ambush St OP/CLY M11	92	A2
Amersham Cl URM M41	78	A4
Amersham Pl BNG/LEV M19	117	D3
Amersham St ORD M5	66	A4
Amesbury Gv RDSH SK5	120	A4
Amesbury Rd BKLY M9	34	B1
Amherst Rd DID/WITH M20	115	D2
Ammon Wrigley Cl OLD OL1 *	23	C2
Amory St WGTN/LGST M12	9	E2
Amos Av NEWH/MOS M40	73	C1
Amos St BKLY M9	54	A2
SLFD M6	65	D3
Ampney Cl ECC M30	61	C4
Amwell St CHH M8	52	A2
Anaconda Dr CSLFD M3	2	C1

Anchorage Quay SALQ M50	83	D1
Anchorage Rd URM M41	95	D4
Anchor Cl BNG/LEV M19	105	D4
Anchor Ct CHH M8 *	32	A4
Anchorside Cl CCHDY M21	112	A2
Anchor St OLD OL1	23	C1
Ancoats Gv ANC M4	71	C4
Ancoats Gv North ANC M4	71	C4
Ancroft St HULME M15	85	D3
Andoc Av ECC M30	63	C4
Andover Av MDTN M24	18	A4
Andover St ECC M30	61	D4
Andre St OP/CLY M11 *	73	D3
Andrew Rd BKLY M9	34	A4
Andrew St CHAD OL9	20	B1
DROY M43	76	B1
FAIL M35	56	B1
MDTN M24	18	B2
Anerley Rd DID/WITH M20	125	C1
Anfield Rd NEWH/MOS M40	37	C4
SALE M33	109	C4
Angela St HULME M15	6	B4
Angel St ANC M4	4	B1
Anglesea Av OFTN SK2	133	C3
Angleside Av BNG/LEV M19	126	B1
Angora Dr CSLFD M3	2	A1
Anita St ANC M4	5	D2
Annable Rd DROY M43	76	A4
GTN M18	91	D3
Annald Sq DROY M43	92	B1
Anne Nuttall Rd HULME M15	6	B4
Annesley Rd NEWH/MOS M40	37	D4
Annie St ORD M5	65	D3
Annisdale Cl ECC M30	61	C3
Annis St BKLY M9	53	D2
Ann St RDSH SK5	129	D1
Anscombe Cl NEWH/MOS M40	71	C2
Ansdell Av CCHDY M21	112	A2
Ansdell Dr DROY M43	74	B3
Ansdell Rd RDSH SK5	107	C4
Ansdell St CHH M8	51	D2
Ansell Cl GTN M18	91	C3
Anselms Ct OLDS OL8	39	D1
Ansleigh Av CHH M8	32	B4
Ansley Gv HTNM SK4	118	B4
Anslow Cl NEWH/MOS M40	53	C4
Anson Av SWIN M27	44	B3
Anson Rd DTN/ASHW M34	107	C3
RUSH/FAL M14	103	C1
SWIN M27	44	B3
Anson St ECC M30	61	C2
Answell Av CHH M8	32	B3
Antares Av BRO M7	50	B4
Anthony Cl WGTN/LGST M12	88	B2
Antilles Cl WGTN/LGST M12	104	B1
Antrim Cl BNG/LEV M19	126	A3
Anvil Wy OLD OL1 *	22	B2
Apfel La CHAD OL9	21	C2
Apperley Gra ECC M30	62	B1
Appian Wy BRO M7	50	B4
Appleby Cl EDGY/DAV SK3	132	A4
Appledore Wk CHAD OL9	21	C3
Appleford Dr CHH M8	52	A3
Appleton Rd HTNM SK4	119	C3
Apple Tree Ct ORD M5	66	B3
Apple Wy MDTN M24	18	A3
Applewood CHAD OL9	19	C2
Appleyard Cl SWIN M27	47	C1
Apsley Gv WGTN/LGST M12	9	F5
Apsley St STKP SK1	130	A4
Aquarius La SLFD M6 *	67	D1
Aquarius St HULME M15	86	B4
Arbor Av BNG/LEV M19	117	D2
Arbor Dr BNG/LEV M19	117	C2
Arbor Gv DROY M43	75	C2
Arbory Av NEWH/MOS M40	55	C1
Arbour Cl SLFD M6	66	A2

Arbroath St *DROY* M43 ....74 B4
Archer Pk *MDTN* M24 ....16 B1
Archer Pl *STRET* M32 ....95 C3
Archer St *OP/CLY* M11 ....72 B3
Archie St *ORD* M5 ....83 D2
Archway *HULME* M15 ....86 A4
Arcon Dr *OLDTF/WHR* M16 ....100 B2
Ardale Av *NEWH/MOS* M40 ....36 B3
Ardcombe Av *BKLY* M9 ....15 D4
Ardeen Wk *BRUN/LGST* M13 ....9 E5
Arden Av *MDTN* M24 ....18 A4
Arden Gv *NEWH/MOS* M40 ....36 A4
Ardens Cl *SWIN* M27 ....25 C3
Arden St *CHAD* OL9 ....38 B2
Ardent Wy *PWCH* M25 ....30 A4
Ardern Gv *STKP* SK1 ....133 C1
Ardern Rd *CHH* M8 ....32 A4
Ardern Wk *STKP* SK1 *.............................129 D4
Ardwick Gn North *WGTN/LGST* M12 ....9 F4
Ardwick Gn South *BRUN/LGST* M13 ....9 E3
Ardwick Ter *WGTN/LGST* M12 ....88 A1
Argus St *OLDS* OL8 ....39 D3
Argyle Av *RUSH/FAL* M14 ....103 C3
    WHTF M45 ....11 D1
Argyle St *DROY* M43 ....75 D4
    GTN M18 ....91 C4
    SWIN M27 ....44 B2
Argyll Av *STRET* M32 ....96 A3
Argyll Cl *FAIL* M35 ....58 A2
Argyll Park Rd *FAIL* M35 ....58 A2
Argyll Rd *CHAD* OL9 ....38 A2
Arkendale Cl *FAIL* M55 * 58 B2
Arkle Dr *CHAD* OL9 ....20 A1
Arkley Wk *BRUN/LGST* M13 ....9 D5
Ark St *BNG/LEV* M19 ....104 B3
Arkwright St *CHAD* OL9 ....21 D1
Arley Av *DID/WITH* M20 ....114 A4
Arley Moss Wk *BRUN/LGST* M13 * 9 D4
Arlington Av *PWCH* M25 ....30 A3
    SWIN M27 ....44 A3
Arlington Rd *STRET* M32 ....96 A4
Arlington St *CHH* M8 ....32 A4
    CSLFD M3 ....2 B1
Arliss Av *BNG/LEV* M19 ....117 D1
Armadale Av *BKLY* M9 ....35 D1
Armitage Cl *MDTN* M24 ....16 A2
    OLDS OL8 ....39 D2
Armitage St *ECC* M30 ....61 D4
Armour Pl *BKLY* M9 ....33 D3
Armoury Dr *EDGY/DAV* SK3 ....132 B1
Arnesby Av *SALE* M33 ....110 B3
Arne St *CHAD* OL9 * 20 B4
Arnfield Rd *DID/WITH* M20 ....9 A1
    EDGY/DAV SK3 ....132 A4
Arnold Dr *DROY* M43 ....75 D4
Arnold Rd *OLDTF/WHR* M16 ....100 B4
Arnold St *EDGY/DAV* SK3 ....132 B2
    OLD OL1 ....23 D1
Arnott Crs *HULME* M15 ....86 A4
Arnside Av *CHAD* OL9 ....20 B4
    HTNM SK4 ....119 C3
Arnside Dr *SLFD* M6 ....64 A3
Arnside Gv *SALE* M33 ....109 C4
Arnside Wk *RUSH/FAL* M14 ....102 A3
Arran Av *OLDS* OL8 ....41 C2
    STRET M32 ....95 C3
Arrandale Ct *URM* M41 * 94 A2
Arran Gdns *URM* M41 ....78 B4
Arran St *BRO* M7 ....50 A3
    NEWH/MOS M40 ....54 A1
Arras Gv *RDSH* SK5 ....107 C2
Arreton Sq *RUSH/FAL* M14 ....103 C2
Arrowfield Rd *CCHDY* M21 ....113 C3
Arrow St *BRO* M7 ....50 A4
Arthog Rd *DID/WITH* M20 ....125 D3
Arthur Rd *OLDTF/WHR* M16 ....99 D2
Arthur St *ECC* M30 ....61 D4

    PWCH M25 ....29 C1
    RDSH SK5 ....119 D2
    SWIN M27 ....44 B3
Artillery St *CSLFD* M3 ....7 D1
Arundale Av *OLDTF/WHR* M16 ....100 B4
Arundel Av *WHTF* M45 ....12 A2
Arundel St *HULME* M15 ....85 B3
    SWIN M27 ....24 B4
Ascension Rd *BRO* M7 ....68 A1
Ascot Av *STRET* M32 ....98 A2
Ascot Cl *CHAD* OL9 ....21 D2
Ascot Pde *BNG/LEV* M19 ....117 C3
Ascot Rd *NEWH/MOS* M40 ....73 C1
Ascroft St *OLD* OL1 ....23 C3
Asgard Dr *ORD* M5 ....84 B1
Asgard Gv *ORD* M5 ....84 B1
Ashbourne Gv *BRO* M7 ....50 B1
    WHTF M45 ....10 B1
Ashbourne Rd *ECC* M30 ....64 B4
    SLFD M6 ....46 B4
    STRET M32 ....95 D1
Ashbourne Sq *OLDS* OL8 * 22 B4
Ashbridge *TRPK* M17 ....81 C3
Ashbridge Rd *FAIL* M35 ....58 A3
Ashbrook Farm Cl *RDSH* SK5 ....107 C3
Ashbrook La *RDSH* SK5 ....107 C3
Ashbrook St *OP/CLY* M11 ....92 B2
Ashburn Av *BNG/LEV* M19 ....117 C4
Ashburn Gv *HTNM* SK4 ....128 B2
Ashburn Rd *HTNM* SK4 ....128 B2
Ashburton Rd *EDGY/DAV* SK3 ....132 B4
Ashburton Rd West *TRPK* M17 ....79 D1
Ashbury Pl *NEWH/MOS* M40 * 71 D1
Ashby Av *BNG/LEV* M19 ....126 B1
Ashby Gv *WHTF* M45 ....11 D2
Ashcroft Av *SLFD* M6 ....65 D1
Ashcroft St *CHAD* OL9 ....20 B4
Ashdale Cl *RDSH* SK5 ....120 A4
Ashdale Dr *DID/WITH* M20 ....116 A4
Ashdene Rd *BNG/LEV* M19 ....126 A3
    DID/WITH M20 ....116 A3
Ashdown Av *BKLY* M9 ....34 A4
Ashdown Dr *SWIN* M27 ....45 D3
Ashdown Gv *BKLY* M9 ....34 A1
Ashdown Rd *HTNM* SK4 ....128 B2
Ashdown Ter *BKLY* M9 ....34 A1
Ash Dr *SWIN* M27 ....24 B3
Ashfield Cl *SLFD* M6 ....65 D1
Ashfield Dr *NEWH/MOS* M40 ....74 A1
Ashfield Gv *GTN* M18 * 107 C1
Ashfield Rd *BRUN/LGST* M13 ....103 D2
    SALE M33 ....109 C4
    URM M41 ....94 A3
Ashfield Sq *DROY* M43 ....75 C4
Ashford Av *ECC* M30 ....78 B1
    RDSH SK5 * 107 C3
    SWIN M27 ....45 D3
Ashford Gv *WALK* M28 ....42 A1
Ashford Rd *DID/WITH* M20 ....114 B2
    HTNM SK4 ....119 C3
Ashford Wk *CHAD* OL9 * 20 B3
Ash Gv *DROY* M43 ....92 B4
    HTNM SK4 ....119 C4
    PWCH M25 ....11 D3
    RUSH/FAL M14 ....103 D1
    STRET M32 ....109 D1
    SWIN M27 ....44 A4
Ashill Wk *CSLFD* M3 ....7 D1
Ashkirk St *GTN* M18 ....91 C4
Ashlands *SALE* M33 ....108 B4
Ashlands Av *NEWH/MOS* M40 ....36 B4
    WALK M28 ....43 D3
Ashlar Dr *WGTN/LGST* M12 ....88 A1
Ashley Av *OLDTF/WHR* M16 ....100 A3
    SWIN M27 ....44 A3
Ashley Court Dr *NEWH/MOS* M40 ....38 A4

Ashley Crs *SWIN* M27	44	A2
Ashley Dr *SWIN* M27	44	A3
Ashley La *BKLY* M9	54	A1
Ashley Ms *WHTF* M45	12	A2
Ashley Rd *DROY* M43	74	B3
Ashley St *ANC* M4	4	C1
CHAD OL9	21	D1
SLFD M6	65	D3
Ashlyn Gv *RUSH/FAL* M14	116	A1
Ashover Av *WGTN/LGST* M12 *	89	C3
Ashover St *STRET* M32	97	D2
Ashridge Dr *ECC* M30	78	B1
Ash Rd *DROY* M43	75	C3
DTN/ASHW M34	107	D1
Ash St *BKLY* M9	53	C2
FAIL M35	56	B1
SLFD M6	66	A3
Ashton Crs *CHAD* OL9	38	B2
Ashton Hill La *DROY* M43	92	B1
Ashton La *MDTN* M24	17	D1
SALE M33	108	A4
Ashton New Rd *OP/CLY* M11	72	A4
Ashton Old Rd *OP/CLY* M11	88	B1
OP/CLY M11	92	A2
Ashton Rd *BKLY* M9	16	A4
DROY M43	75	D4
FAIL M35	58	B3
OLDS OL8	41	C1
Ashton Rd East *FAIL* M35	57	D2
Ashton Rd West *FAIL* M35	56	B2
Ashton St *CHAD* OL9	38	A2
Ash Tree Av *DROY* M43	75	C3
Ash Tree Rd *CHH* M8	32	B4
Ashurst Av *OP/CLY* M11	73	C3
Ashville Ter *NEWH/MOS* M40	35	C4
Ash Wk *CHAD* OL9 *	21	C1
MDTN M24	17	C3
Ashwood *CHAD* OL9	19	D2
Ashwood Av *DID/WITH* M20	123	D1
DTN/ASHW M34	107	D2
Ashworth Cl *CHAD* OL9	39	C1
Ashworth St *CHH* M8	50	B4
FAIL M35	56	A3
OLD OL1	23	C3
Askett Cl *NEWH/MOS* M40	56	A3
Aspell Cl *MDTN* M24	17	C1
Aspenwood Dr *BKLY* M9	33	D4
Aspen Wood Dr *CHAD* OL9	19	D2
Aspinall St *MDTN* M24	18	B2
RUSH/FAL M14	102	B2
Aspin La *ANC* M4	4	B1
Asquith St *RDSH* SK5	107	C4
Assheton Av *DTN/ASHW* M34	76	B4
Assheton Crs *NEWH/MOS* M40	74	A1
Assheton Rd *NEWH/MOS* M40	74	A1
Assheton Wy *MDTN* M24	17	D1
Assisi Gdns *WGTN/LGST* M12	88	B3
Astan Av *DROY* M43	74	A2
Astbury Av *DTN/ASHW* M34	77	C4
Astbury Crs *EDGY/DAV* SK3	132	A3
Astley St *HTNM* SK4	129	D4
OP/CLY M11	73	D4
Aston Av *RUSH/FAL* M14	101	D4
Astor Rd *BNG/LEV* M19	116	B2
SALQ M50	64	B4
Atcham Gv *BKLY* M9	15	C3
Athenian Gdns *BRO* M7	49	D4
Athens St *STKP* SK1	130	B4
Atherley Gv *NEWH/MOS* M40	38	A3
Atherstone Av *CHH* M8	32	B3
Atherton Cl *FAIL* M35	58	A4
Atherton St *CSLFD* M3	6	C1
ECC M30	61	D4
EDGY/DAV SK3	132	A1
Atherton Wy *ECC* M30	61	D4
Athlone Av *NEWH/MOS* M40	54	B1
Athole St *ORD* M5	66	A4

Atholl Av *STRET* M32	95	D3
Athol Rd *OLDTF/WHR* M16	100	B4
Athol St *ECC* M30	61	D4
GTN M18	106	D2
HTNM SK4	129	C2
Atkinson Rd *SALE* M33	108	B3
URM M41	94	A3
Atkinson St *CHAD* OL9	22	A1
CSLFD M3	3	D1
STKP SK1	133	D2
Atlas St *OLDS* OL8	22	B3
Attercliffe Rd *CCHDY* M21	111	D2
Attewell St *OP/CLY* M11 *	89	D1
Attleboro Rd *NEWH/MOS* M40	54	B2
Attlee Wy *WGTN/LGST* M12	71	D4
Attock Cl *CHAD* OL9	21	C4
Attwood St *WGTN/LGST* M12	104	B3
Atwood Rd *DID/WITH* M20	125	D2
Atwood St *CMANE* M1	8	A2
Aubrey Rd *RUSH/FAL* M14	116	B3
Aubrey St *SALQ* M50	83	D2
Auburn Dr *URM* M41	94	B4
Auburn Rd *OLDTF/WHR* M16	99	C1
Auburn St *CMANE* M1	8	C1
Auckland Dr *SLFD* M6	48	B4
Auckland Rd *BNG/LEV* M19	117	C1
Audax Wk *NEWH/MOS* M40	73	C1
Auden Cl *OP/CLY* M11	74	A4
Audenshaw Hall Gv *DTN/ASHW* M34	93	C1
Audenshaw Rd *DTN/ASHW* M34	93	D2
Audiem Cl *NEWH/MOS* M40	71	C3
Audley Av *STRET* M32	95	C1
Audley Rd *BNG/LEV* M19 *	105	C3
Audrey Av *GTN* M18	91	D4
Audrey St *BKLY* M9	54	A1
Augustine Webster Cl *BKLY* M9	53	D1
Augustus St *ANC* M4	69	D1
Augustus Wy *HULME* M15	100	A1
Auriga Wk *BRO* M7	67	D2
Austen Rd *ECC* M30	62	A4
Austin Dr *DID/WITH* M20	125	D1
Austin Gv *BNG/LEV* M19	117	C1
Autumn St *BRUN/LGST* M13	102	B1
Avebury Cl *BRO* M7	51	C3
Avenue St *STKP* SK1 *	130	A3
The Avenue *BRO* M7	49	D4
ECC M30	62	A4
Averill St *NEWH/MOS* M40	56	A4
Aveson Av *CCHDY* M21	112	A3
Avian Dr *RUSH/FAL* M14	115	C1
Avonbrook Dr *NEWH/MOS* M40	38	A3
Avoncourt Dr *DID/WITH* M20	124	B1
Avondale *SWIN* M27	26	B3
Avondale Dr *SLFD* M6	46	A4
Avondale Rd *STRET* M32	97	D1
Avondale St *CHH* M8	51	D2
OLDS OL8	40	B1
Avon Gdns *BNG/LEV* M19	117	D3
Avonlea Dr *BNG/LEV* M19	116	B3
Avonlea Rd *DROY* M43	74	B3
Avon Rd *BNG/LEV* M19	117	C3
CHAD OL9	20	A1
Avon St *EDGY/DAV* SK3	132	B2
OLDS OL8	41	C1
Avril Cl *RDSH* SK5	120	A1
Avro Cl *RUSH/FAL* M14	102	A4
Axbridge Wk *NEWH/MOS* M40	71	C3
Axford Cl *BRO* M7	51	C3
Axon Sq *OLDTF/WHR* M16	101	C1
Aycliffe Av *CCHDY* M21	113	C4
Aycliffe Gv *BRUN/LGST* M13	103	D2
Aylesbury Av *URM* M41	94	B3
Aylesbury Cl *ORD* M5	66	B4
Aylesby Av *GTN* M18	105	C1
Aylesford Rd *RUSH/FAL* M14	103	C3
Aylsham Ms *SWIN* M27	44	A4
Ayr Av *OLDS* OL8	41	C2

Ayres Rd *OLDTF/WHR* M16 ....**99** D1
Ayrshire Rd *BRO* M7 ....**48** B3
Aysgarth Av *GTN* M18 ....**91** D3
Ayton Gv *RUSH/FAL* M14 ....**103** D1
Aytoun St *CMANE* M1 ....**4** C5
Azalea Av *GTN* M18 ....**91** C3

B

Babbacombe Gv *BKLY* M9 ....**15** C4
Back Acton St *CMANE* M1 * **8** C1
Back Adcroft St *STKP* SK1 * **133** C2
Back Ashley St *ANC* M4 ....**4** C1
Back Balloon St *ANC* M4 * **4** A2
Back Bank St *CHH* M8 ....**69** D1
Back Bridge St *CSLFD* M3 ....**3** E4
Back Camp St *BRO* M7 * **50** A4
Back Chapel St *BNG/LEV* M19 ....**104** B4
Back China La *CMANE* M1 ....**4** C5
Back College Land *CSLFD* M3 * **3** E4
Back Duncan St *BRO* M7 ....**49** D2
Back Elsworth St *CSLFD* M3 ....**69** D2
Back George St *CMANE* M1 ....**4** C4
Back Gilmour St *MDTN* M24 ....**17** D1
Back Greaves St *OLD* OL1 ....**23** C2
Back Halliwell La *CHH* M8 * **51** C2
Back Hamilton St *BRO* M7 * **50** A3
Back Hampson St *NEWH/MOS* M40 ....**71** C1
Back Hilton St *BRO* M7 * **50** A2
Back Hope St *BRO* M7 ....**50** A2
Back Howe St *BRO* M7 ....**49** D2
Back Hulme St *ORD* M5 ....**67** D4
Back Junction St *CMANE* M1 ....**5** D4
Back King St *OLDS* OL8 ....**22** B3
Back La *AULW* OL7 ....**77** D1
   DROY M43 ....**59** C4
Back Piccadilly *CMANE* M1 ....**4** C4
Back Pool Fold *CMANW* M2 * **3** F4
Back Quay St *CSLFD* M3 ....**2** C5
Back Red Bank *ANC* M4 ....**69** D2
Back St George's Rd *ANC* M4 ....**4** C1
Back St Mark's La *CHH* M8 * **51** C1
Back Scott St *OLDS* OL8 * **23** C4
Back South Pde *CSLFD* M3 ....**3** E4
Back Spear St *ANC* M4 * **4** C3
Back Thomas St *ANC* M4 * **4** B3
Back Turner St *ANC* M4 ....**4** B3
Back Water St *STKP* SK1 * **130** A3
Bacup St *NEWH/MOS* M40 ....**54** B1
Badby Cl *ANC* M4 ....**71** C4
Baddeley Cl *EDGY/DAV* SK3 ....**132** A4
Bagot St *OP/CLY* M11 ....**73** D3
   SWIN M27 ....**24** B4
Baguley Crs *EDGY/DAV* SK3 ....**132** A3
   MDTN M24 ....**14** B3
Baguley St *DROY* M43 ....**76** A4
Baildon St *NEWH/MOS* M40 ....**35** D4
Bailey Rd *TRPK* M17 ....**80** B2
Bailey St *OLD* OL1 * **23** D2
   OP/CLY M11 ....**74** A4
   PWCH M25 ....**12** B4
The Bails *BRO* M7 ....**49** D3
Bainbridge Cl *WGTN/LGST* M12 * **88** A3
Bain St *SWIN* M27 ....**45** C2
Baird St *CMANE* M1 ....**9** D1
Baker St *HTNM* SK4 ....**129** D1
   MDTN M24 ....**18** A1
Bakewell Rd *DROY* M43 ....**74** B3
   ECC M30 ....**78** A1
   STRET M32 ....**95** D2
Bakewell St *EDGY/DAV* SK3 ....**132** A1
   GTN M18 ....**105** D1
Bala Cl *ORD* M5 ....**66** B3
Baldock Cl *DID/WITH* M20 ....**126** A2

Baldwin Rd *BNG/LEV* M19 ....**117** C3
Bale St *CMANW* M2 ....**7** F1
Balfour Gv *RDSH* SK5 ....**107** C4
   RDSH SK5 ....**120** A1
Balfour St *CHH* M8 ....**51** D1
   SLFD M6 ....**48** A3
Balham Wk *WGTN/LGST* M12 ....**89** A3
Ballantine St *NEWH/MOS* M40 ....**73** D1
Ballbrook Av *DID/WITH* M20 ....**114** B4
Balleratt St *BNG/LEV* M19 ....**104** B4
Ball Gn *STRET* M32 ....**81** C4
Balliol St *CHH* M8 ....**51** D1
   SWIN M27 ....**44** B1
Balloon St *ANC* M4 ....**4** A2
Balmain Av *GTN* M18 ....**105** D2
Balmfield St *CHH* M8 ....**51** D1
Balmforth St *HULME* M15 * **6** B3
Balmoral Av *STRET* M32 ....**97** C2
   WHTF M45 ....**11** D2
Balmoral Dr *DTN/ASHW* M34 ....**107** D1
Balmoral Gra *PWCH* M25 ....**31** D2
Balmoral Rd *HTNM* SK4 ....**127** D2
   RUSH/FAL M14 ....**116** A1
   SWIN M27 ....**26** B3
Balmoral St *GTN* M18 ....**105** D1
Balsam Cl *BRUN/LGST* M13 ....**9** D4
Baltic St *ORD* M5 ....**65** D3
Baltimore St *NEWH/MOS* M40 ....**54** A4
Bamber St *BKLY* M9 ....**16** A4
Bamburgh Dr *AULW* OL7 ....**59** D4
Bamford Gv *DID/WITH* M20 ....**124** B2
Bamford Rd *DID/WITH* M20 ....**124** B2
Bamford St *CHAD* OL9 ....**21** D1
   OP/CLY M11 ....**73** C3
   STKP SK1 ....**133** C1
Banbury Ms *SWIN* M27 ....**25** C4
Banbury Rd *FAIL* M35 ....**74** B1
   MDTN M24 ....**17** C4
Banbury St *STKP* SK1 ....**130** A3
Bancroft Rd *SWIN* M27 ....**25** D4
Banff Rd *RUSH/FAL* M14 ....**102** A3
Bangor St *HULME* M15 ....**85** C4
   RDSH SK5 ....**130** A1
Bank Bridge Rd *OP/CLY* M11 ....**72** B2
Bankfield Av *BRUN/LGST* M13 ....**103** D1
   DROY M43 ....**75** D3
   HTNM SK4 ....**128** B3
Bankfield St *BKLY* M9 ....**34** A4
   HTNM SK4 ....**129** D1
Bankhall Rd *HTNM* SK4 ....**127** D3
Bankhirst Cl *CHH* M8 ....**32** B4
Bank House Rd *BKLY* M9 ....**33** D2
Bank La *SLFD* M6 ....**47** C3
Bankley St *BNG/LEV* M19 ....**104** B4
Bankmill Cl *BRUN/LGST* M13 ....**9** D4
Bank Pl *CSLFD* M3 ....**2** A3
Bank Rd *CHH* M8 ....**32** B3
Bankside *CHAD* OL9 ....**22** A3
Bankside Cl *HTNM* SK4 * **127** D3
Bank St *BRO* M7 ....**51** C1
   CSLFD M3 ....**2** A3
   DROY M43 ....**92** A1
   OP/CLY M11 ....**72** B3
   SALE M33 ....**109** D4
Bankwell St *HULME* M15 ....**85** D4
Bannach Dr *CHAD* OL9 ....**20** B1
Bannatyne Cl *NEWH/MOS* M40 ....**37** D4
Banner Dale Cl *BRUN/LGST* M13 ....**104** A1
Bannerman Av *PWCH* M25 ....**30** A2
Bannerman Rd *DROY* M43 ....**76** A4
Banner Wk *OP/CLY* M11 ....**72** A4
Bannister St *OFTN* SK2 ....**133** C2
Bann St *EDGY/DAV* SK3 ....**132** A1
Bantry Av *BKLY* M9 ....**33** C2
Baptist St *ANC* M4 ....**4** C1
Barbeck Cl *NEWH/MOS* M40 ....**71** D2
Barber St *OP/CLY* M11 * **91** D2

Barbican St *DID/WITH* M20..............**115** C2
Barbirolli Sq *CMANW* M2........................**7** F2
Barbon Wk *ANC* M4...............................**5** E3
Barcicroft Rd *BNG/LEV* M19..........**126** B1
Barclays Av *SLFD* M6...........................**47** C3
Barcliffe Av *NEWH/MOS* M40.............**36** B3
Barcombe Cl *STRET* M32.....................**95** C2
Bardsley Av *FAIL* M35..........................**57** C2
Bardsley St *CHAD* OL9.........................**38** A2
  HTNM SK4..............................**129** C2
  NEWH/MOS M40.........................**56** A4
Barff Rd *ORD* M5...................................**64** B3
Barfoot Aqueduct *STRET* M32.........**109** D2
Bar Gap Rd *OLD* OL1...........................**23** C1
Baring St *CMANE* M1..............................**9** D2
Barkan Wy *SWIN* M27...........................**46** A1
Barker's La *SALE* M33........................**108** A4
Barker St *CSLFD* M3.............................**69** C1
Barking St *NEWH/MOS* M40.................**71** D2
Bark Wk *HULME* M15.............................**11** F5
Barkway Rd *STRET* M32.......................**95** D4
Barlea Av *NEWH/MOS* M40...................**37** C4
Barleycroft St *OLDTF/WHR* M16........**101** C1
Barlow Fold Rd *RDSH* SK5................**120** A1
Barlow Hall Rd *CCHDY* M21...............**112** B4
Barlow La *ECC* M30...............................**61** D3
Barlow La North *RDSH* SK5...............**120** A1
Barlow Moor Ct *DID/WITH* M20.........**124** A1
Barlow Moor Rd *CCHDY* M21.............**112** A2
  DID/WITH M20.........................**123** D1
Barlow Pl *BRUN/LGST* M13.....................**9** E4
Barlow Rd *BNG/LEV* M19....................**105** D4
  STRET M32...............................**98** A1
Barlow's Cft *CSLFD* M3...........................**3** D3
Barlow St *ECC* M30...............................**62** A4
  OLDE OL4................................**23** D3
Barmouth St *OP/CLY* M11......................**89** C1
Barmouth Wk *OLDS* OL8........................**39** C3
Barnard Av *HTNM* SK4.........................**128** A3
  WHTF M45.................................**12** A2
Barnard Rd *GTN* M18...........................**105** C2
Barnby St *WGTN/LGST* M12................**104** B2
Barnes Av *STKP* SK1...........................**127** D3
Barneswell St *NEWH/MOS* M40...........**55** D4
Barnett Av *DID/WITH* M20..................**115** C3
Barnett Dr *CSLFD* M3..............................**2** B2
Barnfield Cl *ORD* M5.............................**66** A4
Barnfield Crs *SALE* M33.....................**108** A4
Barnfield Rd *BNG/LEV* M19................**126** B1
  SWIN M27.................................**25** C3
Barnhill Av *PWCH* M25.........................**30** A3
Barnhill Dr *PWCH* M25.........................**30** A3
Barnhill Rd *PWCH* M25.........................**29** D2
Barnsdale Dr *CHH* M8..........................**51** D4
Barnsfold Av *RUSH/FAL* M14.............**115** D1
Barnside Wy *FAIL* M35..........................**58** B2
Barnstable Dr *NEWH/MOS* M40...........**52** B3
Barnstead Av *DID/WITH* M20.............**116** A4
Barnston Av *RUSH/FAL* M14...............**102** A3
Barn St *OLDS* OL8.................................**22** B3
  WHTF M45.................................**11** C2
Baroness Av *BRO* M7...........................**67** D1
Barons Ct *FAIL* M35..............................**56** A3
Barrack St *HULME* M15...........................**6** A4
Barra Dr *URM* M41.................................**79** C4
Barrass St *OP/CLY* M11.......................**91** C2
Barrfield Rd *SLFD* M6...........................**65** D1
Barr Hill Av *SLFD* M6............................**47** D4
Barrhill Cl *HULME* M15...........................**6** C5
Barrington Av *DROY* M43......................**75** C4
Barrington St *OP/CLY* M11....................**73** D3
Barrow Hill Rd *CHH* M8........................**51** C4
Barrow St *ORD* M5...................................**2** A4
Barry Lawson Cl *CHH* M8 *..................**51** C2
Barry Rd *NTHM/RTH* M23....................**122** A3

  RDSH SK5................................**120** A4
Bartlam Pl *OLD* OL1..............................**23** C2
Bartlett St *OP/CLY* M11.........................**90** A2
Barton Dock Rd *STRET* M32..................**95** D1
  URM M41..................................**79** D3
Barton Hall Av *ECC* M30......................**60** B4
Barton Highlevel Br *TRPK* M17............**78** D4
Barton La *ECC* M30...............................**79** C1
Barton Rd *ECC* M30..............................**78** B4
  HTNM SK4..............................**126** B4
  MDTN M24................................**17** C1
  STRET M32...............................**95** D2
  STRET M32...............................**96** A2
  SWIN M27.................................**45** D2
  URM M41..................................**78** B4
  WALK M28.................................**42** A4
Barton St *CHAD* OL9.............................**22** A1
  CSLFD M3..................................**7** D2
Barway Rd *CCHDY* M21........................**98** A4
Basechurch Wk *WGTN/LGST* M12 *.....**89** C3
Basford Rd *OLDTF/WHR* M16...............**99** C2
Basildon Cl *BRUN/LGST* M13................**88** A4
Basil St *HTNM* SK4..............................**129** C2
  RUSH/FAL M14 *.....................**102** B2
Baslow Av *BNG/LEV* M19....................**105** C3
Baslow Gv *RDSH* SK5..........................**120** A4
Baslow Rd *DROY* M43............................**74** B3
  STRET M32...............................**95** D2
Baslow St *OP/CLY* M11.........................**71** D4
Basset Av *SLFD* M6...............................**49** D4
Basten Dr *BRO* M7................................**50** A3
Batchelor Cl *CCHDY* M21....................**113** D2
Bateson St *STKP* SK1..........................**130** B3
Bateson Wy *OLDS* OL8 *.......................**23** C4
Bates St *BRUN/LGST* M13...................**104** A1
Bath Crs *OLDTF/WHR* M16....................**84** B4
Bath St *CHAD* OL9.................................**21** D4
Batley St *BKLY* M9................................**53** D1
Batsmans Dr *SWIN* M27........................**25** D1
Battersby St *OP/CLY* M11 *..................**91** D2
Battersea Rd *HTNM* SK4....................**126** B4
Batty St *CHH* M8....................................**52** B4
Baxter St *OLDS* OL8..............................**39** C3
Baydon Av *BRO* M7...............................**51** C3
Bayfield Gv *NEWH/MOS* M40 *.............**35** D4
Bayston Wk *WGTN/LGST* M12..............**89** C3
Bay St *CHAD* OL9..................................**22** A1
Bayswater Av *NEWH/MOS* M40............**73** D1
Baytree Av *CHAD* OL9...........................**19** C3
Bay Tree Av *WALK* M28.........................**42** B4
Baytree La *MDTN* M24...........................**19** C1
Baywood St *BKLY* M9............................**53** C1
Bazaar St *SLFD* M6...............................**66** B1
Bazley Rd *WYTH/NTH* M22..................**123** C4
Beacon Rd *TRPK* M17............................**79** D2
Beaconsfield *RUSH/FAL* M14 *...........**115** D2
Beadham Dr *BKLY* M9...........................**14** B4
Beal Cl *HTNM* SK4...............................**126** A2
Beale Gv *CCHDY* M21..........................**112** A1
Bealey Cl *GTN* M18...............................**90** A3
Beaminster Rd *HTNM* SK4..................**127** C2
Beaminster Wk *BRUN/LGST* M13 *.......**87** D4
Beamish Cl *BRUN/LGST* M13...................**9** F5
Beanfields *WALK* M28...........................**42** A4
Beard Rd *GTN* M18 *............................**105** D1
Beard St *DROY* M43...............................**75** C4
Beardwood Rd *BKLY* M9........................**34** A3
Beatrice Av *GTN* M18...........................**107** C1
Beatrice Rd *WALK* M28.........................**43** C2
Beatrice St *SWIN* M27...........................**25** D4
Beatrice Wignall St *DROY* M43 *..........**92** B1
Beatson Wk *ANC* M4................................**5** E4
Beattock Cl *HULME* M15 *.......................**6** B4
Beattock St *HULME* M15..........................**6** B4
Beaufort Av *DID/WITH* M20................**114** B4
  SWIN M27.................................**44** A2
Beaufort St *CSLFD* M3.............................**6** C2

ECC M30	61	C2
PWCH M25	30	B1
Beaumont Rd CCHDY M21	112	A2
Beaver Rd OLDTF/WHR M20	125	C2
Beaver St CMANE M1	8	A2
Bebbington St OP/CLY M11 *	73	D2
Beckenham Rd CHH M8	51	D2
Becket Av BRO M7	50	B3
Beckett St GTN M18	105	D1
Beckfoot Dr BRUN/LGST M13	103	D2
Beckford Cl NEWH/MOS M40	53	D4
Beckhampton Cl BRUN/LGST M13	87	D4
Beckley Av PWCH M25	29	D3
Beckside RDSH SK5	107	D4
Beck St CSLFD M3	2	C3
OP/CLY M11 *	91	D2
Bedford Av OLDTF/WHR M16	100	A3
SWIN M27 *	44	B2
Bedford Rd ECC M30	62	B2
OLDTF/WHR M16	98	B3
Bedfordshire Cl CHAD OL9	21	C4
Bedford St PWCH M25	12	B4
RDSH SK5	119	D2
Bednal Av NEWH/MOS M40	71	D1
Bedwell St OLDTF/WHR M16	101	D1
Beech Dr DROY M43	75	C4
EDGY/DAV SK3	133	C3
SLFD M6	65	D1
WHTF M45	11	C2
Beech Cl PWCH M25	30	B2
Beechcroft PWCH M25	30	B3
Beechdale Cl NEWH/MOS M40	55	D1
The Beeches DID/WITH M20	123	D1
The Beeches DID/WITH M20	124	A1
Beechey Sq OLD OL1 *	23	D2
Beechfield Rd SWIN M27	44	B4
Beechfield St CHH M8	51	D3
Beech Gv RUSH/FAL M14	116	A1
SLFD M6	65	D1
Beech Hurst Cl OLDTF/WHR M16 *	100	A3
OFTN SK2	133	D4
Beech Ms CCHDY M21	111	D1
Beech Mt BKLY M9	53	C1
Beech Rd CCHDY M21	112	A1
EDGY/DAV SK3	132	B3
Beech St ECC M30	61	C4
FAIL M35	56	B1
MDTN M24 *	17	C1
OLD OL1	23	D1
SWIN M27	45	C2
Beech Wk MDTN M24	17	C3
STRET M32	109	D1
Beechwood Av CCHDY M21	112	B2
Beechwood Dr WALK M28	43	C3
Beechwood Rd OLDS OL8	41	C3
PWCH M25	31	C2
Beede St OP/CLY M11	90	A1
Beehive St OLDS OL8	41	C2
Beeley St SLFD M6	49	C4
Beeston Av BRO M7	49	C3
Beeston Gv EDGY/DAV SK3	132	B4
WHTF M45	12	A2
Beeston St BKLY M9	53	D2
Beeth St OP/CLY M11	91	D3
Beeton Gv BRUN/LGST M13	103	D1
Beever St OLD OL1	23	D2
OLDTF/WHR M16	84	B4
Belding Av NEWH/MOS M40	38	A4
Beldon Rd BKLY M9	33	C1
Belfield Rd DID/WITH M20	125	C2
PWCH M25	31	D1
Belford Av DTN/ASHW M34	107	D2
Belford Rd STRET M32	97	C2
Belfort Dr BRO M7	84	A1
Belgate Cl WGTN/LGST M12	104	B1
Belgrave Av FAIL M35	58	A1
OLDS OL8	41	D1
Belgrave Ct OLDS OL8	41	C1
Belgrave Crs ECC M30	63	C2
Belgrave Rd NEWH/MOS M40	37	D4
OLDS OL8	41	C1
Belgravia Gdns CCHDY M21	111	D1
Belhaven Rd CHH M8	32	A3
Bell Clough Rd DROY M43	76	A2
Bell Crs OP/CLY M11	89	C1
Belldale Cl HTNM SK4	127	D3
Bellerby Cl WHTF M45	10	B1
Belle Vue Av WGTN/LGST M12	89	C4
Belle Vue St WGTN/LGST M12	89	D3
Bellfield Av OLDS OL8	41	C3
Bellfield Cl BKLY M9	33	D3
Bellhill Gdns SLFD M6	66	A2
Bellis Cl WGTN/LGST M12	71	D4
Bellott St CHH M8	51	D3
Bellott Wk OLD OL1 *	22	B1
Bells Croft Av NEWH/MOS M40	55	C2
Bell St DROY M43	76	A3
OLD OL1	23	D2
Bell Ter ECC M30	78	B1
Belmont Av SLFD M6	63	D2
Belmont Cl HTNM SK4	129	D2
Belmont Rd SALE M33	108	B3
Belmont St ECC M30	62	A2
HTNM SK4	129	D2
OLD OL1	22	B1
SALQ M50	65	C4
Belmont Wk BRUN/LGST M13	9	E5
Belmont Wy CHAD OL9	21	D1
HTNM SK4	129	D2
Belper Rd ECC M30	78	A1
HTNM SK4	127	C4
Belroy Ct PWCH M25 *	30	A2
Belsay Cl AULW OL7	59	D4
Belthorne Av BKLY M9	35	D3
Beltone Cl STRET M32	96	A4
Belton Wk CHAD OL9 *	22	A3
Belvedere Av RDSH SK5	107	C3
Belvedere Ct PWCH M25 *	29	D2
Belvedere Dr MPL/ROM SK6	131	D2
Belvedere Rd RUSH/FAL M14	116	B1
SLFD M6	66	B2
Belvedere St SLFD M6 *	67	C2
Belvoir Av BNG/LEV M19 *	104	B3
Belwood Rd CCHDY M21	111	D2
Bembridge Cl RUSH/FAL M14	102	B2
Bemsley Pl ORD M5 *	83	D1
Benbecula Wy URM M41	78	B4
Benbow Av WGTN/LGST M12	89	C4
Benbow St SALE M33	109	C4
Ben Brierley Wy OLD OL1	23	C2
Bendall St OP/CLY M11	91	D1
Bendix St ANC M4	4	C2
Benedict Cl BRO M7	49	D4
Benfield Av NEWH/MOS M40	36	B3
Benfleet Cl WGTN/LGST M12 *	89	D3
Bengal St ANC M4	5	D2
EDGY/DAV SK3	132	B1
Benmore Rd BKLY M9	35	C2
Bennett Dr BRO M7	50	B3
Bennett Rd CHH M8	32	A4
Bennett St STRET M32 *	96	B4
WGTN/LGST M12	88	B3
Benny La DROY M43	77	C2
Benson Cl BRO M7	50	B4
Ben St OP/CLY M11	73	C3
Bentcliffe Wy ECC M30	63	D4
Bentinck St HULME M15	6	A4
Bent La CHH M8	51	C2
PWCH M25	30	B1
Bentley Rd BRO M7	50	B1
CCHDY M21	98	B4
Bentley St CHAD OL9	21	C2
Benton St BKLY M9	54	A2
Bent St CHH M8	51	D4

Bentworth Wk *BKLY* M9 ....53 D2
Beresford Crs *RDSH* SK5 ....106 B2
Beresford Rd *BRUN/LGST* M13 ......104 A2
   STRET M32 ....97 D1
Beresford St *FAIL* M35 ....56 B2
   RUSH/FAL M14 ....101 C2
Berigan Cl *WGTN/LGST* M12 ....88 B2
Berkeley Av *CHAD* OL9 ....38 C1
   RUSH/FAL M14 ....103 D1
   STRET M32 ....95 D1
Berkley Av *BNG/LEV* M19 ....104 B3
Berkshire Cl *CHAD* OL9 ....21 C4
Berkshire Pl *CHAD* OL9 * 21 D4
Berkshire Rd *NEWH/MOS* M40 ......71 C2
Berlin Rd *EDGY/DAV* SK3 ....132 A3
Bermondsay St *ORD* M5 ....84 A1
Bernard St *BKLY* M9 ....53 C1
Berne Cl *CHAD* OL9 ....21 D3
Bernice Av *CHAD* OL9 ....21 C3
Berriedale Cl *OLDTF/WHR* M16 * ..100 A3
Berrie Gv *BNG/LEV* M19 ....117 D1
Berry Brow *NEWH/MOS* M40 ....74 B1
Berry St *CMANE* M1 ....9 D2
   ECC M30 ....78 A1
   SWIN M27 ....26 A3
Bertha St *OP/CLY* M11 ....90 A2
Bertram St *WGTN/LGST* M12 * 89 D3
Berwick Av *HTNM* SK4 ....126 A3
   URM M41 ....95 D3
   WHTF M45 ....11 D2
Berwyn Av *BKLY* M9 ....15 D4
   MDTN M24 ....18 B1
Berwyn Cl *OLDS* OL8 ....40 B2
Bessemer Av *OP/CLY* M11 ....90 B2
Bessemer Wy *OLD* OL1 * 22 B2
Beswick Dr *FAIL* M35 ....57 D3
Beswick Rw *ANC* M4 ....4 A2
Beswick St *ANC* M4 ....71 C3
   DROY M43 ....76 A4
Beta Av *STRET* M32 ....96 B4
Bethel Av *FAIL* M35 ....56 B2
Bethesda St *OLDS* OL8 ....41 C1
Bethnall Dr *RUSH/FAL* M14 ....114 B1
Betley Rd *RDSH* SK5 ....107 C4
Betley St *HULME* M15 ....9 E1
Betnor Av *STKP* SK1 ....131 C4
Betsham St *HULME* M15 ....86 A4
Bettwood Dr *CHH* M8 ....32 A3
Betula Gv *BRO* M7 ....50 A2
Bevan Cl *WGTN/LGST* M12 ....71 D4
Bevendon Sq *BRO* M7 ....50 B3
Beveridge St *RUSH/FAL* M14 ....101 D2
Beverley Av *URM* M41 ....94 B1
Beverley Rd *SWIN* M27 ....46 A3
Beverley St *BKLY* M9 ....34 B4
Beverley Wk *OLDS* OL8 * 22 B4
Beverly Rd *RUSH/FAL* M14 ....116 A4
Beverston Dr *BRO* M7 ....50 B3
Bevill Sq *CSLFD* M3 ....2 C1
Bewley St *OLDS* OL8 ....40 A3
Bexhill Dr *BRUN/LGST* M13 ....103 D2
Bexhill Wk *CHAD* OL9 ....21 C3
Bexington Rd *OLDTF/WHR* M16 ....100 A2
Bexley Sq *CSLFD* M3 ....2 B5
Bexley St *CHAD* OL9 ....21 D4
Beyer Cl *CTN* M18 ....90 B4
Bibby La *BNG/LEV* M19 ....117 C3
Bickerdike Av *WGTN/LGST* M12 ..105 C2
Biddisham Wk *NEWH/MOS* M40 * ..71 C1
Bideford Rd *OFTN* SK2 ....131 D4
Bidston Av *RUSH/FAL* M14 ....102 A3
Bignor St *CHH* M8 ....51 D3
Bilbrook St *ANC* M4 ....70 A2
Billberry Cl *WHTF* M45 ....12 A1
Billing Av *WGTN/LGST* M12 ....9 E3
Billington Rd *SWIN* M27 ....47 D1
Bill Williams Cl *OP/CLY* M11 ....90 B1

Billy La *SWIN* M27 ....26 A3
Bindloss Av *ECC* M30 ....63 D2
Bingham St *SWIN* M27 ....45 C1
Bingley Cl *OP/CLY* M11 ....89 C1
Bingley Wk *BRO* M7 ....48 A1
Binns Pl *ANC* M4 ....5 D4
Binstead Cl *RUSH/FAL* M14 ....103 D2
Birchacre Gv *RUSH/FAL* M14 ......116 A2
Birch Av *FAIL* M35 ....57 C4
   HTNM SK4 ....128 A1
   MDTN M24 ....17 D2
   OLDS OL8 ....40 A3
   OLDTF/WHR M16 ....98 B1
   SLFD M6 ....65 D1
   WHTF M45 ....11 C3
Birch Dr *SWIN* M27 ....46 A1
Birchell Wy *HULME* M15 ....7 F5
Birchenall St *NEWH/MOS* M40 ......54 A1
Birchenlea St *CHAD* OL9 ....38 B2
Birchfields Av *BRUN/LGST* M13 ..103 D3
Birchfields Rd *BRUN/LGST* M13 ..103 D2
Birch Gv *PWCH* M25 ....11 D3
   RUSH/FAL M14 ....103 C2
Birch Hall La *BRUN/LGST* M13 ....103 D3
Birchington Rd *DID/WITH* M20 ....114 B1
Birchin Pl *ANC* M4 * 4 B1
Birch La *BRUN/LGST* M13 ....103 D1
Birchleaf Gv *ORD* M5 ....64 B3
Birch Polygon *RUSH/FAL* M14 ....103 C2
Birch Rd *CHH* M8 ....33 C4
   SWIN M27 ....44 A4
Birch St *AULW* OL7 ....77 D4
   DROY M43 * 93 C1
   WGTN/LGST M12 ....89 D5
Birchvale Cl *HULME* M15 ....6 C4
Birchwood *CHAD* OL9 ....19 D2
   DROY M43 ....76 A3
Birchwood Dr *NEWH/MOS* M40 ....53 C3
Birchwood Rd *MDTN* M24 ....18 B1
Birdhall Gv *BNG/LEV* M19 ....117 D3
Birkdale Av *WHTF* M45 ....10 A3
Birkdale Gv *ECC* M30 ....63 C3
   RDSH SK5 ....120 A4
Birkdale Pl *SALE* M33 * 108 A3
Birkdale Rd *RDSH* SK5 ....120 A4
Birkdale St *CHH* M8 ....51 D2
Birley Pk *DID/WITH* M20 ....124 A2
Birtles Av *RDSH* SK5 ....107 C3
Birtley Wk *NEWH/MOS* M40 * 5 F1
Birt St *NEWH/MOS* M40 ....71 C1
Birwood Rd *CHH* M8 ....33 C3
Biscay Cl *OP/CLY* M11 ....72 A4
Bishop Rd *OLDTF/WHR* M16 ....100 B1
Bishopgate St *CHAD* OL9 ....20 B4
Bishop Marshall St *NEWH/MOS* M40 * ...53 C4
Bishop Rd *SLFD* M6 ....64 B1
Bishopsgate *CMANW* M2 ....7 F1
Bishops Rd *PWCH* M25 ....30 B2
Bishop St *MDTN* M24 ....19 C2
   STKP SK1 ....130 B4
Bishopton Cl *BNG/LEV* M19 ....105 D4
Bisley St *OLDS* OL8 ....22 A3
Bismarck St *OLDE* OL4 ....23 D4
Bispham Gv *BRO* M7 ....50 B2
Bittern Dr *DROY* M43 ....76 B2
Blackberry La *RDSH* SK5 ....121 C2
Black Brook Rd *HTNM* SK4 ....119 C2
Blackburn Gdns *DID/WITH* M20 ..124 B1
Blackburn Pl *ORD* M5 ....67 D4
Blackburn St *CSLFD* M3 ....2 A1
   OLDTF/WHR M16 ....84 B4
   PWCH M25 ....30 B1
Blackcroft Cl *SWIN* M27 ....44 B1
Blackdown Gv *OLDS* OL8 ....40 B2
Blackfield La *BRO* M7 ....49 D1
Blackfields Av *BRO* M7 * 50 A1
Blackford Rd *BNG/LEV* M19 ....118 A2

Blackford Wk *NEWH/MOS* M40 ....**71** C2
Blackfriars Rd *CSLFD* M3 ....**2** C1
Blackfriars St *CSLFD* M3 ....**3** E3
Blackhill Cl *BRUN/LGST* M13 ....**9** D4
Blackley New Rd *BKLY* M9 ....**32** A2
Blackley Park Rd *BKLY* M9 ....**34** A4
Blackley St *WGTN/LGST* M24 ....**15** C2
  OLDTF/WHR M16 ....**84** B4
Blacklock St *CSLFD* M3 ....**69** C1
Blackmore Rd *STRET* M32 ....**81** C4
Blackpool St *OP/CLY* M11 ....**73** D3
Blackrock St *OP/CLY* M11 ....**72** A4
Blackshaw St *EDGY/DAV* SK3 ....**132** B1
Blackstock St *BRUN/LGST* M13 ....**102** B1
Blackthorn Av *BNG/LEV* M19 ....**117** D2
Blackthorn Rd *OLDS* OL8 ....**58** B1
Blackwin St *WGTN/LGST* M12 ....**89** D3
Bladon St *CMANE* M1 * **8** C1
Blairhall Av *NEWH/MOS* M40 ....**54** B2
Blair Rd *OLDTF/WHR* M16 ....**100** B2
Blair St *OLDTF/WHR* M16 ....**85** C4
Blakedown Wk *WGTN/LGST* M12 ....**88** D2
Blakemore Wk *WGTN/LGST* M12 * **71** D4
Blakey St *WGTN/LGST* M12 ....**104** B1
Blanchard St *HULME* M15 ....**85** D4
Blanche Wk *OLD* OL1 * **23** D1
Bland Cl *FAIL* M35 ....**56** B2
Blandford Av *WALK* M28 ....**42** B1
Blandford Dr *NEWH/MOS* M40 ....**36** B3
Blandford Rd *ECC* M30 ....**61** C3
  HTNM SK4 ....**128** B3
  SLFD M6 ....**49** C4
Bland Rd *PWCH* M25 ....**30** A3
Bland St *OLDTF/WHR* M16 * **100** B1
Blanefield Cl *CCHDY* M21 ....**113** D2
Blantyre Rd *SWIN* M27 ....**46** A3
Blantyre St *ECC* M30 ....**60** B2
  HULME M15 ....**6** B3
  SWIN M27 ....**44** A1
Blanwood Dr *CHH* M8 ....**52** B1
Blaven Cl *EDGY/DAV* SK3 ....**133** C4
Bledlow Cl *ECC* M30 ....**62** B1
Blenheim Av *OLDTF/WHR* M16 ....**100** A3
Blenheim Rd *OLDTF/WHR* M16 ....**98** B2
Bletchley Cl *BRUN/LGST* M13 ....**88** A4
Bletchley Rd *HTNM* SK4 ....**126** B1
Blinco Rd *URM* M41 ....**95** C4
Blind La *WGTN/LGST* M12 ....**88** A2
Blisworth Av *ECC* M30 ....**79** D1
Blisworth Cl *ANC* M4 ....**71** C4
Block La *CHAD* OL9 ....**21** C4
Blodwell St *SLFD* M6 ....**66** A3
Bloom St *CMANE* M1 ....**8** B1
  CSLFD M3 ....**2** C3
Blossoms St *OFTN* SK2 ....**133** C2
Blossom St *ANC* M4 ....**5** D3
  CSLFD M3 ....**3** D2
Blucher St *ORD* M5 ....**67** D4
  WGTN/LGST M12 ....**88** B3
Blue Bell Av *NEWH/MOS* M40 ....**35** D4
Blue Ribbon Wk *SWIN* M27 ....**26** B4
Bluestone Dr *HTNM* SK4 ....**126** B2
Bluestone Rd *NEWH/MOS* M40 ....**54** B1
  RDSH SK5 ....**107** D3
Blunn St *OLDS* OL8 ....**41** C1
Blyborough Cl *SLFD* M6 ....**67** C4
Blyton St *HULME* M15 ....**87** C4
Boad St *CMANE* M1 ....**9** D1
Boardman Cl *RDSH* SK5 ....**129** D1
Boardman Fold Cl *MDTN* M24 ....**17** D4
Boardman Fold Rd *MDTN* M24 ....**17** D4
Boardman La *MDTN* M24 ....**15** C1
Boardman Rd *CHH* M8 ....**32** A3
Boardman St *ECC* M30 ....**62** B4
Boar Green Cl *NEWH/MOS* M40 ....**55** D2
Boat La *WYTH/NTH* M22 ....**123** D4
Bobbin Wk *ANC* M4 * **5** E4

OLDE OL4 ....**23** D3
Bob Brook Cl *NEWH/MOS* M40 ....**55** D3
Bob Massey Cl *OP/CLY* M11 ....**90** B1
Boddens Hill Rd *HTNM* SK4 ....**127** D4
Boddington Rd *ECC* M30 ....**60** A4
Bodley St *OP/CLY* M11 ....**73** D3
Bodmin Crs *RDSH* SK5 ....**121** C4
Boland Dr *RUSH/FAL* M14 ....**116** A1
Bolbury Crs *SWIN* M27 ....**47** C1
Bolderod Pl *OLD* OL1 ....**23** D1
Bolesworth Cl *CCHDY* M21 ....**111** C1
Bolivia St *ORD* M5 ....**64** B3
Bollin Ct *HULME* M15 ....**85** C3
Bollington Rd *HTNM* SK4 ....**119** C4
  NEWH/MOS M40 ....**71** C3
Bolton Av *BNG/LEV* M19 ....**126** A3
Bolton Cl *PWCH* M25 ....**29** C3
Bolton Rd *SLFD* M6 ....**46** B3
  SLFD M6 ....**47** D1
  SWIN M27 ....**46** B1
Bolton St *CSLFD* M3 ....**2** C4
  OLDE OL4 ....**23** D5
  RDSH SK5 ....**119** D2
Bombay St *CMANE* M1 ....**8** B2
Bonchurch Wk *WGTN/LGST* M12 ....**90** A3
Bondmark Rd *GTN* M18 ....**90** B3
Bond Sq *BRO* M7 * **50** B3
Bond St *WGTN/LGST* M12 ....**9** E2
Bonhill Wk *OP/CLY* M11 ....**73** C3
Bonny Brow St *MDTN* M24 ....**15** C2
Bonsall St *HULME* M15 ....**7** F5
  HULME M15 ....**86** A3
Boond St *ANC* M4 ....**71** C4
  CSLFD M3 ....**3** D2
Booth Av *RUSH/FAL* M14 ....**116** A2
Booth Bridge Cl *MDTN* M24 * **15** D2
Boothby Rd *SWIN* M27 ....**25** D3
Boothfield *ECC* M30 ....**60** B2
Booth Hall Rd *BKLY* M9 ....**35** D2
Booth Rd *DTN/ASHW* M34 ....**92** B2
  OLDTF/WHR M16 ....**99** D2
  SALE M33 ....**109** C3
Boothroyden Rd *BKLY* M9 ....**15** D3
Boothroyden Ter *BKLY* M9 ....**15** D3
Booth St *CHAD* OL9 ....**22** B3
  CMANW M2 ....**3** F5
  CSLFD M3 ....**3** E2
  EDGY/DAV SK3 ....**132** B2
  MDTN M24 ....**19** C3
Booth St East *BRUN/LGST* M13 ....**8** C5
Booth St West *HULME* M15 ....**8** B5
Bootle St *CMANW* M2 ....**3** E5
Bordale Av *BKLY* M9 ....**54** A2
Bordan St *OP/CLY* M11 ....**89** C2
Boringdon Cl *NEWH/MOS* M40 * **55** C3
Borland Av *NEWH/MOS* M40 ....**37** D4
Borough Av *SWIN* M27 ....**26** B4
Borough Rd *SALQ* M50 ....**65** C4
Borron St *STKP* SK1 ....**130** B3
Borrowdale Crs *DID/WITH* M20 ....**123** D1
Borsden St *SWIN* M27 ....**25** C4
Borwell St *GTN* M18 ....**91** C4
Boscombe Av *ECC* M30 ....**78** B1
Boscombe St *RDSH* SK5 ....**107** C3
  RUSH/FAL M14 ....**102** A3
Bosden Fold *STKP* SK1 ....**133** C1
Bosley Av *DID/WITH* M20 ....**114** B1
Bossall Av *BKLY* M9 ....**34** B1
Bostock Wk *BRUN/LGST* M13 ....**9** D4
Boston Cl *FAIL* M35 ....**57** C1
Boston Ct *SALQ* M50 ....**82** B1
Boston St *HULME* M15 ....**86** A4
  OLDS OL8 ....**41** C1
Boswell Av *DTN/ASHW* M34 ....**77** C4

ne.

Bosworth Cl *WHTF* M45 ....12 B1
Bosworth St *OP/CLY* M11 ....89 D1
Botanical Av *OLDTF/WHR* M16 ....83 D4
Botany Rd *ECC* M50 ....60 B1
Botham Cl *HULME* M15 ....86 B4
Bothwell Rd *NEWH/MOS* M40 ....5 F1
Bottesford Av *DID/WITH* M20 ....114 A4
Bottomley Side *BKLY* M9 ....33 D3
Bottom o' th' Moor *OLD* OL1 ....23 D2
The Boulevard *DID/WITH* M20 ....113 D3
Boundary Gdns *OLD* OL1 ....22 B1
Boundary Rd *SWIN* M27 ....45 C1
Boundary St *WGTN/LGST* M12 ....89 D4
Boundary St East *CMANE* M1 * 8 B4
Boundary St West *HULME* M15 ....8 A5
The Boundary *SWIN* M27 ....25 C1
Bourdon St *NEWH/MOS* M40 ....71 C2
Bourget St *BRO* M7 ....51 C1
Bourne Av *SWIN* M27 ....45 C2
Bourne Dr *NEWH/MOS* M40 ....36 A4
Bournelea Av *BNG/LEV* M19 ....116 B3
Bourne St *CHAD* OL9 ....39 C3
  HTNM SK4 ....129 D1
Bournville Av *HTNM* SK4 ....129 D1
Bournville Gv *BNG/LEV* M19 ....105 C4
Bourton Dr *GTN* M18 ....105 C1
Bowden Rd *SWIN* M27 ....45 D2
Bowdon Av *RUSH/FAL* M14 ....101 C4
Bowdon St *EDGY/DAV* SK3 ....132 B1
Bower Av *HTNM* SK4 ....128 B2
Bowerfold La *HTNM* SK4 ....128 B3
Bowers St *RUSH/FAL* M14 ....116 A2
Bower St *BRO* M7 * 50 B2
  NEWH/MOS M40 ....54 A4
  RDSH SK5 ....107 C3
Bower Ter *DROY* M43 ....76 B2
Bowes St *RUSH/FAL* M14 ....101 C2
Bowfell Gv *RUSH/FAL* M14 ....33 C2
Bowgreen Wk *HULME* M15 ....85 C3
Bowker Bank Av *CHH* M8 ....32 A3
Bowker St *BRO* M7 ....50 A3
Bowland Av *GTN* M18 ....107 D1
Bow La *CMANW* M2 ....3 F5
Bowler St *BNG/LEV* M19 ....118 A1
Bowling Green Cl *CHAD* OL9 ....38 B1
Bowling Rd *GTN* M18 ....106 B2
Bowling St *CHAD* OL9 ....39 C3
Bow Meadow Gra *WGTN/LGST* M12 ..104 A1
Bowness Av *HTNM* SK4 ....119 D3
Bowness Dr *SALE* M33 ....108 A4
Bowness St *OP/CLY* M11 ....92 A2
  STRET M32 ....97 C2
Bowring Rd *BRO* M7 * 49 D4
Bowscale Cl *BRUN/LGST* M13 ....104 A1
Bow St *CMANW* M2 ....3 E5
  OLD OL1 ....23 C3
Boxtree Av *GTN* M18 ....106 A2
Boyd St *WGTN/LGST* M12 ....89 D2
Boyer St *OLDTF/WHR* M16 ....84 A4
Boyle St *CHH* M8 ....52 A3
Brabham Cl *CCHDY* M21 ....112 A1
Brabham Ms *SWIN* M27 ....43 D2
Bracadale Dr *EDGY/DAV* SK3 ....132 B4
Bracewell Cl *WGTN/LGST* M12 ....89 D4
Bracken Cl *DROY* M43 ....76 B3
Brackenlea Dr *BKLY* M9 ....33 D3
Brackenlea Pl *EDGY/DAV* SK3 ....132 A4
Brackenside *RDSH* SK5 ....120 B1
Brackley Av *HULME* M15 ....6 A4
Brackley Dr *MDTN* M24 ....17 D4
Brackley Ldg *ECC* M30 ....63 C2
Brackley Rd *ECC* M30 ....62 A1
  HTNM SK4 ....119 C4
Brackley Sq *OLD* OL1 * 23 D1
Brackley St *OLD* OL1 ....23 D1
Bradburn Cl *ECC* M30 ....62 A4
Bradburn St *ECC* M30 ....62 A4

Bradburn Wk *CHH* M8 ....52 A3
Bradden Cl *ORD* M5 ....66 B4
Braddon Av *URM* M41 ....94 A2
Braddon St *OP/CLY* M11 ....73 D4
Brade Cl *OP/CLY* M11 ....90 B1
Bradfield Av *SLFD* M6 ....64 B3
Bradfield Cl *RDSH* SK5 ....106 B3
Bradfield Rd *STRET* M32 ....96 A3
  URM M41 ....95 C3
Bradford Rd *ECC* M30 ....62 B1
  NEWH/MOS M40 ....71 C3
Bradford St *OLD* OL1 ....22 B1
Bradgreen Rd *ECC* M30 ....61 D2
Bradley Av *BRO* M7 ....49 C2
Bradley La *STRET* M32 ....108 B2
Bradleys Count *CMANE* M1 * 4 C3
Bradley St *CMANE* M1 ....4 C3
Bradney Cl *BKLY* M9 ....33 C1
Bradshaw Av *DID/WITH* M20 ....115 C1
  FAIL M35 ....56 B4
Bradshaw Fold Av *NEWH/MOS* M40 ..37 C3
Bradshaw La *STRET* M32 ....110 A1
Bradshaw St *ANC* M4 * 4 A2
  BRO M7 ....50 B3
  OLD OL1 ....23 C2
Bradshaw St North *BRO* M7 ....50 A2
Bradstock Rd *OLDTF/WHR* M16 ....100 B3
Bradstone Rd *CHH* M8 ....51 C4
Bradwell Av *DID/WITH* M20 ....114 A4
  STRET M32 ....95 D2
Bradwen Av *CHH* M8 ....32 A3
Brady St *STKP* SK1 ....130 B3
Braemar Av *STRET* M32 ....95 D3
Braemar Rd *RUSH/FAL* M14 ....116 B3
Brae Side *OLDS* OL8 ....40 B3
Braeside *STRET* M32 * 95 D4
Bragenham St *GTN* M18 ....90 B4
Brailsford Rd *RUSH/FAL* M14 ....116 B1
Brakenhurst Dr *BRO* M7 * 51 C3
Braley St *WGTN/LGST* M12 * 9 D3
Bramble Av *ORD* M5 ....84 B2
Brambling Cl *DTN/ASHW* M34 ....76 B3
Bramfield Wk *HULME* M15 * 6 B4
Bramhall La *EDGY/DAV* SK3 ....133 C4
Bramhall St *GTN* M18 * 91 D4
Bramley Av *BNG/LEV* M19 ....117 D1
  STRET M32 ....96 A3
Bramley Cl *SWIN* M27 ....43 D3
Bramley Crs *HTNM* SK4 ....128 A4
Bramley Meade *BRO* M7 ....50 B2
Bramley St *BRO* M7 ....50 B4
Bramwell Dr *BRUN/LGST* M13 ....9 E5
Brancaster Rd *CMANE* M1 ....8 B3
Brandish Cl *BRUN/LGST* M13 ....103 C1
Brandon Av *DTN/ASHW* M34 ....107 C2
  ECC M30 ....63 D1
Brandon Brow *OLD* OL1 * 22 B1
Brandon Rd *SLFD* M6 ....46 A4
Brandram Rd *PWCH* M25 * 30 A1
Brandsby Gdns *ORD* M5 * 83 D1
Brandwood Av *CCHDY* M21 ....123 C1
Branksome Av *PWCH* M25 ....29 D1
Branksome Dr *BKLY* M9 ....15 C3
  SLFD M6 ....45 D4
Branksome Rd *HTNM* SK4 ....128 A4
Brannach Dr *CHAD* OL9 ....20 B1
Bransby Av *BKLY* M9 ....34 B1
Bransford Rd *OP/CLY* M11 ....91 C1
Branson St *ANC* M4 ....71 C4
Branston Rd *NEWH/MOS* M40 ....37 C3
Brantingham Rd *CCHDY* M21 ....99 C4
Brantwood Av *BRO* M7 ....50 A1
  HTNM SK4 ....128 B1
Brantwood Ter *BKLY* M9 * 54 A2
Brassica Cl *ECC* M30 ....60 B3
Brassington Av *CCHDY* M21 ....112 A2
  ORD M5 ....84 A1

Brassington Rd *HTNM* SK4	126	B1
Brathay Cl *WHTF* M45	12	B1
Brattice Dr *SWIN* M27	46	B1
Bratton Wk *BRUN/LGST* M13 *	88	A3
Braunston Cl *ECC* M30	79	D1
Bray Av *ECC* M30	61	C2
Brayside Rd *DID/WITH* M20	126	A1
Brayston Fold *MDTN* M24	15	D1
Brayton Av *DID/WITH* M20	125	D3
Brazennose St *CMANW* M2	3	E5
Brazil Pl *CMANE* M1	8	B2
Brazil St *CMANE* M1	8	B2
Bread St *GTN* M18	91	D3
Breck Rd *ECC* M30	61	C3
Brecon Av *BNG/LEV* M19	117	C2
Brecon Wk *OLDS* OL8 *	39	C3
Bredbury Rd *RUSH/FAL* M14	102	A3
Bredbury St *CHAD* OL9	21	C3
Bredon Wy *OLDS* OL8	40	B2
Breeze Mt *PWCH* M25	30	A3
Brendon Av *NEWH/MOS* M40	54	B2
RDSH SK5	120	A3
Brendon Dr *DTN/ASHW* M34	77	C4
Brennan Cl *HULME* M15	86	B4
Brennan Ct *OLDS* OL8	39	D3
Brennock Cl *OP/CLY* M11	89	C1
Brentbridge Rd *DID/WITH* M20	115	C2
Brentfield Av *CHH* M8	51	C3
Brentford Rd *RDSH* SK5	120	A3
Brentford St *BKLY* M9	53	D2
Brentnall St *STKP* SK1	133	C2
Brentnor Rd *NEWH/MOS* M40	36	B3
Brent Rd *HTNM* SK4	128	B4
Brentwood *SLFD* M6	65	D2
Brentwood Av *URM* M41	94	A3
WALK M28	43	C3
Brentwood Cl *OLDTF/WHR* M16	101	C2
Brentwood Ct *PWCH* M25	29	C2
Brentwood Dr *ECC* M30	62	A1
Brentwood Rd *SWIN* M27	44	A3
Brereton Dr *WALK* M28	42	A2
Brereton Rd *ECC* M30	60	A4
Breslyn St *CSLFD* M3	3	F1
Brethren's Ct *DROY* M43	92	B1
Brettargh St *SLFD* M6	66	B1
Brett St *WYTH/NTH* M22	123	D4
Brewer St *CMANE* M1	4	C4
Brewery St *SLFD* M6	66	B1
Brewster St *BKLY* M9 *	53	C1
Brian Av *DROY* M43 *	76	B2
Brian Redhead Ct *HULME* M15	6	C4
Briarfield Rd *DID/WITH* M20	116	A3
HTNM SK4	119	D3
WALK M28	42	A2
Briar Hill Wy *SLFD* M6 *	66	B2
Briar Hollow *HTNM* SK4	128	A4
Briarlea Gdns *BNG/LEV* M19	116	B4
Briarmere Wk *CHAD* OL9	21	D2
Briars Mt *HTNM* SK4	127	D3
Briarwood Av *DROY* M43	74	B2
Brickley St *CSLFD* M3	69	D2
Brick St *ANC* M4 *	4	B3
Bridcam St *CHH* M8	51	D4
Briddon St *CSLFD* M3	69	C2
Brideoak St *CHH* M8	51	D3
Bridgefield St *STKP* SK1	129	D4
Bridgelea Ms *DID/WITH* M20	115	C3
Bridgelea Rd *DID/WITH* M20	115	C3
Bridgend Cl *WGTN/LGST* M12	89	D3
Bridgenorth Av *URM* M41	95	C3
Bridge St *CSLFD* M3	3	D4
DROY M43	91	D1
MDTN M24 *	17	D1
OLD OL1	23	D1
STKP SK1	130	A3
SWIN M27	45	D1
Bridge St Brow *STKP* SK1 *	130	A3
Bridgewater Cir *TRPK* M17	78	B3
Bridgewater Pl *CMANE* M1	4	A4
Bridgewater Rd *SWIN* M27	46	A2
Bridgewater St *CSLFD* M3	6	C2
ECC M30	61	C3
OLD OL1	23	D1
SALE M33	109	C4
STRET M32 *	97	D3
Bridgewater Viad *CSLFD* M3	7	D3
Bridgewater Wy *OLDTF/WHR* M16	84	B3
Bridgnorth Rd *BKLY* M9	32	B2
Bridle Cl *DROY* M43	76	B2
Bridle Rd *PWCH* M25	13	D2
Bridlington Av *SLFD* M6 *	64	B2
Bridlington Cl *NEWH/MOS* M40	55	D3
Bridport Av *NEWH/MOS* M40	56	A1
Bridson St *ORD* M5	65	D4
Briercliffe Cl *GTN* M18	90	B3
Brierley Av *FAIL* M35	57	D2
Brierley Dr *MDTN* M24	16	A1
Brierley Rd East *SWIN* M27	25	D4
Brierley Rd West *SWIN* M27	25	D4
Brierley St *CHAD* OL9	21	D1
OLDS OL8	41	C2
Brierley Wk *CHAD* OL9	21	D1
Brigade Dr *STRET* M32	96	B2
Brigadier Cl *DID/WITH* M20	115	C3
Brigantine Cl *ORD* M5	83	D1
Briggs Rd *STRET* M32 *	98	A1
Briggs St *CSLFD* M3	2	B1
Brigham St *OP/CLY* M11	90	B1
Bright Cir *URM* M41	79	D3
Brightgate Wy *STRET* M32	80	B4
Brightman St *GTN* M18	91	C3
Brighton Av *BNG/LEV* M19	117	C2
BRO M7	50	B3
RDSH SK5	107	C3
Brighton Gv *RUSH/FAL* M14	103	C3
SALE M33	108	B4
Brighton Pl *BRUN/LGST* M13	7	C3
Brighton Range *GTN* M18 *	107	C1
Brighton Rd *HTNM* SK4	128	B4
Brighton St *ANC* M4	69	D2
Bright Rd *ECC* M30	62	B3
Brightstone Wk *RUSH/FAL* M14	103	D1
Bright St *CHAD* OL9	38	B2
DROY M43	76	A4
OLDS OL8	22	A4
Brightwater Cl *WHTF* M45	11	D1
Brightwell Wk *ANC* M4	4	B3
Brigstock Av *GTN* M18	90	B4
Brimelow St *MPL/ROM* SK6	131	D2
Brindale Rd *RDSH* SK5	131	D1
Brindle Cl *SLFD* M6	66	A1
Brindle Heath Rd *SLFD* M6	66	A1
Brindley Av *BKLY* M9	15	C4
SALE M33	109	D3
Brindley Rd *OLDTF/WHR* M16	84	A4
Brindley St *ECC* M30	61	C2
SWIN M27	26	A3
Brinklow Cl *OP/CLY* M11	91	D2
Brinksway *EDGY/DAV* SK3	129	C4
Brinnington Crs *RDSH* SK5	131	C1
Brinnington Rd *RDSH* SK5	131	D1
STKP SK1	130	B2
Brinsop Sq *WGTN/LGST* M12	90	A3
Brinsworth Dr *CHH* M8	51	D3
Brisbane St *BRUN/LGST* M13	87	C3
Briscoe La *NEWH/MOS* M40	72	B1
Briscoe St *OLD* OL1	23	C1
Bristle St *HULME* M15	8	A5
Bristol Av *BNG/LEV* M19	118	A1
Bristol St *BRO* M7	50	B2
Bristowe St *OP/CLY* M11	74	A2
Britannia Rd *SALE* M33	109	C4
Britannia St *OLD* OL1	23	D2
SLFD M6	48	B3

Britnall Av *WGTN/LGST* M12 ....88 B4
Brixham Rd *OLDTF/WHR* M16 ....99 C1
Brixham Wk *BRUN/LGST* M13 ....87 D4
Brixton Av *DID/WITH* M20 ....114 B3
Broadbent St *SWIN* M27 ....44 A2
Broadfield Gv *RDSH* SK5 ....106 B2
Broadfield Rd *RDSH* SK5 ....106 B2
    RUSH/FAL M14 ....101 D2
Broadgate *CHAD* OL9 ....37 D1
    MDTN M24 ....19 C3
Broadgate Meadow *SWIN* M27 * 45 C2
Broadhill Rd *BNG/LEV* M19 ....116 B3
Broadhurst Av *SWIN* M27 ....26 A2
Broadhurst St *EDGY/DAV* SK3 ....132 B2
Broadlands Rd *WALK* M28 ....43 D3
Broadlea Rd *BNG/LEV* M19 ....116 B4
Broadmeadow Av *OLDTF/WHR* M16 ...101 C4
Broadmoss Dr *BKLY* M9 ....35 D2
Broadmoss Rd *BKLY* M9 ....35 D2
Broadmount Ter *CHAD* OL9 * 39 C1
Broad Oak Crs *OLDS* OL8 ....41 D3
Broad Oak Pk *ECC* M30 ....62 A1
    WALK M28 ....43 C3
Broad Rd *SALE* M33 ....109 D4
Broadstone Cl *PWCH* M25 ....29 D3
Broadstone Hall Rd North *HTNM* SK4 ...119 C3
Broadstone Hall Rd South *HTNM* SK4 ...119 D3
Broadstone Rd *HTNM* SK4 ....119 C3
Broad St *MDTN* M24 ....15 D2
    SLFD M6 ....47 D4
Broadway *CHAD* OL9 ....38 A2
    DROY M43 ....92 B1
    FAIL M35 ....56 A1
    SALE M33 ....108 A3
    SALQ M50 ....82 B1
Broadway North *DROY* M43 ....92 B1
Broadway St *OLDS* OL8 ....41 C1
Broadwell Dr *BKLY* M9 ....53 D2
Brocade Cl *CSLFD* M3 ....2 A1
Brock Cl *OP/CLY* M11 ....91 C2
Brockford Dr *BKLY* M9 ....16 B4
Brocklebank Rd *RUSH/FAL* M14 ....115 D1
Brocklehurst St *BKLY* M9 ....54 B1
Brockley Av *RUSH/FAL* M14 ....102 A3
Brock St *CMANE* M1 * 5 D4
Brodick St *NEWH/MOS* M40 ....54 A1
Brodie Cl *ECC* M30 ....61 C3
Brogan St *GTN* M18 ....91 C4
Bromborough Av *DID/WITH* M20 ....114 B1
Bromfield Av *BKLY* M9 ....34 A4
Bromley St *ANC* M4 ....70 A2
    CHAD OL9 ....38 B3
Bromlow St *OP/CLY* M11 ....73 D4
Brompton Av *FAIL* M35 ....58 A1
Brompton Rd *HTNM* SK4 ....127 D5
    RUSH/FAL M14 ....102 A3
    STRET M32 ....95 C2
Brompton St *OLDE* OL4 ....23 D4
Bromsgrove Av *ECC* M30 ....61 C3
Bromshill Dr *BRO* M7 ....50 B3
Bronte St *HULME* M15 ....86 B4
Brook Av *BNG/LEV* M19 ....105 C3
    DROY M43 * 74 B4
    HTNM SK4 ....119 C4
    SWIN M27 ....45 C2
Brookbank Cl *MDTN* M24 ....18 A2
Brookburn Rd *CCHDY* M21 ....111 D2
Brook Cl *WHTF* M45 ....12 A1
Brookdale Av *NEWH/MOS* M40 ....74 A1
Brookdale St *FAIL* M35 ....56 B2
Brookdene Rd *BNG/LEV* M19 ....116 B3
Brook Dr *WHTF* M45 ....12 A1
Brookfield *PWCH* M25 ....30 A1
Brookfield Av *CCHDY* M21 ....112 B2
    SLFD M6 ....64 B2
    STKP SK1 ....133 D2
Brookfield Cl *STKP* SK1 ....133 D2

Brookfield Dr *SWIN* M27 ....25 D4
Brookfield Rd *CHH* M8 ....32 B4
    ECC M30 ....61 C1
Brookfield St *OL8* 23 C4
Brookfold *FAIL* M35 ....56 B1
Brookfold Rd *HTNM* SK4 ....119 C4
Brook Green La *GTN* M18 ....107 C2
Brookhead Av *DID/WITH* M20 * 114 A2
Brookhill St *NEWH/MOS* M40 ....71 D2
Brookhouse Av *ECC* M30 ....60 B4
Brookhurst Rd *GTN* M18 ....106 A1
Brooklands Av *OLD* OL9 ....21 C4
    DID/WITH M20 ....114 B3
Brooklands Cl *HTNM* SK4 ....119 C4
Brooklands Dr *DROY* M43 ....76 B2
Brooklands Rd *PWCH* M25 ....31 D3
    RDSH SK5 ....106 B3
    SWIN M27 ....44 A3
Brook La *OLDS* OL8 ....41 D1
Brooklawn Dr *DID/WITH* M20 ....125 C1
    PWCH M25 ....12 B3
Brookleigh Rd *DID/WITH* M20 ....116 A3
Brooklyn Av *OLDTF/WHR* M16 ....99 C3
Brook Rd *HTNM* SK4 ....118 B4
    RUSH/FAL M14 ....115 D2
Brooks Dr *FAIL* M35 ....56 B3
Brookshaw St *OP/CLY* M11 ....72 A3
Brookside Av *DROY* M43 ....76 B2
Brookside Crs *MDTN* M24 ....18 B3
Brookside Dr *PWCH* M25 ....31 C4
Brookside Rd *NEWH/MOS* M40 ....35 C4
Brook's Rd *OLDTF/WHR* M16 ....99 C3
Brookstone Cl *CCHDY* M21 ....113 C3
Brook St *CHAD* OL9 ....21 C1
    CMANE M1 ....8 B3
    FAIL M35 ....56 A3
    OLD OL1 ....23 D1
    SALE M33 ....109 D4
    SLFD M6 ....67 C1
    SWIN M27 ....44 A1
Brookthorpe Av *BNG/LEV* M19 ....116 B3
Brookway Cl *BNG/LEV* M19 ....126 B1
Brookwood Av *CHH* M8 ....52 B1
Broom Av *BNG/LEV* M19 ....118 A1
    BRO M7 ....50 B3
    RDSH SK5 ....120 B3
Broome Gv *FAIL* M35 ....57 C3
Broome St *CHAD* OL9 ....22 A3
Broomfield *SWIN* M27 ....47 C3
Broomfield Cl *RDSH* SK5 ....120 A3
Broomfield Dr *CHH* M8 ....51 C2
    RDSH SK5 ....120 A3
Broomfield Rd *HTNM* SK4 ....128 B1
Broomhall Rd *BKLY* M9 ....14 B4
    SWIN M27 ....47 C3
Broomhurst Av *OLDS* OL8 ....40 A3
Broom La *BNG/LEV* M19 ....118 A1
    BRO M7 ....50 A3
Broom St *SWIN* M27 ....45 C2
Broomwood Wk *HULME* M15 * 7 F5
Broseley Av *DID/WITH* M20 ....126 A2
Broseley Rd *OLDTF/WHR* M16 ....98 B3
Brotherton Cl *HULME* M15 ....6 A4
Brotherton Dr *CSLFD* M3 ....2 B1
Broughton La *BRO* M7 ....50 A4
Broughton Rd *RDSH* SK5 ....130 A3
    SLFD M6 ....66 B2
Broughton Rd East *SLFD* M6 ....67 C1
Broughton St *CHH* M8 ....51 C4
Brow Av *MDTN* M24 ....18 A3
Browfield Av *ORD* M5 ....84 A2
Browmere Dr *DID/WITH* M20 ....124 A1
Brownacre St *DID/WITH* M20 ....115 C3
Browncross St *CSLFD* M3 ....2 C4
Brownhills Ct *CCHDY* M21 * 112 A1
Brownhill St *OP/CLY* M11 * 89 D1

Name	Area/Grid	Page	Ref
Browning Av *DROY* M43		75	D4
Browning Rd *RDSH* SK5		106	A4
SWIN M27		44	B1
Browning St *CSLFD* M3		2	B1
HULME M15		85	C3
Brownslow Wk *BRUN/LGST* M13 *		9	D4
Brown St *CHAD* OL9		20	B2
CSLFD M3		3	D4
FAIL M35		56	B2
OLD OL1		23	D2
SLFD M6		66	A4
STKP SK1		129	D4
Brownsville Rd *HTNM* SK4		118	A4
Brownwood Av *STKP* SK4		131	C4
Broxton St *NEWH/MOS* M40		72	A2
Broxwood Cl *GTN* M18 *		91	C4
Brundretts Rd *CCHDY* M21		112	A1
Brundrett St *STKP* SK1		133	D1
Brunel Av *ORD* M5		67	C4
Brunel Cl *STRET* M32		97	D3
Brunet Wk *WGTN/LGST* M12 *		89	C3
Brunswick Rd *BRUN/LGST* M20		115	D3
Brunswick Sq *OLD* OL1 *		23	C3
Brunswick St *BRUN/LGST* M13		9	D5
OLD OL1		22	B3
STRET M32		109	D1
Brunton Rd *RDSH* SK5		120	A3
Brunt St *RUSH/FAL* M14		102	A2
Brussels St *EDGY/DAV* SK3		132	A3
Bruton Av *STRET* M32		96	A4
Bryan Rd *CCHDY* M21		99	C3
Bryant Cl *BRUN/LGST* M13 *		87	D4
Brydon Av *WGTN/LGST* M12		9	F3
Brydon Cl *SLFD* M6		66	B3
Brynden Av *DID/WITH* M20		115	D4
Bryn Dr *RDSH* SK5		120	A4
Brynford Av *BKLY* M9		14	B4
Brynorme Rd *CHH* M8		32	B3
Brynton Rd *BRUN/LGST* M13		103	D3
Buchanan St *SWIN* M27		26	A4
Buchan St *OP/CLY* M11		73	C3
Buckden Rd *HTNM* SK4		119	C2
Buckfast Cl *CCHDY* M21		99	C4
Buckfield Av *ORD* M5		84	A2
Buckhurst Rd *BNG/LEV* M19		104	B4
Buckingham Av *SLFD* M6		65	C3
WHTF M45		11	D2
Buckingham Rd West *HTNM* SK4		127	D1
Buckingham Rd *CCHDY* M21		99	C2
DROY M43		74	B4
HTNM SK4		118	B4
PWCH M25 *		30	A3
STRET M32		83	C4
SWIN M27		26	B3
Buckland Av *BKLY* M9		32	B2
Buckland Rd *SLFD* M6		65	C1
Buckley Av *GTN* M18		105	D1
Buckley La *WHTF* M45		28	B2
Buckley Rd *GTN* M18		105	C1
Buckley St *CHAD* OL9		20	B2
DROY M43		92	B1
OP/CLY M11		91	D2
RDSH SK5		106	B3
Bucklow Av *RUSH/FAL* M14		102	A4
Buckthorn Cl *CCHDY* M21		113	C3
Buckthorn La *ECC* M30		60	A4
Buddleia Gv *BRO* M7 *		50	A3
Bude Av *RDSH* SK5		121	C4
Budsworth Av *DID/WITH* M20		115	C2
Buerton Av *BKLY* M9		14	B4
Bugle St *CMANE* M1 *		7	D2
Buile Dr *BKLY* M9		35	C1
Buile Hill Dr *ORD* M5		65	C2
Buile St *BRO* M7		50	B2
Bulkeley St *EDGY/DAV* SK3		132	A2
Buller Rd *BRUN/LGST* M13		104	A3
Buller St *DROY* M43		93	C1
Bullock St *STKP* SK1		133	C2
Bulteel St *ECC* M30		61	C2
Bunkers HI *WHTF* M45		28	B2
Bunsen St *CMANE* M1 *		4	C4
Bunyard St *CHH* M8		52	A3
Burbridge Cl *OP/CLY* M11		88	B3
Burdale Dr *SLFD* M6		64	A1
Burder St *OLDS* OL8		39	D3
Burdett Wy *WGTN/LGST* M12		88	B4
Burdith Av *RUSH/FAL* M14		101	D3
Burford Av *OLDTF/WHR* M16		100	A3
URM M41		94	B2
Burford Dr *OLDTF/WHR* M16		100	A3
SWIN M27		25	D3
Burford Rd *OLDTF/WHR* M16		100	A3
Burgess Dr *FAIL* M35		57	C2
Burgin Wk *NEWH/MOS* M40		70	B1
Burland St *BRO* M7		66	A4
Burleigh Ms *CCHDY* M21		112	A3
Burleigh Rd *STRET* M32		97	D3
Burleigh St *HULME* M15		87	C4
Burley Ct *HTNM* SK4 *		128	B3
Burlington Av *OLDS* OL8		40	B1
Burlington Cl *HTNM* SK4		126	B3
Burlington Rd *DID/WITH* M20		115	D2
ECC M30		62	B1
Burlington St *BRUN/LGST* M13		87	C4
HULME M15		87	C4
Burman St *OP/CLY* M11		92	A2
Burnaby St *OLDS* OL8 *		21	D4
Burnage Av *BNG/LEV* M19		117	C1
Burnage Hall Rd *BNG/LEV* M19		116	B2
Burnage La *BNG/LEV* M19		126	A3
Burnage Range *BNG/LEV* M19		104	B4
Burnbray Av *BNG/LEV* M19		116	B3
Burnell Cl *NEWH/MOS* M40		5	F1
Burnett Av *ORD* M5		84	A1
Burnett Cl *NEWH/MOS* M40		53	C4
Burnfield Rd *GTN* M18		106	C2
Burnham Av *RDSH* SK5		107	C4
Burnham Dr *BNG/LEV* M19		117	C2
Burnham Rd *DTN/ASHW* M34		107	D2
Burnley Rd *CHAD* OL9		21	C2
FAIL M35		57	D2
Burnsall Av *WHTF* M45		10	A1
Burns Av *SWIN* M27		25	C4
Burns Cl *OP/CLY* M11		72	A4
Burns Gdns *PWCH* M25 *		29	C2
Burns Gv *DROY* M43		75	D3
Burnside Av *HTNM* SK4		119	D3
SLFD M6		46	A4
Burnside Dr *BNG/LEV* M19		116	B2
Burnthorp Av *BKLY* M9		33	D2
Burrows Av *CCHDY* M21		112	A3
Burslem Av *DID/WITH* M20		114	B1
Burstead St *GTN* M18		91	D3
Burstock St *ANC* M4		70	A2
Burston St *GTN* M18		90	B3
Burton Av *DID/WITH* M20		115	C3
Burton Gv *WALK* M28		43	D1
Burton Rd *DID/WITH* M20		124	A1
Burton St *HTNM* SK4		129	D2
MDTN M24		17	C1
Burton Wk *CSLFD* M3 *		2	B1
HTNM SK4		129	D1
Burtree St *WGTN/LGST* M12 *		89	D3
Bury Av *OLDTF/WHR* M16		99	D3
Bury New Rd *BRO* M7		50	A2
PWCH M25		11	D4
Bury Old Rd *BRO* M7		31	D4
WHTF M45		11	D3
Bury Pl *OP/CLY* M11		73	D3
Bury St *CSLFD* M3		3	D2
RDSH SK5		130	A2
Bush St *NEWH/MOS* M40		53	D4

Busk Rd *CHAD* OL9 ....21 D2
Busk Wk *CHAD* OL9 * 21 D1
Bute Av *OLDS* OL8 ....41 C2
Bute St *NEWH/MOS* M40 ....35 C4
   SALQ M50 ....65 C4
Butler Gn *CHAD* OL9 ....38 B1
Butler La *ANC* M4 ....5 F1
Butler St *ANC* M4 ....5 F2
Butman St *GTN* M18 ....92 A3
Buttercup Dr *EDGY/DAV* SK3 ....132 A4
Butter La *CSLFD* M3 * 3 E4
Buttermere Av *SWIN* M27 ....45 C3
Buttermere Cl *STRET* M32 ....96 B2
Butterstile Av *PWCH* M25 ....29 C4
Butterstile Cl *PWCH* M25 ....29 C4
Butterstile La *PWCH* M25 ....29 D2
Butterwick Cl *WGTN/LGST* M12 ......105 C2
Butterworth La *CHAD* OL9 ....37 D2
Butterworth St *CHAD* OL9 * 21 C2
   MDTN M24 ....18 B2
   OP/CLY M11 ....89 D1
Butt Hill Av *PWCH* M25 ....30 A2
Butt Hill Dr *PWCH* M25 ....30 A2
Butt Hill Rd *PWCH* M25 ....30 A3
Buttress St *GTN* M18 ....90 B3
Buxton *DID/WITH* M20 ....114 A3
Buxton La *DROY* M43 ....91 D1
Buxton Pl *OLDS* OL8 * 22 B3
Buxton Rd *STRET* M32 ....95 D2
Buxton St *CMANE* M1 ....9 D2
Byrcland Cl *WGTN/LGST* M12 ....88 B1
Byrom Av *BNG/LEV* M19 ....105 D4
Byrom St *CSLFD* M3 ....7 D1
   OLDTF/WHR M16 ....100 A1
   ORD M5 ....83 D1
Byron Av *DROY* M43 ....75 D3
   PWCH M25 ....29 C2
   SWIN M27 ....44 B1
Byron Gv *RDSH* SK5 ....106 B4
Byron Rd *STRET* M32 ....97 D2
Byron St *ECC* M30 ....62 A3
   OLDS OL8 ....39 C3

C

Cablestead Wk *OP/CLY* M11 ....89 C1
Cable St *ANC* M4 ....4 B2
   CSLFD M3 ....3 D2
Cabot Pl *RDSH* SK5 ....130 A1
Cabot St *BRUN/LGST* M13 ....9 D5
Caddington Rd *CCHDY* M21 ....112 B1
Cadogan Pl *BRO* M7 * 31 D4
Cadogan St *RUSH/FAL* M14 ....101 D1
Cadum Wk *BRUN/LGST* M13 ....9 E5
Caen Av *NEWH/MOS* M40 ....36 B2
Cairn Dr *SLFD* M6 ....67 D1
Cairn Wk *OP/CLY* M11 * 72 A4
Cairnwell Rd *CHAD* OL9 ....20 B1
Caister Av *WHTF* M45 ....11 D2
Caistor Cl *OLDTF/WHR* M16 ....113 D1
Caistor St *STKP* SK1 ....131 C2
Caistor Wk *OLD* OL1 ....23 C2
Cakebread St *HTNM* SK4 ....9 E3
Calbourne Crs *WGTN/LGST* M12 ....105 C2
Caldbeck Av *SALE* M33 ....110 B4
Caldecott Rd *BKLY* M9.....................14 B4
Calder Cl *RDSH* SK5 ....120 B4
Calder Dr *SWIN* M27 ....25 D4
Calder St *ORD* M5 ....6 A2
Caldervale Av *CCHDY* M21 ....122 B1
Caldon Cl *ECC* M30 ....79 C1
Caldwell St *RDSH* SK5 ....107 C4
Caldy Rd *SLFD* M6 ....65 C1
Caledon Av *NEWH/MOS* M40 ....54 B1

Caledonian Dr *ECC* M30 ....79 D1
Caledonia Wy *STRET* M32 ....80 B4
Cale Gn *OFTN* SK2 ....133 C3
Cale St *OFTN* SK2 ....133 C2
Caley St *CMANE* M1 ....8 A3
Calgary St *GTN* M18 ....90 B4
Calico Cl *CSLFD* M3 ....2 A1
Callingdon Rd *CCHDY* M21 ....113 C4
Callum Wk *BRUN/LGST* M13 * 87 D3
Calluna Ms *DID/WITH* M20 * 124 B1
Caithorpe Av *BKLY* M9 ....52 B2
Calton Av *BRO* M7 ....48 B2
Calver Av *ECC* M30 ....78 B1
Calverley Av *BNG/LEV* M19 ....117 C2
Calverton Dr *NEWH/MOS* M40 ....55 D2
Calvert St *ORD* M5 ....65 C3
Calver Wk *NEWH/MOS* M40 * 5 F1
Calvine Wk *NEWH/MOS* M40 * 70 B2
Cambell Rd *ECC* M30 ....61 C3
Cambert La *GTN* M18 ....90 B4
Camberwell St *CHH* M8 ....69 D1
   OLDS OL8 * 40 B1
Camborne St *RUSH/FAL* M14 ....102 A3
Cambo St *HTNM* SK4 ....127 C2
Cambrai Crs *ECC* M30 ....60 A3
Cambrian Rd *CHAD* OL9 ....71 D3
Cambridge Av *OLDTF/WHR* M16 ....99 D3
Cambridge Dr *DTN/ASHW* M34 ....107 D2
Cambridge Gv *ECC* M30 ....63 D3
   WHTF M45 ....11 D1
Cambridge Rd *BKLY* M9 ....34 A4
   DROY M43 ....75 C2
   FAIL M35 ....57 C4
   HTNM SK4 ....118 B4
Cambridge St *BRO* M7 ....68 B1
   CHAD OL9 ....39 D1
   CMANE M1 ....7 F3
   OFTN SK2 ....133 D3
Camden Av *NEWH/MOS* M40 ....73 D1
Camelford Cl *HULME* M15 * 86 B3
Camelia Rd *BKLY* M9 ....52 B2
Cameron St *CMANE* M1 * 7 E2
Campbell Rd *BRUN/LGST* M13 ....104 A3
   SWIN M27 ....44 B3
Campbell St *RDSH* SK5 ....107 C4
Camp St *BRO* M7 ....67 D1
   CSLFD M3 ....7 D1
Camrose Wk *BRUN/LGST* M13 * 88 B1
Canada St *NEWH/MOS* M40 ....71 D1
   OFTN SK2 ....133 C3
Canal Bank *ECC* M30 ....61 D2
Canal Bridge La *DROY* M43 ....74 A4
Canal Cottages Yd *ANC* M4 * 5 F5
Canal Side *ECC* M30 ....61 D2
Canal St *CHAD* OL9 ....39 C2
   CMANE M1 ....8 B1
   DROY M43 ....92 B1
   ORD M5 * 67 D4
   STKP SK1 ....133 D3
Canary Wy *SWIN* M27 ....47 D2
Canberra St *OP/CLY* M11 ....73 D3
Candleford Rd *DID/WITH* M20 * 115 C3
Canisp Cl *CHAD* OL9 ....20 B1
Canley Cl *STKP* SK1 ....133 C1
Canning St *HTNM* SK4 ....129 D1
Cannock Dr *HTNM* SK4 ....127 D3
Cannon Ct *CSLFD* M3 ....3 F3
Cannon St *CHAD* OL9 ....22 B2
   CSLFD M3 ....2 A2
   ECC M30 ....62 B4
Canon Green Dr *CSLFD* M3 ....2 C2
Canons Gv *NEWH/MOS* M40 ....53 D4
Canonsleigh Cl *CHH* M8 ....50 B4
Canonsway *SWIN* M27 ....44 B2
Canon Tighe Ct *CHAD* OL9 * 20 B2
Canterbury Dr *PWCH* M25 ....30 B3
Canterbury Gdns *ORD* M5 ....63 D3

Canterbury Pk *DID/WITH* M20..........**124** A2
Canterbury Rd *STKP* SK1..................**131** C4
    URM M41....................................**94** A3
Canterfield Cl *DROY* M43..................**77** C3
Cantrell St *OP/CLY* M11....................**73** C3
Canute Rd *STRET* M32......................**97** D2
Canute St *ORD* M5 *..........................**67** C4
Capella Wk *BRO* M7..........................**67** D1
Cape St *DID/WITH* M20......................**115** C4
Capital Rd *OP/CLY* M11....................**92** A2
Capricorn Rd *BKLY* M9......................**36** A2
Capricorn Wy *SLFD* M6 *....................**67** D1
Capstan St *BKLY* M9..........................**53** D1
Carberry Rd *GTN* M18........................**91** D4
Carden Av *SWIN* M27..........................**44** A3
Carder Cl *SWIN* M27..........................**45** C2
Cardiff Cl *OLDS* OL8..........................**39** C4
Cardiff St *BRO* M7..............................**50** B2
Cardigan Rd *OLDS* OL8......................**39** C3
Cardigan St *SLFD* M6 *........................**65** D4
Cardinal St *CHH* M8............................**52** A3
    OLD OL1..**23** C2
Carding Gv *CSLFD* M3..........................**2** C1
Cardroom Rd *ANC* M4............................**5** E4
Cardus St *BNG/LEV* M19....................**104** B4
Cardwell Rd *ECC* M30..........................**60** B4
Cardwell St *OLDS* OL8........................**41** C2
Caremine Av *BNG/LEV* M19................**105** C3
Carey Cl *BRO* M7 *..............................**68** A1
Carey Wk *HULME* M15........................**86** A4
Carfax St *GTN* M18..............................**91** C4
Carill Av *NEWH/MOS* M40....................**35** D4
Carill Dr *RUSH/FAL* M14....................**116** A1
Carina Pl *BRO* M7................................**67** D1
Carisbrook Av *WHTF* M45....................**11** D3
Carisbrook Dr *SWIN* M27....................**45** D3
Carisbrook St *BKLY* M9......................**53** C2
Carlburn St *OP/CLY* M11....................**74** A3
Carley Gv *BKLY* M9..............................**33** D1
Carlford Gv *PWCH* M25........................**29** C2
Carlile St *EDGY/DAV* SK3..................**132** B2
Carlingford Cl *EDGY/DAV* SK3............**132** B4
Carlisle Cl *WHTF* M45........................**12** A4
Carlisle Cl *CHAD* OL9..........................**39** D1
    SWIN M27......................................**26** A3
Carloon Rd *NTHM/RTH* M23................**122** A4
Carlton Av *PWCH* M25........................**31** D3
Carlton Crs *STKP* SK1......................**130** B3
    URM M41......................................**94** A4
Carlton Dr *PWCH* M25........................**31** D3
Carlton Range *GTN* M18 *..................**107** C1
Carlton Rd *HTNM* SK4........................**127** D3
    OLDTF/WHR M16............................**100** A3
    SALE M33....................................**108** B3
    SLFD M6..**65** D1
Carlton St *ECC* M30..............................**62** A2
    OLDTF/WHR M16..............................**99** D1
Carlyle Cl *CHH* M8..............................**51** D3
Carlyn Av *SALE* M33..........................**110** A4
Carmel Av *ORD* M5..............................**84** B2
Carmel Cl *ORD* M5..............................**84** B1
Carmel St *BKLY* M9..............................**34** A4
Carmichael St *EDGY/DAV* SK3............**132** A1
Carmona Dr *PWCH* M25......................**29** D1
Carmona Gdns *BRO* M7........................**30** B4
Carmoor Rd *BRUN/LGST* M13..............**87** D4
Carnaby St *BKLY* M9............................**35** C4
Carna Rd *RDSH* SK5..........................**106** B3
Carnarvon St *BRO* M7 *......................**50** B2
    CSLFD M3......................................**69** C2
    OLDS OL8......................................**39** C3
    STKP SK1....................................**133** D1
Carnegie Av *BNG/LEV* M19................**105** C4
Carnforth Av *CHAD* OL9......................**20** B3
Carnforth Rd *HTNM* SK4....................**118** B3
Carnforth St *RUSH/FAL* M14..............**102** A2
Carnoustie Cl *NEWH/MOS* M40............**55** D2

Carnwood Cl *NEWH/MOS* M40..............**74** A1
Carolina Wy *SALQ* M50........................**65** D2
Caroline St *BRO* M7............................**68** B1
    EDGY/DAV SK3............................**132** A2
Carpenters La *ANC* M4..........................**4** B3
Carpenters Wk *DROY* M43....................**75** C4
Carr Av *PWCH* M25..............................**29** C3
Carr Bank Av *BKLY* M9........................**32** A2
Carrgreen Cl *BNG/LEV* M19................**117** C4
Carriage Dr *NEWH/MOS* M40................**53** C4
Carriage St *OLDTF/WHR* M16..............**85** C4
Carrigart *PWCH* M25............................**29** D2
Carrill Gv East *BNG/LEV* M19............**104** B4
Carrington Field St *OFTN* SK2............**133** C2
Carrington Rd *RUSH/FAL* M14............**115** D1
    STKP SK1....................................**131** C3
Carrington St *CHAD* OL9......................**39** C2
    SWIN M27......................................**27** C4
Carrington Ter *SWIN* M27 *..................**26** B4
Carron Av *BKLY* M9..............................**34** B4
Carrsdale Dr *BKLY* M9........................**33** D3
Carr St *SWIN* M27................................**44** A2
Carruthers St *ANC* M4........................**71** C4
Carslake Rd *NEWH/MOS* M40..............**53** C4
Carson Rd *BNG/LEV* M19..................**117** D1
Carstairs Cl *CHH* M8............................**51** C2
Carter St *BRO* M7 *............................**50** A4
    SALQ M50....................................**64** B4
Carthage St *OLDS* OL8........................**41** C1
Cartmel Av *HTNM* SK4......................**119** C3
Cartmel Cl *OLDS* OL8..........................**40** A2
Cartmel Crs *CHAD* OL9........................**38** A3
Cartmel Gv *WALK* M28........................**43** C2
Cartwright Rd *CCHDY* M21................**111** D1
Carver Av *PWCH* M25..........................**12** B4
Carver Cl *OLDTF/WHR* M16..................**84** A4
Carver St *OLDTF/WHR* M16..................**84** A4
Carver Wk *HULME* M15 *......................**86** A4
Carville Rd *BKLY* M9............................**36** B2
Cascade Dr *BRO* M7............................**50** B2
Cashgate Ct *OLDS* OL8........................**39** D2
Cashmoor Wk *WGTN/LGST* M12............**88** B3
Caspian Rd *BKLY* M9............................**36** A4
Cass Av *ORD* M5..................................**83** D1
Cassidy Cl *ANC* M4................................**5** D1
Casson St *FAIL* M35............................**57** C2
Castle Cl *DROY* M43............................**76** A3
Castledene Av *SLFD* M6......................**65** D2
Castlefield Av *BRO* M7........................**50** B1
Castlefield Br *ORD* M5..........................**6** A1
Castle Hill Dr *BKLY* M9........................**33** D4
Castle Hill Rd *PWCH* M25....................**31** C3
Castlemere Rd *BKLY* M9......................**33** D2
Castlemill St *OLD* OL1..........................**23** D2
Castlemoor Av *BRO* M7........................**49** C1
Castle Quay *HULME* M15........................**6** C3
Castlerea Cl *ECC* M30..........................**79** C4
Castlerigg Cl *HTNM* SK4....................**119** C2
Castle St *CSLFD* M3..............................**6** C2
    ECC M30..**63** C3
    EDGY/DAV SK3............................**132** B2
    MDTN M24......................................**19** C2
Castleton Av *STRET* M32......................**96** A2
Castleton Rd *BRO* M7..........................**50** B1
    STRET M32....................................**95** D1
Castleton Cl *OLD9* OL9 *......................**21** D3
Castleton Wk *OP/CLY* M11 *................**72** A4
Castleway *SLFD* M6..............................**65** D1
Castle Wy *SWIN* M27............................**26** B3
Castlewood Rd *BRO* M7........................**48** A1
Catchdale Cl *BKLY* M9........................**15** D4
Cateaton St *CSLFD* M3..........................**3** F3
Caterham St *ANC* M4..........................**71** C4
Catfield Wk *HULME* M15 *......................**6** A4
Cathedral Ap *CSLFD* M3........................**3** F2
Cathedral Gdns *ANC* M4 *......................**3** F2
Cathedral Gates *CSLFD* M3 *................**3** F3

Cathedral St *CSLFD* M3 ....3 F3
Catherine Houses *HTNM* SK4 * 127 C3
Catherine Rd *CHH* M8 ....31 D4
   SWIN M27 ....43 D2
Catherine St *ECC* M30 ....60 B2
   OP/CLY M11 ....91 D1
Catherston Cl *OLDTF/WHR* M16 ....100 B2
Catlow La *ANC* M4 * 4 A3
Catlow St *BRO* M7 ....68 B1
Catterick Av *DID/WITH* M20 ....125 D2
Catterick Rd *DID/WITH* M20 ....125 D2
Cattlin Wy *OLDS* OL8 ....39 D3
The Causeway *CHAD* OL9 ....19 C4
Cavanagh Cl *BRUN/LGST* M13 ....88 A3
Cavell St *CMANE* M1 * 4 C4
Cavell Wy *ORD* M5 ....66 B4
Cavendish Av *DID/WITH* M20 ....114 A3
   SWIN M27 ....27 D2
Cavendish Gv *ECC* M30 ....62 B2
Cavendish Rd *BRO* M7 ....31 C4
   DID/WITH M20 ....114 A3
   ECC M30 ....62 B2
   HTNM SK4 ....127 C3
   STRET M32 ....97 D1
   URM M41 ....94 B3
   WALK M28 ....43 C3
Cavendish St *HULME* M15 ....8 B4
   OLDS OL8 ....22 B3
Caversham Dr *BKLY* M9 ....53 D1
Cawdor Rd *RUSH/FAL* M14 ....102 B4
Cawdor St *ECC* M30 ....61 D4
   HULME M15 ....6 A4
   SWIN M27 ....44 A1
Cawley Av *PWCH* M25 ....29 C3
Cawley Ter *BKLY* M9 * 14 B4
Cawood Sq *RDSH* SK5 ....121 D3
Cawston Wk *CHH* M8 ....51 D3
Caxton Rd *RUSH/FAL* M14 ....102 A4
Caxton St *CSLFD* M3 * 3 D3
Caxton Wy *ORD* M5 ....67 C4
Caygill St *CSLFD* M3 ....3 D2
Caythorpe St *RUSH/FAL* M14 ....101 D2
Cayton St *WGTN/LGST* M12 ....104 B2
Cecil Gv *GTN* M18 ....106 A1
Cecil Rd *BKLY* M9 ....34 A1
   ECC M30 ....62 B4
   STRET M32 ....96 B4
Cecil St *EDGY/DAV* SK3 * 132 B2
   HULME M15 ....87 C4
   OLDS OL8 ....22 B4
Cedar Av *WHTF* M45 ....11 C3
Cedar Crs *CHAD* OL9 ....21 C1
Cedar Dr *DROY* M43 ....76 A3
   SWIN M27 ....25 C1
Cedar Gv *HTNM* SK4 ....118 B4
   PWCH M25 ....11 C3
   RUSH/FAL M14 ....116 A1
Cedar Pl *BRO* M7 ....67 D1
Cedar Rd *FAIL* M35 ....57 C3
   MDTN M24 ....18 B1
Cedarwood Av *HTNM* SK4 ....127 D4
Cedric Rd *CHH* M8 ....31 D3
Cedric St *ORD* M5 ....65 C3
Celia St *CHH* M8 ....52 B1
Celtic St *STKP* SK1 ....133 D1
Cemetery Rd *DROY* M43 ....75 C4
   FAIL M35 ....57 C4
   ORD M5 ....65 D4
   SWIN M27 ....25 D4
Cemetery Rd North *SWIN* M27 ....25 D3
Centaur Cl *SWIN* M27 ....26 A3
Centenary Wy *SALQ* M50 ....63 D4
   TRPK M17 ....80 B1
Central Av *BNG/LEV* M19 ....104 B3
   SLFD M6 ....47 D3
   SWIN M27 ....28 A3
   URM M41 ....79 D3

Central Dr *CHH* M8 ....33 C4
   RDSH SK5 ....120 B4
   SWIN M27 ....46 A2
   URM M41 ....94 A3
Central Park Est *TRPK* M17 * 81 D3
Central Rd *DID/WITH* M20 ....114 B4
Central St *CMANW* M2 ....7 F1
Centurion Gv *BRO* M7 ....50 B4
Ceylon St *NEWH/MOS* M40 ....54 B3
Chadderton Prec *CHAD* OL9 * 21 C2
Chadderton St *ANC* M4 ....4 C2
Chadderton Wy *OLDS* OL8 ....22 A1
Chaddesley Wk *OP/CLY* M11 * 89 D1
Chadwick Cl *RUSH/FAL* M14 * 102 A2
Chadwick Rd *ECC* M30 ....62 B3
   URM M41 ....95 C3
Chadwick St *STKP* SK1 ....133 C1
   SWIN M27 ....45 C1
Chaffinch Cl *DROY* M43 ....76 B2
Chain Rd *BKLY* M9 ....16 A4
Chain St *CMANE* M1 ....4 A5
Chalcombe Gra *WGTN/LGST* M12 * 104 A1
Chale Cl *NEWH/MOS* M40 ....71 C2
Chale Dr *MDTN* M24 ....18 B3
Chalfont Av *URM* M41 * 94 B3
Chalfont Dr *CHH* M8 ....51 D2
Challenor Sq *WGTN/LGST* M12 * 89 D1
Challum Dr *CHAD* OL9 ....20 B1
Chamber Hall Cl *OLDS* OL8 ....40 A1
Chamber Rd *OLDS* OL8 ....39 D2
Chambers Field Ct *ORD* M5 ....66 B4
Chancel Av *ORD* M5 ....84 B1
Chancellor La *WGTN/LGST* M12 ....88 A1
Chancel Ms *STKP* SK1 ....130 B4
Chancel Pl *CMANE* M1 * 5 E5
Chancery La *CMANW* M2 ....3 F5
Chancery St *CHAD* OL9 ....21 D1
Chancery Wk *CHAD* OL9 ....21 D1
Chandos Gv *ORD* M5 ....65 C3
Chandos Rd *CCHDY* M21 ....99 D4
   HTNM SK4 ....118 A3
   PWCH M25 ....30 A3
Chandos Rd South *CCHDY* M21 ....99 D4
Change Wy *CSLFD* M3 ....2 C1
Chantry Cl *RDSH* SK5 ....119 D3
Chapelfield Rd *WGTN/LGST* M12 ....9 F2
Chapel Gv *URM* M41 ....94 B3
Chapelhill Dr *BKLY* M9 ....33 D2
Chapel La *BKLY* M9 ....33 C2
Chapel Pl *URM* M41 ....79 C1
Chapel Rd *OLDS* OL8 ....39 D1
   PWCH M25 ....29 C4
   SALE M33 ....109 C4
   SWIN M27 ....43 D2
Chapel St *BNG/LEV* M19 ....104 B4
   CSLFD M3 ....2 C3
   DROY M43 ....76 A4
   ECC M30 ....60 D4
   HTNM SK4 ....126 A4
   MDTN M24 * 15 D2
   MDTN M24 ....17 C1
   PWCH M25 ....29 D1
   SWIN M27 ....26 B4
Chapeltown St *CMANE* M1 ....9 E1
Chapel Wks *CMANW* M2 ....3 F4
Chaplin Cl *SLFD* M6 ....65 D1
Chapman Ms *GTN* M18 * 91 C4
Chapman St *GTN* M18 ....91 C3
Chappell Rd *DROY* M43 ....75 D3
Chapter St *NEWH/MOS* M40 ....72 A1
Chariot St *OP/CLY* M11 ....91 C1
Charlbury Av *PWCH* M25 ....31 C2
   RDSH SK5 ....120 A3
Charles Av *DTN/ASHW* M34 ....92 B2
Charles Halle Rd *RUSH/FAL* M14 ....86 B4
Charles Morris Cl *FAIL* M35 ....58 A1
Charles St *CHAD* OL9 ....21 D3

CMANE M1 .... 8 B2
DROY M43 * 74 B4
SLFD M6 .... 66 A1
STKP SK1 .... 133 C2
SWIN M27 .... 25 C4
WHTF M45 .... 11 C2
Charleston St *OLDS* OL8 .... 41 C1
Charlestown Rd *BKLY* M9 .... 34 A3
Charlesworth St *OP/CLY* M11 .... 89 C1
STKP SK1 * 133 C2
Charlotte St *CMANW* M2 .... 4 A5
STKP SK1 .... 131 C2
Charlton Av *ECC* M30 .... 62 A4
PWCH M25 .... 30 A2
Charlton Dr *SWIN* M27 .... 25 C3
Charlton Pl *CMANE* M1 .... 9 D3
Charlton Rd *BNG/LEV* M19 .... 105 C3
Charminster Dr *CHH* M8 .... 52 A1
Charnley Cl *NEWH/MOS* M40 .... 71 D2
Charnley St *WHTF* M45 .... 11 C1
Charnwood Rd *BKLY* M9 .... 16 A4
Charter St *CSLFD* M3 .... 69 C2
OLD OL1 .... 23 D1
Chartwell Cl *SLFD* M6 .... 66 A3
Chaseley Rd *SLFD* M6 .... 65 D1
The Chase *WALK* M28 .... 42 B4
Chasewood *BNG/LEV* M19 * 104 A3
Chataway Rd *CHH* M8 .... 52 A1
Chatburn Rd *CCHDY* M21 .... 112 B1
Chatfield Rd *CCHDY* M21 .... 112 A1
Chatford Cl *BRO* M7 .... 68 B1
Chatham Ct *DID/WITH* M20 * 114 B3
Chatham Gv *DID/WITH* M20 .... 114 B3
Chatham Rd *GTN* M18 * 106 B2
OLDTF/WHR M16 .... 99 D2
Chatham St *CMANE* M1 .... 4 C5
EDGY/DAV SK3 .... 132 A1
Chatley Rd *ECC* M30 .... 60 A4
Chatley St *CSLFD* M3 .... 69 C1
Chatsworth Av *PWCH* M25 .... 30 A1
Chatsworth Cl *DROY* M43 .... 74 A2
URM M41 .... 94 B3
Chatsworth Gv *OLDTF/WHR* M16 .... 100 A3
Chatsworth Rd *DROY* M43 .... 74 B3
ECC M30 .... 63 C1
GTN M18 .... 90 B4
STRET M32 .... 95 C2
WALK M28 .... 43 C4
Chatterton Cl *DID/WITH* M20 .... 115 D3
Chattock St *OLDTF/WHR* M16 .... 100 B3
Chatwood Rd *NEWH/MOS* M40 .... 37 C3
Chaucer Av *DROY* M43 .... 75 D4
RDSH SK5 .... 119 C1
Chaucer Ms *STKP* SK1 .... 131 C4
Chaucer St *OLD* OL1 .... 22 B5
Chaucer Wk *BRUN/LGST* M13 .... 87 C1
Chauncy Rd *NEWH/MOS* M40 .... 56 B1
Chaytor Av *NEWH/MOS* M40 .... 55 C2
Cheadle Av *BRO* M7 .... 48 B2
Cheadle Old Rd *EDGY/DAV* SK3 .... 132 A2
Cheadle St *OP/CLY* M11 .... 91 C1
Cheapside *CMANW* M2 .... 3 F4
OLD OL1 .... 22 C2
Cheddar St *GTN* M18 .... 91 C4
Cheeryble St *DROY* M43 .... 4 A1
Cheetham Hill Rd *ANC* M4 .... 51 D2
CHH M8 .... 51 D2
Cheetham Rd *SWIN* M27 .... 45 D2
Cheetham St *FAIL* M35 .... 57 D1
MDTN M24 .... 17 C1
NEWH/MOS M40 * 53 D4
Cheetwood Rd *CHH* M8 .... 51 C4
Cheetwood St *BRO* M7 .... 68 B1
Chelbourne Dr *OLDS* OL8 * 39 C3
Chelford Dr *SWIN* M27 .... 25 D3
Chelford Rd *OLDTF/WHR* M16 .... 99 D2

Chell St *BRUN/LGST* M13 .... 104 A1
Chelmsford Av *NEWH/MOS* M40 .... 73 C1
Chelmsford St *OLDS* OL8 .... 22 B4
Chelsea Rd *NEWH/MOS* M40 .... 55 D4
Chelsfield Gv *CCHDY* M21 .... 113 C1
Chelston Av *NEWH/MOS* M40 .... 37 C3
Cheltenham Crs *BRO* M7 .... 50 B2
Cheltenham Gn *MDTN* M24 .... 17 C3
Cheltenham Rd *CCHDY* M21 .... 99 C3
MDTN M24 .... 17 D3
Cheltenham St *SLFD* M6 .... 66 B1
Chelwood Dr *DROY* M43 .... 75 C3
Chendre Rd *BKLY* M9 .... 36 A2
Cheney Cl *OP/CLY* M11 * 91 C2
Chepstow Rd *CCHDY* M21 .... 98 B4
SWIN M27 .... 26 B3
Chepstow St *CMANE* M1 .... 7 F2
Chepstow St South *CMANE* M1 * 7 F2
Chequers Rd *CCHDY* M21 .... 112 A1
Cherington Cl *NTHM/RTH* M23 .... 122 A3
Cheriton Av *SALE* M33 .... 109 D4
Cherry Dr *SWIN* M27 .... 45 D1
Cherry Hinton *OLD* OL1 * 22 A1
Cherry Holt Av *HTNM* SK4 .... 127 C1
Cherry St *PWCH* M25 * 12 B4
Cherryton Wk *BRUN/LGST* M13 .... 87 D5
Cherry Tree Wk *STRET* M32 .... 96 A4
Cherrywood *CHAD* OL9 .... 19 C2
Chertsey Cl *GTN* M18 .... 102 A4
Chervil Cl *RUSH/FAL* M14 .... 88 D1
Chervil Cl *RUSH/FAL* M14 .... 115 D1
Cherwell Cl *OLDS* OL8 .... 39 D4
WHTF M45 .... 11 D1
Chesham Rd *ECC* M30 * 78 B1
Cheshire Cl *STRET* M32 .... 96 A4
Chesney Av *CHAD* OL9 .... 37 D5
Chesshyre Av *ANC* M4 * 71 C4
Chessington Ri *SWIN* M27 .... 26 B2
Chester Av *URM* M41 .... 94 B3
WHTF M45 .... 11 D2
Chestergate *EDGY/DAV* SK3 .... 129 D1
Chester Rd *HULME* M15 .... 6 A4
OLDTF/WHR M16 .... 84 B1
STRET M32 .... 109 D1
Chester St *CHAD* OL9 .... 21 D4
EDGY/DAV SK3 .... 129 C4
HULME M15 .... 7 F4
PWCH M25 .... 11 D4
SWIN M27 .... 44 B2
Chesterton Gv *DROY* M43 .... 75 D3
Chestnut Av *CCHDY* M21 .... 112 A1
DROY M43 .... 74 B2
WHTF M45 .... 11 C2
Chestnut Crs *OLDS* OL8 .... 41 D3
Chestnut Gv *FAIL* M35 .... 57 C3
Chestnut Rd *ECC* M30 .... 60 B1
Chestnut St *CHAD* OL9 .... 38 B2
Chesworth Cl *STKP* SK1 * 133 C1
Chesworth Fold *STKP* SK1 .... 133 C1
Chetham St *ORD* M5 * 84 A2
Chevassut St *HULME* M15 .... 6 C5
Chevington Dr *BKLY* M9 .... 53 C3
HTNM SK4 .... 126 A2
Cheviot Av *OLDS* OL8 .... 40 B2
Cheviot Cl *CHAD* OL9 .... 129 C2
HTNM SK4 .... 19 C1
MDTN M24 .... 19 C1
SLFD M6 .... 65 D2
Cheviot St *CSLFD* M3 .... 69 C2
Chevril Cl *HULME* M15 .... 8 A5
Chevron Cl *SLFD* M6 .... 67 C3
Chichester Rd *HULME* M15 .... 85 D4
Chichester Rd South *HULME* M15 * 85 D4
Chidlow Av *DID/WITH* M20 .... 114 B2
Chief St *OLDE* OL4 .... 23 D3
Chiffon Wy *CSLFD* M3 .... 2 A1
Chilham Rd *ECC* M30 .... 63 C1

Chilham St *SWIN* M27....................44 B3
Chiltern Dr *SWIN* M27...................45 C3
Chilton Av *CHAD* OL9...................20 B3
Chilton Dr *MDTN* M24...................18 B2
Chilworth St *RUSH/FAL* M14........102 A3
Chime Bank *CHH* M8......................52 B2
China La *CMANE* M1.........................4 C5
Chingford Wk *BRUN/LGST* M13 *...104 A1
Chinley Av *NEWH/MOS* M40..........54 B1
    STRET M32..................................95 D1
Chinley Cl *HTNM* SK4..................128 A2
Chinley St *SLFD* M6......................49 C4
Chinwell Vw *BNG/LEV* M19 *.......104 B4
Chippenham Av *ANC* M4................71 C3
Chippenham Rd *ANC* M4..................5 F3
Chipstead Av *WGTN/LGST* M12.....88 B4
Chiselhurst St *CHH* M8..................51 D2
Chisholm St *OP/CLY* M11...............91 C2
Chisledon Av *BRO* M7 *.................51 C3
Chislehurst Av *URM* M41...............94 A2
Chiswick Rd *DID/WITH* M20.........125 D2
Choir St *BRO* M7............................68 B1
Cholmondeley Rd *SLFD* M6............64 B1
Chomlea Mnr *SLFD* M6 *................64 A1
Choral Gv *BRO* M7.........................50 A4
Chorley Rd *SWIN* M27....................25 C4
Chorley St *STRET* M32...................83 C4
Chorley Wood Av *BNG/LEV* M19 *...117 C3
Choriton Fold *ECC* M30.................44 A4
Choriton Pl *CCHDY* M21.................99 C3
Choriton Rd *HULME* M15...................6 B4
Choriton St *CMANE* M1....................4 B5
    OLDTF/WHR M16........................84 B4
Choriton Ter *BRUN/LGST* M13 *......8 C5
Chretien Rd *WYTH/NTH* M22........123 D3
Christchurch Av *ORD* M5................67 C3
Christie Rd *STRET* M32..................97 D3
Christleton Av *HTNM* SK4.............119 C4
Christopher St *NEWH/MOS* M40....74 A1
    ORD M5.......................................66 B4
Chudleigh Rd *CHH* M8....................32 B3
Church Av *NEWH/MOS* M40...........55 D4
    SLFD M6.......................................65 C3
Churchdale Rd *BKLY* M9................33 C1
Church Dr *PWCH* M25.....................29 C1
Churchfield Rd *SLFD* M6................47 C4
Churchfield Wk *OP/CLY* M11 *.......89 D1
Churchgate *STKP* SK1..................130 A4
    URM M41......................................94 B4
Churchgate Buildings *CMANE* M1 *...9 E1
Church Gn *SLFD* M6 *....................66 A2
Churchill Crs *RDSH* SK5...............106 B4
Churchill St *HTNM* SK4................129 C2
    OLDE OL4.....................................23 D3
Churchill St East *OLDE* OL4...........23 D3
Churchill Wy *SLFD* M6...................66 B3
    TRPK M17.....................................81 D2
Church La *BKLY* M9.........................53 D2
    BKLY M9.......................................54 A2
    BNG/LEV M19.............................117 C3
    BRO M7...30 A4
    OLD OL1..23 C2
    PWCH M25....................................29 D1
    WHTF M45.....................................10 B1
Church Rd *ECC* M30........................63 C3
    HTNM SK4..................................129 D3
    MDTN M24....................................19 C2
    URM M41.......................................94 A4
    WYTH/NTH M22...........................123 D4
Churchside Cl *BKLY* M9..................34 A3
Church St *ANC* M4............................4 B3
    DROY M43.....................................76 A4
    ECC M30..62 B3
    FAIL M35.......................................57 C1
    HTNM SK4...................................129 D1
    OLD OL1..23 C2
    STRET M32....................................96 B4

    SWIN M27......................................44 B1
    SWIN M27......................................46 A1
Church Ter *SALE* M33....................108 B3
Church Wk *SWIN* M27.....................26 A1
Churchwood Rd *DID/WITH* M20...125 C2
Churnet St *NEWH/MOS* M40..........53 C4
Churston Av *BKLY* M9.....................34 B1
Churton Rd *GTN* M18....................105 D2
Churwell Av *NEWH/MOS* M40........36 A3
Cicero St *BKLY* M9..........................53 D1
Cinder St *ANC* M4..............................5 E2
Cipher St *ANC* M4.............................5 E1
Circle South *TRPK* M17..................82 B3
The Circuit *DID/WITH* M20...........115 C3
Circular Rd *DID/WITH* M20...........115 C4
    PWCH M25.....................................30 A4
Circus St *CMANE* M1 *......................4 C5
Ciss La *URM* M41............................94 B3
Citrus Wy *SLFD* M6.........................66 B3
City Rd *HULME* M15.........................85 C3
City Rd East *HULME* M15................7 E4
City Wk *SWIN* M27...........................46 A1
Clacton Wk *BRUN/LGST* M13..........9 E5
Clague St *OP/CLY* M11....................72 B3
Claife Av *NEWH/MOS* M40.............36 A3
Clandon Av *ECC* M30.......................61 C3
Clapham St *NEWH/MOS* M40.........55 D1
Clara St *CHAD* OL9.........................39 D1
Claremont Av *DID/WITH* M20.......114 B4
    HTNM SK4...................................118 B4
Claremont Gv *DID/WITH* M20......124 B2
Claremont Range *GTN* M18 *........107 C1
Claremont Rd *OLDTF/WHR* M16...101 C2
    SALE M33.....................................109 C4
    SLFD M6..64 B1
Claremont St *FAIL* M35...................57 C1
    OLDS OL8......................................41 C3
    SLFD M6..46 B3
Clarence Av *OLDS* OL8....................40 A3
    TRPK M17......................................80 A3
    WHTF M45.....................................11 D2
Clarence Rd *BRUN/LGST* M13......103 D2
    HTNM SK4...................................118 A4
    SWIN M27......................................43 D2
Clarence St *BRO* M7........................68 A1
    CMANW M2 *..................................3 F5
Clarendon Av *HTNM* SK4..............128 A2
Clarendon Crs *ECC* M30..................63 C2
    SALE M33.....................................110 A4
Clarendon Rd *DTN/ASHW* M34......93 C2
    ECC M30..63 C2
    OLDTF/WHR M16..........................99 D3
    SWIN M27......................................45 C1
Clarendon Rd West *CCHDY* M21....99 C3
Clarendon St *HULME* M15.................7 D5
    RDSH SK5....................................130 A2
    WHTF M45.....................................11 C1
Clare Rd *BNG/LEV* M19.................117 D1
    RDSH SK5....................................130 A1
Clare St *CMANE* M1...........................9 D3
    ORD M5...67 D4
Claribel St *OP/CLY* M11..................88 B1
Claridge Rd *CCHDY* M21.................98 B3
Clarion St *ANC* M4.............................5 E1
Clark Av *BKLY* M9............................91 D4
Clarke Av *ORD* M5...........................84 A2
Clark's HI *PWCH* M25......................29 D1
Clarkwell Cl *OLD* OL1 *..................22 B1
Claude Av *SWIN* M27.......................44 B3
Claude Rd *CCHDY* M21..................111 D3
Claude St *CHH* M8...........................32 B4
    ECC M30..61 C1
    SWIN M27......................................44 A1
Claxton Av *BKLY* M9........................34 A2
Clay Bank *DROY* M43.......................74 B4
Claybar Dr *ECC* M30........................62 B2
Claybrook Wk *OP/CLY* M11 *..........72 B4

Clayburn Rd *HULME* M15......................**7** D5
Claycourt Av *ECC* M30.........................**61** C1
Claygate Dr *BKLY* M9...........................**16** A4
Claymore St *GTN* M18..........................**91** D3
Clay St *OLDS* OL8................................**40** B1
Claythorpe Wk *PWCH* M25.................**31** D3
Clayton Av *DID/WITH* M20................**125** C2
Claytonbrook Rd *OP/CLY* M11............**73** D4
Clayton Cl *HULME* M15.......................**85** C4
Clayton Hall Rd *OP/CLY* M11..............**73** D4
Clayton La *OP/CLY* M11.......................**90** A1
Clayton La South *WGTN/LGST* M12...**89** D2
Clayton St *CHAD* OL9.........................**38** B2
   FAIL M35 *...**56** B2
   OP/CLY M11.......................................**73** C2
Cleadon Av *GTN* M18.........................**105** D1
Clearwater Dr *DID/WITH* M20...........**114** A4
Cleavley St *ECC* M30..........................**61** C3
Clee Av *BRUN/LGST* M13...................**104** A3
Cleethorpes Av *BKLY* M9....................**33** C2
Clegg St *DROY* M43 *...........................**75** C4
   OLD OL1...**23** C3
   WHTF M45...**11** C1
Clementine Cl *SLFD* M6......................**67** C1
Clement Stott Cl *BKLY* M9.................**35** C1
Clement St *HTNM* SK4.......................**129** D2
Cleminson St *CSLFD* M3........................**2** B3
Clevedon Av *URM* M41........................**95** D3
Clevedon St *BKLY* M9.........................**53** D2
Cleveland Av *BNG/LEV* M19...............**105** C3
   SLFD M6..**64** B2
Cleveland Rd *CHH* M8.........................**33** C3
   HTNM SK4...**127** D1
Cleveleys Av *CCHDY* M21...................**112** B2
Cleveleys Gv *BRO* M7...........................**50** B2
Cleworth St *HULME* M15 *....................**6** A4
Cleworth Wk *HULME* M15......................**6** A4
Clibran St *CHH* M8..............................**52** A3
Cliff Av *BRO* M7..................................**49** D3
Cliff Crs *BRO* M7.................................**50** A2
Cliffdale Dr *CHH* M8...........................**32** B4
Cliff Gv *HTNM* SK4............................**128** A1
Clifford St *ECC* M30............................**78** A1
   SWIN M27...**46** A1
Clifton Av *ECC* M30............................**62** A2
   RUSH/FAL M14.................................**116** A1
Clifton Cl *OLDTF/WHR* M16...............**85** C4
Clifton Dr *SWIN* M27...........................**25** C3
Clifton Gv *OLDTF/WHR* M16...............**85** C4
   SWIN M27...**25** C3
Clifton House Rd *SWIN* M27...............**25** D1
Clifton Park Rd *OFTN* SK2................**133** D4
Clifton Pl *PWCH* M25 *.......................**11** C3
Clifton Rd *CCHDY* M21.......................**112** B1
   ECC M30...**62** A2
   HTNM SK4...**127** D1
   PWCH M25..**28** B1
Clifton Vw *SWIN* M27..........................**25** D1
Cliftonville Dr *SWIN* M27....................**46** A3
Clinton Av *RUSH/FAL* M14.................**101** D3
Clinton Gdns *RUSH/FAL* M14.............**101** D3
Clinton Wk *OLDE* OL4 *......................**23** D3
Clippers Quay *SALQ* M50....................**83** D3
Clitheroe Rd *BRUN/LGST* M13..........**104** A2
Clito St *BKLY* M9.................................**54** A1
Clively Av *SWIN* M27...........................**27** C4
Clive Rd *FAIL* M35...............................**56** B2
Clive St *ANC* M4....................................**4** C1
   OLDS OL8..**40** A3
Clivia Gv *BRO* M7 *.............................**50** A3
Cloak St *CMANE* M1..............................**8** A1
Clock House Av *DROY* M43..................**74** B2
Clockhouse Ms *DROY* M43 *.................**74** B2
Clock St *CHAD* OL9..............................**39** C3

Cloister Rd *HTNM* SK4.......................**126** A3
Cloister St *BKLY* M9............................**54** A1
Clopton Wk *HULME* M15.......................**85** D3
Clothorn Rd *DID/WITH* M20.............**125** C1
Clough Bank *BKLY* M9 *.......................**34** A3
Clough Dr *PWCH* M25..........................**29** C1
Cloughfield Av *ORD* M5.......................**84** A1
Clough Ga *OLDS* OL8............................**40** A4
Clough La *PWCH* M25...........................**29** C1
Clough Rd *BKLY* M9..............................**54** A1
   DROY M43..**76** A3
   FAIL M35..**57** D2
Cloughs Av *CHAD* OL9.........................**19** C1
Clough St *NEWH/MOS* M40.................**71** D1
The Clough *RDSH* SK5........................**121** C3
Clough Top Rd *BKLY* M9......................**55** D3
Clovelly Av *OLDS* OL8..........................**39** D3
Clovelly Rd *CCHDY* M21.....................**112** B1
   SWIN M27...**43** D2
Clovelly St *NEWH/MOS* M40 *.............**56** A4
Clover Av *EDGY/DAV* SK3..................**132** A4
Cloverbank Av *BNG/LEV* M19............**126** A1
Clowes St *CHAD* OL9............................**38** B3
   CSLFD M3...**3** D3
   WGTN/LGST M12.............................**89** D3
Club St *OP/CLY* M11.............................**92** A2
Clumber Rd *GTN* M18........................**107** C1
Clwyd Av *EDGY/DAV* SK3..................**132** A2
Clyde Av *WHTF* M45............................**11** C3
Clyde Rd *DID/WITH* M20...................**124** A4
Clydesdale St *OLDS* OL8......................**40** B1
Clyne St *STRET* M32............................**83** C4
Coalbrook Wk *WGTN/LGST* M12........**88** A1
Coalburn St *WGTN/LGST* M12............**89** D4
Coal Pit La *OLDS* OL8...........................**59** C2
Coalshaw Green Rd *CHAD* OL9............**38** B2
Coatbridge St *OP/CLY* M11..................**73** D4
Cobalt Av *URM* M41............................**80** A3
Cobb Cl *CHH* M8..................................**31** D2
Cobble Bank *BKLY* M9.........................**33** D2
Cobden St *BKLY* M9.............................**34** B4
   CHAD OL9..**21** C2
   SLFD M6...**66** A1
Cob Hall Rd *STRET* M32......................**96** B4
Cobham Av *NEWH/MOS* M40..............**36** B3
Cobourg St *CMANE* M1...........................**8** C1
Coburg Av *BRO* M7..............................**68** A3
Cochrane Av *WGTN/LGST* M12...........**88** B4
Cockcroft Rd *ORD* M5..........................**67** D3
Cockcroft St *BKLY* M9.........................**34** A4
Coconut Gv *SLFD* M6...........................**66** B3
Coddington Av *OP/CLY* M11................**91** D1
Coghlan Cl *OP/CLY* M11 *....................**73** C3
Colborne Av *ECC* M30.........................**61** C3
   RDSH SK5...**107** C2
Colbourne Av *CHH* M8........................**32** A4
Colchester Pl *HTNM* SK4...................**128** A2
Colchester Wk *OLD* OL1 *.....................**23** C2
Colc: lough Cl *NEWH/MOS* M40..........**55** C3
Coldhurst St *OLD* OL1..........................**22** B1
Coldstream Av *BKLY* M9......................**34** A1
Colebrook Dr *NEWH/MOS* M40...........**54** B3
Coleby Av *OLDTF/WHR* M16................**99** D1
Colemore Av *DID/WITH* M20.............**126** A2
Colenso Gv *HTNM* SK4.......................**128** A2
Colenso St *OLDS* OL8...........................**40** A2
Coleridge Cl *RDSH* SK5......................**106** B4
Coleridge Rd *OLDTF/WHR* M16..........**99** D2
   RDSH SK5...**106** B4
Coleshill St *NEWH/MOS* M40...............**71** D2
Cole St *NEWH/MOS* M40.....................**54** A1
Colgate Crs *RUSH/FAL* M14..............**115** C1
Colgate La *ORD* M5.............................**83** D3
Colgrove Av *NEWH/MOS* M40.............**36** B3
Colina Dr *BRO* M7...............................**50** B4
Colindale Av *BKLY* M9.........................**34** B1
Colin Murphy Rd *HULME* M15..............**6** C5

Colin Rd *HTNM* SK4 ....129 D1
Coll Dr *URM* M41 ....79 C4
College Av *OLDS* OL8 ....40 A2
College Cl *OFTN* SK2 ....133 D3
College Dr *OLDTF/WHR* M16......99 D3
College Rd *ECC* M30 ....63 D3
    OLDS OL8 ....40 A1
    OLDTF/WHR M16 ....100 A3
Collegiate Wy *SWIN* M27 ....26 A2
Colley St *STRET* M32 ....83 C4
Collie Av *SLFD* M6 ....49 D4
Collier Hl *OLDS* OL8 ....40 A2
Collier Hill Av *OLDS* OL8 ....39 D2
Collier St *CSLFD* M3 ....3 D1
    CSLFD M3 ....7 D2
    SWIN M27 ....44 B2
Colliery St *OP/CLY* M11 ....72 B4
Collin Av *GTN* M18 ....105 D1
Collingburn Av *ORD* M5 ....84 A2
Collinge Av *MDTN* M24 ....18 B1
Collinge St *MDTN* M24 ....19 C2
Collingham St *CHH* M8 ....69 D1
Collingwood Av *DROY* M43 ....74 B2
Collingwood Dr *SWIN* M27 ....45 D2
Collingwood Rd *BNG/LEV* M19...104 A4
Collingwood Wy *OLD* OL1 * 23 C1
Collins Wy *CHAD* OL9 ....39 D2
Collyhurst Rd *NEWH/MOS* M40...70 A1
Collyhurst St *NEWH/MOS* M40....70 B1
Colman Gdns *ORD* M5 ....84 A2
Colmore Dr *BKLY* M9 ....35 D1
Colonial Rd *OFTN* SK2 ....133 D3
Colson Dr *MDTN* M24 ....17 C2
Columbia Av *GTN* M18 ....107 C1
Columbia St *OLDS* OL8 * 41 C1
Columbine St *OP/CLY* M11 ....91 C2
Colwell Av *STRET* M32 ....96 A4
Colwyn Av *MDTN* M24 ....17 D3
    RUSH/FAL M14 ....116 B1
Colwyn Crs *RDSH* SK5 ....120 A4
Colwyn Rd *SWIN* M27 ....43 D3
Colwyn St *CHAD* OL9 ....22 A2
    SLFD M6 ....66 A2
Combe Cl *OP/CLY* M11 ....73 C2
Combermere Av *DID/WITH* M20...114 B2
Comet St *CMANE* M1 ....5 D5
Commercial Rd *OLD* OL1 * 23 C3
Commercial St *CHAD* OL9 ....21 D3
    CSLFD M3 ....7 D3
Como Wk *GTN* M18 ....90 A3
Compass St *OP/CLY* M11 ....90 B2
Compstall Av *RUSH/FAL* M14....102 A4
Compstall St *GTN* M18 * 91 D3
Compton Wy *MDTN* M24 ....18 B2
Comus St *ORD* M5 ....84 B1
Concert La *CMANW* M2 ....4 A5
Concord Pl *SLFD* M6 ....48 B4
Condor Cl *DROY* M43 * 76 B2
Condor Pl *SLFD* M6 ....48 B4
Condor Wk *BRUN/LGST* M13 * 87 C3
Conewood Wk *BRUN/LGST* M13...87 C3
Congleton Av *RUSH/FAL* M14....101 D3
Congou St *CMANE* M1 ....9 E1
Congreave St *OLD* OL1 * 22 B1
Coningsby Dr *BKLY* M9 ....53 C1
Conisborough Pl *WHTF* M45 ....12 A2
Coniston Av *BKLY* M9 ....53 C1
    OLDS OL8 ....40 A1
    WHTF M45 ....11 C1
Coniston Cl *CHAD* OL9 ....20 B2
Coniston Rd *RDSH* SK5 ....120 A3
    STRET M32 ....96 B2
    SWIN M27 ....45 C3
Coniston St *NEWH/MOS* M40 .....55 D4
    SLFD M6 ....67 C1
Conmere Sq *HULME* M15 ....7 F4

Connaught Av *BNG/LEV* M19.....117 C2
    WHTF M45 ....11 D2
Connaught St *OLDS* OL8 ....22 B3
Connie St *OP/CLY* M11 ....90 B1
Connington Av *BKLY* M9 ....34 A4
Conran St *BKLY* M9 ....53 C2
Constable St *GTN* M18 ....91 D3
Constance Gdns *ORD* M5 ....66 A4
Constance St *HULME* M15 * 7 D3
Consul St *WYTH/NTH* M22 ....123 D4
Conway Av *SWIN* M27 ....27 C3
    WHTF M45 ....11 C2
Conway Cl *MDTN* M24 ....17 D2
    OLDTF/WHR M16 ....98 B2
Conway Gv *CHAD* OL9 ....20 A1
Conway Rd *URM* M41 ....94 A1
Conway St *RDSH* SK5 ....129 D1
Conyngham Rd *RUSH/FAL* M14..103 C1
Cooke St *FAIL* M35 ....57 C1
Cook St *CSLFD* M3 ....2 C3
    ECC M30 ....61 D3
    EDGY/DAV SK3 * 129 C4
Coomassie St *SLFD* M6 * 66 A2
Co-operation St *FAIL* M35 ....38 A4
Co-operative St *SLFD* M6 ....66 A3
Cooper Av *BKLY* M9 ....16 A4
Cooper St *CMANW* M2 ....3 F5
    DROY M43 * 74 B4
    OFTN SK2 ....133 C2
    STRET M32 ....97 C3
Coop St *ANC* M4 * 4 C2
Cope Cl *OP/CLY* M11 * 91 D2
Copeland Av *SWIN* M27 ....27 D4
Copeman Cl *BRUN/LGST* M13.....87 D3
Copenhagen St *NEWH/MOS* M40..54 B3
Copgrove Rd *CCHDY* M21 ....112 A2
Copley Rd *CCHDY* M21 ....98 B3
Copperas La *DROY* M43 ....91 D1
Copperas St *ANC* M4 ....4 B1
Copperbeech Cl *WYTH/NTH* M22..123 D4
Coppice Dr *WYTH/NTH* M22 .....123 C4
Coppice St *OLDS* OL8 ....22 A4
The Coppice *BKLY* M9 ....35 D3
    PWCH M25 ....29 D1
    WALK M28 ....42 A1
    WALK M28 ....43 D4
Copping St *WGTN/LGST* M12 .....89 C3
Coppleridge Dr *CHH* M8 ....32 B3
Copson St *DID/WITH* M20 ....115 C2
Copster Av *OLDS* OL8 ....40 B2
Copster Hill Rd *OLDS* OL8 ....40 B2
Copster Pl *OLDS* OL8 ....40 B2
Copthall La *CHH* M8 ....51 C1
Copthorne Crs *BRUN/LGST* M13..103 C3
Coral St *BRUN/LGST* M13 ....9 E4
Coram St *GTN* M18 ....92 A3
Corbel Wy *ECC* M30 ....62 B2
Corbett St *OP/CLY* M11 ....72 B4
Corby St *WGTN/LGST* M12 ....89 C3
Cordingley Av *DROY* M43 ....92 A1
Cordova Av *DTN/ASHW* M34 .....107 C2
Corelli St *NEWH/MOS* M40 ....72 A1
Corinthian Av *BRO* M7 ....49 D4
Corkland Rd *CCHDY* M21 ....112 A1
Cork St *WGTN/LGST* M12 ....88 C1
Corley Wk *OP/CLY* M11 * 72 A4
Cormallen Gv *FAIL* M35 ....57 D2
Cornbrook Arches *HULME* M15....84 B2
Cornbrook Gv *OLDTF/WHR* M16..85 C3
Cornbrook Park Rd *HULME* M15...84 B3
Cornbrook St *OLDTF/WHR* M16...85 C3
Cornbrook Wy *OLDTF/WHR* M16..85 C4
Corn Cl *BRUN/LGST* M13 ....87 C4
Cornell St *ANC* M4 ....5 D2
Cornet St *BRO* M7 ....50 A4
Cornford Av *GTN* M18 ....105 C2
Corn Hill La *DTN/ASHW* M34 ......92 B4

Corn St *FAIL* M35 ....**55** D3
  OLDE OL4.................................**23** D2
Cornwall Av *BNG/LEV* M19 ....**118** A1
Cornwall Crs *RDSH* SK5 ....**121** D3
Cornwall Rd *DROY* M43.................**75** D2
Cornwall St *CHAD* OL9 ....**21** C4
  ECC M30..................................**61** D4
  OP/CLY M11..............................**91** C2
Corona Av *OLDS* OL8....................**40** A2
Coronation Rd *DROY* M43............**75** C2
  FAIL M35.................................**56** B3
Coronation Sq *CMANE* M1............**9** F2
Coronation St *OP/CLY* M11 *........**90** B1
  ORD M5..................................**84** A1
  RDSH SK5................................**129** D1
  SWIN M27................................**26** B4
Corporation St *ANC* M4 ....**4** A3
  CMANW M2...............................**3** F4
  MDTN M24..............................**17** D1
  STKP SK1..............................**130** A3
Corran Cl *ECC* M30 ....**61** C3
Corrie Crs *FWTH* BL4.....................**25** D1
Corrie Dr *FWTH* BL4 ....**25** C1
Corrie Rd *SWIN* M27.....................**26** B2
Corrigan St *GTN* M18....................**91** C1
Corringham Rd *BNG/LEV* M19 ....**118** B2
Corriss Av *BKLY* M9.......................**14** B3
Corwen Av *BKLY* M9......................**53** D1
Corwen Cl *OLDS* OL8....................**39** C3
Cosgrove Crs *FAIL* M35.................**56** B4
Cosgrove Rd *FAIL* M35.................**56** B4
Cotham St *CSLFD* M3....................**69** C2
Cotswold Av *CHAD* OL9.................**20** B4
Cotswold Cl *PWCH* M25 ....**12** B4
Cotswold Dr *SLFD* M6..................**66** A2
Cotswold Dr *HTNM* SK4..............**129** C2
Cottam Gv *SWIN* M27...................**45** D2
Cottam St *OLD* OL1 ....**22** A1
Cottenham La *BRO* M7..................**68** B1
Cottenham St *BRUN/LGST* M13 ....**9** D5
Cotterdale Cl *OLDTF/WHR* M16........**100** A3
Cotterill St *SLFD* M6.....................**66** B5
Cotter St *WGTN/LGST* M12.............**9** E5
Cottesmore Dr *CHH* M8................**52** B1
Cottingham Rd *WGTN/LGST* M12 .....**88** B3
Cottonfield Rd *DID/WITH* M20........**115** D5
Cotton Hl *DID/WITH* M20..............**115** D4
Cotton La *DID/WITH* M20...............**115** D4
Cotton Mill Crs *CHAD* OL9 ....**39** C1
Cotton St *ANC* M4..........................**5** D3
Cotton Tree St *HTNM* SK4...........**129** D4
Coulsden Dr *BKLY* M9....................**34** A2
Coulton Cl *OL1* OL1.......................**23** C4
Councillor St *WGTN/LGST* M12 .....**71** D4
Countess Gv *BRO* M7....................**50** A4
Countess Pl *PWCH* M25................**30** B1
Countess Rd *DID/WITH* M20.......**125** C2
Countess St *OFTN* SK2.................**133** D4
Counthill Dr *HTNM* **3** F5
County St *CMANW* M2........................**39** D3
  OLDS OL8................................**86** B4
Coupland St *HULME* M15..............**86** B4
Courier St *GTN* M18.......................**91** D3
Court Dr *NEWH/MOS* M40............**74** B1
Courtfield Av *BKLY* M9 *...............**34** A1
Courthill St *STKP* SK1..................**133** D1
Courts Vw *SALE* M33...................**109** D4
Covent Gdn *STKP* SK1..................**130** A4
Covent Gdns *STKP* SK1................**130** A4
Coverdale Crs *WGTN/LGST* M12....**88** A3
Cowan St *NEWH/MOS* M40...........**71** C3
Cowburn St *CSLFD* M3..................**69** D2
Cowesby St *RUSH/FAL* M14.........**56** B2
Cow La *FAIL* M35...........................**55** D3
  ORD M5....................................**67** D4
  SALE M33...............................**110** B3
Cowley St *NEWH/MOS* M40..........**55** D3

Cowling St *BRO* M7........................**48** A1
  OLDS OL8..................................**23** C4
Cowper St *MDTN* M24...................**19** C2
Crabbe St *ANC* M4..........................**69** D2
Crab La *BKLY* M9.............................**33** C1
Crabtree La *OP/CLY* M11................**91** C1
Cradley Av *OP/CLY* M11.................**91** C1
Cragie St *CHH* M8..........................**51** C4
Craig Cl *HTNM* SK4......................**128** A4
Craighall Av *BNG/LEV* M19..........**117** C1
Craigmore Av *DID/WITH* M20......**123** C1
Craignair Ct *SWIN* M27 *...............**46** B1
Craig Rd *GTN* M18.......................**105** D1
  HTNM SK4...............................**127** D4
Craigslands Av *NEWH/MOS* M40 .....**54** B3
Craig Wk *OLDS* OL8 *.....................**22** B4
Craigweil Av *DID/WITH* M20.......**125** D2
Craigweil Rd *PWCH* M25................**31** C3
Cramer St *NEWH/MOS* M40 *........**54** A4
Crammond Cl *NEWH/MOS* M40.....**54** A3
Cranage Rd *BNG/LEV* M19..........**118** A1
Cranberry Rd *CCHDY* M21............**112** A1
  HTNM SK4...............................**128** A1
  OLDTF/WHR M16......................**91** D1
Cranbourne St *ORD* M5.................**67** D4
Cranbrook Dr *PWCH* M25...............**30** B3
Cranbrook Rd *ECC* M30.................**60** B1
  GTN M18................................**106** B2
Cranbrook Wk *CHAD* OL9 *............**20** B3
Crane St *WGTN/LGST* M12..............**9** F2
Cranfield Cl *NEWH/MOS* M40.........**71** C3
Cranford Av *DID/WITH* M20.......**126** A1
  SALE M33...............................**109** D3
  STRET M32................................**98** A2
Cranford Cl *SWIN* M27...................**46** A3
Cranleigh Av *HTNM* SK4..............**127** C1
Cranleigh Dr *SALE* M33...............**108** B4
Cranlington Dr *CHH* M8................**51** C3
Cranmere Av *BNG/LEV* M19........**105** D3
Cranmer Rd *DID/WITH* M20.......**125** C1
Cranswick St *RUSH/FAL* M14.......**101** D2
Crantock St *WGTN/LGST* M12.....**105** C2
Cranwell Dr *BNG/LEV* M19.........**126** B1
Craston Rd *BRUN/LGST* M13......**103** D3
Craven Av *ORD* M5.........................**84** A1
Craven Dr *ORD* M5..........................**83** D3
Cravenhurst Av *NEWH/MOS* M40 ....**73** C1
Craven Pl *OP/CLY* M11...................**73** D5
Crayfield Rd *RDSH* SK5...............**120** A3
Craven St *ORD* M5.........................**67** D4
Cravenwood Rd *CHH* M8..............**51** D1
Crawford Av *WALK* M28.................**42** A1
Crawford St *ECC* M30....................**62** A2
  NEWH/MOS M40 *...................**55** D4
Crawley Av *ECC* M30......................**63** D2
Craydon St *OP/CLY* M11...............**90** B1
Crayfield Rd *BNG/LEV* M19.........**118** A1
Crayford Rd *NEWH/MOS* M40........**73** C1
Cray Wk *BRUN/LGST* M13...............**8** C4
Crediton Cl *HULME* M15................**86** A4
Cresbury St *WGTN/LGST* M12 *.....**88** A2
Crescent *ORD* M5............................**2** A3
Crescent Av *CHH* M8 *...................**51** D1
  PWCH M25................................**30** A3
  SWIN M27................................**46** A1
Crescent Dr *CHH* M8......................**33** C4
Crescent Gv *BNG/LEV* M19 *.......**104** B3
  PWCH M25................................**30** A3
Crescent Pk *HTNM* SK4..............**128** A4
Crescent Range *RUSH/FAL* M14 ....**102** B2
Crescent Rd *CHAD* OL9.................**37** D3
  CHH M8....................................**51** D1
  STKP SK1...............................**131** C2
Crescent St *CHH* M8......................**52** B1
The Crescent *BNG/LEV* M19.......**104** B4
  DROY M43................................**75** C4

MDTN M24	...16	B1
PWCH M25	...30	A1
Crescent Wy *EDGY/DAV* SK3	...133	D4
Cressfield Av *CCHDY* M21	...113	C2
Cressingham Rd *STRET* M32	...96	A4
Cressington Cl *ORD* M5 *	...65	D3
Cresswell Gv *DID/WITH* M20	...114	B4
Crest St *CSLFD* M3	...3	F1
The Crest *DROY* M43	...92	B2
Crete St *OLDS* OL8	...41	C1
Criccieth St *OLDTF/WHR* M16	...101	C1
Crime La *OLDS* OL8	...59	C2
Crimsworth Av *OLDTF/WHR* M16	...99	C3
Crinan Wk *NEWH/MOS* M40	...71	C2
Cringleford Wk *WGTN/LGST* M12	...89	C4
Cringle Hall Rd *BNG/LEV* M19	...117	C1
Cringle Rd *BNG/LEV* M19	...118	A2
Criterion St *RDSH* SK5	...107	C3
Croasdale Av *RUSH/FAL* M14	...102	A4
Croft Av *PWCH* M25 *	...14	A1
Croft Bank *BRO* M7 *	...49	D4
GTN M18	...91	D4
Croft Brow *OLDS* OL8	...40	B3
Croft Gates Rd *MDTN* M24	...16	A2
Croft Hill Rd *NEWH/MOS* M40	...35	D4
Crofton St *OLDS* OL8	...40	B2
OLDTF/WHR M16	...100	A1
RUSH/FAL M14	...102	A2
Croft St *BRO* M7	...49	D4
FAIL M35	...38	B4
OP/CLY M11	...73	C4
The Croft *OLDS* OL8	...40	B3
Cromarty Av *CHAD* OL9	...38	C4
Cromarty Wk *OP/CLY* M11	...72	A4
Cromer Av *DID/WITH* M20	...115	C3
DTN/ASHW M34	...107	D2
Cromer Av *OP/CLY* M11 *	...74	A4
STKP SK1	...130	B3
Cromford Av *STRET* M32	...96	A2
Cromford St *OLD* OL1	...23	D1
Cromhurst St *CHH* M8	...51	D1
Crompton Rd *BNG/LEV* M19	...117	D2
Crompton St *CHAD* OL9	...21	D2
OLD OL1	...22	B1
SWIN M27	...44	B1
Cromwell Av *OLDTF/WHR* M16	...99	D3
RDSH SK5	...107	D3
Cromwell Gv *BNG/LEV* M19	...104	B4
BRO M7	...49	D4
Cromwell Range *RUSH/FAL* M14	...103	C3
Cromwell Rd *ECC* M30	...61	D3
PWCH M25	...30	B1
SLFD M6	...66	B1
STRET M32	...97	D4
SWIN M27	...25	D4
Cromwell St *HTNM* SK4	...129	C2
OLD OL1	...23	C3
Crondall St *RUSH/FAL* M14	...101	D2
Cronshaw St *BNG/LEV* M19	...118	A1
Crookhill Dr *CHH* M8	...51	C2
Crookilley Wy *STKP* SK1	...131	C2
Crosby Av *PWCH* M25	...11	D3
Crosby Rd *NEWH/MOS* M40	...56	A4
SLFD M6 *	...47	C4
Crosby St *OFTN* SK2	...133	C2
Crosfield Gv *GTN* M18	...106	A1
Cross Av *PWCH* M25	...11	D3
Crossbank Cl *BRUN/LGST* M13	...88	A4
Crossbank St *OLDS* OL8	...22	B4
Crossby Cl *MDTN* M24	...17	C4
Crosscliffe St *OLDTF/WHR* M16	...101	C1
Crossdale Rd *BKLY* M9	...34	B1
Crossfell Av *BKLY* M9	...15	C4
Crossfield Dr *SWIN* M27	...25	D4
WALK M28	...42	A2
Crossford Br *SALE* M33	...109	D2
Crossford Ct *SALE* M33 *	...109	C3
Crossford St *STRET* M32	...97	C4
Crossgate Ms *HTNM* SK4	...126	B3
Crosshill St *OLDTF/WHR* M16	...101	C1
Cross Keys St *ANC* M4	...4	C2
Crossland Rd *CCHDY* M21	...111	D1
DROY M43	...75	D3
Crosslands *PWCH* M25	...29	D2
Cross La *DROY* M43	...75	D3
GTN M18	...91	C4
ORD M5	...66	B4
Crosslee Rd *BKLY* M9	...35	C1
Crossley Ct *ANC* M4	...71	C4
Crossley Rd *BNG/LEV* M19	...117	C2
SALE M33	...108	B3
Crossley St *GTN* M18	...90	A3
Crossmead Dr *BKLY* M9	...16	B4
Cross Rd *CCHDY* M21	...112	A2
Cross St *CMANW* M2	...3	F4
CSLFD M3	...3	D5
MDTN M24	...17	C1
OLDTF/WHR M16	...85	C4
SALE M33	...109	C4
STRET M32	...97	C3
SWIN M27	...28	A3
WALK M28	...43	D2
Crossway *DID/WITH* M20	...125	C2
DROY M43	...92	B2
Crossways *OLDS* OL8	...41	D4
Croston Wk *OP/CLY* M11	...71	D4
Croton St *HTNM* SK4	...126	B3
Croughton Cl *OP/CLY* M11 *	...91	C2
Crowborough Wk *HULME* M15	...86	A4
Crowcroft Rd *BRUN/LGST* M13	...104	B3
Crowden Rd *NEWH/MOS* M40	...36	A3
Crow Hl North *MDTN* M24	...17	C3
Crow Hl South *MDTN* M24	...17	C3
Crowley Rd *BKLY* M9	...54	A1
Crowngreen Rd *ECC* M30	...62	B4
Crownhill Dr *DROY* M43	...75	D3
Crown La *ANC* M4	...4	B1
Crown Point Av *NEWH/MOS* M40 *	...55	D4
Crown Sq *CSLFD* M3	...3	D5
Crown St *CSLFD* M3	...3	D2
FAIL M35	...57	C1
HULME M15	...6	C1
NEWH/MOS M40	...55	D4
Crowther Av *ORD* M5	...83	D1
Crowther St *GTN* M18	...91	D4
Crowthorn Rd *HTNM* SK4	...119	C2
Croxdale Cl *AULW* OL7	...59	D4
Croydon Dr *NEWH/MOS* M40	...73	D1
Crumpsall La *CHH* M8	...32	A4
Crumpsall V *CHH* M8	...33	D3
Crumpsall Wy *CHH* M8	...33	C4
Cryer St *DROY* M43	...76	B1
Cubley Rd *BRO* M7	...50	B1
Cuckoo Gv *PWCH* M25	...12	A3
Cuckoo La *PWCH* M25	...12	B1
Cuddington Av *DID/WITH* M20	...114	B1
Cuddington Crs *EDGY/DAV* SK3	...132	A3
Cudworth Rd *BKLY* M9	...14	B4
Culand St *WGTN/LGST* M12	...88	B3
Culbert Av *DID/WITH* M20	...125	D2
Culcheth La *NEWH/MOS* M40	...73	D1
Culford Cl *WGTN/LGST* M12	...88	B4
Cullen Gv *BKLY* M9	...34	B2
Cullercoats Wk *WGTN/LGST* M12 *	...105	C2
Culross Av *NEWH/MOS* M40	...37	D4
Culvercliff Wk *CSLFD* M3	...7	D1
Culver Rd *EDGY/DAV* SK3	...132	A4
Culverwell Dr *ORD* M5	...67	C3
Cumberland Av *RDSH* SK5	...131	D1
SWIN M27	...26	A3
Cumberland Rd *BKLY* M9 *	...34	A4
Cumberland St *BRO* M7	...68	A1
Cumbrae Gdns *ORD* M5	...65	D4
Cumbrae Rd *BNG/LEV* M19	...105	D4
Cumbrian Cl *BRUN/LGST* M13 *	...87	D3

Cumbria Wk *SLFD* M6..........................**67** C1
Cummings St *OLDS* OL8........................**39** D3
Cunard Cl *BRUN/LGST* M13.....................**9** E5
Cundiff Rd *CCHDY* M21.........................**112** A3
Cunningham Wy *OLD* OL1 *....................**22** B1
Curate St *STKP* SK1..............................**130** B4
Curtels Cl *WALK* M28............................**43** D2
Curtis Rd *BNG/LEV* M19........................**105** D4
   HTNM SK4................................**127** D3
Curzon Av *RUSH/FAL* M14......................**103** D1
Curzon Rd *BRO* M7.................................**50** A2
   SALE M33...................................**109** C4
   STRET M32.................................**95** D2
Curzon St *OLD* OL1................................**23** C2
Cuthbert Av *BNG/LEV* M19.....................**105** C3
Cutland St *NEWH/MOS* M40.....................**54** B3
Cutler Hill Rd *FAIL* M35...........................**58** B2
Cutter Cl *ORD* M5..................................**83** D1
Cycle St *OP/CLY* M11.............................**90** A1
Cyclone St *OP/CLY* M11..........................**89** C1
Cygnus Av *BRO* M7.................................**67** D2
Cymbal Ct *RDSH* SK5............................**129** D2
Cypress Av *CHAD* OL9.............................**21** C1
Cypress Rd *DROY* M43.............................**75** D2
   ECC M30....................................**60** B3
Cypress St *MDTN* M24.............................**18** B1
Cyprus Cl *ORD* M5...................................**66** A4
Cyprus St *STRET* M32..............................**97** C3
Cyril St *RUSH/FAL* M14..........................**102** A2
Cyrus St *NEWH/MOS* M40.........................**71** D2

D

Daccamill Dr *SWIN* M27..........................**45** C2
Dacre Av *OLDTF/WHR* M16........................**99** C3
Dagenham Rd *RUSH/FAL* M14 *................**102** B2
Dagnall Av *CCHDY* M21..........................**112** A3
Dahlia Cl *BNG/LEV* M19.........................**117** C3
Daimler St *CHH* M8.................................**51** D3
Daine Av *NTHM/RTH* M23........................**122** A4
Dainton St *WGTN/LGST* M12.....................**88** A2
Daintry Cl *HULME* M15 *............................**7** E5
Daintry Rd *CHAD* OL9.............................**21** D3
Dairy St *CHAD* OL9.................................**21** C2
Daisy Av *BRUN/LGST* M13......................**103** D1
Daisy Bank *NEWH/MOS* M40.....................**55** D4
Daisy Bank Av *SWIN* M27.........................**46** B3
Daisy Bank Rd *RUSH/FAL* M14.................**103** D1
Daisy St *CHAD* OL9.................................**20** B1
   CHAD OL9...................................**22** A2
   OFTN SK2..................................**133** C2
Dakerwood Cl *NEWH/MOS* M40.................**55** D4
Dakley St *OP/CLY* M11............................**90** B2
Dakota Av *SALQ* M50..............................**82** B1
Dakota South *SALQ* M50..........................**83** C1
Dalbeattie St *BKLY* M9............................**53** D1
Dalberg St *WGTN/LGST* M12.....................**88** A2
Dalbury Dr *NEWH/MOS* M40......................**52** B4
Dalby Av *SWIN* M27................................**44** B2
Dalby Gv *STKP* SK1...............................**130** B4
Dale Av *ECC* M30....................................**61** D2
Dalebeck Cl *WHTF* M45............................**12** A1
Dalebrook Ct *HTNM* SK4 *.......................**128** B4
Daleford Sq *BRUN/LGST* M13 *...................**9** D4
Dales Av *CHH* M8....................................**32** A3
Dales Brow *SWIN* M27 *...........................**44** A3
Dalesman Cl *BKLY* M9..............................**54** A1
Dalesman Wk *HULME* M15...........................**8** A5
Dales Park Dr *SWIN* M27 *........................**44** A3
Dale St *CMANE* M1....................................**4** A4
   EDGY/DAV SK3...........................**132** A2
   MDTN M24..................................**18** A2
   SWIN M27...................................**44** B3
Dalham Av *BKLY* M9................................**35** D3

Dalkeith Rd *RDSH* SK5...........................**120** A2
Dalkeith St *GTN* M18...............................**90** A3
Dallas St *SALQ* M50................................**82** B1
Dalley Av *BRO* M7...................................**68** A1
Dalmahoy Cl *NEWH/MOS* M40....................**55** D3
Dalmain Cl *CHH* M8.................................**51** C3
Dalmorton Rd *CCHDY* M21.......................**113** C1
Dalny St *BNG/LEV* M19..........................**105** C4
Daiston Av *FAIL* M35................................**58** A1
Dalston Dr *DID/WITH* M20.......................**125** D3
Dalton Av *RUSH/FAL* M14.......................**101** D3
   STRET M32.................................**95** C1
   WHTF M45..................................**11** D2
Dalton Dr *SWIN* M27................................**47** C2
Dalton Gv *HTNM* SK4..............................**128** B1
Dalton Rd *BKLY* M9..................................**16** A4
   MDTN M24...................................**15** C2
Dalton St *ANC* M4....................................**70** A2
   CHAD OL9....................................**22** A2
   ECC M30.....................................**62** A2
   FAIL M35....................................**56** B1
   SALE M33..................................**109** D3
Daltry St *OLD* OL1...................................**23** D1
Damask Av *CSLFD* M3.................................**2** A2
Dameral Cl *CHH* M8 *..............................**51** D3
Dame St *CHAD* OL9.................................**22** A1
Dam Head Dr *BKLY* M9.............................**34** B2
Damien St *BNG/LEV* M19........................**105** C3
Damson Gn *MDTN* M24............................**18** A3
Danby Ct *OLD* OL1 *................................**22** B1
Dane Bank *MDTN* M24..............................**18** A2
Danebank Wk *BRUN/LGST* M13 *.................**9** D4
Danecroft Cl *BRUN/LGST* M13...................**88** A4
Danefield Rd *SALE* M33..........................**109** D3
Daneholme Rd *BNG/LEV* M19...................**116** B4
Dane Ms *SALE* M33 *.............................**109** C3
Dane Rd *DTN/ASHW* M34........................**107** D3
   SALE M33..................................**109** D3
Daneshill *PWCH* M25................................**12** A3
Danesmoor Rd *DID/WITH* M20.................**114** B4
Danes Rd *RUSH/FAL* M14.......................**103** C3
Dane St *OP/CLY* M11...............................**91** D2
Danesway *PWCH* M25................................**31** C3
   SWIN M27....................................**46** B3
Daneswood Av *BKLY* M9...........................**35** C1
Danett Cl *WGTN/LGST* M12......................**89** D3
Dan Fold *OLD* OL1 *................................**22** B2
Danforth Gv *BNG/LEV* M19......................**118** A1
Daniel Adamson Rd *SALQ* M50..................**82** A1
Daniel's La *STKP* SK1.............................**130** A3
Danson St *NEWH/MOS* M40.......................**71** D2
Dantall Av *BKLY* M9.................................**35** D3
Dante Cl *ECC* M30...................................**63** D1
Dantzic St *ANC* M4....................................**4** A3
Darden Cl *HTNM* SK4..............................**126** B2
Darell Wk *CHH* M8...................................**52** A3
Daresbury Cl *EDGY/DAV* SK3..................**132** A4
Daresbury Rd *CCHDY* M21........................**98** A3
Daresbury St *CHH* M8...............................**52** A3
Dargai St *OP/CLY* M11.............................**74** A4
Dargle Rd *SALE* M33..............................**109** C3
Dark La *WGTN/LGST* M12.........................**88** A1
Darley Av *CCHDY* M21............................**123** D1
   DID/WITH M20............................**125** D1
   ECC M30....................................**78** D1
Darley Rd *OLDTF/WHR* M16........................**99** C4
Darley St *OP/CLY* M11.............................**71** D4
   STRET M32.................................**97** D1
Darlington Rd *DID/WITH* M20..................**114** B3
Darliston Av *BKLY* M9..............................**14** B4
Darnall Av *DID/WITH* M20.......................**114** B1
Darncombe Cl *OLDTF/WHR* M16...............**101** C1
Darnley St *OLDTF/WHR* M16....................**100** A1
Darras Rd *GTN* M18...............................**105** D2
Dart Cl *CHAD* OL9..................................**20** A1
Dartford Av *ECC* M30...............................**61** C3
   RDSH SK5.................................**121** C3

Dartford Cl *WGTN/LGST* M12 ....88 A3
Dartmouth Cl *OLDS* OL8 ....41 C1
Dartmouth Crs *RDSH* SK5 ....121 D4
Dartmouth Rd *CCHDY* M21 ....112 B1
  WHTF M45 ....11 D2
Darton Av *NEWH/MOS* M40 ....71 D2
Darwell Av *ECC* M30 ....78 B1
Darwen St *OLDTF/WHR* M16 ....84 B4
Dashwood Rd *PWCH* M25 ....11 C4
Dauntesy Av *SWIN* M27 * 47 C2
Davenfield Gv *DID/WITH* M20 ....125 C2
Davenfield Rd *DID/WITH* M20 ....125 C2
Davenham Rd *RDSH* SK5 ....107 C3
Davenhill Rd *BNG/LEV* M19 ....117 D1
Davenport Av *DID/WITH* M20 ....115 C2
Davenport Park Rd *OFTN* SK2 ....133 D4
Davenport St *DROY* M43 * 74 B4
Daventry Rd *CCHDY* M21 ....113 C1
David's Farm Cl *MDTN* M24 ....18 B2
Davidson Dr *MDTN* M24 ....18 B3
David's Rd *DROY* M43 ....74 B3
David St *RDSH* SK5 ....119 D1
Davies Sq *RUSH/FAL* M14 ....101 D1
Davies St *OLD* OL1 ....22 A1
Davis St *ECC* M30 ....62 B4
Davy Av *SWIN* M27 ....28 A3
Davyhulme Rd *STRET* M32 ....96 B2
Davyhulme Rd East *STRET* M32 ....97 C2
Davy St *NEWH/MOS* M40 * 70 A1
Dawlish Av *DROY* M43 ....74 B3
  RDSH SK5 ....121 D4
Dawlish Rd *CCHDY* M21 ....112 B1
Dawnay St *OP/CLY* M11 * 90 A2
Dawson St *CSLFD* M3 * 3 E2
  CSLFD M3 ....6 B2
  STKP SK1 ....131 C2
  SWIN M27 ....45 D1
Day Dr *FAIL* M35 ....57 C3
Deacons Cl *STKP* SK1 ....130 B4
Deacons Dr *SLFD* M6 ....47 C3
Deal Av *RDSH* SK5 ....121 C3
Deal Cl *NEWH/MOS* M40 ....56 A4
Deal St *CSLFD* M3 * 3 D3
Deal Wk *CHAD* OL9 ....20 B3
Dean Av *NEWH/MOS* M40 ....55 C3
  OLDTF/WHR M16 ....99 C2
Deanbank Av *BNG/LEV* M19 ....117 C1
Dean Brook Cl *NEWH/MOS* M40 ....55 D2
Dean Cl *WHTF* M45 ....10 A2
Dean Ct *HULME* M15 * 85 C3
Deanery Wy *STKP* SK1 ....130 A3
Dean La *NEWH/MOS* M40 ....55 C3
Dean Rd *CSLFD* M3 ....3 D1
  GTN M18 ....106 B3
Deanscourt Av *SWIN* M27 ....44 B2
Deansgate *HULME* M15 ....7 D4
Deanshut Rd *OLDS* OL8 ....41 D3
Deans Rd *SWIN* M27 ....44 B2
Dean St *CMANE* M1 ....5 D4
  FAIL M35 ....56 B2
Deansway *SWIN* M27 ....44 B2
Deanswood Dr *BKLY* M9 ....14 B4
Deanwater Cl *BRUN/LGST* M13 ....9 D1
Deanwater Ct *STRET* M32 * 109 D1
Deanway *NEWH/MOS* M40 ....54 B1
Dearden St *WHTF* M15 ....7 D5
Dearmans Pl *CSLFD* M3 ....3 D1
Dearnalay Wy *CHAD* OL9 ....21 C4
Dearne Dr *STRET* M32 ....97 C3
Debdale Av *GTN* M18 ....107 C1
Debdale La *GTN* M18 ....107 C1
Debenham Av *NEWH/MOS* M40 ....73 D1
Debenham Rd *STRET* M32 ....95 D4
Deepcar St *BNG/LEV* M19 ....104 B3
Deepdale Av *DID/WITH* M20 ....114 B1
Deepdale Cl *RDSH* SK5 ....107 C4
Deepdale Dr *SWIN* M27 ....47 C2

Deeping Av *OLDTF/WHR* M16 ....100 A3
Deerfold Cl *GTN* M18 * 91 C4
Deerhurst Dr *CHH* M8 ....51 C3
Deeroak Cl *GTN* M18 ....90 A3
Deerpark Rd *OLDTF/WHR* M16 ....100 B2
Deganwy Gv *RDSH* SK5 ....120 A4
Degas Cl *BRO* M7 ....49 C1
Delacourt Rd *RUSH/FAL* M14 ....114 A1
Delafield Av *WGTN/LGST* M12 ....108 B3
Delahays Range *WYTH* M18 ....107 C1
Delaine Rd *DID/WITH* M20 ....115 D3
Delamere Av *SLFD* M6 ....46 B3
  STRET M32 ....97 C3
  SWIN M27 ....27 C3
  WHTF M45 ....10 B1
Delamere Rd *BNG/LEV* M19 ....117 D1
Delamere St *OP/CLY* M11 ....92 A2
Delaunays Rd *CHH* M8 ....33 C3
Dell Av *SWIN* M27 ....47 C2
Dellcot Cl *PWCH* M25 ....31 C3
  SLFD M6 ....46 A4
Dellcot La *WALK* M28 ....42 A4
The Delph *WALK* M28 * 42 A3
Delside Av *NEWH/MOS* M40 ....54 B1
Delvino Wk *RUSH/FAL* M14 ....101 D1
Demesne Rd *OLDTF/WHR* M16 ....100 B3
Denbigh Pl *ORD* M5 ....66 B3
Denbigh Rd *SWIN* M27 ....26 B3
Denbigh St *HTNM* SK4 ....129 C2
  OLDS OL8 * 41 C2
Denbigh Wk *HULME* M15 ....85 C3
Denby La *HTNM* SK4 ....129 C1
Dencombe St *BRUN/LGST* M13 ....104 A1
Dene Ct *HTNM* SK4 ....128 B3
Dene Dr *MDTN* M24 ....17 C2
Deneford Rd *DID/WITH* M20 ....124 B3
Dene Hollow *RDSH* SK5 ....107 D4
Denehurst St *WGTN/LGST* M12 * 89 C3
Dene Pk *DID/WITH* M20 ....124 B3
Dene Rd *DID/WITH* M20 ....124 B2
Dene Rd West *DID/WITH* M20 ....124 A2
Deneway *HTNM* SK4 ....128 B3
Deneway Cl *HTNM* SK4 ....128 B3
Deneway Ms *HTNM* SK4 * 128 B3
Denewell Cl *BRUN/LGST* M13 ....88 A4
Denham St *BRUN/LGST* M13 ....103 C1
Denhill Rd *HULME* M15 ....101 C1
Denis Av *OLDTF/WHR* M16 ....100 B3
Denison Rd *RUSH/FAL* M14 ....102 B2
Denison St *RUSH/FAL* M14 ....102 B2
Deniston Rd *HTNM* SK4 ....118 A4
Denmark Rd *HULME* M15 ....101 C1
  SALE M33 ....109 C3
Denmark St *CHAD* OL9 ....21 C1
Denmark Wy *CHAD* OL9 ....21 C1
Denmore Rd *NEWH/MOS* M40 ....36 B3
Dennison Av *DID/WITH* M20 ....115 C2
Denshaw Cl *BNG/LEV* M19 ....126 B2
Densmead Wk *NEWH/MOS* M40 ....5 C1
Densmore St *FAIL* M35 * 56 B2
Denstone Av *ECC* M30 ....62 B4
Denstone Rd *RDSH* SK5 ....107 C4
  SLFD M6 ....47 C4
Denton La *CHAD* OL9 ....20 B4
Denver Av *NEWH/MOS* M40 ....71 C2
Deramore St *RUSH/FAL* M14 ....102 A2
Derby Av *SLFD* M6 ....65 D3
Derby Ct *CHAD* OL9 ....21 D4
Derby Gv *BNG/LEV* M19 ....105 C3
Derby Range *HTNM* SK4 ....128 A1
Derby Rd *HTNM* SK4 ....128 B1
  ORD M5 ....65 D3
  RUSH/FAL M14 ....115 D2
  URM M41 ....95 C4
  WHTF M45 ....11 D3
Derbyshire Av *STRET* M32 ....96 A2
Derbyshire Crs *STRET* M32 ....96 A2

Derbyshire Gv *STRET* M32 ....**95** D2
Derbyshire La *STRET* M32 ....**96** B3
Derbyshire La West *STRET* M32 ....**95** D2
Derbyshire Rd *NEWH/MOS* M40 ....**74** A1
Derbyshire St *OP/CLY* M11 ....**39** D1
Derby St *CHAD* OL9 ....**39** C1
   CHH M8 ....**50** B4
   EDGY/DAV SK3 * **132** A1
   FAIL M35 ....**38** D4
   PWCH M25 ....**29** D1
Derg St *SLFD* M6 ....**66** A3
Derker St *OLD* OL1 ....**23** D1
Dermot Murphy CI *DID/WITH* M20 ....**114** A3
Dernford Av *BNG/LEV* M19 ....**117** C2
Derwent Av *CCHDY* M21 ....**113** C4
   DROY M43 ....**74** C4
   WHTF M45 ....**12** A1
Derwent CI *WHTF* M45 ....**12** A2
Derwent Dr *OLDS* **20** B2
Derwent Rd *STRET* M32 ....**97** C2
Derwent St *CHH* M8 ....**52** B3
   DROY M43 * **74** A4
   ORD M5 ....**84** D1
Dettingen St *SLFD* M6 ....**47** D3
Deva Sq *CHAD* OL9 * **21** D4
Devas St *HULME* M15 ....**87** C4
Deverill Av *GTN* M18 ....**107** C1
Devine CI *CSLFD* M3 ....**2** A2
Devon Av *BNG/LEV* M19 ....**117** C1
Devon CI *RDSH* SK5 ....**131** D1
   SLFD M6 ....**63** D2
Devon Rd *DROY* M43 ....**75** D2
   FAIL M35 ....**56** B3
Devonshire CI *URM* M41 ....**94** B3
Devonshire Park Rd *OFTN* SK2 ....**133** D4
Devonshire PI *PWCH* M25 ....**11** D4
Devonshire Rd *CCHDY* M21 ....**112** B1
   ECC M30 ....**62** B3
   HTNM SK4 ....**128** A3
   SLFD M6 ....**63** D2
Devonshire St *BRO* M7 ....**50** B3
   BRUN/LGST M13 ....**88** B3
Devonshire St East *FAIL* M35 * **56** A4
Devonshire St North *WGTN/LGST* M12..**88** A2
Devonshire St South *BRUN/LGST* M13..**88** A4
Devon St *CHAD* OL9 ....**39** C1
   SWIN M27 ....**26** A3
Devon Wy *OLDS* OL8 ....**39** D3
Dewar CI *OP/CLY* M11 ....**72** B4
Dewes Av *SWIN* M27 ....**27** C3
Dewey St *OP/CLY* M11 ....**91** C2
Dewhurst St *CHH* M8 ....**69** C1
Dew Wy *CHAD* OL9 ....**22** A2
Dexter Rd *BKLY* M9 ....**14** B4
Deyne Av *PWCH* M25 ....**30** A1
   RUSH M14 ....**102** B1
Deyne St *ORD* M5 ....**65** D3
Diamond St *OFTN* SK2 ....**133** D3
Dickenson Rd *RUSH/FAL* M14 ....**103** C2
Dickens Rd *ECC* M30 ....**62** A4
Dickinson St *CMANE* M1 ....**8** A1
Didley Sq *WGTN/LGST* M12 * **89** D3
Didsbury Pk *DID/WITH* M20 ....**125** D4
Didsbury Rd *HTNM* SK4 ....**127** D3
Dillmoss Wk *HULME* M15 * **85** C1
Dillon Dr *WGTN/LGST* M12 ....**88** B4
Dilworth St *HULME* M15 ....**87** C4
Dingle Dr *DROY* M43 ....**76** A2
Dingle Rd *MDTN* M24 ....**16** B3
Dinnington Dr *CHH* M8 ....**51** C3
Dinorwic CI *CHH* M8 ....**32** B3
Dinting Av *DID/WITH* M20 ....**114** B2
Dinton St *HULME* M15 ....**84** B2
Discovery Pk *HTNM* SK4 * **118** B4
Disley Av *DID/WITH* M20 ....**114** A3
Dixon Av *BRO* M7 ....**50** A3

Dixon Dr *SWIN* M27 ....**25** D1
Dixon St *NEWH/MOS* M40 ....**55** C3
   OLD OL1 ....**22** B1
   SLFD M6 ....**48** A3
Dobcross CI *BRUN/LGST* M13 ....**104** B3
Dobroyd St *CHH* M8 ....**51** D1
Dobson CI *BRUN/LGST* M13 ....**88** A3
Doddington La *ORD* M5 ....**83** D1
Dodd St *ORD* M5 ....**65** C3
Dodge HI *HTNM* SK4 ....**129** D3
Dodworth CI *HULME* M15 ....**86** A3
Doe Brow *SWIN* M27 ....**25** D1
Dolbey St *ORD* M5 ....**65** D4
Dolefield *CSLFD* M3 ....**3** D5
Dollond St *BKLY* M9 ....**34** B4
Dolphin PI *WGTN/LGST* M12 ....**9** F4
Dolphin St *WGTN/LGST* M12 ....**9** F4
Domett St *BKLY* M9 ....**33** D3
Donald St *CMANE* M1 * **8** B2
Dona St *STKP* SK1 ....**133** D1
Don Av *SLFD* M6 ....**64** B3
Doncaster Av *DID/WITH* M20 ....**114** B2
Doncaster Wk *OLD* OL1 * **23** C2
Donhead Wk *BRUN/LGST* M13 * **87** D3
Donleigh St *NEWH/MOS* M40 ....**56** A4
Donnington Rd *GTN* M18 ....**91** D4
Donnison St *WGTN/LGST* M12 ....**89** D1
Donovan Av *NEWH/MOS* M40 ....**56** A4
Dorchester Av *PWCH* M25 ....**30** B3
   URM M41 ....**94** A3
Dorchester Rd *SWIN* M27 ....**45** C3
Dorclyn Av *URM* M41 ....**94** A3
Doric CI *OP/CLY* M11 ....**72** A4
Dorking Av *NEWH/MOS* M40 ....**72** B1
Dorlan Av *GTN* M18 ....**107** C1
Dorman St *OP/CLY* M11 ....**91** C1
Dorney St *GTN* M18 ....**91** C4
Dorning Rd *SWIN* M27 ....**45** D2
Dorning St *ECC* M30 ....**62** A4
Dorothy St *BRO* M7 ....**51** C2
Dorris St *BNG/LEV* M19 ....**118** A1
Dorset Av *DTN/ASHW* M34 ....**93** D1
   RDSH SK5 ....**121** D1
   RUSH/FAL M14 ....**101** D3
Dorset Rd *BNG/LEV* M19 ....**105** D3
   DROY M43 ....**75** C2
   FAIL M35 ....**57** C4
Dorset St *CHAD* OL9 ....**21** D4
   STRET M32 ....**97** C3
   SWIN M27 ....**26** A3
Dorsey St *ANC* M4 * **4** C5
Dorstone CI *NEWH/MOS* M40 ....**73** D1
Dorwood Av *BKLY* M9 ....**15** D4
Dougall Wk *WGTN/LGST* M12 ....**89** D3
Doughty Av *ECC* M30 ....**63** C2
Douglas Av *STRET* M32 ....**97** C3
Douglas Gn *SLFD* M6 ....**48** B4
Douglas Rd *WALK* M28 ....**43** D2
Douglas St *BRO* M7 ....**50** A3
   FAIL M35 ....**57** D2
   NEWH/MOS M40 ....**54** B3
   OLD OL1 ....**23** D1
   SWIN M27 ....**45** D2
Doulton St *NEWH/MOS* M40 ....**55** D1
Dounby Av *ECC* M30 ....**61** D2
Douro St *NEWH/MOS* M40 ....**54** A4
Dovecote *DROY* M43 ....**77** C2
Dovecote Ms *CCHDY* M21 ....**111** D2
Dovedale Av *DID/WITH* M20 ....**114** B2
   DROY M43 ....**74** B3
   ECC M30 ....**62** B3
   PWCH M25 ....**31** C2
   URM M41 ....**94** A3
Dovedale St *FAIL* M35 ....**56** B2
Dovehouse CI *WHTF* M45 ....**10** A1
Doveleys Rd *SLFD* M6 ....**65** C1
Dovercort Av *HTNM* SK4 ....**127** C1

Dovercourt Av *HTNM* SK4 *	127	C2
Doveridge Gdns *SLFD* M6	66	A2
Dover Pk *URM* M41	94	A1
Dover Rd *SWIN* M27	26	B3
Dover St *BRUN/LGST* M13	87	C3
CHAD OL9	21	D1
ECC M30	61	C3
RDSH SK5 *	119	D2
Dovestone Wk *NEWH/MOS* M40 *	37	D4
Doveston Rd *SALE* M33	109	C3
Downfields *RDSH* SK5	107	C3
Downham Crs *PWCH* M25	31	D2
Downham Gdns *PWCH* M25	31	D2
Downham Rd *HTNM* SK4	119	C4
Downing St *CMANE* M1	9	D3
Downley Dr *ANC* M4	5	F3
The Downs *MDTN* M24	18	A3
PWCH M25	29	D2
Dowry St *OLDS* OL8	41	C2
Drake Cl *OLD* OL1	23	C1
Drake Ct *RDSH* SK5	129	D1
Drayfields *DROY* M43	77	C3
Drayton Av *ECC* M30	85	D4
Drayton Wk *OLDTF/WHR* M16	84	B4
Dresden St *NEWH/MOS* M40	55	D1
Drewett St *NEWH/MOS* M40	71	D1
Dreyfus Av *OP/CLY* M11	73	D3
Driffield St *ECC* M30	78	B1
RUSH/FAL M14	101	D2
Drill Wk *ANC* M4	5	F1
Drinkwater Rd *PWCH* M25	29	C4
Driscoll St *BRUN/LGST* M13	104	A4
The Drive *BRO* M7	49	D1
DID/WITH M20	125	D2
PWCH M25	30	A1
RDSH SK5	131	D1
Droitwich Rd *NEWH/MOS* M40	71	C1
Dronfield Rd *SLFD* M6	65	C1
Droughts La *PWCH* M25	13	C1
Droylsden Rd *DTN/ASHW* M34	76	A4
NEWH/MOS M40	56	A4
Drury La *CHAD* OL9	38	B2
Drury St *BNG/LEV* M19	104	B4
Dryad Cl *SWIN* M27	26	A3
Drybrook Cl *BRUN/LGST* M13	88	B4
Dryden Av *SWIN* M27	44	A2
Dryden Rd *OLDTF/WHR* M16	99	D2
Dryden St *BRUN/LGST* M13	87	D3
Dryhurst Wk *HULME* M15	86	B3
Drymoss *OLDS* OL8	41	C4
Drywood Av *WALK* M28	42	B4
Ducal St *ANC* M4	70	A1
Duchess Rd *CHH* M8	52	A1
Duchy Rd *SLFD* M6	47	C3
Duchy Rd *SLFD* M6	47	D4
Duchy St *EDGY/DAV* SK3	132	A2
SLFD M6	66	A3
Ducie St *CMANE* M1	4	C5
OLDS OL8	41	D4
WHTF M45	11	C1
Duckworth Rd *PWCH* M25	29	C2
Duddon Cl *WHTF* M45	12	A1
Dudley Av *WHTF* M45	11	C1
Dudley Cl *HULME* M15	85	D4
Dudley Rd *OLDTF/WHR* M16	100	A2
SALE M33	109	D3
SWIN M27	26	A4
Dudley St *BRO* M7	51	C3
ECC M30	61	D4
Dudlow Wk *HULME* M15 *	85	C3
Duffield Ct *MDTN* M24 *	17	C4
Duffield Gdns *MDTN* M24	17	C4
Duffield Rd *MDTN* M24	17	C4
SLFD M6	47	C4
Dugdale Av *BKLY* M9	34	B1
Duke Ct *OLDTF/WHR* M16	85	C4
Duke Pl *CSLFD* M3	6	C2
Duke St *BRO* M7	50	A4
CSLFD M3	3	E2
CSLFD M3	6	C2
ECC M30	61	D1
FAIL M35	57	D1
STKP SK1	129	D4
WALK M28	24	B1
Dulford Wk *BRUN/LGST* M13 *	87	D4
Dulgar St *OP/CLY* M11 *	90	A1
Dulverton St *NEWH/MOS* M40	55	C3
Dulwich St *ANC* M4	70	A2
Dumbarton Cl *RDSH* SK5	120	A3
Dumbarton Rd *RDSH* SK5	120	A3
Dumbell St *SWIN* M27	26	A3
Dumber La *SALE* M33	108	A3
Dunbar St *OLD* OL1	22	B1
Dunblane Av *HTNM* SK4	129	C3
Duncan Rd *BRUN/LGST* M13	104	A2
Duncan St *BRO* M7	49	D3
ORD M5	84	B1
Dun Cl *CSLFD* M3	2	B1
Duncombe Dr *NEWH/MOS* M40	55	C2
Duncombe St *BRO* M7	50	B3
Dundonald Rd *DID/WITH* M20	125	D2
Dundonald St *OFTN* SK2	133	C3
Dunedin Dr *SLFD* M6	48	A4
Dunham St *HULME* M15	85	D3
Dunkerley Av *FAIL* M35	57	C2
Dunkirk St *DROY* M43	76	A4
Dunley Cl *WGTN/LGST* M12	89	D3
Dunlop St *CSLFD* M3 *	3	E4
Dunoon Rd *RDSH* SK5	120	A3
Dunscar Cl *WHTF* M45	10	A2
Dunsley Av *NEWH/MOS* M40	37	C3
Dunsmore Cl *OLDTF/WHR* M16	100	A1
Dunstable St *BNG/LEV* M19	105	C4
Dunster Av *BKLY* M9	34	B1
RDSH SK5	121	D4
SWIN M27	27	C3
Dunston St *OP/CLY* M11	90	B1
Dunton Gn *RDSH* SK5	121	C3
Dunworth Rd *RUSH/FAL* M14	102	A2
Durant St *ANC* M4 *	4	C1
Durban St *AULW* OL7	77	D4
OLDS OL8	39	D2
Durham Av *URM* M41	94	B2
Durham Crs *FAIL* M35	57	C2
Durham Rd *SLFD* M6	66	B3
Durham St *BKLY* M9 *	53	D2
CHAD OL9	39	D1
DROY M43	92	B1
RDSH SK5	106	B3
Durley Av *CHH* M8	52	A1
Durling St *WGTN/LGST* M12	9	F4
Durnford Av *URM* M41	95	D3
Dutton St *CSLFD* M3	69	C2
Dyche St *ANC* M4	4	C2
Dyer St *OP/CLY* M11	89	D1
ORD M5	84	B2
Dymchurch St *NEWH/MOS* M40	73	D1
Dyserth Gv *RDSH* SK5	120	A4

E

Eades St *SLFD* M6	66	B2
Eadington St *CHH* M8	32	B4
Eagar St *NEWH/MOS* M40	55	D3
Eagle Dr *SLFD* M6	48	B3
Eagle St *ANC* M4	4	B2
CHAD OL9	22	B3
Ealing Av *RUSH/FAL* M14	102	A3
Ealinger Wy *SWIN* M27	26	A3
Ealing Pl *BNG/LEV* M19 *	117	D3
Ealing Rd *EDGY/DAV* SK3	132	A1

Earby Gv *BKLY* M9.................................**35** C2
Earl Rd *HTNM* SK4.................................**128** B1
Earlston Av *DTN/ASHW* M34......**107** D2
Earl St *BRO* M7....................................**68** A1
  DTN/ASHW M34............................**107** A1
  EDGY/DAV SK3.............................**132** A1
  PWCH M25.......................................**30** B1
  SALE M33 *....................................**109** D4
Earls Wy *FAIL* M35..............................**56** A3
Earl Wk *WGTN/LGST* M12 *.........**104** A1
Earnshaw Av *STKP* SK1.................**131** C4
Easedale Rd *NEWH/MOS* M40.........**55** D1
East Aisle Rd *TRPK* M17.................**96** B1
East Av *BNG/LEV* M19.....................**117** C2
Eastburn Av *NEWH/MOS* M40.........**70** B2
East Central Dr *SWIN* M27.............**46** A2
Eastcombe Av *BRO* M7....................**49** C2
Eastcote Rd *RDSH* SK5..................**120** A4
East Crs *MDTN* M24.........................**17** C3
East Dr *SLFD* M6..............................**47** D4
  SWIN M27.......................................**46** A2
Eastern Av *SWIN* M27......................**28** A3
Eastern By-Pass *OP/CLY* M11.......**73** D3
  OP/CLY M11.....................................**91** C1
Eastern Cir *BNG/LEV* M19.............**117** C1
Eastfield *SLFD* M6...........................**65** D1
Eastfield Av *MDTN* M24...................**17** D2
  NEWH/MOS M40...............................**71** D2
Eastford Sq *NEWH/MOS* M40.........**70** A1
East Gra *OP/CLY* M11......................**73** D2
East Gv *BRUN/LGST* M13.................**87** D4
Eastham Av *RUSH/FAL* M14..........**102** A4
Easthaven Av *OP/CLY* M11..............**73** D3
East Hill St *OLDE* OL4 *..................**23** D3
Eastholme Dr *BNG/LEV* M19.........**118** A2
Easthope Cl *DID/WITH* M20...........**115** C2
East Lancashire Rd *SWIN* M27......**44** B3
Eastlands Rd *BKLY* M9.....................**16** A4
Eastleigh Av *BRO* M7.......................**50** B1
Eastleigh Dr *NEWH/MOS* M40.........**71** C2
Eastleigh Rd *PWCH* M25.................**31** D2
East Meade *CCHDY* M21.................**112** A2
  PWCH M25.......................................**31** C3
  SWIN M27.......................................**44** B3
Eastmoor Dr *NEWH/MOS* M40.........**74** A1
East Newton St *ANC* M4.....................**5** F1
Easton Cl *MDTN* M24........................**18** B2
Easton Rd *DROY* M43.......................**74** B3
East Ordsall La *CSLFD* M3................**2** B4
East Park Cl *BRUN/LGST* M13 *..........**9** F5
Eastpark Cl *BRUN/LGST* M13.........**87** D3
East Philip St *CSLFD* M3.................**68** B2
East Rd *GTN* M18............................**105** C2
  STRET M32......................................**96** A1
  URM M41..**80** A4
  WGTN/LGST M12............................**104** B2
Eastry Av *RDSH* SK5......................**121** C4
East Union St *OLDTF/WHR* M16......**84** B3
Eastville Gdns *BNG/LEV* M19......**116** B4
East Vw *MDTN* M24..........................**17** C1
Eastwood Av *DROY* M43...................**74** B4
  NEWH/MOS M40...............................**38** A4
  URM M41..**94** A3
Eastwood Rd *NEWH/MOS* M40.........**38** A4
Eaton Rd *CHH* M8.............................**32** A4
Eaves La *CHAD* OL9.........................**20** B4
Ebbdale Cl *STKP* SK1....................**133** D1
Ebberstone St *RUSH/FAL* M14.....**101** D3
Ebden St *CMANE* M1 *.......................**8** C2
Ebenezer St *HULME* M15....................**7** F4
Ebsworth St *NEWH/MOS* M40.........**54** A1
Eccles Cl *OP/CLY* M11.....................**90** B1
Eccleshall St *OP/CLY* M11..............**73** D4
Eccles New Rd *SALQ* M50................**64** A3
Eccles Old Rd *SLFD* M6...................**64** B2
Eccles Rd *SWIN* M27........................**45** C3
Eccleston Av *RUSH/FAL* M14........**101** D4

Eccleston Pl *NEWH/MOS* M7 *.........**44** A2
Eccleston St *FAIL* M35 *...................**50** A1
Echo St *CMANE* M1.............................**8** C2
Eckford St *CHH* M8...........................**52** A3
Edale Av *NEWH/MOS* M40...............**54** B1
  RDSH SK5.....................................**107** D3
Edale Rd *STRET* M32.......................**96** A2
Edale St *SLFD* M6............................**49** C4
Edbrook Wk *BRUN/LGST* M13 *.......**88** A4
Eddie Colman Cl *NEWH/MOS* M40 *..**55** C4
Eddisbury Av *DID/WITH* M20..........**114** A1
Eddystone Cl *ORD* M5......................**66** B4
Edenbridge Rd *NEWH/MOS* M40.......**73** C1
Eden Cl *HULME* M15........................**86** B4
  STKP SK1.......................................**133** D1
Edenfield La *WALK* M28...................**60** A1
Edenfield Rd *PWCH* M25..................**31** D2
Edenhall Av *BNG/LEV* M19............**117** C1
Eden St *OLD* OL1..............................**22** B2
Edgbaston Dr *OLDTF/WHR* M16......**98** B2
Edgedale Av *BNG/LEV* M19............**116** B4
Edgefield Av *BKLY* M9......................**34** B1
Edgehill Cl *ORD* M5..........................**66** A3
Edgehill Rd *SLFD* M6.......................**64** B2
Edgehill St *ANC* M4 *..........................**4** B3
Edge La *DROY* M43...........................**74** B4
  STRET M32......................................**96** A2
Edge Lane Rd *OLD* OL1...................**23** D1
Edgeley Rd *EDGY/DAV* SK3...........**132** A2
Edge St *ANC* M4..................................**4** B3
Edgeware Av *PWCH* M25..................**32** A1
Edgeware Rd *CHAD* OL9...................**37** D2
  ECC M30..**61** B1
Edgewater *ORD* M5...........................**65** C3
Edgeworth Dr *RUSH/FAL* M14......**116** B2
Edgware Rd *NEWH/MOS* M40.........**73** C1
Edilom Rd *CHH* M8...........................**31** D3
Edinburgh Sq *NEWH/MOS* M40.......**71** C1
Edison Rd *ECC* M30..........................**78** B1
Edison St *OP/CLY* M11.....................**91** D2
Edith Av *RUSH/FAL* M14................**101** D3
Edith Cavell Cl *OP/CLY* M11............**73** D4
Edith St *OLDS* OL8...........................**41** C2
Edlin Cl *WGTN/LGST* M12................**88** B4
Edmonton Rd *NEWH/MOS* M40.......**72** B1
Edmund Cl *HTNM* SK4....................**129** D1
Edmund St *CSLFD* M3 *......................**2** D1
  DROY M43.......................................**92** B1
  FAIL M35 *......................................**57** D2
  SLFD M6...**65** D2
Edson Rd *CHH* M8............................**32** A2
Edward Av *CCHDY* M21...................**111** C2
  SLFD M6...**64** B2
Edward Charlton Rd *OLDTF/WHR* M16..**98** B3
Edward Ms *CHAD* OL9 *...................**21** D4
Edward Rd *BKLY* M9.........................**16** A4
Edwards Dr *WHTF* M45.....................**12** A1
Edward St *BKLY* M9..........................**53** D1
  BRO M7...**68** B1
  CHAD OL9.......................................**20** B2
  DROY M43 *....................................**92** A1
  PWCH M25......................................**11** D4
  STKP SK1......................................**133** C1
Edwin Rd *OP/CLY* M11......................**71** D4
Eeasbrook *URM* M41.........................**94** A4
Egbert St *NEWH/MOS* M40...............**55** C2
Egerton Cl *WALK* M28.......................**42** B1
Egerton Crs *DID/WITH* M20 *.........**115** C2
Egerton Dr *SALE* M33 *..................**109** C4
Egerton Ms *DROY* M43 *...................**92** B1
  RUSH/FAL M14.............................**116** A1
Egerton Pk *WALK* M28......................**43** C2
Egerton Rd *ECC* M30........................**62** A1
  RUSH/FAL M14.............................**116** A1
  WHTF M45.......................................**11** C2
Egerton Rd North *CCHDY* M21........**99** D4

HTNM SK4 ....**118**	B4
Egerton Rd South *CCHDY* M21 ....**112**	B1
HTNM SK4 ....**128**	B1
Egerton St *CSLFD* M3 ....**2**	B4
DROY M43 ....**76**	A4
ECC M30 ....**61**	C3
HULME M15 ....**6**	B3
MDTN M24 * **15**	D2
OLD OL1 ....**23**	D2
PWCH M25 ....**30**	B1
Egerton Ter *RUSH/FAL* M14 ......**116**	A2
Eggington St *NEWH/MOS* M40 ....**52**	B4
Egmont St *CHH* M8 ....**51**	D1
SLFD M6 ....**47**	D3
Egremont Av *DID/WITH* M20 .....**114**	B2
Egremont Ct *BRO* M7 * **49**	D1
Eida Wy *TRPK* M17 ....**81**	D1
Eighth Av *OLDS* OL8 ....**40**	A4
Eighth St *TRPK* M17 ....**81**	D3
Eileen Gv *RUSH/FAL* M14 ....**102**	B3
Eileen Gv West *RUSH/FAL* M14 ....**102**	A3
Elaine Av *BKLY* M9 ....**36**	A3
Elbe St *WGTN/LGST* M12 * **9**	F2
Elbow St *BNG/LEV* M19 ....**104**	B4
Elcot Cl *NEWH/MOS* M40 * **52**	B4
Elder Gv *NEWH/MOS* M40 ....**38**	A3
Eldermount Rd *BKLY* M9 ....**34**	A3
Elderwood *CHAD* OL9 ....**19**	D2
Eldon Pl *ECC* M30 ....**61**	D4
Eldon Prec *OLDS* OL8 ....**22**	B4
Eldon St *OLDS* OL8 ....**23**	C4
Eldridge Dr *NEWH/MOS* M40 ....**54**	B4
Eleanor Rd *CCHDY* M21 ....**111**	C1
Eleanor St *OLD* OL1 ....**22**	A1
Electo St *OP/CLY* M11 ....**91**	D2
Elevator Rd *TRPK* M17 ....**82**	B3
Eleventh St *TRPK* M17 ....**82**	A3
Elf Mill Cl *EDGY/DAV* SK3 ....**132**	B3
Elford Gv *GTN* M18 ....**107**	D1
Elgar St *WGTN/LGST* M12 ....**104**	B2
Elgin Av *DID/WITH* M20 * **126**	A2
Elgol Cl *EDGY/DAV* SK3 ....**133**	C4
Eliot Rd *ECC* M30 ....**62**	A4
Eli St *CHAD* OL9 ....**38**	B2
Eliza Ann St *ECC* M30 ....**61**	D4
NEWH/MOS M40 ....**70**	B1
Elizabeth Av *CHAD* OL9 ....**38**	B1
STKP SK1 * **133**	C1
Elizabeth Cl *STRET* M32 ....**97**	C3
Elizabeth Ct *HTNM* SK4 ....**128**	B3
Elizabeth Slinger Rd *DID/WITH* M20..**123**	D1
Elizabeth St *CHH* M8 ....**51**	D4
SWIN M27 ....**26**	B4
WHTF M45 ....**11**	C2
Eliza St *HULME* M15 ....**6**	C5
Elkanagh Gdns *SLFD* M6 ....**66**	A2
Elladene Pk *CCHDY* M21 ....**112**	B1
Ellanby Cl *RUSH/FAL* M14 ....**102**	A2
Ellaston Dr *URM* M41 * **94**	A3
Ellastone Rd *SLFD* M6 ....**64**	B1
Ellbourne Rd *BKLY* M9 ....**32**	B2
Ellenbrook Cl *WGTN/LGST* M12 ....**90**	A3
Ellenhall Cl *BKLY* M9 ....**53**	C1
Ellen St *CHAD* OL9 ....**22**	A1
DROY M43 ....**93**	C1
HTNM SK4 ....**128**	C2
Ellen Wilkinson Crs *WGTN/LGST* M12...**89**	D4
Elleray Rd *MDTN* M24 ....**17**	C4
SLFD M6 ....**47**	C4
Ellerby Av *SWIN* M27 ....**26**	B2
Ellesmere Av *ECC* M30 ....**62**	B3
Ellesmere Cir *URM* M41 ....**79**	C2
Ellesmere Rd *CCHDY* M21 ....**99**	D3
ECC M30 ....**62**	B1
Ellesmere Rd North *HTNM* SK4 ....**118**	B4
Ellesmere Rd South *CCHDY* M21 ..**112**	B1
Ellesmere St *ECC* M30 ....**62**	A4

FAIL M35 ....**57**	C1
SWIN M27 ....**26**	B4
SWIN M27 ....**44**	A2
Ellesmere Ter *RUSH/FAL* M14 .....**116**	C2
Ellingham Cl *OP/CLY* M11 ....**72**	A4
Elliot Sq *OLD* OL1 * **23**	D1
Ellis Dr *CHH* M8 ....**33**	C4
Ellis La *MDTN* M24 ....**15**	C1
Ellis St *CHH* M8 ....**68**	B1
HULME M15 ....**85**	D3
Elliston Sq *WGTN/LGST* M12 ....**89**	D3
Ellor St *SLFD* M6 ....**66**	C4
Ellwood Rd *STKP* SK1 ....**131**	C4
Elmbank Av *DID/WITH* M20 ....**123**	D1
Elmbank Rd *MDTN* M24 ....**18**	B1
Elm Crs *WALK* M28 ....**42**	B2
Elmdale Wk *HULME* M15 * **8**	A4
Elm Dr *STRET* M32 ....**96**	A4
STRET M32 ....**109**	D1
Elmfield Rd *DTN/ASHW* M34 ....**93**	D1
EDGY/DAV SK3 ....**133**	C4
Elmfield St *CHH* M8 ....**51**	D3
Elmgate Gv *BNG/LEV* M19 ....**104**	B4
Elm Gv *DID/WITH* M20 ....**125**	C2
DROY M43 ....**74**	A3
PWCH M25 ....**11**	D3
SALE M33 ....**109**	C3
SWIN M27 ....**24**	A4
URM M41 ....**94**	B3
Elmham Wk *NEWH/MOS* M40 ....**70**	B1
Elmhurst Dr *BNG/LEV* M19 ....**117**	C4
Elmira Wy *ORD* M5 ....**83**	D3
Elm Rd *DID/WITH* M20 ....**124**	B1
OLDS OL8 ....**40**	A4
Elmscott Wk *BRUN/LGST* M13 ....**88**	A4
Elmsdale Av *BKLY* M9 ....**15**	D4
Elmsmere Rd *DID/WITH* M20 ....**126**	A2
Elms Rd *HTNM* SK4 ....**118**	A4
Elmstead Av *DID/WITH* M20 ....**114**	B3
Elmstone Cl *BKLY* M9 ....**33**	D3
Elm St *ECC* M30 ....**62**	A4
FAIL M35 ....**57**	C1
MDTN M24 ....**18**	B1
SWIN M27 ....**25**	D4
Elmswood Av *RUSH/FAL* M14 ....**101**	C1
Elmsworth Av *BNG/LEV* M19 ....**105**	C4
Elmton Rd *BKLY* M9 ....**34**	B2
Elm Tree Cl *FAIL* M35 ....**58**	A2
Elmtree Dr *HTNM* SK4 ....**128**	A3
Elm Tree Rd *MPL/ROM* SK6 ....**131**	D2
Elmwood Gv *BKLY* M9 ....**54**	A2
Elsa Rd *BNG/LEV* M19 ....**105**	D4
Elsdon Dr *GTN* M18 ....**91**	C3
Elsdon Rd *BRUN/LGST* M13 ....**104**	A3
Elsham Gdns *GTN* M18 ....**104**	B1
Elsie St *BKLY* M9 ....**53**	D1
Elsinore Cl *FAIL* M35 ....**58**	A2
Elsinore Rd *OLDTF/WHR* M16 ....**98**	B3
Elsma Rd *NEWH/MOS* M40 ....**74**	A3
Elsmore Rd *RUSH/FAL* M14 ....**101**	D4
Elstree Av *NEWH/MOS* M40 ....**73**	C1
Elswick Av *CCHDY* M21 ....**123**	C1
Elsworth St *CSLFD* M3 ....**69**	D2
Eltham Dr *URM* M41 ....**94**	A3
Eltham St *BNG/LEV* M19 ....**104**	B3
Elton Av *BNG/LEV* M19 ....**117**	D1
Elton Cl *WHTF* M45 ....**11**	D1
Elton St *BRO* M7 ....**68**	A2
STRET M32 ....**83**	C4
Elton's Yd *BRO* M7 ....**68**	A2
Elvate Crs *CHH* M8 ....**50**	B4
Elverdon Cl *HULME* M15 ....**85**	D4
Elverston St *WYTH/NTH* M22 ....**123**	C4
Elverston Wy *CHAD* OL9 * **21**	D1
Elvey St *NEWH/MOS* M40 ....**54**	A4
Elwick Cl *OLDTF/WHR* M16 ....**101**	C2
Ely Av *STRET* M32 ....**95**	C2

Ely Crs *FAIL* M35 ....**57** C4
Elysian St *OP/CLY* M11 ....**90** B1
Ely St *CHAD* OL9.............................**21** C1
Emaline Gra *SLFD* M6......................**65** D3
Ember St *OP/CLY* M11 * **74** A3
Emerson Av *ECC* M30......................**63** D2
Emerson St *ORD* M5.........................**65** C3
Emery Av *CCHDY* M21 ....**112** B3
Emery Cl *HTNM* SK4.......................**127** D1
Emily Beavan Cl *OP/CLY* M11......**73** C4
Emily Cl *FAIL* M35............................**38** B4
Emily Pl *DROY* M43..........................**75** C4
Emley St *BNG/LEV* M19................**105** C4
Emlyn St *SWIN* M27.........................**44** A1
Emma St *OLDS* OL8.........................**41** C2
Emmerson St *SWIN* M27.................**26** A4
Emmett St East *NEWH/MOS* M40......**53** D4
Emmott St *OLD* OL1.........................**23** C3
Emmott Wy *OLD* OL1.......................**23** C3
Emperor St *STKP* SK1 * **130** B3
Empire St *CHH* M8...........................**69** C4
Empress Dr *HTNM* SK4..................**129** C1
Empress St *CHH* M8,.......................**51** C1
    OLDTF/WHR M16.......................**84** B3
Enbridge St *ORD* M5 * **83** D1
Encombe Pl *CSLFD* M3....................**2** A1
Endcott Cl *GTN* M18.......................**90** A3
Enderby Rd *NEWH/MOS* M40.........**36** B4
Endon Dr *CCHDY* M21...................**114** A1
Endsleigh Rd *DID/WITH* M20.......**115** D3
Energy St *NEWH/MOS* M40 * **71** D2
Enfield Av *BNG/LEV* M19..............**117** D3
    OLDS OL8...**40** B2
Enfield Cl *ECC* M30.........................**79** C1
Enfield Dr *OP/CLY* M11..................**73** C3
Enfield Rd *ECC* M30.........................**62** A1
    SWIN M27...**44** B3
Engell Cl *GTN* M18...........................**90** B4
Engine St *CHAD* OL9........................**39** C1
Enid Cl *BRO* M7.................................**50** B4
Ennerdale Av *CCHDY* M21...........**123** C1
    SWIN M27...**45** C3
Ennerdale Rd *STRET* M32 * **96** B2
Ennismore Av *ECC* M30...................**63** D3
Enstone Dr *NEWH/MOS* M40.........**37** C4
Entwisle St *SWIN* M27......................**25** C4
Enver Rd *CHH* M8.............................**52** A1
Enville Rd *NEWH/MOS* M40............**36** A4
    SLFD M6..**47** D3
Enville St *BKLY* M9..........................**34** A2
Epping Cl *CHAD* OL9.......................**19** D1
Epping St *HULME* M15.......................**7** F5
Eppleworth Ri *SWIN* M27................**26** B2
Epsom Av *BNG/LEV* M19...............**117** C3
Epworth St *ANC* M4...........................**5** F5
Ercall Av *WGTN/LGST* M12............**88** B3
Erica Cl *RDSH* SK5.........................**120** A1
Erica Dr *BNG/LEV* M19..................**126** B1
Eric Brook Cl *RUSH/FAL* M14......**101** D2
Erin Cl *CHAD* OL9............................**21** C4
Erin St *OP/CLY* M11 * **91** D1
Erith Cl *RDSH* SK5.........................**121** C3
Erlington Av *OLDTF/WHR* M16......**99** C2
Ermen Rd *ECC* M30..........................**78** B1
Ermington Dr *CHH* M8.....................**51** C1
Erneley Cl *WGTN/LGST* M12.......**105** C2
Ernest St *OFTN* SK2.......................**133** D3
    PWCH M25.......................................**29** C1
Ernocroft Gv *GTN* M18 * **91** D3
Errington Dr *BRO* M7......................**68** A1
Errol Av *BKLY* M9............................**14** B4
Errwood Crs *BNG/LEV* M19..........**117** D1
Errwood Rd *BNG/LEV* M19...........**117** D1
Erwin St *NEWH/MOS* M40...............**55** C3
Erwood Rd *BNG/LEV* M19............**117** D3

Eryngo St *STKP* SK1 ....**130** B4
Escott St *OLDTF/WHR* M16...........**101** C2
Eskdale Av *DID/WITH* M20...........**114** B2
    OLDS OL8...**40** A1
Eskrigge Cl *BRO* M7........................**51** C1
Esmond Rd *CHH* M8........................**51** D2
Essex Av *DID/WITH* M20................**125** C1
    DROY M43.......................................**75** D2
Essex Cl *FAIL* M35............................**57** C3
Essex Rd *GTN* M18.........................**107** C2
    RDSH SK5.......................................**121** D4
Essex St *CMANW* M2.........................**3** F5
Essex Wy *OLDTF/WHR* M16...........**85** C4
Essington Dr *NEWH/MOS* M40.......**53** C3
Estate Av *OLDS* OL8........................**41** C1
Estate St South *OLDS* OL8...............**41** C1
Estonfield Dr *URM* M41....................**95** C3
Eston St *BRUN/LGST* M13.............**103** C1
Eswick St *OP/CLY* M11....................**73** D4
Etchells St *STKP* SK1 * **130** A4
Etchell St *NEWH/MOS* M40 * **52** B4
Ethel Av *BKLY* M9............................**34** A1
    SWIN M27...**46** A1
Ethel St *OLDS* OL8...........................**41** C2
Ethel Ter *BNG/LEV* M19................**104** B4
Etherow Av *NEWH/MOS* M40 * **38** A3
Etherstone St *CHH* M8......................**52** B1
Eton Av *OLDS* OL8............................**40** B2
Eton Cl *OLDTF/WHR* M16...............**85** C4
Eton Ct *OLDTF/WHR* M16 * **85** C4
Etruria Cl *BRUN/LGST* M13............**88** B4
Ettrick Cl *OP/CLY* M11....................**91** C2
Euclid Cl *OP/CLY* M11.....................**71** D4
Europa Ga *TRPK* M17......................**82** A4
Europa Wy *TRPK* M17......................**82** A4
Euston Av *BKLY* M9..........................**35** D2
Evan Cl *DID/WITH* M20..................**124** B2
Evans Cl *DID/WITH* M20................**124** B2
Evans Rd *ECC* M30...........................**60** B4
Evans St *CSLFD* M3............................**3** D1
    MDTN M24..**18** A1
    OLD OL1...**23** C1
Evan St *NEWH/MOS* M40.................**53** D4
Eva St *RUSH/FAL* M14...................**102** B2
Evelyn St *RUSH/FAL* M14.............**116** A1
Evening St *FAIL* M35........................**57** C1
Evenley Cl *OP/CLY* M11 * **91** C1
Everard St *ORD* M5...........................**84** B2
Everett Rd *DID/WITH* M20............**115** C3
Everglade *OLDS* OL8........................**41** C3
Everleigh Dr *BRO* M7.......................**51** C3
Eversden Ct *BRO* M7 * **68** B1
Everside Dr *CHH* M8.........................**50** B3
Eversley Rd *DID/WITH* M20..........**124** B2
Everton Rd *OLDS* OL8......................**40** A2
    RDSH SK5.......................................**107** C3
Everton St *SWIN* M27.......................**27** B1
Every St *ANC* M4...............................**71** C4
Evesham Av *HTNM* SK4................**128** D1
Evesham Cl *MDTN* M24....................**18** A4
Evesham Gdns *MDTN* M24 * **17** D4
Evesham Rd *BKLY* M9.......................**35** D3
    MDTN M24..**17** D4
Evesham Wk *MDTN* M24..................**18** A4
    OLDS OL8 * **22** B4
Eve St *OLDS* OL8..............................**41** C3
Ewan St *GTN* M18.............................**91** C3
Ewart Av *ORD* M5.............................**65** C3
Ewhurst Av *SWIN* M27.....................**44** A3
Ewing Cl *CHH* M8..............................**32** B4
Exbury St *RUSH/FAL* M14.............**116** A4
Exchange Quay *ORD* M5...................**83** D3
Exchange Sq *CSLFD* M3.....................**3** F3
Exchange St *CSLFD* M3 * **3** F4
    EDGY/DAV SK3.............................**129** D4
Exeter Av *ECC* M30..........................**63** D1
Exeter Rd *RDSH* SK5.......................**121** D4

URM M41.....................................**94** A1
Exeter St *SLFD* M6.......................**65** D3
Exford CI *NEWH/MOS* M40..........**71** C2
RDSH SK5...................................**120** A3
Exmouth Av *RDSH* SK5.............**121** D4
Exmouth Wk *OLDTF/WHR* M16....**100** B2
Eynford Av *RDSH* SK5.................**121** C4
Eyre St *HULME* M15....................**86** B4

F

Faber St *ANC* M4.........................**69** D2
Factory Brow *MDTN* M24.............**15** D2
Factory La *BKLY* M9....................**34** A4
CSLFD M3 *.....................................**2** A1
Factory St *MDTN* M24................**17** C1
Failsworth Rd *FAIL* M35.............**58** A2
Fairbottom St *OLD* OL1..............**23** C2
Fairbourne Rd *BNG/LEV* M19.....**105** D4
Fairbrook Dr *SLFD* M6.................**65** D3
Fairbrother St *ORD* M5...............**84** B2
Fairclough St *OP/CLY* M11.........**72** B3
Fairfax Av *DROY* M43..................**92** B2
Fairfax Rd *PWCH* M25................**11** D4
Fairfield Av *DROY* M43................**92** B2
Fairfield Rd *DROY* M43...............**92** B1
OP/CLY M11...................................**91** D2
Fairfields *OLDS* OL8...................**40** B3
Fairfield Sq *DROY* M43...............**92** B1
Fairfield St *CMANE* M1................**9** D2
SLFD M6..**47** C4
Fairford CI *RDSH* SK5................**120** A4
Fairford Wy *RDSH* SK5...............**120** A4
Fairhaven Av *CCHDY* M21..........**112** A2
WHTF M45......................................**10** A2
Fairhaven St *WGTN/LGST* M12...**89** C3
Fairholme Rd *DID/WITH* M20......**115** D3
HTNM SK4....................................**128** B2
Fairhope Av *SLFD* M6..................**64** A1
Fairisle CI *OP/CLY* M11...............**72** A4
Fairlawn *HTNM* SK4...................**129** C2
Fairlawn CI *RUSH/FAL* M14........**101** D1
Fairlea Av *DID/WITH* M20...........**125** D3
Fairlee Av *DTN/ASHW* M34.........**76** B4
Fairleigh Av *SLFD* M6.................**64** B2
Fairless Rd *ECC* M30...................**62** A4
Fairman Dr *OLDTF/WHR* M16......**101** C2
Fairmead Rd *NTHM/RTH* M23.....**122** B4
Fairmount Rd *SWIN* M27............**43** C3
Fair Oak Rd *BNG/LEV* M19.........**117** C4
Fairstead Wk *OP/CLY* M11..........**92** A2
Fair St *CMANE* M1.......................**5** E5
SWIN M27.....................................**26** B4
Fairview Av *BNG/LEV* M19..........**104** A3
DTN/ASHW M34............................**107** D4
Fairview CI *CHAD* OL9................**19** D1
Fairview Rd *DTN/ASHW* M34.......**107** D4
Fairway *DROY* M43......................**92** B1
PWCH M25....................................**31** C3
SWIN M27.....................................**46** B2
The Fairways *WHTF* M45.............**11** C3
The Fairway *NEWH/MOS* M40.....**56** A1
Fairy La *CHH* M8.........................**50** B4
SALE M33....................................**122** A2
Falcon Av *URM* M41....................**94** B3
Falcon Crs *SWIN* M27.................**27** C3
Falcon Dr *CHAD* OL9...................**21** D1
Falcon St *OLDS* OL8....................**22** B4
Falfield Dr *CHH* M8......................**52** A4
Fallons Wk *WALK* M28................**24** B4
Fallowfield Av *ORD* M5................**84** A1
Fallow Fields Dr *RDSH* SK5........**107** D4

The Fallows *CHAD* OL9...............**20** B4
Falmer CI *GTN* M18....................**92** A3
Falmouth Crs *RDSH* SK5...........**121** D4
Falmouth St *NEWH/MOS* M40....**72** A1
OLDS OL8......................................**41** C1
Falsgrave CI *NEWH/MOS* M40....**54** B4
Falston Av *NEWH/MOS* M40........**37** C3
Faraday Av *CHH* M8.....................**51** D3
SWIN M27.....................................**28** A3
Faraday St *CMANE* M1..................**4** C4
Far La *GTN* M18.........................**106** A1
Farley Av *GTN* M18....................**107** D1
Farley Wy *RDSH* SK5.................**106** D4
Farm Av *STRET* M32....................**95** D1
Farm CI *HTNM* SK4....................**118** B3
Farmer St *HTNM* SK4.................**129** C2
Farm HI *PWCH* M25 *...................**11** D4
Farm La *PWCH* M25....................**13** D1
WALK M28.....................................**42** A4
Farm Rd *OLDS* OL8......................**58** B1
Farmstead CI *FAIL* M35..............**58** B3
Farm St *FAIL* M35........................**56** A3
Farmway *MDTN* M24...................**17** C2
Farm Yd *BNG/LEV* M19..............**104** B4
Farn Av *RDSH* SK5.....................**106** B3
Farnborough Rd *NEWH/MOS* M40...**71** C2
Farndon Rd *RDSH* SK5..............**106** B3
Farnham Av *BKLY* M9...................**16** A4
Farnley St *WGTN/LGST* M12 *.....**89** D3
Farnworth Dr *RUSH/FAL* M14......**102** B3
Farrand Rd *OLDS* OL8..................**39** C3
Farrant Rd *WGTN/LGST* M12......**104** B2
Farrar Rd *DROY* M43....................**92** A1
Farrell St *BRO* M7........................**68** B2
Farrer Rd *BRUN/LGST* M13........**104** A3
Farringdon St *SLFD* M6 *.............**65** D2
Farr St *EDGY/DAV* SK3..............**132** A1
Farwood CI *OLDTF/WHR* M16......**84** B4
Fastnet St *OP/CLY* M11...............**89** D1
Faulkner Rd *STRET* M32..............**97** D4
Faulkner St *CMANE* M1..................**8** A1
Faversham Brow *OLD* OL1 *........**22** B1
Faversham St *NEWH/MOS* M40...**55** C2
Fay Av *BKLY* M9...........................**36** A3
Featherstall Rd North *CHAD* OL9...**22** A3
Featherstall Rd South *CHAD* OL9...**22** A3
Federation St *ANC* M4...................**4** C1
PWCH M25....................................**11** C4
Fellbrigg CI *GTN* M18................**105** D2
Felltop Dr *RDSH* SK5.................**120** B1
Felthorpe Dr *CHH* M8..................**51** C3
Fencegate Av *HTNM* SK4...........**119** C4
Fenchurch Av *NEWH/MOS* M40...**73** D1
Fencot Dr *WGTN/LGST* M12.......**104** B1
Fenella St *BRUN/LGST* M13.......**103** D1
Fenham CI *NEWH/MOS* M40 *......**52** B4
Fenmore Av *GTN* M18................**105** C2
Fennel St *ANC* M4.........................**3** F2
Fenney St *BRO* M7.......................**50** A4
Fenney St East *BRO* M7..............**50** B3
Fenn St *HULME* M15......................**6** C5
Fenton St *WGTN/LGST* M12........**89** C4
Fenwick Dr *HTNM* SK4...............**126** B2
Fenwick St *HULME* M15................**8** A5
Ferdinand St *NEWH/MOS* M40 *...**71** C1
Fernacre *SALE* M33...................**109** D4
Fern Bank *NEWH/MOS* M40 *......**55** D2
Fernbray Av *BNG/LEV* M19........**126** A1
Fernbrook CI *BRUN/LGST* M13....**88** C3
Fern CI *MDTN* M24........................**19** C1
Fernclough Rd *BKLY* M9..............**53** C3
Ferndale Gdns *BNG/LEV* M19....**116** B3
Ferndene Rd *DID/WITH* M20.......**115** C4
WHTF M45.....................................**12** B2
Ferndown Av *CHAD* OL9..............**19** C2
Ferney Field Rd *MDTN* M24.........**19** D3
Ferngate Dr *DID/WITH* M20........**115** C3

Fernhill Dr *GTN* M18	105	C1
Fernholme Ct *OLDS* OL8	39	D1
Fernhurst Rd *DID/WITH* M20	115	D4
Fernie St *ANC* M4 *	69	D2
Fernlea Crs *SWIN* M27	44	A4
Fernleigh Av *BNG/LEV* M19	105	D4
Fernleigh Dr *OLDTF/WHR* M16 *	84	B4
Fernside Av *DID/WITH* M20	116	A4
Fern St *CHAD* OL9	20	B1
CHH M8	69	D1
OLDS OL8	22	A4
Fernwood Av *GTN* M18	106	A2
Ferring Wk *CHAD* OL9 *	21	C3
Ferris St *OP/CLY* M11	91	C1
Ferry St *OP/CLY* M11	88	B1
Fettler Cl *SWIN* M27	44	B3
Feversham Cl *ECC* M30	63	C1
Field Bank Gv *BNG/LEV* M19	105	C4
Fielden Av *CCHDY* M21	99	C4
Fielden Ct *CCHDY* M21	113	C4
Fielden Rd *DID/WITH* M20	114	A4
Fielders Wy *SWIN* M27	25	D3
Fieldfare Av *NEWH/MOS* M40	73	C1
Fielding St *ECC* M30	61	D4
Field Pl *DID/WITH* M20	125	C2
Fields New Rd *CHAD* OL9	20	B4
Field St *DROY* M43	92	A1
FAIL M35	56	D3
GTN M18	91	D3
SLFD M6	66	B3
Fieldsway *OLDS* OL8	40	B3
Field Vale Dr *RDSH* SK5	107	D4
Field View Wk *OLDTF/WHR* M16 *	101	C3
Fife Av *CHAD* OL9	38	A3
Fifield Cl *OLDS* OL8	41	D2
Fifth Av *OLDS* OL8	39	D3
OP/CLY M11	73	D3
TRPK M17	81	D4
Fifth St *TRPK* M17	81	D4
Filby Wk *NEWH/MOS* M40	71	D4
Fildes St *MDTN* M24	19	C2
Filey Av *OLDTF/WHR* M16	100	A3
Filey Dr *SLFD* M6	47	C3
Filey Rd *RUSH/FAL* M14	116	A1
Finborough Cl *OLDTF/WHR* M16	100	B1
Finchley Av *NEWH/MOS* M40	73	D1
Finchley Gv *NEWH/MOS* M40	35	D4
Finchley Rd *RUSH/FAL* M14	115	C1
Finishing Wk *ANC* M4	5	F4
Finland Rd *EDGY/DAV* SK3	132	A4
Finney Dr *CCHDY* M21	111	D2
Finningley Rd *BKLY* M9	15	C3
Finny Bank Rd *SALE* M33	108	B3
Finsbury Av *NEWH/MOS* M40	73	D1
Finsbury Rd *RDSH* SK5	119	D1
Finstock Cl *ECC* M30	61	C4
Fintry Gv *ECC* M30	62	A4
Firbeck Dr *ANC* M4	71	C3
Fircroft Rd *OLDS* OL8	41	D3
Firdale Av *NEWH/MOS* M40	37	D4
Firdale Wk *CHAD* OL9	21	D2
Firefly Cl *CSLFD* M3	2	A4
Fire Station Sq *ORD* M5 *	67	D3
Firethorn Av *BNG/LEV* M19	117	C3
Fir Gv *BNG/LEV* M19	104	B4
CHAD OL9	21	C1
Fir Rd *SWIN* M27	44	B3
Firs Av *FAIL* M35	56	B2
OLDTF/WHR M16	99	C3
Firsby St *BNG/LEV* M19	104	B4
First Av *OLDS* OL8	40	A3
OP/CLY M11	74	A3
SWIN M27	44	A4
TRPK M17	82	A4
Fir St *ECC* M30	62	A4
FAIL M35	56	B2
HTNM SK4	129	D3
NEWH/MOS M40	71	C1
OLDTF/WHR M16 *	99	D1
SLFD M6	66	A3
Firswood Dr *SWIN* M27	44	B3
Firth St *OLD* OL1	23	C3
Fir Tree Av *OLDS* OL8	41	D3
Firwood Av *URM* M41	95	D4
Firwood Pk *CHAD* OL9	19	D2
Fishbourne Sq *RUSH/FAL* M14 *	102	B2
Fisher St *OLD* OL1	23	C1
Fitton Av *CCHDY* M21	112	A3
Fitton Crs *SWIN* M27	26	A3
Fitton Hill Rd *OLDS* OL8	41	D2
Fitzgeorge St *NEWH/MOS* M40	52	B4
Fitzgerald Cl *PWCH* M25	29	C3
Fitzgerald Wy *SLFD* M6 *	66	A2
Fitzroy St *DROY* M43	93	C1
Fitzwarren St *SLFD* M6	66	A3
Fitzwilliam St *BRO* M7	68	A1
Flag Rw *ANC* M4 *	70	A2
Flagship Av *ORD* M5 *	84	A1
Flamborough Wk *RUSH/FAL* M14 *	102	A2
Flamingo Cl *WGTN/LGST* M12	89	D3
Flashfields *PWCH* M25	29	C4
Flash St *NEWH/MOS* M40	55	D3
Flatley Cl *HULME* M15	86	B3
Flavian Wk *OP/CLY* M11 *	90	A1
Flaxpool Cl *OLDTF/WHR* M16	100	B3
Flax St *CSLFD* M3	2	B1
Fleeson St *RUSH/FAL* M14	102	B1
Fleet St *GTN* M18	92	A3
Fleming Pl *CHAD* OL9 *	22	B3
Fletcher Av *SWIN* M27	26	B3
Fletcher Cl *CHAD* OL9	22	A3
Fletcher Sq *CMANE* M1 *	5	E5
Fletcher St *NEWH/MOS* M40	54	A4
STKP SK1	130	A4
Flint Cl *OP/CLY* M11 *	73	C3
Flint St *DROY* M43	76	A3
EDGY/DAV SK3	132	B2
Flora St *BKLY* M9	33	D2
OLD OL1	22	B2
Florence Park Ct *DID/WITH* M20	125	D1
Florence St *DROY* M43	93	C1
ECC M30	61	C4
FAIL M35	57	C1
HTNM SK4	129	D3
SALE M33	109	C3
Florida St *OLDS* OL8	22	B4
Florin Gdns *SLFD* M6	66	A2
Florist St *EDGY/DAV* SK3	132	B2
Floyd Av *CCHDY* M21	112	B3
Floyer Rd *BKLY* M9	34	B1
Fog La *BNG/LEV* M19	126	A1
DID/WITH M20	125	C1
Fold Av *DROY* M43	76	A3
Fold Gn *CHAD* OL9	20	B3
Fold St *NEWH/MOS* M40	54	B1
The Fold *BKLY* M9	34	A2
Fold Vw *OLDS* OL8	41	D3
Foleshill Av *BKLY* M9	53	C2
Foliage Crs *RDSH* SK5	121	C4
Foliage Gdns *RDSH* SK5	121	C4
Foliage Rd *RDSH* SK5	131	C1
Folkestone Rd *OP/CLY* M11	74	A3
Folkestone Rd East *OP/CLY* M11	74	A3
Folkestone Rd West *OP/CLY* M11	73	D3
Follows St *GTN* M18	91	C3
Folly La *SWIN* M27	44	A4
Fontwell Cl *OLDTF/WHR* M16	99	D2
Fooley Cl *DROY* M43	91	D1
Forber Crs *GTN* M18	105	D2
Forbes Rd *STKP* SK1	131	C4
Fordbank Rd *DID/WITH* M20	124	B3
Ford La *SLFD* M6	66	B1
WYTH/NTH M22	123	D4
WYTH/NTH M22	124	A4

Ford Ldg *DID/WITH* M20 ....**125** C3
Ford St *CSLFD* M3 ....**2** B3
   EDGY/DAV SK3 ....**129** C4
   WGTN/LGST M12 ....**88** A3
Foreland Cl *NEWH/MOS* M40 ......**53** C4
Forest Range *BNG/LEV* M19 ....**104** B3
Forest St *ECC* M30 ....**60** B1
   OLDS OL8 ....**41** C3
Formby Av *CCHDY* M21 ....**113** C2
Formby Rd *SLFD* M6 ....**47** C4
Forresters Gn *TRPK* M17 ....**82** B3
Forrester St *WALK* M28 ....**42** B1
Forshaw Av *GTN* M18 ....**92** A4
Fortran Cl *ORD* M5 ....**66** B4
Fort Rd *PWCH* M25 ....**31** C3
Fortrose Av *BKLY* M9 ....**33** C2
Fortuna Gv *BNG/LEV* M19 ....**117** C1
Forum Gv *BRO* M7 ....**50** B4
Fosbrook Av *DID/WITH* M20 ......**125** D1
Fotherby Dr *BKLY* M9 ....**34** A2
Foundry La *ANC* M4 ....**4** C3
Foundry St *OLDS* OL8 ....**22** B3
Fountain Pl *WHTF* M45 ....**11** C2
Fountains Rd *STRET* M32 ....**95** C2
Fountain St *CMANW* M2 ....**4** A5
   ECC M30 ....**79** C1
   MDTN M24 ....**17** C1
   OLD OL1 ....**22** B2
Fountains Wk *CHAD* OL9 * **20** B4
Fourth Av *CHAD* OL9 ....**20** B4
   OLDS OL8 ....**39** D3
   OP/CLY M11 ....**73** D2
   SWIN M27 ....**44** B4
Fourth St *TRPK* M17 ....**81** D4
Fourways *TRPK* M17 ....**80** B3
Four Yards *CMANW* M2 ....**3** F5
Fovant Crs *RDSH* SK5 ....**106** B4
Fowler Av *GTN* M18 ....**92** A4
Fowler St *OLDS* OL8 ....**39** A2
Foxall Cl *MDTN* M24 ....**15** D2
Foxall St *MDTN* M24 ....**15** D2
Foxbank St *BRUN/LGST* M13 .....**103** D1
Foxdale St *OP/CLY* M11 ....**73** D4
Foxdenton Dr *STRET* M32 ....**95** C2
Foxdenton La *MDTN* M24 ....**19** D3
Foxfield Dr *OLDS* OL8 ....**39** D4
Foxham Dr *BRO* M7 ....**50** B3
Foxhill Rd *ECC* M30 ....**60** A4
Fox Park Rd *OLDS* OL8 ....**39** D4
Fox St *ECC* M30 ....**63** C3
   EDGY/DAV SK3 ....**132** A1
   OLDS OL8 ....**39** D3
Foxton St *MDTN* M24 ....**15** D2
Foxwood Gdns *BNG/LEV* M19 ....**116** B4
Foynes Cl *NEWH/MOS* M40 * **53** C4
Frampton Cl *MDTN* M24 ....**18** A2
Fram St *BKLY* M9 ....**54** A1
   SLFD M6 * **65** D3
Frances James Leech St
   EDGY/DAV SK3 * **133** C1
Frances St *BRUN/LGST* M13 * **9** D5
   EDGY/DAV SK3 * **132** A3
Francis Av *ECC* M30 ....**62** B3
Francis Rd *DID/WITH* M20 ....**115** D4
Francis St *CSLFD* M3 ....**69** C2
   ECC M30 ....**62** A2
   FAIL M35 ....**57** C2
Frankby Cl *SWIN* M27 * **46** B2
Frankland Cl *OP/CLY* M11 ....**73** C3
Franklin Cl *OLD* OL1 ....**22** B1
Franklin Rd *DROY* M43 ....**75** D4
Franklin St *ECC* M30 ....**62** A3
   OLD OL1 ....**22** B1
Franklyn Rd *GTN* M18 ....**91** D3
Frank St *FAIL* M35 ....**56** B2
   SLFD M6 ....**66** B1

Frankton Rd *WHTF* M45 ....**11** C2
Franton Rd *OP/CLY* M11 ....**73** C3
Fraser Pl *TRPK* M17 ....**82** A4
Fraser Rd *CHH* M8 ....**32** A4
Fraser St *SWIN* M27 ....**26** B4
Freckleton Av *CCHDY* M21 ....**122** B1
Frederick Rd *SLFD* M6 ....**67** C2
Frederick St *CHAD* OL9 ....**21** C1
   CSLFD M3 ....**2** C1
   OLDS OL8 ....**40** A1
Frederick Ter *BKLY* M9 * **34** A4
Fred Tilson Cl *RUSH/FAL* M14 ....**101** D2
Freeman Sq *HULME* M15 * **86** B3
Freetown Cl *RUSH/FAL* M14 ......**101** D1
Fremantle Av *GTN* M18 ....**106** A2
French Barn La *BKLY* M9 ....**33** D2
Freshfield Av *PWCH* M25 ....**12** B3
Freshfield Cl *FAIL* M35 ....**57** D3
Freshfield Rd *HTNM* SK4 ....**127** C3
Freshville St *CMANE* M1 * **9** D1
Freshwater St *GTN* M18 ....**91** D3
Freya Gv *ORD* M5 ....**84** B1
Friendship Av *GTN* M18 ....**106** B1
Frinton Av *NEWH/MOS* M40 * **37** C2
Frith Rd *DID/WITH* M20 ....**115** D4
Frobisher Cl *BRUN/LGST* M13 .....**88** A4
Frobisher Pl *RDSH* SK5 ....**129** D1
Frodesley Wk *WGTN/LGST* M12 * ..**89** C3
Frodsham Av *HTNM* SK4 ....**128** B3
Frodsham St *RUSH/FAL* M14 * ...**102** A2
Frome Dr *CHH* M8 ....**52** A2
Frostlands St *OLDTF/WHR* M16 ..**100** B2
Frost St *ANC* M4 * **71** C4
   OLDS OL8 ....**40** B1
Froxmer St *GTN* M18 ....**90** B3
Fulford St *OLDTF/WHR* M16 ....**99** D1
Fulham Av *NEWH/MOS* M40 ....**55** C4
Fullerton Rd *HTNM* SK4 ....**128** A3
Fulmer Dr *ANC* M4 ....**5** F2
Fulmere Ct *SWIN* M27 ....**44** A3
Fulneck Sq *DROY* M43 ....**92** B1
Fulwood Av *BKLY* M9 ....**35** C1
Furness Av *WHTF* M45 ....**11** D1
Furness Gv *HTNM* SK4 ....**127** D4
Furness Quay *SALO* M50 ....**83** D2
Furness Rd *RUSH/FAL* M14 ....**102** B4
   URM M41 ....**94** A2
Furnival Rd *GTN* M18 ....**90** B3
Furnival St *RDSH* SK5 ....**106** B3
Furrow Dr *ECC* M30 ....**61** C1
Fushia Gv *BRO* M7 * **50** A3
Fylde Rd *HTNM* SK4 ....**127** D3

G

Gable St *OP/CLY* M11 ....**89** C1
Gabriel's Ter *MDTN* M24 ....**18** B2
Gaddum Rd *DID/WITH* M20 ....**125** D2
Gail Av *HTNM* SK4 ....**129** C3
Gail Cl *FAIL* M35 ....**56** B4
Gainford Gdns *NEWH/MOS* M40 ..**36** A4
Gainford Rd *RDSH* SK5 ....**107** C4
Gainsborough Av *DID/WITH* M20 * ..**115** D4
   OLDS OL8 ....**40** B1
   STRET M32 * **98** A2
Gainsborough Rd *CHAD* OL9 ....**19** D1
   DTN/ASHW M34 ....**77** C4
Gainsborough St *BRO* M7 ....**50** B2
Gairloch Av *STRET* M32 ....**96** A3
Gair Rd *RDSH* SK5 ....**130** A1
Gaitskell Cl *WGTN/LGST* M12 ....**71** D4
Galbraith Rd *DID/WITH* M20 .....**125** D2
Galbraith St *CMANE* M1 * **8** B2
Gale Rd *PWCH* M25 ....**29** C2

Galgate Cl *HULME* M15........................6 C4
Galloway Dr *SWIN* M27.......................26 A1
Galloway Rd *SWIN* M27 *....................44 A3
Galston St *OP/CLY* M11.......................89 D1
Galsworthy Av *CHH* M8.......................51 B4
Galvin Rd *BKLY* M9............................33 C2
Galway St *OLD* OL1............................23 C3
Gamma Wk *OP/CLY* M11.....................73 C3
Gantock Wk *RUSH/FAL* M14..............102 B2
Ganton Av *WHTF* M45........................10 A2
Garbrook Av *BKLY* M9.........................15 C3
Garden Av *DROY* M43.........................76 A3
  STRET M32.....................................97 C3
  SWIN M27......................................44 A2
Gardenfold Wy *DROY* M43...................76 A3
Garden La *CSLFD* M3............................3 D1
  CSLFD M3...3 E4
Garden St *ECC* M30............................62 B4
  OLD OL1..23 D4
Garden Wall Cl *ORD* M5......................84 B1
Gardner Rd *PWCH* M25.......................29 C1
Gardner St *SLFD* M6...........................66 B2
  WGTN/LGST M12.............................90 A3
Garfield Av *BNG/LEV* M19.................105 C4
Garfield St *STKP* SK1 *.....................130 B3
Garforth Av *ANC* M4..............................5 F2
Garforth Crs *DROY* M43......................76 B2
Garforth St *CHAD* OL9........................21 D2
Gargrave St *BRO* M7..........................48 A1
Garlick St *CHAD* OL9 *.......................22 B3
  GTN M18...91 C4
Garnant Cl *BKLY* M9...........................54 A1
Garner Dr *ECC* M30 *.........................61 D2
  ORD M5...65 C2
Garner's La *EDGY/DAV* SK3..............133 C4
Garnett St *STKP* SK1 *......................130 A4
Garratt Wy *GTN* M18...........................90 B4
Garston Cl *HTNM* SK4.......................128 B2
Garswood Rd *RUSH/FAL* M14...........101 D3
Garthorne Cl *OLDTF/WHR* M16..........100 B1
The Garth *ORD* M5.............................65 D4
Garthwaite Av *OLDS* OL8....................40 B2
Gartside St *AULW* OL7 *......................77 D4
  CSLFD M3...3 D5
Garwood St *HULME* M15.......................7 D4
Gascoyne St *RUSH/FAL* M14..............102 A2
Gaskell Rd *ECC* M30...........................62 B4
Gaskell St *NEWH/MOS* M40...............55 D4
  SWIN M27......................................26 A3
Gas St *HTNM* SK4.............................129 D4
Gatcombe Sq *RUSH/FAL* M14...........102 B2
Gateshead Cl *RUSH/FAL* M14...........102 A1
Gate St *OP/CLY* M11...........................90 B1
Gateway Crs *CHAD* OL9.......................37 D1
Gateway Rd *GTN* M18 *.......................90 B3
The Gateways *SWIN* M27....................26 A4
The Gateway *NEWH/MOS* M40...........54 A3
Gathurst St *GTN* M18..........................91 D3
Gatley Av *RUSH/FAL* M14..................101 D4
Gatley Brow *OLD* OL1 *.......................22 B1
Gatling Av *WGTN/LGST* M12.............104 B3
Gavin Av *ORD* M5...............................66 B4
Gawsworth Av *DID/WITH* M20............125 D4
Gawsworth Cl *EDGY/DAV* SK3...........132 A4
Gaythorn St *ORD* M5...........................67 C3
Gee La *ECC* M30.................................61 C2
Gee St *EDGY/DAV* SK3.....................132 A2
Gemini Rd *SLFD* M6............................67 D1
Geneva Wk *CHAD* OL9 *.....................21 D3
Genista Gv *BRO* M7 *..........................50 A3
George Leigh St *ANC* M4......................4 C3
George's Rd *HTNM* SK4.....................129 C3
George St *CHAD* OL9..........................20 B2
  CMANE M1..8 A1
  ECC M30...61 C4
  FAIL M35...57 C1
  OLDS OL8..22 B3

PWCH M25...30 A4
STKP SK1..130 B4
URM M41...94 B3
George St North *BRO* M7......................7 C1
George St South *BRO* M7....................50 B1
Georgette Dr *CSLFD* M3........................3 D1
Georgia Av *DID/WITH* M20.................114 A3
Gerald Av *CHH* M8...............................51 D1
Gerald Rd *SLFD* M6.............................48 B4
Germain Cl *BKLY* M9...........................15 D4
Gerrard St *SLFD* M6............................66 B2
Gertrude Cl *ORD* M5............................83 D1
Gervis Cl *NEWH/MOS* M40 *................53 C4
Giants Seat Gv *SWIN* M27...................47 C1
Gibbon St *OP/CLY* M11........................72 B3
Gibb Rd *WALK* M28..............................42 C3
Gibbs St *ORD* M5..................................2 A4
Gibson Av *GTN* M18.............................92 A2
Gibson Pl *ANC* M4...............................69 D2
Gibsons Rd *HTNM* SK4......................128 A1
Gidlow St *GTN* M18..............................91 D3
Gifford Av *BKLY* M9.............................35 C1
Gilbert St *ECC* M30.............................78 A1
  HULME M15......................................7 D3
  SLFD M6 *.......................................66 A4
Gilda Brook Rd *ECC* M30......................63 D4
Gilda Crs *ECC* M30..............................63 D2
Gildenhall *FAIL* M35............................37 C3
Gildersdale Dr *BKLY* M9......................15 C3
Gildridge Rd *OLDTF/WHR* M16..........100 B4
Gilesgate *RUSH/FAL* M14..................102 A2
Giles St *WGTN/LGST* M12.................104 B1
Gillbrook Rd *DID/WITH* M20...............125 C3
Gillford Av *BKLY* M9............................54 A1
Gillingham Rd *ECC* M30......................61 C3
Gillingham Sq *OP/CLY* M11.................89 C1
Gill St *BKLY* M9...................................35 D4
  STKP SK1.......................................131 C2
Gilman Cl *BKLY* M9 *...........................33 D3
Gilman St *BKLY* M9..............................33 D3
Gilmerton Dr *NEWH/MOS* M40 *.........55 D1
Gilmore Dr *PWCH* M25........................12 A4
Gilmore St *EDGY/DAV* SK3...............132 B2
Gilmour St *MDTN* M24.........................17 D1
Gilmour Ter *BKLY* M9...........................35 D4
Gilpin Rd *URM* M41.............................95 C4
Giltbrook Av *NEWH/MOS* M40............71 D1
Girton St *BRO* M7................................68 B1
Girvan Av *NEWH/MOS* M40.................37 C3
Gisborn Dr *SLFD* M6............................48 A4
Gisburne Av *NEWH/MOS* M40.............37 C3
Givendale Dr *CHH* M8..........................32 B3
The Glade *HTNM* SK4........................127 D4
Gladstone Ct *HULME* M15..................100 B1
Gladstone Gv *HTNM* SK4...................127 D2
Gladstone Ms *HTNM* SK4 *................129 D2
Gladstone Rd *ECC* M30.......................62 B3
  URM M41...94 B3
Gladstone St *SWIN* M27......................45 D1
Gladwyn Av *DID/WITH* M20................123 D1
Glamis Av *OP/CLY* M11........................73 D2
  STRET M32......................................95 D3
Glamorgan Pl *CHAD* OL9 *..................21 D4
Glanford Av *BKLY* M9..........................32 B2
Glasshouse St *ANC* M4.........................5 E1
Glasson Wk *CHAD* OL9........................20 B3
Glastonbury Rd *STRET* M32................95 C2
Glaswen Gv *RDSH* SK5......................130 A1
Gleaves Rd *ECC* M30...........................62 B3
Gleave St *SALE* M33..........................109 C3
Glebelands Rd *PWCH* M25..................11 D2
  SALE M33......................................108 B3
Glebe Rd *URM* M41.............................94 A3
Glebe St *CHAD* OL9.............................38 B2
  STKP SK1.......................................130 B4
Gleden St *NEWH/MOS* M40.................71 D3
Gledhill Av *ORD* M5.............................83 D2

Gledhill St DID/WITH M20 ......115 C2
Glemsford Cl NEWH/MOS M40 * 55 C3
Glenacre Gdns GTN M18 ......106 B2
Glenart ECC M30 ......62 B2
Glen Av BKLY M9 ......34 B4
  SALE M33 ......108 B3
  SWIN M27 ......44 A1
  WALK M28 ......42 B1
Glenbarry Cl BRUN/LGST M13 ......87 C3
Glenbarry St WGTN/LGST M12 ......88 A1
Glenbrook Rd BKLY M9 ......14 B4
Glencastle Rd GTN M18 ......90 B4
Glencoe St OLDS OL8 * 39 D3
Glencross Av OLDTF/WHR M16 ......98 B3
Glendale SWIN M27 ......27 C4
Glendale Av BNG/LEV M19 ......117 C3
Glendale Ct OLDS OL8 ......41 C1
Glendale Rd ECC M30 ......63 D2
  GTN M18 ......105 D1
Glendene Av DROY M43 ......76 B2
Glendevon Pl WHTF M45 ......12 A2
Glendinning St SLFD M6 ......65 D3
Glendore ORD M5 ......64 B3
Glendower Dr NEWH/MOS M40 ......52 B3
Glenfield Rd HTNM SK4 ......129 C1
Glenfyne Rd SLFD M6 ......47 C4
Glen Gv MDTN M24 ......18 B3
Glenhurst Rd BNG/LEV M19 * 116 B4
Glenmere Cl PWCH M25 ......11 C3
Glenmoor Rd STKP SK1 ......133 D1
Glenmore Av DID/WITH M20 ......123 D1
Glenmore Dr CHH M8 ......52 A2
  FAIL M35 ......58 A1
Glenolden St OP/CLY M11 ......74 A3
Glensdale Dr NEWH/MOS M40 ......37 D4
Glenside Av GTN M18 ......106 A1
Glenside Gdns FAIL M35 ......57 D2
Glen St SALQ M50 ......83 D2
The Glen MDTN M24 ......18 A3
Glenthorn Av BKLY M9 ......16 A3
Glenville Rd CHH M8 ......51 C4
Glenwood Dr BKLY M9 ......53 D2
Glenwyn Av BKLY M9 ......34 B1
Globe Cl OLDTF/WHR M16 ......85 C4
Gloucester Av BNG/LEV M19 ......118 A1
  WHTF M45 ......11 C1
Gloucester Pl SLFD M6 ......66 B2
Gloucester Rd DROY M43 ......75 D2
  DTN/ASHW M34 ......107 D3
  MDTN M24 ......17 D3
  SLFD M6 ......64 B1
  URM M41 ......94 A4
Gloucester St CMANE M1 ......7 F3
  ORD M5 ......84 B1
  SLFD M6 ......66 B1
Gloucester St North CHAD OL9 * 21 D4
Glynrene Dr SWIN M27 ......24 B3
Goadsby St ANC M4 ......4 C4
Godbert Av CCHDY M21 ......112 B4
Goddard St OLDS OL8 ......41 C1
Godfrey Av DROY M43 ......74 A2
Godfrey Range MDTN M18 ......107 C1
Godfrey Rd SLFD M6 ......46 B4
Godlee Dr SWIN M27 ......44 B2
Godley Cl OP/CLY M11 ......90 B2
Godolphin Cl ECC M30 ......62 B1
Godwin St GTN M18 ......91 D3
Golborne Av DID/WITH M20 ......114 A2
Goldenhill Av OP/CLY M11 ......73 C3
Golden St ECC M30 ......62 A4
Goldfinch Wy DROY M43 ......76 B2
Goldsmith Av ORD M5 ......65 C3
Goldsmith Rd RDSH SK5 ......106 A4
Gold St CMANE M1 ......4 B5
Golfview Dr ECC M30 ......62 B1
Goodiers Dr ORD M5 ......83 D1
Goodier St NEWH/MOS M40 ......53 D4

Goodman St BKLY M9 ......34 B4
Goodwill Cl SWIN M27 ......45 C2
Goodwin Sq BKLY M9 * 53 C2
Goodwood Dr SWIN M27 ......46 A2
Goole St OP/CLY M11 ......89 D1
Goostrey Av DID/WITH M20 ......114 A1
Gordon Av BNG/LEV M19 ......105 C3
  CHAD OL9 ......38 B2
Gordon Pl DID/WITH M20 ......115 C4
Gordon Rd ECC M30 ......62 A2
  SALE M33 ......109 C3
  SWIN M27 ......43 D3
Gordon St BRO M7 ......68 A1
  CHAD OL9 ......38 A1
  GTN M18 ......91 D3
  HTNM SK4 ......129 D3
  OLDTF/WHR M16 ......100 A1
Gordon Ter BKLY M9 * 53 D1
Gore Av FAIL M35 ......58 A2
  ORD M5 ......65 C3
Gorebrook Ct WGTN/LGST M12 ......104 B1
Gore Crs ORD M5 ......65 C2
Goredale Av GTN M18 ......106 B2
Gore Dr ORD M5 ......65 C2
Gorelan Rd GTN M18 * 91 C4
Gore St CMANE M1 ......4 C3
  CSLFD M3 ......2 C1
  SLFD M6 ......66 B2
Goring Av GTN M18 ......91 C3
Gorse Av DROY M43 ......76 B3
  STRET M32 ......98 A2
Gorse Crs STRET M32 ......98 A2
Gorse Dr STRET M32 ......98 A2
Gorsefield Dr SWIN M27 ......45 C2
Gorse La STRET M32 ......98 A2
Gorse Rd SWIN M27 ......44 B3
Gorse St CHAD OL9 ......38 A1
  STRET M32 ......97 D2
Gorseway RDSH SK5 ......131 C1
Gorsey Brow STKP SK1 ......130 B1
Gorseyfields DROY M43 ......92 B1
Gorsey Mount St STKP SK1 ......130 B4
Gorton La GTN M18 ......90 B3
  WGTN/LGST M12 ......89 D3
Gorton Rd OP/CLY M11 ......89 C1
  RDSH SK5 ......120 A1
Gorton St CHAD OL9 ......21 D3
  CSLFD M3 * 3 E2
  ECC M30 ......62 A2
Gortonvilla Wk WGTN/LGST M12 ......89 C3
Gosport Sq BRO M7 ......50 A4
Gotha Wk BRUN/LGST M13 ......9 F5
Gough St EDGY/DAV SK3 ......129 C4
Goulden Rd DID/WITH M20 ......114 B4
Goulden St ANC M4 ......4 C2
  SLFD M6 ......65 D3
Goulder Rd GTN M18 ......106 B2
Govan St WYTH/NTH M22 ......123 D4
Gowan Rd OLDTF/WHR M16 ......100 A1
Gowerdale Rd RDSH SK5 ......121 D4
Gower Rd HTNM SK4 ......129 C1
Gower St OLD OL1 ......23 D2
  SWIN M27 ......26 B3
Goyt Crs STKP SK1 ......131 C2
Goyt Rd STKP SK1 ......131 C2
Grace Wk ANC M4 ......71 C4
Gradwell St EDGY/DAV SK3 ......132 A3
Grafton Av ECC M30 ......63 D1
Grafton St BRUN/LGST M13 ......87 C3
  FAIL M35 ......57 C1
  HTNM SK4 ......129 D1
Graham Rd SLFD M6 ......64 B1
Graham St OP/CLY M11 ......89 D1
Grainger Av WGTN/LGST M12 ......104 B2
Grain Vw ORD M5 * 83 D1
Grammar School Rd OLDS OL8 ......39 C3
Grampian Cl CHAD OL9 ......20 B4

Granada Ms *OLDTF/WHR* M16 * **100** B4
Granada Rd *DTN/ASHW* M34 ....**107** D2
Granary La *WALK* M28 ....**60** A1
Granby Rd *STRET* M32 ....**97** D2
   SWIN M27 ....**43** C2
Granby Rw *CMANE* M1 ....**8** C2
Granby St *CHAD* OL9 ....**38** B3
Grandale St *RUSH/FAL* M14 * **102** B2
Grand Central Sq *STKP* SK4 * **132** B1
Grand Union Wy *ECC* M30 ....**79** C1
Grange Av *BNG/LEV* M19 ....**117** C1
   ECC M30 ....**62** A1
   HTNM SK4 ....**118** B4
   OLDS OL8 ....**39** D1
   STRET M32 ....**97** C3
   SWIN M27 ....**25** C3
Grange Ct *OLDS* OL8 * **39** D1
Grange Dr *BKLY* M9 ....**35** C2
   ECC M30 ....**62** A1
Grangeforth Rd *CHH* M8 ....**51** C1
Grange Gv *WHTF* M45 ....**11** C1
Grange La *DID/WITH* M20 ....**125** C3
Grangepark Rd *BKLY* M9 ....**35** C2
Grange Rd *CCHDY* M21 ....**98** B3
   ECC M30 ....**60** A1
Grange St *NEWH/MOS* M40 ....**22** B2
   FAIL M35 ....**56** A3
   SLFD M6 ....**65** D3
The Grange *RUSH/FAL* M14 ....**102** B3
Grangethorpe Dr *BNG/LEV* M19 ....**116** B2
Grangethorpe Rd *RUSH/FAL* M14 ....**102** B3
Grangewood Dr *BKLY* M9 ....**53** C2
Gransden Dr *CHH* M8 ....**52** B3
Granshaw St *NEWH/MOS* M40 ....**71** D2
Gransmoor Av *OP/CLY* M11 ....**92** A2
Gransmoor Rd *OP/CLY* M11 ....**92** A2
Grant Cl *BKLY* M9 ....**34** A3
Grantham Rd *HTNM* SK4 ....**128** B3
Grantham St *OLDE* OL4 ....**23** D4
Granville Av *BRO* M7 ....**50** D1
Granville Cl *CHAD* OL9 ....**21** D2
Granville Gdns *DID/WITH* M20 ....**124** B3
Granville Rd *DTN/ASHW* M34 ....**76** A4
   RUSH/FAL M14 ....**115** D1
   URM M41 ....**94** D2
Granville St *CHAD* OL9 * **21** D1
   ECC M30 ....**62** A2
Granville Wk *CHAD* OL9 ....**21** D1
Grasmere Av *HTNM* SK4 ....**119** D3
   SWIN M27 ....**24** B3
Grasmere Crs *ECC* M50 ....**61** C1
Grasmere Rd *STRET* M32 ....**97** C2
   SWIN M27 ....**45** C3
Grasmere St *WGTN/LGST* M12 ....**105** C3
Grasscroft *RDSH* SK5 ....**121** C3
Grasscroft Cl *RUSH/FAL* M14 ....**101** C3
Grassfield Av *BRO* M7 ....**49** D3
Grassingham Gdns *SLFD* M6 ....**66** A2
Grassingham Av *NEWH/MOS* M40 ....**35** D4
Gratrix Av *ORD* M5 ....**84** A2
Gratrix St *GTN* M18 ....**106** B1
Gravel La *CSLFD* M3 ....**3** F3
Gravenmoor Dr *BRO* M7 ....**50** B3
Graver La *NEWH/MOS* M40 ....**56** A4
Grayson Av *WHTF* M45 ....**11** C1
Graythorpe Wk *ORD* M5 * **66** B4
Graythorp Wk *RUSH/FAL* M14 ....**102** B3
Greame St *OLDTF/WHR* M16 ....**101** C2
Great Ancoats St *ANC* M4 ....**4** C3
   CMANE M1 ....**88** A1
Great Bridgewater St *CMANE* M1 ....**7** E2
Great Cheetham St East *BRO* M7 ....**50** B3
Great Cheetham St West *BRO* M7 ....**49** D4
Great Clowes St *BRO* M7 ....**50** A2
Great Ducie St *CSLFD* M3 ....**3** F1
Great Egerton St *STKP* SK1 ....**129** D3
Great Gable Cl *OLD* OL1 ....**23** D1

Great George St *CSLFD* M3 ....**2** A3
Great Heaton Cl *MDTN* M24 * **18** D2
Great Jackson St *HULME* M15 ....**6** C3
Great John St *CSLFD* M3 ....**6** C1
Great Jones St *WGTN/LGST* M12 ....**89** D3
Great Marlborough St *CMANE* M1 ....**7** F2
Great Newton St *NEWH/MOS* M40 ....**55** D3
Great Portwood St *STKP* SK1 ....**130** B3
Great Southern St *RUSH/FAL* M14 ....**102** A2
Great Stone Rd *STRET* M32 ....**98** A1
Great St *CMANE* M1 ....**9** F1
Great Underbank *STKP* SK1 ....**129** D4
Great Western St *OLDTF/WHR* M16 ....**100** B1
Greaves Av *FAIL* M35 ....**56** B3
Greaves St *OLD* OL1 ....**23** C3
Grecian St *BRO* M7 ....**49** D4
Grecian St North *BRO* M7 ....**49** D4
Grecian Ter *BRO* M7 * **49** D4
Gredle Cl *URM* M41 ....**95** C3
Greek St *CMANE* M1 ....**8** C4
   EDGY/DAV SK3 ....**132** B1
Greenacre La *WALK* M28 ....**60** A1
Greenacres Dr *BNG/LEV* M19 ....**126** B1
Green Av *SWIN* M27 ....**45** C2
Greenbank Av *HTNM* SK4 ....**126** B3
   SWIN M27 * **44** A3
Greenbank Rd *SLFD* M6 ....**65** D2
Green Bank Ter *HTNM* SK4 * **129** D3
Greencroft Rd *ECC* M30 ....**61** C1
Greendale Dr *BKLY* M9 ....**34** B2
Green Dr *BNG/LEV* M19 ....**104** A4
Green End *BNG/LEV* M19 ....**116** B4
Green End Rd *BNG/LEV* M19 ....**116** B4
Greenfield Av *URM* M41 ....**94** A3
Greenfield Cl *EDGY/DAV* SK3 ....**132** B3
Green Fold *GTN* M18 ....**89** C2
Greenfold Rd *CHH* M8 ....**51** D2
Greengate *CSLFD* M3 ....**3** E2
   MDTN M24 ....**18** B4
   NEWH/MOS M40 ....**36** B2
Greengate East *NEWH/MOS* M40 ....**36** B2
Greengate La *PWCH* M25 ....**29** D1
Greengate St *OLDE* OL4 ....**23** D4
Greengate West *CSLFD* M3 ....**2** C1
Greenhalgh St *FAIL* M35 ....**55** D3
   HTNM SK4 ....**129** D3
Greenhalgh Wk *ANC* M4 ....**5** E3
Greenheys *DROY* M43 ....**75** D3
Greenheys La *HULME* M15 ....**86** A4
Greenheys La West *HULME* M15 ....**86** A4
Greenhill *OLD* OL1 ....**23** D3
   PWCH M25 ....**29** D1
Greenhill Av *SALE* M33 ....**108** B3
Greenhill Pas *OLD* OL1 ....**23** D3
Greenhill Rd *CHH* M8 ....**51** D2
   MDTN M24 ....**18** B2
Green Hill St *EDGY/DAV* SK3 ....**132** A2
Green Hill Ter *EDGY/DAV* SK3 ....**132** A2
Greenhill Ter *OLDE* OL4 * **23** D3
Greenholm Cl *NEWH/MOS* M40 ....**37** C4
Greenhow St *DROY* M43 ....**92** A1
Greenhurst Crs *OLDS* OL8 ....**39** D3
Greening Rd *BNG/LEV* M19 ....**105** C3
Greenland St *CHH* M8 ....**51** C2
   SLFD M6 * **65** D3
Green La *ECC* M30 ....**62** D3
   FAIL M35 ....**74** B1
   GTN M18 ....**91** C3
   HTNM SK4 ....**128** B3
   MDTN M24 ....**19** C2
   OLDS OL8 ....**40** B3
Greenlea Av *GTN* M18 ....**106** A2
Greenleach La *WALK* M28 ....**42** A1
Greenpark Rd *WYTH/NTH* M22 ....**123** C4
Green Pastures *HTNM* SK4 ....**126** B4
Greenside *HTNM* SK4 ....**127** D4
   WALK M28 ....**42** B4

Greenside Crs *DROY* M43 ....75 C2
Greenside La *DROY* M43 ....74 B2
  DROY M43 ....75 D3
Greenside St *OP/CLY* M11 ....73 C4
Greenside Wy *MDTN* M24 ....18 B4
Green & Slater Homes *HTNM* SK4 * 127 D1
Greenson Dr *MDTN* M24 ....16 B2
Greenstead Av *CHH* M8 ....51 D1
Greenstone Dr *SLFD* M6 ....48 A4
Green St *ECC* M30 ....78 A1
  EDGY/DAV SK3 ....133 C3
  OLDS OL8 * 22 A3
  RUSH/FAL M14 ....116 B2
  STRET M32 ....109 C1
The Green *HTNM* SK4 ....128 B3
  OLDS OL8 ....41 D2
  SWIN M27 ....27 C3
  WALK M28 ....42 A4
Greenthorne Av *HTNM* SK4 ....119 C2
Green Wk *OLDTF/WHR* M16 ......99 D3
  STRET M32 ....96 A3
Green Wks *PWCH* M25 ....30 B2
Greenway *MDTN* M24 ....16 B4
Greenway Av *BNG/LEV* M19 ......118 A1
Greenways *NEWH/MOS* M40 ....37 C4
Greenwich Cl *NEWH/MOS* M40 ......74 A1
Greenwood Av *SWIN* M27 ....27 C4
Greenwood St *OLDS* OL8 * 41 C4
  SLFD M6 ....66 A1
Greer St *OP/CLY* M11 ....90 B1
Greetland Dr *BKLY* M9 ....35 C1
Gregory St *OLDS* OL8 ....39 C4
  WGTN/LGST M12 ....89 C3
Gregory Wy *RDSH* SK5 ....120 A3
Gregson Rd *RDSH* SK5 ....119 D3
Gregson St *OLD* OL1 ....23 C3
Greg St *RDSH* SK5 ....119 D3
Grelley Wk *RUSH/FAL* M14 ....102 A2
Grendale Av *STKP* SK1 ....131 C4
Grendon Av *OLDS* OL8 ....40 B2
Grendon Wk *WGTN/LGST* M12 ......89 D3
Grenfell Rd *DID/WITH* M20 ....124 B2
Grenham Av *HULME* M15 ....6 A5
Grenville St *EDGY/DAV* SK3 ....132 A1
Gresford Cl *CCHDY* M21 ....111 D1
Gresham Cl *WHTF* M45 ....10 A1
Gresham Dr *CHAD* OL9 ....21 D2
Gresham Wk *HTNM* SK4 ....129 D1
Greton Cl *BRUN/LGST* M13 ....103 D1
Greville St *BRUN/LGST* M13 ....103 D1
Greyhound Dr *SLFD* M6 ....49 C4
Grey Mare La *OP/CLY* M11 ....89 D1
Greystoke Av *BNG/LEV* M19 ....105 C4
Greystoke La *FAIL* M35 ....56 A3
Greystoke St *STKP* SK1 ....130 B4
Greystone Av *CCHDY* M21 ....114 A1
Grey St *PWCH* M25 ....30 B1
  WGTN/LGST M12 ....88 B3
Greyswood Av *CHH* M8 ....51 C3
Greytown Cl *SLFD* M6 ....48 A4
Grierson St *OLDTF/WHR* M16 ......100 B1
Griffin Ct *CSLFD* M3 * 2 C3
Griffin Gv *BNG/LEV* M19 ....117 D1
Griffin Rd *FAIL* M35 ....56 A2
Griffin St *BRO* M7 ....49 D3
Griffiths Cl *BRO* M7 * 68 A1
Griffiths St *NEWH/MOS* M40 ....55 D4
Grimscott Cl *BKLY* M9 ....35 C4
Grimshaw Av *FAIL* M35 ....57 D1
Grimshaw La *MDTN* M24 ....18 A2
  NEWH/MOS M40 ....54 A4
Grimshaw St *FAIL* M35 * 56 B1
  STKP SK1 ....130 B4
Grindall Av *NEWH/MOS* M40 ......36 A3
Grindley Av *CCHDY* M21 ....113 C4
Grindlow St *BRUN/LGST* M13 ......88 B4

Grindon Av *BRO* M7 ....48 B2
Grinton Av *BRUN/LGST* M13 ......103 D3
Grisebeck Wy *OLD* OL1 * 22 B2
Grisedale Cl *GTN* M18 ....105 D1
Grizebeck Cl *GTN* M18 ....90 B3
Groby Rd *CCHDY* M21 ....112 A1
Groby St *OLDS* OL8 ....41 D2
Groom St *CMANE* M1 * 8 C4
Grosvenor Av *WHTF* M45 ....10 B1
Grosvenor Gdns *BRO* M7 ....68 A1
Grosvenor Rd *ECC* M30 ....60 B2
  HTNM SK4 ....127 D2
  OLDTF/WHR M16 ....100 A3
  SALE M33 ....108 A4
  SWIN M27 ....46 A2
Grosvenor St *BRUN/LGST* M13 ......8 C4
  EDGY/DAV SK3 ....133 C2
  PWCH M25 ....30 B1
  STRET M32 ....97 C3
  SWIN M27 ....26 A3
Grove Av *FAIL* M35 ....56 B4
Grove Cl *RUSH/FAL* M14 ....102 B2
Grovehurst *SWIN* M27 ....43 C3
Grove La *DID/WITH* M20 ....125 C3
Grove St *AULW* OL7 ....59 D4
  BRO M7 ....50 B4
  DROY M43 ....92 A1
  OLD OL1 ....23 D2
The Grove *DID/WITH* M20 ....125 C4
  ECC M30 ....63 C4
  OFTN SK2 ....132 B2
Grovewood Cl *AULW* OL7 ....59 D4
Grundy Av *PWCH* M25 ....28 B3
Grundy St *HTNM* SK4 ....126 B3
Guernsey Cl *BNG/LEV* M19 * 117 D3
Guest Rd *PWCH* M25 ....11 D3
Guide Post Sq *BRUN/LGST* M13 * 88 A3
Guide Post St *BRUN/LGST* M13 ......88 A3
Guide St *SALQ* M50 ....64 B4
Guido St *FAIL* M35 ....56 B2
Guildford Rd *BNG/LEV* M19 ....105 C3
  SLFD M6 ....64 A1
  URM M41 ....94 B1
Guildhall Cl *HULME* M15 ....86 B4
Guilford Rd *ECC* M30 ....61 C4
Guinness Rd *TRPK* M17 ....80 B1
Gullane Cl *NEWH/MOS* M40 ......55 D2
Gulvain Pl *CHAD* OL9 ....20 A1
Gunson St *NEWH/MOS* M40 ....5 F1
Gun St *ANC* M4 ....5 D3
Gurner Av *ORD* M5 ....84 A2
Gurney St *ANC* M4 ....71 C4
Guy Fawkes St *ORD* M5 ....84 A2
Gwelo St *OP/CLY* M11 ....72 B3
Gwenbury Av *STKP* SK1 ....131 C4
Gwendor Av *CHH* M8 ....32 A2

H

Hacking St *BRO* M7 ....50 B3
  PWCH M25 ....29 D1
Hackle St *OP/CLY* M11 ....73 D3
Hackleton Cl *ANC* M4 ....71 C4
Hackness Rd *CCHDY* M21 ....111 D1
Hackney Av *NEWH/MOS* M40 ......73 D1
Haddington Dr *BKLY* M9 ....34 A2
Haddon Av *NEWH/MOS* M40 ......37 D4
Haddon Gv *RDSH* SK5 ....119 D2
Haddon Hall Rd *DROY* M43 ....74 B3
Haddon Rd *CCHDY* M21 ....113 C4
  ECC M30 ....78 B1
  WALK M28 ....43 C4
Haddon St *SLFD* M6 ....49 C4
  STRET M32 ....97 C1

Hadfield Av *CHAD* OL9 ....**21** C4
Hadfield Cl *RUSH/FAL* M14 ....**103** C2
Hadfield St *BRO* M7 ....**50** B3
   OLDS OL8 ....**40** B2
   OLDTF/WHR M16 ....**84** B3
Hadley Av *BRUN/LGST* M13 ....**103** D3
Hadley St *SLFD* M6 ....**49** C4
Hadlow Gn *RDSH* SK5 ....**121** C3
Hadlow Wk *NEWH/MOS* M40 * **71** D2
Hafton Rd *BRO* M7 ....**49** C3
Hagley Rd *ORD* M5 ....**83** D3
Hague Cl *DID/WITH* M20 ....**114** B4
Hague St *NEWH/MOS* M40 ....**54** A4
Haigh Av *HTNM* SK4 ....**119** D4
Haigh Pk *HTNM* SK4 ....**119** D4
Haig Rd *STRET* M32 ....**97** C2
Haldon Rd *DID/WITH* M20 ....**116** A4
Hale La *FAIL* M35 ....**56** B1
Hale Rd *HTNM* SK4 ....**128** B2
Hales Cl *DROY* M43 ....**75** C2
Halesden Rd *HTNM* SK4 ....**119** C4
Halesworth Wk *NEWH/MOS* M40 * ...**70** B1
Haley Cl *RDSH* SK5 ....**120** A1
Haley St *CHH* M8 ....**51** D2
Half Edge La *ECC* M30 ....**63** C2
Halford Dr *NEWH/MOS* M40 ....**55** C1
Half St *CSLFD* M3 * **3** D1
Hallam Rd *NEWH/MOS* M40 ....**55** C4
Hallam St *OFTN* SK2 ....**133** D3
Hallas Gv *NTHM/RTH* M23 ....**122** A4
Hall Av *RUSH/FAL* M14 ....**103** C2
Hall Bank *ECC* M30 ....**61** D3
Hall Dr *MDTN* M24 ....**17** C3
Hall Gv *RUSH/FAL* M14 ....**103** C2
Halliday Rd *NEWH/MOS* M40 ....**73** C1
Halliford Rd *NEWH/MOS* M40 ....**54** B3
Halliwell Av *OLDS* OL8 ....**40** B2
Halliwell La *CHH* M8 ....**51** C2
Halliwell Rd *PWCH* M25 ....**29** C4
Halliwell St *CHAD* OL9 * **38** B3
Halliwell St West *CHH* M8 * **51** C2
Hall Moss Rd *BKLY* M9 ....**35** D2
Hallows Av *CCHDY* M21 ....**112** B4
Hall Rd *RUSH/FAL* M14 ....**103** C2
Hallroyd Brow *OLD* OL1 * **22** B1
Hall St *CMANW* M2 ....**7** F1
   FAIL M35 ....**56** A3
   MDTN M24 * **17** D1
   STKP SK1 ....**130** B4
   SWIN M27 ....**26** A3
Hallsville Rd *BNG/LEV* M19 ....**105** D4
Hallsworth Rd *ECC* M30 ....**60** B3
Hallwood Av *SLFD* M6 ....**64** B1
Hallworth Av *DTN/ASHW* M34 ....**76** A4
Hallworth Rd *CHH* M8 ....**52** A1
Halmore Rd *NEWH/MOS* M40 ....**71** C3
Halsbury Cl *WGTN/LGST* M12 ....**88** B3
Halsey Cl *CHAD* OL9 ....**37** D2
Halsmere Dr *BKLY* M9 ....**34** B2
Halstead Av *CCHDY* M21 ....**111** D2
   SLFD M6 ....**47** D4
Halstock Wk *NEWH/MOS* M40 ....**53** C4
Halston St *HULME* M15 ....**85** D3
Halton Bank *SLFD* M6 ....**66** A1
Halton Rd *OP/CLY* M11 ....**73** D3
Halvis Gv *OLDTF/WHR* M16 ....**99** C3
Hambridge Cl *CHH* M8 ....**51** D2
Hamer Dr *OLDTF/WHR* M16 ....**85** C4
Hamer Hl *BKLY* M9 ....**33** D2
Hamerton Rd *NEWH/MOS* M40 ....**70** D1
Hamilcar Av *ECC* M30 ....**62** B3
Hamilton Av *ECC* M30 ....**62** B4
Hamilton Cl *PWCH* M25 ....**29** D2
Hamilton Crs *HTNM* SK4 ....**128** A4
Hamilton Gv *OLDTF/WHR* M16 ....**85** C4
Hamilton Ms *ECC* M30 * **61** C2
   PWCH M25 * **29** D2

Hamilton Rd *BRUN/LGST* M13 ....**104** A2
   PWCH M25 ....**29** D2
   WHTF M45 ....**10** B1
Hamilton Sq *HTNM* SK4 ....**129** D2
Hamilton St *BRO* M7 * **50** A2
   CHAD OL9 ....**20** B2
   ECC M30 ....**61** C2
   OLDTF/WHR M16 ....**85** C4
   SWIN M27 ....**25** C4
Hammerstone Rd *GTN* M18 ....**90** B3
Hammett Rd *CCHDY* M21 ....**111** D1
Hammond Av *HTNM* SK4 ....**119** D4
Hamnett St *OP/CLY* M11 ....**74** A4
Hampden Crs *GTN* M18 ....**90** B4
Hampden Gv *ECC* M30 ....**62** A3
Hampden Rd *PWCH* M25 ....**30** A1
Hampshire Rd *CHAD* OL9 ....**21** C4
   DROY M43 ....**75** D2
   RDSH SK5 ....**121** C1
Hampson Cl *ECC* M30 ....**61** C4
Hampson Rd *STRET* M32 ....**96** B3
Hampson St *CSLFD* M3 ....**3** B1
   DROY M43 ....**75** D3
   ECC M30 ....**61** C4
   NEWH/MOS M40 * **71** C1
   SWIN M27 ....**26** B4
Hampton Rd *CCHDY* M21 ....**98** A4
   FAIL M35 ....**57** D1
   URM M41 ....**94** A4
Hampton St *OLDS* OL8 ....**40** A1
Hamsell Rd *BRUN/LGST* M13 ....**9** E4
Hancock Cl *RUSH/FAL* M14 ....**102** A2
Hancock St *STRET* M32 ....**110** A1
Handforth Gv *BRUN/LGST* M13 ....**103** D3
Handforth Rd *RDSH* SK5 ....**120** A4
Handley Av *RUSH/FAL* M14 ....**102** A4
Handsworth St *WGTN/LGST* M12 ......**88** A2
Hankinson Wy *SLFD* M6 ....**66** B2
Hanley Cl *MDTN* M24 ....**17** D4
Hanlith Ms *BNG/LEV* M19 ....**117** C1
Hanlon St *CHH* M8 ....**32** C4
Hannah Baldwin Cl *OP/CLY* M11 ....**89** C1
Hannah St *WGTN/LGST* M12 ....**104** B3
Hanover Ct *BRO* M7 ....**50** A2
   WALK M28 * **43** C3
Hanover Crs *RUSH/FAL* M14 ....**103** C1
Hanover Gdns *BRO* M7 ....**50** B1
Hanover St *ANC* M4 ....**4** C3
Hansdon Cl *CHH* M8 ....**51** D3
Hanson Ms *STKP* SK1 ....**131** C3
Hanson Pk *MDTN* M24 * **18** B1
Hanson Rd *NEWH/MOS* M40 ....**54** B2
Hanson St *MDTN* M24 * **17** D1
Hanworth Cl *BRUN/LGST* M13 ....**9** D4
Hapton Av *STRET* M32 ....**97** C4
Hapton Pl *HTNM* SK4 * **129** D2
Hapton St *BNG/LEV* M19 ....**104** B4
Harbern Cl *ECC* M30 ....**62** A1
Harbord St *MDTN* M24 ....**17** D1
Harcombe Rd *DID/WITH* M20 ....**115** D3
Harcourt Av *URM* M41 ....**95** C4
Harcourt Cl *URM* M41 ....**95** C4
Harcourt Rd *SALE* M33 ....**108** B3
Harcourt St *RDSH* SK5 ....**120** A1
   STRET M32 ....**97** D2
Hardcastle Av *CCHDY* M21 ....**112** B3
Hardcastle Rd *EDGY/DAV* SK3 ....**132** A2
Hardcastle St *OLD* OL1 * **23** D2
Hardfield Rd *MDTN* M24 ....**17** D4
Hardicker St *HTNM* SK4 ....**118** A2
Harding St *ANC* M4 ....**71** C4
   CSLFD M3 ....**3** E2
   SLFD M6 ....**66** B1
   STKP SK1 ....**131** C4
Hardman Av *PWCH* M25 ....**31** C3
Hardman La *FAIL* M35 ....**56** B1
Hardman Rd *RDSH* SK5 ....**120** A1

Hardman's Ms WHTF M45......................**11** C3
Hardman's Rd WHTF M45......................**11** D3
Hardman St CHAD OL9...........................**39** C2
　CSLFD M3..**3** D5
　EDGY/DAV SK3.......................................**129** C4
　FAIL M35...**56** A2
Hardon Gv BRUN/LGST M13..................**104** A3
Hardrush Fold FAIL M35.........................**57** D3
Hardwood Cl CHH M8.............................**51** D2
Hardy Av CCHDY M21.............................**111** D1
Hardy Gv SWIN M27................................**44** A4
　WALK M28...**42** A1
Hardy La CCHDY M21..............................**112** B3
Hardy St ECC M30....................................**61** C4
　OLDE OL4...**23** D4
Harecastle Av ECC M30..........................**79** D1
Haredale Dr CHH M8...............................**52** A3
Harefield Dr DID/WITH M20...................**124** B3
Harehill Cl BRUN/LGST M13...................**9** D3
Hare St ANC M4 *......................................**4** B3
Harewood Gv RDSH SK5........................**119** D1
Harewood Wy SWIN M27........................**26** A3
Hargrave Cl BKLY M9..............................**15** D3
Hargreave's St ANC M4............................**69** D2
　CHAD OL9..**21** D3
　OLD OL1 *...**23** C2
Harkerside Cl CCHDY M21.....................**112** B3
Harkness St WGTN/LGST M12.................**9** F4
Harland Dr CHH M8.................................**52** A2
Harlech Av WHTF M45.............................**12** A3
Harley Av RUSH/FAL M14......................**103** D2
Harley Rd SALE M33...............................**109** D4
Harley St OP/CLY M11...............................**91** C1
Harlow Dr GTN M18.................................**106** A2
Harmer Cl NEWH/MOS M40...................**54** B4
Harmony Cl OLDE OL4.............................**23** D3
Harmsworth Dr HTNM SK4....................**118** A4
Harmsworth St SLFD M6.........................**65** D3
Harold Av GTN M18...................................**91** C1
Harold Priestnall Cl NEWH/MOS M40....**55** C4
Harold St CHAD OL9.................................**22** A2
　FAIL M35 *...**56** B2
　MDTN M24...**16** B1
　OLDTF/WHR M16.................................**84** B3
　PWCH M25...**29** C1
Harper Ct EDGY/DAV SK3.....................**132** B2
Harper St EDGY/DAV SK3 *...................**132** B2
　OLDS OL8..**40** B1
Harp Rd TRPK M17...................................**80** B1
Harp St OP/CLY M11.................................**91** C2
Harpurhey Rd CHH M8............................**52** B1
Harriett St ANC M4....................................**5** F2
Harringay Rd NEWH/MOS M40..............**55** C4
Harrington St GTN M18.............................**91** D4
Harris Av URM M41...................................**79** C4
Harrison Av BNG/LEV M19....................**105** C3
Harrison St ANC M4..................................**71** C4
　BRO M7...**68** A1
　OFTN SK2...**133** C2
　OLD OL1 *...**23** C3
Harris St BRO M7......................................**68** B1
Harrogate Av PWCH M25........................**31** C3
Harrogate Cl OP/CLY M11.......................**91** D2
Harrogate Dr RDSH SK5.........................**119** D1
Harrogate Rd RDSH SK5........................**106** B4
Harrop Fold OLDS OL8............................**41** D4
Harrop St GTN M18...................................**92** A3
Harrow Av BNG/LEV M19......................**117** D3
　OLDS OL8..**40** A2
Harrowby Dr NEWH/MOS M40...............**53** C4
Harrowby Rd SWIN M27..........................**44** B3
Harrow St CHH M8....................................**33** C4
Harry Hall Gdns BRO M7 *......................**67** D1
Harry Rd RDSH SK5................................**120** A1
Harry St CHAD OL9..................................**21** D3
Harry Thorneycroft Wk OP/CLY M11.....**88** B1

Hart Av DROY M43...................................**76** A4
Harter St CMANE M1..................................**8** A1
Hartfield Cl BRUN/LGST M13....................**9** E5
Hartford Av HTNM SK4...........................**119** C3
Hartford Rd URM M41..............................**94** B1
Hartford Sq OP/CLY M11 *.......................**21** D3
Hart Hill Dr ORD M5.................................**65** C2
Harthill St CHH M8...................................**51** C4
Hartington Cl URM M41...........................**94** B3
Hartington Dr OP/CLY M11.......................**73** C2
Hartington Rd CCHDY M21...................**112** A1
　ECC M30..**60** B2
Hartington St RUSH/FAL M14...............**101** C2
Hartis Av BRO M7.....................................**50** B3
Hartlepool Cl RUSH/FAL M14...............**102** A2
Hartley Av PWCH M25..............................**30** B2
Hartley Rd CCHDY M21............................**98** B4
Hartley St EDGY/DAV SK3 *..................**132** A1
　NEWH/MOS M40.................................**54** A1
Harton Av GTN M18................................**105** D2
Hart Rd RUSH/FAL M14.........................**102** A4
Hartshead Cl OP/CLY M11.......................**92** B2
Hartshead Crs FAIL M35...........................**58** B3
Hartspring Av SWIN M27.........................**45** C2
Hart St CMANE M1......................................**8** B1
　DROY M43..**75** D3
Hartswood Rd DID/WITH M20...............**116** A3
Hartwell Cl OP/CLY M11..........................**89** C1
Harvard Gv SLFD M6................................**64** B2
Harvard Rd GTN M18................................**90** A4
Harvest Cl SLFD M6.................................**47** D4
Harvey Av DID/WITH M20......................**114** B2
Harvey St STKP SK1...............................**130** A4
Harwich Cl BNG/LEV M19 *....................**104** B4
　RDSH SK5..**121** D3
Harwood Ct SLFD M6................................**67** C1
Harwood Rd BNG/LEV M19...................**116** B3
　HTNM SK4...**126** B3
Harwood St HTNM SK4..........................**129** D2
Haslam Rd EDGY/DAV SK3...................**132** B3
Haslam St MDTN M24 *............................**18** B2
Haslemere Rd DID/WITH M20...............**116** A3
Hasper Av DID/WITH M20.....................**114** B2
Hassall Av DID/WITH M20.....................**114** A1
Hassop Av BRO M7...................................**48** B3
Hassop Cl OP/CLY M11............................**71** C4
Hassop Rd RDSH SK5............................**107** D4
Hastings Av CCHDY M21........................**111** D1
　WHTF M45..**12** A2
Hastings Cl WHTF M45............................**12** A2
Hastings Rd ECC M30..............................**60** B1
　PWCH M25..**12** B4
Haston Cl RDSH SK5..............................**130** A1
Hatfield Av BNG/LEV M19......................**117** C3
Hatherley Rd DID/WITH M20.................**116** A3
Hatherop Cl ECC M30...............................**61** C4
Hathersage Rd BRUN/LGST M13..........**102** B3
Hathersage St CHAD OL9........................**21** D3
Hathershaw La OLDS OL8........................**41** C2
Hatro Ct URM M41....................................**95** D4
Hatters Ct STKP SK1..............................**133** C1
Hatter St ANC M4.......................................**4** C2
Hattons Ct STRET M32.............................**96** B2
Hattons Rd TRPK M17..............................**81** C3
Hatton St STKP SK1................................**129** D3
　WGTN/LGST M12...............................**104** B2
Haughton Dr WYTH/NTH M22..............**123** C4
Havana Cl OP/CLY M11.............................**72** A4
Havelock Dr BRO M7................................**68** A1
Havelock St OLDS OL8.............................**23** C4
Haven Dr DROY M43.................................**74** B3
Havenscroft Av ECC M30.........................**79** C1
Haven St SLFD M6....................................**65** D4
Haverfield Rd BKLY M9...........................**34** B2
Haverford St WGTN/LGST M12..............**89** C1
Haversham Rd CHH M8............................**31** D3
Havers Rd GTN M18..................................**91** D4

Hawarden Av OLDTF/WHR M16	99	D3
Hawes Av RUSH/FAL M14	116	B2
SWIN M27 *	45	C3
Hawes Cl OFTN SK2	133	D3
Haweswater Cl DTN/ASHW M34	107	D3
Hawkeshead Rd CHH M8	52	A3
Hawkhurst Rd BRUN/LGST M13	104	A2
Hawkins St RDSH SK5	129	D1
Hawkshaw Ct ORD M5	66	B4
Hawksley St OLB	39	D2
Hawkstone Av DROY M43	74	B2
WHTF M45	10	A2
Hawley St BNG/LEV M19	118	A1
Haworth Dr STRET M32	95	D2
Haworth Rd GTN M18	105	D1
Hawthorn Av ECC M30	62	A2
URM M41	95	C4
Hawthorn Crs OLDS OL8	41	C3
Hawthorn Dr BNG/LEV M19	117	C2
SLFD M6	63	D1
SWIN M27	46	B2
Hawthorne Dr WALK M28	43	C2
Hawthorn Gv CHAD OL9	21	C1
Hawthorn Gv HTNM SK4	128	A2
Hawthorn La CCHDY M21 *	111	C1
Hawthorn Rd DROY M43	76	B3
HTNM SK4	126	B3
NEWH/MOS M40	37	D4
OLDS OL8	39	C4
STRET M32	110	B1
Hawthorn Rd South DROY M43	76	B3
Hawthorn St GTN M18	91	C3
Hawthorn Ter HTNM SK4 *	128	A2
Haxby Rd GTN M18	106	A2
Haydn Av RUSH/FAL M14	102	A1
Haydock Cl STRET M32	98	A1
Hayfield Cl WGTN/LGST M12	88	B3
Hayfield Rd SLFD M6	64	A1
Hayley St WGTN/LGST M12 *	103	D1
Haymans Wk BRUN/LGST M13	9	D3
Haymond Cl SLFD M6	48	B3
Hazel Av OLDTF/WHR M16	100	A3
SWIN M27	45	D2
Hazelbank Av DID/WITH M20	115	C2
Hazelbottom Rd CHH M8	52	A2
Hazel Cl DROY M43	76	B3
Hazeldene Rd NEWH/MOS M40	37	D4
Hazelfields WALK M28	43	C2
Hazel Gv CHAD OL9	21	C1
ORD M5	64	B3
URM M41	94	B3
Hazelhurst Fold WALK M28	43	D2
Hazelhurst Rd WALK M28	43	C2
Hazel La OLDS OL8	40	A3
Hazelmere Av ECC M30	61	C1
Hazel Rd WHTF M45	12	A1
Hazel Ter BKLY M9 *	34	A1
Hazelwood CHAD OL9	19	D2
Headingley Dr OLDTF/WHR M16	98	B2
Headingley Rd RUSH/FAL M14	116	A2
Headlands Dr PWCH M25	29	D3
Heald Av RUSH/FAL M14	102	A2
Heald Gv RUSH/FAL M14	102	A2
Heald Pl RUSH/FAL M14	102	A2
Heald St STKP SK1	130	B3
Healey Cl BRO M7	49	D1
Heap St WHTF M45 *	11	C2
Heath Av BRO M7	67	D1
Heathbank Rd BKLY M9	15	D4
Heathcliffe Wk BRUN/LGST M13	87	D4
Heathcote Av HTNM SK4	128	B2
Heathcote Rd GTN M18	105	D1
Heath Crs OFTN SK2	133	C4
Heather Av DROY M43	76	B3
Heatherdale Dr CHH M8	51	D3
Heather Gv DROY M43	93	C1
Heatherside RDSH SK5	107	D4

Heather St OP/CLY M11	73	C3
Heathfield WALK M28	42	A4
Heathfield Av HTNM SK4	118	B4
Heathfield Dr SWIN M27	45	D3
Heathfield Rd OFTN SK2	133	C3
Heathfield St NEWH/MOS M40	55	D4
Heathland Av BRO M7	30	A4
Heathlands Dr PWCH M25	29	D4
Heathland Ter EDGY/DAV SK3	132	B2
Heath Pl BRO M7	67	D1
Heath Rd OFTN SK2	133	C3
Heathside Rd DID/WITH M20	115	D4
Heath St CHH M8	51	C2
The Heath MDTN M24	18	A3
Heathwood Rd BNG/LEV M19	126	B1
Heaton Cl HTNM SK4	127	D2
Heaton La HTNM SK4	129	D4
Heaton Moor Rd HTNM SK4	128	A2
Heaton Park Rd BKLY M9	14	B4
Heaton Park Rd West BKLY M9	14	B4
Heaton Rd DID/WITH M20	115	D2
HTNM SK4	129	C2
Heaton St BRO M7	50	B2
MDTN M24	15	C2
PWCH M25	30	B1
Heaviley Gv OFTN SK2	133	D3
Hebburn Wk RUSH/FAL M14	102	A1
Hebden Av SLFD M6	65	D1
Hebden Wk HULME M15	86	A4
Hector Rd BRUN/LGST M13	104	A2
Heddon Cl HTNM SK4	126	B2
Hedges St FAIL M35	57	D1
Helena St SLFD M6	66	B4
Helen St BRO M7	50	B2
ECC M30	78	A1
Helensville Av SLFD M6	48	A4
Helga St NEWH/MOS M40	71	C1
Helmet St CMANE M1	9	F2
Helmshore Wk BRUN/LGST M13	9	D4
Helsby Wk WGTN/LGST M12	88	B1
Hembury Av BNG/LEV M19	117	C3
Hemlock Av OLDS OL8	82	B2
Hemming Dr ECC M30	62	B4
Hemmington Dr BKLY M9	53	C2
Hemmons Rd WGTN/LGST M12	105	C3
Hempshaw La STKP SK1	133	D1
Hemsley St BKLY M9	34	B4
Hemsley St South BKLY M9	34	B4
Hemswell Cl SLFD M6	65	D1
Hemsworth Rd GTN M18	106	A2
Henbury Dr RUSH/FAL M14	101	D2
Henderson Av SWIN M27	26	A4
Henderson St BNG/LEV M19	118	A1
Hendham V BKLY M9	52	B2
Hendon Rd BKLY M9	33	D1
Hengist St GTN M18	106	A1
Henley Av OLDTF/WHR M16	99	C2
Henley Pl BNG/LEV M19	117	D3
Henley St CHAD OL9	38	B2
OLD OL1	22	A1
Henniker St SWIN M27	44	B3
Henrietta St OLDTF/WHR M16	84	B4
Henry St ANC M4	4	C3
DROY M43	75	D4
ECC M30	61	D4
FAIL M35	57	D4
MDTN M24	17	C1
OLDTF/WHR M16	84	B4
PWCH M25	12	B4
Henshaw St OLDTF/WHR M16	99	C1
Henshaw La CHAD OL9	38	A3
Henshaw St OLD OL1	22	B2
STRET M32	97	C3
Henton Wk NEWH/MOS M40	70	B2
Henty Cl ECC M30	61	C4
Henwood Rd DID/WITH M20	115	D4
Hepple Cl HTNM SK4	127	C2

Heppleton Rd *NEWH/MOS* M40	37	C3
Hepple Wk *AULW* OL7 *	59	D4
Hepton St *OLD* OL1	22	B1
Herbert St *CHAD* OL9	21	C2
CHH M8 *	51	C4
DROY M43	75	C4
EDGY/DAV SK3	132	A2
PWCH M25	29	C1
STRET M32	97	C3
Hereford Dr *PWCH* M25	30	B3
SWIN M27	45	C3
Hereford Rd *ECC* M30	45	D4
RDSH SK5	121	D4
Hereford St *CHAD* OL9	21	C4
SALE M33	109	C4
Heritage Gdns *DID/WITH* M20	125	C3
Hermitage Rd *CHH* M8	32	B4
Hermon Av *OLDS* OL8	40	B2
Herne St *OP/CLY* M11	89	D1
Heron Ct *SLFD* M6	64	A2
Herondale Cl *NEWH/MOS* M40	55	C4
Heron Dr *DTN/ASHW* M34	76	B4
Heron Ml *OLDS* OL8 *	40	A2
Heron St *EDGY/DAV* SK3	132	A1
HULME M15	85	C4
OLDS OL8	39	D2
SWIN M27	26	B4
Herristone Rd *CHH* M8	32	B3
Herrod Av *HTNM* SK4	119	D1
Herschel St *NEWH/MOS* M40	54	B1
Hersey St *SLFD* M6 *	65	D3
Hertford Rd *BKLY* M9	34	A4
Hesford Av *BKLY* M9	54	A2
Hesketh Av *DID/WITH* M20	124	B2
Hesketh St *HTNM* SK4	129	D2
Hessel St *SALQ* M50	65	C4
Hester Wk *HULME* M15 *	86	A3
Heston Av *BRUN/LGST* M13	103	D3
Heswall Av *DID/WITH* M20	115	C2
Heswall Rd *RDSH* SK5	107	C4
Hetherington Wk *WGTN/LGST* M12	104	A1
Hethorn St *NEWH/MOS* M40	55	D4
Hetton Av *BRUN/LGST* M13	103	D3
Hewart Cl *NEWH/MOS* M40	70	B1
Hewitt Av *DTN/ASHW* M34	107	C2
Hewitt St *HULME* M15	7	D3
Hewlett Rd *CCHDY* M21	98	B4
Hexham Cl *CHAD* OL9	21	D2
Hexham Rd *GTN* M18	105	C1
Hexon Cl *SLFD* M6	65	D2
Heybrook Cl *WHTF* M45	12	B1
Heybury Cl *OP/CLY* M11	89	C1
Heyford Av *NEWH/MOS* M40	37	C3
Heyridge Dr *WYTH/NTH* M22	123	C4
Heyrod St *CMANE* M1	9	E1
Heyrose Wk *HULME* M15	85	C3
Heys Av *SWIN* M27	25	C3
Heys Cl North *SWIN* M27	24	B3
Heyscroft Rd *DID/WITH* M20	115	D3
HTNM SK4	127	D3
Heysham Av *DID/WITH* M20	114	A2
Heys Rd *PWCH* M25	12	A4
The Heys *PWCH* M25	12	A4
RDSH SK5	107	C4
Heys Vw *PWCH* M25	30	A1
Heywood Av *SWIN* M27	27	C3
Heywood Gdns *PWCH* M25	30	A1
Heywood Gv *SALE* M33	108	B3
Heywood Old Rd *MDTN* M24	14	B1
Heywood Rd *PWCH* M25	30	A2
CHH M8	51	D3
FAIL M35	56	A2
SWIN M27	44	B1
Heywood Wy *SLFD* M6	66	A2
Heyworth St *ORD* M5 *	65	D4
Hibbert Crs *FAIL* M35	57	D2
Hibbert St *HTNM* SK4	119	D4
RUSH/FAL M14	102	B2
Hibernia Wy *STRET* M32	80	B3
Higginson Rd *RDSH* SK5	119	D2
Higham Vw *SLFD* M6	66	B2
High Bank *GTN* M18	91	D4
High Bank Crs *PWCH* M25	30	B2
High Bank Gv *PWCH* M25	30	B2
High Bank Rd *DROY* M43	92	A1
SWIN M27	46	A1
High Bank Side *STKP* SK1 *	130	A4
High Barn Rd *MDTN* M24	17	D2
Highbury Rd *HTNM* SK4	118	B3
OLDTF/WHR M16	100	B4
Highclere Av *CHH* M8	51	C3
Highclere Rd *CHH* M8	32	A3
Highcliffe Rd *BKLY* M9	32	B2
Highcroft Av *DID/WITH* M20	123	D1
Higher Ardwick *WGTN/LGST* M12 *	9	F4
Higher Barlow Rw *STKP* SK1	133	C3
Higher Bury St *HTNM* SK4	129	C3
Higher Cambridge St *HULME* M15	8	A5
Higher Chatham St *HULME* M15	8	A5
Higher Cft *ECC* M30	78	B1
Higher Hillgate *STKP* SK1	133	C2
Higher House Cl *CHAD* OL9	38	B1
Higher La *WHTF* M45	10	B1
Higher Lime Rd *OLDS* OL8	58	B3
Higher Mdw *BNG/LEV* M19	105	D4
Higher Ormond St *BRUN/LGST* M13 *	8	B5
Higher Oswald St *ANC* M4	4	B2
Higher Rd *URM* M41	94	B3
Higher York St *BRUN/LGST* M13 *	8	B5
Highfield Cl *STRET* M32	109	D1
Highfield Dr *ECC* M30	62	A2
MDTN M24	17	C2
SWIN M27	46	B2
Highfield Pk *HTNM* SK4	127	C3
Highfield Pl *GTN* M18 *	107	C1
PWCH M25	11	D4
Highfield Range *GTN* M18 *	107	C1
Highfield Rd *BNG/LEV* M19	105	D4
ECC M30	62	A1
PWCH M25	11	D3
SLFD M6	66	A2
STRET M32	109	D1
Highfield St *BRO* M7	51	C2
CHAD OL9	22	A3
MDTN M24	18	A1
Highfield Ter *BKLY* M9	53	C3
Highgate Crs *GTN* M18	106	A1
High Gates *SALE* M33	110	B4
High Hurst Cl *MDTN* M24 *	15	D2
High La *CCHDY* M21	112	A1
High Legh Rd *OP/CLY* M11	91	C1
Highmead St *GTN* M18	91	C4
Highmead Wk *OLDTF/WHR* M16 *	85	C4
Highmore Dr *BKLY* M9	34	B2
High Peak St *NEWH/MOS* M40	55	C3
Highshore Dr *CHH* M8	51	C2
Highstone Dr *CHH* M8	52	B3
High St *ANC* M4	4	B3
DROY M43	75	D4
OLD OL1	23	C2
STKP SK1	130	A4
Highworth Dr *NEWH/MOS* M40	37	C3
Higson Av *CCHDY* M21	112	A2
ECC M30	78	B1
Hilary Av *OLDS* OL8	41	C4
Hilary Cl *HTNM* SK4	129	C3
Hilbury Av *BKLY* M9	34	A4
Hilda Gv *RDSH* SK5	130	A1
Hilda St *CHAD* OL9	22	A2
Hilden Ct *OLDTF/WHR* M16 *	100	A1
Hillam Cl *URM* M41	95	C4
Hillbrook Av *NEWH/MOS* M40 *	36	A3
Hillcote Wk *GTN* M18 *	90	A3
Hillcourt St *CMANE* M1	8	B4

Hill Crs *BKLY* M9 ....**32** B2
Hillcrest *SLFD* M6 * **63** D2
Hill Crest Av *HTNM* SK4 ....**127** D3
Hillcrest Dr *BNG/LEV* M19 ....**118** D3
Hillcrest Rd *PWCH* M25 ....**29** C3
Hillcroft Cl *CHH* M8 ....**51** D1
Hilldale Av *BKLY* M9 ....**34** A1
Hillfield *ORD* M5 ....**65** C3
Hillfield Cl *BRUN/LGST* M13 ....**88** A4
Hillfoot Wk *HULME* M15 * **85** C3
Hillgate Av *ORD* M5 ....**84** A2
Hillier St *BKLY* M9 ....**53** D1
Hillier St North *BKLY* M9 ....**53** D1
Hillingdon Cl *OLDS* OL8 ....**39** C4
Hillingdon Dr *NEWH/MOS* M40 ....**36** A3
Hillingdon Rd *STRET* M32 ....**97** D3
Hillkirk St *OP/CLY* M11 ....**71** D4
Hill La *BKLY* M9 ....**34** A2
Hillman Cl *NEWH/MOS* M40 ....**53** C4
Hillside Av *BRO* M7 ....**48** B1
Hillside Cl *NEWH/MOS* M40 ....**35** D4
Hillside Dr *SWIN* M27 ....**47** C3
Hill St *BRO* M7 ....**50** A3
DID/WITH M20 ....**115** C2
Hilltop Av *BKLY* M9 ....**34** A2
Hill Top Av *PWCH* M25 ....**30** A4
Hilltop Av *WHTF* M45 ....**12** A1
Hilltop Gv *WHTF* M45 ....**12** A1
Hillview Rd *DTN/ASHW* M34 ....**107** D4
Hillwood Av *CHH* M8 ....**32** A2
Hilrose Av *URM* M41 ....**95** C3
Hilton Av *URM* M41 ....**94** A3
Hilton Ct *EDGY/DAV* SK3 * **132** B1
Hilton Crs *PWCH* M25 ....**30** A3
Hilton Dr *PWCH* M25 ....**30** A3
Hilton La *PWCH* M25 ....**29** C3
Hiltons Cl *OLDS* OL8 ....**22** B4
Hilton Sq *SWIN* M27 ....**26** B4
Hilton St *ANC* M4 ....**4** B3
BRO M7 ....**50** B4
EDGY/DAV SK3 ....**132** A1
Hilton St North *BRO* M7 ....**50** A3
Himley Rd *OP/CLY* M11 ....**73** D2
Hinchley Rd *BKLY* M9 ....**36** A2
Hinchley Wk *SWIN* M27 ....**26** A3
Hinckley St *OP/CLY* M11 ....**89** C1
Hindburn Dr *WHTF* M45 ....**12** A1
Hinde St *NEWH/MOS* M40 ....**54** B1
Hindley St *STKP* SK1 ....**133** C1
Hinton St *ANC* M4 * **5** D1
OLDS OL8 ....**23** C4
Hitchin Wk *BRUN/LGST* M13 ....**87** D4
Hive St *OLDS* OL8 ....**39** C3
Hobart St *GTN* M18 ....**91** C4
Hobson St *FAIL* M35 ....**56** A3
OLD OL1 ....**23** C4
OP/CLY M11 ....**92** B2
RDSH SK5 ....**107** C3
Hodder Wy *WHTF* M45 ....**12** B1
Hoddesdon St *CHH* M8 ....**52** A2
Hodge La *SLFD* M6 ....**66** A4
Hodge St *BKLY* M9 ....**35** C4
Hodgson St *CHH* M8 ....**51** C4
Hodson Fold *OLDS* OL8 ....**41** D4
Hodson Rd *SWIN* M27 ....**25** D3
Holbeck Gv *RUSH/FAL* M14 ....**103** D1
Holbeton Cl *CHH* M8 ....**50** B4
Holborn Av *FAIL* M35 ....**58** A2
Holborn Dr *CHH* M8 ....**52** A4
Holborn St *STKP* SK1 * **130** A4
Holbrook St *CMANE* M1 * **8** A2
Holcombe Cl *SLFD* M6 ....**66** B3
Holcombe Rd *RUSH/FAL* M14 ....**116** B2
Holden Av *OLDTF/WHR* M16 ....**100** B4
Holden Rd *BRO* M7 ....**31** C4
Holden St *OLDS* OL8 ....**41** C2

Holdgate Cl *HULME* M15 ....**85** D4
Holdsworth St *SWIN* M27 ....**44** A2
Holford Av *RUSH/FAL* M14 ....**102** A3
Holker Cl *BRUN/LGST* M13 ....**103** C1
Holkham Cl *ANC* M4 * **5** F3
Holland Rd *CHH* M8 ....**32** A3
Holland St *NEWH/MOS* M40 ....**71** C3
SLFD M6 ....**48** A4
The Hollies *DID/WITH* M20 ....**124** A2
Hollin Bank *HTNM* SK4 ....**119** C2
Hollingworth Av *NEWH/MOS* M40 ....**38** A3
Hollingworth Cl *STKP* SK1 * **133** C1
Hollingworth St *CHAD* OL9 ....**39** C2
Hollins Gv *WGTN/LGST* M12 ....**104** B2
Hollins Rd *OLDS* OL8 ....**39** D3
OLDS OL8 ....**41** C2
Hollinwood Av *CHAD* OL9 ....**38** B3
NEWH/MOS M40 ....**37** C3
Holloway Dr *WALK* M28 ....**24** B4
Hollow End *RDSH* SK5 ....**121** C2
Hollow Vale Dr *RDSH* SK5 ....**120** B1
Holly Bank *DROY* M43 ....**76** B2
NEWH/MOS M40 * **55** D2
Hollybush St *GTN* M18 ....**91** D3
Hollyedge Dr *PWCH* M25 ....**29** D3
Holly Gv *CHAD* OL9 ....**21** C1
Hollyhey Dr *NTHM/RTH* M23 ....**122** A4
Hollyhurst *WALK* M28 ....**43** C3
Holly La *OLDS* OL8 ....**39** D3
Holly Rd *HTNM* SK4 ....**118** B4
SWIN M27 ....**44** A3
Holly Royde Cl *DID/WITH* M20 ....**114** B3
Holly St *DROY* M43 ....**74** A3
STKP SK1 ....**130** B4
WGTN/LGST M12 ....**88** B1
Hollywood Wy *HTNM* SK4 ....**129** C4
Holmbrook Wk *CHH* M8 ....**51** D3
Holm Ct *SLFD* M6 * **66** B2
Holmcroft Rd *GTN* M18 ....**106** A3
Holmdale Av *BNG/LEV* M19 ....**116** B4
Holme Park Wy *FAIL* M35 ....**58** A2
Holme Rd *DID/WITH* M20 ....**124** A2
Holmes St *OFTN* SK2 * **132** B2
Holmfield Av *BKLY* M9 ....**54** A3
PWCH M25 ....**30** B2
Holmfield Av West *BKLY* M9 ....**54** A3
Holmfield Cl *HTNM* SK4 ....**129** C2
Holmfirth St *BRUN/LGST* M13 ....**104** A1
Holmlea Rd *DROY* M43 ....**74** B3
Holmleigh Av *BKLY* M9 ....**34** B4
Holmpark Rd *OP/CLY* M11 ....**92** A2
Holmside Gdns *BNG/LEV* M19 ....**126** A1
Holmwood Rd *DID/WITH* M20 ....**115** C4
Holroyd St *OP/CLY* M11 * **89** D1
Holst Av *CHH* M8 ....**51** D3
Holtby St *BKLY* M9 ....**34** B4
Holt La *FAIL* M35 ....**58** A2
Holt Lane Ms *FAIL* M35 ....**58** A2
Holt St *ECC* M30 ....**78** B1
NEWH/MOS M40 ....**54** A4
STKP SK1 ....**133** C1
SWIN M27 ....**26** A3
Holt Town *NEWH/MOS* M40 ....**71** D3
Holwood Dr *OLDTF/WHR* M16 ....**113** D1
Holyoake Av *DROY* M43 ....**76** B3
Holyoak St *NEWH/MOS* M40 ....**55** D3
Holyrood Cl *PWCH* M25 ....**12** B3
Holyrood Dr *PWCH* M25 ....**12** B3
SWIN M27 ....**43** D2
Holyrood Gv *PWCH* M25 ....**12** B3
Holyrood Rd *PWCH* M25 ....**12** B4
Holyrood St *NEWH/MOS* M40 ....**54** A1
Holywood St *RUSH/FAL* M14 ....**102** A2
Homebury Dr *OP/CLY* M11 * **73** C3
Home Dr *MDTN* M24 ....**17** C3
Homerton Rd *NEWH/MOS* M40 ....**73** C1
Homestead Crs *BNG/LEV* M19 ....**126** A2

Hometel *RUSH/FAL* M14 ....**102** B4
Homewood Av *WYTH/NTH* M22 ....**123** C4
Homewood Rd *WYTH/NTH* M22 ....**122** B4
Honduras St *OLDE* OL4 ....**23** D2
Honey St *CHH* M8 ....**69** D1
Honeywell La *OLDS* OL8 ....**41** C2
Honister Rd *BKLY* M9 ....**54** A2
Honor St *BRUN/LGST* M13 ....**103** D2
Hood St *ANC* M4 ....**5** D3
Hooley Range *HTNM* SK4 ....**128** A2
Hooper St *EDGY/DAV* SK3 ....**129** D4
   OLDE OL4 ....**23** C3
   WGTN/LGST M12 ....**88** A1
Hooton St *NEWH/MOS* M40 ....**71** D2
Hopcroft Cl *BKLY* M9 ....**15** D3
Hope Av *STRET* M32 ....**96** A2
Hopecourt Cl *SLFD* M6 ....**64** A1
Hopedale Rd *RDSH* SK5 ....**120** A3
Hopelea St *DID/WITH* M20 ....**115** C3
Hope Park Cl *PWCH* M25 ....**30** A2
Hope Park Rd *PWCH* M25 ....**30** A2
Hope Rd *PWCH* M25 ....**29** D3
   RUSH/FAL M14 ....**103** C1
Hopes Carr *STKP* SK1 ....**130** A4
Hope St *BRO* M7 ....**50** A2
   CMANE M1 ....**4** A4
   HTNM SK4 ....**129** C4
   ORD M5 ....**67** D4
   SWIN M27 ....**45** D1
Hope Ter *EDGY/DAV* SK3 ....**132** B1
Hopkinson Rd *BKLY* M9 ....**16** A4
Hopkin St *OLD* OL1 ....**23** C2
   WGTN/LGST M12 ....**104** B2
Hoppet La *DROY* M43 ....**76** B3
Hopwood Av *ECC* M30 ....**62** A2
Hopwood Cl *CSLFD* M3 * **3** D1
   NEWH/MOS M40 ....**55** C3
   SWIN M27 ....**45** D1
Horace Barnes Cl *RUSH/FAL* M14 ...**101** D2
Horace Gv *HTNM* SK4 ....**129** D1
Horatio St *GTN* M18 ....**92** A3
Horbury Rd *GTN* M18 ....**106** A2
Hornbeam Ct *SLFD* M6 ....**66** B2
Hornbeam Rd *BNG/LEV* M19 ....**105** C3
Hornby Av *BKLY* M9 ....**16** B4
Hornby Rd *STRET* M32 ....**98** A1
Hornby St *CHH* M8 ....**69** D1
   MDTN M24 ....**17** D1
   OLDS OL8 * **22** A4
Horncastle Rd *NEWH/MOS* M40 ....**36** A4
Hornchurch St *HULME* M15 ....**85** D3
Horne Dr *ANC* M4 ....**5** F3
Hornsea Wk *OP/CLY* M11 * **72** B4
Horsedge St *OLD* OL1 ....**23** C1
Horsefield Cl *CCHDY* M21 ....**113** D2
Horseshoe La *MDTN* M24 ....**20** A3
Horsham St *SLFD* M6 ....**65** D3
Horstead Wk *BNG/LEV* M19 ....**104** B3
Horton Rd *RUSH/FAL* M14 ....**101** D1
Horton St *STKP* SK1 ....**133** C2
Hortree Rd *STRET* M32 ....**97** A3
Horwood Crs *DID/WITH* M20 ....**116** A4
Hoscar Dr *BNG/LEV* M19 ....**116** B2
Hoskins Cl *WGTN/LGST* M12 ....**89** D4
Hospital Rd *SWIN* M27 ....**46** A2
Hothersall Rd *RDSH* SK5 ....**120** A2
Hotspur Cl *RUSH/FAL* M14 ....**114** B1
Hough Cl *OLDS* OL8 ....**41** D3
Hough End Av *CCHDY* M21 ....**112** B3
Houghend Crs *CCHDY* M21 ....**113** D2
Hough Hall Rd *NEWH/MOS* M40 ......**54** A1
Houghton Av *OLDS* OL8 ....**40** A3
Houghton La *SWIN* M27 ....**44** A4
Houghton Rd *CHH* M8 ....**32** B4
Houghton St *SWIN* M27 ....**47** C3
Hough Wk *BRO* M7 ....**67** D2
Houldsworth Ml *RDSH* SK5 * **119** D2

Houldsworth St *CMANE* M1 ....**4** C3
   RDSH SK5 ....**119** D2
Houseley Av *CHAD* OL9 ....**38** B2
Houson St *OLDS* OL8 ....**23** C4
Houston Pk *SALO* M50 ....**66** A4
Hoveden St *CHH* M8 ....**69** C1
Hove Dr *RUSH/FAL* M14 ....**116** B2
Hovey Cl *CHH* M8 * **51** C2
Hovis St *OP/CLY* M11 ....**90** B1
Howard Av *ECC* M30 ....**61** D1
   HTNM SK4 ....**118** B3
Howardian Cl *OLDS* OL8 ....**40** B3
Howard Rd *WYTH/NTH* M22 ....**122** C4
Howard St *CHH* M8 ....**68** B1
   ORD M5 ....**83** D1
   STKP SK1 ....**130** A3
   STRET M32 ....**97** C3
Howarth Av *WALK* M28 ....**43** D2
Howarth St *OLDTF/WHR* M16 ....**99** D1
Howbro Dr *AULW* OL7 ....**59** D4
Howden Cl *RDSH* SK5 ....**106** B3
Howden Rd *BKLY* M9 ....**15** D4
Howells Av *SALE* M33 ....**108** B4
Howe St *BRO* M7 ....**49** D2
Howgill Crs *OLDS* OL8 ....**40** B2
Howgill St *OP/CLY* M11 ....**74** A4
Howton Cl *WGTN/LGST* M12 ....**104** B1
Hoy Dr *URM* M41 ....**79** C4
Hoylake Cl *NEWH/MOS* M40 ....**56** A1
Hoyland Cl *WGTN/LGST* M12 ....**89** C3
Hoyle Av *OLDS* OL8 ....**23** B4
Hoyle St *WGTN/LGST* M12 * **9** F2
Hoyle Wk *BRUN/LGST* M13 ....**9** E5
Huddart Cl *ORD* M5 ....**84** A1
Hudson St *CHAD* OL9 ....**38** B3
Hudswell Cl *WHTF* M45 ....**10** B1
Hughes Cl *FAIL* M35 ....**56** B1
Hughes St *OP/CLY* M11 ....**88** B1
Hugh Oldham Dr *BRO* M7 ....**49** D3
Hugo St *NEWH/MOS* M40 ....**54** B2
Hull Sq *CSLFD* M3 ....**2** A2
Hulme Hall La *NEWH/MOS* M40 ....**71** D1
Hulme Hall Rd *HULME* M15 ....**6** A4
Hulme Pl *ORD* M5 * **67** D4
Hulme Rd *HTNM* SK4 ....**119** C4
Hulmes Rd *NEWH/MOS* M40 ....**56** A4
Hulme St *HULME* M15 ....**7** D4
   OLDS OL8 ....**40** B1
   ORD M5 ....**67** D4
Hulton Dr *OLDTF/WHR* M16 ....**100** B1
Hulton St *FAIL* M35 ....**56** A2
   ORD M5 ....**83** D2
Humberstone Av *HULME* M15 ....**7** D5
Humber St *CHH* M8 ....**51** D2
   SALO M50 ....**65** C4
Hume St *BNG/LEV* M19 * **118** A1
Humphrey Crs *URM* M41 ....**95** D3
Humphrey La *URM* M41 ....**95** D3
Humphrey Pk *URM* M41 ....**95** D4
Humphrey Rd *OLDTF/WHR* M16 ......**84** A4
Humphrey St *CHH* M8 ....**51** C1
Huncoat Av *HTNM* SK4 ....**119** C4
Huncote Dr *BKLY* M9 ....**34** B4
Hunmanby Av *HULME* M15 ....**7** E4
Hunter's La *OLD* OL1 ....**23** C2
Hunterston Av *ECC* M30 ....**63** D3
Huntingdon Av *CHAD* OL9 ....**21** C4
Huntingdon Crs *RDSH* SK5 ....**121** D4
Huntington Av *DID/WITH* M20 ....**114** A1
Hunt La *CHAD* OL9 ....**20** B2
Huntley Rd *CHH* M8 ....**31** D3
Hunts Bank *CSLFD* M3 ....**3** F2
Hunts Rd *SLFD* M6 ....**47** C4
Hunt St *BKLY* M9 ....**34** A4
Hurdlow Av *BRO* M7 ....**48** B3
Hurford Av *GTN* M18 ....**91** C3
Hurstbank Av *BNG/LEV* M19 * **126** A1

Hurstbourne Av *OP/CLY* M11 ....**73** C2
Hurstbrook Dr *STRET* M32 ....**95** C3
Hurstfold Av *BNG/LEV* M19 ....**126** A2
Hursthead Wk *BRUN/LGST* M13 .....**9** A4
Hurst St *CHAD* OL9 ....**22** A2
   RDSH SK5 ....**119** D2
Hurstville Rd *CCHDY* M21 ....**112** A3
Hurstway Dr *BKLY* M9 ....**34** B2
Hus St *DROY* M43 ....**92** A1
Huxley Av *CHH* M8 ....**51** D3
Hyacinth Cl *EDGY/DAV* SK3 ....**132** A4
Hyde Fold Cl *BNG/LEV* M19 ....**117** C3
Hyde Gv *BRUN/LGST* M13 ....**87** D4
Hyde Pl *BRUN/LGST* M13 ....**87** D4
Hyde Rd *GTN* M18 ....**107** C1
   MDTN M24 ....**19** D3
   WGTN/LGST M12 ....**9** F4
Hyde Sq *MDTN* M24 ....**16** B1
Hyde St *DROY* M43 ....**76** B1
Hydra Cl *BRO* M7 ....**67** D2
Hythe Cl *RUSH/FAL* M14 ....**102** B2
Hythe Wk *CHAD* OL9 * **21** C3

Iceland St *SLFD* M6 ....**65** D3
Ilex Gv *BRO* M7 ....**50** A3
Ilford St *OP/CLY* M11 ....**73** C3
Ilfracombe St *NEWH/MOS* M40 ......**56** A3
Ilkley Cl *CHAD* OL9 ....**21** C3
Ilkley Crs *RDSH* SK5 ....**119** D1
Ilkley St *NEWH/MOS* M40 ....**35** D4
Ilk St *OP/CLY* M11 ....**73** C3
Illona Dr *BRO* M7 ....**48** B1
Imperial Ter *SALE* M33 * **108** B3
Ince Cl *DID/WITH* M20 ....**115** C2
   HTNM SK4 ....**129** D2
Ince St *HTNM* SK4 ....**129** D2
Inchcape Dr *BKLY* M9 ....**33** C1
Inchfield Rd *NEWH/MOS* M40 ....**35** D4
Inchley Rd *BRUN/LGST* M13 ....**8** C4
Incline Rd *OLDS* OL8 ....**39** C4
Indigo St *SLFD* M6 ....**48** A4
Indus Pl *BRO* M7 ....**67** D1
Industry St *CHAD* OL9 ....**38** B1
Infant St *PWCH* M25 * **30** B1
Ingham St *NEWH/MOS* M40 * **74** B1
Inghamwood Cl *BRO* M7 ....**51** C2
Ingleby Av *BKLY* M9 ....**35** C1
Ingleby Ct *STRET* M32 ....**97** D4
Ingledene Av *BRO* M7 ....**31** D4
Ingleton Av *CHH* M8 ....**33** C4
Inglewood Cl *BRUN/LGST* M13 * **9** E5
Ingoldsby Av *BRUN/LGST* M13 ......**103** C1
Ingram Dr *HTNM* SK4 ....**126** B2
Inkerman St *NEWH/MOS* M40 ....**53** C4
Innes St *WGTN/LGST* M12 ....**105** C2
Innis Av *NEWH/MOS* M40 ....**55** D4
Instow Cl *BRUN/LGST* M13 ....**88** C4
Invar Rd *WALK* M28 ....**25** C4
Inverness Av *BKLY* M9 ....**35** D1
Inwood Wk *CHH* M8 ....**52** B3
Iona Wy *URM* M41 ....**79** C4
Ionian Gdns *BRO* M7 ....**49** D4
Iqbal St *WGTN/LGST* M12 ....**89** D4
Iredine St *OP/CLY* M11 ....**73** D4
Iris St *OLDS* OL8 ....**41** C3
Irkdale St *CHH* M8 ....**52** B3
Irlam Av *ECC* M30 ....**62** A4
Irlam Rd *SALE* M33 ....**109** D4
Irlam Sq *SLFD* M6 ....**47** C4
Irlam St *NEWH/MOS* M40 ....**53** C4
Iron St *NEWH/MOS* M40 ....**71** D2
Irving St *OLDS* OL8 ....**39** C3

Irvin St *NEWH/MOS* M40 ....**55** D3
Irwell Av *ECC* M30 ....**63** C4
Irwell Gv *ECC* M30 ....**63** C4
Irwell Pl *ECC* M30 ....**63** C4
   ORD M5 ....**67** D4
Irwell Sculpture Trail *BRO* M7 ....**49** D3
Irwell St *CSLFD* M3 ....**2** C4
   CSLFD M3 ....**68** B1
Isaac Cl *ORD* M5 ....**83** D1
Isabella Cl *OLDTF/WHR* M16 ....**99** D1
Isaiah St *OLDS* OL8 * **41** C1
Isca St *OP/CLY* M11 ....**72** A1
Isis Cl *BRO* M7 ....**48** B1
Islington St *CSLFD* M3 ....**2** B3
Islington Wy *CSLFD* M3 ....**2** A4
Isobel Cl *ECC* M30 ....**61** C4
   OLDTF/WHR M16 ....**101** D1
Ivybridge Cl *BRUN/LGST* M13 ....**88** A4
Ivy Cl *DROY* M43 ....**75** C3
Ivy Dr *MDTN* M24 ....**17** C3
Ivygreen Rd *CCHDY* M21 ....**111** C1
Ivyleaf Sq *BRO* M7 ....**50** B3
Ivylea Rd *BNG/LEV* M19 ....**126** A3
Ivy St *ECC* M30 ....**62** A4
   NEWH/MOS M40 ....**54** B1

Jack La *DROY* M43 ....**76** B3
   URM M41 ....**94** B3
Jackroom Dr *ANC* M4 * **5** E4
Jackson Cl *OLDS* OL8 ....**22** B4
Jackson Crs *HULME* M15 ....**7** D4
Jacksons Rw *CMANW* M2 ....**3** E5
Jackson St *FAIL* M35 ....**56** A3
   SALE M33 ....**110** A4
   STRET M32 ....**96** B4
   WHTF M45 ....**11** C2
Jacobite Cl *BRO* M7 ....**30** B4
James Brindley Basin *CMANE* M1 ....**5** E5
James Corbett Rd *SALQ* M50 ....**64** B4
James Henry Av *ORD* M5 ....**84** A1
James Leech St *EDGY/DAV* SK3 ......**132** B1
James Leigh St *CMANE* M1 ....**8** A2
James St *DROY* M43 ....**76** A3
   EDGY/DAV SK3 ....**132** B1
   FAIL M35 ....**57** D1
   NEWH/MOS M40 ....**71** C2
   ORD M5 ....**2** A4
   PWCH M25 ....**11** D4
James St South *OLDS* OL9 * **20** B2
Jamieson Cl *CHH* M8 ....**50** B4
Jammy La *CHAD* OL9 ....**21** D3
Jane St *CHAD* OL9 ....**21** C3
Japan St *BRO* M7 ....**51** C2
Jardine Wy *CHAD* OL9 ....**38** A1
Jarvis St *OLDE* OL4 ....**23** D3
Jasmine Av *DROY* M43 ....**76** B3
Jason St *ANC* M4 ....**70** A2
Jean Cl *BNG/LEV* M19 ....**104** A2
Jehlum Cl *CHH* M8 ....**52** A2
Jenkinson St *HULME* M15 ....**8** B4
Jennings Av *ORD* M5 ....**83** D1
Jennings Cl *ORD* M5 ....**83** D1
Jennings St *EDGY/DAV* SK3 ....**132** A2
Jennison Cl *WGTN/LGST* M12 ....**90** A3
Jenny St *OLDS* OL8 ....**39** D3
Jepson St *OFTN* SK2 ....**133** D1
Jersey Rd *RDSH* SK5 ....**130** A1
Jersey St *ANC* M4 ....**5** D3
Jerusalem Pl *CMANW* M2 * **7** E1
Jesmond Av *PWCH* M25 ....**30** A1
Jespersen St *OLD* OL1 ....**23** C2
Jessamine Av *BRO* M7 ....**68** A1

Jessel Cl *BRUN/LGST* M13.............9 E5
Jessie St *NEWH/MOS* M40.............54 B3
Jessop St *GTN* M18.............91 C4
Jetson St *GTN* M18.............92 A3
Jimmy McMullen Wk
  RUSH/FAL M14 *.............101 D2
Jinnah Cl *OP/CLY* M11.............90 B1
J J Thomson Ms *RUSH/FAL* M14 *.............102 B4
Joan St *NEWH/MOS* M40.............54 B2
Jobling St *OP/CLY* M11.............89 C1
Jocelyn St *NEWH/MOS* M40.............53 D3
Joddrell St *CSLFD* M3.............3 D5
John Atkinson Ct *ORD* M5 *.............65 C3
John Beeley Av *OP/CLY* M11.............91 C1
John Clynes Av *NEWH/MOS* M40 *.............70 B2
John Dalton St *CMANW* M2.............3 E5
John Foran Cl *NEWH/MOS* M40.............55 C3
John Gilbert St *TRPK* M17.............82 B4
John Heywood St *OP/CLY* M11.............73 C3
John Nash Crs *HULME* M15.............85 D3
Johnny King Cl *NEWH/MOS* M40.............53 C3
Johns Cl *CCHDY* M21.............112 A1
Johnson Gv *MDTN* M24.............16 B1
Johnson's Sq *NEWH/MOS* M40.............71 C1
Johnson St *CSLFD* M3.............3 D3
  HULME M15.............85 C3
  SWIN M27.............47 C3
John Smeaton Ct *CMANE* M1.............5 E5
John St *ANC* M4.............4 B3
  BRO M7.............68 A1
  CSLFD M3.............3 D2
  DROY M43.............92 A1
  ECC M30.............61 C4
  FAIL M35.............38 A4
  OLDS OL8.............22 B3
  PWCH M25.............13 D1
  SALE M33.............109 C4
  STKP SK1.............133 C1
  SWIN M27.............45 D1
John William St *ECC* M30.............63 C3
  OP/CLY M11 *.............73 D4
Joiner St *ANC* M4.............4 B4
  ORD M5.............67 C3
Jonas St *BKLY* M9.............53 D1
  CSLFD M3.............68 B2
Jones Sq *STKP* SK1.............133 C2
Jones St *OLD* OL1.............23 D1
  SLFD M6.............66 A2
Jordan St *HULME* M15.............7 D3
Josephine Dr *SWIN* M27.............45 D2
Joseph Johnson Ms
  WYTH/NTH M22 *.............123 D4
Joseph St *ECC* M30.............61 C4
  FAIL M35.............57 D1
Joshua La *MDTN* M24.............19 C2
Josslyn Rd *ORD* M5.............65 C2
Jo St *ORD* M5.............66 B4
Joule Cl *ORD* M5.............83 C1
Joules Ct *STKP* SK1.............133 C1
Joule St *BKLY* M9.............34 B4
Jowett St *RDSH* SK5.............130 A1
Joyce St *NEWH/MOS* M40.............55 C3
Joynson Av *BRO* M7.............68 A1
Joynson St *SALE* M33.............109 C4
Jubilee St *SLFD* M6.............66 A3
Judson Av *CCHDY* M21.............112 B4
Julia St *CSLFD* M3.............69 C2
Julius St *BNG/LEV* M19.............118 A1
Junction Rd *OFTN* SK2.............133 C2
Junction St *MDTN* M24.............19 C3
  OLDS OL8 *.............40 B1
June Av *HTNM* SK4 *.............128 A3
Juniper Bank *RDSH* SK5.............120 B1
Juniper Cl *SALE* M33.............108 B3
Jura Dr *URM* M41.............79 D4
Jurby Av *BKLY* M9.............33 D1
Jury St *CHH* M8.............69 C1

Justin Cl *BRUN/LGST* M13.............8 C4
Jutland St *CMANE* M1.............5 D5

K

Kale St *BRUN/LGST* M13.............9 D4
Kalima Gv *BRO* M7.............50 A3
Kansas Av *SALQ* M50.............82 B1
Kara St *SLFD* M6.............65 D3
Kathleen Gv *RUSH/FAL* M14.............102 B3
Kay's Av *STKP* SK1.............131 C4
Kays Gdns *CSLFD* M3.............2 B2
Kay St *OP/CLY* M11.............89 C2
  SLFD M6.............48 A3
Keadby Cl *ECC* M30.............79 C1
Kearsley Rd *CHH* M8.............32 B3
Kearsley St *ECC* M30.............61 C3
Kearton Dr *ECC* M30.............63 D3
Keary Cl *GTN* M18.............91 C3
Keaton Cl *SLFD* M6.............65 D1
Keats Av *DROY* M43.............75 D3
Keats Rd *ECC* M30.............62 A4
Keble Av *OLDS* OL8.............40 B2
Kedleston Av *RUSH/FAL* M14.............103 C3
Keele Cl *NEWH/MOS* M40.............70 B2
Keele St *ECC* M30.............61 C3
Keele Wk *NEWH/MOS* M40.............70 B2
Keighley Av *DROY* M43.............75 D2
Keith Wk *NEWH/MOS* M40.............71 C2
Kelbrook Rd *OP/CLY* M11.............90 A1
Kelbrook Crs *BRO* M7 *.............48 B1
Kelling Wk *HULME* M15.............6 A1
Kelmarsh Cl *OP/CLY* M11 *.............91 C2
Kelsall Crs *EDGY/DAV* SK3.............132 A3
Kelsall Dr *DROY* M43.............75 C2
Kelsall St *CHAD* OL9.............22 A3
  WGTN/LGST M12.............89 C3
Kelso Cl *OLDS* OL8.............41 C4
Kelstern Av *BRUN/LGST* M13.............103 D2
Kelstern Sq *BRUN/LGST* M13.............103 D2
Kelton Cl *RDSH* SK5.............120 A4
Kelvin Av *MDTN* M24.............15 C2
Kelvin Gv *CHH* M8.............51 D3
Kelvington Dr *BKLY* M9.............53 C3
Kelvin St *ANC* M4.............4 B3
Kemble Av *NTHM/RTH* M23.............122 B4
Kempnough Hall Rd *WALK* M28.............42 A2
Kempsey Ct *CHAD* OL9.............20 B2
Kempster St *BRO* M7.............68 A1
Kemp St *MDTN* M24.............17 C1
Kempton Cl *DROY* M43.............76 B3
Kempton Wy *CHAD* OL9.............21 D2
Kemsing Wk *ORD* M5 *.............66 B3
Kenchester Av *OP/CLY* M11.............91 C1
Kendal Gv *WHTF* M45.............11 C1
Kendall Rd *CHH* M8.............32 A2
Kendal Rd *SLFD* M6.............46 B3
  STRET M32.............97 C2
Kenilworth Av *DID/WITH* M20.............114 A1
  SWIN M27.............27 C2
  WHTF M45.............11 D3
Kenilworth Gv *DTN/ASHW* M34.............93 C1
Kenley Wk *CHH* M8 *.............52 B3
Kenmere Gv *NEWH/MOS* M40.............36 A4
Kenmore Cl *WHTF* M45.............12 A1
Kenmore Rd *WHTF* M45.............12 A1
Kenmore Wy *WHTF* M45.............12 A1
Kennard Cl *BKLY* M9.............35 C4
Kennedy Rd *ORD* M5.............64 B3
Kennedy St *CMANW* M2.............3 F5
  OLDS OL8 *.............22 B4
Kennedy Wy *HTNM* SK4.............128 B3
Kennerley Rd *OFTN* SK2.............133 C4
Kenneth Sq *BRO* M7.............50 B3
Kennington Av *NEWH/MOS* M40.............73 C1

Kensington Av *CHAD* OL9 ....**19** D1
   RUSH/FAL M14 ....**103** C1
Kensington Dr *ORD* M5 ....**65** C2
Kensington Rd *CCHDY* M21 ....**98** B3
   FAIL M35 ....**58** A1
   OLDS OL8 ....**40** A1
Kensington St *RUSH/FAL* M14 ....**101** D2
Kenslow Av *CHH* M8 ....**32** A3
Kent Av *CHAD* OL9 ....**20** B3
   DROY M43 ....**74** B4
Kentford Dr *NEWH/MOS* M40 ....**70** B1
Kentmore Cl *HTNM* SK4 ....**126** B3
   WGTN/LGST M12 ....**89** D2
Kenton Av *GTN* M18 ....**105** D2
Kent Rd *DTN/ASHW* M34 ....**107** D3
   FAIL M35 ....**56** B3
Kent Rd East *RUSH/FAL* M14 ....**103** C2
Kent Rd West *RUSH/FAL* M14 ....**102** B2
Kentstone Av *BNG/LEV* M19 ....**126** A2
Kent St *BRO* M7 ....**68** A1
   CMANW M2 * **3** F4
   OLDS OL8 ....**41** C1
   SWIN M27 ....**26** A3
Kenwick Dr *NEWH/MOS* M40 ....**37** D3
Kenwood Av *BNG/LEV* M19 ....**117** C3
Kenwood Cl *STRET* M32 ....**97** D3
Kenwood La *WALK* M28 ....**42** A4
Kenwood Rd *RDSH* SK5 ....**106** B3
   STRET M32 ....**97** D4
Kenworthy La *WYTH/NTH* M22 ....**123** C3
Kenwright St *ANC* M4 ....**4** B2
Kenwyn St *NEWH/MOS* M40 ....**71** D2
Kenyon Av *OLDS* OL8 ....**41** C2
Kenyon La *MDTN* M24 ....**18** B1
   NEWH/MOS M40 ....**54** B1
   PWCH M25 ....**30** B1
Kenyon St *GTN* M18 ....**91** D3
Keppel Rd *CCHDY* M21 ....**99** C4
Kerrera Dr *ORD* M5 * **65** C4
Kerr St *BKLY* M9 ....**34** A2
Kershaw Av *PWCH* M25 ....**29** C3
Kershaw Dr *CHAD* OL9 ....**37** C1
Kershaw Gv *DTN/ASHW* M34 ....**93** C1
Kershaw La *DTN/ASHW* M34 ....**93** C1
Kershaw Rd *FAIL* M35 ....**57** C1
Kershaw St *DROY* M43 ....**75** C4
Kershaw Wk *WGTN/LGST* M12 ....**88** A3
Kershope Gv *ORD* M5 ....**83** C1
Kerwin Wk *OP/CLY* M11 * **89** D1
Kesteven Rd *BKLY* M9 ....**53** C2
Keston Av *BKLY* M9 ....**35** D2
   DROY M43 ....**74** B4
Keston Crs *RDSH* SK5 ....**121** C3
Kestrel Av *DTN/ASHW* M34 ....**76** B4
   SWIN M27 ....**27** C3
Kestrel Cl *PWCH* M25 ....**11** D3
Kestrel Rd *TRPK* M17 ....**80** A1
Kestrel Wk *WGTN/LGST* M12 ....**89** D3
Keswick Av *CHAD* OL9 ....**20** B2
   OLDS OL8 ....**41** D1
Keswick Cl *BRUN/LGST* M13 ....**103** C1
Keswick Gv *SLFD* M6 ....**66** A2
Keswick Rd *HTNM* SK4 ....**119** C2
   STRET M32 ....**96** B2
Kettering Rd *BNG/LEV* M19 ....**105** C3
Ketton Cl *OP/CLY* M11 ....**91** D2
Kevin St *BNG/LEV* M19 ....**118** A1
Kew Gdns *NEWH/MOS* M40 ....**35** D4

Kew Rd *FAIL* M35 ....**57** D1
Keymer St *OP/CLY* M11 ....**71** D3
Keynsham Rd *OP/CLY* M11 ....**73** C2
Keystone Cl *SLFD* M6 ....**65** D1
Key West Cl *OP/CLY* M11 ....**72** A4
Keyworth Wk *NEWH/MOS* M40 ....**71** D1
Khartoum St *OLDTF/WHR* M16 ....**100** A1
   OP/CLY M11 ....**74** A3
Kibworth Cl *WHTF* M45 ....**10** A1
Kiel Cl *ECC* M30 ....**79** D1
Kilburn Av *BKLY* M9 ....**16** A4
Kilcoby Av *SWIN* M27 ....**47** D1
Kildare Rd *CCHDY* M21 ....**113** C1
   SWIN M27 ....**44** B2
Kilmaine Av *BKLY* M9 ....**36** A2
Kilmington Dr *CHH* M8 ....**51** C3
Kilner Wk *NEWH/MOS* M40 ....**70** B1
Kilnside Dr *BKLY* M9 ....**53** C2
Kilnwick Cl *GTN* M18 ....**105** C2
Kilrush Av *ECC* M30 ....**79** C1
Kilsby Wk *NEWH/MOS* M40 ....**71** C1
Kilton Wk *NEWH/MOS* M40 * **70** B1
Kilvert Dr *SALE* M33 ....**108** A4
Kilvert St *TRPK* M17 ....**83** D4
Kimberley St *BRO* M7 * **50** B2
   EDGY/DAV SK3 ....**132** B2
   OLDS OL8 ....**39** D2
Kimberley Wk *HULME* M15 ....**6** B4
Kimbolton Cl *WGTN/LGST* M12 ....**89** D2
Kinburn Rd *BNG/LEV* M19 ....**126** A3
Kincardine Rd *BRUN/LGST* M13 ....**8** C4
Kincraig Cl *OP/CLY* M11 ....**74** D4
Kinder St *EDGY/DAV* SK3 ....**132** B2
Kinderton Av *DID/WITH* M20 ....**115** C2
Kineton Wk *BRUN/LGST* M13 ....**87** D3
King Edward St *BNG/LEV* M19 ....**105** C4
   ECC M30 ....**61** D3
   ORD M5 ....**84** A1
Kingfisher Av *DTN/ASHW* M34 ....**76** B4
Kingfisher Cl *WGTN/LGST* M12 ....**88** B2
Kingham Dr *ANC* M4 ....**5** F2
Kings Av *CHH* M8 ....**51** D1
Kingsbridge Rd *BKLY* M9 ....**52** B2
Kingsbrook Rd *OLDTF/WHR* M16 ....**113** D1
Kingsbury Rd *OP/CLY* M11 ....**73** D3
Kingscliffe St *BKLY* M9 ....**53** D2
King's Cl *GTN* M18 ....**92** A3
   PWCH M25 ....**12** B4
Kings Ct *RDSH* SK5 ....**130** A2
Kings Crs *OLDTF/WHR* M16 ....**99** C2
Kingsdale Rd *GTN* M18 ....**107** D1
King's Dr *HTNM* SK4 ....**127** D2
   MDTN M24 ....**16** A1
Kingsfield Dr *DID/WITH* M20 ....**125** D3
Kingsfold Av *NEWH/MOS* M40 * **70** B1
Kingsford St *ORD* M5 ....**65** C3
Kings Gv *STRET* M32 ....**98** A2
Kingsheath Av *OP/CLY* M11 ....**73** C2
Kingshill Rd *CCHDY* M21 ....**111** D1
Kingsland Cl *NEWH/MOS* M40 ....**71** C2
Kings La *STRET* M32 ....**98** A2
Kingslea Rd *DID/WITH* M20 ....**115** D4
Kingsleigh Rd *HTNM* SK4 ....**127** C1
Kingsley Av *BKLY* M9 ....**54** A2
   BRO M7 ....**48** B2
   HTNM SK4 ....**129** D1
   STRET M32 ....**98** A2
   WHTF M45 ....**11** D2
Kingsley Gv *DTN/ASHW* M34 ....**93** D1
Kingsley Rd *SWIN* M27 ....**53** C4
King's Lynn Cl *DID/WITH* M20 ....**125** C2
Kingsmead Ms *BKLY* M9 ....**15** D4
Kingsmere Av *BNG/LEV* M19 ....**104** A4
Kingsmill Av *BNG/LEV* M19 ....**118** A1
Kings Rd *CCHDY* M21 ....**113** C1
   CHAD OL9 ....**37** D2
   DTN/ASHW M34 ....**92** B4

OLDS OL8 ....23 C4
OLDTF/WHR M16 ....98 B2
PWCH M25 ....30 B3
STRET M32 ....97 D3
Kings Ter STRET M32 ....98 A2
Kingston Av CHAD OL9 ....38 B1
DID/WITH M20 ....125 C4
Kingston Cl BRO M7 ....50 A1
Kingston Dr SALE M33 ....110 A4
Kingston Gv BKLY M9 ....35 C3
Kingston MI EDGY/DAV SK3 * 129 C4
Kingston Rd DID/WITH M20 ....125 C4
FAIL M35 ....58 A2
Kingston St EDGY/DAV SK3 ....129 C4
King St BRO M7 ....50 B2
CMANW M2 ....3 F4
CSLFD M3 ....3 D2
DROY M43 ....92 B1
ECC M30 ....63 C4
FAIL M35 ....54 A3
OLDS OL8 ....22 B3
SLFD M6 ....46 C4
King St East STKP SK1 * 130 A3
King St West SLFD M3 ....3 E4
Kings Vw HTNM SK4 * 128 B4
Kingsway BNG/LEV M19 ....116 B2
DID/WITH M20 ....126 A3
MDTN M24 ....17 C3
STKP SK1 ....130 A3
STRET M32 ....96 B4
SWIN M27 ....46 B3
Kingsway Av BNG/LEV M19 ....104 A4
Kingsway Cl OLDS OL8 ....22 B4
Kingsway Crs BNG/LEV M19 ....116 B4
Kingsway Pk URM M41 ....94 A1
Kingswood Gv RDSH SK5 ....107 C4
Kingswood Rd ECC M30 ....61 C1
PWCH M25 ....11 C4
RUSH/FAL M14 ....116 B2
King William St ECC M30 ....60 B2
SALQ M50 ....83 D1
Kinley St WGTN/LGST M12 ....89 C3
Kinloch Gdns OLDS OL8 ....41 C1
Kinloch St OLDS OL8 ....41 D1
OP/CLY M11 ....72 B3
Kinmel Av RDSH SK5 ....131 D1
Kinnaird Rd DID/WITH M20 ....115 D4
Kinross Rd RUSH/FAL M14 ....103 D2
Kintyre Av ORD M5 ....65 D4
Kintyre Cl OP/CLY M11 * 73 D1
Kinver Rd NEWH/MOS M40 ....36 B3
Kipling Av DROY M43 ....75 D2
Kipling St BRO M7 ....50 A3
Kippax St RUSH/FAL M14 ....102 A2
Kirby Av CHAD OL9 ....37 C2
SWIN M27 ....44 A4
Kirkbank St CHAD OL9 ....22 A3
Kirkby Av NEWH/MOS M40 ....55 C2
Kirkdale Av NEWH/MOS M40 ....37 C3
Kirkgate Cl NEWH/MOS M40 * 5 F1
Kirkham Av GTN M18 ....91 C3
Kirkham St CHAD OL9 ....22 B2
SALQ M50 ....65 D4
Kirkhaven Sq NEWH/MOS M40 ....71 D1
Kirklinton Dr BKLY M9 ....53 C3
Kirkman Av ECC M30 ....78 B1
Kirkman Cl GTN M18 ....106 A1
Kirkmanshulme La GTN M18 * 90 A4
WGTN/LGST M12 ....104 B1
Kirk Rd BNG/LEV M19 ....118 A2
Kirkstall Rd URM M41 ....94 B2
Kirkstall Sq BRUN/LGST M13 ....9 E5
Kirkstead Cl OP/CLY M11 ....89 D1
Kirkstile Pl SWIN M27 ....25 D1
Kirkstone Rd NEWH/MOS M40 ....36 B3

Kirk St GTN M18 ....91 C4
Kirkway BKLY M9 ....35 D1
MDTN M24 ....17 D3
Kirkwood Dr NEWH/MOS M40 ....70 B1
Kirtley Av ECC M30 ....62 A2
Kitepool St ECC M30 * 60 B2
Kitty Wheeldon Gdns SALE M33 * 108 B4
Kiwi St SLFD M6 ....67 C3
Knaresborough Cl RDSH SK5 ....106 B4
Knightley Wk NEWH/MOS M40 ....53 C4
Knightsbridge STKP SK1 ....130 A3
Knightsbridge Cl BRO M7 ....50 A1
Knight's Cl PWCH M25 ....12 A4
Knight St DID/WITH M20 ....125 C3
Knightswood Rd CHH M8 ....51 D2
Kniveton Cl DTN/ASHW M34 ....107 C3
Kniveton Rd WGTN/LGST M12 ....89 C3
Knoll St BRO M7 ....50 A2
Knott Lanes OLDS OL8 ....59 D1
Knott St ORD M5 ....65 C4
Knowl Cl DTN/ASHW M34 ....107 C3
Knowldale Wy WGTN/LGST M12 ....88 B4
Knowle Dr PWCH M25 ....29 D3
Knowles Pl HULME M15 ....7 F4
The Knowles OLDS OL8 ....39 C4
Knowl St OLDS OL8 ....39 D3
Knowsley Av ORD M5 ....84 A1
Knowsley Dr SWIN M27 ....44 A3
Knowsley Gn ORD M5 * 84 A1
Knowsley Rd WHTF M45 ....11 C1
Knowsley St CHH M8 ....69 D1
Knutsford Av HTNM SK4 ....119 C2
Knutsford Rd GTN M18 ....105 D1
Knutsford St SLFD M6 ....65 D3
Krokus Sq CHAD OL9 * 20 B2

L

Labrador Quay SALQ M50 ....83 C2
Labtec St SWIN M27 ....27 C4
Laburnum Av DTN/ASHW M34 ....76 B4
FAIL M35 ....57 C3
SWIN M27 ....44 B3
WHTF M45 * 11 C3
Laburnum Gv PWCH M25 ....11 D4
Laburnum Rd DTN/ASHW M34 ....107 C2
GTN M18 ....106 A1
MDTN M24 ....18 B1
OLDS OL8 ....58 B1
Laburnum St SLFD M6 ....66 A3
Lacerta Ms BRO M7 ....67 D2
Lackford Dr NEWH/MOS M40 ....70 B1
Lacrosse Av OLDS OL8 ....39 D1
Lacy Gv STRET M32 ....97 D2
Lacy St STKP SK1 ....133 C1
STRET M32 ....97 D2
Lacy Wk WGTN/LGST M12 ....88 A1
Ladybarn Crs RUSH/FAL M14 ....88 A1
Ladybarn La RUSH/FAL M14 ....116 A2
Ladybarn Rd RUSH/FAL M14 ....116 A1
Ladyshore Cl ORD M5 ....66 A4
Ladysmith Rd DID/WITH M20 ....125 D3
Ladysmith St EDGY/DAV SK3 ....132 B2
OLDS OL8 ....39 D2
Ladythorn Ct PWCH M25 ....29 C3
Ladythorne Av PWCH M25 ....29 C3
Ladythorne Dr PWCH M25 ....29 C3
Lagos Cl RUSH/FAL M14 ....101 D1
Laindon Rd RUSH/FAL M14 ....103 D2
Lake Dr MDTN M24 ....17 C2
Lake Rd TRPK M17 ....81 D2
Lakeside Cl GTN M18 ....92 A3
Lakeside Ri BKLY M9 ....32 B2
Lake Vw BKLY M9 ....35 D3

Lakin St *NEWH/MOS* M40..............**54** B2
Lamb Cl *WGTN/LGST* M12 *...........**89** C4
Lamb Ct *CSLFD* M3 *.........................**2** C3
Lambeth Av *FAIL* M35....................**57** D1
Lambeth Rd *NEWH/MOS* M40..........**73** D1
  RDSH SK5...................................**120** A2
Lamb La *CSLFD* M3...........................**2** C3
Lambton Rd *CCHDY* M21.................**113** C1
  WALK M28.....................................**43** D3
Lambton St *ECC* M30.....................**61** C1
Lamburn Av *NEWH/MOS* M40 *........**37** C3
Lamorna Cl *BRO* M7.......................**49** C1
Lamplight Wy *SWIN* M27................**47** D2
Lamport Cl *CMANE* M1......................**8** C3
Lamport Ct *CMANE* M1 *...................**8** C3
Lampson St *CHH* M8.......................**68** B1
Lamsholme Cl *BNG/LEV* M19.........**104** B3
Lanbury Dr *CHH* M8........................**51** C2
Lancashire Ct *CHAD* OL9 *..............**21** D4
Lancashire Hl *HTNM* SK4..............**129** D2
Lancashire St *NEWH/MOS* M40.......**54** A4
Lancaster Av *FAIL* M35...................**56** B4
  MDTN M24......................................**18** B2
  URM M41..**94** B2
  WHTF M45.....................................**11** D2
Lancaster Dr *PWCH* M25.................**30** B3
Lancaster Rd *DID/WITH* M20..........**124** B2
  DROY M43......................................**75** C2
  SLFD M6...**64** A1
Lancaster St *CHAD* OL9..................**38** C3
  STKP SK1......................................**130** B3
Lanchester St *NEWH/MOS* M40.......**71** D2
Lancing Av *DID/WITH* M20.............**126** A2
Lancing Wk *CHAD* OL9 *.................**20** B3
Landcross Rd *RUSH/FAL* M14.........**102** B4
Lander Gv *BKLY* M9........................**35** C2
Landos Rd *NEWH/MOS* M40...............**5** F1
Landsberg Rd *FAIL* M35..................**58** A1
Landseer St *OLDE* OL4....................**23** D4
Lands End Rd *MDTN* M24................**15** C2
Lane End *ECC* M30..........................**63** C4
Lane End Cl *FAIL* M35....................**57** D3
Lane End Rd *BNG/LEV* M19............**126** A1
Lanfield Dr *CHH* M8.......................**51** C2
Langcroft St *NEWH/MOS* M40.........**55** D4
Langdale Av *BNG/LEV* M19............**118** A1
  OLDS OL8.......................................**40** A1
Langdale Rd *HTNM* SK4.................**118** B3
  RUSH/FAL M14............................**103** C1
  STRET M32.....................................**96** B2
Langfield Av *OLDTF/WHR* M16.......**100** A2
Langfield Crs *DROY* M43 *...............**76** B3
Langford Rd *DID/WITH* M20...........**114** B3
  HTNM SK4....................................**128** B1
Langham Ct *STRET* M32..................**95** D1
Langham Rd *HTNM* SK4.................**128** A4
  OLDS OL8.......................................**40** B1
  SLFD M6...**66** A3
Langholme Cl *HULME* M15 *..............**6** B4
Langholme Pl *ECC* M30...................**61** C3
Langland Cl *BNG/LEV* M19............**106** A3
Langland Dr *ECC* M30.....................**78** B2
Langley Av *PWCH* M25...................**12** A4
Langley Cl *URM* M41.......................**94** B3
Langley Gdns *PWCH* M25...............**12** A3
Langley Hall Rd *PWCH* M25...........**12** A3
Langley Rd *PWCH* M25...................**11** D4
  RUSH/FAL M14............................**102** B4
  SWIN M27.......................................**48** A1
Langley Rd South *SLFD* M6............**48** B4
Langness St *OP/CLY* M11................**73** D4
Lango St *OLDTF/WHR* M16 *.............**99** D1
Langport Av *WGTN/LGST* M12........**88** B2
Langsett Av *SLFD* M6......................**64** B2
Langshaw St *OLDTF/WHR* M16.......**99** D1
  SLFD M6...**66** A4
Langside Av *BKLY* M9.....................**34** B1

Langston St *CSLFD* M3 *.................**69** C2
Langthorne St *BNG/LEV* M19........**118** A1
Langton Cl *FAIL* M35.......................**58** A1
Langton St *MDTN* M24....................**17** D1
  SLFD M6...**65** D3
Langworthy Rd *NEWH/MOS* M40....**54** B2
  SLFD M6...**66** A2
Lanhill Dr *CHH* M8.........................**52** B3
Lankro Wy *TRPK* M17......................**63** C4
Lansdale Gdns *BNG/LEV* M19.......**116** B4
Lansdowne Av *DTN/ASHW* M34......**76** B3
Lansdowne Ct *CHAD* OL9................**21** C3
Lansdowne Rd *CHAD* OL9...............**21** D3
  CHH M8...**51** D1
  ECC M30..**62** A2
  SALE M33....................................**108** B3
Lanstead Dr *NEWH/MOS* M40.........**71** D3
Lapwing La *DID/WITH* M20...........**118** B4
  RDSH SK5.......................................**97** C4
Larch Av *STRET* M32........................**97** C4
  SWIN M27.......................................**43** D3
Larch Cl *FAIL* M35...........................**57** C3
Larch Gv *CHAD* OL9........................**21** C1
  SWIN M27.......................................**24** A3
Larch Rd *ECC* M30...........................**60** B1
Larch St *OLDS* OL8..........................**22** A3
Larchview Rd *MDTN* M24................**18** B1
Larchwood *CHAD* OL9.....................**19** D2
Larchwood Av *BKLY* M9..................**54** A2
Larke Ri *DID/WITH* M20................**124** A2
Larkhill Wk *CHH* M8......................**52** A3
Larks Ri *DROY* M43.........................**77** C2
Larmuth Av *CCHDY* M21...............**112** B3
Larne Av *STRET* M32.......................**96** B3
Larne St *OP/CLY* M11......................**89** D1
Larwood Av *HTNM* SK4.................**127** D4
Lascar Av *ORD* M5...........................**83** D1
Lashbrook Cl *NEWH/MOS* M40.........**71** D3
Lassell St *OP/CLY* M11 *..................**92** A2
Lastingham St *NEWH/MOS* M40......**55** D3
Latchmere Rd *RUSH/FAL* M14.......**115** D1
Latham St *OP/CLY* M11...................**92** A2
Lathbury Rd *BKLY* M9.....................**53** C3
Lathom Rd *DID/WITH* M20............**116** A2
Latimer St *OLDE* OL4......................**23** D3
Latrobe St *DROY* M43......................**92** B1
Lauderdale Crs *BRUN/LGST* M13....**87** D3
Laundry St *SLFD* M6........................**66** A3
Laurel Av *CHAD* OL9.......................**19** C1
  RUSH/FAL M14............................**101** D3
Laurel Bank Gdns *BKLY* M9...........**34** A1
Laurel End La *HTNM* SK4..............**127** D2
Laurel Gv *SLFD* M6 *.......................**64** B3
Laurel Rd *HTNM* SK4....................**128** A1
Laurel St *HTNM* SK4.....................**129** D3
  MDTN M24......................................**31** C1
Laurence Cl *WGTN/LGST* M12.......**89** D3
Lausanne Rd *DID/WITH* M20.........**115** C2
Lavenders Brow *STKP* SK1............**130** A4
Lavenham Av *OP/CLY* M11..............**74** A4
Lavington Gv *GTN* M18.................**106** A1
Lavinia St *ECC* M30.........................**61** C3
Lavister Av *BNG/LEV* M19............**126** A2
Lawers Av *CHAD* OL9......................**20** B1
Lawler Av *ORD* M5..........................**84** A3
Lawn Dr *SWIN* M27.........................**44** B2
Lawngreen Av *CCHDY* M21............**111** D2
Lawnside Ms *DID/WITH* M20.........**114** B4
Lawnswood Dr *SWIN* M27..............**45** D3
Lawnswood Park Rd *SWIN* M27......**45** D3
Lawrence St *EDGY/DAV* SK3.........**129** D4
  CSL WALK M28.............................**43** D2
Lawson Cl *WALK* M28.....................**43** D2
Lawson Gv *SALE* M33....................**108** B3
Lawson St *BKLY* M9.........................**33** D3
Lawton Moor Rd *NTHM/RTH* M23.**122** A4
Lawton Rd *HTNM* SK4...................**128** B1
Lawton St *DROY* M43.......................**76** A3

OP/CLY M11 ....91 C2
Laxey St NEWH/MOS M40 * 55 C2
Laxley Cl CHAD OL9 ....21 C4
Laycock Crs FAIL M35 ....57 C3
Laycock Gv FAIL M35 ....57 C2
Laystall St CMANE M1 ....5 D4
Layton Cl STKP SK1 ....133 D1
Layton St NEWH/MOS M40 ....71 C3
Leabank St BNG/LEV M19 ....104 B4
Leabrook St NEWH/MOS M40 ....56 B1
Leaburn Dr BNG/LEV M19 ....126 B1
Leach St GTN M18 ....90 A4
PWCH M25 ....9 C1
Leaconfield Dr WALK M28 ....42 A2
Lea Ct FAIL M35 ....56 B2
Leacroft Rd CCHDY M21 ....113 C4
Lea Dr BKLY M9 ....35 D4
Leafield Av DID/WITH M20 ....126 A1
Leaf St HULME M15 ....7 E5
RDSH SK5 ....119 D2
Leagate URM M41 ....94 B4
Leaholme Cl NEWH/MOS M40 ....56 A4
Leak St OLDTF/WHR M16 ....84 B3
Leamington Av DID/WITH M20 ....124 A1
Leamington Rd ECC M30 ....61 C2
RDSH SK5 ....119 D2
Leamington St OP/CLY M11 ....91 C2
Leander Cl BKLY M9 ....34 B3
Lea Rd HTNM SK4 ....128 A1
Leaside Dr DID/WITH M20 ....116 A4
Lecester Rd CHH M8 ....52 A3
Leconfield Dr BKLY M9 ....34 B2
Leconfield Rd ECC M30 ....60 A1
Ledbrooke Cl ORD M5 ....84 A2
Ledbury Cl MDTN M24 ....17 D3
Ledbury Rd FAIL M35 * 74 B1
Ledsham Av BKLY M9 ....14 B4
Lee Crs STRET M32 ....97 D3
Leegate Cl HTNM SK4 ....127 C1
Leegate Dr BKLY M9 ....35 C1
Leegate Gdns HTNM SK4 ....127 C1
Leegate Rd HTNM SK4 ....127 D1
Leegrange Rd BKLY M9 ....34 B4
Lees Hall Crs RUSH/FAL M14 ....116 A1
Leeside HTNM SK4 ....127 C4
Lees Park Av DROY M43 ....76 B3
Lees Rd OLDE OL4 ....23 D2
Lees St DROY M43 ....76 A3
GTN M18 ....91 D5
MDTN M24 ....19 C2
SWIN M27 ....26 A4
Lee St OLDS OL8 ....22 B4
Leeswood Av CCHDY M21 ....112 B3
Leewood SWIN M27 ....25 C1
Left Bank CSLFD M3 ....3 D4
Legh Dr DTN/ASHW M34 ....76 A4
Legh Rd BRO M7 ....50 A1
Legh St BRO M7 ....50 A1
ECC M30 ....61 D4
Legion Gv BRO M7 ....50 B3
Leicester Av BRO M7 * 51 C1
DROY M43 ....75 C2
Leicester Rd BRO M7 ....50 B2
FAIL M35 ....57 D4
SALE M33 ....109 C4
Leicester St RDSH SK5 ....106 B3
Leigh Av SWIN M27 ....44 A4
Leighbrook Rd RUSH/FAL M14 ....115 C1
Leighton Rd OLDTF/WHR M16 ....99 D1
Leighton St NEWH/MOS M40 ....54 B1
Leinster Rd SWIN M27 ....44 B2
Leith Pl OLDS OL8 ....40 B3
Lemnos St OLD OL1 ....23 D2
Lena St CMANE M1 ....4 C5
Len Cox Wk ANC M4 * 4 C3
Leng Rd NEWH/MOS M40 ....56 A4

Lenham Cl RDSH SK5 ....121 C3
Lentmead Dr BKLY M9 ....35 D4
Leominster Rd MDTN M24 * 18 A3
Leopold Av DID/WITH M20 ....114 B4
Leroy Dr BKLY M9 ....34 A3
Lesley Rd URM M41 ....95 D4
Leslie Av CHAD OL9 ....21 C4
Leslie Hough Wy SLFD M6 ....67 C2
Leslie St RUSH/FAL M14 ....102 A2
Lester St STRET M32 ....97 C3
Letchworth St RUSH/FAL M14 ....102 A2
Letham St OLDS OL8 ....41 C3
Levedale Rd BKLY M9 ....34 B1
Levenhurst Rd CHH M8 ....51 C2
Levenshulme Rd GTN M18 ....106 A1
Levenshulme Ter BNG/LEV M19 * ..104 B4
Levens St NEWH/MOS M40 ....54 B2
SLFD M6 ....49 C4
Levens Wk CHAD OL9 ....20 B3
Lever Av SWIN M27 ....27 C3
Lever St CMANE M1 ....4 C4
Lever Wk MDTN M24 ....17 C2
Lewis Av BKLY M9 ....34 B4
URM M41 ....79 C4
Lewisham Av NEWH/MOS M40 ....73 C1
Lewis Dr DROY M43 ....74 B3
RDSH SK5 ....107 C4
Lewis St ECC M30 ....62 A4
NEWH/MOS M40 ....71 C2
Lewtas St CHH M8 ....33 C3
Lexton Av CHH M8 ....33 C4
Leybourne Av BNG/LEV M19 ....105 C3
Leyburn Av STRET M32 ....96 B3
Leyburn Cl WHTF M45 ....10 B1
Leyburn Rd NEWH/MOS M40 ....36 B3
Leycroft St CMANE M1 * 5 D5
CMANE M1 * 9 D1
Leyland Av DID/WITH M20 ....126 A2
Leyland St HTNM SK4 ....129 D4
Leyton Av NEWH/MOS M40 ....55 C2
Leywell Rd BKLY M9 ....54 A1
Library La CHAD OL9 ....22 A1
Lichens Crs OLDS OL9 ....41 D2
Lichfield Av RDSH SK5 ....119 D2
Lichfield Dr CHH M8 ....52 A2
PWCH M25 ....30 B3
SWIN M27 ....45 C3
Lichfield Rd ECC M30 ....63 C1
URM M41 ....94 A1
Lichfield St SLFD M6 ....48 B4
Lidbrook Wk WGTN/LGST M12 ....88 B3
Lidiard St CHH M8 ....32 B4
Lifton Av NEWH/MOS M40 ....71 D1
Lightbourne Av SWIN M27 ....45 C2
Lightbowne Rd NEWH/MOS M40 .....54 B3
Light Oaks Rd SLFD M6 ....64 A1
Lignum Av CHAD OL9 ....21 C1
Lilac Av SWIN M27 ....45 D1
Lilac Ct SLFD M6 ....66 B3
Lilac Gv CHAD OL9 ....21 C1
NEWH/MOS M40 ....35 D4
PWCH M25 ....11 D3
Lilac La OLDS OL8 ....40 A3
Lilac St OFTN SK2 ....133 C2
Lila St BKLY M9 ....54 A2
Lilford Cl WGTN/LGST M12 ....89 D3
Lillian Gv RDSH SK5 ....120 A1
Lillian St OLDTF/WHR M16 ....99 D1
Lilmore Av CHH M8 ....52 B3
NEWH/MOS M40 ....55 D3
Lily Cl EDGY/DAV SK3 ....132 A4
Lily La BKLY M9 ....54 A4
Lily St ECC M30 ....61 C4
MDTN M24 ....18 B3
Limbert Cir CHH M8 ....33 D4
Lime Av SWIN M27 ....43 D3
WHTF M45 ....11 C2

Lime Bank St *WGTN/LGST* M12 ....88 A1
Limebrook Cl *OP/CLY* M11 ....91 D1
Lime Cl *SLFD* M6 ....66 B2
Lime Ct *SLFD* M6 * 66 B2
Lime Crs *OLDTF/WHR* M16 ....99 C1
Limeditch Rd *FAIL* M35 ....58 A1
Limefield *MDTN* M24 ....16 B2
Limefield Rd *BRO* M7 ....31 C4
Limefield Ter *BNG/LEV* M19 ....104 B4
Lime Gdns *MDTN* M24 ....16 B1
Lime Ga *OLDS* OL8 ....39 D3
Lime Gn *OLDS* OL8 ....40 A4
Lime Green Rd *OLDS* OL8 ....58 B1
Lime Gv *OLDTF/WHR* M16 ....99 C1
  PWCH M25 ....11 D3
Limehurst Av *RUSH/FAL* M14 ....114 A1
Limehurst Ct *OLDS* OL8 ....40 A4
Limekiln La *WGTN/LGST* M12 ....88 B2
Lime La *FAIL* M35 ....39 D4
  OLDS OL8 ....39 D4
Lime Rd *STRET* M32 ....97 C4
Limerston Dr *NEWH/MOS* M40 ....54 A4
Limeside Rd *OLDS* OL8 ....58 B1
Limestead Av *CHH* M8 ....62 A4
Lime St *ECC* M30 ....61 D4
  NEWH/MOS M40 ....71 C2
Lime Tree Cl *URM* M41 ....94 B4
Lime Tree Gv *FAIL* M35 ....58 A2
Limetrees Rd *MDTN* M24 ....17 C1
Limley Gv *CCHDY* M21 ....112 B2
Linby St *HULME* M15 ....6 C4
Lincoln Av *BNG/LEV* M19 ....105 C4
  DROY M43 ....75 D2
  STRET M32 ....95 C2
Lincoln Cl *BRUN/LGST* M13 ....87 D4
Lincoln Rd *FAIL* M35 ....57 D3
  MDTN M24 ....18 B4
Lincoln St *BRUN/LGST* M13 ....104 A1
  CHAD OL9 ....21 C4
  ECC M30 ....61 D4
Lindale Av *CHAD* OL9 ....20 B3
  NEWH/MOS M40 ....37 C3
Linden Av *SLFD* M6 ....47 D3
  SWIN M27 ....44 A2
Linden Dr *ORD* M5 ....83 D1
Linden Gv *RUSH/FAL* M14 ....116 A1
Linden Pk *BNG/LEV* M19 ....117 D1
Linden Rd *DID/WITH* M20 ....124 B1
Lindenwood *CHAD* OL9 ....19 D1
Lindeth Av *GTN* M18 ....106 A1
Lindfield Rd *RDSH* SK5 ....107 C4
Lindinis Av *ORD* M5 ....68 B3
Lindisfarne Rd *AULW* OL7 ....59 D4
Lindley Gv *EDGY/DAV* SK3 ....132 A4
Lindleywood Rd *RUSH/FAL* M14 ....116 B1
Lindon Wy *DROY* M43 ....91 C1
Lindow Rd *OLDTF/WHR* M16 ....99 C3
Lindrick Av *WHTF* M45 ....10 A3
Lindum Av *OLDTF/WHR* M16 ....99 D1
Lindum St *RUSH/FAL* M14 ....102 A2
Lindwall Cl *NTHM/RTH* M23 ....122 A3
Linehan Cl *HTNM* M18 ....126 A3
Linen Ct *CSLFD* M3 ....2 A1
Lines Rd *DROY* M43 ....76 A4
Linfield St *OP/CLY* M11 ....73 C4
Linford Av *NEWH/MOS* M40 ....36 B3
Lingard St *WYTH/NTH* M22 ....123 C4
Lingard Rd *RDSH* SK5 ....120 A1
Lingcrest Rd *HTNM* SK4 ....118 B2
Lingfield Rd *OP/CLY* M11 ....73 D3
Lingmoor Wk *HULME* M15 * 86 A4
Linhope Cl *HTNM* SK4 ....126 B2

Link Av *URM* M41 ....95 D4
Link La *OLDS* OL8 ....40 B3
Links Av *FAIL* M35 ....57 C4
Links Crs *PWCH* M25 ....31 D3
The Links *NEWH/MOS* M40 ....55 D2
Links Vw *PWCH* M25 ....29 D4
Linksway *PWCH* M25 ....31 C3
  SWIN M27 ....45 D3
Linksway Cl *HTNM* SK4 ....117 D4
The Link *RDSH* SK5 ....121 D3
Linley Rd *SALE* M33 ....109 C4
Linnet Cl *DTN/ASHW* M34 ....76 B3
  WGTN/LGST M12 ....104 A1
Linn St *CHH* M8 ....32 B4
Linsley Gv *CSLFD* M3 * 3 D3
Linstead Dr *CHH* M8 ....51 C3
Linton Av *DTN/ASHW* M34 ....107 D2
Linton Cl *ANC* M4 ....88 A1
Linton Rd *SALE* M33 ....109 D3
Linton Wk *BRO* M7 ....48 A1
Linwood Gv *WGTN/LGST* M12 ....104 B3
Linwood St *NEWH/MOS* M40 ....55 D3
Lion Brow *BKLY* M9 ....34 A3
Lion Fold La *BKLY* M9 ....34 A3
Lions Dr *SWIN* M27 ....45 D2
Lion St *BKLY* M9 ....34 A3
Lisburn Av *OLDTF/WHR* M16 ....99 D4
Lisburn Rd *NEWH/MOS* M40 ....54 B1
Liscard Av *RUSH/FAL* M14 ....102 A4
Lismore Wy *URM* M41 ....79 C4
Lissadel St *SLFD* M6 ....66 B1
Lister Rd *MDTN* M24 ....15 C3
Litcham Cl *CMANE* M1 ....8 C3
Litchfield Gv *WALK* M28 ....43 C2
Little Ancoats St *CMANE* M1 ....4 C3
Little David St *CMANE* M1 ....8 C1
Little Ees La *SALE* M33 ....108 A2
Little Egerton St *STKP* SK1 ....129 D3
Littlegreen Gdns *SLFD* M6 ....66 A2
Littlehaven Cl *WGTN/LGST* M12 ....88 B4
Little Holme St *ANC* M4 ....71 C4
Little John St *CSLFD* M3 ....6 C1
Little Lever St *CMANE* M1 ....4 C4
Little Moss La *SWIN* M27 ....26 A3
Littlemoss Rd *DROY* M43 ....76 B2
Little Nelson St *ANC* M4 * 4 B1
Little Peter St *HULME* M15 ....7 D3
Little Pitt St *CMANE* M1 * 5 D1
Little Quay St *CSLFD* M3 ....3 C5
Littleton Rd *BRO* M7 ....48 B1
Little Underbank *STKP* SK1 * 130 A3
Littlewood St *SLFD* M6 ....65 D3
Liverpool Cl *RDSH* SK5 ....119 D2
Liverpool Rd *CSLFD* M3 ....6 B1
  ECC M30 ....61 C4
Liverpool St *ORD* M5 ....67 C4
  RDSH SK5 ....119 D2
  SLFD M6 ....65 D4
Liverstudd Av *RDSH* SK5 ....120 A1
Livesey St *ANC* M4 ....70 B2
  BNG/LEV M19 ....117 D1
Livsey St *WHTF* M45 ....11 C1
Lizmar St *BKLY* M9 ....54 A1
Lloyd Rd *BNG/LEV* M19 ....118 A2
Lloyd St *CMANW* M2 ....3 F5
  HTNM SK4 ....129 C3
Lloyd St South *RUSH/FAL* M14 ....101 D4
Lockett Gdns *CSLFD* M3 ....2 D4
Lockett St *CHH* M8 ....68 B1
  SLFD M6 ....48 B4
Lockhart Cl *WGTN/LGST* M12 ....89 D2
Lock Keepers Ms *SWIN* M27 ....47 C1
Locksley Cl *HTNM* SK4 ....128 B3
Lockton Cl *CMANE* M1 ....9 D3
  RDSH SK5 ....119 D3
Lockton Ct *CMANE* M1 ....8 C3

Lockwood St *WGTN/LGST* M12 ....105 C2
Lodge Av *URM* M41 ....94 B3
Lodge Ct *HTNM* SK4 ....127 C3
Lodge Fold *DROY* M43 ....76 A3
Lodgeside Cl *DROY* M43 ....76 A3
Lodge St *NEWH/MOS* M40 ....53 D4
Lodge Vw *DROY* M43 ....76 A3
Loganberry Av *SLFD* M6 ....66 B2
Lokfu Gdns *CHH* M8 ....50 B4
Lomas Cl *BNG/LEV* M19 ....126 A2
Lomas St *EDGY/DAV* SK3 ....132 A2
 FAIL M35 ....38 B4
Lomax St *CMANE* M1 ....5 E4
Lombard Gv *RUSH/FAL* M14 ....115 D1
Lombard St *OLD* OL1 ....22 B2
Lombardy Ct *SLFD* M6 * 66 B2
Lomond Av *STRET* M32 ....97 C2
London Pl *STKP* SK1 ....130 A4
London Rd *CMANE* M1 ....9 D2
London Sq *STKP* SK1 ....130 A4
London St *SLFD* M6 ....67 C1
 WHTF M45 ....11 C2
Longacre St *CMANE* M1 ....9 E1
Longbow Ct *BRO* M7 * 68 A1
Longbridge Rd *TRPK* M17 ....80 B3
Longcrag Wk *HULME* M15 * 86 A4
Longcroft Gv *DTN/ASHW* M34 ....93 C1
Longden Rd *WGTN/LGST* M12 ....104 B3
Longford Av *STRET* M32 ....97 D3
Longford Cl *STRET* M32 ....97 D2
Longford Pk *STRET* M32 ....98 A3
Longford Rd *RUSH/FAL* M14 ....103 D1
Longford Rd *GTN* M18 ....91 C3
Longford Rd West *BNG/LEV* M19 ....106 A4
Longford St *GTN* M18 ....91 C3
 MDTN M24 ....17 C1
 SWIN M27 ....45 C2
Longham Cl *OP/CLY* M11 ....71 D4
Longhurst Rd *BKLY* M9 ....33 C1
Long La *CHAD* OL9 ....38 A2
Longley Dr *WALK* M28 ....43 C3
Longley St *OLD* OL1 * 23 C3
Longmead Rd *SLFD* M6 ....47 C4
Long Millgate *CSLFD* M3 ....3 F2
Longport Av *DID/WITH* M20 ....114 B2
Longshaw Av *SWIN* M27 ....26 A4
Longshut La *OFTN* SK2 ....133 C2
Longshut La West *OFTN* SK2 ....133 C2
Longsight Rd *GTN* M18 ....105 C2
Longsight St *HTNM* SK4 ....129 C3
Long St *GTN* M18 ....91 D3
 MDTN M24 ....17 C1
 SWIN M27 ....45 C2
Longton Av *DID/WITH* M20 ....114 B4
Longton Rd *BKLY* M9 ....33 D1
 SLFD M6 ....46 B4
Longview Dr *SWIN* M27 ....24 B4
Longwood Rd *TRPK* M17 ....81 C3
Longworth St *CSLFD* M3 ....7 D1
Lonsdale Av *RDSH* SK5 ....107 C2
 SWIN M27 ....44 A4
Lonsdale Rd *BNG/LEV* M19 ....105 C3
 OLDS OL8 ....39 C3
Lonsdale St *NEWH/MOS* M40 ....55 D3
Loom St *ANC* M4 ....5 D3
Lord Byron Sq *SALQ* M50 ....83 C1
Lord La *FAIL* M35 ....74 B1
Lord Napier Dr *ORD* M5 ....83 D2
Lord North St *NEWH/MOS* M40 ....71 D1
Lord's Av *ORD* M5 ....65 C3
Lord Sheldon Wy *AULW* OL7 ....77 D3
Lordship Cl *BKLY* M9 ....35 C4
Lordsmead St *HULME* M15 ....6 B5
Lord St *ANC* M4 ....69 D2
 DTN/ASHW M34 ....107 D1
 OLD OL1 ....23 C2
 STKP SK1 ....129 D4

Loretto Rd *URM* M41 ....95 C4
Loring St *NEWH/MOS* M40 ....55 D4
Lorne Gv *EDGY/DAV* SK3 ....132 B3
 URM M41 ....94 B3
Lorne Rd *RUSH/FAL* M14 ....115 D1
Lorne St *BRUN/LGST* M13 ....87 D4
 ECC M30 ....78 A1
 OLDS OL8 ....40 B1
Lostock Av *BNG/LEV* M19 ....105 C4
Lostock Gv *STRET* M32 ....96 A3
Lostock Rd *ORD* M5 ....65 D3
 URM M41 ....94 A1
Lostock St *NEWH/MOS* M40 ....71 C2
Lothian Av *ECC* M30 ....61 C2
Lottery St *EDGY/DAV* SK3 ....129 C4
Lottie St *SWIN* M27 ....45 D1
Louisa St *OP/CLY* M11 ....91 C1
Louvain St *FAIL* M35 ....56 B2
Love La *HTNM* SK4 ....129 D3
Lowbrook Av *BKLY* M9 ....36 A2
Lowcroft Crs *CHAD* OL9 ....20 A1
Lowcross Rd *NEWH/MOS* M40 ....54 B3
Lower Albion St *CMANE* M1 ....8 C2
Lower Brook La *WALK* M28 * 42 B4
Lower Brook St *CMANE* M1 * 8 C1
Lower Broughton Rd *BRO* M7 ....49 D4
Lower Bury St *HTNM* SK4 ....129 C3
Lower Byrom St *CSLFD* M3 ....6 C1
Lower Carrs *STKP* SK1 ....130 A4
Lower Chatham St *CMANE* M1 ....8 A3
Lower Edge Av *OLD* OL1 ....22 B1
Lower Gn *MDTN* M24 ....17 C4
Lower Hardman St *CSLFD* M3 ....2 C5
Lower Hillgate *STKP* SK1 ....130 A4
Lower Lime Rd *OLDS* OL8 ....58 B2
Lower Moat Cl *HTNM* SK4 ....129 D2
Lower Monton Rd *ECC* M30 ....62 B3
Lower Mosley St *CMANE* M1 ....7 E2
Lower Moss La *HULME* M15 ....6 B4
 WHTF M45 ....11 C2
Lower Ormond St *CMANE* M1 ....8 A3
Lower Park Rd *RUSH/FAL* M14 ....102 B1
Lower Seedley Rd *SLFD* M6 ....65 D2
Lower Sutherland St *SWIN* M27 ....44 B1
Lower Victoria St *CHAD* OL9 ....21 C2
Lowestead Rd *OP/CLY* M11 ....73 D3
Lowestoft St *RUSH/FAL* M14 ....102 A3
Lowe St *STKP* SK1 ....130 A4
Lowfield Av *DROY* M43 ....75 C2
Lowfield Gv *OFTN* SK2 ....133 C2
Lowfield Rd *EDGY/DAV* SK3 ....132 B3
Lowlands Cl *MDTN* M24 ....36 B1
Lowndes Wk *BRUN/LGST* M13 * 87 D3
Lowry Dr *SWIN* M27 ....26 A4
Lowry Houses *ECC* M30 * 62 B3
Lowther Av *GTN* M18 ....105 C2
Lowther Cl *PWCH* M25 ....29 C3
Lowther Rd *CHH* M8 ....32 B4
 PWCH M25 ....29 C2
Lowthorpe St *RUSH/FAL* M14 ....101 D3
Lowton Av *BKLY* M9 ....54 A2
Low Wood Rd *DTN/ASHW* M34 ....107 D1
Loxford Ct *HULME* M15 * 7 F4
Loxford St *HULME* M15 ....7 F5
Lubeck St *BKLY* M9 ....53 D1
Lucas Wk *OP/CLY* M11 ....89 C1
Lucerne Cl *CHAD* OL9 ....21 D3
Lucien Ct *WGTN/LGST* M12 ....88 B3
Lucy St *BRO* M7 ....50 A4
 EDGY/DAV SK3 ....132 B1
 HULME M15 ....85 C3
Ludgate Hl *ANC* M4 ....4 C1
Ludgate Rd *NEWH/MOS* M40 ....73 D1
Ludgate St *ANC* M4 ....4 B1
Ludlow Av *SWIN* M27 ....26 B3
 WHTF M45 ....12 A3
Luke Rd *DROY* M43 ....76 A4

Lullington Rd *SLFD* M6 ....**65** C1
Lulworth Crs *FAIL* M35 ....**58** A1
Lulworth Rd *ECC* M30 ....**61** D3
Lumb La *DROY* M43 ....**59** C4
  DTN/ASHW M34 ....**76** B3
Lumley Cl *RUSH/FAL* M14 ....**102** A1
Lumn's La *SWIN* M27 ....**27** D3
Lumsdale Rd *STRET* M32 ....**95** D1
Luna St *ANC* M4 ....**4** C3
Lund St *OLDTF/WHR* M16 .....**84** B3
Lundy Av *GTN* M21 ....**112** B4
Lune Cl *WHTF* M45 ....**11** D1
Lune Dr *WHTF* M45 ....**11** D1
Lune St *OLDS* OL8 ....**40** B1
Lune Wy *RDSH* SK5 ....**120** A4
Lunn Av *GTN* M18 ....**92** A3
Lupton St *CSLFD* M3 * **2** B3
Lurden Wk *CHAD* OL9 * **38** B1
Luton Rd *RDSH* SK5 ....**120** A1
Luxhall Wk *NEWH/MOS* M40 ....**55** C4
Luxor Gv *DTN/ASHW* M34 ......**107** C2
Lyceum Pl *HULME* M15 * **8** A4
Lychgate Ms *HTNM* SK4 * **126** B3
Lydden Av *OP/CLY* M11 * **74** A2
Lydford St *SLFD* M6 ....**67** C1
Lydford Wk *BRUN/LGST* M13 * ...**87** D3
Lydgate Cl *WHTF* M45 ....**11** D1
Lydgate Rd *DROY* M43 ....**74** B2
Lyme Gv *DROY* M43 ....**92** A1
  OFTN SK2 ....**133** C2
Lyme St *HTNM* SK4 ....**126** B3
Lymington Cl *MDTN* M24 ....**18** A4
Lymm Cl *EDGY/DAV* SK3 ....**132** A3
Lyndale Av *RDSH* SK5 ....**107** C2
  SWIN M27 ....**44** A3
Lyndene Av *WALK* M28 ....**42** B1
Lyndhurst Av *CHAD* OL9 ....**20** A4
  PWCH M25 ....**31** D2
Lyndhurst Rd *DID/WITH* M20 ..**124** B1
  OLDS OL8 ....**40** A2
  RDSH SK5 * **106** B3
  STRET M32 ....**96** A3
Lyndhurst St *SLFD* M6 ....**65** D3
Lynmouth Av *DID/WITH* M20 ..**114** B3
  OLDS OL8 ....**41** C1
  RDSH SK5 ....**119** D2
Lynmouth Gv *PWCH* M25 ....**29** C2
Lynn Av *SALE* M33 ....**109** D3
Lynn Dr *DROY* M43 ....**74** B3
Lynn St *CHAD* OL9 ....**39** D1
Lynnwood Rd *BNG/LEV* M19 ..**126** A3
Lynthorpe Rd *NEWH/MOS* M40 ...**37** C3
Lynton Av *OLDS* OL8 ....**39** D3
  SWIN M27 ....**26** A4
Lynton Dr *BNG/LEV* M19 ....**117** C2
  PWCH M25 ....**12** B3
Lynton Rd *CCHDY* M21 ....**98** B4
  HTNM SK4 ....**118** A4
  SWIN M27 ....**26** A4
Lynton St *RUSH/FAL* M14 * **102** A3
Lynway Dr *DID/WITH* M20 ......**115** C4
Lynwell Rd *ECC* M30 ....**62** A3
Lynwood Av *ECC* M30 ....**62** A3
  OLDTF/WHR M16 ....**99** D3
Lynwood Gv *DTN/ASHW* M34 ...**58** B4
  HTNM SK4 ....**118** B3
  SALE M33 ....**109** D4
Lyon Gv *WALK* M28 ....**42** B1
Lyons Fold *SALE* M33 ....**109** C3
Lyons Rd *TRPK* M17 ....**80** B2
Lyon St *SWIN* M27 ....**44** B2
Lyra Pl *BRO* M7 ....**67** D2
Lysander Cl *RUSH/FAL* M14 ..**114** B1
Lytham Av *CCHDY* M21 ....**112** B2
Lytham Rd *RUSH/FAL* M14 ....**104** A4
Lytham St *EDGY/DAV* SK3 .....**133** C3
Lyth St *RUSH/FAL* M14 ....**116** A2

Lytton Av *CHH* M8 ....**51** D3
Lytton Rd *DROY* M43 ....**75** D3

M

Mabel Av *WALK* M28 ....**42** B2
Mabel Rd *FAIL* M35 ....**38** B4
Mabel St *NEWH/MOS* M40 ......**56** A4
Mabfield Rd *RUSH/FAL* M14 ..**102** B4
Macauley Rd *OLDTF/WHR* M16 ...**99** C3
  RDSH SK5 ....**106** A4
Macdonald St *OLDS* OL8 ....**41** C1
Macefin Av *CCHDY* M21 ....**123** C1
Macfarren St *WGTN/LGST* M12 ...**104** B2
Mackenzie Rd *BRO* M7 ....**49** C3
Mackenzie St *WGTN/LGST* M12 ...**104** B2
Mackintosh Wy *OLD* OL1 ....**23** C2
Mackworth St *HULME* M15 ......**85** C4
Maclaren Dr *CHH* M8 ....**31** D4
Maddison Rd *DROY* M43 ....**92** A1
Madeley Dr *CHAD* OL9 ....**21** C3
Maden Wk *CHAD* OL9 * **21** C1
Madison Av *DTN/ASHW* M34 ....**93** D1
Madison St *GTN* M18 ....**91** D3
Mafeking St *OLDS* OL8 ....**39** D2
Magdala St *OLD* OL1 ....**22** B1
Magnolia Dr *CHH* M8 * **51** D3
Magpie Cl *DROY* M43 ....**76** B2
Magpie Wk *OP/CLY* M11 * **72** A4
Maher Gdns *HULME* M15 ....**100** B1
Mahood St *EDGY/DAV* SK3 ....**132** A2
Maida St *BNG/LEV* M19 ....**105** C3
Maidford Cl *ANC* M4 * **71** C4
  STRET M32 ....**97** D3
Maidstone Av *CCHDY* M21 ....**98** B4
Maidstone Ms *CCHDY* M21 ......**98** B4
Maidstone Rd *BNG/LEV* M19 ..**126** A3
Main Av *BNG/LEV* M19 ....**117** C2
  TRPK M17 ....**96** B1
Maine Rd *RUSH/FAL* M14 ......**101** D3
Mainprice Cl *SLFD* M6 ....**66** A1
Main Rd *CHAD* OL9 ....**21** D2
  SWIN M27 ....**28** A2
Main St *FAIL* M35 ....**57** C1
Mainway *MDTN* M24 ....**17** C3
Mainway East *MDTN* M24 ....**18** B3
Maitland Av *CCHDY* M21 ....**122** B1
Maitland Wk *CHAD* OL9 * **21** C1
Major St *CMANE* M1 ....**8** B1
Makin St *CMANE* M1 * **8** B2
Makkah Cl *NEWH/MOS* M40 ....**54** B4
Malbrook Wk *BRUN/LGST* M13 * ...**9** E5
Malby St *OLD* OL1 ....**23** C1
Malcolm Av *SWIN* M27 ....**26** B3
Malcolm Dr *SWIN* M27 ....**26** B3
Maldon Crs *SWIN* M27 ....**45** C3
Maldon Dr *ECC* M30 ....**62** B1
Maldwyn Av *CHH* M8 ....**32** B3
Maleham St *BRO* M7 * **50** B3
Mallard Cl *OLDS* OL8 ....**40** A3
Mallard St *CMANE* M1 * **8** A3
Mallowdale Av *RUSH/FAL* M14 ...**115** C1
Mallow St *HULME* M15 ....**6** C5
Malpas St *OLD* OL1 ....**23** C2
  WGTN/LGST M12 ....**89** D3
Malpas Wk *OLDTF/WHR* M16 * ...**85** C4
Malta Cl *MDTN* M24 ....**19** C2
Malta St *ANC* M4 ....**71** C4
Malton Av *CCHDY* M21 ....**112** C2
Malton Rd *HTNM* SK4 ....**127** D1
Malton St *OLDS* OL8 ....**40** B3
Malt St *HULME* M15 ....**6** A4
Malus Ct *SLFD* M6 ....**66** B2

Malvern Av *DROY* M43 ....76 B3
Malvern Cl *HTNM* SK4 ....129 C2
  PWCH M25 ....12 B4
  SWIN M27 ....47 C3
Malvern Dr *SWIN* M27 ....47 C3
Malvern Gv *DID/WITH* M20 ....114 B3
  SLFD M6 ....64 B2
Malvern Rd *MDTN* M24 ....17 D4
Malvern Rw *HULME* M15 * 84 B3
Malvern St *OLDS* OL8 ....22 A4
Manby Rd *GTN* M18 ....105 C1
Manby Sq *GTN* M18 ....105 C1
Manchester New Rd *MDTN* M24 ....17 C3
Manchester Old Rd *MDTN* M24 ....15 D2
Manchester Rd *AULW* OL7 ....77 C1
  CCHDY M21 ....99 C4
  CCHDY M21 ....111 D1
  DROY M43 ....74 B4
  DTN/ASHW M34 ....93 C2
  DTN/ASHW M34 ....107 C1
  HTNM SK4 ....119 C4
  OLDS OL8 ....39 D1
  SWIN M27 ....25 C4
  SWIN M27 ....26 A2
  SWIN M27 ....46 A3
Manchester St *OLDTF/WHR* M16 ....84 B4
Mancroft Wk *CMANE* M1 ....8 C3
Mancunian Wy *WGTN/LGST* M12 ....9 F3
Mandarin Wk *SLFD* M6 * 66 B2
Mandeville St *BNG/LEV* M19 ....118 A1
Mandley Av *NEWH/MOS* M40 * 37 C3
Mandley Park Av *BRO* M7 ....50 B2
Manet Cl *BRO* M7 ....49 C1
Mangle St *CMANE* M1 ....4 C4
Mango Pl *SLFD* M6 ....66 B3
Manifold St *SLFD* M6 ....49 C4
Manilla Wk *OP/CLY* M11 ....72 A4
Manipur St *OP/CLY* M11 ....88 B1
Manley Av *SWIN* M27 ....26 A1
Manley Rd *CCHDY* M21 ....99 D4
  OLDS OL8 ....40 B1
  OLDTF/WHR M16 ....100 B3
Manley St *BRO* M7 ....50 A3
Mannington Dr *BKLY* M9 ....52 B3
Mannock St *OLDS* OL8 ....22 A3
Manor Av *OLDTF/WHR* M16 ....100 A3
  URM M41 ....94 A4
Manor Cl *CHAD* OL9 ....21 C1
Manor Ct *STRET* M32 ....96 A4
Manor Dr *CCHDY* M21 ....123 C1
Manor Ml *CHAD* OL9 * 21 C1
Manor Pk *URM* M41 ....94 A4
Manor Rd *BNG/LEV* M19 ....105 C3
  DROY M43 ....74 B4
  DTN/ASHW M34 ....93 C2
  MDTN M24 ....17 C3
  RDSH SK5 ....121 C4
  SALE M33 ....109 C4
  SLFD M6 ....65 C1
  STRET M32 ....96 A4
  SWIN M27 ....45 C3
Manor St *WGTN/LGST* M12 ....9 E3
Mansfield Av *BKLY* M9 ....34 A1
Mansfield Dr *BKLY* M9 ....34 B1
Mansfield Rd *BKLY* M9 ....34 B1
Mansford Dr *NEWH/MOS* M40 ....54 A4
Manshaw Crs *DTN/ASHW* M34 ....92 B2
Manshaw Rd *OP/CLY* M11 ....92 B2
Manson Av *HULME* M15 ....6 A4
Manstead Wk *NEWH/MOS* M40 * 71 D3
Manswood Dr *CHH* M8 ....51 D2
Manthorpe Av *WALK* M28 ....42 B2
Manton Av *BKLY* M9 ....36 A2
  DTN/ASHW M34 ....107 C3
Manton Cl *BRO* M7 ....51 C3
Manvers St *RDSH* SK5 ....129 D2
Manwaring St *FAIL* M35 ....56 B1

Maple Av *CCHDY* M21 ....112 A1
  DTN/ASHW M34 ....76 A4
  ECC M30 ....60 B1
  STRET M32 ....97 C4
  WHTF M45 ....11 C2
Maple Cl *MDTN* M24 ....19 C1
  SLFD M6 ....66 B4
Mapledon Rd *BKLY* M9 ....54 A1
Maple Gv *FAIL* M35 ....56 B4
  NEWH/MOS M40 ....37 D3
  PWCH M25 ....11 D3
Maple Rd *SWIN* M27 ....44 B3
Maple St *OLDS* OL8 ....39 D2
Maplewood Cl *BKLY* M9 ....33 D3
Maplewood Ct *BRO* M7 ....50 A2
Maplin Cl *BRUN/LGST* M13 ....9 E4
Marble St *CMANW* M2 ....4 A4
Marbury Av *RUSH/FAL* M14 ....102 A4
Marbury Rd *HTNM* SK4 ....119 C2
Marcer Rd *NEWH/MOS* M40 ....71 C3
March Av *HTNM* SK4 ....128 A3
Marchers Ms *ECC* M30 ....61 C4
Marchioness St *GTN* M18 * 92 A3
Marchmont Cl *BRUN/LGST* M13 ....88 A3
Marchwood Av *CCHDY* M21 ....100 A4
Marcliffe Dr *BNG/LEV* M19 ....105 D4
Marcliff Gv *HTNM* SK4 ....128 A3
Marcus Gv *RUSH/FAL* M14 ....102 B3
Mardale Av *DID/WITH* M20 ....115 D4
  SWIN M27 ....24 B3
Mardale Cl *PWCH* M25 ....12 B2
Mardale Rd *SWIN* M27 ....44 A3
Marfield *BKLY* M9 * 34 B4
Marfield Av *CHAD* OL9 ....20 B4
Margaret Ashton Cl *BKLY* M9 ....54 A2
Margaret Rd *DROY* M43 ....74 B3
Margaret Sands St *HULME* M15 ....85 C3
Margaret St *OLDS* OL8 ....39 C3
  RDSH SK5 ....119 D2
Margate Av *NEWH/MOS* M40 ....55 C4
Margate Rd *RDSH* SK5 ....120 A2
Margrove Cl *FAIL* M35 ....58 B2
Margrove Rd *SLFD* M6 ....64 B1
Marguerita Rd *NEWH/MOS* M40 ....74 A1
Marham Cl *CCHDY* M21 * 113 D3
Marie St *BRO* M7 * 50 B2
Mariman Dr *CHH* M8 ....32 B3
Marina Crs *OP/CLY* M11 ....73 C2
Marina Rd *DROY* M43 ....76 A3
Marion St *OLDS* OL8 ....41 C2
Marjorie Cl *GTN* M18 ....90 A3
Mark Av *SLFD* M6 ....67 C1
Market Pl *OLD* OL1 * 22 B2
  STKP SK1 ....130 A4
Market St *CMANE* M1 ....4 A4
  DROY M43 ....92 B1
  SWIN M27 ....26 B4
Market Wy *SLFD* M6 ....66 A2
Markfield Av *BRUN/LGST* M13 ....88 A3
Markham Cl *WGTN/LGST* M12 ....88 B1
Markington St *RUSH/FAL* M14 ....101 D2
Mark St *CHAD* OL9 ....22 A2
Marland Av *OLDS* OL8 ....41 D4
Marland Crs *RDSH* SK5 ....120 A1
Marland Fold La *OLDS* OL8 ....41 C4
Marland St *CHAD* OL9 ....38 B2
Marland Wy *STRET* M32 ....97 C2
Marlborough Av *OLDTF/WHR* M16 ....99 D4
Marlborough Dr *FAIL* M35 ....56 B3
  HTNM SK4 ....129 C1
Marlborough Rd *BRO* M7 ....51 C3
  ECC M30 ....63 D1
  STRET M32 ....96 B2
Marlborough St *OLDE* OL4 ....23 D3
Marlcroft Av *HTNM* SK4 ....128 A3
Marley Dr *SALE* M33 ....108 B3
Marleyer Cl *NEWH/MOS* M40 ....55 D2

Marley Rd *BNG/LEV* M19 ....**118** A1
Marlfield St *BKLY* M9 ....**34** B4
Marlinford Dr *NEWH/MOS* M40 ....**55** D4
Marlow Dr *SWIN* M27 ....**44** B3
Marlowe Dr *DID/WITH* M20 ....**125** C1
Marlow Rd *BKLY* M9 ....**35** C4
Marmion Dr *CCHDY* M21 ....**111** D1
Marple Cl *OLDS* OL8 ....**40** A3
Marple Gv *STRET* M32 ....**96** B2
Marple St *HULME* M15 ....**85** C4
Marquis St *BNG/LEV* M19 ....**106** A4
Marriotts Ct *CMANW* M2 ....**4** A4
Marriott St *DID/WITH* M20 ....**115** C3
   STKP SK1..**133** C1
Marron Pl *CMANW* M2 * **7** E1
Marsden Cl *AULW* OL7 ....**59** D4
Marsden St *CMANW* M2 ....**3** F4
   ECC M30 ....**61** D2
   MDTN M24 ....**18** B2
Marshall Ct *OLD* OL1 * **22** B1
Marshall Rd *BNG/LEV* M19 ....**104** B4
Marshall Stevens Wy *TRPK* M17 ....**81** C4
Marshall St *ANC* M4 ....**4** C2
   WGTN/LGST M12 ....**9** F5
Marsham Cl *BRUN/LGST* M13 ....**103** D1
Marshbrook Dr *BKLY* M9 ....**33** D4
Marsh Cl *EDGY/DAV* SK3 ....**132** A3
Marshfield Wk *BRUN/LGST* M13 ....**87** D3
Marsland St *STKP* SK1 ....**130** A3
Marsland St North *BRO* M7 ....**50** B2
Marsland St South *BRO* M7 ....**51** C2
Mars St *CHAD* OL9 ....**21** D2
Marston Cl *FAIL* M35 ....**58** A3
   WHTF M45 ....**12** B1
Marston Rd *BRO* M7 ....**50** B1
   STRET M32 ....**97** D3
Marston Wy South *CMANE* M1 * **3** F4
Marsworth Dr *ANC* M4 * **5** F3
Martha St *OLD* OL1 ....**22** A1
Martindale Crs *WGTN/LGST* M12 ....**88** B3
Martingale Wy *DROY* M43 ....**77** C2
Martin Rd *SWIN* M27 ....**27** C3
Martin St *ORD* M5 ....**65** C3
Martlesham Wk *ANC* M4 * **4** B2
Martlet Cl *RUSH/FAL* M14 ....**101** D4
Marton Av *DID/WITH* M20 ....**125** D3
Marton Gra *PWCH* M25 ....**31** D3
Marton Gn *EDGY/DAV* SK3 ....**132** A3
Marton Gv *HTNM* SK4 ....**119** D3
Maryfield Ct *OLDTF/WHR* M16 * **113** D1
Mary France St *HULME* M15 ....**6** C5
Mary St *CSLFD* M3 ....**69** C2
   DROY M43 ....**76** A4
   STKP SK1...**130** B3
Masboro St *CHH* M8 ....**51** C4
Masefield Av *PWCH* M25 ....**29** C2
Masefield Crs *DROY* M43 ....**75** D4
Masefield Dr *HTNM* SK4 ....**127** D3
Masefield Gv *RDSH* SK5 ....**106** B4
Masefield Rd *DROY* M43 ....**75** D4
Mason St *ANC* M4 ....**4** C2
Massey Av *FAIL* M35 ....**58** A1
Massey St *STKP* SK1 ....**130** A4
Matham Wk *HULME* M15 ....**8** A4
Mather Av *ECC* M30 ....**62** B3
   PWCH M25 ....**30** B4
Mather Rd *ECC* M30 ....**62** B3
Mather St *FAIL* M35 ....**56** A2
Mather Wy *SLFD* M6 * **66** B2
Matisse Wy *BRO* M7 ....**49** C1
Matley Gn *RDSH* SK5 ....**121** D3
Matlock Av *BRO* M7 ....**48** B2
   DID/WITH M20 ....**114** A3
Matlock Rd *RDSH* SK5 ....**107** C4
   STRET M32 ....**95** D2
Matlock St *ECC* M30 ....**78** B1
Matt Busby Cl *SWIN* M27 ....**46** A2

Matthews La *BNG/LEV* M19 ....**105** C3
Matthew's St *WGTN/LGST* M12 ....**89** C2
Mattison St *OP/CLY* M11 ....**91** D2
Mauldeth Cl *HTNM* SK4 ....**127** D2
Mauldeth Rd *BNG/LEV* M19 ....**127** C1
   DID/WITH M20 ....**126** A1
   RUSH/FAL M14 ....**116** A2
Mauldeth Rd West *CCHDY* M21 ....**113** D1
Maureen Av *CHH* M8 ....**51** D1
Maurice Dr *SLFD* M6 ....**66** A1
Maurice St *SLFD* M6 ....**66** A1
Mawdsley Dr *CHH* M8 ....**52** B1
Max Woosnam Wk *RUSH/FAL* M14 ......**101** D2
Mayan Av *CSLFD* M3 ....**2** A2
May Av *HTNM* SK4 ....**128** B3
Mayberth Av *CHH* M8 ....**32** B3
Mayburn Cl *MDTN* M24 ....**18** B4
Maybury St *GTN* M18 ....**91** D3
Maycroft Av *DID/WITH* M20 ....**115** D4
May Dr *BNG/LEV* M19 ....**117** C3
Mayes Gdns *ANC* M4 ....**71** C4
Mayes St *ANC* M4 ....**4** B2
Mayfair Av *SLFD* M6 ....**64** A2
   WHTF M45 ....**11** C2
Mayfair Crs *FAIL* M35 ....**58** A1
Mayfair Ms *DID/WITH* M20 * **124** A1
Mayfair Pk *DID/WITH* M20 * **124** A1
Mayfield Av *RDSH* SK5 ....**120** A4
   STRET M32 ....**96** A4
   WALK M28 ....**43** D3
Mayfield Gv *GTN* M18 ....**107** C2
   RDSH SK5 ....**120** A4
Mayfield Rd *BRO* M7 ....**30** A4
   OLDTF/WHR M16 ....**100** B2
Mayflower Av *ORD* M5 ....**83** D1
Mayford Rd *BNG/LEV* M19 ....**104** B3
Maygate *CHAD* OL9 ....**22** A1
May Gv *BNG/LEV* M19 ....**118** A3
Mayhill Dr *SLFD* M6 ....**63** D1
   WALK M28 ....**42** D1
Mayhurst Av *CCHDY* M21 ....**123** C2
Mayorlowe Av *RDSH* SK5 ....**131** D1
Mayor St *CHAD* OL9 ....**21** D2
Mayo St *WGTN/LGST* M12 ....**88** A1
Maypool Dr *RDSH* SK5 ....**120** A3
May Rd *OLDTF/WHR* M16 ....**100** A2
   SWIN M27 ....**46** A3
May St *ECC* M30 ....**61** D1
   NEWH/MOS M40 ....**55** D4
   OLDS OL8 ....**39** D1
Mayton St *OP/CLY* M11 ....**89** D1
Mayville Dr *DID/WITH* M20 ....**115** C4
McConnell Rd *NEWH/MOS* M40 ....**54** B2
McCready Dr *ORD* M5 * **84** A1
McDonough Cl *OLDS* OL8 ....**41** D4
McKie Cl *OLDS* OL8 ....**41** D2
McLaren Ct *CCHDY* M21 ....**98** B4
Meachin Av *CCHDY* M21 ....**112** B4
Meade Gv *BRUN/LGST* M13 ....**104** A2
Meade Hill Rd *CHH* M8 ....**32** A2
   PWCH M25 ....**31** D2
Meadfoot Av *PWCH* M25 ....**30** B2
Meadfoot Rd *GTN* M18 ....**91** C3
Meadow Av *SWIN* M27 ....**27** C4
Meadow Bank *CCHDY* M21 ....**111** D2
   HTNM SK4 ....**128** A3
Meadowbank Cl *FAIL* M35 ....**57** D3
Meadow Bank Ct *STRET* M32 ....**96** A4
Meadow Cl *STRET* M32 ....**97** D4
Meadow Ct *CCHDY* M21 ....**111** C1
Meadowgate *URM* M41 ....**94** A4
   WALK M28 ....**42** A1
Meadowgate Rd *SLFD* M6 ....**64** B3
Meadow La *OLDS* OL8 ....**42** A4
   WALK M28 ....**42** A4
Meadow Rd *BRO* M7 ....**67** D3
   MDTN M24 ....**16** B3

URM M41..**94** A4
Meadows Rd *HTNM* SK4..................**118** B3
SALE M33..**109** D3
The Meadows *MDTN* M24..................**18** A3
PWCH M25..**30** A1
Meadow Wy *NEWH/MOS* M40..........**35** D4
The Meads *CHAD* OL9..........................**20** B3
The Mead *CCHDY* M21 *....................**112** A2
ORD M5..**65** D3
Meadway *CHAD* OL9..............................**37** D3
Mealhouse Brow *STKP* SK1 *..........**130** A4
Meal St *HTNM* SK4..............................**129** D2
Measham Ms *CMANE* M1 *..................**8** A3
Medlock Dr *OLDS* OL8..........................**41** D4
Medlock Rd *FAIL* M35..........................**57** D4
Medlock St *DROY* M43..........................**75** D3
HULME M15..**7** E3
OLD OL1..**23** D2
Medlock Wy *WHTF* M45........................**12** B1
Medway Cl *OLDS* OL8............................**39** D2
ORD M5..**65** D3
Medway Rd *OLDS* OL8............................**39** D2
Medway Wk *NEWH/MOS* M40..............**71** C2
Meech St *OP/CLY* M11..........................**90** B1
Mee's Sq *ECC* M30..............................**79** C1
Megna Cl *CHAD* OL9............................**22** A2
Melanie Dr *RDSH* SK5........................**120** A1
Melba St *OP/CLY* M11..........................**91** D1
Melbourne Av *CHAD* OL9....................**20** B2
STRET M32..**97** C3
Melbourne St *BKLY* M9........................**53** D1
BRO M7..**50** A4
CHAD OL9..**21** C2
HULME M15..**7** D4
RDSH SK5..**120** A1
SWIN M27..**46** A1
Melbury Av *DID/WITH* M20................**126** A1
Meldon Rd *BRUN/LGST* M13..............**103** D3
Meldrum St *OLDS* OL8..........................**41** C1
Melford Av *NEWH/MOS* M40..............**37** D4
Melfort Av *STRET* M32........................**97** D4
Melksham Cl *ORD* M5............................**67** C3
Melland Av *CCHDY* M21......................**112** B4
Melland Rd *GTN* M18..........................**105** D2
Meller Rd *BRUN/LGST* M13..............**104** A3
Melling Av *HTNM* SK4........................**119** D3
Melling St *WGTN/LGST* M12..............**104** B1
Mellors Rd *TRPK* M17............................**81** C2
Mellor St *DROY* M43..........................**75** C4
ECC M30..**62** A4
FAIL M35..**56** A2
NEWH/MOS M40..**71** C2
OLDS OL8..**39** D3
PWCH M25..**29** C1
STRET M32..**97** C1
Mellor Wy *CHAD* OL9............................**38** B1
Mellowstone Dr *CCHDY* M21............**114** A1
Melloy Pl *CHH* M8..................................**69** D1
Melon Pl *SLFD* M6..................................**67** C1
Melrose Av *DID/WITH* M20................**125** D2
ECC M30..**60** B1
Melrose Ct *CHAD* OL9 *........................**38** B1
Melrose Rd *NEWH/MOS* M40..............**55** D4
Meltham Av *DID/WITH* M20................**114** B3
Meltham Cl *HTNM* SK4......................**126** B4
Meltham Rd *HTNM* SK4......................**126** B4
Melton Av *DTN/ASHW* M34................**107** D2
Melton Rd *CHH* M8................................**31** D4
Melton St *BKLY* M9..............................**35** C4
RDSH SK5..**130** A1
Melverley Rd *BKLY* M9........................**14** B4
Melville Cl *OP/CLY* M11......................**91** D2
Melville Rd *STRET* M32........................**96** A2
Melville St *CSLFD* M3..............................**2** B3
Memorial Cottages *SWIN* M27 *..........**26** A2
Menai Rd *EDGY/DAV* SK3..................**132** B3
Mendip Cl *CHAD* OL9 *..........................**20** B4

HTNM SK4..**129** D2
Mendip Rd *OLDS* OL8............................**40** A2
Menston Av *NEWH/MOS* M40..............**37** D4
Mentone Rd *HTNM* SK4......................**128** A2
Mentor St *BRUN/LGST* M13..............**104** A3
Mercer Rd *GTN* M18..............................**91** C4
Mercer St *BNG/LEV* M19....................**105** C3
DROY M43..**76** A3
Merchants Quay *SALQ* M50................**83** D3
Mercian Wy *EDGY/DAV* SK3..............**132** B2
Mercury Pk *URM* M41 *........................**80** A3
Mercury Wy *URM* M41............................**80** A4
Mere Av *DROY* M43................................**91** D1
MDTN M24..**17** D3
SLFD M6..**65** D3
Meredew Av *SWIN* M27........................**44** B3
Meredith St *RUSH/FAL* M14..............**116** A2
Mere Dr *DID/WITH* M20......................**125** C1
SWIN M27..**26** B3
Mereland Av *DID/WITH* M20..............**125** D1
Meridian Pl *DID/WITH* M20................**124** B1
Merlewood Av *BNG/LEV* M19............**118** B3
DTN/ASHW M34 *......................................**76** A4
Merlewood Dr *SWIN* M27....................**43** D3
Merlin Dr *SWIN* M27............................**27** C3
Merlyn Av *DID/WITH* M20..................**125** D1
SALE M33..**109** D4
Merridale Rd *NEWH/MOS* M40..........**36** B3
Merrill St *ANC* M4................................**71** C4
Merriman St *OLDTF/WHR* M16..........**100** B1
Merrow Wk *CMANE* M1............................**8** C3
Merrybower Rd *BRO* M7......................**50** B1
Merrydale Av *ECC* M30........................**62** B1
Merseybank Av *CCHDY* M21..............**123** C1
Mersey Crs *DID/WITH* M20................**123** C2
Mersey Mdw *DID/WITH* M20..............**124** A2
Mersey Rd *DID/WITH* M20..................**124** A2
HTNM SK4..**127** C3
SALE M33..**109** C3
Mersey Rd North *FAIL* M35................**38** B4
Mersey Sq *STKP* SK1..........................**129** D4
Mersey St *DROY* M43............................**91** D1
STKP SK1..**130** B3
Merseyway *STKP* SK1..........................**129** D3
Merton Av *OLDS* OL8............................**40** A2
Merton Dr *DROY* M43............................**74** B4
Merton Gv *CHAD* OL9............................**37** C3
Merton Rd *PWCH* M25..........................**12** B4
SALE M33..**108** B3
Merville Av *NEWH/MOS* M40..............**35** C4
Mervyn Rd *BRO* M7..............................**48** B3
Merwood Gv *RUSH/FAL* M14..............**103** D1
Mesnefield Rd *BRO* M7........................**48** B1
Methuen St *WGTN/LGST* M12............**105** C2
The Mews *NEWH/MOS* M40..................**71** D2
PWCH M25..**30** A2
WHTF M45..**10** A1
Meyer St *EDGY/DAV* SK3 *................**133** C3
Meyrick Rd *SLFD* M6............................**66** B2
Michael St *MDTN* M24..........................**17** C3
Michigan Av *SALQ* M50........................**83** C1
Mickleby Wk *NEWH/MOS* M40 *..........**5** F1
Micklehurst Av *DID/WITH* M20..........**123** D1
Middlebourne St *SLFD* M6..................**65** D3
Middlegate *NEWH/MOS* M40................**37** C2
Middle Ga *OLDS* OL8............................**40** B3
Middleham St *RUSH/FAL* M14............**101** D3
Middle Hillgate *STKP* SK1..................**133** C1
Middlesex Rd *BKLY* M9........................**34** A3
RDSH SK5..**121** D3
Middlesex Wk *CHAD* OL9 *..................**22** A3
Middlestone Dr *BKLY* M9......................**53** C2
Middleton Av *FAIL* M35........................**57** C2
Middleton Old Rd *BKLY* M9................**34** A3
Middleton Rd *BKLY* M9........................**14** A4
CHAD OL9..**20** A1
CHH M8..**32** A3

RDSH SK5..**107** C3
Middleton Wy *MDTN* M24 ....**17** C1
Middlewood Dr *HTNM* SK4...........**127** D4
Middlewood Gn *CHAD* OL9 ....**20** B2
Middlewood St *ORD* M5 ....**67** D4
Midford Av *ECC* M30.......................**61** C3
Midgley Av *GTN* M18 ....**91** D3
Midgley St *SWIN* M27 ....**44** A3
Midhurst Av *NEWH/MOS* M40 * **73** C1
Midland Rd *RDSH* SK5 ....**107** C3
Midlothian St *OP/CLY* M11 ....**73** C3
Midville Rd *OP/CLY* M11.................**73** D2
Midway St *WGTN/LGST* M12 ....**104** B3
Milan St *BRO* M7 ....**50** B3
Milburn Av *NTHM/RTH* M23 ....**122** A3
Milden Cl *DID/WITH* M20 * **125** D1
Mildred Av *PWCH* M25 ....**30** B3
Mildred St *BRO* M7 ....**49** D4
Miles St *WGTN/LGST* M12 ....**89** D2
Milford Av *OLDS* OL8........................**39** D3
Milford Dr *BNG/LEV* M19................**118** B2
Milford St *BKLY* M9..........................**33** C2
SLFD M6...**65** D4
Milk St *CMANW* M2...........................**4** A4
Milkwood Gv *GTN* M18...................**106** A1
Millais St *NEWH/MOS* M40 ....**54** B1
Millard St *CHAD* OL9 ....**20** B2
Millbank St *CMANE* M1 ....**5** E5
Millbrook St *STKP* SK1...................**133** C1
Mill Brow *CHH* M8.............................**33** D3
WALK M28.....................................**42** A3
Miller Rd *OLDS* OL8..........................**40** B2
Millers Ct *ORD* M5 ....**63** D3
Millers St *ECC* M30...........................**61** D4
Miller St *ANC* M4 ....**4** B2
Mill Fold Rd *MDTN* M24...................**17** C2
Millgate *ANC* M4 * **4** A3
Mill Ga *OLDS* OL8 ....**40** A2
Millgate *STKP* SK1...........................**130** A3
Millgate La *DID/WITH* M20...........**125** C4
Mill Green St *WGTN/LGST* M12 *......**88** C1
Millhall Cl *HULME* M15....................**85** D4
Millhead Av *NEWH/MOS* M40 ....**71** D3
Millington Wk *HULME* M15 *..............**6** B5
Mill La *CHAD* OL9 ....**39** D1
FAIL M35.......................................**55** D2
RDSH SK5....................................**120** B2
WYTH/NTH M22..........................**123** D4
Millom Av *NTHM/RTH* M23 ....**122** A4
Millow St *ANC* M4 ....**4** A1
Mills Farm Cl *OLDS* OL8..................**41** D4
Millstream La *NEWH/MOS* M40.......**74** B2
Mill St *FAIL* M35 ....**55** D2
OP/CLY M11 ....**89** D1
SLFD M6...**66** B1
Millwall Cl *GTN* M18 ....**91** C4
Millwright St *NEWH/MOS* M40 ....**55** C4
Milne Cl *WGTN/LGST* M12...............**89** D3
Milner St *OLDTF/WHR* M16 ....**100** A1
SWIN M27 ....**45** D1
Milne St *CHAD* OL9 ....**21** C2
CHAD OL9 ....**21** D4
Milnrow Cl *BRUN/LGST* M13 ....**9** C3
Milnthorpe St *SLFD* M6 ....**48** B4
Milnthorpe Wy *WGTN/LGST* M12 ....**88** B3
Milo St *BKLY* M9 * **34** A2
Milton Av *DROY* M43 ....**75** D4
ORD M5 * **65** C3
Milton Cl *STRET* M32 ....**97** D2
Milton Ct *BNG/LEV* M19 ....**126** B1
Milton Dr *OLDS* OL9 ....**20** B3
SALE M33.....................................**108** B3
Milton Gv *OLDTF/WHR* M16 ....**99** D3
SALE M33.....................................**108** B3
Milton Pl *SLFD* M6..............................**66** B2
Milton Rd *DTN/ASHW* M34 ....**77** C4

PWCH M25 ....**12** B4
STRET M32 ....**97** D2
SWIN M27 ....**25** C4
Milton St *BRO* M7 ....**68** B1
ECC M30 ....**62** A3
Milverton Rd *RUSH/FAL* M14.........**103** C2
Milwain Rd *BNG/LEV* M19...............**117** C1
STRET M32 ....**96** B4
Mimosa Dr *SWIN* M27.......................**26** A3
Mincing St *ANC* M4 * **4** B1
Minden Cl *DID/WITH* M20.................**125** D1
Minden St *SLFD* M6...........................**47** D3
Minehead Av *DID/WITH* M20...........**114** A2
Minor St *FAIL* M35 ....**57** D1
OLDS OL8 ....**22** B4
Minshull St *CMANE* M1 ....**4** B5
Minshull St South *CMANE* M1 ....**8** C1
Minster Rd *BKLY* M9 ....**54** A1
Minstrel Cl *SWIN* M27 ....**44** A2
Minton St *NEWH/MOS* M40 ....**53** D1
OLDE OL4.....................................**23** D4
Mirabel St *CSLFD* M3...........................**3** E1
Mirfield Av *BKLY* M9 ....**34** A1
HTNM SK4...................................**128** A3
OLDS OL8 ....**40** B1
Mirfield Dr *ECC* M30..........................**62** A3
Mirfield Rd *BKLY* M9 ....**34** A1
Miriam St *FAIL* M35 ....**57** C1
Missouri Av *SALQ* M50.......................**65** D4
Mistletoe Gv *CSLFD* M3 * **2** B1
Mitcham Av *BKLY* M9..........................**35** D2
Mitchells Quay *FAIL* M35...................**56** B2
Mitchell St *ECC* M30..........................**61** D2
NEWH/MOS M40.........................**55** C4
OLD OL1.......................................**22** A1
OP/CLY M11 * **89** C2
Mitcheson Gdns *SLFD* M6..................**66** A2
Mitford Rd *RUSH/FAL* M14..............**115** D2
Mitford St *STRET* M32........................**96** B4
Mitre Rd *BRUN/LGST* M13................**104** A1
Mitre St *FAIL* M35...............................**57** C1
Mobberley Cl *BNG/LEV* M19 ....**126** B1
Mocha Pde *BRO* M7............................**68** A2
Mode Hill La *WHTF* M45....................**12** A1
Mode Wheel Rd South *SALQ* M50.....**65** C4
Modwen Rd *ORD* M5 * **84** A3
Mold St *OLD* OL1................................**22** B1
Molyneux Rd *BNG/LEV* M19............**117** C1
Mona Av *STRET* M32...........................**96** B2
Monaco Dr *WYTH/NTH* M22.............**123** C3
Mona Rd *CHAD* OL9 ....**21** C4
Monart Rd *BKLY* M9............................**34** B4
Mona St *SLFD* M6.................................**66** B1
Monica Av *CHH* M8.............................**32** A3
Monica Gv *BNG/LEV* M19.................**117** C1
Monks Hall Gv *ECC* M30....................**63** C3
Monkton Av *GTN* M18 ....**105** D2
Monkwood Dr *BKLY* M9 * **53** D1
Monmouth Av *SALE* M33..................**108** A4
Monmouth St *CHAD* OL9...................**21** D4
GTN M18.......................................**91** D3
MDTN M24....................................**31** B1
Monroe Cl *SLFD* M6............................**65** D1
Monsal Av *BRO* M7..............................**51** C1
Monsall Rd *NEWH/MOS* M40.............**53** D3
Monsall St *NEWH/MOS* M40..............**53** D4
OLDS OL8 ....**40** B2
Montague Rd *OLDTF/WHR* M16........**83** D4
Montana Sq *OP/CLY* M11...................**91** D2
Montcliffe Crs *OLDTF/WHR* M16......**101** C4
Monteagle St *BKLY* M9.......................**33** C1
Montford St *SALQ* M50 ....**83** C1
Montgomery Rd *BRUN/LGST* M13....**104** A3
Montgomery St *OLDS* OL8.................**39** C3
Monton Av *ECC* M30............................**62** B2

Montondale *ECC* M30 ....**61** D2
Montonfields Rd *ECC* M30 ....**61** D2
Monton Gn *ECC* M30 ....**62** A1
Monton La *ECC* M30 ....**62** B3
Monton Mill Gdns *ECC* M30 ....**61** D2
Monton Rd *ECC* M30 ....**62** A2
   RDSH SK5 ....**131** D1
Monton St *RUSH/FAL* M14 ....**101** D1
Montreal St *BNG/LEV* M19 ....**105** C4
   OLDS OL8 ....**41** C1
Montrose Av *DID/WITH* M20 ....**114** A4
   STRET M32 ....**96** A3
Montrose Crs *BNG/LEV* M19 ....**104** B4
Moon Gv *RUSH/FAL* M14 ....**103** C3
Moon St *CHAD* OL9 * **21** D2
Moorby Av *BNG/LEV* M19 ....**126** B1
Moorby St *OLD* OL1 ....**23** D1
Moorclose St *MDTN* M24 ....**18** B1
Moorcock Av *SWIN* M27 ....**46** A1
Moorcroft Dr *BNG/LEV* M19 ....**127** C1
Moorcroft St *DROY* M43 * **75** D4
   OLDS OL8 ....**39** D3
Moordale St *DID/WITH* M20 ....**114** B4
Moordown Cl *CHH* M8 ....**52** A3
Moor End St *BRO* M7 ....**49** D1
Moorfield *WALK* M28 ....**42** A1
Moorfield Av *DID/WITH* M20 ....**115** D2
Moorfield Cl *SWIN* M27 ....**44** A3
Moorfield Gv *HTNM* SK4 ....**128** A1
Moorfield Rd *DID/WITH* M20 ....**124** A1
   OLDS OL8 ....**39** C3
   SLFD M6 ....**47** C4
   SWIN M27 ....**43** D3
Moorfield St *DID/WITH* M20 ....**115** C2
Moorgate Av *DID/WITH* M20 ....**114** A3
Moorhead St *ANC* M4 ....**5** D1
The Moorings *TRPK* M17 ....**81** C1
The Moorings *WALK* M28 ....**42** B4
Moorland Av *CHH* M8 ....**32** A3
   DROY M43 ....**74** B4
Moorland Rd *DID/WITH* M20 ....**125** C2
Moor La *BRO* M7 ....**48** B1
Moor Park Rd *DID/WITH* M20 * **125** D4
Moorsholme Av *NEWH/MOS* M40 ......**54** B2
Moorside *SWIN* M27 ....**44** A2
Moorside Av *DROY* M43 ....**76** B3
Moorside Crs *DROY* M43 ....**76** B3
Moorside Rd *BRO* M7 ....**30** B4
   CHH M8 * **32** B4
   HTNM SK4 ....**127** D3
   SWIN M27 ....**43** D2
Moorside St *DROY* M43 ....**76** A3
Moorsley Dr *BKLY* M9 ....**35** C1
Moor St *ECC* M30 ....**61** C4
   SWIN M27 ....**45** C2
Moorton Av *BNG/LEV* M19 ....**117** C2
Moorton Pk *BNG/LEV* M19 ....**117** C2
Moortop Cl *BKLY* M9 ....**15** D4
Moor Top Pl *HTNM* SK4 ....**128** A2
Moorville Rd *SLFD* M6 ....**46** B4
Moorway Dr *BKLY* M9 ....**35** D1
Moran Wk *HULME* M15 ....**86** A3
Mora St *BKLY* M9 ....**54** A2
Moravian Fld *DROY* M43 * **92** B1
Moray Rd *CHAD* OL9 ....**38** B1
Morbourne Cl *WGTN/LGST* M12 ....**88** B3
Morecambe Cl *NEWH/MOS* M40 ....**55** C3
Moreton Av *STRET* M32 ....**97** C3
Moreton St *CHAD* OL9 ....**20** A1
Morgan Pl *RDSH* SK5 ....**130** A1
Morland Rd *OLDTF/WHR* M16 ....**99** D1
Morley Av *RUSH/FAL* M14 ....**101** D4
   SWIN M27 ....**44** B3
Morley St *WHTF* M45 ....**11** C1
Morna Wk *WGTN/LGST* M12 ....**88** A1
Morningside Cl *OP/CLY* M11 ....**92** A1
Mornington Crs *RUSH/FAL* M14 ....**114** B1

Mornington Rd *SALE* M33 ....**110** A4
Morpeth Cl *AULW* OL7 ....**77** D1
   WGTN/LGST M12 ....**88** B4
Morpeth St *SWIN* M27 ....**44** B3
Morris St *DID/WITH* M20 ....**115** C2
   OLDE OL4 ....**23** D4
Morrowfield Av *CHH* M8 ....**51** C2
Morse Rd *NEWH/MOS* M40 ....**55** C4
Mortimer Av *BKLY* M9 ....**34** B1
Mortlake Dr *NEWH/MOS* M40 ....**55** C4
Morton St *FAIL* M35 ....**55** D2
   HTNM SK4 ....**129** D1
Morville Dr *BNG/LEV* M19 ....**100** A4
Morville St *CMANE* M1 * **9** E1
Moscow Rd *EDGY/DAV* SK3 ....**132** A2
Moscow Rd East *EDGY/DAV* SK3.......**132** B2
Moseley Av *BNG/LEV* M19 ....**117** C1
   RUSH/FAL M14 ....**116** B1
Moseley St *EDGY/DAV* SK3 ....**132** B1
Mosley Rd *TRPK* M17 ....**96** B1
Mosley Rd North *TRPK* M17 ....**81** D1
Mosley St *CMANW* M2 * **3** F5
Moss Bank *CHH* M8 ....**51** C2
Moss Bank Av *DROY* M43 ....**76** B3
Moss Bank Ct *DROY* M43 * **76** B3
Moss Bank Gv *SWIN* M27 ....**24** B3
Moss Bank Rd *SWIN* M27 ....**25** C3
Mossbray Av *BNG/LEV* M19 ....**126** A1
Moss Brook Rd *BKLY* M9 ....**53** D2
Mossclough Ct *BKLY* M9 ....**53** D2
Moss Colliery Rd *SWIN* M27 ....**25** D2
Mosscot Wk *BRUN/LGST* M13 ....**9** D1
Moss Farm Cl *MDTN* M24 ....**18** A3
Mossfield Cl *HTNM* SK4 ....**128** A3
Mossfield Dr *BKLY* M9 ....**35** D1
Mossfield Rd *SWIN* M27 ....**25** D3
Moss Grange Av *OLDTF/WHR* M16 * ...**100** A2
Mosshall Cl *HULME* M15 ....**85** C3
Moss Hey Dr *NTHM/RTH* M23 ....**122** B4
Moss House Ter *BKLY* M9 * **33** D4
Moss La *AULW* OL7 ....**77** D3
   MDTN M24 ....**17** C4
   SWIN M27 ....**25** C4
   URM M41 ....**79** D4
   WHTF M45 ....**11** C1
Moss La East *OLDTF/WHR* M16 ....**100** B3
Moss La West *HULME* M15 ....**100** A3
   RUSH/FAL M14 ....**101** D1
Mosslee Av *CHH* M8 ....**32** A2
Moss Meadow Rd *SLFD* M6 * **64** B1
Moss Park Rd *STRET* M32 ....**95** D3
Moss Rd *STRET* M32 ....**96** B2
Moss St *BRO* M7 ....**50** A4
   DROY M43 ....**76** A3
The Moss *MDTN* M24 ....**18** A3
Moss Vale Crs *STRET* M32 ....**95** C1
Moss Vale Rd *STRET* M32 ....**95** C2
   URM M41 ....**94** B3
Mossway *MDTN* M24 ....**17** C4
Mossylea Cl *MDTN* M24 ....**18** A4
Moston Bank Av *BKLY* M9 ....**53** D3
Moston La *BKLY* M9 ....**53** D1
   NEWH/MOS M40 ....**54** B1
Moston La East *NEWH/MOS* M40 ....**37** D4
Moston Rd *MDTN* M24 ....**19** C3
   RDSH SK5 ....**120** A2
Moston St *BRO* M7 ....**51** C2
Mostyn Av *RUSH/FAL* M14 ....**116** B1
Motherwell Av *BNG/LEV* M19 ....**104** B3
Mottram Av *CCHDY* M21 ....**112** B4
Mottram Fold *STKP* SK1 ....**133** C1
Mottram St *STKP* SK1 ....**133** C1
Mough La *CHAD* OL9 ....**37** C2
Mouldsworth Av *DID/WITH* M20 ......**114** B2
   HTNM SK4 ....**119** C3
Moulton St *CHH* M8 ....**68** B1
Mouncey St *CMANE* M1 * **8** A3

Mountain St *NEWH/MOS* M40.................**74** A1
   STKP SK1 *...**130** B3
Mountbatten St *GTN* M18......................**90** B4
Mount Carmel Crs *ORD* M5 *..............**84** B2
Mount Dr *URM* M41...............................**95** C3
Mountfield *PWCH* M25...........................**30** A1
Mountfield Wk *OP/CLY* M11..................**72** A4
Mount Fold *MDTN* M24.........................**17** D2
Mountford Av *CHH* M8..........................**32** A3
Mount Pleasant *MDTN* M24..................**15** D1
   PWCH M25..**13** D1
Mount Rd *GTN* M18...............................**90** A4
   HTNM SK4.......................................**128** B3
   MDTN M24..**17** D2
   PWCH M25..**12** B2
Mountside Crs *PWCH* M25....................**29** C1
Mount St *CMANW* M2..............................**7** F1
   CSLFD M3..**2** B2
   ECC M30...**78** B1
   SWIN M27...**45** C2
Mousell St *CHH* M8..............................**69** D1
Mowbray Av *PWCH* M25........................**30** B3
Mowbray St *OLD* OL1 *.........................**23** C3
   STKP SK3..**133** C1
Moxley Rd *CHH* M8...............................**31** D4
Mozart Cl *ANC* M4...................................**5** F2
Muirfield Cl *NEWH/MOS* M40................**55** D2
Mulberry Ct *SLFD* M6 *.........................**66** B2
Mulberry Ms *HTNM* SK4.......................**129** D3
Mulberry Mount St *EDGY/DAV* SK3......**132** B3
Mulberry Rd *SLFD* M6...........................**66** B3
Mulberry St *CMANW* M2..........................**3** E5
Mulberry Wk *DROY* M43........................**91** D1
Mulgrave Rd *WALK* M28........................**42** B1
Mulgrave St *SWIN* M27..........................**25** C4
Mull Av *WGTN/LGST* M12.....................**88** B4
Mullion Cl *BNG/LEV* M19......................**106** A3
Mullion Wk *CHH* M8...............................**52** A3
Mulmount Cl *OLDS* OL8.........................**39** D2
Munday St *ANC* M4................................**71** C4
Munn Rd *BKLY* M9.................................**15** C4
Munster St *ANC* M4 *...............................**4** C1
Muriel St *ANC* M4....................................**5** E3
Murray St *ANC* M4...................................**5** E3
   BRO M7...**50** A3
Museum St *CMANW* M2...........................**7** F1
Muslin St *ORD* M5..................................**67** D4
Myerscroft Cl *NEWH/MOS* M40............**56** A1
Myrtle Bank *PWCH* M25.........................**29** D4
Myrtle Cl *OLDS* OL8..............................**22** B4
Myrtle Gv *DROY* M43.............................**76** B3
   DTN/ASHW M34.............................**107** C2
   PWCH M25..**30** A3
Myrtleleaf Gv *ORD* M5 *.........................**65** C3
Myrtle Pl *BRO* M7...................................**67** D1
Myrtle St *OLDTF/WHR* M16 *.................**99** D1
   OP/CLY M11.....................................**88** B1
My St *ORD* M5..**65** D4
Mytton St *HULME* M15...........................**85** D4

N

Naburn Cl *RDSH* SK5...........................**121** D3
Naburn St *BRUN/LGST* M13.................**103** C1
Nada Rd *CHH* M8...................................**32** A4
Nadine St *SLFD* M6...............................**65** D2
Nadin St *OLDS* OL8................................**40** B2
Nairn Cl *NEWH/MOS* M40 *..................**71** D2
Nall St *BNG/LEV* M19...........................**118** A2
Nameplate Cl *ECC* M30.........................**61** C3
Nancy St *HULME* M15..............................**6** A5
Nangreave Rd *OFTN* SK2.....................**133** C3
Nansen Av *ECC* M30..............................**61** D2
Nansen Cl *STRET* M32...........................**97** D1
Nansen St *OP/CLY* M11.........................**88** B1
   SLFD M6...**65** D3
   STRET M32......................................**97** D1
Nantwich Rd *RUSH/FAL* M14................**101** D4
Napier Ct *HULME* M15 *.........................**84** B3
Napier Gn *ORD* M5................................**84** A2
Napier Rd *CCHDY* M21.........................**112** A1
   ECC M30...**61** D3
   HTNM SK4.......................................**128** A2
Napier St *SWIN* M27...............................**44** A2
Napier St East *OLDS* OL8......................**22** A4
Napier St West *OLDS* OL8......................**22** A4
Naples St *ANC* M4....................................**4** C1
Narbonne Av *ECC* M30...........................**63** D1
Narbuth Dr *CHH* M8...............................**51** C2
Naseby Av *BKLY* M9..............................**35** C1
Naseby Pl *PWCH* M25............................**12** B4
Naseby Rd *RDSH* SK5..........................**119** D1
Naseby Wk *WHTF* M45............................**12** B1
Nash Rd *TRPK* M17................................**97** B4
Nash St *HULME* M15...............................**85** D3
Nasmyth Rd *ECC* M30............................**78** B1
Nasmyth St *CHH* M8..............................**52** B4
Nately Rd *OLDTF/WHR* M16 *...............**98** B3
Nathan Dr *CSLFD* M3..............................**2** C2
National Dr *ORD* M5................................**85** D1
Naunton Rd *MDTN* M24.........................**18** A2
Naval St *ANC* M4......................................**3** E3
Nave Ct *SLFD* M6...................................**66** A1
Navenby Av *OLDTF/WHR* M16..............**99** D1
Naylor St *NEWH/MOS* M40....................**71** C2
   OLD OL1..**22** B2
Nazeby Wk *CHAD* OL9 *........................**21** D4
Naze Ct *OLD* OL1 *................................**22** B1
Neale Rd *CCHDY* M21..........................**111** D2
Neary Wy *URM* M41...............................**88** B4
Neath Cl *WHTF* M45...............................**12** B2
Neath St *CHAD* OL9...............................**22** A2
Neden Cl *OP/CLY* M11...........................**90** A1
Needham Av *CCHDY* M21.....................**112** A1
Needwood Cl *NEWH/MOS* M40.............**53** C4
Neenton Sq *WGTN/LGST* M12...............**89** D2
Neild St *CMANE* M1..................................**9** D2
   OLDS OL8...**40** B1
Neill St *BRO* M7.....................................**68** B1
Neilson Cl *MDTN* M24............................**18** B2
Nell La *CCHDY* M21.............................**113** D3
   DID/WITH M20...............................**114** A4
Nelson Av *ECC* M30...............................**62** A2
Nelson Dr *DROY* M43............................**74** A3
Nelson Fold *SWIN* M27..........................**26** B4
Nelson Rd *BKLY* M9...............................**16** A4
Nelson St *BRO* M7.................................**50** A4
   BRUN/LGST M13............................**87** D4
   ECC M30...**62** A3
   MDTN M24..**18** B2
   NEWH/MOS M40............................**71** C1
   ORD M5...**65** D4
   STRET M32......................................**97** C4
Nelson Wy *CHAD* OL9 *.........................**38** B1
Nelstrop Crs *HTNM* SK4.......................**119** C3
Nelstrop Rd *HTNM* SK4.........................**118** B3
Nelstrop Rd North *BNG/LEV* M19.........**119** C1
Nepaul Rd *BKLY* M9...............................**34** B4
Neptune Gdns *BRO* M7..........................**67** D1
Neston Av *DID/WITH* M20.....................**114** B3
Neston Gv *EDGY/DAV* SK3...................**132** A4
Neston St *OP/CLY* M11...........................**92** A2
Netherbury Cl *GTN* M18.......................**105** D2
Netherfield Cl *OLDS* OL8.......................**39** D1
Netherland St *SALQ* M50.......................**66** A4
Nether St *WGTN/LGST* M12 *..................**9** E2
Netherton Rd *RUSH/FAL* M14..............**101** D4
Nethervale Dr *BKLY* M9.........................**53** D2
Netherwood *FAIL* M35............................**58** A1
Nettleford Rd *CCHDY* M21...................**113** D1
Nettleton Gv *BKLY* M9...........................**35** C4

Nevile Rd *BRO* M7	.49	C1
Neville Cardus Wk *RUSH/FAL* M14	.102	B3
Neville St *CHAD* OL9	.21	D2
Nevin Rd *NEWH/MOS* M40	.37	C4
New Allen St *NEWH/MOS* M40	.70	B1
Newall St *CHAD* OL9	.39	C3
Newark Av *RUSH/FAL* M14	.102	A2
Newark Rd *RDSH* SK5	.120	A2
SWIN M27	.27	C3
New Bailey St *SLFD* M3	.2	C4
Newbank Cha *CHAD* OL9	.20	B1
Newbank Cl *MDTN* M24	.18	A2
New Bank St *WGTN/LGST* M12	.88	B4
New Barns St *CCHDY* M21	.112	B3
New Barton St *SLFD* M6	.46	B4
Newbeck St *ANC* M4 *	.4	B2
New Beech Rd *HTNM* SK4	.126	B3
Newberry Gv *EDGY/DAV* SK3	.132	A4
Newbold Cl *HULME* M15	.7	F5
New Bridge La *STKP* SK1	.130	B3
New Bridge St *CSLFD* M3	.3	F1
Newbrook Av *CCHDY* M21	.123	C2
Newburn Av *BKLY* M9	.35	C1
Newbury Dr *ECC* M30	.61	C2
URM M41	.78	B4
Newbury Wk *CHAD* OL9 *	.21	D2
Newby Rd *HTNM* SK4 *	.128	B4
Newcastle St *HULME* M15	.7	F4
New Church Ct *WHTF* M45 *	.11	C2
Newchurch St *OP/CLY* M11	.89	C1
Newcliffe Rd *BKLY* M9	.35	C1
Newcombe Cl *OP/CLY* M11	.72	A4
Newcombe St *CSLFD* M3 *	.69	C2
Newcroft *FAIL* M35	.58	A3
Newcroft Crs *URM* M41	.95	C4
Newcroft Dr *BKLY* M9	.33	D4
EDGY/DAV SK3	.132	A3
URM M41	.95	C4
Newcroft Rd *URM* M41	.95	C4
New Cross St *ORD* M5	.64	B3
SWIN M27	.45	D2
Newdale Rd *WGTN/LGST* M12	.105	C3
New Elm Rd *CSLFD* M3	.6	B2
New Hall Av *BRO* M7	.50	A1
New Hall Rd *BRO* M7	.50	A2
Newhall Rd *RDSH* SK5	.107	D3
Newham Av *OP/CLY* M11	.73	C3
Newhaven Av *OP/CLY* M11	.92	A2
New Herbert St *SLFD* M6	.46	B4
Newholme Rd *DID/WITH* M20	.113	D4
Newington Av *CHH* M8	.32	A2
New Islington *ANC* M4	.5	F3
New Kings Head Yd *CSLFD* M3 *	.3	E2
Newlands *FAIL* M35	.74	B1
Newlands Dr *PWCH* M25	.11	D4
SWIN M27	.46	B3
Newland St *CHH* M8	.33	C4
New La *ECC* M30	.61	C4
New Lawns *RDSH* SK5	.107	D4
Newlyn St *RUSH/FAL* M14	.102	A3
New Market *CMANW* M2	.3	F4
Newmarket Gv *AULW* OL7	.59	D4
New Market La *CMANW* M2	.3	F4
Newmarket Rd *AULW* OL7	.59	D4
New Mount St *ANC* M4 *	.4	B1
New Park Rd *ORD* M5	.84	A2
Newpark Wk *CHH* M8	.51	D3
Newport Av *RDSH* SK5	.119	D2
Newport Rd *CCHDY* M21	.98	B4
Newport St *OLDS* OL8	.22	A4
RUSH/FAL M14	.102	A2
SLFD M6	.65	D3
Newquay Av *RDSH* SK5	.119	D2
New Quay St *CSLFD* M3	.2	C4
New Radcliffe St *OLD* OL1	.22	B2
New Rd *OLDS* OL8	.40	B1
Newry Rd *ECC* M30	.79	D1
Newsham Rd *EDGY/DAV* SK3	.132	B3
Newsham Wk *WGTN/LGST* M12 *	.105	C2
Newsholme St *CHH* M8	.51	C2
Newstead Av *DID/WITH* M20	.116	A4
Newstead Rd *URM* M41	.94	B2
New St *DROY* M43	.92	B1
ECC M30	.61	D4
NEWH/MOS M40	.71	D1
SWIN M27	.26	B4
New Thomas St *SLFD* M6 *	.66	B1
Newton Av *DID/WITH* M20	.114	B3
WGTN/LGST M12	.104	A1
Newton Rd *FAIL* M35	.56	B4
MDTN M24	.15	C2
Newton St *CMANE* M1	.4	C4
DROY M43	.76	B2
EDGY/DAV SK3	.132	B2
FAIL M35 *	.55	D3
STRET M32	.97	C2
Newtown Cl *OP/CLY* M11	.90	A1
SWIN M27	.26	A3
Newtown St *PWCH* M25	.30	B1
New Union St *ANC* M4	.5	E3
New Viaduct St *NEWH/MOS* M40	.71	D4
Newville Dr *DID/WITH* M20	.116	A4
New Vine St *HULME* M15	.7	E5
New Wakefield St *CMANE* M1	.7	F5
New Welcome St *HULME* M15	.7	E5
New Zealand Rd *STKP* SK1	.130	B4
Niagara St *OFTN* SK2	.133	D3
Nicholas Cft *ANC* M4	.4	A3
Nicholas Owen Cl *OP/CLY* M11	.90	B1
Nicholas Rd *OLDS* OL8	.40	B1
Nicholas St *CMANW* M2	.4	A5
Nicholls St *SLFD* M6 *	.66	B2
Nicholson St *HTNM* SK4	.129	D3
Nichols St *SLFD* M6	.67	C2
Nicolas Rd *CCHDY* M21	.98	B4
Nigel Rd *BKLY* M9	.54	A2
Nightingale Dr *DTN/ASHW* M34	.76	B3
Nile St *OLD* OL1	.22	B1
Nile Ter *BRO* M7	.50	A4
Nimble Nook *CHAD* OL9	.20	B4
Nina Dr *NEWH/MOS* M40	.36	B2
Nine Acre Dr *ORD* M5	.84	A2
Ninth Av *OLDS* OL8	.40	A4
Niven St *WGTN/LGST* M12	.9	E3
Nixon St *EDGY/DAV* SK3	.132	B1
FAIL M35	.56	B2
No 11 Pas *DID/WITH* M20 *	.114	A4
Noble St *OLDS* OL8	.41	C1
Nolan St *BKLY* M9	.53	D2
Nona St *SLFD* M6	.65	D3
The Nook *ECC* M30	.60	B2
URM M41	.94	A4
WALK M28	.42	A1
Norbet Wk *BKLY* M9 *	.53	D2
Norbreck Av *CCHDY* M21	.112	A2
Norburn Rd *BRUN/LGST* M13	.104	A3
Norbury Av *SLFD* M6	.47	C4
Norbury Cl *NEWH/MOS* M40 *	.71	C1
Norbury Gv *SWIN* M27	.26	A4
Norbury St *BRO* M7	.50	B3
STKP SK1	.130	A4
Norcot Wk *HULME* M15 *	.6	B5
Norden Av *DID/WITH* M20	.114	B3
Nordens Rd *CHAD* OL9	.20	A1
Nordens St *CHAD* OL9	.20	B1
Noreen Av *PWCH* M25	.12	B4
Norfolk Av *DROY* M43	.75	C2
DTN/ASHW M34	.107	D2
GTN M18	.105	D1
HTNM SK4	.118	B3
WHTF M45	.11	D1
Norfolk Crs *FAIL* M35	.56	B3
Norfolk Rd *GTN* M18	.105	D1
Norfolk St *CHAD* OL9	.39	D1

CMANW M2 ....3 F4
SLFD M6 ....48 B4
Norgate St DID/WITH M20 ....125 C2
Norley Av STRET M32 ....98 A2
Norley Dr BNG/LEV M19 ....105 D3
Normanby Gv SWIN M27 ....25 D4
Normanby St RUSH/FAL M14 ......101 D1
SWIN M27 ....25 D4
Norman Gv RDSH SK5 ....119 D2
WGTN/LGST M12 * 104 B1
Norman Rd BRO M7 * 50 B2
HTNM SK4 ....128 A2
RUSH/FAL M14 ....103 C3
Norman Rd West BKLY M9 * 54 A2
Norman St FAIL M35 ....38 B4
OLD OL1 ....22 A1
WGTN/LGST M12 ....90 A4
Normanton Av SLFD M6 ....64 B2
Normanton Dr BKLY M9 ....34 B1
Norris Av HTNM SK4 ....128 B4
Norris Bank Ter HTNM SK4 ....128 B3
Norris Hill Dr HTNM SK4 ....128 B3
Northallerton Rd BRO M7 ....49 C3
Northampton Rd NEWH/MOS M40...53 D3
North Av BNG/LEV M19 ....117 C2
URM M41 ....79 D2
Northbank Gdns BNG/LEV M19 ....116 B3
North Blackfield La BRO M7 ....49 D1
Northbourne St SLFD M6 ....65 D5
Northbrook Av CHH M8 ....32 A1
North Cir WHTF M45 ....11 D3
North Clifden La BRO M7 ....50 B3
Northcombe Rd EDGY/DAV SK3 ...132 B4
North Crs NEWH/MOS M40 ....37 C2
OP/CLY M11 ....74 A2
North Cft OLDS OL8 ....41 D2
Northdale Rd BKLY M9 ....15 C4
North Dean St SWIN M27 ....26 B4
Northdown Av HULME M15 ....6 A5
North Dr DTN/ASHW M34 ....76 B4
SWIN M27 ....46 A2
Northen Gv DID/WITH M20 ....124 A1
Northern Av SWIN M27 ....27 D2
Northfield Av NEWH/MOS M40 ....38 A3
Northfield Rd NEWH/MOS M40 ....38 A3
North Ga OLDS OL8 ....40 B2
North George St CSLFD M3 ....2 A1
North Gv BRUN/LGST M13 ....88 A4
North Harvey St STKP SK1 * 130 A4
North Hill St CSLFD M3 ....2 B1
Northland Rd BKLY M9 ....35 D2
Northleigh Dr PWCH M25 * 31 C2
Northleigh Rd OLDTF/WHR M16 ......99 C2
North Lonsdale St STRET M32 * 97 D2
North Md CCHDY M21 ....112 A2
Northmoor Rd WGTN/LGST M12 ....104 B1
Northolme Gdns BNG/LEV M19 ....126 B1
Northolt Ct OP/CLY M11 * 74 A3
North Pde CSLFD M3 ....3 E4
North Phoebe St ORD M5 ....84 A1
North Pl STKP SK1 ....130 A1
Northridge Rd BKLY M9 ....16 A3
North Rd DTN/ASHW M34 ....77 C4
OP/CLY M11 ....73 D3
PWCH M25 ....11 C4
STRET M32 ....96 A1
TRPK M17 ....81 D4
North Star Dr CSLFD M3 ....2 B4
North St CHH M8 ....69 D1
Northumberland Cl OLDTF/WHR M16...84 B4
Northumberland Crs
OLDTF/WHR M16 * 84 B4
Northumberland Rd OLDTF/WHR M16...99 D1
RDSH SK5 ....121 C3
Northumberland St BRO M7 ....50 B3
Northurst Dr CHH M8 ....32 A2
Northway DROY M43 ....92 B1

North Wy RDSH SK5 ....121 D3
North Western St BNG/LEV M19 ...117 C2
CMANE M1 ....9 E1
Northwold Dr BKLY M9 ....36 A2
Norton Av DTN/ASHW M34 ....107 D2
URM M41 ....79 C4
WGTN/LGST M12 ....105 C2
Norton Crs PWCH M25 ....30 A3
Norton Gv HTNM SK4 ....128 A4
Norton St BRO M7 ....50 B2
CMANE M1 * 5 F5
CSLFD M3 ....3 E2
NEWH/MOS M40 ....71 D1
Norville Av NEWH/MOS M40 ....36 A4
Norway Gv RDSH SK5 * 130 A1
Norway St SLFD M6 ....65 D3
STRET M32 ....97 D2
Norwich Rd STRET M32 ....95 C2
Norwood Av PWCH M25 ....30 A3
Norwood Av BRO M7 ....50 B2
DID/WITH M20 ....126 A1
Norwood Dr SWIN M27 ....46 A2
Norwood Rd STRET M32 ....97 D4
Nottingham Av RDSH SK5 ....121 D4
Nottingham Cl RDSH SK5 ....121 D3
Nottingham Dr FAIL M35 ....57 D4
RDSH SK5 ....121 D3
Nuneaton Dr NEWH/MOS M40 ....71 D1
Nuneham Av DID/WITH M20 ....115 D2
Nunfield Cl NEWH/MOS M40 ....36 A3
Nunthorpe Dr CHH M8 ....52 B1
Nursery Rd FAIL M35 ....57 D3
HTNM SK4 ....128 B3
PWCH M25 ....11 D3
Nursery St OLDTF/WHR M16 ....101 C2
SLFD M6 ....65 C4
Nuthurst Rd NEWH/MOS M40 ....36 B4
Nutsford V WGTN/LGST M12 ....90 B1
Nuttall Av WHTF M45 ....11 C1
Nuttall Ms WHTF M45 ....11 C1
Nuttall St OLDTF/WHR M16 ....84 B4
OP/CLY M11 ....89 D2
Nutt La PWCH M25 ....13 D1

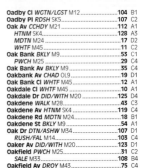

Oadby Cl WGTN/LGST M12 ....104 B1
Oadby Pl RDSH SK5 ....107 C2
Oak Av CCHDY M21 ....112 A1
HTNM SK4 ....128 A3
MDTN M24 ....17 D2
WHTF M45 ....11 C2
Oak Bank BKLY M9 ....55 C4
PWCH M25 ....29 C4
Oak Bank Av BKLY M9 ....35 C4
Oak Bank Cl WHTF M45 ....10 A1
Oakdale Cl WHTF M45 ....10 A1
Oakdale Dr DID/WITH M20 ....125 D4
Oakdene WALK M28 ....43 C3
Oakdene Av HTNM SK4 ....119 C4
Oakdene Rd MDTN M24 ....18 B1
Oakdene St BKLY M9 ....55 C4
Oak Dr DTN/ASHW M34 ....107 D1
RUSH/FAL M14 ....103 C4
Oaker Av DID/WITH M20 ....123 C4
Oakfield PWCH M25 ....31 C2
SALE M33 ....108 B4
Oakfield Av DROY M43 ....75 C4
OLDTF/WHR M16 ....98 B2
OLDTF/WHR M16 ....100 A2
Oakfield Gv GTN M18 ....106 A1
Oakfield Rd DID/WITH M20 ....124 B2
EDGY/DAV SK3 ....133 C4

Oakfield St *CHH* M8 ....**51** D3
Oak Gv *ECC* M30 ....**61** C4
  URM M41 ....**94** B3
Oakham Av *DID/WITH* M20 ....**114** B1
Oakham Ms *BRO* M7 ....**30** B4
Oakhill Wy *CHH* M8 ....**51** C2
Oakhouse Dr *CCHDY* M21 ....**112** A2
Oakhurst Gdns *PWCH* M25 ....**29** D1
Oakington Av *RUSH/FAL* M14 * ...**102** A2
Oakland Av *BNG/LEV* M19 ....**126** B1
  SLFD M6 ....**63** D1
Oaklands Dr *PWCH* M25 ....**12** A4
  SALE M33 ....**108** B4
Oaklands Rd *BRO* M7 ....**48** B2
  SWIN M27 ....**44** A3
Oak La *WHTF* M45 ....**12** A1
Oakleigh Av *BNG/LEV* M19 ....**117** C2
Oakley Cl *NEWH/MOS* M40 ....**55** D4
Oakley St *ORD* M5 ....**65** C4
Oakley Vls *HTNM* SK4 ....**128** A2
Oakmere Av *ECC* M30 ....**61** D1
Oakmoor Dr *BRO* M7 ....**48** B1
Oak Mt *DID/WITH* M20 * **125** C3
Oak Rd *BRO* M7 ....**49** D3
  DID/WITH M20 ....**115** C4
  FAIL M35 ....**57** C3
  OLDS OL8 ....**39** D3
Oak Shaw Cl *BKLY* M9 ....**34** A3
Oak St *ANC* M4 ....**4** C3
  ECC M30 ....**62** A4
  MDTN M24 * **19** C2
  SWIN M27 ....**26** B4
Oakville Dr *SLFD* M6 ....**63** D1
Oakville Ter *NEWH/MOS* M40 ......**35** C4
Oakwell Dr *BRO* M7 ....**31** D4
Oakwell Man *BRO* M7 ....**31** D4
Oakwood *CHAD* OL9 ....**19** D2
Oakwood Av *NEWH/MOS* M40 .....**37** C4
  SWIN M27 ....**25** D1
Oakwood Dr *SLFD* M6 ....**46** A4
Oakworth St *BKLY* M9 ....**33** D2
Oat St *STKP* SK1 ....**133** D2
Oban Av *NEWH/MOS* M40 ....**73** C1
Ockendon Dr *BKLY* M9 ....**53** D2
Octavia Dr *NEWH/MOS* M40 ....**73** D1
Odell St *OP/CLY* M11 * **90** A2
Odessa Av *SLFD* M6 ....**64** A1
Odette St *GTN* M18 ....**105** D1
Offerton St *STKP* SK1 ....**131** C3
Ogbourne Wk *BRUN/LGST* M13 ...**87** D3
Ogden La *OP/CLY* M11 ....**91** C2
Ogden Rd *FAIL* M35 ....**56** B3
Ogden St *CHAD* OL9 ....**21** C1
  DID/WITH M20 ....**125** C2
  MDTN M24 ....**17** D1
  PWCH M25 ....**30** B1
  SWIN M27 ....**45** C2
Ogwen Dr *PWCH* M25 ....**12** A4
Ohio Av *SALQ* M50 ....**83** C1
Okeover Rd *BRO* M7 ....**50** A1
Olanyian Dr *CHH* M8 ....**50** B4
Old Bank St *CMANW* M2 ....**3** F4
Old Barton Rd *ECC* M30 ....**78** B2
Old Birley St *HULME* M15 ....**86** A4
Old Broadway *DID/WITH* M20 ....**115** D4
Oldbury Cl *NEWH/MOS* M40 ....**71** C2
Oldcastle Av *DID/WITH* M20 ......**114** B2
Old Chapel St *EDGY/DAV* SK3 ...**132** A2
Old Church St *NEWH/MOS* M40 ....**55** C3
Old Clough La *WALK* M28 ....**42** A1
Old Elm St *BRUN/LGST* M13 * **9** F5
Oldershaw Dr *BKLY* M9 ....**53** C3
Old Farm Crs *DROY* M43 ....**92** A1
Oldfield Gv *SALE* M33 ....**109** D4
Oldfield Rd *ORD* M5 ....**84** B2
  PWCH M25 ....**12** B2
  SALE M33 ....**109** D4

Oldfield St *OP/CLY* M11 ....**73** C4
Old Gardens St *STKP* SK1 * **133** C1
Oldgate Wk *HULME* M15 * **85** C3
Old Hall Dr *GTN* M18 ....**106** A1
Old Hall La *PWCH* M25 ....**14** A2
  RUSH/FAL M14 ....**103** C4
Old Hall Rd *BRO* M7 ....**50** A1
  NEWH/MOS M40 ....**55** C2
  STRET M32 ....**95** D1
Old Hall St *MDTN* M24 ....**17** D1
  OP/CLY M11 * **91** D2
Oldham Av *STKP* SK1 ....**131** C4
Oldham Rd *ANC* M4 ....**5** D2
  FAIL M35 ....**57** C1
  MDTN M24 ....**17** C1
  NEWH/MOS M40 ....**55** D3
Oldham St *CMANE* M1 ....**4** B4
  DROY M43 ....**76** A3
  ORD M5 ....**2** A5
  RDSH SK5 * **119** D2
Oldham Wy *CHAD* OL9 ....**22** A2
  OLDE OL4 ....**23** C3
Old La *CHAD* OL9 ....**39** C1
  OP/CLY M11 ....**91** C2
Old Lansdowne Rd *DID/WITH* M20 ..**124** A1
Old Malt La *DID/WITH* M20 ....**114** B2
Old Market St *BKLY* M9 ....**33** D3
Old Medlock St *CSLFD* M3 * **6** B1
Old Mill Cl *SWIN* M27 ....**46** A1
Old Mill St *ANC* M4 ....**5** F4
Old Moat La *DID/WITH* M20 ......**115** C3
Old Mount St *ANC* M4 ....**4** B1
Old Oak St *DID/WITH* M20 ....**125** C2
Old Park La *TRPK* M17 ....**78** B3
Old Parrin La *ECC* M30 ....**61** C2
Old Rd *BKLY* M9 ....**34** A3
  FAIL M35 ....**56** B2
  HTNM SK4 ....**129** D2
Old School Dr *BKLY* M9 * **33** D3
Old Shaw St *ORD* M5 * **83** D1
Old Station St *ECC* M30 ....**61** D4
Old Wellington Rd *ECC* M30 ....**62** B3
Old York St *HULME* M15 ....**6** C5
Olebrook Cl *WGTN/LGST* M12 ......**88** A3
Olga Ter *BKLY* M9 * **34** A3
Oliver St *EDGY/DAV* SK3 ....**133** C1
  OP/CLY M11 ....**89** C1
Olive Shapley Av *DID/WITH* M20 ..**125** C2
Olive St *FAIL* M35 ....**56** B1
Olivia Gv *RUSH/FAL* M14 ....**103** C2
Ollerton St *FAIL* M35 ....**57** C3
Ollier Av *WGTN/LGST* M12 ....**104** B3
Olney St *BRUN/LGST* M13 ....**103** C1
Olwen Crs *RDSH* SK5 ....**120** A1
Olympic Ct *SALQ* M50 ....**83** C1
Omer Av *BRUN/LGST* M13 ....**104** A3
Omer Dr *BNG/LEV* M19 ....**116** B2
Onslow Av *NEWH/MOS* M40 ....**37** D4
Onslow Cl *OLD* OL1 ....**22** A1
Opal Ct *RUSH/FAL* M14 * **116** A1
Opal St *BNG/LEV* M19 ....**118** A3
Orama Av *SLFD* M6 ....**63** D1
Orange Hill Rd *PWCH* M25 ....**12** B4
Orange St *SLFD* M6 ....**66** B2
Orchard Av *GTN* M18 ....**106** B1
Orchard Gv *DID/WITH* M20 ....**114** A4
Orchard Pl *SALE* M33 ....**109** C4
Orchard Rd *FAIL* M35 ....**57** C2
Orchard Rd East *WYTH/NTH* M22 ..**123** C3
Orchard Rd West *WYTH/NTH* M22 ..**123** C3
Orchard St *DID/WITH* M20 ....**114** A4
  SLFD M6 ....**66** B3
  STKP SK1 ....**130** A4
Orchid St *BKLY* M9 ....**53** C2
Ordsall Dr *ORD* M5 ....**84** A2
Ordsall La *ORD* M5 ....**6** A1
  ORD M5 ....**83** D3

Oregon Cl BRUN/LGST M13......................9 E5
Orford Rd NEWH/MOS M40...................55 D4
　　PWCH M25..................................11 D4
Oriel Av OLDS OL8.............................40 B2
Oriel Cl CHAD OL9.............................38 B1
Oriel Rd DID/WITH M20.....................124 B1
Orient Rd SLFD M6.............................63 D1
Orient St BRO M7..............................51 C2
Orion Pl BRO M7 *.............................67 D1
Orkney Dr URM M41............................79 C4
Orlanda Av SLFD M6...........................63 D1
Orlanda Dr BRO M7.............................51 C3
Orleans Wy OLD OL1 *.........................22 B2
Orme Av MDTN M24.............................17 D2
　　SLFD M6....................................64 A1
Orme Cl OP/CLY M11............................71 D4
　　URM M41....................................95 C3
Orme St OLDE OL4..............................23 D4
　　STKP SK1...................................131 C3
Ormonde Av SLFD M6...........................64 A1
Ormsby Av GTN M18............................105 C1
Ormsgill Cl HULME M15........................86 A3
Ormsgill St HULME M15........................86 A3
Ormskirk Av DID/WITH M20....................114 A3
Ormskirk Rd RDSH SK5........................120 A3
Orphanage St HTNM SK4.......................129 D2
Orpington Rd BKLY M9..........................53 D2
Orrell St OP/CLY M11 *.........................91 C1
Orrel St SLFD M6...............................65 D3
Orsett Cl NEWH/MOS M40.......................70 B2
Orthes Gv HTNM SK4...........................119 C4
Orvietto Av SLFD M6...........................63 D1
Orville Dr BNG/LEV M19.......................117 C2
Orwell Av DTN/ASHW M34......................107 C2
Osborne Dr SWIN M27...........................46 B2
Osborne Rd BKLY M9 *...........................53 D2
　　BNG/LEV M19...............................104 A4
　　OFTN SK2...................................133 C3
　　OLDS OL8....................................22 A4
　　SLFD M6 *...................................63 D2
Osborne St CHAD OL9...........................21 D1
　　MPL/ROM SK6...............................131 D4
　　NEWH/MOS M40..............................70 B1
　　SLFD M6....................................66 A2
Osbourne St DID/WITH M20....................124 B2
Oscar St NEWH/MOS M40.......................54 B2
Oscroft Cl CHH M8..............................51 C3
Osprey Cl HULME M15...........................85 D4
Osprey Dr DROY M43............................76 B2
Osprey Wk BRUN/LGST M13 *...................87 D3
Ossory St RUSH/FAL M14.......................102 A2
Osterley Av BKLY M9............................35 D2
Ostlers Ga DROY M43...........................77 C3
Ostrich La PWCH M25...........................30 B2
Oswald Cl SLFD M6..............................88 B4
Oswald La CCHDY M21...........................99 C4
Oswald Rd CCHDY M21..........................99 C3
Oswald St ANC M4................................4 A1
　　ANC M4 *....................................71 C4
　　CHAD OL9....................................22 A1
　　RDSH SK5...................................107 C2
Othello Dr ECC M30.............................62 B3
Otley Av SLFD M6...............................64 B2
Otley Cl CHAD OL9..............................21 C3
Otranto Av SLFD M6............................64 A1
Ott Cl HULME M15...............................86 A3
Otter Dr CHH M8................................50 B4
Oulton Av SALE M33...........................110 B4
Oulton Wk NEWH/MOS M40......................71 C3
Oundle Cl RUSH/FAL M14......................102 B2
Ouse St SALQ M50...............................64 B4
Outram Sq DROY M43 *..........................92 B1
Outrington Dr OP/CLY M11.....................89 D1
Outwood Av SWIN M27...........................25 C1
Overbridge Rd BRO M7..........................68 B1
Overbrook Av NEWH/MOS M40...................53 C4
Overbrook Dr PWCH M25.........................30 A2

Overdale SWIN M27..............................45 D3
Overhill Rd CHAD OL9...........................20 A1
Overlea Dr BNG/LEV M19.......................116 B4
Overlinks Dr SLFD M6...........................46 A4
Overstone Dr CHH M8...........................51 C2
Owens Cl CHAD OL9..............................19 D1
Owens Pk RUSH/FAL M14 *.....................103 C4
Owen St ECC M30................................61 C4
　　EDGY/DAV SK3...............................129 C4
　　SLFD M6....................................48 B4
Owler La CHAD OL9..............................37 C2
Oxbrow Wy WHTF M45............................11 D1
Oxford Av DROY M43.............................75 C2
　　WHTF M45...................................11 D1
Oxford Ct CMANW M2 *............................7 F2
　　OLDTF/WHR M16.............................85 C4
Oxford Pl RUSH/FAL M14......................102 B1
Oxford Rd BRUN/LGST M13.......................87 C4
　　CMANE M1.....................................8 A3
　　SLFD M6....................................63 D1
Oxford St CHAD OL9.............................21 C4
　　CMANE M1....................................7 F1
　　ECC M30....................................84 B4
Oxford Wy HTNM SK4...........................129 C2
Oxney Rd RUSH/FAL M14.......................102 B1
Oxton St OP/CLY M11............................92 A2

P

Pacific Wy SALQ M50............................81 D1
Packwood Cha CHAD OL9.........................20 A1
Paddington Av NEWH/MOS M40 *...............55 C4
Paddington Cl SLFD M6..........................66 B3
Paddison St SWIN M27...........................44 B2
Paddock La FAIL M35.............................57 C4
The Paddocks EDGY/DAV SK3...................133 D4
Paddock St NEWH/MOS M40 *....................71 D2
Padstow St NEWH/MOS M40 *.....................55 C4
Paget St CHAD OL9...............................21 C4
Pagnall Ct CHAD OL9 *...........................21 C4
Paignton Av BNG/LEV M19......................117 C1
Paignton Gv RDSH SK5.........................119 D2
Pailin Dr DROY M43..............................76 B3
Palace Rd SALE M33............................108 B4
Palace St CHAD OL9.............................21 D2
Palatine Av DID/WITH M20.....................115 C3
Palatine Crs DID/WITH M20....................115 C4
Palatine Rd DID/WITH M20.....................124 A2
　　WYTH/NTH M22..............................123 D3
Paldfrey Pl WGTN/LGST M12......................9 F4
Palgrave Av NEWH/MOS M40.....................53 C4
Pall Ml CMANW M2................................3 F5
Palmer Cl OLDS OL8.............................41 C1
Palmerston Av OLDTF/WHR M16.................100 A3
Palmerston St WGTN/LGST M12..................88 B1
Palmer St BRO M7...............................49 D4
Palm Gv CHAD OL9...............................21 C1
Palm St BRUN/LGST M13........................104 A2
　　DROY M43...................................74 A3
Pandora St DID/WITH M20......................114 B4
Pangbourne Av URM M41..........................94 B2
Pankhurst Wk RUSH/FAL M14...................102 A2
Panmure St OLDS OL8.............................41 C1
Paprika Cl OP/CLY M11...........................91 C1
Parbold Av DID/WITH M20......................114 B2
Paris Av ORD M5................................84 A2
Parish Vw ORD M5...............................84 A1
Park Av BNG/LEV M19..........................104 A4
　　BRO M7.....................................51 C1
　　FAIL M35...................................56 A1
　　OLDTF/WHR M16.............................85 D4
　　PWCH M25...................................30 A1
　　SALE M33..................................108 B3
　　WHTF M45...................................10 A3

Park Brow Cl CCHDY M21 ....112 B2
Park Cl WHTF M45 ....11 C3
Park Crs RUSH/FAL M14 ....102 B2
Parkdale Av GTN M18 ....90 B4
Park Dr ECC M30 ....62 A1
  HTNM SK4 ....128 A3
  OLDTF/WHR M16 ....99 D3
Parker St CMANE M1 ....4 B5
Parkfield DROY M43 ....75 D3
  ORD M5 ....65 C3
Parkfield Av OLDS OL8 ....39 C3
  PWCH M25 ....31 C2
  RUSH/FAL M14 ....102 A2
Parkfield Dr MDTN M24 ....16 B1
Parkfield Rd North NEWH/MOS M40 ....37 D3
Parkfield Rd South DID/WITH M20 ....124 B1
Parkfield St RUSH/FAL M14 ....102 A2
Park Gate Av DID/WITH M20 ....115 C3
Parkgate Dr SWIN M27 ....46 A2
Park Gv BNG/LEV M19 ....104 B3
  HTNM SK4 ....128 A1
Park HI PWCH M25 * 31 C3
Parkhill Av CHH M8 ....33 C3
Park Hill Dr WHTF M45 ....10 B1
Park House Bridge M6 * 48 A2
Park House Bridge Rd SLFD M6 ....48 A3
Parkhouse St OP/CLY M11 ....90 B1
Parkhurst Av NEWH/MOS M40 ....37 D4
Parkin St WGTN/LGST M12 ....104 B4
Parklake Av BRO M7 ....50 B1
Parklands WHTF M45 ....10 B1
The Parklands HTNM SK4 ....129 D4
Park La BRO M7 ....50 A1
  OLDS OL8 ....41 C3
  SLFD M6 ....46 B4
  WHTF M45 ....10 B2
Park Lane Ct WHTF M45 * 10 A2
Park La West SWIN M27 ....47 C2
Parkleigh Dr NEWH/MOS M40 ....37 D3
Park Ldg BNG/LEV M19 ....104 B4
Park Ms OLDTF/WHR M16 ....99 D3
Parkmount Rd BKLY M9 ....34 B4
Park PI ANC M4 ....69 C2
  HTNM SK4 ....127 C3
  PWCH M25 ....12 B4
  SLFD M6 ....63 D2
Park Range RUSH/FAL M14 ....103 C2
Park Rd ECC M30 ....62 A1
  HTNM SK4 ....118 A4
  MDTN M24 ....17 C4
  OLDS OL8 ....23 C4
  PWCH M25 ....31 C2
  SALE M33 ....108 B3
  SLFD M6 ....63 D1
  STRET M32 ....96 B3
Park Rw HTNM SK4 ....127 C4
Park Seventeen WHTF M45 ....11 C1
Parkside MDTN M24 ....16 B3
Parkside Av BRO M7 ....50 B1
  ECC M30 ....61 D4
  FAIL M35 ....56 B4
Parkside Rd RUSH/FAL M14 ....101 C3
Parkside Av WGTN/LGST M12 * 9 F3
Park Sq OLDTF/WHR M16 ....98 B3
Parkstone Av GTN M18 ....92 A3
  WHTF M45 ....10 A3
Parkstone Dr SWIN M27 ....46 A3
Parkstone La WALK M28 ....60 A1
Park St BRO M7 ....49 D1
  CSLFD M3 ....2 A4
  CSLFD M3 ....69 C2
  DROY M43 ....76 B3
  OLDS OL8 ....22 B4
  PWCH M25 ....30 B1
  STKP SK1 ....130 A3
  SWIN M27 ....45 D2

Parksway BKLY M9 ....15 C3
  PWCH M25 ....30 B3
  SWIN M27 ....46 B3
Park Vw BKLY M9 ....52 B3
  RUSH/FAL M14 * 116 B2
Park View Ct PWCH M25 * 30 A2
Park View Rd PWCH M25 ....30 A2
Parkville Rd DID/WITH M20 ....115 D4
  WHTF M45 ....12 B2
Park Wy STRET M32 ....95 C1
Parrenthorn Rd PWCH M25 ....12 B2
Parrfield Rd WALK M28 ....42 B2
Parrin La ECC M30 ....61 D2
Parrot St OP/CLY M11 ....73 D4
Parrs Mount Ms HTNM SK4 ....127 C3
Parr St ECC M30 ....62 A4
  OP/CLY M11 * 91 D2
Parrs Wood Av DID/WITH M20 ....125 D4
Parrs Wood La DID/WITH M20 ....126 A4
Parrs Wood Rd DID/WITH M20 ....125 D4
Parry Rd WGTN/LGST M12 ....104 B3
Parslow Av CHH M8 ....51 D1
Parsonage Cl ORD M5 ....84 B1
Parsonage Gdns CSLFD M3 * 3 E4
Parsonage La CSLFD M3 * 3 E3
Parsonage Rd DID/WITH M20 ....115 D2
  HTNM SK4 ....128 A1
Parsonage St CHH M8 ....32 A4
  HTNM SK4 ....129 D3
  HULME M15 ....85 D4
Parsons Fld SLFD M6 * 48 B4
Parsons Wy BKLY M9 ....53 D2
Partington La SWIN M27 ....44 B2
Partington PI SALE M33 ....109 C4
Partington St ECC M30 ....62 A2
  FAIL M35 ....57 C2
  NEWH/MOS M40 ....54 A4
  OLD OL1 ....23 D2
  WALK M28 ....43 D1
Partridge Ri DROY M43 ....77 C2
Partridge Rd FAIL M35 ....58 B3
Partridge St STRET M32 ....83 C4
Partridge Wy CHAD OL9 ....19 C1
Parvet Av DROY M43 ....75 C2
Pascal St BNG/LEV M19 ....117 C1
Pass St CHAD OL9 ....22 A3
Patchett St WGTN/LGST M12 ....89 C3
Patey St WGTN/LGST M12 ....104 B2
Paton Ct BRO M7 ....67 D1
Paton St CMANE M1 ....5 C5
Patten St DID/WITH M20 ....115 C3
Patterson Av CCHDY M21 ....98 B4
Pattishall Cl ANC M4 ....71 C4
Paulden Dr FAIL M35 ....57 D2
Paulhan Rd DID/WITH M20 ....126 A1
Peace St FAIL M35 * 38 B4
Peaceville Rd BNG/LEV M19 ....104 A4
Peach Bank MDTN M24 ....17 D1
Peach St PWCH M25 ....12 B4
Peach Tree Cl BRO M7 * 51 C3
Peach Tree Ct SLFD M6 * 66 B3
Peacock Av SLFD M6 ....47 D4
Peacock Cl GTN M18 ....90 B4
Peacock Gv GTN M18 ....106 A1
Peakdale Rd DROY M43 ....74 B2
Peaknaze Cl SWIN M27 ....46 A1
Peak St CHAD OL9 ....21 D3
  CMANE M1 ....5 D5
  STKP SK1 ....130 B4
Pear Cl MDTN M24 ....18 A3
Peardale Cl ECC M30 ....78 B1
Pearl Av BRO M7 ....31 D4
Pearn Rd BNG/LEV M19 ....117 C4
Pearson St RDSH SK5 ....130 A2
Pear Tree Cl SLFD M6 ....66 B3
Pear Tree Ct SLFD M6 ....66 B3
Peary St ANC M4 ....70 A2

Peatfield Av SWIN M27 ....**25** C3
Peatfield Wk HULME M15 * **86** A4
Pebworth Cl MDTN M24 ....**17** C4
Peckford Dr NEWH/MOS M40 ....**54** B4
Pedley Wk BRUN/LGST M13 ....**9** D3
Peebles Dr NEWH/MOS M40 ....**74** A1
Peel Cir URM M41 ....**79** D3
Peel Cross Rd ORD M5 ....**66** B4
Peel Green Rd ECC M30 ....**78** B1
Peel Gv WGTN/LGST M12 ....**104** B1
Peel La CHH M8 ....**69** D1
Peel Moat Rd HTNM SK4 ....**118** A4
Peel Mt SLFD M6 ....**67** C2
Peel St CHAD OL9 ....**21** C3
    DROY M43 ....**92** A1
    ECC M30 ....**63** C3
    FAIL M35 ....**56** A3
    OFTN SK2 ....**133** C3
Pegasus Sq BRO M7 ....**67** D2
Pegwell Dr BRO M7 ....**50** B4
Pelham Pl CHH M8 ....**33** C3
Pelham St OLDS OL8 ....**41** C3
Pellowe Rd OLDS OL8 ....**40** B2
Pelton Av SWIN M27 ....**25** C3
Pembridge Fold MDTN M24 ....**18** B1
Pembridge Rd BKLY M9 ....**35** C1
Pembroke Av ECC M30 ....**62** A3
    SALE M33 ....**108** A4
Pembroke Cl BRUN/LGST M13 ....**88** A3
Pembroke St BRO M7 ....**50** B3
    OLDS OL8 ....**22** A3
    SLFD M6 ....**65** D4
Pembry Cl RDSH SK5 ....**121** C4
Pencarrow Cl DID/WITH M20 ....**124** A2
Pencombe Cl WGTN/LGST M12 ....**104** B1
Pencroft Wy HULME M15 ....**86** B4
Pendale Av CHH M8 ....**52** A1
Pendennis Rd HTNM SK4 ....**128** B2
Pendlebury Cl PWCH M25 ....**29** C3
Pendlebury Rd SWIN M27 ....**45** D1
Pendlecroft Av SWIN M27 ....**46** B2
Pendlegreen Cl OP/CLY M11 ....**89** C1
Pendleton Gn SLFD M6 * **66** A2
Pendleton Wy SLFD M6 ....**66** B2
Pendleway SWIN M27 ....**26** B4
Pendragon Pl FAIL M35 ....**57** D2
Penelope Rd SLFD M6 ....**47** C4
Penerly Dr BKLY M9 ....**53** C3
Penfield Cl CMANE M1 ....**8** C3
Penfold Wk WGTN/LGST M12 * **89** C3
Penistone Av BKLY M9 ....**35** D2
    SLFD M6 ....**64** B2
Penketh Av GTN M18 ....**105** C1
Pennant Dr PWCH M25 ....**11** D4
Pennell St OP/CLY M11 ....**74** A4
Pennine Av CHAD OL9 ....**20** B4
Pennine Cl BKLY M9 ....**35** C1
Pennington St CHAD OL9 ....**39** C2
    WGTN/LGST M12 ....**104** B3
Pennon Cl BRO M7 ....**50** B3
Penn St NEWH/MOS M40 ....**54** A1
    OLDS OL8 ....**22** A4
Penny La RDSH SK5 ....**130** A3
Penrhyn Av MDTN M24 ....**17** D2
Penrhyn Dr PWCH M25 ....**30** A1
Penrith Av OLDS OL8 ....**39** D2
    RDSH SK5 ....**107** C4
    WHTF M45 ....**12** A2
Penrod Pl SLFD M6 ....**67** C1
Penrose Cl CHH M8 ....**51** D3
Penroy Av DID/WITH M20 ....**123** C2
Penruddock Wk BRUN/LGST M13 * ...**104** A1
Pensarn Av RUSH/FAL M14 ....**116** B1
Pensarn Gv RDSH SK5 ....**130** A1
Pensby Cl SWIN M27 ....**46** B2
Penshurst Rd RDSH SK5 ....**121** C3
Pentland Av NEWH/MOS M40 ....**36** B3

Pentlands Av BRO M7 ....**50** A3
Penwortham St NEWH/MOS M40 ....**72** A1
Penzance St NEWH/MOS M40 ....**71** D2
Penzance St NEWH/MOS M40 * **71** D2
Pepler Av NTHM/RTH M23 ....**122** A3
Pepperhill Rd OLDTF/WHR M16 ....**101** C1
Percival Cl CHH M8 * **51** C3
Percival Rd DROY M43 ....**76** A4
Percy Dr ORD M5 ....**84** A2
Percy St HULME M15 ....**85** C3
    STKP SK1 * **130** A3
Peregrine Crs DROY M43 ....**76** B2
Peregrine St HULME M15 ....**86** A4
Perrygate Av DID/WITH M20 ....**114** B3
Perrymead PWCH M25 ....**12** A3
Perth Av CHAD OL9 ....**38** B1
Perth St SWIN M27 ....**44** A2
Peru St CSLFD M3 ....**2** A2
Peterborough St GTN M18 ....**92** A3
Peterhead Wk ORD M5 * **6** B3
Peterloo Ct SLFD M6 * **65** D3
Peter Moss Wy BNG/LEV M19 ....**105** D4
Peter St CMANE M1 ....**7** F1
    ECC M30 ....**62** A4
    OLD OL1 ....**23** C3
    STKP SK1 ....**130** B3
Peterwood Gdns STRET M32 ....**95** D4
Petrel Cl DROY M43 ....**76** B2
    EDGY/DAV SK3 ....**132** A3
Petworth Rd CHAD OL9 ....**21** C3
Pevensey Rd SLFD M6 ....**47** D4
Pevensey Wk CHAD OL9 * **21** C3
Peveril Cl WHTF M45 ....**12** B2
Peveril Crs CCHDY M21 ....**98** B3
Peveril Rd ORD M5 ....**65** C3
Pheasant Dr CCHDY M21 ....**113** C2
Phelan Cl NEWH/MOS M40 ....**52** B4
Philips Park Rd OP/CLY M11 ....**71** D3
    WHTF M45 ....**10** B3
Philip St ECC M30 ....**62** A4
Phillips Park Rd WHTF M45 ....**11** C3
Phoebe St ORD M5 ....**83** D1
Phoenix Wy CMANW M2 * **4** A4
    OLD OL1 ....**23** C3
Phoenix Wy HULME M15 ....**86** A4
    URM M41 ....**79** D3
Phyllis St MDTN M24 ....**18** B2
Piccadilly CMANE M1 ....**4** A4
    STKP SK1 ....**130** A4
Piccadilly Plaza CMANE M1 ....**4** B5
Piccadilly South CMANE M1 ....**8** C1
Piccard Cl ANC M4 ....**5** E1
Pickering Ct HULME M15 ....**85** D4
Pickford's Brow STKP SK1 ....**130** A4
Pickford St ANC M4 ....**5** D3
Pickmere Av DID/WITH M20 ....**115** C1
Pickmere Cl DROY M43 ....**76** A4
Picton Cl CSLFD M3 ....**6** C3
Picton Sq OLDE OL4 ....**23** D3
Picton St BRO M7 ....**68** A2
Picton Wk OLDTF/WHR M16 ....**101** C2
Piercy St ANC M4 ....**71** C4
    FAIL M35 * **56** B2
Pigeon St CMANE M1 ....**5** D4
Pike Av FAIL M35 ....**58** B3
Pike Fold La BKLY M9 ....**33** D2
Pilgrim Dr OP/CLY M11 ....**72** A4
Pilkington Rd BKLY M9 ....**35** D3
Pilling St NEWH/MOS M40 ....**54** A4
Pimblett St CSLFD M3 ....**69** C2
Pimlico Cl BRO M7 * **50** A3
Pimlott Gv PWCH M25 ....**28** B3
Pine Av WHTF M45 ....**11** C2
Pine Gv ECC M30 ....**61** D3
    PWCH M25 ....**11** D3
    RUSH/FAL M14 ....**103** D1
    SWIN M27 ....**44** A2

Pinehurst Rd NEWH/MOS M40 ....53 D4
Pine Rd DID/WITH M20 ....124 B1
Pine St CHAD OL9 ....20 B1
   CMANE M1 ....4 A5
   MDTN M24 ....18 B2
Pinetop Cl CCHDY M21 ....113 C2
Pine Tree Rd OL8 ....40 A4
Pinetree St GTN M18 ....90 B4
Pinewood CHAD OL9 ....19 D2
Pinewood Cl HTNM SK4 ....127 D2
Pinewood Cl SALE M33 ....110 A4
Pinewood Rd CCHDY M21 * 111 D2
Pinfold Av BKLY M9 ....35 D3
Pinfold La WHTF M45 ....10 B1
Pingot Av NTHM/RTH M23 ....122 A4
Pink Bank La WGTN/LGST M12 ....104 B1
Pinner Pl BNG/LEV M19 ....117 D2
Pinnington La STRET M32 * 97 C3
Pinnington Rd GTN M18 ....91 C3
Pintail Av EDGY/DAV SK3 ....132 A3
Pioneer Av SWIN M27 ....28 A3
Pioneer St OP/CLY M11 ....73 C2
Piperhill Av WYTH/NTH M22 ....123 C4
Pipewell Av GTN M18 ....90 B4
Pipit Cl DTN/ASHW M34 ....76 B3
Pitman Cl OP/CLY M11 ....89 D1
Pitsford Rd NEWH/MOS M40 ....53 D4
Pit St CHAD OL9 ....39 C1
Pittbrook St WGTN/LGST M12 ....88 C3
Pitt St EDGY/DAV SK3 ....132 A1
   OLDE OL4 ....23 D3
Plainsfield Cl OLDTF/WHR M16 ....101 C1
Plainsfield St OLDTF/WHR M16 ....100 B1
Plane Ct SLFD M6 * 66 B3
Plane Rd FAIL M35 ....57 C4
Plantation St GTN M18 ....91 D4
Plant Cl SALE M33 ....108 D4
Plant Hill Rd BKLY M9 ....15 D4
Plant St CMANE M1 * 4 C5
Plant Ter BKLY M9 * 16 A4
Plate St OLD OL1 ....23 C3
Plato St CHAD OL9 ....22 A2
Plattbrook Cl RUSH/FAL M14 ....102 A4
Platt La RUSH/FAL M14 ....101 C4
Plattwood Wk HULME M15 * 85 C3
Playfair St RUSH/FAL M14 ....102 A1
Pleachway HTNM SK4 ....127 C4
Pleasant Rd ECC M30 ....62 B4
Pleasant St BKLY M9 ....53 D1
Pleasington Dr NEWH/MOS M40 ....36 B3
Ploughbank Dr CCHDY M21 ....113 C3
Plowley Cl DID/WITH M20 ....125 C3
Plumbley Dr OLDTF/WHR M16 ....99 D2
Plumbley St OP/CLY M11 * 91 D2
Plumley Cl EDGY/DAV SK3 ....133 C4
Plummer Av CCHDY M21 ....112 A3
Plumpton Wk BRUN/LGST M13 * 104 A1
Plum St OLDS OL8 ....22 A4
Plum Tree Ct SLFD M6 ....66 B3
Pluto Cl SLFD M6 * 67 D1
Plymouth Av BRUN/LGST M13 ....88 B4
Plymouth Gv BRUN/LGST M13 ....88 A4
Plymouth Gv West BRUN/LGST M13 ....88 B4
Plymouth St OLDS OL8 ....41 C1
Plymouth Vw BRUN/LGST M13 ....87 D3
Plymtree Cl CHH M8 ....31 D3
Pochin St NEWH/MOS M40 ....71 C3
Poland St ANC M4 ....5 E2
Polden Cl OLDS OL8 ....40 B2
Polebrook Cl WGTN/LGST M12 ....88 C3
Polefield Ap PWCH M25 ....12 A3
Polefield Cir PWCH M25 ....12 A3
Polefield Gdns PWCH M25 ....12 A3
Polefield Gra PWCH M25 ....12 A3
Polefield Gv PWCH M25 ....12 A3
Polefield Hall Rd PWCH M25 ....12 A3
Polefield Rd BKLY M9 ....34 A3

PWCH M25 ....12 A2
Pole La FAIL M35 ....57 C1
Polesworth Cl WGTN/LGST M12 ....89 D3
Police St CMANW M2 ....3 E4
   ECC M30 ....61 D3
Pollard Ct OLD OL1 * 22 B1
Pollard St ANC M4 ....5 F5
Pollard St East ANC M4 ....71 C3
Polletts Av RDSH SK5 ....121 D3
Pollitt Cl WGTN/LGST M12 * 89 C3
Pollitts Cl ECC M30 ....61 C3
Polonia Ct OLDS OL8 ....39 D2
Polruan Rd BKLY M9 ....98 B3
Polworth Rd BKLY M9 ....34 B4
Polygon Av BRUN/LGST M13 ....87 D3
Polygon Rd CHH M8 ....32 A4
Polygon St BRUN/LGST M13 ....9 E4
The Polygon BRO M7 ....49 D3
   ECC M30 ....63 D3
Pomfret St SLFD M6 * 46 B4
   WGTN/LGST M12 ....89 D3
Pomona Crs ORD M5 ....84 A2
Pomona Strd HULME M15 ....84 B3
ORD M5 ....83 D4
Ponds Cl CCHDY M21 * 99 C4
Ponsford Av BKLY M9 ....35 D2
Ponsonby Rd STRET M32 ....97 C2
Pontefract Cl SWIN M27 ....46 A2
Pool Bank St MDTN M24 ....15 D2
Pool Fold FAIL M35 ....57 D3
Pool St OLDS OL8 ....41 C1
Poolton Rd BKLY M9 ....33 C1
Poorfield St OLDS OL8 ....22 B4
Poplar Av EDGY/DAV SK3 ....133 C4
   OLDS OL8 ....40 A3
Poplar Dr PWCH M25 ....29 D3
Poplar Gv GTN M18 ....106 A1
   URM M41 ....94 B3
Poplar Rd BNG/LEV M19 ....126 A2
   ECC M30 ....62 B1
   STRET M32 ....109 D1
   SWIN M27 ....44 A2
Poplar St FAIL M35 ....56 A3
   HTNM SK4 ....126 B3
Poplar Wk CHAD OL9 * 21 C1
Poplin Dr CSLFD M3 ....3 D1
Poppy Cl CHAD OL9 ....19 C2
Poppythorn La PWCH M25 ....11 D4
Porchfield Sq CSLFD M3 ....7 D1
Porlock Av DTN/ASHW M34 ....93 D1
Porter Dr NEWH/MOS M40 ....53 C3
Porter St CHAD OL9 ....21 D4
Portland Crs BRUN/LGST M13 ....103 C1
Portland Gv HTNM SK4 ....128 A1
Portland Rd BRUN/LGST M13 ....104 A2
   ECC M30 ....63 C2
   STRET M32 ....97 D2
   SWIN M27 ....45 D2
Portland St CMANE M1 ....8 A1
Portman Rd OLDTF/WHR M16 ....100 B2
Portrea Cl EDGY/DAV SK3 ....132 B4
Portree Cl ECC M30 ....61 C3
Portsmouth Cl BRO M7 ....50 A4
Portsmouth St BRUN/LGST M13 ....87 C3
Port Soderick Av ORD M5 ....66 B4
Portstone Cl OLDTF/WHR M16 ....100 B1
Portstone St OLDTF/WHR M16 * 100 B1
Port St CMANE M1 ....4 C4
   OLDS OL8 ....41 C1
   STKP SK1 ....129 D4
Portugal Rd PWCH M25 ....30 A3
Portugal St ANC M4 ....5 F1
Portugal St East CMANE M1 ....9 E1
Portville Rd BNG/LEV M19 ....104 A3
Portwood Pl STKP SK1 ....130 A3
Postal St CMANE M1 * 4 C4

Postbridge Cl *BRUN/LGST* M13 ....**87** D3
Potato Whf *CSLFD* M3 ....**6** B2
Potters La *BKLY* M9 ....**53** D2
Pottery La *OP/CLY* M11 ....**89** D1
Pott St *SWIN* M27 ....**26** A3
Poulton St *OP/CLY* M11 ....**91** D2
Powell St *OLDTF/WHR* M16 ....**99** D1
  OP/CLY M11 ....**74** A3
Pownall Av *DID/WITH* M20 ....**114** B1
Poynter St *NEWH/MOS* M40 ....**36** B4
Poynton St *HULME* M15 ....**86** A3
Praed Rd *TRPK* M17 ....**81** D4
The Precinct *EDGY/DAV* SK3 * **132** B2
Premier Rd *CHH* M8 ....**69** C1
Premier St *OLDTF/WHR* M16 ....**100** A1
Prenton St *OP/CLY* M11 ....**91** D1
Prescot Rd *BKLY* M9 ....**53** C2
Press St *OP/CLY* M11 ....**91** C2
Presswood Ct *SLFD* M6 ....**46** B3
Prestage St *OLDTF/WHR* M16 ....**100** A1
  WGTN/LGST M12 ....**105** C3
Prestbury Av *RUSH/FAL* M14 ....**101** C4
Prestfield Rd *WHTF* M45 ....**11** D2
Preston Av *ECC* M30 ....**63** D2
Preston Cl *ECC* M30 * **63** D2
Preston Rd *BNG/LEV* M19 ....**117** D1
Preston St *MDTN* M18 ....**90** B3
  MDTN M24 ....**17** D1
  OLDE OL4 ....**23** D3
Prestwich Hills *PWCH* M25 ....**29** D3
Prestwich Park Rd South *PWCH* M25 .....**29** D2
Prestwood Rd *SLFD* M6 ....**64** B1
Pretoria Rd *OLDS* OL8 ....**39** D2
Price St *ANC* M4 * **71** C4
Prichard St *STRET* M32 ....**97** C3
Pridmouth Rd *DID/WITH* M20 ....**115** D3
Priestley Rd *WALK* M28 ....**43** D1
Priestnall Rd *HTNM* SK4 ....**127** C2
Priest St *STKP* SK1 ....**133** C2
Primrose Av *URM* M41 * **94** A3
Primrose Bank *OLDS* OL8 ....**22** B4
Primrose Cl *ORD* M5 ....**66** A3
Primrose Dr *DROY* M43 ....**76** B2
Primrose St *ANC* M4 ....**5** D2
  OLDS OL8 ....**22** B4
Primrose Wk *OLDS* OL8 * **22** B4
Prince Albert Av *BNG/LEV* M19 * **104** D1
Princedom St *BKLY* M9 ....**53** D1
Prince Mead Pl *TRPK* M17 ....**81** C4
Prince's Av *DID/WITH* M20 ....**125** D1
Princes Ct *ECC* M30 * **62** A2
Princes Rd *HTNM* SK4 ....**127** C1
Princess Av *PWCH* M25 ....**30** B3
Princess Dr *MDTN* M24 ....**16** B1
Princess Pde *RUSH/FAL* M14 ....**101** C4
Princess Pkwy *WYTH/NTH* M22 ....**122** B4
Princess Rd *OLDS* OL9 ....**37** D2
  DID/WITH M20 ....**114** A2
  DID/WITH M20 ....**123** C2
  HULME M15 ....**7** F5
  PWCH M25 * **30** B1
Princess St *CMANW* M2 ....**3** F5
  ECC M30 ....**61** D3
  FAIL M35 ....**56** B2
  HULME M15 ....**6** A5
  SLFD M6 ....**66** B1
  SWIN M27 ....**45** D2
Prince's St *STKP* SK1 ....**129** D4
Prince St *OLD* OL1 * **23** D2
Princeton Cl *SLFD* M6 ....**64** B2
Printers Cl *BNG/LEV* M19 ....**126** A3
Printer St *OLD* OL1 ....**23** C3
  OP/CLY M11 ....**91** C1
Printon Av *BKLY* M9 ....**33** C2
Printworks La *BNG/LEV* M19 ....**105** D4
Priory Av *BRO* M7 ....**49** D3
  CCHDY M21 ....**112** A1

Priory Cl *OLDS* OL8 ....**40** A2
  SALE M33 ....**110** A3
Priory Ct *RDSH* SK5 ....**119** D1
Priory Gv *BRO* M7 ....**49** D3
  CHAD OL9 ....**38** B1
Priory La *RDSH* SK5 ....**119** D1
Priory Rd *SALE* M33 ....**110** A4
  SWIN M27 ....**44** B1
The Priory *BRO* M7 ....**49** D3
Pritchard St *CMANE* M1 * **8** B2
Propps Hall Dr *FAIL* M35 ....**56** B3
Prospect Dr *FAIL* M35 ....**57** C4
Prospect Rd *CHAD* OL9 ....**20** B2
Prospect Vw *SWIN* M27 ....**45** D2
Prout St *WGTN/LGST* M12 ....**104** B2
Providence St *ANC* M4 ....**71** C4
Provident Av *BNG/LEV* M19 ....**105** D4
Provis Rd *CCHDY* M21 ....**112** A2
Pryme St *HULME* M15 ....**6** C3
Pulford Av *CCHDY* M21 ....**123** C1
Pullman Cl *BNG/LEV* M19 ....**118** A1
Pullman Dr *STRET* M32 ....**95** C3
Purcell St *WGTN/LGST* M12 ....**104** B2
Purley Av *NTHM/RTH* M23 ....**122** A4
Purslow Cl *WGTN/LGST* M12 ....**71** D4
Pym St *ECC* M30 ....**62** A3
  NEWH/MOS M40 * **54** A1
Pyramid Ct *BRO* M7 ....**50** A3
Pytha Fold Rd *DID/WITH* M20 ....**116** A4

Q

The Quadrant *BKLY* M9 ....**35** D2
  DROY M43 ....**75** C4
  STKP SK1 ....**131** C4
Quantock Cl *HTNM* SK4 ....**129** D3
Quantock Dr *OLDS* OL8 ....**41** C2
Quantock St *OLDTF/WHR* M16 * **100** B1
Quarmby Rd *GTN* M18 ....**107** C1
Quarry Wk *OP/CLY* M11 * **72** A4
The Quays *SALQ* M50 ....**83** C2
Quay St *CSLFD* M3 ....**2** C5
  CSLFD M3 ....**3** D3
Quay Vw *ORD* M5 ....**83** D1
Quebec St *CHAD* OL9 ....**21** D1
Queen Alexandra Cl *ORD* M5 * **84** B1
Queenhill Rd *WYTH/NTH* M22 ....**123** D4
Queensbury Pde *NEWH/MOS* M40 * **71** D2
Queens Cl *HTNM* SK4 ....**127** D3
Queens Ct *NEWH/MOS* M40 ....**53** C4
Queens Dr *HTNM* SK4 ....**127** D3
  PWCH M25 ....**30** B3
Queensferry St *NEWH/MOS* M40 ....**55** C3
Queen's Gv *WGTN/LGST* M12 ....**104** B1
Queensland Rd *GTN* M18 ....**90** A4
Queensmere Dr *SWIN* M27 ....**26** B3
Queens Rd *CHAD* OL9 ....**20** B2
  CHH M8 ....**52** A4
  NEWH/MOS M40 ....**53** C4
  OLDS OL8 ....**23** D4
  URM M41 ....**94** A4
Queenston Rd *DID/WITH* M20 ....**124** B1
Queen St *CSLFD* M3 ....**3** D2
  CSLFD M3 ....**3** E5
  ECC M30 ....**63** C4
  FAIL M35 ....**56** B2
  MDTN M24 ....**18** B1
  OLD OL1 ....**23** C2
  SLFD M6 ....**47** C4
Queen St West *DID/WITH* M20 ....**115** C2
Queensway *BNG/LEV* M19 ....**126** A3
  SWIN M27 ....**26** B3
  URM M41 ....**94** B1
Queen Victoria St *ECC* M30 ....**61** D3

Quenby St *HULME* M15...........................6 B5
Quendon Av *BRO* M7.............................68 B1
Quilter Gv *BKLY* M9.............................33 D3
Quinney Crs *OLDTF/WHR* M16..............100 B1
Quinn St *OP/CLY* M11............................72 B4
Quinton Wk *BRUN/LGST* M13.................9 D5

R

Raby St *OLDTF/WHR* M16.......................100 B1
  RUSH/FAL M14...................................101 C1
Rachel St *WGTN/LGST* M12.....................9 F3
Rackhouse Rd *NTHM/RTH* M23.............122 A4
Radbourne Cl *WGTN/LGST* M12.............89 D3
Radcliffe Park Crs *SLFD* M6...................46 B4
Radcliffe Park Rd *SLFD* M6....................46 B4
Radcliffe St *OLD* OL1...........................23 C2
Radclyffe St *CHAD* OL9.........................21 C1
Radford Dr *BKLY* M9.............................53 D1
Radford St *BRO* M7..............................49 D1
Radium St *ANC* M4................................5 D2
Radlett Wk *BRUN/LGST* M13 *................87 D4
Radley St *DROY* M43.............................91 D1
  OLDTF/WHR M16...............................101 C2
Radnor St *CHAD* OL9............................21 D4
  GTN M18..105 D1
  HULME M15......................................86 A4
  STRET M32.......................................97 C4
Radstock Cl *RUSH/FAL* M14..................102 A4
Radstock Rd *STRET* M32........................96 B3
Raglan Av *SWIN* M27.............................27 C3
  WHTF M45.......................................12 A2
Raglan Rd *STRET* M32............................96 A2
Raglan St *HULME* M15 *.........................86 A3
Railton Av *OLDTF/WHR* M16..................100 A3
Railton Ter *BKLY* M9 *...........................54 A2
Railway Rd *CHAD* OL9............................22 A3
  CHAD OL9...38 B3
  STKP SK1..132 B1
  STRET M32..83 C4
  URM M41..94 A3
Railway St *GTN* M18.............................90 B3
  HTNM SK4.......................................129 C3
Rainbow Cl *CHDY* M21.........................112 A2
Raincliff Av *BRUN/LGST* M13................104 A3
Rainford Av *DID/WITH* M20..................114 B1
Rainforth St *BRUN/LGST* M13...............104 A2
Rainham Dr *CHH* M8..............................51 D2
Rainham Wy *CHAD* OL9.........................21 C3
  RDSH SK5..121 C3
Rainow Av *DROY* M43............................91 D1
Rainsough Av *PWCH* M25.......................29 C4
Rainsough Brow *PWCH* M25...................29 C4
Rainsough Cl *PWCH* M25.......................29 D4
Rainwood *CHAD* OL9.............................19 D1
Raja Cl *CHH* M8...................................52 A2
Rake La *SWIN* M27...............................26 A2
Raleigh Cl *DID/WITH* M20....................114 B4
  OLD OL1...23 C1
Raleigh St *RDSH* SK5...........................129 C3
  STRET M32...97 C3
Ralli Cts *CSLFD* M3................................2 C1
Ralph Green St *CHAD* OL9......................39 C3
Ralph St *OP/CLY* M11............................74 A4
Ralston Cl *BRO* M7...............................51 C1
Ralstone Av *OLDS* OL8..........................41 C1
Ramage Wk *WGTN/LGST* M12................71 D4
Ramsbury Dr *NEWH/MOS* M40...............37 C3
Ramsdale St *CHAD* OL9.........................20 B2
Ramsden Cl *OLD* OL1............................22 B2
Ramsden Crs *OLD* OL1..........................22 B2
Ramsden Fold *SWIN* M27......................26 A3
Ramsden St *OLD* OL1............................22 B2
Ramsey Av *BNG/LEV* M19.....................106 A4

Ramsey St *CHAD* OL9............................21 C4
  NEWH/MOS M40................................55 C2
Ramsgate Rd *NEWH/MOS* M40..............73 D1
  RDSH SK5.......................................120 A2
Ramsgate St *BRO* M7............................50 B4
Ranby Av *BKLY* M9...............................35 C1
Randerson St *WGTN/LGST* M12 *.............9 E3
Randlesham St *PWCH* M25.....................30 B1
Randolph Pl *EDGY/DAV* SK3.................132 B2
Randolph St *BNG/LEV* M19...................104 B3
  OLDS OL8...39 D3
Ranelagh Rd *SWIN* M27........................46 B2
Ranelagh St *OP/CLY* M11.......................73 C3
Ranford Rd *BNG/LEV* M19....................117 D1
Range Rd *EDGY/DAV* SK3.....................132 B3
  OLDTF/WHR M16...............................100 B2
Range St *OP/CLY* M11............................90 B1
Ransfield Rd *CCHDY* M21.......................98 B3
Ranulph Ct *SLFD* M6 *...........................47 C4
Ranworth Av *HTNM* SK4.......................127 C3
Ratcliffe St *BNG/LEV* M19....................105 C4
  STKP SK1..133 C1
Rathbourne Av *BKLY* M9.......................34 A2
Rathen Rd *DID/WITH* M20....................115 C4
Rathmore Av *NEWH/MOS* M40...............53 D4
Rattenbury Ct *SLFD* M6.........................46 B4
Raveley Av *RUSH/FAL* M14...................116 A1
Ravelston Dr *BKLY* M9..........................53 C4
Raven Av *CHAD* OL9.............................20 B4
Raven Cl *DROY* M43.............................76 B2
Ravenhead Cl *RUSH/FAL* M14...............116 A1
Ravenoak Av *BNG/LEV* M19..................118 A1
Ravenoak Dr *FAIL* M35..........................57 D1
Ravensbury St *OP/CLY* M11....................73 C3
Ravens Cl *PWCH* M25............................31 D3
Ravensdale Gdns *ECC* M30.....................62 B2
Ravensdale St *RUSH/FAL* M14...............102 B2
Ravenside Pk *CHAD* OL9........................20 B4
Ravenstone Dr *SALE* M33.....................110 B4
Raven St *WGTN/LGST* M12......................9 F2
Ravensway *PWCH* M25...........................31 C3
Ravenswood Av *HTNM* SK4...................127 D4
Ravenswood Dr *BKLY* M9........................34 B2
Ravenswood Rd *STRET* M32....................83 C4
Raven Wy *SLFD* M6...............................66 A2
Ravenwood *CHAD* OL9..........................19 C2
Ravine Av *BKLY* M9..............................53 D2
Rawcliffe St *RUSH/FAL* M14..................102 A2
Rawdon Cl *BNG/LEV* M19......................105 C4
Rawkin Cl *HULME* M15..........................85 D4
Rawsthorne Av *GTN* M18......................106 A3
Raycroft Av *BKLY* M9...........................35 D3
Raydon Av *NEWH/MOS* M40 *.................53 C4
Rayleigh Av *OP/CLY* M11.......................92 A2
Raymond Av *CHAD* OL9.........................39 C2
Raymond Rd *NTHM/RTH* M23...............122 A3
Raymond St *SWIN* M27..........................26 A4
Rayner La *AULW* OL7.............................77 C4
Raynham Av *DID/WITH* M20..................125 C2
Rayson Hill Dr *BKLY* M9........................33 D3
Reabrook Av *WGTN/LGST* M12...............89 C3
Reading Cl *OP/CLY* M11.........................90 B1
Reading St *SLFD* M6.............................49 C4
Readitt Wk *OP/CLY* M11........................73 C3
Reaney Wk *WGTN/LGST* M12 *...............89 D3
Reather Wk *NEWH/MOS* M40.................70 B2
Rebecca St *CHH* M8..............................51 D1
Recreation Rd *FAIL* M35.........................38 B4
Recreation St *PWCH* M25.......................30 B1
Rectory Av *CHH* M8..............................32 B4
  PWCH M25..30 A1
Rectory Flds *STKP* SK1........................130 B4
Rectory Gdns *PWCH* M25.......................30 A1
Rectory Gn *PWCH* M25..........................29 D1
  STKP SK1..130 B4
Rectory Gv *PWCH* M25..........................30 A2
Rectory La *PWCH* M25...........................29 D1

Rectory Rd *CHH* M8.............................32 A4
Redacre Rd *GTN* M18..........................91 D4
Red Bank *ANC* M4...............................69 D2
Redbrook Av *NEWH/MOS* M40............53 D4
Redby St *OP/CLY* M11 *.......................90 A2
Redcar Av *DID/WITH* M20...................115 C3
Redcar Rd *SWIN* M27...........................46 B2
Redclyffe Av *RUSH/FAL* M14..............102 B2
Redclyffe Rd *DID/WITH* M20...............114 B4
  ECC M30..79 C1
Redcote St *NEWH/MOS* M40................54 B1
Redcourt Av *DID/WITH* M20................125 C1
Redcroft Gdns *BNG/LEV* M19.............126 B1
Reddaway Cl *SLFD* M6.........................48 B4
Reddish La *GTN* M18..........................106 B2
Reddish Rd *RDSH* SK5........................120 A3
Reddish Vale Rd *RDSH* SK5................120 B2
Redesmere Dr *DROY* M43.....................76 A4
Redfern St *ANC* M4...............................4 A2
Redfield Cl *OP/CLY* M11......................72 A4
Redford Rd *CHH* M8............................32 A1
Redgate La *WGTN/LGST* M12..............89 D4
Redgates Wk *CCHDY* M21 *.................99 C4
Redhill St *ANC* M4................................5 D4
Redland Av *RDSH* SK5.......................120 A4
Redland Crs *CCHDY* M21...................112 A3
Red Lion St *ANC* M4 *...........................4 B3
Redmans Cl *ECC* M30..........................61 C4
Redmere Gv *RUSH/FAL* M14...............115 D1
Redmoor Sq *BRUN/LGST* M13 *............9 C3
Redmoss Rw *SWIN* M27........................47 C1
Red Pike Wk *OLD* OL1..........................23 D1
Red Rose Crs *BNG/LEV* M19...............118 B2
Redruth St *RUSH/FAL* M14.................102 A3
Redshaw Cl *RUSH/FAL* M14................103 C1
Redstone Rd *BNG/LEV* M19................126 A2
Redthorn Av *BNG/LEV* M19................117 C2
Redvale Rd *BRO* M7.............................50 B3
Redvers St *OLD* OL1.............................22 A1
Redwood *CHAD* OL9..............................19 C2
Redwood Dr *CHH* M8............................52 A4
Redwood St *SLFD* M6...........................66 B1
Reed Ct *OLD* OL1 *...............................22 B1
Reedham Wk *CHAD* OL9 *....................39 D1
  NEWH/MOS M40............................71 C1
Reedshaw Rd *BKLY* M9........................52 B3
Reed St *GTN* M18.................................91 C3
Reeves Rd *CCHDY* M21.......................112 A2
Reform Wk *OP/CLY* M11.......................90 A1
Regal Cl *WHTF* M45.............................12 A1
Regan Av *CCHDY* M21........................113 C2
Regatta Cl *CHAD* OL9..........................38 B2
Regatta St *SLFD* M6............................48 A3
Regency Cl *NEWH/MOS* M40................53 C4
  OLDS OL8..40 A1
Regency Ldg *PWCH* M25.......................29 D2
Regent Av *RUSH/FAL* M14..................101 C3
Regent Ct *HTNM* SK4..........................118 B4
Regent Crs *FAIL* M35............................56 B3
Regent Pl *RUSH/FAL* M14...................102 B1
Regent Rd *OFTN* SK2..........................133 D3
  ORD M5...84 A1
Regents Pk *ORD* M5 *...........................84 B1
Regent Sq *ORD* M5..............................84 A1
Regent St *ECC* M30..............................63 D3
  NEWH/MOS M40..............................56 A4
  OLD OL1...23 D2
Reginald St *OP/CLY* M11......................92 A2
  SWIN M27...25 C4
Reilly St *HULME* M15.............................7 E5
Reins Lee Av *OLDS* OL8........................41 D3
Reliance St *NEWH/MOS* M40................55 D3
Rena Cl *HTNM* SK4.............................129 C2
Rendel Cl *STRET* M32...........................97 C3
Rennie Cl *STRET* M32...........................97 C3
Renshaw Av *ECC* M30..........................62 A4
Renshaw St *ECC* M30...........................62 A4

Renton Rd *STRET* M32..........................97 D3
Repton Av *DROY* M43............................43 A2
  DTN/ASHW M34..............................107 D2
  NEWH/MOS M40..............................37 D4
  OLDS OL8...40 A2
Reservoir Rd *EDGY/DAV* SK3..............132 A2
Reservoir St *CSLFD* M3...........................3 D1
  SLFD M6...3 A3
The Residences *PWCH* M25...................30 B2
Retiro St *OLD* OL1................................23 C2
Reuben St *HTNM* SK4.........................129 D1
Reynard Rd *CCHDY* M21.....................112 A2
Reynell Rd *BRUN/LGST* M13...............104 A3
Reyner St *CMANE* M1.............................8 A1
Reynolds Dr *GTN* M18...........................91 C3
Reynolds Rd *OLDTF/WHR* M16.............99 D1
Rhine Dr *CHH* M8.................................50 B4
Rhodes Bank *OLD* OL1..........................23 D3
Rhodes St *NEWH/MOS* M40..................71 D1
  OLD OL1...23 D2
Rhos Av *MDTN* M24.............................17 D2
  RUSH/FAL M14..............................116 B1
Rialto Gdns *BRO* M7 *..........................50 B3
Ribble Rd *OLDS* OL8............................39 D2
Ribblesdale Dr *NEWH/MOS* M40............52 B4
Ribchester Wk *HULME* M15....................7 E5
Ribston St *HULME* M15.........................85 D3
Rice St *CSLFD* M3..................................2 C2
Richardson Rd *ECC* M30.......................62 B3
Richardson St *OP/CLY* M11..................91 D2
  STKP SK1..133 D2
Richard St *FAIL* M35.............................57 C2
  STKP SK1..130 A3
Richborough Cl *BRO* M7.......................50 B4
Richmond Av *CHAD* OL9......................38 B1
  PWCH M25..30 B4
  URM M41..94 B3
Richmond Cl *WHTF* M45.......................10 A2
Richmond Dr *WALK* M28.......................43 D1
Richmond Gv *BRUN/LGST* M13...........103 D1
Richmond Gv East *WGTN/LGST* M12.....88 B3
Richmond Rd *DTN/ASHW* M34 *..........107 D2
  FAIL M35..57 D1
  HTNM SK4.......................................127 C3
  RUSH/FAL M14..............................116 A1
  TRPK M17...8 B2
Richmond St *CMANE* M1........................8 B1
  CSLFD M3...2 C1
  DROY M43 *.......................................76 B3
Richmond Wk *CHAD* OL9......................22 A3
Ridge Crs *WHTF* M45............................12 A1
Ridgefield *CMANW* M2...........................3 E5
Ridgefield St *FAIL* M35..........................56 B3
Ridge Gv *WHTF* M45.............................12 A1
Ridgemont Av *HTNM* SK4....................128 A3
Ridgeway *SWIN* M27.............................27 C4
Ridgeway St *NEWH/MOS* M40...............71 C3
Ridgewood Av *CHAD* OL9......................10 B4
  NEWH/MOS M40..............................53 D4
Riding Fold *DROY* M43...........................76 B2
Riding Fold La *WALK* M28......................42 B4
Ridings St *NEWH/MOS* M40..................54 A4
  OP/CLY M11....................................90 A1
Riding St *CSLFD* M3................................2 C4
Ridings Wy *CHAD* OL9...........................21 D3
Ridley Cl *OLDE* OL4 *............................23 D3
Ridley Wk *HULME* M15 *.......................86 A4
Ridsdale Av *DID/WITH* M20.................114 B3
Rifle Rd *SALE* M33..............................111 C4
Rifle St *OLD* OL1.................................23 C1
Riga Rd *RUSH/FAL* M14......................102 B4
Riga St *ANC* M4.....................................4 B2
Rigby St *BRO* M7.................................50 A2
Rigel St *ANC* M4....................................5 F1
Rigton Cl *WGTN/LGST* M12..................89 D4
Rimmer Cl *OP/CLY* M11........................88 B1
Rimmington Cl *BKLY* M9........................35 D3

Rimworth Dr *NEWH/MOS* M40	**70**	B1
Ringcroft Gdns *NEWH/MOS* M40	**36**	A4
Ringley Cha *WHTF* M45	**10**	B1
Ringley Cl *WHTF* M45	**10**	A1
Ringley Dr *WHTF* M45	**10**	A2
Ringley Hey *WHTF* M45	**10**	A1
Ringley Pk *WHTF* M45	**10**	A1
Ringley Rd *WHTF* M45	**10**	B1
Ringley St *BKLY* M9 *	**53**	C1
Ringlow Av *SWIN* M27	**43**	D2
Ringlow Park Rd *SWIN* M27	**43**	D3
Ringmere Ct *OLD* OL1 *	**22**	B1
Rings Cl *FAIL* M35	**57**	C3
Ringstead Dr *NEWH/MOS* M40	**70**	B2
Ringstone *PWCH* M25	**29**	D2
Ringwood Av *DTN/ASHW* M34	**76**	B4
WGTN/LGST M12	**105**	C3
Ringwood Wy *CHAD* OL9 *	**21**	C1
Rink St *RUSH/FAL* M14	**116**	A1
Ripley Cl *ANC* M4 *	**88**	A4
Ripon Cl *CHAD* OL9	**21**	C3
STKP SK1 *	**133**	C3
Ripon Crs *STRET* M32	**95**	C2
Ripon Gv *SALE* M33	**108**	A3
Ripon Rd *STRET* M32	**95**	D2
Ripon St *OLD* OL1	**22**	A1
Rippenden Av *CCHDY* M21	**98**	B3
Rippingham Rd *DID/WITH* M20	**115**	C2
Rishworth Dr *NEWH/MOS* M40	**56**	B1
Rising La *OLDS* OL8	**40**	B3
Risley Av *BKLY* M9	**53**	C1
Risley St *OLD* OL1	**23**	C1
Rita Av *RUSH/FAL* M14 *	**102**	A2
Ritson Cl *GTN* M18	**90**	A3
Riva Rd *BNG/LEV* M19	**126**	A3
Riverdale Rd *BKLY* M9	**32**	B2
Rivermead Wy *WHTF* M45	**11**	D1
Riverpark Rd *NEWH/MOS* M40	**72**	B2
River Pl *HULME* M15	**7**	D3
Riversdale Dr *OLDS* OL8	**41**	D4
Rivershill *SALE* M33	**108**	B3
Riverside *BRO* M7	**67**	D2
Riverside Gdns *SALE* M33	**108**	B3
Rivers La *URM* M41	**78**	B4
River St *HULME* M15	**7**	E4
STKP SK1	**131**	C2
WGTN/LGST M12	**9**	F2
River Vw *RDSH* SK5	**120**	A2
River View Cl *PWCH* M25	**29**	C3
Rivington Av *SWIN* M27	**46**	B2
Rivington Gv *DTN/ASHW* M54	**93**	D1
Rivington Rd *SLFD* M6	**64**	B1
Rivington St *OLD* OL1	**23**	C1
Rivington Wk *WGTN/LGST* M12 *	**88**	B4
Roachwood Cl *CHAD* OL9	**19**	D2
Robert Hall St *ORD* M5	**2**	A2
Robert Malcolm Cl *NEWH/MOS* M40	**53**	C4
Robertshaw Av *CCHDY* M21	**112**	A3
Roberts St *ECC* M30	**62**	A4
Robert St *CSLFD* M3	**69**	C2
FAIL M35	**38**	B4
NEWH/MOS M40	**54**	A4
OLDS OL8	**39**	C3
PWCH M25	**30**	B1
Robin Hood St *CHH* M8	**51**	C1
Robins Cl *DROY* M43	**76**	B2
Robinson St *CHAD* OL9	**21**	C3
EDGY/DAV SK3	**132**	A2
OLDS OL8	**41**	C2
Robin St *OLD* OL1 *	**22**	B1
Robson Av *URM* M41	**79**	D2
Robson St *OLD* OL1	**23**	C3
Roby Rd *ECC* M30	**78**	B1
Roby St *CMANE* M1	**4**	C5
Roch Bank *BKLY* M9	**32**	A2
Rochdale Rd *ANC* M4	**4**	C2
BKLY M9	**53**	C2
NEWH/MOS M40	**70**	B1
OLD OL1	**22**	B1
Rochester Av *CCHDY* M21	**113**	C3
PWCH M25	**30**	B3
Rochester Rd *URM* M41	**94**	A1
Rochester Wy *CHAD* OL9	**21**	C5
Rochford Av *WHTF* M45	**10**	A2
Rochford Cl *WHTF* M45	**10**	A2
Rockall Wk *OP/CLY* M11 *	**72**	A4
Rock Bank *BRO* M7 *	**49**	D3
Rockdove Av *HULME* M15	**7**	E4
Rocket Wy *CSLFD* M3	**2**	B4
Rockfield Dr *BKLY* M9 *	**53**	D1
Rockhampton St *GTN* M18	**91**	D4
Rockhouse Cl *ECC* M30	**79**	C1
Rockingham Cl *WGTN/LGST* M12	**88**	A3
Rockley Gdns *SLFD* M6	**67**	C1
Rocklyn Av *NEWH/MOS* M40	**36**	B3
Rockmead Dr *BKLY* M9	**34**	B2
Rock Rd *URM* M41	**95**	C3
Rock St *BRO* M7	**50**	A3
OLD OL1	**23**	C2
OP/CLY M11	**91**	D2
Rocky La *ECC* M30	**62**	A1
Roda St *BKLY* M9	**54**	A2
Rodenhurst Dr *NEWH/MOS* M40	**54**	B3
Rodmell Av *NEWH/MOS* M40 *	**53**	C4
Rodmill Ct *RUSH/FAL* M14	**102**	B4
Rodney Ct *ANC* M4	**5**	E1
Rodney St *ANC* M4	**5**	F2
CSLFD M3	**2**	A4
Roe Gn *WALK* M28	**42**	B1
Roe Green Av *WALK* M28	**42**	B1
Roe St *ANC* M4	**5**	E1
Roger St *ANC* M4	**69**	D2
Rokeby Av *STRET* M32	**97**	C4
Roker Av *BRUN/LGST* M13	**104**	A3
Roland Rd *RDSH* SK5	**120**	A2
Rolla St *CSLFD* M3	**3**	D2
Rolleston Av *ANC* M4	**71**	C3
Rolls Crs *HULME* M15	**85**	D3
Rollswood Dr *NEWH/MOS* M40	**54**	B3
Roman Rd *FAIL* M35	**57**	D1
HTNM SK4	**129**	D3
OLDS OL8	**39**	C4
PWCH M25	**29**	C4
Romer Av *NEWH/MOS* M40 *	**37**	C4
Rome Rd *NEWH/MOS* M40	**5**	E1
Romford Cl *OLDS* OL8	**22**	B4
Romiley St *SLFD* M6	**47**	C4
STKP SK1	**131**	C3
Romley Rd *URM* M41	**94**	A1
Romney Av *NEWH/MOS* M40	**54**	B1
SLFD M6	**48**	B4
Romney Wk *CHAD* OL9	**21**	C3
Romney Wy *RDSH* SK5	**121**	C3
Romsley Cl *WGTN/LGST* M12	**89**	D3
Rona Cl *WGTN/LGST* M12	**89**	C4
Ronaldsay Gdns *ORD* M5	**65**	D4
Ronald St *OP/CLY* M11	**74**	A4
Rondin Cl *WGTN/LGST* M12	**88**	B2
Rondin Rd *WGTN/LGST* M12	**88**	B2
Rookery Av *GTN* M18	**92**	A3
Rookfield Av *SALE* M33	**109**	C4
Rookley Wk *RUSH/FAL* M14 *	**102**	B2
Rook St *HULME* M15	**85**	D4
Rookway *MDTN* M24	**17**	C2
Rooth St *HTNM* SK4	**129**	C3
Rope Wk *CSLFD* M3	**3**	D1
Rosa St *BRO* M7	**50**	A3
Rosamond Dr *CSLFD* M3	**2**	B3
Rosamond St *HULME* M15	**8**	A5
Rosamond St West *HULME* M15	**8**	A5
Rosary Cl *OLDS* OL8	**41**	C4
Rosary Rd *OLDS* OL8	**41**	D4
Roscoe St *EDGY/DAV* SK3	**132**	A1
OLD OL1	**23**	D3

Rosebank Rd *NEWH/MOS* M40	**73**	C1	
Roseberry St *OLDS* OL8	**22**	A3	
Rosebery St *RUSH/FAL* M14	**101**	C2	
Rose Cottage Rd *DID/WITH* M20	**115**	C2	
Rosedale Rd *NEWH/MOS* SK4	**119**	C4	
RUSH/FAL M14	**101**	D3	
Rosefield Cl *EDGY/DAV* SK3	**132**	B4	
Rosegarth Av *DID/WITH* M20	**123**	C1	
Rose Hey La *FAIL* M35	**74**	B1	
Rose Hill Av *NEWH/MOS* M40 *	**75**	C1	
Rosehill Cl *SLFD* M6	**66**	A3	
Rosehill Rd *SWIN* M27	**26**	A3	
Roseland Av *DID/WITH* M20	**125**	C1	
Roseland Dr *PWCH* M25	**12**	B3	
Rosemary Gv *BRO* M7	**49**	D4	
Rosemary La *STKP* SK1	**130**	B4	
Rosemary Rd *CHAD* OL9	**19**	D1	
Roseneath Av *BNG/LEV* M19	**105**	C3	
Rosen Sq *CHAD* OL9 *	**21**	C2	
Rose St *CHAD* OL9	**38**	B2	
MDTN M24	**18**	B1	
RDSH SK5	**130**	A2	
Rosevale Av *BNG/LEV* M19	**116**	B4	
Rosewell Cl *NEWH/MOS* M40	**71**	C1	
Rosewood Av *DROY* M43	**76**	B2	
HTNM SK4	**127**	D4	
Rosford Av *RUSH/FAL* M14	**102**	A3	
Rosgill Cl *HTNM* SK4	**126**	B3	
Rosina St *OP/CLY* M11	**92**	A2	
Roslin St *OP/CLY* M11	**74**	A3	
Roslyn Rd *EDGY/DAV* SK3	**132**	B4	
Rossall Av *STRET* M32	**96**	B2	
Rossall Wy *SLFD* M6	**66**	B2	
Ross Av *CHAD* OL9	**38**	A2	
EDGY/DAV SK3	**132**	B4	
WHTF M45	**11**	C3	
Ross Dr *SWIN* M27	**25**	D1	
Rossendale Av *BKLY* M9	**35**	C4	
Rosshill Wk *HULME* M15	**6**	B5	
Rossington St *NEWH/MOS* M40	**56**	A4	
Ross Lave La *RDSH* SK5	**121**	D1	
Rosslyn Rd *NEWH/MOS* M40	**35**	D4	
OLDTF/WHR M16	**98**	B3	
Ross St *OLDS* OL8	**22**	A4	
Rostherne Av *RUSH/FAL* M14	**101**	D4	
Rostherne Rd *EDGY/DAV* SK3	**132**	B4	
Rostherne St *SLFD* M6 *	**65**	D4	
Roston Rd *BRO* M7	**50**	B1	
Rostrevor Rd *EDGY/DAV* SK3	**132**	B4	
Rostron Av *WGTN/LGST* M12	**88**	B3	
Rostron St *BNG/LEV* M19	**105**	C4	
Rothay Cl *WHTF* M45	**12**	B1	
Rothay Dr *RDSH* SK5	**120**	A1	
Rothbury Av *AULW* OL7	**59**	D4	
Rotherwood Av *STRET* M32	**97**	D2	
Rothesay Rd *CHH* M8	**31**	D3	
Rothman Cl *NEWH/MOS* M40	**55**	D3	
Rothwell St *FAIL* M35	**56**	B5	
NEWH/MOS M40	**55**	D3	
Roughlee Av *SWIN* M27	**44**	A2	
Round Thorn Rd *MDTN* M24	**18**	A2	
Rousdon Cl *NEWH/MOS* M40 *	**53**	C4	
Roving Bridge Ri *SWIN* M27	**47**	C1	
Rowan Av *OLDTF/WHR* M16	**99**	D2	
URM M41	**94**	A2	
Rowan Cl *FAIL* M35	**57**	C4	
Rowanlea *PWCH* M25 *	**30**	B1	
Rowan Pl *PWCH* M25	**30**	A2	
Rowan Tree Rd *OLDS* OL8	**40**	A4	
Rowanwood *CHAD* OL9	**19**	D2	
Rowany Cl *PWCH* M25	**29**	D3	
Rowbottom Wk *OLDS* OL8 *	**22**	B4	
Rowendale St *HULME* M15 *	**7**	E2	
Rowland Av *URM* M41	**94**	B2	
Rowland St *ORD* M5	**83**	D1	
Rowood Av *CHH* M8	**52**	A3	
RDSH SK5	**107**	C3	
Rowsley Av *DID/WITH* M20	**123**	D1	
Rowsley Gv *RDSH* SK5	**119**	D2	
Rowsley Rd *ECC* M30	**78**	B1	
STRET M32	**95**	D2	
Rowsley St *OP/CLY* M11	**71**	D3	
SLFD M6	**49**	C4	
Roxburgh St *GTN* M18	**91**	C4	
Roxton Rd *HTNM* SK4	**118**	B3	
Royal Av *CCHDY* M21	**111**	D2	
DROY M43	**76**	A3	
URM M41	**94**	A3	
Royal Ex *CMANW* M2 *	**3**	F4	
Royal Exchange Ar *CMANW* M2 *	**3**	F4	
Royal George St *EDGY/DAV* SK3	**132**	B1	
Royal Oak Yd *STKP* SK1 *	**130**	A4	
Royce Rd *HULME* M15	**6**	C5	
Roydale St *NEWH/MOS* M40	**71**	D2	
Royden Av *BKLY* M9	**16**	A4	
Royds Cl *BRUN/LGST* M13	**88**	A4	
Royd St *OLDS* OL8	**39**	D1	
Royle Cl *OFTN* SK2	**133**	D4	
OLDS OL8	**41**	C2	
Royle St *RUSH/FAL* M14	**116**	A2	
SLFD M6 *	**66**	A4	
STKP SK1	**133**	C2	
Royley Rd *OLDS* OL8	**40**	B1	
Royston Av *DTN/ASHW* M34	**107**	C2	
OLDTF/WHR M16	**100**	A2	
Royston Rd *OLDTF/WHR* M16	**99**	C2	
URM M41	**94**	B2	
Rozel Sq *CSLFD* M3	**2**	D1	
Ruabon Rd *DID/WITH* M20	**125**	D3	
Ruby St *HULME* M15	**85**	B3	
Rudcroft Cl *BRUN/LGST* M13	**9**	D5	
Rudd St *NEWH/MOS* M40	**54**	B2	
Rudheath Av *DID/WITH* M20	**114**	B2	
Rudman Dr *ORD* M5	**84**	B1	
Rudston Av *NEWH/MOS* M40	**36**	A3	
Rudyard Gv *HTNM* SK4	**119**	C3	
Rudyard Rd *SLFD* M6	**46**	B4	
Rudyard St *BRO* M7	**50**	A3	
Rufford Pl *GTN* M18 *	**107**	C1	
Rufford Rd *OLDTF/WHR* M16	**100**	A2	
Rufus St *RUSH/FAL* M14	**116**	B2	
Rugby Rd *SLFD* M6	**63**	D2	
Rugby St *CHH* M8	**68**	B1	
Rugeley St *SLFD* M6	**49**	C4	
Ruislip Av *NEWH/MOS* M40	**53**	D4	
Runcorn St *HULME* M15	**84**	B2	
Runhall Cl *WGTN/LGST* M12	**89**	D3	
Runnymeade *SWIN* M27	**45**	D3	
Rupert St *NEWH/MOS* M40	**74**	B1	
RDSH SK5	**119**	D2	
Rushbrooke Av *OP/CLY* M11	**73**	D2	
Rushden Rd *BNG/LEV* M19	**105**	C3	
Rushen St *OP/CLY* M11	**73**	D4	
Rushfield Dr *BRUN/LGST* M13	**103**	D2	
Rushford Av *BNG/LEV* M19	**104**	B3	
Rushford St *WGTN/LGST* M12	**104**	B1	
Rushley Av *BRO* M7	**49**	C3	
Rushmere Av *BNG/LEV* M19	**105**	C4	
Rushmere Wk *OLDTF/WHR* M16	**85**	C4	
Rusholme Gv *RUSH/FAL* M14	**102**	B2	
Rusholme Pl *RUSH/FAL* M14	**102**	B1	
Rushton Gv *OP/CLY* M11	**91**	D2	
Rushton St *DID/WITH* M20	**125**	C3	
Rushway Av *BKLY* M9	**36**	A3	
Rushwick Av *NEWH/MOS* M40	**53**	D4	
Rushworth Ct *HTNM* SK4	**118**	B4	
Ruskin Av *CHAD* OL9	**38**	A2	
DTN/ASHW M34	**93**	D2	
RUSH/FAL M14	**102**	A1	
Ruskin Crs *PWCH* M25	**29**	C2	
Ruskington Dr *BKLY* M9	**53**	C2	
Ruskin Rd *DROY* M43	**75**	D3	
OLDTF/WHR M16	**99**	D2	
PWCH M25	**28**	B2	

RDSH SK5...**106** B4
Ruskin St *OLD* OL1...**22** A1
Russell Av *OLDTF/WHR* M16.........................**100** A3
   SALE M33...**110** A4
Russell Gdns *HTNM* SK4...............................**128** A4
Russell Rd *OLDTF/WHR* M16........................**100** A2
   SLFD M6...**46** A4
Russell St *CHAD* OL9 *....................................**21** C2
   CHH M8...**69** C1
   ECC M30..**62** B3
   OFTN SK2..**133** D3
   OLDTF/WHR M16..................................**101** C2
   PWCH M25..**30** B1
Russet Rd *BKLY* M9..**34** A4
Ruth Av *NEWH/MOS* M40..............................**37** D4
Ruthen La *OLDTF/WHR* M16.........................**99** C1
Rutherford Av *RUSH/FAL* M14....................**102** A2
Rutherglade Cl *NEWH/MOS* M40..................**52** B3
Rutherglen Wk *NEWH/MOS* M40..................**53** D4
Ruthin Av *BKLY* M9...**15** D4
   MDTN M24..**17** D3
Ruthin Cl *OLDS* OL8.......................................**39** C3
Ruth St *GTN* M18..**106** A2
   OLD OL1...**23** C1
Rutland Av *DID/WITH* M20...........................**114** B4
   OLDTF/WHR M16....................................**98** B2
   SWIN M27..**26** A3
   URM M41...**94** B3
Rutland Dr *BRO* M7..**49** D1
Rutland La *SALE* M33...................................**111** D4
Rutland Rd *DROY* M43...................................**74** B3
   ECC M30..**63** C2
Rutland St *CHAD* OL9......................................**21** D4
   FAIL M35 *...**57** C1
   GTN M18..**91** D3
   SWIN M27..**25** D4
Ryall Av *ORD* M5..**84** A1
Ryall Av South *ORD* M5.................................**84** A1
Ryan St *OP/CLY* M11......................................**91** D2
Rydal Av *DROY* M43..**74** B4
   ECC M30..**61** C1
   MDTN M24..**17** C3
   SALE M33..**108** A4
Rydal Crs *SWIN* M27.......................................**45** C3
Rydal Gv *WHTF* M45..**11** C1
Rydal Rd *STRET* M32......................................**97** C2
Ryde Av *HTNM* SK4......................................**128** A3
Ryder Brow *GTN* M18...................................**106** A1
Ryderbrow Rd *GTN* M18...............................**106** A1
Ryder St *NEWH/MOS* M40.............................**71** C1
Ryebank Ms *CCHDY* M21 *............................**98** A4
Ryebank Rd *CCHDY* M21.................................**98** A4
Rye Bank Rd *OLDTF/WHR* M16......................**98** B3
Rye Croft *SLFD* M6..**64** B2
Ryecroft Cl *CHAD* OL9....................................**38** B2
Ryecroft La *WALK* M28...................................**60** A1
Ryecroft Rd *STRET* M32..................................**96** B4
Ryecroft Vw *DTN/ASHW* M34........................**93** D1
Ryedale Av *NEWH/MOS* M40.........................**53** C4
Ryedale Cl *HTNM* SK4..................................**128** A2
Rylance St *OP/CLY* M11..................................**71** C4
Rylands St *GTN* M18......................................**91** D3
Rylane Wk *NEWH/MOS* M40...........................**53** D4
Rylstone Gv *CCHDY* M21...............................**123** C2
Ryther Gv *BKLY* M9...**15** C4
Ryton Av *GTN* M18.......................................**105** D2

S

Sabden Cl *NEWH/MOS* M40............................**71** D2
Sabrina St *CHH* M8..**50** B4
Sackville St *CMANE* M1....................................**8** B2
   CSLFD M3...**2** C3
Saddlecote *WALK* M28......................................**60** B1

Saddlecote Cl *CHH* M8.....................................**52** A1
Saddle Gv *DROY* M43.......................................**77** C2
Saddlewood Av *BNG/LEV* M19.....................**126** A3
Sadie Av *STRET* M32..**95** D1
Sadler Ct *HULME* M15......................................**85** D4
Sagar St *CHH* M8...**69** C1
St Agnes Rd *BRUN/LGST* M13......................**104** A3
St Agnes St *RDSH* SK5...................................**107** C2
St Aidan's Gv *BRO* M7.....................................**49** C3
St Alban's Av *HTNM* SK4..............................**118** B4
   NEWH/MOS M40...................................**55** C4
St Albans Cl *OLDS* OL8...................................**41** C1
St Alban's Ter *CHH* M8....................................**51** C4
St Aldwyn's Rd *DID/WITH* M20...................**115** C4
St Ambrose Gdns *SLFD* M6 *..........................**66** A3
St Andrew's Av *DROY* M43.............................**74** B4
   ECC M30..**62** B4
St Andrews Cl *HTNM* SK4.............................**128** A1
St Andrews Rd *HTNM* SK4...........................**128** A1
   STRET M32..**96** A3
St Andrew's Sq *CMANE* M1..............................**9** F1
St Andrew's St *CMANE* M1...............................**9** E1
St Anne's *SLFD* M6..**65** D2
St Annes Cl *SLFD* M6 *....................................**66** A1
St Annes Rd *CCHDY* M21..............................**112** A2
St Anns Cl *PWCH* M25.....................................**29** D2
St Anns Pas *CMANW* M2....................................**3** F4
St Ann's Rd *PWCH* M25....................................**29** C2
St Ann's Sq *CMANW* M2.....................................**3** F4
St Ann's St *CMANW* M2......................................**3** E4
   SWIN M27..**44** B1
St Augustine St *NEWH/MOS* M40..................**53** D4
St Austell Rd *OLDTF/WHR* M16...................**113** D1
St Austells Dr *PWCH* M25................................**12** A4
   SWIN M27..**46** B3
St Barnabas Sq *OP/CLY* M11.........................**90** A1
St Bartholomew's Dr *ORD* M5.........................**84** B1
St Bees Cl *RUSH/FAL* M14............................**101** D1
St Benedicts Av *WGTN/LGST* M12 *...............**89** C3
St Benedict's Sq *WGTN/LGST* M12................**89** C3
St Bernard's Av *SLFD* M6................................**49** D4
St Boniface Rd *BRO* M7...................................**67** C1
St Brannocks Rd *CCHDY* M21........................**99** D4
St Brelades Dr *BRO* M7...................................**51** C1
St Brendans Rd *DID/WITH* M20...................**115** C2
St Brendans Rd North *DID/WITH* M20.......**115** C2
St Brides Wy *OLDTF/WHR* M16......................**85** C2
St Catherine's Rd *DID/WITH* M20................**115** C2
St Chads Crs *OLDS* OL8...................................**40** A4
St Chad's Rd *DID/WITH* M20........................**116** A2
St Chad's St *CHH* M8 *.....................................**69** D1
St Christophers Cl *DID/WITH* M20...............**114** A3
St Clements Cl *OLDS* OL8 *.............................**22** B4
St Clement's Dr *ORD* M5.................................**84** A2
St Clements Fold *URM* M41 *..........................**94** B3
St Clements Rd *CCHDY* M21.........................**111** D2
St Cuthberts Fold *OLDS* OL8..........................**41** D4
St Domingo St *OLD* OL1 *................................**22** B2
St Dominics Wy *MDTN* M24...........................**17** D2
St Edmund's Rd *NEWH/MOS* M40..................**53** D3
St Elisabeth's Wy *RDSH* SK5.......................**119** D2
St Georges Av *HULME* M15.............................**6** B5
St Georges Ct *STRET* M32 *............................**96** B4
St George's Crs *SLFD* M6 *.............................**63** D2
St George's Dr *NEWH/MOS* M40....................**55** C2
St George's Rd *DROY* M43..............................**75** C2
   RUSH/FAL M14......................................**116** B2
   STRET M32..**96** A3
St George's Sq *CHAD* OL9...............................**37** D2
St George's Wy *SLFD* M6................................**66** B1
St Gregorys Rd *WGTN/LGST* M12....................**9** F3
St Helier's Dr *BRO* M7.....................................**51** C1
St Hilda's Dr *OLD* OL1.....................................**22** A1
St Hilda's Rd *OLDTF/WHR* M16......................**84** A4
   WYTH/NTH M22...................................**125** C4
St Ignatius Wk *ORD* M5 *................................**84** A1
St Ives Rd *RUSH/FAL* M14............................**102** A3

St James' Ct *SLFD* M6 * **64** A2
St James Rd *HTNM* SK4 ....**118** A4
St James's Rd *BRO* M7 ....**50** B3
St James's Sq *CMANW* M2 ....**3** F5
St James St *CMANE* M1 ....**8** A1
   ECC M30 * **62** B3
St John's Av *DROY* M43 ....**76** A3
St John's Cl *BRO* M7 ....**50** A3
St Johns Ct *BRO* M7 * **50** A3
St John's Rd *BRUN/LGST* M13 ....**104** A1
   HTNM SK4 ....**126** B3
   OLDTF/WHR M16 ....**99** D1
St John's St *BRO* M7 ....**50** A3
   CHAD OL9 ....**21** D4
St John St *CSLFD* M3 ....**7** D1
   ECC M30 * **62** A4
   SWIN M27 ....**47** C3
St John's Wk *CHAD* OL9 * **21** D1
St Josephs Av *WHTF* M45 ....**12** B2
St Joseph's Dr *ORD* M5 ....**84** A1
St Kildas Av *DROY* M43 ....**75** C2
St Kilda's Dr *BRO* M7 ....**51** C1
St Lawrence Quay *SALQ* M50 ....**83** C2
St Leonard's Rd *HTNM* SK4 ....**119** C4
St Lukes Ct *CHAD* OL9 ....**20** B2
St Luke's Rd *SLFD* M6 ....**65** C3
St Margaret's Av *BNG/LEV* M19 ....**117** C3
St Margaret's Cl *PWCH* M25 ....**12** B3
St Margarets Gdns *OLDS* OL8 * **39** D2
St Margaret's Rd *NEWH/MOS* M40 ....**37** C2
   PWCH M25 ....**12** B4
St Mark's La *BRO* M7 ....**51** C1
St Mark's St *BNG/LEV* M19 ....**105** D4
St Martin's Av *HTNM* SK4 ....**128** B3
St Martins Dr *DROY* M43 ....**75** C2
St Martin's Dr *BRO* M7 ....**51** C1
St Martin's Rd *OLDS* OL8 ....**41** D3
St Marys Cl *PWCH* M25 ....**29** D1
   STKP SK1 ....**130** B4
St Marys Ct *NEWH/MOS* M40 ....**55** C1
   OLD OL1 * **22** B2
St Mary's Dr *RDSH* SK5 ....**120** A4
St Marys Est *OLD* OL1 ....**23** C2
St Mary's Ga *CMANE* M1 ....**3** F3
St Mary's Hall Rd *CHH* M8 ....**32** A4
St Mary's Parsonage *CSLFD* M3 ....**3** E4
St Mary's Rd *ECC* M30 ....**63** C3
   NEWH/MOS M40 ....**55** C2
   PWCH M25 ....**29** D1
   SALE M33 ....**108** A4
St Mary's Wy *OLD* OL1 * **22** B2
   STKP SK1 ....**130** B4
   STKP SK1 ....**133** D1
St Matthews Ct *STRET* M32 * **96** B4
St Matthew's Rd *EDGY/DAV* SK3 ....**132** A1
St Matthews Ter *EDGY/DAV* SK3 * **132** A1
St Michael's Sq *ANC* M4 * **4** B1
St Modwen Rd *STRET* M32 ....**80** A4
St Nicholas Rd *HULME* M15 ....**6** C4
St Oswald's Rd *BNG/LEV* M19 ....**105** C3
St Paul's Rd *BRO* M7 ....**30** B3
   DID/WITH M20 ....**115** D3
   HTNM SK4 ....**128** A1
St Pauls St *STKP* SK1 ....**130** B2
St Peters Ct *STRET* M32 * **97** D2
St Petersgate *STKP* SK1 ....**130** A4
St Peters Rd *SWIN* M27 ....**44** B2
St Peters Sq *CMANE* M1 * **7** F1
   CMANW M2 ....**7** F1
   STKP SK1 ....**129** D4
St Philip's Pl *CSLFD* M3 * **2** A3
St Philip's Rd *GTN* M18 ....**106** A1
St Simon St *CSLFD* M3 ....**2** C1

St Stephen's Cl *BRUN/LGST* M13 ....**88** A4
St Stephens Ct *BKLY* M9 * **53** C2
St Stephens St *OLD* OL1 * **23** D1
St Stephen St *CSLFD* M3 ....**2** C1
   OLD OL1 ....**23** D1
St Stephens Vw *DROY* M43 ....**75** D3
St Teresa's Rd *OLDTF/WHR* M16 ....**98** B2
St Thomas' Pl *CHH* M8 ....**8** D1
St Thomas's Cir *OLDS* OL8 ....**22** A4
St Thomas's Pl *STKP* SK1 ....**133** C1
St Thomas St North *OLDS* OL8 * **22** A4
St Thomas St South *OLDS* OL8 ....**22** A4
St Vincent St *ANC* M4 ....**5** F3
St Werburghs Rd *CCHDY* M21 ....**112** B3
St Wilfrids Rd *HULME* M15 ....**6** C5
Salcombe Rd *OP/CLY* M11 ....**91** C1
Salcot Wk *NEWH/MOS* M40 * **70** B2
Salisbury Dr *PWCH* M25 ....**30** B3
Salisbury Rd *CCHDY* M21 ....**99** C4
   ECC M30 ....**63** C1
   SWIN M27 ....**44** B2
   URM M41 ....**94** A1
   WHTF M45 ....**11** C1
Salisbury St *RDSH* SK5 ....**120** A1
   RUSH/FAL M14 ....**101** D1
Salmon St *ANC* M4 ....**8** A3
Salop St *SLFD* M6 ....**66** B1
Saltergate Ms *ORD* M5 * **91** C1
Salteye Rd *ECC* M30 ....**60** B4
Saltford Av *ANC* M4 ....**5** F3
Saltford Ct *ANC* M4 ....**5** F3
Saltire Gdns *BRO* M7 ....**50** B1
Saltney Av *DID/WITH* M20 ....**114** A2
Sam Cowan Cl *RUSH/FAL* M14 ....**101** D2
Samian Gdns *BRO* M7 ....**49** D4
Samlesbury Cl *DID/WITH* M20 ....**124** A2
Samouth Cl *NEWH/MOS* M40 ....**71** C2
Sampson Sq *RUSH/FAL* M14 ....**101** D1
Sam Swire St *HULME* M15 ....**85** D4
Samuel Ogden St *CMANE* M1 ....**8** B2
Samuel St *BNG/LEV* M19 ....**118** A1
   FAIL M35 ....**57** C1
   HTNM SK4 ....**129** C2
Sanby Av *GTN* M18 ....**105** D1
Sanby Rd *GTN* M18 ....**105** D1
Sanctuary Cl *HULME* M15 ....**87** C4
The Sanctuary *HULME* M15 ....**7** D5
Sandal St *NEWH/MOS* M40 ....**71** C1
Sandbach Av *RUSH/FAL* M14 ....**114** A1
Sandbach Rd *RDSH* SK5 * **106** B3
Sanderson Cl *WALK* M28 ....**43** C1
Sanderson St *NEWH/MOS* M40 ....**53** D4
Sanderstead Dr *BKLY* M9 ....**34** B2
Sandfold La *BNG/LEV* M19 ....**105** D3
Sandford Av *GTN* M18 * **91** C3
Sandford Station La *RDSH* SK5 ....**106** A3
Sandgate Av *OP/CLY* M11 ....**74** A3
Sandgate Dr *URM* M41 ....**94** A4
Sandgate Rd *CHAD* OL9 ....**21** C3
   WHTF M45 ....**12** A2
Sandheys Gv *GTN* M18 ....**106** B1
Sandhurst Av *DID/WITH* M20 ....**114** B3
Sandhurst Rd *DID/WITH* M20 ....**125** C3
Sandhutton Rd *BKLY* M9 ....**34** A4
Sandileigh Av *DID/WITH* M20 ....**115** C4
   RDSH SK5 ....**131** C1
Sandiway Dr *DID/WITH* M20 ....**124** B2
Sandown Av *SLFD* M6 ....**66** B3
Sandown Crs *GTN* M18 ....**106** A2
Sandown St *GTN* M18 ....**91** D3
Sandpiper Dr *EDGY/DAV* SK3 ....**132** A3
Sandray Gv *ORD* M5 ....**65** D4
Sandridge Wk *WGTN/LGST* M12 ....**88** B3
Sandringham Av *DTN/ASHW* M34 ....**107** D2
Sandringham Dr *HTNM* SK4 ....**127** D4
Sandringham Gra *PWCH* M25 ....**31** D2
Sandringham Rd *MPL/ROM* SK6 ....**131** D2

Sandringham St *GTN* M18 ....**105** D1
Sands Av *CHAD* OL9 ....**19** D1
Sandsend Cl *CHH* M8 ....**50** B4
Sandstone Wy *CCHDY* M21 ....**113** C3
Sand St *NEWH/MOS* M40 ....**70** B1
Sandwell Dr *SALE* M33 ....**109** C3
Sandwich Rd *ECC* M30 ....**63** C2
Sandy Bank Rd *CHH* M8 ....**51** C1
Sandybrook Dr *BKLY* M9 ....**33** D3
Sandy Brow *BKLY* M9 ....**34** A3
Sandygate Cl *SWIN* M27 ....**44** B2
Sandy Gv *SLFD* M6 ....**65** D2
   SWIN M27 ....**45** C1
Sandyhill Rd *BKLY* M9 ....**32** B2
Sandylands Dr *PWCH* M25 ....**29** C4
Sandy La *CCHDY* M21 ....**112** A1
   DROY M43 ....**76** B2
   MDTN M24 ....**18** A3
   OLDS OL8 * **22** A3
   PWCH M25 ....**29** D3
   RDSH SK5 ....**129** D2
   SLFD M6 ....**65** D2
   STRET M32 ....**96** A4
Sandy Meade *PWCH* M25 ....**29** D2
Sandyway *PWCH* M25 * **29** D2
Sandywell Cl *OP/CLY* M11 ....**91** C2
Sandywell St *OP/CLY* M11 ....**91** C1
Sandy Wd *SLFD* M6 ....**65** D2
Sangster Ct *ORD* M5 ....**83** D1
Sankey Gv *BKLY* M9 ....**33** C2
Santiago St *RUSH/FAL* M14 ....**102** A2
Santley St *WGTN/LGST* M12 ....**104** B2
Santon Av *RUSH/FAL* M14 ....**116** B1
Sapling Rd *SWIN* M27 ....**44** A4
Sarah St *ECC* M30 ....**61** C4
   MDTN M24 ....**17** C1
   OP/CLY M11 ....**89** C1
Sargent Dr *OLDTF/WHR* M16 ....**100** B1
Sark Rd *CCHDY* M21 ....**98** B3
Saturn Gv *SLFD* M6 ....**67** C1
Saunton Rd *OP/CLY* M11 ....**91** C1
Saville St *MDTN* M24 ....**19** C2
Savio Wy *MDTN* M24 ....**17** D2
Sawley Rd *NEWH/MOS* M40 ....**71** C1
Saxby St *SLFD* M6 ....**46** B4
Saxelby Dr *CHH* M8 ....**52** A3
Saxon Av *CHH* M8 ....**32** B3
Saxon Dr *OLDS* OL9 ....**19** D1
   DROY M43 ....**75** D3
Saxon St *DROY* M43 ....**76** A3
   MDTN M24 ....**18** A1
   NEWH/MOS M40 ....**71** D2
Saxthorpe Wk *WGTN/LGST* M12 ....**88** B4
Saxwood Av *BKLY* M9 ....**34** A4
Scale St *ORD* M5 ....**67** C4
Scarborough St *NEWH/MOS* M40 ....**54** B1
Scarcroft Rd *WGTN/LGST* M12 ....**89** D4
Scargill Cl *BNG/LEV* M19 ....**115** D1
Scarisbrick Av *DID/WITH* M20 ....**126** A2
Scarisbrick Rd *BNG/LEV* M19 ....**117** C1
Scarsdale Rd *RUSH/FAL* M14 ....**103** D1
Scarsdale St *SLFD* M6 ....**67** C2
Schofield Rd *DROY* M43 ....**76** A4
   ECC M30 ....**60** B4
Schofield St *FAIL* M35 * **57** C1
   OLDS OL8 ....**40** B2
   OP/CLY M11 ....**73** D3
Scholar Green Rd *STRET* M32 ....**80** B4
Scholars Dr *DID/WITH* M20 ....**114** B2
Scholars Wy *MDTN* M24 ....**17** C1
Scholes Dr *NEWH/MOS* M40 ....**37** D3
Scholes La *PWCH* M25 ....**30** B2
Scholes St *CHAD* OL9 ....**38** B1
   FAIL M35 ....**38** B4
   OLD OL1 * **23** D2
   SWIN M27 ....**45** D1
Scholes Wk *PWCH* M25 ....**30** B2

Scholfield Av *URM* M41 ....**95** C4
School Av *STRET* M32 ....**98** A2
School Brow *WALK* M28 ....**42** A3
School Ct *ANC* M4 ....**5** E3
   EDGY/DAV SK3 ....**133** C3
School Gv *DID/WITH* M20 ....**115** D3
   PWCH M25 ....**29** D3
School Gv West *DID/WITH* M20 * **115** D3
School House Flats *OLDS* OL8 * **39** D5
School La *BKLY* M9 ....**33** D5
   DID/WITH M20 ....**125** D2
   HTNM SK4 ....**118** B4
School Rd *ECC* M30 ....**78** B1
   FAIL M35 ....**57** C2
   OLDS OL8 ....**39** C3
   SALE M33 ....**108** B4
   STRET M32 ....**96** B3
Schoolside Cl *CHH* M8 ....**52** A3
Schoolside La *MDTN* M24 ....**15** D2
Schools Rd *GTN* M18 ....**91** D4
School St *ANC* M4 ....**4** B1
   ECC M30 ....**61** C2
   OLDS OL8 ....**22** A4
School Wk *OLDTF/WHR* M16 ....**85** C4
Schuter Rd *RUSH/FAL* M14 ....**102** B2
Schwabe St *MDTN* M24 ....**15** D1
Scoltock Wy *OLD* OL1 ....**23** C2
Score St *OP/CLY* M11 ....**72** B4
Scotforth Cl *HULME* M15 ....**6** C1
Scotland Hall Rd *NEWH/MOS* M40 ....**73** C1
Scotland St *NEWH/MOS* M40 ....**55** D4
Scott Av *CCHDY* M21 ....**99** C3
   ECC M30 ....**61** D2
Scott Cl *RDSH* SK5 ....**130** A1
Scottfield *OLDS* OL8 ....**22** B4
Scottia Rd *ECC* M30 ....**78** A1
Scott Rd *DROY* M43 ....**75** D4
   PWCH M25 ....**29** C2
Scott St *OLDS* OL8 ....**23** C4
Scovell St *BRO* M7 ....**50** A3
Scropton St *NEWH/MOS* M40 ....**55** C4
Seabright Wk *OP/CLY* M11 * **72** A4
Seabrook Crs *URM* M41 ....**94** A1
Seabrook Rd *NEWH/MOS* M40 ....**73** D1
Seacombe Av *RUSH/FAL* M14 ....**101** D4
Seaford Rd *SLFD* M6 ....**49** C4
Seaford Wk *CHAD* OL9 * **21** C1
Seaham Wk *RUSH/FAL* M14 ....**102** A3
Sealey Wk *NEWH/MOS* M40 * **71** D1
Searby Rd *GTN* M18 ....**91** C3
Searle Rd *GTN* M18 ....**91** C3
Seascale Av *OP/CLY* M11 ....**73** C2
Seaton Ms *AULW* OL7 ....**77** D1
Sebastopol Wk *ANC* M4 ....**5** E3
Second Av *OLDS* OL8 ....**39** D3
   OP/CLY M11 ....**74** A3
   SWIN M27 ....**44** A4
   TRPK M17 ....**82** A4
Sedan Cl *ORD* M5 ....**66** B4
Seddon Av *GTN* M18 ....**91** C3
Seddon St *BNG/LEV* M19 ....**105** C3
Sedgeborough Rd *OLDTF/WHR* M16 ....**100** B4
Sedge Cl *RDSH* SK5 ....**120** B1
Sedgefield Cl *ORD* M5 ....**66** B3
Sedgeford Rd *NEWH/MOS* M40 ....**53** C4
Sedgemoor Wy *OLD* OL1 * **22** B2
Sedgley Av *PWCH* M25 ....**30** B3
Sedgley Park Rd *PWCH* M25 ....**30** B3
Sedgley Cl *MDTN* M24 ....**18** B2
Sedgley Rd *CHH* M8 ....**51** D1
Sedgley St *MDTN* M24 ....**18** B2
Seedley Park Rd *SLFD* M6 ....**65** D3
Seedley Rd *SLFD* M6 ....**65** D3
Seedley St *RUSH/FAL* M14 ....**102** A2
Seedley Ter *SLFD* M6 ....**65** D2
Seedley View Rd *ORD* M5 ....**65** D2
Sefton Cl *BRUN/LGST* M13 ....**9** D5
   MDTN M24 ....**16** B1

Sefton Crs *SALE* M33 ....109 C3
Sefton Dr *SWIN* M27 ....44 A4
   WALK M28 ....42 B3
Sefton Rd *CCHDY* M21 ....112 A1
   MDTN M24 ....16 B1
   SALE M33 ....109 C4
   SWIN M27 ....26 A4
Sefton St *CHAD* OL9 ....38 B3
   CHH M8 ....51 D1
   WHTF M45 ....11 C2
Segal Cl *BRO* M7 ....50 A2
Selborne Rd *CCHDY* M21 ....99 C4
Selby Cl *STRET* M32 ....95 C3
Selby Dr *SLFD* M6 ....64 A2
Selby Rd *STRET* M32 ....95 D2
Selby St *HTNM* SK4 ....129 D1
   OP/CLY M11 ....89 D1
Selham Wk *BRUN/LGST* M13 * 9 E4
Selhurst Av *OP/CLY* M11 ....73 D3
Selkirk Av *OLDS* OL8 ....40 A1
Selkirk Dr *BKLY* M9 ....35 C2
Selkirk Rd *CHAD* OL9 ....38 A1
Sellars Sq *DROY* M43 ....92 B1
Sellers Wy *CHAD* OL9 ....38 B2
Selsby Av *ECC* M30 ....61 C3
Selside Wk *RUSH/FAL* M14 ....115 D1
Selston Rd *BKLY* M9 ....33 C1
Selworthy Rd *OLDTF/WHR* M16 ....100 B1
Selwyn Av *BKLY* M9 ....53 C1
Selwyn Cl *OLDS* OL8 * 22 B4
Selwyn St *OLDS* OL8 ....22 B4
Senior Av *RUSH/FAL* M14 ....116 B2
Senior St *CSLFD* M3 ....3 D1
Sepal Cl *RDSH* SK5 ....107 C4
Sequoia St *BKLY* M9 ....53 D1
Sevenoaks Av *HTNM* SK4 ....117 C4
   URM M41 ....94 A1
Sevenoaks Dr *SWIN* M27 ....45 D3
Sevenoaks Wk *BRUN/LGST* M13 * 87 C1
Seventh Av *OLDS* OL8 ....39 D4
Severn Rd *CHAD* OL9 ....20 A1
   OLDS OL8 ....39 C4
Severn Wy *RDSH* SK5 ....120 A4
Sewerby Cl *OLDTF/WHR* M16 ....101 C1
Sewerby St *OLDTF/WHR* M16 ....100 B1
Sexa St *OP/CLY* M11 ....91 C1
Seymour Av *OP/CLY* M11 ....74 A3
Seymour Cl *OLDTF/WHR* M16 ....84 B4
Seymour Gv *OLDTF/WHR* M16 ....99 C1
Seymour Pl *OLDTF/WHR* M16 * 84 A4
Seymour Rd *CHH* M8 ....32 A4
Seymour Rd South *OP/CLY* M11 ....74 A3
Seymour St *GTN* M18 ....91 C3
Shackleton St *ECC* M30 ....61 C2
Shackliffe Rd *NEWH/MOS* M40 ....36 A3
Shaftesbury Av *ECC* M30 ....78 B1
Shaftesbury Rd *CHH* M8 ....51 D1
   SWIN M27 ....45 C2
Shakespeare Crs *DROY* M43 ....75 D3
   ECC M30 ....62 A3
Shakespeare Rd *DROY* M43 ....75 D3
   PWCH M25 ....29 C2
   SWIN M27 ....44 A1
Shakespeare Wk *BRUN/LGST* M13 ....87 C4
Shakleton Av *BKLY* M9 ....35 D2
Shaldon Dr *NEWH/MOS* M40 ....74 B1
Shambles Sq *CMANE* M1 ....3 F3
Shandon Av *WYTH/NTH* M22 ....123 C4
Shanklin Cl *CCHDY* M21 ....98 B3
Shanley Ct *CHH* M8 ....21 C1
Sharcott Cl *OLDTF/WHR* M16 ....101 C1
Shardlow Av *OLDTF/WHR* M16 ....71 C1
Sharnford Sq *WGTN/LGST* M12 ....89 D3
Sharon Cl *AULW* OL7 ....77 D4
Sharples St *HTNM* SK4 ....129 D1
Sharp St *ANC* M4 ....4 C1
   MDTN M24 ....17 D1

   PWCH M25 * 29 D1
Shawbrook Rd *BNG/LEV* M19 ....117 D4
Shawbury St *MDTN* M24 ....18 B2
Shawcross Fold *STKP* SK1 ....130 A3
Shawcross St *SLFD* M6 ....66 A4
   STKP SK1 ....133 C1
Shawfield Cl *RUSH/FAL* M14 ....114 B1
Shawford Rd *NEWH/MOS* M40 ....36 B3
Shawgreen Cl *HULME* M15 ....6 B5
Shaw Head Dr *FAIL* M35 ....57 C3
Shaw Heath *EDGY/DAV* SK3 ....132 B2
   OFTN SK2 ....133 C2
Shawhill Wk *NEWH/MOS* M40 ....71 D3
Shawlea Av *BNG/LEV* M19 ....116 B3
Shaw Rd *HTNM* SK4 ....118 A4
Shaw Rd South *EDGY/DAV* SK3 ....132 B3
Shaw St *CSLFD* M3 ....3 F1
   OLD OL1 ....23 C1
Shayfield Av *CHAD* OL9 ....19 D2
Sheader Dr *ORD* M5 ....83 B3
Shearer Wy *SWIN* M27 ....47 C2
Shearsby Cl *HULME* M15 ....85 D3
Sheepfoot La *PWCH* M25 ....31 C2
Sheerness St *GTN* M18 ....91 C4
Sheffield St *CMANE* M1 ....9 D1
   HTNM SK4 ....129 D2
Shefford Cl *OP/CLY* M11 ....89 C1
Shelderton Cl *NEWH/MOS* M40 ....54 B2
Sheldon Cl *OP/CLY* M11 ....73 C3
Shelford Av *GTN* M18 ....105 C1
Shelley Gv *DROY* M43 ....75 D4
Shelley Rd *CHAD* OL9 ....38 A2
   PWCH M25 ....29 C2
   RDSH SK5 ....106 A4
   SWIN M27 ....44 A1
Shelley St *NEWH/MOS* M40 ....55 D1
Shenfield Wk *NEWH/MOS* M40 ....71 C2
Shepherd St *BKLY* M9 * 34 A4
Shepley St *FAIL* M35 ....38 B4
Sheraton Rd *OLDS* OL8 ....40 B1
Sherborne Rd *URM* M41 ....94 B2
Sherborne St *CHH* M8 ....69 C1
Sherborne St West *CSLFD* M3 ....68 B2
Sherbourne St *PWCH* M25 * 29 C1
Sherdley Ct *CHH* M8 ....32 B4
Sherdley Rd *CHH* M8 ....32 B4
Sheridan Wy *CHAD* OL9 * 19 D1
Sheringham Dr *SWIN* M27 ....45 C3
Sheringham Rd *DID/WITH* M20 ....116 A2
Sherlock St *RUSH/FAL* M14 ....116 A2
Sherratt St *ANC* M4 ....5 D2
Sherrington St *WGTN/LGST* M12 ....104 B2
Sherwell Rd *BKLY* M9 ....33 C2
Sherwood Av *BRO* M7 ....49 C2
   DROY M43 ....76 B3
   HTNM SK4 ....127 D4
   RUSH/FAL M14 ....115 D1
   SALE M33 ....109 C4
Sherwood Cl *ORD* M5 ....65 C2
Sherwood Dr *SWIN* M27 ....46 A3
Sherwood St *OLD* OL1 ....22 A1
   RUSH/FAL M14 ....115 D1
Shetland Rd *NEWH/MOS* M40 ....71 C2
Shetland Wy *URM* M41 ....79 C4
Shevington Gdns *NTHM/RTH* M23 ....122 A4
Shieldborn Dr *BKLY* M9 ....53 C2
Shield Cl *OLDS* OL8 ....22 B3
Shield Dr *WALK* M28 ....43 D1
Shield St *EDGY/DAV* SK3 ....132 B1
Shilford Dr *ANC* M4 ....5 D1
Shipla Cl *CHAD* OL9 ....22 B2
Shipley Av *SLFD* M6 ....64 B2
Shippey St *RUSH/FAL* M14 ....116 A2
Shiredale Dr *BKLY* M9 ....53 C2
Shiregreen Av *NEWH/MOS* M40 ....52 B4
Shirehills *PWCH* M25 ....29 D2
Shireoak Rd *DID/WITH* M20 ....116 A2

The Shires *DROY* M43 ....**77** C2
Shirley Av *BRO* M7 ....**48** B2
   CHAD OL9 ....**37** D3
   DTN/ASHW M34 ....**93** D1
   DTN/ASHW M34 ....**107** D1
   ECC M30 ....**78** B3
   STRET M32 ....**98** A2
   SWIN M27 ....**46** B2
Shirley Gv *EDGY/DAV* SK3 ....**132** B4
Shirley Rd *CHH* M8 ....**51** D2
Shoreditch Cl *HTNM* SK4 ....**118** A4
Shoreham Wk *CHAD* OL9 * **20** B3
Shore St *OLD* OL1 ....**23** D2
Shorland St *SWIN* M27 ....**43** D2
Short Av *DROY* M43 ....**92** A1
Shortcroft St *HULME* M15 ....**7** E3
Shortland Crs *BNG/LEV* M19 ....**126** A2
Short St *BRO* M7 ....**68** B2
   CMANE M1 ....**4** B4
   HTNM SK4 ....**129** D2
Short St East *HTNM* SK4 ....**129** D2
Shotton Wk *RUSH/FAL* M14 * **102** A2
Shrewsbury Ct *OLDTF/WHR* M16 * **85** C4
Shrewsbury Rd *DROY* M43 ....**75** D3
   PWCH M25 ....**29** D2
Shrewsbury St *OLDTF/WHR* M16 .....**85** C4
Shropshire Av *RDSH* SK5 ....**121** D3
Shropshire Rd *FAIL* M35 ....**57** D3
Shropshire Sq *WGTN/LGST* M12 * ..**88** B3
Shrowbridge Wk *WGTN/LGST* M12 ..**89** D3
Shudehill *ANC* M4 ....**4** B2
Shuttle St *ECC* M30 * **63** C3
Shuttleworth Cl *OLDTF/WHR* M16 ..**113** D1
Siam St *OP/CLY* M11 ....**89** C1
Sibley Rd *HTNM* SK4 ....**128** A2
Sibley St *GTN* M18 ....**91** C4
Sibson Rd *CCHDY* M21 ....**98** B4
Sickle St *CMANW* M2 * **4** C4
   OLDE OL4 ....**23** D4
Sidbury Rd *CCHDY* M21 ....**112** B3
Siddall St *OLD* OL1 ....**23** C1
   WGTN/LGST M12 ....**104** B3
Siddington Av *DID/WITH* M20 ......**114** B2
Sidebottom St *DROY* M43 * **75** C4
Side Av *OLDS* OL8 ....**39** D3
   OP/CLY M11 ....**73** C4
The Sidings *WALK* M28 ....**42** B4
Sidlaw Cl *OLDS* OL8 ....**41** C3
Sidley Av *BKLY* M9 ....**35** C1
Sidmouth Av *BKLY* M9 ....**34** A3
Sidmouth St *CHAD* OL9 ....**21** D3
Sidney Rd *BKLY* M9 ....**34** A4
Sidney St *CMANE* M1 ....**8** B4
   CSLFD M3 ....**2** B3
   CSLFD M3 * **3** E5
Sidwell Wk *ANC* M4 * **71** C4
Signal Cl *ECC* M30 * **61** C3
Signal Dr *NEWH/MOS* M40 ....**53** C3
Signet Wk *CHH* M8 ....**52** A4
Silburn Wy *MDTN* M24 ....**15** D2
Silchester Dr *NEWH/MOS* M40 ......**53** C3
Silfield Cl *OP/CLY* M11 ....**71** D4
Silikin Cl *BRUN/LGST* M13 ....**8** C4
Silkstone St *OP/CLY* M11 ....**90** B2
Silk St *ANC* M4 ....**5** D2
   CSLFD M3 ....**2** A1
   MDTN M24 ....**17** C1
   NEWH/MOS M40 ....**55** D3
Sillavan Wy *CSLFD* M3 ....**2** C3
Silsden Av *BKLY* M9 ....**15** C4
Silton St *BKLY* M9 ....**54** A2
Silver Birch Gv *SWIN* M27 ....**46** A3
Silverbirch Wy *FAIL* M35 ....**57** C2
Silvercroft St *HULME* M15 ....**6** C3
Silverdale *SWIN* M27 ....**26** B3
Silverdale Av *CHAD* OL9 ....**20** B4
   PWCH M25 ....**31** D3

Silverdale Rd *CCHDY* M21 ....**99** D4
   HTNM SK4 ....**128** B1
Silverdale St *OP/CLY* M11 ....**92** A2
Silver Jubilee Wk *ANC* M4 ....**4** C1
Silverlea Dr *BKLY* M9 ....**33** D3
Silverstone Dr *NEWH/MOS* M40 ....**74** A1
Silver St *CMANE* M1 ....**4** B5
   CMANE M1 * **8** A1
   OLD OL1 ....**23** B3
Silverwell St *NEWH/MOS* M40 ....**56** A4
Silverwood *CHAD* OL9 ....**19** D2
Silverwood Av *CCHDY* M21 ....**112** A1
Simeon St *ANC* M4 * **4** C1
Simister Gn *PWCH* M25 ....**13** D1
Simister La *PWCH* M25 ....**13** C1
Simister Rd *FAIL* M35 ....**57** C2
Simister St *BKLY* M9 ....**53** D1
Simkin Wy *OLDS* OL8 ....**41** D4
Simms Cl *CSLFD* M3 ....**2** A3
Simon Freeman Cl *BNG/LEV* M19 ..**118** B3
Simpson Av *SWIN* M27 ....**27** D3
Simpson St *ANC* M4 ....**4** C1
   CHAD OL9 ....**39** C1
   EDGY/DAV SK3 ....**132** B1
   OP/CLY M11 ....**72** B4
Sindsley Rd *SWIN* M27 ....**25** C3
Singleton Cl *BRO* M7 ....**30** B4
Singleton Rd *BRO* M7 ....**30** B4
   HTNM SK4 ....**128** A1
Sirdar St *OP/CLY* M11 * **92** A1
Sirius Pl *BRO* M7 ....**68** A2
Sir Matt Busby Wy *TRPK* M17 ....**83** C4
Sir Richard Fairey Rd *HTNM* SK4 ...**117** D2
Sir Robert Thomas Ct *BKLY* M9 * **53** C1
Sisley Cl *BRO* M7 ....**49** C1
Sisson St *FAIL* M35 ....**56** B2
Sisters' St *DROY* M43 ....**92** B1
Sixth Av *OLDS* OL8 ....**39** D4
Sixth St *TRPK* M17 ....**82** A4
Skarratt Cl *WGTN/LGST* M12 ....**89** C3
Skelton Gv *BRUN/LGST* M13 ....**104** A3
Skelton Rd *STRET* M32 ....**97** C2
Skerry Cl *BRUN/LGST* M13 ....**9** D4
Skerton Rd *OLDTF/WHR* M16 ....**99** C1
Skip Pl *ANC* M4 ....**69** D2
Skipton Av *NEWH/MOS* M40 ....**37** C4
Skipton Cl *RDSH* SK5 ....**119** D1
Skye Rd *URM* M41 ....**79** C4
Slack La *SWIN* M27 ....**26** B4
Slack Rd *BKLY* M9 ....**33** D4
Slade Gv *BRUN/LGST* M13 ....**104** A2
Slade Hall Rd *WGTN/LGST* M12 ....**104** B3
Slade La *BNG/LEV* M19 ....**117** C1
Slade Mt *BNG/LEV* M19 * **117** C1
Slaithwaite Dr *OP/CLY* M11 ....**73** D3
Slate Av *ANC* M4 ....**5** F4
Slate La *AULW* OL7 ....**77** D4
   DTN/ASHW M34 ....**93** D1
Slater St *ECC* M30 ....**61** C3
   FAIL M35 ....**38** A4
   OLDS OL8 * **22** B3
Slate Whf *HULME* M15 * **6** B2
Sleaford Cl *NEWH/MOS* M40 ....**71** C2
Sledmere Cl *OP/CLY* M11 ....**72** B4
Sloane St *OP/CLY* M11 ....**72** B3
Smaildale Av *OLDTF/WHR* M16 ....**101** C3
Smallfield Dr *BKLY* M9 ....**53** C1
Smallridge Cl *NEWH/MOS* M40 ......**71** C2
Smallwood St *NEWH/MOS* M40 .....**55** D3
Smart St *WGTN/LGST* M12 ....**104** B2
Smeaton Cl *STRET* M32 ....**97** D3
Smeaton St *CHH* M8 ....**52** B3
Smedley La *CHH* M8 ....**52** A3
Smedley Rd *CHH* M8 ....**52** A3
Smedley St *CHH* M8 ....**51** D3
Smethurst St *BKLY* M9 ....**34** A4
   MDTN M24 ....**19** C2

Smith St *OLDTF/WHR* M16 ....84 B3
Smithy La *CSLFD* M3 * 3 E4
Smyrna St *ORD* M5 ....65 D4
Snell St *ANC* M4 ....71 C4
Snipe Wy *AULW* OL7 ....77 C4
Snowden St *OLDS* OL8 ....41 C1
Snowdon Rd *ECC* M30 ....63 D2
Soap St *ANC* M4 ....4 B3
Solent Av *CHH* M8 ....32 B3
Solway Cl *OLDS* OL8 ....22 B4
   SWIN M27 ....25 D1
Somerfield Rd *BKLY* M9 ....34 A4
Somerford Av *DID/WITH* M20 ....114 B1
Somerford Rd *RDSH* SK5 ....107 D3
Somerset Cl *RDSH* SK5 ....131 D1
Somerset Pl *SALE* M33 ....109 C3
Somerset Rd *DROY* M43 ....75 D2
   ECC M30 ....63 D1
   FAIL M35 ....56 B3
Somers Rd *RDSH* SK5 ....107 C4
Somerwood Wk *WGTN/LGST* M12 * 89 C3
Sopwith Dr *RUSH/FAL* M14 ....101 D4
Sorrel Bank *SLFD* M6 ....66 A1
Sorrell Bank *RDSH* SK5 ....120 B1
Sorrel St *HULME* M15 ....6 C5
Sorton St *CMANE* M1 * 8 B3
Soudan Rd *OFTN* SK2 ....133 D3
Southall St *CSLFD* M3 ....69 C2
Southampton Cl *BRO* M7 ....50 A4
Southam St *BRO* M7 ....51 D2
South Av *BNG/LEV* M19 ....117 C2
   SWIN M27 ....44 A4
   URM M41 ....79 D3
Southbank Rd *BNG/LEV* M19 ....116 A4
Southbourne Av *URM* M41 ....95 C3
Southbourne St *SLFD* M6 ....65 D3
Southbrook Av *CHH* M8 ....32 A2
Southcliffe Rd *RDSH* SK5 ....120 A3
South Cliffe St *OP/CLY* M11 ....92 A3
South Cres *NEWH/MOS* M40 ....37 C2
   OP/CLY M11 ....74 A3
Southcross Rd *GTN* M18 ....106 A2
South Croston St *OLDTF/WHR* M16 ....100 A1
Southdene Av *DID/WITH* M20 ....123 D1
Southdown Cl *HTNM* SK4 ....129 C3
Southdown Crs *BKLY* M9 ....35 D3
South Dr *CCHDY* M21 ....112 A3
Southern Ap *SWIN* M27 ....27 D3
Southernby Cl *BRUN/LGST* M13 * 104 A1
Southern Rd *SALE* M33 ....108 B3
Southern St *CSLFD* M3 ....7 D2
   SLFD M6 ....65 D3
Southfields Av *OP/CLY* M11 ....73 D3
Southgarth Rd *SLFD* M6 ....65 D2
Southgate *CCHDY* M21 ....112 A2
   HTNM SK4 ....118 B4
Southgate Av *NEWH/MOS* M40 * 72 B1
Southgate College Land *CSLFD* M3 * 3 E4
Southgate Rd *CHAD* OL9 ....37 D3
Southgate St *OLD* OL1 ....23 C3
South Gv *BRUN/LGST* M13 ....88 A4
South Hill St *OLDE* OL4 ....23 D3
South King St *CMANW* M2 ....3 F4
   CSLFD M3 ....3 E4
   ECC M30 ....61 C3
South Langworthy Rd *ORD* M5 ....66 A4
Southlea Rd *DID/WITH* M20 ....116 A4
Southlink *OLDE* OL4 ....23 D3
South Lonsdale St *STRET* M32 ....97 D2
South Meade *CCHDY* M21 ....112 A2
   PWCH M25 ....31 C3
Southmere Cl *BKLY* M9 ....36 B3
South Mesnefield Rd *BRO* M7 ....48 B2
Southmill St *CMANW* M2 ....7 E1
South Pump St *CMANE* M1 * 8 C1
South Radford St *BRO* M7 ....48 B2
South Rd *DID/WITH* M20 ....125 C3

STRET M32 ....95 D1
SWIN M27 ....28 A3
TRPK M17 ....96 B1
South Rw *PWCH* M25 ....29 C4
Southsea St *OP/CLY* M11 ....91 C2
South St *OLDS* OL8 ....39 D3
   OP/CLY M11 ....90 B2
   WGTN/LGST M12 ....88 B4
South Vw *RDSH* SK5 ....107 C2
Southway *DROY* M43 ....92 B1
   NEWH/MOS M40 ....38 A3
South Wy *OLDS* OL8 ....40 B3
Southwell Ct *STRET* M32 * 96 B4
Southwell St *BKLY* M9 ....53 D2
Southwood Dr *BKLY* M9 ....37 C4
Southyard St *BNG/LEV* M19 * 118 A1
Sovereign St *SLFD* M6 ....66 B1
Spa Cl *RDSH* SK5 ....119 D1
Sparkle St *CMANE* M1 ....3 D5
Sparrow Cl *RDSH* SK5 ....106 B3
Sparta Wk *OP/CLY* M11 ....90 B2
Sparthfield Rd *HTNM* SK4 ....129 C2
Sparth La *HTNM* SK4 ....129 C2
Sparth Rd *NEWH/MOS* M40 ....56 A4
Spa St *HULME* M15 ....6 C5
Spath Rd *DID/WITH* M20 ....124 B2
Spaw St *CSLFD* M3 ....3 C3
Spear St *CMANE* M1 ....4 C4
Spectator St *ANC* M4 ....71 C3
Spencer Av *OLDTF/WHR* M16 ....99 D3
Spencer St *CHAD* OL9 ....39 C1
   ECC M30 ....61 D4
   OLD OL1 ....23 D2
   RDSH SK5 ....120 A1
Spenden Av *CHH* M8 ....51 D3
Speyside Cl *WHTF* M45 * 11 D1
The Spinney *WALK* M28 * 43 D3
Spinning Jenny Wk *ANC* M4 ....5 F3
Spire Wk *WGTN/LGST* M12 * 88 D1
Sportsmans Dr *OLDS* OL8 ....41 D1
Spreadbury St *NEWH/MOS* M40 ....54 B2
Springbank *CHAD* OL9 * 20 B2
Spring Bank Pl *STKP* SK1 * 132 B1
Spring Bank St *OLDS* OL8 ....39 D1
Spring Bridge Rd *OLDTF/WHR* M16 ....101 C2
Spring Clough *WALK* M28 ....43 C4
Springdale Gdns *DID/WITH* M20 ....124 B2
Springfield Av *CHH* M8 ....52 A1
   HTNM SK4 ....119 D2
Springfield Cl *FAIL* M35 ....56 B1
Springfield La *CSLFD* M3 ....3 D1
Springfield Rd *DROY* M43 ....75 C2
Spring Gdns *CMANW* M2 ....4 A4
   SLFD M6 ....66 A2
   STKP SK1 ....130 B4
Springhead Av *DID/WITH* M20 ....114 B2
Springside *HTNM* SK4 ....119 C2
Springside Wk *HULME* M15 * 85 C3
Springs Rd *MDTN* M24 ....19 D3
Spring St *WGTN/LGST* M12 ....104 B3
Spring Ter *CHAD* OL9 ....20 B2
Spring V *MDTN* M24 ....17 D1
   PWCH M25 ....29 D3
Springville Av *BKLY* M9 ....54 A2
Springwell Cl *SLFD* M6 * 65 D3
Springwood Av *CHAD* OL9 ....19 D3
   SWIN M27 ....43 D3
Springwood Hall Rd *OLDS* OL8 ....41 D5
Spruce Ct *SLFD* M6 ....67 C3
Spruce St *HULME* M15 ....85 D3
Sprucewood *CHAD* OL9 ....19 C1
The Spur *OLDS* OL8 ....41 D5
The Square *HTNM* SK4 ....128 B3
   SWIN M27 ....44 B4
   WHTF M45 ....10 B1
Squire Rd *CHH* M8 ....51 C2

Stablefold *WALK* M28 ....**42** B4
Stableford Av *ECC* M30 ....**61** D1
The Stables *DROY* M43 ....**77** C2
Stable St *CHAD* OL9 ....**38** B3
Stafford Rd *ECC* M30 ....**62** B2
   FAIL M35 ....**57** D4
   SWIN M27 ....**45** C1
Stafford St *CHAD* OL9 ....**39** D1
Stag Pasture Rd *OLDS* OL8 ....**40** A4
Stainburn Rd *OP/CLY* M11 ....**90** A1
Stainer St *WGTN/LGST* M12 ....**104** B2
Stainforth St *OP/CLY* M11 ....**89** C2
Stainton Av *GTN* M18 ....**106** B1
Stakeford Dr *CHH* M8 ....**52** B1
Stalham Cl *NEWH/MOS* M40 ....**71** C2
Stamford Dr *FAIL* M35 ....**58** A4
Stamford Rd *BRO* M7 ....**49** C3
   BRUN/LGST M13 ....**104** A2
Stamford St *OLDTF/WHR* M16 ....**100** A1
   SALE M33 ....**108** B3
   SWIN M27 ....**26** B4
Stanage Av *BKLY* M9 * **35** C1
Stanbank St *HTNM* SK4 ....**129** D4
Stanbrook St *BNG/LEV* M19 ....**118** B1
Stanbury Wk *NEWH/MOS* M40 * **71** C2
Standish Rd *RUSH/FAL* M14 ....**116** A1
Standmoor Ct *WHTF* M45 * **10** A2
Standmoor Rd *WHTF* M45 ....**10** A2
Stanhope Av *PWCH* M25 ....**11** D4
Stanhope Ct *PWCH* M25 ....**11** D3
Stanhope Rd *SLFD* M6 ....**47** D4
Stanhope St *BNG/LEV* M19 ....**105** C1
   RDSH SK5 * **119** D2
Stanhope Wy *FAIL* M35 ....**56** B1
Stanhorne Av *CHH* M8 ....**32** B3
Stanier Av *ECC* M30 ....**62** A2
Stanier St *BKLY* M9 ....**53** D1
Stan Jolly Wk *OP/CLY* M11 ....**90** A1
Stanley Av *RUSH/FAL* M14 ....**102** B2
Stanley Av North *PWCH* M25 ....**11** D3
Stanley Av South *PWCH* M25 ....**11** D3
Stanley Ct *OLDTF/WHR* M16 ....**84** B4
Stanley Dr *WHTF* M45 ....**11** C3
Stanley Gv *GTN* M18 ....**105** C1
   HTNM SK4 ....**128** A1
   URM M41 ....**94** A3
   WGTN/LGST M12 ....**104** B1
Stanley Rd *BRO* M7 ....**50** B1
   CHAD OL9 ....**39** D2
   ECC M30 ....**61** D4
   HTNM SK4 ....**128** A1
   OLDTF/WHR M16 ....**84** B4
   OLDTF/WHR M16 ....**100** B3
   SWIN M27 ....**45** D1
Stanley St *BKLY* M9 * **53** D1
   CHAD OL9 ....**21** C2
   CHH M8..**69** D1
   CSLFD M3 ....**2** C4
   NEWH/MOS M40 ....**54** A4
   OP/CLY M11 ....**91** D2
   PWCH M25 ....**30** B1
   STKP SK1 * **130** B3
Stanmore Av *STRET* M32 ....**96** A3
Stannard Rd *ECC* M30 ....**60** A4
Stannybrook Rd *FAIL* M35 ....**59** C3
Stansby Gdns *WGTN/LGST* M12 ....**88** B3
Stansfield Rd *FAIL* M35 ....**38** B4
Stansfield St *CHAD* OL9 ....**21** C4
   NEWH/MOS M40 ....**74** A1
   OLD OL1 ....**22** B1
   OP/CLY M11 ....**91** C1
Stanthorne Av *DID/WITH* M20 ....**114** B2
Stanton Av *BRO* M7 ....**49** C3
   DID/WITH M20 ....**123** D1
Stanton Gdns *HTNM* SK4 ....**128** A4
Stanton St *CHAD* OL9 ....**39** C2
   OP/CLY M11 ....**73** D3

Stanway Cl *MDTN* M24 ....**18** A3
Stanway Rd *WHTF* M45 ....**12** A1
Stanway St *BKLY* M9 ....**53** D1
   STRET M32 ....**97** C2
Stanwell Rd *NEWH/MOS* M40 ....**36** B4
   SWIN M27 ....**44** B2
Stanwick Av *BKLY* M9 ....**32** B1
Stanworth Cl *OLDTF/WHR* M16 ....**100** B2
Stanyard Ct *ORD* M5 ....**83** D1
Stapleford Cl *SALE* M33 ....**110** B4
Staplehurst Rd *NEWH/MOS* M40 ....**72** B1
Stapleton St *SLFD* M6 ....**46** B4
Star Gv *BRO* M7 ....**50** B3
Starkie St *WALK* M28 ....**42** B1
Starling Cl *DROY* M43 ....**77** C2
Starmoor Dr *CHH* M8 ....**51** D3
Statford Av *ECC* M30 ....**78** B1
Statham St *SLFD* M6 ....**67** C3
Station Ap *CMANE* M1 ....**4** C5
   CMANE M1 ....**8** A2
Station Cl *CHH* M8 ....**32** B4
   ECC M30 ....**61** D4
   EDGY/DAV SK3 ....**132** B1
   HTNM SK4..**126** B4
   RDSH SK5 ....**106** B3
   STKP SK1..**129** D4
   STRET M32 ....**97** C2
   SWIN M27 ....**26** A4
   URM M41 ....**94** A4
Station Vw *BNG/LEV* M19 ....**104** B4
Staton St *OP/CLY* M11 ....**90** B1
Staverton Cl *BRUN/LGST* M13 ....**9** E5
Staycott St *OLDTF/WHR* M16 ....**101** C1
Stedman Cl *OP/CLY* M11 ....**71** D4
Steeple Cl *CHH* M8 ....**51** C4
Steeple Dr *ORD* M5 ....**83** D1
Stelfox Av *RUSH/FAL* M14 ....**101** D4
Stelfox St *ECC* M30 ....**78** A1
Stella St *BKLY* M9 ....**33** C1
Stelling St *GTN* M18 ....**91** C4
Stenbury Cl *RUSH/FAL* M14 ....**102** B2
Stenner La *DID/WITH* M20 ....**124** B3
Stephenson Av *DROY* M43 ....**75** D4
Stephenson Rd *STRET* M32 ....**97** D3
Stephenson St *FAIL* M35 ....**38** B4
Stephens Rd *DID/WITH* M20 ....**115** D4
Stephen St *CSLFD* M3 ....**69** C1
   URM M41 ....**94** B3
Stern Av *ORD* M5 * **83** D1
Sterndale Rd *EDGY/DAV* SK3 ....**132** B4
Stevenson Pl *CMANE* M1 * **4** C4
Stevenson Rd *SWIN* M27 ....**44** B1
Stevenson Sq *CMANE* M1 ....**4** C4
Stevenson St *ORD* M5 * **2** A4
Stillwater Dr *OP/CLY* M11 ....**72** B3
Stilton Dr *OP/CLY* M11 * **89** C1
Stirling Av *DID/WITH* M20 ....**114** A1
Stirling Gv *WHTF* M45 ....**11** C3
Stirling Rd *CHAD* OL9 ....**38** A1
Stirling St *CHAD* OL9 ....**21** D2
Stirrup Ga *WALK* M28 ....**42** B4
Stitch La *HTNM* SK4 ....**129** C2
Stobart Av *PWCH* M25 ....**30** B3
Stockburn Dr *FAIL* M35 ....**58** A2
Stockdale Av *EDGY/DAV* SK3 ....**133** C4
Stockdale Rd *BKLY* M9 ....**34** B1
Stockfield Mt *CHAD* OL9 ....**21** C3
Stockfield Rd *CHAD* OL9 ....**21** C2
Stockholm Rd *EDGY/DAV* SK3 ....**132** A3
Stockholm St *OP/CLY* M11 ....**73** C1
Stockland Cl *BRUN/LGST* M13 ....**8** C4
Stock La *CHAD* OL9 ....**21** C2
Stockley Wk *HULME* M15 * **85** C3
Stockport Rd *BNG/LEV* M19 ....**117** D1
   BRUN/LGST M13 ....**9** F5
   WGTN/LGST M12 ....**103** D1

Stockport Rd West *MPL/ROM* SK6........**131** D2
Stockport Village *STKP* SK1 *............**129** D4
Stocksfield Dr *BKLY* M9.....................**34** B2
Stocks St *CHH* M8.............................**69** D1
Stocks St East *CHH* M8......................**69** D1
Stockton Rd *CCHDY* M21...................**111** D3
Stockton St *OLDTF/WHR* M16.............**100** B1
  SWIN M27....................................**44** B2
Stokes St *OP/CLY* M11.......................**74** A4
Stonall Av *HULME* M15 *.....................**6** B5
Stoneacre Ct *SWIN* M27.....................**45** C2
Stonechat Cl *DROY* M43 *...................**76** B2
Stonefield Dr *CHH* M8.......................**50** B4
Stonehead St *BKLY* M9.......................**54** A2
Stonehurst Cl *WGTN/LGST* M12...........**89** D3
Stonelow Cl *HULME* M15......................**7** F5
Stonemead Dr *BKLY* M9......................**34** A1
Stone Pale *WHTF* M45........................**11** C2
Stonesby Cl *OLDTF/WHR* M16.............**100** B1
Stone St *CSLFD* M3.............................**7** D2
Stoneyfield Cl *OLDTF/WHR* M16..........**101** C3
Stoneygate Wk *OP/CLY* M11...............**91** C2
Stoneyhurst Cl *HULME* M15.................**86** A3
Stopford St *EDGY/DAV* SK3................**132** A1
  OP/CLY M11...............................**91** D2
Stores St *PWCH* M25.........................**30** B1
Store St *CMANE* M1.............................**5** E5
  OP/CLY M11...............................**90** A2
Stortford Dr *NTHM/RTH* M23..............**122** A3
Stothard Rd *STRET* M32......................**96** A4
Stott La *OLD* M....................................**64** A2
Stott Milne St *CHAD* OL9.....................**20** B4
Stott Rd *CHAD* OL9............................**37** D2
  SWIN M27....................................**44** A3
Stott's La *NEWH/MOS* M40..................**56** A3
Stott St *FAIL* M35..............................**56** A3
Stovell Av *WGTN/LGST* M12................**104** B3
Stovell Rd *NEWH/MOS* M40..................**54** B1
Stowell St *ORD* M5............................**65** D4
Stowfield Cl *BKLY* M9.........................**33** C1
Stow Gdns *DID/WITH* M20..................**114** B3
Stracey St *NEWH/MOS* M40 *..............**71** D2
Stradbroke St *GTN* M18.......................**90** A4
Strain Av *BKLY* M9.............................**34** A1
Strand Ct *STRET* M32........................**109** C1
Stranton Dr *WALK* M28.......................**43** D1
Stratford Av *DID/WITH* M20...............**114** A4
  OLDS OL8...................................**40** B2
Stratford Rd *MDTN* M24......................**18** A4
Strathblane Cl *DID/WITH* M20............**115** C2
Strathfield Dr *OP/CLY* M11..................**73** C3
Strathmere Av *STRET* M32...................**97** C3
Strathmore Av *CCHDY* M21..................**99** C3
Stratton Rd *OLDTF/WHR* M16...............**99** C3
  SWIN M27....................................**26** A4
Strawberry Bank *SLFD* M6 *.................**67** C2
Strawberry Hl *SLFD* M6.......................**67** C2
Strawberry Rd *SLFD* M6......................**66** B2
Stray St *OP/CLY* M11..........................**91** D1
Stream Ter *STKP* SK1........................**131** C4
Stretford Rd *OLDTF/WHR* M16.............**84** B4
  URM M41.....................................**94** A4
Stretton Av *DID/WITH* M20................**125** D2
  STRET M32..................................**95** D2
Stretton Cl *NEWH/MOS* M40................**53** C4
Stringer St *STKP* SK1........................**130** B5
Stroma Gdns *URM* M41.......................**78** B4
Strong St *BRO* M7..............................**68** B1
Stroud Av *ECC* M30............................**61** C2
Stroud Cl *MDTN* M24...........................**17** D4
Stuart Rd *STRET* M32..........................**97** C3
Stuart St *MDTN* M24...........................**18** B1
  OLDS OL8...................................**22** B4
  OP/CLY M11...............................**72** B3
Stuart St East *OP/CLY* M11..................**72** B3
Stuart Wk *MDTN* M24..........................**17** C2

Stubbs Cl *BRO* M7..............................**49** C1
Studforth Wk *HULME* M15 *.................**86** A4
Styal Av *RDSH* SK5...........................**120** A4
  STRET M32...................................**95** D2
Style St *ANC* M4.................................**4** B1
Sudell St *ANC* M4...............................**5** D1
Suffield St *MDTN* M24.........................**17** C1
Suffolk Av *DROY* M43..........................**75** D2
Suffolk Dr *RDSH* SK5.........................**121** D3
Suffolk St *CHAD* OL9.........................**21** C4
  SLFD M6.....................................**48** B4
Sugar Mill Sq *ORD* M5 *.....................**65** C3
Sulby Av *STRET* M32..........................**97** D3
Sulby St *NEWH/MOS* M40....................**54** B1
Sullivan St *WGTN/LGST* M12..............**104** B2
Sulway Cl *SWIN* M27 *........................**45** D2
Sumac St *OP/CLY* M11.........................**74** A3
Summer Av *URM* M41..........................**A** B3
Summercroft *CHAD* OL9......................**39** C2
Summerfield Av *DROY* M43..................**74** B2
Summerfield Rd *WALK* M28..................**42** B2
Summer Pl *RUSH/FAL* M14..................**102** B3
Summerseat Cl *ORD* M5 *....................**83** D1
Summers St *CHAD* OL9........................**21** D2
Summerville Av *BKLY* M9.....................**54** A2
Summerville Rd *SLFD* M6......................**47** D4
Sumner Rd *SLFD* M6...........................**47** C4
Sumner Wy *URM* M41..........................**94** B3
Sunbury Dr *NEWH/MOS* M40.................**74** A1
Sundew Pl *MDTN* M24..........................**19** C2
Sunfield Rd *OLD* OL1..........................**22** B1
Sunk La *MDTN* M24.............................**17** D2
Sunningdale Av *OP/CLY* M11................**73** C3
Sunningdale Dr *PWCH* M25..................**11** D4
  SLFD M6.....................................**45** D4
Sunny Bank Av *DROY* M43....................**75** C2
Sunnybank Av *ECC* M30.......................**63** C2
  HTNM SK4.................................**127** C1
Sunny Bank Rd *BRUN/LGST* M13.........**103** D2
Sunnybank Rd *DROY* M43.....................**75** C4
Sunny Brow Rd *GTN* M18.....................**90** B4
  MDTN M24..................................**31** B1
Sunny Dr *PWCH* M25...........................**29** C1
Sunnyfield Rd *HTNM* SK4....................**127** C3
  PWCH M25..................................**12** B2
Sunnylea Av *BNG/LEV* M19.................**116** B2
Sunnyside *AULW* OL7..........................**59** D4
Sunnyside Ct *DROY* M43 *....................**75** C2
Sunnyside La *DROY* M43......................**75** C1
Sunnyside Rd *DROY* M43......................**75** D2
Sunset Av *WYTH/NTH* M22.................**123** C4
Surbiton Rd *NEWH/MOS* M40................**54** A4
Surma Cl *CHAD* OL9...........................**22** A2
Surrey Av *DROY* M43...........................**75** C2
Surrey Rd *BKLY* M9.............................**34** A3
Surrey St *BKLY* M9 *............................**33** D3
  CHAD OL9..................................**21** D4
Surrey Wy *RDSH* SK5.........................**131** D1
Sussex Av *DID/WITH* M20...................**125** C1
Sussex Cl *CHAD* OL9..........................**21** C3
  SWIN M27....................................**26** B3
Sussex Dr *DROY* M43..........................**75** D2
Sussex St *BRO* M7..............................**68** A2
  CMANW M3...................................**3** F4
Sutcliffe Av *WGTN/LGST* M12.............**104** B3
Sutcliffe St *MDTN* M24........................**18** B1
  OLDS OL8...................................**22** B4
Sutherland Cl *OLDS* OL8......................**41** C4
Sutherland Rd *OLDTF/WHR* M16...........**98** C2
Sutherland St *ECC* M30........................**61** C2
  SWIN M27....................................**25** D4
Suthers St *CHAD* OL9.........................**21** D3
Sutton Dr *DROY* M43...........................**74** B2
Sutton Dwellings *SLFD* M6...................**65** A2
Sutton Rd *GTN* M18...........................**105** D2
  HTNM SK4.................................**128** B2
Swaine St *EDGY/DAV* SK3..................**129** D4

Swainsthorpe Dr *BKLY* M9 ....**53** D1
Swallow St *OLDS* OL8 ....**40** A3
  OP/CLY M11 ....**72** A4
  STKP SK1 ....**133** C2
  WGTN/LGST M12 * **104** B3
Swanage Rd *ECC* M30 ....**61** C2
Swanhill Cl *GTN* M18 ....**92** A3
Swanley Av *NEWH/MOS* M40 ....**53** D4
Swan St *ANC* M4 ....**4** B2
Swarbrick Dr *PWCH* M25 ....**29** C3
Swayfield Av *BRUN/LGST* M13 ....**104** A2
Sweetnam Dr *OP/CLY* M11 ....**73** C3
Swinbourne Gv *DID/WITH* M20 ....**115** D2
Swinburne Av *DROY* M43 ....**75** D2
Swinburne Gn *RDSH* SK5 ....**106** A4
Swinburn St *BKLY* M9 ....**35** C4
Swindell's St *OP/CLY* M11 * **91** D2
Swindon Cl *GTN* M18 ....**91** C4
Swinfield Av *CCHDY* M21 ....**111** C1
Swinstead Av *NEWH/MOS* M40 ....**53** D4
Swinton Gv *BRUN/LGST* M13 ....**87** D4
Swinton Hall Rd *SWIN* M27 ....**45** C1
Swinton Park Rd *SLFD* M6 ....**46** B4
Sycamore Av *SWIN* M27 ....**38** A2
Sycamore Cl *DID/WITH* M20 * **115** D2
Sycamore Ct *SLFD* M6 ....**66** B2
Sycamore Gv *FAIL* M35 ....**58** A2
Sycamore Pl *WHTF* M45 ....**11** C3
Sycamore Rd *ECC* M30 ....**60** B1
Sydney Av *ECC* M30 ....**62** A3
Sydney Jones Ct *NEWH/MOS* M40 ....**36** B4
Sydney St *FAIL* M35 ....**56** B2
  SLFD M6 ....**65** D3
  STRET M32 ....**97** C3
  SWIN M27 ....**44** A1
Sykes Meadow *EDGY/DAV* SK3 ....**132** A3
Sykes St *RDSH* SK5 ....**120** A1
Sylvan Av *FAIL* M35 ....**56** B4
  URM M41 ....**94** A2
Sylvandale Av *BNG/LEV* M19 ....**104** B4
Sylvan St *CHAD* OL9 ....**21** D2
Sylvia Gv *RDSH* SK5 ....**119** D2
Symms St *SLFD* M6 ....**67** C1
Symond Rd *BKLY* M9 ....**16** B4
Symons Rd *SALE* M33 ....**109** C4
Symons St *BRO* M7 ....**50** B2
Syndall Av *WGTN/LGST* M12 ....**88** A3
Syndall St *WGTN/LGST* M12 ....**88** A3

T

Tabley Av *RUSH/FAL* M14 ....**102** A3
Tabley Gv *BRUN/LGST* M13 ....**104** A3
  RDSH SK5 ....**119** D2
Tabley St *SLFD* M6 ....**49** C4
Tackler Cl *SWIN* M27 ....**45** C2
Tadcaster Dr *NEWH/MOS* M40 ....**53** D2
Tagore Cl *BRUN/LGST* M13 ....**103** D1
Tahir Cl *CHH* M8 ....**52** A2
Tait Ms *HTNM* SK4 ....**127** C3
Talavera St *BRO* M7 ....**50** A4
Talbot Pl *OLDTF/WHR* M16 ....**84** A4
Talbot Rd *RUSH/FAL* M14 ....**116** B2
  STRET M32 ....**98** A1
Talbot St *ECC* M30 ....**62** B4
Talford Gv *DID/WITH* M20 ....**114** B4
Talgarth Rd *NEWH/MOS* M40 ....**70** B1
Talland Wk *BRUN/LGST* M13 ....**88** A4
Tallarn Cl *DID/WITH* M20 ....**115** D2
Tallis St *WGTN/LGST* M12 ....**104** B2
Tallyman Wy *SWIN* M27 ....**47** D2
Tamar Cl *WHTF* M45 ....**11** D1
Tamar Ct *HULME* M15 ....**85** C3
Tamarin Cl *SWIN* M27 ....**24** B4

Tamerton Dr *CHH* M8 ....**51** D3
Tame St *ANC* M4 ....**71** C4
Tamworth Av *ORD* M5 ....**84** A1
  WHTF M45 ....**12** A2
Tamworth Ave West *ORD* M5 * **83** D1
Tamworth Cl *HULME* M15 ....**85** D1
Tamworth Gn *STKP* SK1 ....**131** C3
Tamworth St *CHAD* OL9 ....**21** D4
  STKP SK1 ....**131** C3
Tamworth Wk *ORD* M5 ....**83** D1
Tandis Ct *SLFD* M6 * **63** D2
Tandlewood Ms *NEWH/MOS* M40 ....**55** D4
Tangmere Cl *NEWH/MOS* M40 * **36** B2
Tanhill La *OLDS* OL8 ....**41** D3
Tanners Fold *OLDS* OL8 ....**41** D3
Tanners Gn *SLFD* M6 ....**66** A2
Tansey Gv *BRO* M7 ....**51** C3
Tansley Rd *CHH* M8 ....**32** B3
Tan Yard Brow *GTN* M18 ....**106** B1
Tanyard Gn *RDSH* SK5 ....**120** A4
Taplin Dr *GTN* M18 ....**90** B4
Taplow Wk *RUSH/FAL* M14 ....**103** D2
Tariff St *CMANE* M1 ....**5** D4
Tarleton Wk *BRUN/LGST* M13 * **87** D3
Tarnbrook Cl *WHTF* M45 ....**12** B1
Tarnbrook Wk *HULME* M15 ....**86** A4
Tarporley Av *RUSH/FAL* M14 ....**114** B1
Tarrington Cl *WGTN/LGST* M12 ....**89** D4
Tartan St *OP/CLY* M11 ....**73** D2
Tarvin Av *DID/WITH* M20 ....**114** B2
  HTNM SK4 ....**119** C2
Tarvington Cl *NEWH/MOS* M40 * **52** B3
Tasle Aly *CMANW* M2 ....**3** F5
Tatchbury Rd *FAIL* M35 ....**57** D2
Tatham Cl *BRUN/LGST* M13 ....**104** A2
Tattersall St *CHAD* OL9 ....**22** A3
Tatton Gv *DID/WITH* M20 ....**115** C3
Tatton Mere Dr *DROY* M43 ....**76** A4
Tatton Pl *SALE* M33 ....**109** C4
Tatton Rd *SALE* M33 ....**109** C4
Tatton Rd North *HTNM* SK4 ....**118** B4
Tatton Rd South *HTNM* SK4 ....**128** B1
Tatton St *HULME* M15 ....**6** A5
  ORD M5 ....**84** A1
  STKP SK1 * **130** A4
Taunton Av *ECC* M30 ....**61** C2
  RDSH SK5 ....**121** D4
Taunton Brook La *AULW* OL7 ....**59** D4
Taunton Gv *WHTF* M45 ....**11** D3
Taunton St *ANC* M4 ....**71** C4
Tavern Court Av *FAIL* M35 ....**57** D2
Tavery Cl *ANC* M4 * **5** F3
Tay Cl *OLDS* OL8 ....**22** B4
Taylor Rd *URM* M41 ....**79** D2
Taylorson St *ORD* M5 ....**84** A2
Taylorson St South *ORD* M5 ....**83** D3
Taylor's Rd *STRET* M32 ....**97** D1
Taylor St *CHAD* OL9 ....**20** B2
  DROY M43 ....**75** D2
  GTN M18 ....**90** B3
  MDTN M24 ....**17** D1
  PWCH M25 ....**30** B1
  RUSH/FAL M14 ....**102** B2
Teak Dr *FWTH* BL4 ....**25** C1
Tealby Av *OLDTF/WHR* M16 ....**99** D1
Tealby Rd *GTN* M18 ....**105** C1
Teasdale Cl *CHAD* OL9 ....**37** D2
Tebbutt St *ANC* M4 ....**5** D1
Teddington Rd *NEWH/MOS* M40 ....**36** B4
Ted Jackson Wk *OP/CLY* M11 * **89** C1
Teer St *ANC* M4 ....**71** C3
Teignmouth Av *NEWH/MOS* M40 * **70** B1
Teignmouth St *NEWH/MOS* M40 ....**70** B1
Telfer Av *BRUN/LGST* M13 ....**103** D3
Telfer Rd *BRUN/LGST* M13 ....**103** D3
Telford St *CHH* M8 ....**52** B4
Telford Wk *OLDTF/WHR* M16 ....**100** A1

Tellson Cl *SLFD* M6	**47**	C3
Tellson Crs *SLFD* M6	**47**	C3
Temperance St *WGTN/LGST* M12	**9**	F3
Temple Dr *SWIN* M27	**46**	A2
Temple Sq *CHH* M8	**51**	D4
Ten Acre Ct *WHTF* M45 *	**10**	A2
Ten Acre Dr *WHTF* M45	**10**	A2
Ten Acres La *NEWH/MOS* M40	**72**	B1
Tenax Rd *TRPK* M17	**81**	C2
Tenbury Cl *SLFD* M6 *	**66**	A2
Tenbury Dr *MDTN* M24	**17**	D4
STRET M32	**97**	D1
Tenby Av *DID/WITH* M20	**115**	C3
Tenby Ct *OLDTF/WHR* M16 *	**84**	B3
Tenby Dr *SLFD* M6	**47**	C3
Tenby Rd *OLDS* OL8	**39**	C3
Teneriffe St *BRO* M7	**50**	A4
Tennis St *OLDTF/WHR* M16	**99**	C1
Tennyson Cl *HTNM* SK4	**127**	D4
Tennyson Gdns *PWCH* M25	**29**	C2
Tennyson Rd *DROY* M43	**75**	D3
RDSH SK5	**106**	A4
SWIN M27	**44**	A1
Tennyson St *BRUN/LGST* M13	**87**	D4
Tenth St *TRPK* M17	**82**	A3
Terence St *NEWH/MOS* M40	**56**	A4
The Terrace *PWCH* M25	**30**	A2
Terrington Cl *M21*	**113**	D2
Tetlow Gv *ECC* M30	**61**	D4
Tetlow La *BRO* M7	**50**	B4
Tetlow St *MDTN* M24	**17**	D1
NEWH/MOS M40	**55**	D4
Teviot St *BRUN/LGST* M13	**103**	D1
Tewkesbury Av *DROY* M43	**75**	D2
URM M41	**94**	A1
Tewkesbury Dr *PWCH* M25	**30**	B3
Tewkesbury Rd *NEWH/MOS* M40	**71**	C2
Textile St *WGTN/LGST* M12	**89**	D2
Textilose Rd *TRPK* M17	**81**	C4
Thackeray Cl *CHH* M8	**51**	D3
Thackeray Gv *DROY* M43	**75**	D3
Thames Ct *OP/CLY* M11	**90**	A1
Thames Ct *HULME* M15	**85**	C3
Thames St *OLD* OL1	**23**	D1
Thanet Cl *BRO* M7	**50**	B4
Thankerton Av *DTN/ASHW* M34	**77**	C4
Thatcher St *OLDS* OL8	**41**	D2
Thatch Leach *CHAD* OL9	**20**	A4
Thatch Leach La *WHTF* M45	**11**	D2
Thaxmead Dr *NEWH/MOS* M40	**74**	A1
Theatre St *OLD* OL1 *	**23**	C2
Thekla St *OLD* OL9	**22**	A1
Thelwall Av *RUSH/FAL* M14	**114**	A1
Theta Cl *OP/CLY* M11	**73**	C3
Thetford Dr *CHH* M8	**52**	A2
Third Av *OLDS* OL8	**39**	D3
OP/CLY M11	**73**	D3
SWIN M27	**44**	B4
TRPK M17	**82**	A4
Thirlmere Av *STRET* M32	**96**	B3
SWIN M27	**45**	D2
Thirsfield Dr *OP/CLY* M11	**73**	D3
Thirsk St *WGTN/LGST* M12	**9**	E3
Thistle Bank Cl *BKLY* M9	**33**	D4
Thistledown Cl *ECC* M30	**78**	B1
Thomas Gibbon Cl *STRET* M32 *	**96**	B4
Thomas Johnson Cl *ECC* M30 *	**61**	D4
Thomas St *ANC* M4	**4**	B3
CHH M8	**51**	C1
STKP SK1	**133**	C2
STRET M32	**97**	C2
Thomas St West *STKP* SK1	**133**	C2
Thompson Av *WHTF* M45	**11**	D4
Thompson La *CHAD* OL9	**38**	B1
Thompson Rd *TRPK* M17	**79**	D1
Thompson St *ANC* M4	**4**	C2

CHAD OL9	**22**	A2
CSLFD M3 *	**68**	B2
NEWH/MOS M40	**54**	A4
Thomson Rd *GTN* M18	**105**	D1
Thomson St *BRUN/LGST* M13	**87**	D3
EDGY/DAV SK3	**132**	B1
Thoralby Cl *WGTN/LGST* M12	**89**	D4
Thoresway Rd *BRUN/LGST* M13	**103**	D1
Thor Gv *ORD* M5	**84**	B1
Thorley Cl *CHAD* OL9	**37**	D3
Thorley Dr *URM* M41	**94**	A3
Thorley St *FAIL* M35	**57**	C1
Thornage Dr *NEWH/MOS* M40	**70**	B1
Thorn Av *FAIL* M35	**57**	C3
Thorn Bank *DROY* M43 *	**75**	C2
Thornbridge Av *CCHDY* M21	**112**	A1
Thornbury Rd *STRET* M32	**97**	D1
Thornbury Wy *GTN* M18	**90**	B4
Thorncliff Av *OLDS* OL8	**40**	B2
Thorncliffe Gv *BNG/LEV* M19	**105**	D4
Thorncombe Rd *OLDTF/WHR* M16	**100**	B2
Thorn Ct *SLFD* M6	**67**	C3
Thorncross Cl *HULME* M15	**84**	B2
Thorneycroft Av *CCHDY* M21	**112**	B4
Thorney Hill Cl *OLDE* OL4	**23**	D3
Thornfield Dr *SWIN* M27	**44**	B2
Thornfield Rd *BNG/LEV* M19	**116**	B4
HTNM SK4	**127**	D2
Thornfield St *ORD* M5	**65**	C4
Thorngate Rd *CHH* M8	**51**	D4
Thorn Gv *RUSH/FAL* M14	**116**	A1
Thornhill Rd *DROY* M43	**76**	A3
HTNM SK4	**127**	C3
Thornholme Cl *GTN* M18	**105**	C2
Thorniley Brow *ANC* M4	**4**	A3
Thornlea *DROY* M43	**74**	B4
Thornlea Av *OLDS* OL8	**39**	D4
SWIN M27	**44**	A3
Thornleigh Rd *RUSH/FAL* M14	**102**	A4
Thorley La North *RDSH* SK5	**107**	C2
Thorley La South *RDSH* SK5	**107**	D4
Thornley Rd *PWCH* M25	**12**	B2
Thornmere Cl *SWIN* M27	**24**	B3
Thorn Rd *SWIN* M27	**44**	B3
Thornsett Cl *BKLY* M9 *	**53**	D1
The Thorns *CCHDY* M21	**112**	A2
Thornton Av *DTN/ASHW* M34	**93**	D1
Thornton Crs *PWCH* M25	**11**	C4
Thornton Pl *HTNM* SK4	**128**	A1
Thornton Rd *RUSH/FAL* M14	**101**	D3
Thornton St *NEWH/MOS* M40	**70**	B1
OLDE OL4	**23**	C4
Thornton St North *NEWH/MOS* M40	**71**	C1
Thorntree Cl *BKLY* M9	**53**	D2
Thornwood Av *GTN* M18	**106**	B1
Thorpe Av *SWIN* M27	**25**	D4
Thorpebrook Rd *NEWH/MOS* M40	**54**	B3
Thorpe Gv *HTNM* SK4	**119**	C3
Thorpeness Sq *GTN* M18	**91**	C3
Thorpe St *MDTN* M24	**15**	D2
OLDTF/WHR M16	**99**	D1
Thorp Rd *NEWH/MOS* M40	**54**	B3
Thorp St *ECC* M30	**78**	A1
Thrapston Av *DTN/ASHW* M34	**77**	C4
Throstles Cl *DROY* M43	**76**	B2
Thruxton Cl *OLDTF/WHR* M16	**100**	B2
Thurland St *CHAD* OL9	**19**	D1
Thurlby Av *BKLY* M9	**16**	B4
Thurlby St *BRUN/LGST* M13	**103**	C1
Thurleigh Rd *DID/WITH* M20	**125**	C1
Thurloe St *RUSH/FAL* M14	**102**	B2
Thurlow St *SALQ* M50	**83**	C1
Thurlston Crs *CHH* M8	**52**	A2
Thurlwood Av *DID/WITH* M20	**114**	B2
Thursfield St *SLFD* M6	**49**	C4
Tiber St *OLDS* OL8	**39**	D4
Tib La *CMANW* M2	**3**	F5

Tib St CMANE M1....4 B4
Tideswell Av NEWH/MOS M40....71 C2
Tideswell Rd DROY M43....74 B2
Tideway Cl BRO M7....48 A1
Tidworth Av ANC M4....5 F3
Tilbury St OLD OL1....22 B3
Tillerman Cl SWIN M27....47 C1
Tilney Av STRET M32....97 D2
Tilshead Wk BRUN/LGST M13 *....87 D3
Times St MDTN M24....18 A1
Timothy Cl SLFD M6....64 A2
Timperley Cl OLDS OL8....41 D3
Timperley St CHAD OL9....22 A2
  OP/CLY M11 *....90 B1
Timson St FAIL M35....57 C2
Tindall St ECC M30....78 A1
  RDSH SK5....107 C2
Tinningham Cl OP/CLY M11....91 C2
Tinshill Cl WGTN/LGST M12....89 D4
Tinsley St NEWH/MOS M40....71 D3
Tintern Av DID/WITH M20....114 A4
Tintern Gv STKP SK1....131 C4
Tintern St RUSH/FAL M14....102 A3
Tirza Av BNG/LEV M19....117 C2
Tithe Barn Rd HTNM SK4....127 C1
Titherington Cl BNG/LEV M19 *....106 A4
Titterington Av CCHDY M21....99 C3
Tiverton Rd URM M41....94 B1
Tiviot Dl STKP SK1....130 A3
Tiviot Wy RDSH SK5....130 A2
Tivoli Cl CSLFD M3....3 E5
Tobermory Cl OP/CLY M11....74 A4
Todd St BRO M7....50 A3
  CSLFD M3....4 A2
Toft Rd GTN M18....105 D1
Toledo St OP/CLY M11....74 A4
Tollard Av NEWH/MOS M40....53 C4
Toll Bar St WGTN/LGST M12....88 B3
Tollesbury Cl NEWH/MOS M40....71 C1
Toll Gate Cl BRUN/LGST M13....103 D1
Tolworth Dr CHH M8....52 A2
Tomlinson Cl OLDS OL8....22 B4
Tomlinson St HULME M15....85 D3
  NEWH/MOS M40....36 B2
Tommy Browell Cl RUSH/FAL M14....101 D2
Tommy Johnson Wk RUSH/FAL M14....101 D2
Tommy Taylor Cl NEWH/MOS M40 *....55 D4
Tonbridge Rd BNG/LEV M19....118 A1
  RDSH SK5....120 A1
Tonge Hall Cl MDTN M24....18 A1
Tonge Meadow MDTN M24....18 A1
Tonge Roughs MDTN M24....19 C1
Tonge St WGTN/LGST M12 *....88 A2
Tonman St CSLFD M3....7 D1
Tootal Dr SLFD M6....64 B2
Tootal Gv SLFD M6....64 B3
Tootal Rd ORD M5....64 B3
Topgate Brow SWIN M27....47 C1
Topley St BKLY M9....52 B1
Top o' th' Gn CHAD OL9....39 D1
Top Schwabe St MDTN M24....15 D1
Torah St CHH M8....69 D1
Torbay Rd CCHDY M21....112 B1
  URM M41....94 B4
Torcross Rd BKLY M9....15 C4
Torkington Av SWIN M27....26 A4
Torkington St EDGY/DAV SK3....132 A2
Torness Wk OP/CLY M11....73 C4
Toronto Rd OFTN SK2....133 D3
Torquay Dr BRUN/LGST M13....88 A4
Torrax Cl SLFD M6....46 A3
Torrens St SLFD M6....47 C4
Torrin Cl EDGY/DAV SK3....133 C4
Torrington Av BKLY M9....35 D3
Torrington Rd SWIN M27....46 A3
Torside Wy SWIN M27....26 A3
Totland Cl WGTN/LGST M12....104 B2

Totnes Rd CCHDY M21....112 B1
Tottington La PWCH M25....10 B4
Tottington St OP/CLY M11....73 D3
Totton Rd FAIL M35....57 C2
Towcester Cl ANC M4....71 C4
Tower Sq BRUN/LGST M13....9 E5
Towey Cl GTN M18....91 C3
Towncliffe Wk HULME M15 *....85 C3
Townfield Wk HULME M15....6 B5
Town Hall La CMANW M2 *....3 F1
Townley St CHH M8....51 C4
  OP/CLY M11 *....89 C1
Townsend Rd SWIN M27....26 A4
Towton St BKLY M9....53 D1
Towyn Av ORD M5....66 B3
Toxteth St OP/CLY M11....91 D2
Tracey St CHH M8....32 B4
Traders Av URM M41....79 D2
Trafalgar Av DTN/ASHW M34....93 D2
Trafalgar Gv BRO M7 *....50 A4
Trafalgar Pl DID/WITH M20....124 B1
Trafalgar Rd SALE M33....109 D3
  SLFD M6....63 D2
Trafalgar St BRO M7....50 B4
  OLD OL1....22 B1
Trafford Av URM M41....94 B2
Trafford Bank Rd OLDTF/WHR M16 *....84 B4
Trafford Bvd URM M41....78 B3
Trafford Gv STRET M32....97 C3
Trafford Park Rd TRPK M17....81 D2
Trafford Pl OLDTF/WHR M16....85 C3
Trafford Rd ECC M30....79 C1
  SALQ M50....83 D1
Trafford St CSLFD M3....7 D2
  OLDS OL8....22 B4
Trafford Wharf Rd TRPK M17....81 D2
Trail St SLFD M6....65 D3
Tram St OP/CLY M11....90 B2
Tranmere Cl GTN M18....90 A4
Transvaal St OP/CLY M11....74 A4
Travis Brow HTNM SK4....129 C4
Travis St CMANE M1....9 E1
Tree Av DROY M43....75 D2
Treelands Wk ORD M5....84 A3
Tregaer Fold MDTN M24....18 B1
Trenam Pl ORD M5....67 C3
Trenant Rd SLFD M6....65 C1
Trent Av CHAD OL9....19 D1
Trent Bridge Wk OLDTF/WHR M16....98 B2
Trent Cl RDSH SK5....121 D4
Trent Ct HULME M15 *....85 C3
Trentham Av URM M41....94 B2
Trentham Gv NEWH/MOS M40....35 D2
Trentham Lawns SLFD M6....66 B1
Trentham Rd OLDTF/WHR M16....98 B2
Trentham St HULME M15....84 B2
  SWIN M27 *....25 D1
Trent Wk DROY M43....93 C3
Tresco Av STRET M32....97 D4
Trevelyan St ECC M30....63 D3
Trevor Dr NEWH/MOS M40....37 D3
Trevor Rd ECC M30....61 C2
  SWIN M27....44 B3
Trevor St OP/CLY M11....91 D2
Trimdon Cl OP/CLY M11....73 C3
Trimley Av NEWH/MOS M40....53 C4
Trinity St MDTN M24 *....17 C1
  OLD OL1....22 B1
Trinity Wy CSLFD M3....2 B5
Tripps Ms DID/WITH M20....124 A1
Triscombe Wy OLDTF/WHR M16....100 B2
Tristam Cl BRUN/LGST M13....9 E5
Trojan Gdns BRO M7....49 D4
Trough Ga OLDS OL8....40 A3
Troutbeck Av ANC M4....5 F3
Trowbridge Dr NEWH/MOS M40....36 B4
Trowtree Av WGTN/LGST M12....88 B3

Troydale Dr *NEWH/MOS* M40 ...... **54** B3
Troy Av *ORD* M5 * **84** A2
Trumpet St *CMANE* M1 ...... **7** E2
Truro Av *RDSH* SK5 ...... **121** D4
   STRET M32 ...... **97** D3
Trust Rd *GTN* M18 ...... **105** D2
Tucana Av *BRO* M7 ...... **67** D2
Tudbury Wy *CSLFD* M3 ...... **2** B2
Tudor Av *BKLY* M9 ...... **34** B4
   CHAD OL9 ...... **37** C2
Tudor Cl *RDSH* SK5 ...... **119** D2
Tudor Ct *PWCH* M25 ...... **30** B2
Tudor St *MDTN* M24 ...... **18** A1
   OLDS OL8 ...... **22** A4
Tugford Cl *OLDTF/WHR* M16 ...... **100** B2
Tuley St *OP/CLY* M11 ...... **89** C2
Tulip Cl *CHAD* OL9 ...... **19** D2
   EDGY/DAV SK3 ...... **132** A4
Tully Pl *BRO* M7 ...... **68** B1
Tully St *BRO* M7 ...... **50** B2
Tully St South *BRO* M7 ...... **50** B3
Tulpen Sq *CHAD* OL9 ...... **21** C2
Tunbridge Sq *ORD* M5 ...... **66** B3
Tunstall St *HTNM* SK4 * **129** D2
   OP/CLY M11 * **91** D2
Tunstead Av *DID/WITH* M20 ...... **114** A3
Turf La *CHAD* OL9 ...... **38** A3
Turley St *CHH* M8 ...... **52** A3
Turnbull Av *PWCH* M25 ...... **12** A3
Turnbull Rd *BRUN/LGST* M13 ...... **104** A3
   GTN M18 ...... **107** C2
Turnbury Cl *SALE* M33 ...... **109** C3
Turncroft La *STKP* SK1 ...... **130** B4
Turnell Wy *WALK* M28 ...... **42** B4
Turner Av *FAIL* M35 ...... **56** B3
Turner Dr *URM* M41 ...... **95** C3
Turner St *ANC* M4 ...... **4** B3
   BRO M7 ...... **50** B2
   GTN M18 ...... **91** C4
   OLDTF/WHR M16 ...... **84** B3
   OP/CLY M11 ...... **73** D4
   STKP SK1 ...... **130** A3
Turn Moss Rd *STRET* M32 ...... **111** C1
Turnpike Gn *SLFD* M6 * **66** A2
Turnpike Wk *OP/CLY* M11 ...... **72** A4
Turton La *PWCH* M25 ...... **11** C4
Turton St *OP/CLY* M11 * **91** C2
Tuscany Vw *BRO* M7 ...... **49** C4
Tutbury St *ANC* M4 ...... **71** C4
Tuxford Wk *NEWH/MOS* M40 ...... **53** C4
Tweedale Av *BKLY* M9 ...... **15** D4
Tweedale Wy *CHAD* OL9 ...... **38** A3
Tweed Cl *OLDS* OL8 ...... **22** B4
Tweedle Hill Rd *BKLY* M9 ...... **33** D1
Twillbrook Dr *CSLFD* M3 * **3** D1
Twining Rd *ECC* M30 ...... **79** C1
Twyford Cl *DID/WITH* M20 ...... **124** A2
Tydden St *OLDS* OL8 ...... **41** C2
Tyldesley St *RUSH/FAL* M14 ...... **101** D2
Tymm St *NEWH/MOS* M40 ...... **55** D1
Tyndall Av *NEWH/MOS* M40 ...... **35** D4
Tynedale Cl *RDSH* SK5 ...... **119** D4
Tyrol Wk *OP/CLY* M11 ...... **89** C1
Tyro St *OLDS* OL8 * **41** C2
Tyrrel Rd *RDSH* SK5 ...... **107** C4
Tysoe Gdns *CSLFD* M3 ...... **2** B2
Tyson St *CHH* M8 ...... **51** C1
Tytherington Dr *BNG/LEV* M19 ...... **106** A4

U

Ukraine Rd *BRO* M7 ...... **48** B3
Ulverston Av *CHAD* OL9 ...... **20** B3
   DID/WITH M20 ...... **114** A2

Underhill Wk *NEWH/MOS* M40 ...... **73** C1
Under La *CHAD* OL9 ...... **39** C2
Underwood Cl *GTN* M18 ...... **92** A3
Unicorn St *ECC* M30 ...... **78** A1
Union St *ANC* M4 ...... **4** B3
   CHAD OL9 ...... **39** C1
   GTN M18 ...... **91** D3
   OLD OL1 ...... **75** D1
   RUSH/FAL M14 * **102** A2
   SLFD M6 ...... **66** B1
   STKP SK1 ...... **133** C1
   SWIN M27 ...... **44** B1
   SWIN M27 ...... **45** D1
   WGTN/LGST M12 ...... **9** F3
Union St West *OLDS* OL8 ...... **22** B4
Union Ter *BRO* M7 ...... **51** C1
United Rd *OLDTF/WHR* M16 ...... **82** B4
Unity Dr *BRO* M7 ...... **50** B3
Unity Wy *STKP* SK1 ...... **133** C1
University Rd *ORD* M5 ...... **67** C3
University Rd West *ORD* M5 * **67** C3
Unsworth Wy *OLD* OL1 * **22** B1
Unwin Av *GTN* M18 ...... **106** A1
Upland Rd *OLDS* OL8 ...... **40** B1
Uplands *MDTN* M24 ...... **17** D2
Upper Brook St *BRUN/LGST* M13 ...... **8** C5
   STKP SK1 ...... **130** B4
Upper Camp St *BRO* M7 ...... **50** A4
Upper Chorlton Rd *OLDTF/WHR* M16 ...... **99** D2
Upper Cleminson St *CSLFD* M3 ...... **2** A3
Upper Conran St *BKLY* M9 ...... **53** D1
Upper Gloucester St *SLFD* M6 ...... **66** B2
Upper Helena St *NEWH/MOS* M40 ...... **71** D3
Upper Kent Rd *RUSH/FAL* M14 ...... **103** C2
Upper Kirby St *ANC* M4 ...... **5** F4
Upper Lloyd St *RUSH/FAL* M14 ...... **101** D2
Upper Medlock St *HULME* M15 ...... **7** F5
Uppermill Dr *BNG/LEV* M19 ...... **126** A2
Upper Monsall St *NEWH/MOS* M40 ...... **53** D3
Upper Moss La *HULME* M15 ...... **85** D1
Upper Park Rd *BRO* M7 ...... **31** D4
   RUSH/FAL M14 ...... **102** B1
Upper West Gv *BRUN/LGST* M13 ...... **88** A4
Upper Wharf St *ORD* M5 ...... **66** B3
Upper Wilton St *PWCH* M25 ...... **30** B1
Upton Av *HTNM* SK4 ...... **126** A1
Upton Cl *MDTN* M24 ...... **17** D4
Urmson St *OLDS* OL8 ...... **41** C2
Urmston La *STRET* M32 ...... **95** D4
Urmston Pk *URM* M41 ...... **94** B3
Usk Cl *WHTF* M45 ...... **12** B2
Uxbridge Av *OP/CLY* M11 ...... **73** D3

V

Vaal St *OLDS* OL8 ...... **39** D2
Valance Cl *WGTN/LGST* M12 ...... **89** D3
Vale Av *SALE* M33 ...... **110** B4
   SWIN M27 ...... **26** B4
Vale Cl *HTNM* SK4 ...... **127** C3
Vale Dr *CHAD* OL9 ...... **22** A3
   PWCH M25 ...... **29** D3
Vale La *FAIL* M35 ...... **75** D1
Valencia Rd *BRO* M7 ...... **49** C3
Valentia Rd *BKLY* M9 ...... **34** A1
Valentine St *FAIL* M35 ...... **56** B2
Vale Park Wy *CHH* M8 ...... **52** B2
Valerie Wk *HULME* M15 ...... **7** F4
Vale Rd *DROY* M43 ...... **76** A2
   HTNM SK4 ...... **127** C4
Vale St *MDTN* M24 ...... **18** A1
   OP/CLY M11 ...... **73** D3
Vale Top Av *BKLY* M9 ...... **53** D2
Valetta Cl *RUSH/FAL* M14 ...... **115** C1

Valewood Av *HTNM* SK4 ....127 D4
Valley Park Rd *PWCH* M25 ....11 C4
Valley Wk *OP/CLY* M11 ....72 A4
Vancouver Quay *SALQ* M50 ....85 C2
Vandyke St *SLFD* M6 ....64 A2
Vane St *ECC* M30 ....61 D3
Varden Gv *EDGY/DAV* SK3 * 132 A4
Varey St *GTN* M18 ....91 C1
Varley St *NEWH/MOS* M40 ....71 C4
Varna St *OP/CLY* M11 ....91 A4
Vauban Dr *SLFD* M6 ....64 A2
Vaughan Av *NEWH/MOS* M40 ....54 B1
Vaughan Rd *CCHDY* M21 ....113 C1
    HTNM SK4 ....129 C2
Vaughan St *ECC* M30 ....61 C2
    WGTN/LGST M12 ....89 C2
Vauxhall St *NEWH/MOS* M40 ....70 A1
Vega St *CHH* M8 ....68 B1
Vela Wk *BRO* M7 ....67 D2
Velmere Av *BKLY* M9 ....14 B4
Velour Cl *CSLFD* M3 ....2 A1
Vendale Av *SWIN* M27 ....44 A3
Venetia St *NEWH/MOS* M40 * 55 D4
Venice St *CMANE* M1 * 8 B2
Ventnor Av *BNG/LEV* M19 ....118 B1
    SALE M33 ....109 C3
Ventnor Rd *DID/WITH* M20 ....125 D2
    HTNM SK4 ....127 D3
Ventnor St *SLFD* M6 ....49 C4
Ventor St *BKLY* M9 ....53 C1
Ventura Cl *RUSH/FAL* M14 ....101 D4
Venture Scout Wy *CHH* M8 ....51 C3
Venwood Ct *PWCH* M25 * 29 C3
Venwood Rd *PWCH* M25 ....29 C3
Verdun Av *SLFD* M6 ....64 A2
Verdun Rd *ECC* M30 ....61 C1
Verdure Cl *FAIL* M35 ....58 A1
Vere St *SALQ* M50 ....66 A4
Verity Cl *DID/WITH* M20 ....115 C3
Verne Av *SWIN* M27 ....44 B1
Vernon Av *ECC* M30 * 63 C3
    STKP SK1 ....131 C3
    STRET M32 ....97 C4
Vernon Dr *PWCH* M25 ....29 D3
Vernon Rd *BRO* M7 ....30 B4
    DROY M43 ....74 B3
Vernon St *BKLY* M9 ....53 D2
    BRO M7 ....50 A4
    OLDTF/WHR M16 ....84 B4
Verona Dr *NEWH/MOS* M40 ....73 D1
Veronica Rd *DID/WITH* M20 ....125 D2
Verrill Av *NTHM/RTH* M23 ....122 B4
Vesper St *FAIL* M35 ....57 D1
Vesta St *ANC* M4 ....5 F4
Vestris Dr *SLFD* M6 ....64 A2
Viaduct St *CSLFD* M3 ....3 D2
    EDGY/DAV SK3 ....129 D4
    WGTN/LGST M12 ....88 B1
Vicarage Cl *SLFD* M6 ....64 A2
Vicarage Gdns *EDGY/DAV* SK3 * 132 B1
Vicarage Gv *ECC* M30 ....63 C3
Vicarage La *MDTN* M24 ....19 C2
Vicarage Rd *EDGY/DAV* SK3 ....132 B3
    SWIN M27 ....44 B1
Vicarage St *OLDS* OL8 ....39 D3
Vicars Rd *CCHDY* M21 ....111 D1
Vicars St *ECC* M30 ....63 C3
Vicker Cl *SWIN* M27 ....26 A3
Vicker Gv *DID/WITH* M20 ....114 A4
Vickers St *NEWH/MOS* M40 ....71 D2
Victoria Av *BKLY* M9 ....15 D4
    BNG/LEV M19 ....117 D1
    DID/WITH M20 ....124 B2
    ECC M30 ....63 C2
    SWIN M27 ....45 D1
    WHTF M45 ....11 D1
Victoria Av East *BKLY* M9 ....35 C1

Victoria Bridge St *CSLFD* M3 ....3 E2
Victoria Cl *EDGY/DAV* SK3 * 132 B2
Victoria Crs *ECC* M30 ....63 C2
Victoria Gv *HTNM* SK4 ....118 B4
    RUSH/FAL M14 ....115 D2
Victoria La *SWIN* M27 ....44 A1
    WHTF M45 ....11 C2
Victoria Ldg *BRO* M7 * 49 D4
Victoria Pl *TRPK* M17 ....83 C2
Victoria Rd *ECC* M30 ....62 B2
    OLDTF/WHR M16 ....100 A3
    RUSH/FAL M14 ....115 C1
    SLFD M6 ....63 D1
    STKP SK1 ....131 C4
    STRET M32 ....97 C3
Victoria Sq *ANC* M4 * 5 D2
Victoria Station Ap *CSLFD* M3 ....3 F2
Victoria St *CHAD* OL9 ....21 D1
    CSLFD M3 ....3 F2
    FAIL M35 ....56 A3
    MDTN M24 ....17 D1
    OLDE OL4 ....23 D3
    OP/CLY M11 ....90 B1
Victoria Ter *WGTN/LGST* M12 ....104 A1
Victor Mann St *OP/CLY* M11 ....92 B2
Victor St *CSLFD* M3 ....3 B3
    NEWH/MOS M40 ....70 B1
    OLDS OL8 ....39 C4
Victory Gv *DTN/ASHW* M34 ....93 D2
Victory St *RUSH/FAL* M14 ....102 B2
Vienna Rd *EDGY/DAV* SK3 ....132 A3
Vienna Rd East *EDGY/DAV* SK3 ....132 A3
Viking Cl *OP/CLY* M11 ....72 A4
Village Ct *TRPK* M17 ....81 D3
Village St *BRO* M7 ....49 D4
Village Wy (Ashburton Rd East)
    TRPK M17 ....81 D3
Villa Rd *OLDS* OL8 ....41 C1
Villiers Ct *WHTF* M45 * 11 D3
Villiers Dr *OLDS* OL8 ....22 B4
Vinca Gv *BRO* M7 ....50 A3
Vincent Av *CCHDY* M21 ....98 B4
Vincent St *BRO* M7 ....50 B2
    OP/CLY M11 ....90 B1
Vine Av *SWIN* M27 ....46 A1
Vine Ct *STRET* M32 ....97 C4
Vine Fold *NEWH/MOS* M40 ....38 A4
Vine St *BRO* M7 ....49 C1
    CHAD OL9 ....39 C2
    ECC M30 ....61 D4
    OP/CLY M11 ....91 D2
    PWCH M25 ....12 B4
Viola St *OP/CLY* M11 ....74 A3
Violet St *GTN* M18 ....92 A3
    OFTN SK2 ....133 C3
Violet Wy *MDTN* M24 ....19 C2
Virgil St *OLDTF/WHR* M16 ....84 B3
Viscount St *RUSH/FAL* M14 ....102 B2
Vixen Cl *CCHDY* M21 ....113 C2
Voltaire Av *SLFD* M6 ....64 A2
Vorlich Dr *CHAD* OL9 ....20 A1
Vyner Gv *SALE* M33 ....108 A3

W

Waddington St *CHAD* OL9 ....21 D1
Wadeford Cl *ANC* M4 ....5 F2
Wadesmill Wk *BRUN/LGST* M13 * 8 C1
Wadeson Rd *BRUN/LGST* M13 ....9 D4
Wade St *MDTN* M24 ....19 C3
Wade Wk *OP/CLY* M11 ....89 D1
Wadhurst Wk *BRUN/LGST* M13 * 87 D4
Wadlow Cl *CSLFD* M3 * 2 C1
Wadsworth Ms *DROY* M43 ....75 C4

Waggoners Ct *SWIN* M27......................**45** C2
Wagstaffe Dr *FAIL* M35 ....**57** C2
Wainclffe Av *CCHDY* M21.................**123** C1
Wainman St *SLFD* M6.............................**49** C4
Wainwright Av *DTN/ASHW* M34.......**107** C2
Wainwright Cl *OFTN* SK2...................**133** D2
Wainwright St *OLDS* OL8.....................**22** B4
Wakefield Dr *SWIN* M27........................**25** C1
Wakefield St *CMANE* M1 *......................**8** A3
Walcott Cl *BRUN/LGST* M13................**88** A4
Wald Av *RUSH/FAL* M14.....................**116** B2
Walden Cl *RUSH/FAL* M14...................**114** B1
Walderton Av *NEWH/MOS* M40..........**54** B3
Walker Av *FAIL* M35 *...........................**58** A3
    WHTF M45..**11** D1
Walker Rd *BKLY* M9...............................**34** B1
    CHAD OL9...**38** A3
    ECC M30..**60** B1
Walker's Cft *SLFD* M3..............................**3** F2
Walker's Rd *OLDS* OL8.........................**39** D3
Walker St *CHAD* OL9 *..........................**22** A3
    MDTN M24...**15** D2
    STKP SK1 *..**129** D4
Wallace Av *RUSH/FAL* M14................**103** C3
Wallace St *OLDS* OL8...........................**41** C1
Wallasey Av *RUSH/FAL* M14...............**101** D4
Wallbrook Dr *BKLY* M9...........................**33** D3
The Walled Gdn *SWIN* M27.................**44** A3
Waller Av *RUSH/FAL* M14...................**115** D1
Wallingford Rd *URM* M41......................**94** B2
Wallis St *CHAD* OL9................................**38** B1
    NEWH/MOS M40...............................**55** D4
Wallness La *SLFD* M6.............................**67** C2
Wallshaw Pl *OLD* OL1..........................**23** D2
Wallshaw St *OLD* OL1...........................**23** D2
Wall St *OLDS* OL8....................................**23** C4
    SLFD M6..**66** A3
Wall Wy *OLD* OL1..................................**106** B1
Wallwork St *OP/CLY* M11.....................**91** D1
    RDSH SK5 *.......................................**107** C3
Wallworth Av *GTN* M18..........................**91** C4
Wally Sq *BRO* M7...................................**50** B3
Walmersley Rd *NEWH/MOS* M40.......**37** C3
Walmer St *GTN* M18................................**91** D3
    RUSH/FAL M14.................................**102** A2
Walmer St East *RUSH/FAL* M14.......**102** B2
Walmsley Gv *URM* M41..........................**94** A3
Walmsley St *RDSH* SK5 *..................**129** D2
Walnut Cl *SWIN* M27..............................**25** C1
Walnut Rd *ECC* M30................................**60** B1
Walnut St *GTN* M18.................................**91** C3
Walnut Wk *STRET* M32.........................**109** D1
Walsall *SLFD* M6.......................................**48** B4
Walsden St *OP/CLY* M11.......................**73** D3
Walsh Av *BKLY* M9..................................**33** D3
Walshaw Dr *SWIN* M27...........................**45** C2
Walsh St *CHAD* OL9................................**21** D3
Walsingham Av *DID/WITH* M20..........**124** A1
    MDTN M24...**17** D4
Walters Dr *OLDS* OL8...........................**41** D2
Walter St *BKLY* M9..................................**53** C1
    GTN M18..**91** D3
    OLDTF/WHR M16...............................**99** D1
    PWCH M25...**29** C1
Waltham Rd *OLDTF/WHR* M16...........**100** B4
Walton Hall Dr *BNG/LEV* M19............**106** A4
Walton Houses *FAIL* M35 *....................**57** C1
Walton Rd *BKLY* M9................................**16** A4
Walton St *STKP* SK1............................**133** C2
Walwyn Cl *STRET* M32...........................**97** D4
Wandsworth Av *OP/CLY* M11................**74** A3
Wansbeck Cl *STRET* M32.......................**97** D4
Wansfell Wk *ANC* M4..............................**71** C3
Wansford St *RUSH/FAL* M14...............**101** D3
Wanstead Av *BKLY* M9...........................**35** D2
Warbeck Cl *RDSH* SK5..........................**107** D3
Warbeck Rd *NEWH/MOS* M40..............**37** C3

Warburton St *DID/WITH* M20..............**125** C2
    ECC M30..**62** B4
    ORD M5..**84** A3
Warden St *NEWH/MOS* M40...................**55** C3
Warde St *HULME* M15..............................**85** D3
Wardle Cl *STRET* M32.............................**97** D3
Wardle St *NEWH/MOS* M40.....................**71** D2
Wardley Av *CCHDY* M21......................**113** D1
Wardley Hall La *WALK* M28....................**42** B1
Wardley Hall Rd *WALK* M28...................**24** A4
Wardley St *SWIN* M27.............................**45** C1
Ward Rd *DID/WITH* M20.......................**125** C2
    DROY M43...**76** B3
Wardsend Wk *HULME* M15 *...................**85** C3
Ward St *BKLY* M9....................................**33** D3
    CHAD OL9...**21** D2
    FAIL M35..**56** B1
    NEWH/MOS M40...............................**54** A1
    OLD OL1...**22** A1
    STKP SK1..**133** D2
Wareham Gv *ECC* M30............................**61** D2
Wareham St *CHH* M8 *............................**53** C4
Warford St *ANC* M4.................................**70** A1
The Warke *WALK* M28.............................**42** A3
Warley Rd *OLDTF/WHR* M16.................**98** B2
Warmington Dr *WGTN/LGST* M12........**88** B3
Warne Av *DROY* M43................................**76** B3
Warnford Ct *NEWH/MOS* M40...............**74** A1
Warren Bank *BKLY* M9............................**33** D2
Warren Bruce Rd *TRPK* M17...................**82** A3
Warren Dr *SWIN* M27................................**44** A4
Warren Rd *EDGY/DAV* SK3..................**132** B3
    TRPK M17..**81** C3
Warren St *BKLY* M9..................................**33** D3
    BRO M7..**51** C1
    STKP SK1..**130** A3
Warrington Rd *BKLY* M9..........................**33** D1
Warstead Wk *BRUN/LGST* M13 *..........**87** D4
Warwick Av *DID/WITH* M20.................**124** A1
    SWIN M27..**25** C3
    WHTF M45..**12** A2
Warwick Cl *HTNM* SK4..........................**128** B1
    MDTN M24...**17** D4
    WHTF M45..**11** D2
Warwick Ct *MDTN* M24 *.........................**17** D1
    OLDTF/WHR M16...............................**98** B2
Warwick Gv *DTN/ASHW* M34................**93** D1
Warwick Rd *CCHDY* M21........................**99** C4
    FAIL M35..**57** C4
    HTNM SK4..**128** B2
    MDTN M24...**18** A4
    OLDTF/WHR M16...............................**98** B1
    STRET M32...**83** C4
Warwick Rd South *OLDTF/WHR* M16...**98** B2
Warwick St *ANC* M4..................................**4** C3
    CHAD OL9..**39** D1
    HULME M15...**85** D3
    PWCH M25...**25** D3
    SWIN M27..**26** A4
Wasdale Wk *OLD* OL1.............................**23** C1
Washbrook *CHAD* OL9............................**39** C1
Washbrook Dr *STRET* M32......................**96** A4
Washington St *CHAD* OL9......................**21** D2
Wasnidge Wk *HULME* M15 *...................**85** C4
Waterbridge *WALK* M28..........................**42** B4
Waterdale Dr *WHTF* M45.........................**11** D1
Waterfield Wy *FAIL* M35.........................**57** D3
Waterford Av *DID/WITH* M20...............**123** D2
Waterfront Quay *SALQ* M50...................**83** C2
Watergate *DTN/ASHW* M34....................**93** D4
Waterhouse Rd *GTN* M18......................**106** B1
Waterhouse Wy *RDSH* SK5..................**119** C2
Water La *DROY* M43.................................**74** B4
Waterloo Pl *STKP* SK1 *.......................**130** A4
Waterloo Rd *BKLY* M9.............................**34** A4
    CHH M8..**68** B1
    STKP SK1..**130** A4

Waterloo St *CHH* M8	52	B1
CMANE M1	8	A1
OLD OL1	23	C3
Watermans Cl *BKLY* M9	54	A1
Waterpark Rd *BRO* M7	50	B1
Waterside *SALE* M33	109	D4
TRPK M17	83	C3
Waterside Cl *CCHDY* M21	123	C1
Waterside Vw *DROY* M43	91	D1
Waterslea *ECC* M30	61	D3
Watersmeet *STRET* M32	96	B1
Waterson Av *NEWH/MOS* M40	54	B2
Water's Reach *TRPK* M17	83	C3
Water St *BKLY* M9	53	C1
CSLFD M3	6	B2
MDTN M24	17	C1
STKP SK1	130	B2
Watford Av *RUSH/FAL* M14	102	A3
Watkin Cl *BRUN/LGST* M13	87	C3
Watkins Dr *PWCH* M25	31	D2
Watkin St *CSLFD* M3 *	68	A2
Watson Sq *STKP* SK1	130	A4
Watson St *CSLFD* M3	7	E2
ECC M30	61	D3
SWIN M27	26	A4
Watton Cl *SWIN* M27 *	26	A5
Watts St *BNG/LEV* M19	118	A1
CHAD OL9	21	C2
OLDS OL8	40	A3
Waugh Av *FAIL* M35	57	C3
Waverley Av *STRET* M32	97	D2
Waverley Crs *DROY* M43	75	D2
Waverley Rd *BKLY* M9	54	A2
SALE M33	109	D3
SWIN M27	46	B2
Waverley Rd West *BKLY* M9	54	A2
Waverton Av *HTNM* SK4	119	C2
Waverton Rd *RUSH/FAL* M14	101	C3
Wavertree Rd *BKLY* M9	33	D1
Wayfarers Wy *SWIN* M27	44	B2
Wayland Rd *GTN* M18	106	A2
Wayland Rd South *GTN* M18	106	A2
Wayne St *DROY* M43	76	B1
Wayne Sq *OP/CLY* M11	91	D1
Weald Cl *BRUN/LGST* M13	9	E5
Weardale Rd *BKLY* M9	15	C4
Wearste Dr *ORD* M5	65	C2
Weaste La *ORD* M5	65	C2
Weaste Rd *ORD* M5	65	C2
Weatherall St North *BRO* M7	51	C2
Weatherley Cl *OLDS* OL8	41	C4
Weaver Ct *HULME* M15 *	85	C3
Weaverham Cl *BRUN/LGST* M13	104	A3
Webb La *STKP* SK1	133	D1
Webdale Dr *NEWH/MOS* M40	54	B2
Webster Gv *PWCH* M25	29	C3
Webster St *OLDS* OL8	23	C4
Wedgewood St *NEWH/MOS* M40	72	A1
Wedgwood Rd *SWIN* M27	27	D3
Weedall Av *ORD* M5	83	D3
Weir St *FAIL* M35	56	B2
Welbeck Av *CHAD* OL9	37	C2
URM M41	94	B2
Welbeck Gv *BRO* M7	50	B2
Welbeck Rd *ECC* M30	62	B1
RDSH SK5	120	A1
WALK M28	43	C3
Welbeck St *GTN* M18	91	D1
Welby St *BRUN/LGST* M13	103	C1
Welcomb St *OP/CLY* M11	90	A2
Welcroft St *STKP* SK1	133	C1
Weldon Dr *BKLY* M9	16	A4
Weld Rd *DID/WITH* M20	116	A2
Welford Gn *RDSH* SK5	120	A4
Welford Rd *CHH* M8	32	A1
Welford St *SLFD* M6	67	C1
Welkin Rd *MPL/ROM* SK6	131	D2
Welland Cl *HULME* M15 *	85	C3
Welland Ct *HULME* M15	85	C3
Welland St *OP/CLY* M11	91	C1
RDSH SK5	107	C4
Wellbank *PWCH* M25 *	29	C2
Wellbank Cl *OLDS* OL8	41	D1
Wellens Wy *MDTN* M24	15	D2
Weller Av *CCHDY* M21	113	C2
Wellesley Av *GTN* M18	91	C3
Wellfield Rd *CHH* M8	51	D1
Wellgate Av *BNG/LEV* M19	118	A1
Wellhead Cl *HULME* M15	86	A4
Wellhouse Dr *NEWH/MOS* M40	36	B2
Welling Rd *NEWH/MOS* M40	56	B1
Wellington Av *OLDTF/WHR* M16	100	A3
Wellington Cl *SALE* M33	109	D3
Wellington Ct *OLDS* OL8 *	40	A1
Wellington Crs *OLDTF/WHR* M16	99	D2
Wellington Gv *HULME* M15	85	C3
OFTN SK2	133	C2
Wellington Rd *CHH* M8	52	A1
ECC M30	62	B3
OLDS OL8	39	D1
OLDTF/WHR M16	100	B3
RUSH/FAL M14	115	D2
SWIN M27	45	C1
Wellington Rd North *BNG/LEV* M19	118	A2
HTNM SK4	129	C1
Wellington Rd South *HTNM* SK4	129	D2
Wellington St *CHAD* OL9	21	C1
CSLFD M3	2	B2
FAIL M35 *	38	B4
GTN M18	91	C4
OLD OL1	23	C4
STKP SK1	130	A4
STRET M32	96	B4
Wellington St East *BRO* M7	50	A2
Wellington St West *BRO* M7	50	A3
Wellington Ter *ORD* M5	65	C3
Wellmead Cl *CHH* M8	51	C4
Wells Av *PWCH* M25	30	B3
Wells Cl *DROY* M43	92	A1
MDTN M24	15	D2
Wells Dr *HTNM* SK4	126	B3
Wellwood Dr *NEWH/MOS* M40	54	B2
Welney Rd *OLDTF/WHR* M16	99	C2
Welshpool Cl *NTHM/RTH* M23	122	A3
Welton Av *DID/WITH* M20	125	D3
Welwyn Dr *SLFD* M6	78	B4
Welwyn Wk *NEWH/MOS* M40	71	C3
Wembley Cl *EDGY/DAV* SK3	132	A4
Wembley Gv *RUSH/FAL* M14	115	D1
Wembley Rd *GTN* M18	105	D2
Wembury St *BKLY* M9 *	53	D2
Wembury St North *BKLY* M9	53	D1
Wem St *CHAD* OL9	38	B1
Wemyss Av *RDSH* SK5	107	C4
Wenfield Dr *BKLY* M9	35	D2
Wenlock St *SWIN* M27	44	A1
Wenlock Wy *WGTN/LGST* M12	89	C3
Wensley Dr *DID/WITH* M20	115	C4
Wensley Rd *BRO* M7	29	D4
RDSH SK5	130	A1
Wentworth Av *GTN* M18	91	D4
SLFD M6	64	B2
WHTF M45	10	A2
Wentworth Cl *MDTN* M24	16	B1
Wentworth Dr *SALE* M33	108	A4
Wentworth Rd *ECC* M30	63	C1
RDSH SK5	107	C4
SWIN M27	44	A3
Werneth Av *RUSH/FAL* M14	102	A3
Werneth Crs *OLDS* OL8	39	D1
Werneth Hall Rd *OLDS* OL8	22	A4
Werneth St *STKP* SK1	131	C2
Wesley Dr *WALK* M28	42	A1

Wesley Gn *ORD* M5 ....**84** A1
Wesley St *ECC* M30 ....**61** C4
   FAIL M35 ....**38** B4
   OP/CLY M11 ....**89** D1
   STKP SK1 ....**130** A4
   STRET M32 ....**97** D2
   SWIN M27 ....**45** C1
West Ashton St *SALQ* M50 ....**83** C1
West Av *BNG/LEV* M19 ....**117** C2
   GTN M18 * **91** D4
   NEWH/MOS M40 ....**37** C4
West Bank *OP/CLY* M11 ....**92** B2
Westbank Rd *DID/WITH* M20 ....**116** B4
West Bank St *ORD* M5 ....**84** B1
Westbourne Gv *BKLY* M9 ....**53** C3
   DID/WITH M20 ....**114** B3
   RDSH SK5 ....**120** A1
Westbourne Pk *URM* M41 ....**94** A2
Westbourne Range *GTN* M18 ....**107** C2
Westbourne Rd *ECC* M30 ....**61** C1
   RUSH/FAL M14 ....**116** A1
   URM M41 ....**94** A3
Westbourne St *CHAD* OL9 ....**22** A4
Westbrook Rd *SWIN* M27 ....**44** B2
   TRPK M17 ....**81** D2
Westbrook Sq *WGTN/LGST* M12 ..**89** D3
Westbury Rd *CHH* M8 ....**32** B4
West Canteen Rd *TRPK* M17 ....**96** B1
West Central Dr *SWIN* M27 ....**46** A2
West Charles St *ORD* M5 ....**67** C4
Westcott Av *DID/WITH* M20 ....**114** B3
Westcourt Rd *SALE* M33 ....**108** B4
Westcraig Av *NEWH/MOS* M40 .....**36** B2
West Craven St *ORD* M5 ....**84** A2
Westcroft Rd *DID/WITH* M20 ....**126** A1
West Crown Av *ORD* M5 ....**84** A1
Westdale Gdns *BNG/LEV* M19 ......**117** D4
Westdean Crs *BNG/LEV* M19 ....**117** D4
West Dean St *ORD* M5 ....**67** C4
West Dr *DROY* M43 ....**75** C4
   SLFD M6 ....**47** D3
   SWIN M27 ....**46** A2
West Duke St *ORD* M5 ....**2** A5
West Egerton St *ORD* M5 ....**67** C4
West End St *CHAD* OL9 ....**22** A2
Westerham Av *ORD* M5 ....**66** B4
Wester Hill Rd *OLDS* OL8 ....**41** D4
Westerling Wy *OLDTF/WHR* M16 ..**100** B2
Western Access *TRPK* M17 * **80** A1
Western Av *SWIN* M27 ....**28** A3
Western Cir *BNG/LEV* M19 ....**117** C3
Western St *GTN* M18 ....**91** D3
   SLFD M6 ....**65** D2
Westfield *SLFD* M6 ....**65** D1
Westfield Av *MDTN* M24 ....**17** D2
Westfield Rd *CCHDY* M21 ....**99** C4
   DROY M43 ....**74** B3
Westfield St *BRO* M7 ....**31** C4
   CHAD OL9 ....**21** D1
Westgate Av *BKLY* M9 * **33** D3
Westgate Dr *SWIN* M27 ....**45** C3
Westgate Rd *SLFD* M6 ....**64** C1
West Gn *MDTN* M24 ....**15** C2
West Gv *BRUN/LGST* M13 ....**88** A4
West High St *ORD* M5 ....**66** B3
Westholm Av *HTNM* SK4 ....**118** B3
Westholme Rd *DID/WITH* M20 .....**125** C1
   PWCH M25 ....**12** B2
West Hope St *ORD* M5 ....**67** C4
Westinghouse Rd *TRPK* M17 ....**81** D4
West King St *CSLFD* M3 ....**2** C1
Westland Av *STKP* SK1 * **131** C4
Westland Dr *BKLY* M9 ....**34** A1
Westlands *WHTF* M45 ....**11** C3
The Westlands *SWIN* M27 ....**46** A3
Westlea Dr *GTN* M18 ....**106** A2

Westleigh Dr *PWCH* M25 ....**31** C2
Westleigh St *BKLY* M9 ....**34** B4
West Marwood St *BRO* M7 ....**50** B3
West Meade *CCHDY* M21 ....**111** D2
   PWCH M25 * **31** C3
   SWIN M27 ....**44** B3
West Meadow *RDSH* SK5 ....**107** D4
Westmere Dr *BKLY* M9 ....**34** A4
Westminster Av *OLDTF/WHR* M16 ..**99** D3
   RDSH SK5 ....**119** D2
   WHTF M45 ....**11** C1
Westminster Rd *ECC* M30 ....**62** B2
   FAIL M35 ....**58** A1
   URM M41 ....**94** A1
Westminster St *BNG/LEV* M19 * ...**105** C4
   SWIN M27 ....**45** C4
Westmorland Cl *RDSH* SK5 * **121** D3
Westmorland Dr *RDSH* SK5 ....**121** C3
Westmorland Rd *DID/WITH* M20 ..**124** B3
   ECC M30 ....**45** D4
West Mosley St *CMANW* M2 ....**4** A5
Westmount Cl *NEWH/MOS* M40 ....**52** B3
Weston Av *NEWH/MOS* M40 ....**37** D4
   SWIN M27 ....**26** A1
Weston Gv *HTNM* SK4 ....**118** B3
Weston St *NEWH/MOS* M40 * **71** C3
   RDSH SK5 * **129** D1
Westover St *SWIN* M27 ....**45** C4
West Park Rd *STKP* SK1 ....**131** C3
West Park St *ORD* M5 ....**84** A2
West Pl *BNG/LEV* M19 ....**117** C2
Westray Crs *ORD* M5 * **65** C4
Westray Rd *BRUN/LGST* M13 ......**103** D3
West Rd *PWCH* M25 ....**11** C4
   STRET M32 ....**95** D1
West Rw *PWCH* M25 ....**29** C4
West St *CHAD* OL9 ....**22** A3
   EDGY/DAV SK3 ....**129** C4
   FAIL M35 ....**56** B2
   OP/CLY M11 ....**73** C3
West Towers St *SLFD* M6 ....**66** A4
Westville Gdns *BNG/LEV* M19 .....**116** B4
Westway *BKLY* M9 ....**14** B3
   DROY M43 ....**82** B2
Westwood Av *BRO* M7 ....**50** B1
   NEWH/MOS M40 * **37** C4
   URM M41 ....**95** C4
Westwood Crs *ECC* M30 ....**61** C1
Westwood Dr *CHAD* OL9 ....**22** A2
   SWIN M27 ....**46** B3
Westwood Rd *STRET* M32 ....**96** A3
Westwood St *RUSH/FAL* M14 ......**101** C1
West Works Rd *TRPK* M17 ....**96** B1
Wetherall St *BNG/LEV* M19 ....**105** C4
Wetherby St *OP/CLY* M11 ....**91** D2
Weybourne Av *BKLY* M9 ....**33** D3
Weybridge Rd *ANC* M4 ....**5** F3
Weybrook Rd *BNG/LEV* M19 ....**118** B2
Weylands Gv *SLFD* M6 ....**46** A4
Weymouth Rd *ECC* M30 ....**61** C2
Whalley Av *BNG/LEV* M19 ....**105** C3
   CCHDY M21 ....**112** B2
   OLDTF/WHR M16 ....**100** A2
   SALE M33 ....**109** D4
   URM M41 ....**94** B2
Whalley Gv *OLDTF/WHR* M16 ......**100** A3
Whalley Rd *OLDTF/WHR* M16 ......**100** A3
Whalley St *NEWH/MOS* M40 ....**71** C3
Wharf Cl *CMANE* M1 ....**5** D5
Wharfedale Av *NEWH/MOS* M40 ...**35** D2
Wharfedale Rd *RDSH* SK5 ....**119** D1
Wharf End *TRPK* M17 ....**83** D3
Wharf Rd *SALE* M33 ....**109** D4
Wharfside Av *ECC* M30 ....**79** C1
Wharf St *CHAD* OL9 ....**39** C2
   HTNM SK4 ....**129** D2
Wharton Av *CCHDY* M21 ....**113** C2

Wharton Ldg *ECC* M30 ....62 B2
Wheat Cl *BRUN/LGST* M13 ....87 D4
Wheat Cft *EDGY/DAV* SK3 ....133 C4
Wheaters St *BRO* M7 * 67 D1
Wheaters Ter *BRO* M7 ....68 A1
Wheatley Rd *SWIN* M27 ....25 C3
Wheatley Wk *WGTN/LGST* M12 ......89 C3
Wheler St *OP/CLY* M11 ....91 C1
Whernside Av *NEWH/MOS* M40 .....35 D4
Whernside Cl *HTNM* SK4 ....125 D3
Whickham Cl *RUSH/FAL* M14 ....102 A2
Whiley St *BRUN/LGST* M13 ....104 A1
Whimberry Cl *ORD* M5 ....84 B2
Whimberry Wy *DID/WITH* M20 ....116 A3
Whirley Cl *HTNM* SK4 ....119 C4
Whiston Rd *CHH* M8 ....52 A1
Whitaker St *MDTN* M24 ....17 C1
Whitburn Av *BRUN/LGST* M13 ....103 D3
Whitby Av *OLDTF/WHR* M16 ....100 A3
  RUSH/FAL M14 ....116 B1
  SLFD M6 ....64 B2
  URM M41 ....94 B3
Whitby Rd *RUSH/FAL* M14 ....116 A1
Whitchurch Rd *OLDTF/WHR* M16 .....85 C4
Whitchurch Rd *DID/WITH* M20 ....114 A2
Whitchurch St *BRO* M7 ....68 B2
Whiteacres *SWIN* M27 ....43 D2
White Bank Av *RDSH* SK5 ....131 D1
White Bank Rd *OLDS* OL9 ....59 C1
Whitebeam Cl *SLFD* M6 ....66 B2
Whitebeam Ct *SLFD* M6 * 66 B2
Whitebrook Rd *RUSH/FAL* M14 ....102 A4
Whitecar Av *NEWH/MOS* M40 ....37 D4
Whitechapel St *DID/WITH* M20 ....125 C2
White City Wy *OLDTF/WHR* M16 ......83 D4
Whitecliff Cl *RUSH/FAL* M14 ....102 B3
Whitecroft Gdns *BNG/LEV* M19 ....126 B1
Whitefield *HTNM* SK4 ....129 C2
Whitefield Rd *SALE* M33 ....108 A4
Whitegate Av *CHAD* OL9 ....38 A1
Whitegate Cl *NEWH/MOS* M40 ....37 D4
Whitegate Dr *ORD* M5 ....65 C2
  SWIN M27 ....27 C3
Whitegate La *CHAD* OL9 ....38 B1
Whitegate Rd *CHAD* OL9 ....37 C2
Whitehall Rd *DID/WITH* M20 ....125 D2
Whitehall St *OLD* OL1 ....23 C1
Whitehaven Gdns *DID/WITH* M20 ....124 B3
Whitehead Rd *CCHDY* M21 ....111 C1
  SWIN M27 ....27 C3
Whitehill Dr *NEWH/MOS* M40 ....54 B2
Whitehill St *HTNM* SK4 ....129 D1
  RDSH SK5 ....120 A4
Whitehill St West *HTNM* SK4 ....129 C1
Whiteholme Av *CCHDY* M21 ....123 C1
White Horse Gdns *SWIN* M27 * 43 D3
White House Av *PWCH* M25 ....31 D2
Whitehurst Rd *HTNM* SK4 ....127 C1
Whitekirk Cl *BRUN/LGST* M13 ....9 D5
Whitelea Dr *EDGY/DAV* SK3 ....132 A4
Whiteley Dr *MDTN* M24 ....18 B2
Whiteley St *CHAD* OL9 ....39 C1
  OP/CLY M11 ....73 C3
Whitelow Rd *CCHDY* M21 ....111 D1
  HTNM SK4 ....127 D2
White Moss Av *CCHDY* M21 ....112 B4
White Moss Rd *BKLY* M9 ....34 B2
Whitemoss Rd East *BKLY* M9 ....35 C1
Whiteoak Rd *RUSH/FAL* M14 ....115 D1
Whites Cft *SWIN* M27 ....45 C1
Whiteside Cl *ORD* M5 ....65 C3
Whitestone Wk *BRUN/LGST* M13 * ..88 A4
White St *HULME* M15 ....8 B4
  SLFD M6 ....65 D4
White Swallows Rd *SWIN* M27 ....45 D3
Whitethorn Av *BNG/LEV* M19 ....117 D2
  OLDTF/WHR M16 ....100 A2

Whitewater Dr *BRO* M7 ....48 A2
Whiteway St *BKLY* M9 ....53 D2
Whitewillow Cl *FAIL* M35 ....57 D3
Whitfield Cl *CSLFD* M3 ....69 D2
Whitland Dr *OLDS* OL8 ....39 C3
Whit La *SLFD* M6 ....48 B4
Whitley Rd *HTNM* SK4 ....128 B2
  NEWH/MOS M40 ....70 B1
Whitman St *BKLY* M9 ....54 A1
Whitmore Rd *RUSH/FAL* M14 ....102 A4
Whitnall Cl *OLDTF/WHR* M16 ....100 B2
Whitsbury Av *GTN* M18 ....106 A2
Whitstable Cl *OLD* OL9 ....21 C3
Whitstable Rd *NEWH/MOS* M40 * 36 B4
Whittaker La *PWCH* M25 ....30 B1
Whittaker St *OLD* OL9 ....21 C2
  NEWH/MOS M40 ....54 B1
  WGTN/LGST M12 ....88 A1
Whittingham Gv *OLD* OL1 ....22 A1
Whittle's Cft *CMANE* M1 * 5 D5
Whittle St *ANC* M4 * 4 C3
  SWIN M27 ....44 B2
Whitwell Wy *GTN* M18 ....90 B4
Whitworth La *RUSH/FAL* M14 ....103 C3
Whitworth St *CMANE* M1 ....8 C1
  OP/CLY M11 ....90 A2
Whitworth St East *OP/CLY* M11 ....90 B2
Whitworth St West *CMANE* M1 ....7 F2
Whixhall Av *WGTN/LGST* M12 ....88 B3
Wickentree La *FAIL* M35 ....38 B4
Wicket Gv *SWIN* M27 ....25 D1
Wicklow Gv *OLDS* OL8 ....40 B2
Widdop St *CHAD* OL9 ....22 A2
Widgeon Cl *RUSH/FAL* M14 ....115 C1
Widnes St *OP/CLY* M11 * 90 C2
Wiggins Wk *RUSH/FAL* M14 * 102 B2
Wigley St *WGTN/LGST* M12 ....88 B2
Wigmore Rd *CHH* M8 ....52 A2
Wigsby Av *NEWH/MOS* M40 ....36 B4
Wilbraham Rd *CCHDY* M21 ....112 A1
  OLDTF/WHR M16 ....100 B4
  RUSH/FAL M14 ....102 A4
Wilburn St *ORD* M5 ....6 A1
Wilby St *CHH* M8 ....52 A3
Wilcock Cl *OLDTF/WHR* M16 ....100 B1
Wildbrook Crs *OLDS* OL8 ....41 D2
Wildbrook Ter *OLDS* OL8 * 41 D2
Wildcroft Av *NEWH/MOS* M40 ....35 D4
Wilderswood Cl *DID/WITH* M20 ....115 D4
Wild St *OLD* OL1 ....23 D2
Wildwood Cl *OFTN* SK2 ....133 D4
Wilfred St *BRO* M7 ....68 B1
  NEWH/MOS M40 ....54 B1
Wilfrid St *SWIN* M27 ....45 C1
Wilkinson Rd *HTNM* SK4 ....129 D3
Wilkinson St *HTNM* SK4 * 129 D3
  MDTN M24 ....17 C1
Willan Rd *BKLY* M9 ....33 D1
  ECC M30 ....62 B3
Willaston Cl *CCHDY* M21 ....111 D2
Willdale Cl *OP/CLY* M11 ....72 B3
Willenhall Rd *NTHM/RTH* M23 ....122 B3
Willerby Rd *BRO* M7 ....50 B4
Willesden Av *BRUN/LGST* M13 ....103 D2
Will Griffith Wk *OP/CLY* M11 ....88 B1
William Chadwick Cl *NEWH/MOS* M40 ...70 B2
William Jessop Ct *CMANE* M1 ....5 E5
William Kay Cl *OLDS* OL8 ....100 B1
William Lister Cl *NEWH/MOS* M40 * ...74 A1
Williams Crs *CHAD* OL9 ....38 A2
Williamson La *DROY* M43 ....93 C1
Williamson St *ANC* M4 ....70 A2
  RDSH SK5 ....119 D2
Williams Rd *GTN* M18 ....90 B4
  NEWH/MOS M40 ....55 D1
Williams St *GTN* M18 ....105 D1
William St *CSLFD* M3 ....2 C3

DID/WITH M20	125	C2	
FAIL M35	38	B4	
MDTN M24	18	A1	
WGTN/LGST M12	88	A1	
Willingdon Dr *PWCH* M25	12	A4	
Willis Rd *EDGY/DAV* SK3	132	B3	
Willock St *BRO* M7	50	B3	
Willoughby Av *DID/WITH* M20	125	D1	
Willoughby Cl *SALE* M33	108	B4	
Willow Av *MDTN* M24	18	B2	
RDSH SK5	130	A1	
URM M41	94	B3	
Willow Bank *RUSH/FAL* M14	115	D1	
Willowbrook Av *NEWH/MOS* M40	54	B2	
Willow Ct *SALE* M33	110	B4	
Willowdene Cl *NEWH/MOS* M40	52	B4	
Willow Fold *DROY* M43	93	C1	
Willow Gv *CHAD* OL9 *	21	C1	
GTN M18 *	106	B1	
Willow Hill Rd *CHH* M8	32	B4	
Willow Rd *ECC* M30	60	B1	
PWCH M25	11	D3	
Willows Dr *FAIL* M35	75	C1	
Willows Rd *ORD* M5 *	65	C3	
The Willows *CCHDY* M21	111	D2	
Willow St *CHH* M8	68	B1	
OP/CLY M11	72	B4	
SWIN M27	44	A4	
WALK M28	43	D2	
Willow Wy *DID/WITH* M20	125	D2	
Wilma Av *BKLY* M9	33	D1	
Wilmcote Rd *NEWH/MOS* M40	70	B1	
Wilmington Rd *STRET* M32 *	96	A3	
Wilmott St *HULME* M15	7	F4	
Wilmslow Rd *DID/WITH* M20	125	D4	
RUSH/FAL M14	102	B3	
WHTF M45	11	D2	
Wilpshire Av *WGTN/LGST* M12	105	C2	
Wilson Av *SWIN* M27	27	C4	
Wilson Rd *BKLY* M9	34	A4	
HTNM SK4	128	A1	
Wilsons Pk *NEWH/MOS* M40 *	53	D4	
Wilson St *BRUN/LGST* M13	87	D3	
OLDS OL8	40	B1	
OP/CLY M11	89	D1	
STRET M32	97	D1	
Wilson Wy *OLD* OL1	23	C2	
Wilsthorpe Cl *BNG/LEV* M19	118	B3	
Wilton Av *OLDTF/WHR* M16	98	B2	
PWCH M25	31	C3	
SWIN M27	46	B2	
Wilton Ct *GTN* M18	107	D1	
Wilton Gv *DTN/ASHW* M34	107	D1	
Wilton Paddock *DTN/ASHW* M34	107	D1	
Wilton Pl *CSLFD* M3	2	A3	
Wilton Rd *CCHDY* M21	112	A1	
CHH M8	32	B3	
SLFD M6	64	A1	
Wilton St *CHAD* OL9	39	C2	
MDTN M24	15	C2	
PWCH M25	30	B1	
RDSH SK5	107	C3	
WHTF M45	11	C2	
Wiltshire Av *RDSH* SK5	131	D1	
Wiltshire Rd *CHAD* OL9	21	C4	
FAIL M35	57	C3	
Wiltshire St *BRO* M7	50	B3	
Wimbledon Rd *FAIL* M35	58	A1	
Wimborne Av *URM* M41	94	A1	
Wimpole St *OLD* OL1	23	D1	
Wimpory St *OP/CLY* M11	91	C2	
Wince Cl *MDTN* M24	18	B3	
Wincham Cl *HULME* M15	85	C3	
Winchester Av *PWCH* M25	30	B3	
Winchester Dr *HTNM* SK4	128	A3	
Winchester Pk *DID/WITH* M20	124	A2	
Winchester Rd *ECC* M30	63	D1	
SLFD M6	64	B1	
STRET M32	95	C2	
URM M41	94	A2	
Wincombe St *RUSH/FAL* M14	102	A3	
Windcroft Cl *OP/CLY* M11	89	C1	
Winder Dr *ANC* M4	7	F4	
Windermere Av *DTN/ASHW* M34	107	D3	
SWIN M27	45	D2	
Windermere Cl *OP/CLY* M11	89	D1	
PWCH M25	10	B4	
STRET M32	96	B2	
Winders Wy *SLFD* M6	67	C1	
Windle Av *CHH* M8	32	A2	
Windmill Av *ORD* M5	66	A3	
Windmill La *DTN/ASHW* M34	107	D3	
Windmill St *CMANW* M2	7	E1	
Windrush Dr *BKLY* M9	53	C2	
Windsor Av *CHAD* OL9	38	B1	
FAIL M35	58	A1	
HTNM SK4	127	D2	
SALE M33	109	C3	
SWIN M27	26	B3	
WHTF M45	11	D2	
Windsor Crs *PWCH* M25	31	D2	
Windsor Dr *DTN/ASHW* M34	77	C4	
Windsor Rd *BKLY* M9	53	D2	
BNG/LEV M19	104	A4	
DROY M43	74	A3	
DTN/ASHW M34	107	D2	
MPL/ROM SK6	131	D2	
NEWH/MOS M40	74	B1	
OLDS OL8	22	A4	
PWCH M25	31	D2	
Windsor St *FAIL* M35	57	D2	
GTN M18	105	D1	
NEWH/MOS M40	74	B1	
OFTN SK2	133	D3	
ORD M5	67	C4	
Windybank *BKLY* M9	15	D4	
Winfell Dr *NEWH/MOS* M40	91	C2	
Winfield Av *DID/WITH* M20	116	A4	
Winfield Dr *GTN* M18	91	C3	
Winford St *BKLY* M9	53	D1	
Wingate Dr *DID/WITH* M20	125	D3	
Wingate Rd *HTNM* SK4	128	B1	
Wingfield Dr *SWIN* M27	45	D3	
Wingfield St *STRET* M32	97	C1	
Winifred Rd *DID/WITH* M20	125	C2	
NEWH/MOS M40	55	C2	
OFTN SK2	133	D4	
Winifred St *ECC* M30	61	C4	
Winnie St *NEWH/MOS* M40	54	B1	
Winning Hill Cl *GTN* M18	106	A1	
Winnipeg Quay *SALQ* M50	83	C2	
Winscombe Dr *NEWH/MOS* M40	70	B1	
Winser St *CMANE* M1	8	A2	
Winsford Rd *RUSH/FAL* M14	101	D4	
Winslow Pl *BNG/LEV* M19	117	C3	
Winslow St *OP/CLY* M11	89	D1	
Winstanley Rd *NEWH/MOS* M40	71	C2	
SALE M33	109	D4	
Winster Av *BRO* M7	49	C3	
DID/WITH M20	123	D1	
STRET M32	95	D2	
Winster Cl *WHTF* M45	12	A1	
Winster Gv *OFTN* SK2	133	D3	
Winster Rd *ECC* M30	78	A1	
Winston Rd *BKLY* M9	35	C4	
SALE M33	108	A4	
Winswell Cl *OP/CLY* M11	73	C3	
Winterbottom St *CHAD* OL9 *	22	A2	
Winterburn Av *CCHDY* M21	122	B1	
Winterdyne St *BKLY* M9	53	D2	
Winterford Av *BRUN/LGST* M13	88	A4	
Winterford Rd *BRO* M7	51	C2	
Wintermans Rd *CCHDY* M21	113	C3	

Winterton Rd RDSH SK5	107	D4
Winthrop Av NEWH/MOS M40	53	C4
Winton Av NEWH/MOS M40	37	C4
Winton Rd SLFD M6	47	C3
Wirral Cl SWIN M27 *	26	B3
Wiseley St OP/CLY M11	88	B1
Wiseman Ter PWCH M25	30	B1
Wishaw Sq CCHDY M21	113	D3
Wisley Cl RDSH SK5	120	A1
Wistaria Rd GTN M18	91	C4
Withington Rd CCHDY M21	113	C1
OLDTF/WHR M16	100	A2
Withins Hall Rd FAIL M35	58	A3
Withins Rd OLDS OL8	39	C3
Withnell Rd BNG/LEV M19	126	A2
Withycombe Pl SLFD M6	48	B4
Withy Gv ANC M4	4	A3
Wittenbury Rd HTNM SK4	128	A3
Witterage Cl WGTN/LGST M12 *	89	C3
Woburn Cl OLDTF/WHR M16	98	B3
Woburn St OLDTF/WHR M16	101	C2
Wodens Av ORD M5	84	B2
Woden St ORD M5	84	B2
Wolfreton Crs SWIN M27	26	B2
Wolseley Pl DID/WITH M20	115	C4
Wolseley Rd SALE M33	109	C3
Wolverton Av OLDS OL8	40	A2
Wolveton St OP/CLY M11	89	C2
Woodacre OLDTF/WHR M16	100	B4
Woodbine Gdns OFTN SK2	133	C2
Woodbourne Rd HTNM SK4	118	B3
Woodbray Av BNG/LEV M19	116	B4
Woodchurch Wk CHAD OL9 *	21	C3
Woodcock Cl DROY M43	76	B2
Woodcroft Av BNG/LEV M19	126	B1
Woodfield Cl OLDS OL8	39	D1
Woodfield Gv ECC M30	61	D4
SALE M33	108	B3
Woodfield Rd CHH M8	32	B4
MDTN M24	16	B3
SLFD M6	65	C1
Woodfold Av BNG/LEV M19	104	B3
Woodfold Rd FAIL M35	57	D1
Woodford Av ECC M30	61	C3
Woodford Dr SWIN M27	25	D3
Woodford Gdns DID/WITH M20	124	B3
Woodgarth Av NEWH/MOS M40	56	A4
Woodgarth Dr SWIN M27	44	B3
Woodgarth La WALK M28	42	A4
Woodgate Dr PWCH M25	12	B3
Woodgate Rd OLDTF/WHR M16	100	B3
Woodgrange Cl SLFD M6	65	D3
Woodhall Av DID/WITH M20	114	B2
WHTF M45	10	A3
Woodhall Crs RDSH SK5	130	B1
Woodhall Rd RDSH SK5	130	B1
Woodhall St FAIL M35	57	C1
Woodhalt Rd CHH M8	51	D1
Woodhead St OLDTF/WHR M16	100	B1
Woodheys HTNM SK4	127	C2
Woodhill Cl WGTN/LGST M12	105	C1
Woodhill Dr PWCH M25	30	A3
Woodhill Gv PWCH M25	30	A2
Woodhouse St GTN M18	91	D4
Woodlake Av CCHDY M21	122	B1
Woodland Av GTN M18	106	B1
Woodland Crs PWCH M25	30	A3
Woodland Rd BNG/LEV M19	117	D1
GTN M18	106	B1
Woodlands FAIL M35	74	B1
Woodlands Av STRET M32	97	C3
WALK M28	43	D3
Woodlands Rd CHH M8	51	D1
HTNM SK4	126	A3
OLDTF/WHR M16	100	B4
SALE M33	109	D4
WALK M28	42	A2

Woodlands St CHH M8	51	C1
The Woodlands DROY M43 *	74	B2
Woodland St WGTN/LGST M12	90	A4
Woodland Wy MDTN M24	17	C3
Wood La MDTN M24	18	A2
Woodlark Cl CSLFD M3 *	2	B4
Woodlawn Ct OLDTF/WHR M16	99	D2
Woodlea CHAD OL9	19	C2
Woodlea Av BNG/LEV M19	116	B4
Woodleigh Dr DROY M43	76	B1
Woodleigh St BKLY M9	35	C4
Woodman Dr STKP SK1	129	D3
Woodmere Dr BKLY M9	34	B2
Woodnewton Cl GTN M18	105	D1
Woodpark Cl OLDS OL8	41	D2
Wood Rd OLDTF/WHR M16	99	D2
Wood Rd North OLDTF/WHR M16	99	D2
Woodrow Wk WGTN/LGST M12	89	C3
Woodside HTNM SK4	127	C4
Woodside Av BNG/LEV M19	117	C4
Woodside Dr SLFD M6	64	B2
Woodside Rd OLDTF/WHR M16	99	C3
Woodsmoor Rd SWIN M27	44	A2
Wood Sq DROY M43	92	B1
Woodstock Av RDSH SK5	120	A4
Woodstock Dr SWIN M27	45	D3
WALK M28	32	B3
Woodstock Gn RDSH SK5	120	B4
Woodstock Rd NEWH/MOS M40	36	B4
OLDTF/WHR M16	99	D2
Woodstock St OLDE OL4	23	C4
Wood St CSLFD M3	3	D3
CSLFD M3	3	D5
EDGY/DAV SK3	132	A1
OP/CLY M11	90	A2
Woodthorpe Ct PWCH M25	31	C3
Woodthorpe Gra PWCH M25	31	C3
Woodvale Wk OP/CLY M11 *	72	A4
Wood Vw WYTH/NTH M22	123	C4
Woodview Av BNG/LEV M19	117	C4
Woodville Dr SALE M33	108	B4
Woodville Gv RDSH SK5	120	A3
Woodville Rd SALE M33	108	B4
Woodville Ter NEWH/MOS M40	35	C4
Woodward Ct ANC M4	5	F3
Woodward Pl ANC M4	5	F3
Woodward Rd PWCH M25	29	C3
Woodward St ANC M4	5	F3
Woolden St ECC M30	61	C2
Woollacot St OLD OL1	23	C2
Woollam Pl CSLFD M3	6	B1
Woolley St CHH M8	69	C1
Woolpack Gn SLFD M6 *	66	A2
Worcester Av RDSH SK5	131	D1
Worcester Rd MDTN M24	17	C4
SLFD M6	64	B1
SWIN M27	25	C3
Worcester St BRO M7	50	B3
CHAD OL9	21	C4
Wordsworth Av CHH M8	51	D3
DROY M43	75	C3
Wordsworth Crs AULW OL7	59	D4
Wordsworth Gdns PWCH M25	29	C2
Wordsworth Rd OLDTF/WHR M16	99	D2
RDSH SK5	106	A4
SWIN M27	25	C4
Workesleigh St NEWH/MOS M40	55	D4
Worrall St EDGY/DAV SK3	132	B2
NEWH/MOS M40	54	B3
ORD M5	84	B2
Worsefold St NEWH/MOS M40 *	54	B1
Worseley Av NEWH/MOS M40	35	C4
Worsley Brow WALK M28	42	A3
Worsley Gv BNG/LEV M19	104	B4
Worsley Rd ECC M30	61	C3
SWIN M27	44	A3
WALK M28	42	B4

Worsley St *CSLFD* M3 ....**3** D4
   CSLFD M3 * **7** D2
   HULME M15 ....**6** A3
   SWIN M27 ....**26** A3
   SWIN M27 ....**45** D2
Worthenbury Wk *BRUN/LGST* M13 ....**103** D2
Worthing St *RUSH/FAL* M14 ....**102** A3
Worthington Dr *BRO* M7 ....**31** C4
Worthington St *NEWH/MOS* M40 ....**55** D1
Wortley Av *SLFD* M6 ....**64** B2
Wortley Gv *NEWH/MOS* M40 ....**36** A3
Wray Gdns *BNG/LEV* M19 ....**118** B1
Wren Av *SWIN* M27 ....**27** C4
Wrenbury Av *DID/WITH* M20 ....**114** A2
Wren Cl *DTN/ASHW* M34 ....**76** B3
Wren Wy *OP/CLY* M11 ....**88** D1
Wrexham Cl *OLDS* OL8 ....**39** C3
Wright Robinson Cl *OP/CLY* M11 ....**88** B1
Wright St *CHAD* OL9 ....**20** B4
   FAIL M35 ....**57** C1
   OLD OL1 * **23** D2
   OLDTF/WHR M16 ....**84** B4
Wrigley Crs *FAIL* M35 ....**57** C2
Wrigley Head *FAIL* M35 ....**57** C1
Wrigley Head Crs *FAIL* M35 * **57** C1
Wroe St *CSLFD* M5 ....**2** A4
   SWIN M27 ....**26** A2
Wroe Ter *SWIN* M27 * **26** A2
Wrotham Cl *ORD* M5 ....**66** B4
Wroxham Av *DTN/ASHW* M34 ....**107** D2
Wroxham Rd *BKLY* M9 ....**33** D2
Wyatt Av *ORD* M5 * **84** B2
Wyatt St *HTNM* SK4 ....**129** D3
Wychbury St *ORD* M5 ....**65** D3
Wychwood Cl *MDTN* M24 ....**18** A2
Wycliffe St *ECC* M30 ....**61** D3
   HTNM SK4 ....**129** C3
Wycombe Av *GTN* M18 ....**91** D3
Wycombe Cl *URM* M41 ....**78** B4
Wye Av *FAIL* M35 * **57** C2
Wye St *OLDS* OL8 ....**22** A4
Wykeham St *RUSH/FAL* M14 ....**101** D2
Wylam Wk *WGTN/LGST* M12 ....**105** C2
Wyndale Dr *FAIL* M35 ....**57** C4
Wyndale Rd *OLDS* OL8 ....**41** C2
Wyndham Av *SWIN* M27 ....**26** A3
Wynford Sq *SALO* M50 ....**66** A4
Wynne Av *SWIN* M27 ....**26** A2
Wynne Cl *OP/CLY* M11 ....**89** C1
Wynne St *SLFD* M6 ....**67** C1
Wynnstay Gv *RUSH/FAL* M14 ....**115** D1
Wynnstay Rd *SALE* M33 ....**109** C4
Wyre St *CMANE* M1 ....**9** D2
Wythburn Av *CHH* M8 ....**52** B3
Wythburn St *ORD* M5 ....**65** D3
Wythop Gdns *ORD* M5 ....**66** B4
Wyvern Av *HTNM* SK4 ....**119** D4
Wyverne Rd *CCHDY* M21 ....**113** C1
Wyville Dr *BKLY* M9 ....**15** C3
   SLFD M6 ....**66** A2
   SWIN M27 ....**44** B3

Y

Yale Rd *GTN* M18 ....**90** A4
Yarburgh St *OLDTF/WHR* M16 ....**100** B2
Yardley Av *STRET* M32 ....**95** D4
Yardley Cl *STRET* M32 ....**95** D3
Yarmouth Dr *NTHM/RTH* M23 ....**122** A4
Yasmin Gdns *OLD* OL1 ....**22** A1
Yates St *MDTN* M24 ....**15** D2
   OLD OL1 ....**23** D1
   STKP SK1 ....**131** C2
Yeadon Rd *GTN* M18 ....**106** A2

Yealand Av *HTNM* SK4 ....**129** C2
Yeb Fold *NEWH/MOS* M40 * **36** A4
Yeoman Wk *OP/CLY* M11 ....**72** A4
Yeovil St *OLDTF/WHR* M16 ....**101** C2
Yewbarrow Rd *OLD* OL1 ....**23** D1
Yewdale *SWIN* M27 ....**27** C3
Yewdale Dr *FAIL* M35 ....**58** A1
Yewlands Av *BKLY* M9 ....**16** A4
Yew St *BRO* M7 ....**49** D3
   HTNM SK4 ....**128** B4
   HULME M15 ....**85** D4
Yew Tree Av *BNG/LEV* M19 ....**104** B4
   RUSH/FAL M14 ....**101** D2
   WYTH/NTH M22 ....**123** C4
Yew Tree Crs *RUSH/FAL* M14 ....**102** A4
Yew Tree Dr *MDTN* M24 ....**19** C2
   PWCH M25 ....**30** A1
   WYTH/NTH M22 ....**123** C4
Yewtree La *NTHM/RTH* M23 ....**122** A3
   WYTH/NTH M22 ....**123** C4
Yew Tree Rd *RUSH/FAL* M14 ....**102** A3
York Av *OLDS* OL8 ....**40** A1
   OLDTF/WHR M16 ....**99** D3
   PWCH M25 ....**31** C3
   SALE M33 ....**109** C4
   SWIN M27 ....**25** C3
York Rd *CCHDY* M21 ....**112** A1
   CHAD OL9 ....**30** A1
   DROY M43 ....**75** C2
   HTNM SK4 ....**118** A4
   SALE M33 ....**108** B4
York Rd East *MDTN* M24 ....**18** B4
York Rd West *MDTN* M24 ....**18** B4
Yorkshire St *CSLFD* M3 ....**3** D3
   OLD OL1 ....**23** D2
York St *BNG/LEV* M19 ....**117** D1
   CHAD OL9 ....**22** B3
   CMANE M1 ....**8** A2
   CMANE M1 ....**8** B4
   CMANW M2 ....**4** A4
   DID/WITH M20 ....**125** C2
   EDGY/DAV SK3 ....**132** A1
   WHTF M45 ....**11** C1
York Ter *SALE* M33 * **108** B3
Young St *CSLFD* M3 ....**3** D5
Yule St *EDGY/DAV* SK3 ....**132** A1

Z

Zeta St *BKLY* M9 ....**54** A2
Zetland Rd *CCHDY* M21 ....**112** A1
Zyburn Ct *SLFD* M6 * **63** D2

Abbey College Manchester
  CMANW M2 ....3 F5
Abbey Hey Primary School GTN M18 ....91 D4
Abbey Tutorial College CMANE M1 ....4 A4
Abbott Primary School
  NEWH/MOS M40 ....70 B2
Abingdon Primary School
  RDSH SK5 ....120 A1
Abraham Moss High School CHH M8 ....52 A1
Acacias CP School BNG/LEV M19 ....117 C2
Acorn Business Park EDGY/DAV SK3 ....129 C4
Adswood Clinic EDGY/DAV SK3 ....132 B4
Adswood Industrial Estate
  EDGY/DAV SK3 ....132 A4
Adswood Primary School
  EDGY/DAV SK3 ....132 A4
Adult Learning Centre
  RUSH/FAL M14 ....101 C1
Agecroft Crematorium SWIN M27 ....48 A1
Air & Space Museum CSLFD M5 ....7 D1
Al-Afifah High School for Girls
  OLDTF/WHR M16 ....99 C1
Albany Trading Estate CCHDY M21 ....99 C4
Albert Close Trading Estate
  WHTF M45 ....11 D1
Albion Drive Clinic DROY M43 ....75 D2
The Albion High School BRO M7 ....50 A4
Albion Trading Estate SLFD M6 ....66 B1
Alder Park CP School ECC M30 ....61 C4
Aldwyn CP School DTN/ASHW M34 ....76 B4
Alexandra Park Junior School
  OLDS OL8 ....41 D1
Alexandra Retail Park OLDE OL4 ....23 C4
Alkrington Clinic Centre MDTN M24 ....17 D4
Alkrington Moss Primary School
  MDTN M24 ....18 A4
Alkrington Primary School
  MDTN M24 ....17 D3
All Hallows RC High School ORD M5 ....65 C2
Alliance Francaise CMANE M1 ....8 A2
Alliston House Medical Centre
  URM M41 ....94 A3
All Saints CE Primary School
  HTNM SK4 ....129 C1
  NEWH/MOS M40 ....55 D4
All Saints RC Primary School GTN M18 ....90 B1
All Souls RC Primary School ORD M5 ....65 C4
Alma Lodge Hotel OFTN SK2 ....133 D3
Alma Park Primary School
  BNG/LEV M19 ....117 D1
AMC Cinema CSLFD M3 ....7 E2
Ancoats Hospital ANC M4 ....5 F4
Angel Trading Estate ANC M4 ....4 B1
Anson Medical Centre
  RUSH/FAL M14 ....103 C1
Apollo Theatre WGTN/LGST M12 ....9 F5
Arcadia Sports Centre
  BNG/LEV M19 ....104 B4
Armitage CE Primary School
  WGTN/LGST M12 ....88 B3
Arndale Shopping Centre STRET M32 ....96 B4
Ashbury Meadow Primary School
  OP/CLY M11 ....89 C1
Ash Lea School ECC M30 ....62 B2
Aspinal Primary School GTN M18 ....106 B2
Astra Business Park TRPK M17 ....80 A1
Atlas Trading RDSH SK5 ....119 D2
Audenshaw Primary School
  DTN/ASHW M34 ....93 D2
Avenue Medical Centre BKLY M9 ....16 B4
Avicenna Grammar School
  DID/WITH M20 ....124 D1
Bamford Business Park RDSH SK5 ....119 D4
Band on the Wall ANC M4 ....4 B1
Bankfield Trading Estate HTNM SK4 ....129 D1
Bank Meadow Primary School
  WGTN/LGST M12 ....88 A1

Bare Trees J & I School CHAD OL9 ....21 C1
Baring Street Industrial Estate
  CMANE M1 ....9 E2
Barlow Hall Primary School
  CCHDY M21 ....112 B4
Barlow Medical Centre
  DID/WITH M20 ....124 B2
The Barlow RC High School
  DID/WITH M20 ....125 D3
Barton Business Park ECC M30 ....61 D4
Barton Clough Primary School
  STRET M32 ....95 C3
Barton Moss Community Primary
  School ECC M30 ....60 A4
BBC North CMANE M1 ....8 B3
Beaver Road Primary School
  DID/WITH M20 ....125 C2
Beech Street Primary School
  ECC M30 ....61 C4
Beetham Tower CSLFD M3 ....7 D2
Beever Primary School OLD OL1 ....23 D1
Beis Rochel Girls School CHH M8 ....32 A4
The Beis Yaakov Jewish High School
  BRO M7 ....49 D1
Belford College OLDS OL8 ....39 D1
Belle Vue Regional Hockey Centre
  WGTN/LGST M12 ....104 B1
Bentinck Street Industrial Estate
  HULME M15 ....6 A4
Birches Health Centre PWCH M25 ....12 B3
Birchfields Primary School
  RUSH/FAL M14 ....103 C1
Bishop Bilsborrow Memorial RC
  Primary School OLDTF/WHR M16 ....101 C3
Blackbrook Trading Estate
  BNG/LEV M19 ....118 A1
Blackley Cemetery BKLY M9 ....32 B1
Blackley Crematorium BKLY M9 ....32 B1
Blackley Golf Club BKLY M9 ....36 A1
Blue Coat CE School OLD OL1 ....23 C2
Bnos Yisroel Schools BRO M7 ....50 B4
Boarshaw Industrial Estate
  MDTN M24 ....18 A1
B of the Bang OP/CLY M11 ....72 A2
Boggart Hole Clough Track BKLY M9 ....35 C3
Bond Street Industrial Estate
  WGTN/LGST M12 ....9 E2
Booth Hall Hospital School BKLY M9 ....35 C2
The Borchardt Medical Centre
  DID/WITH M20 ....114 A3
Bowker Bank Industrial Park
  CHH M8 ....33 C3
Bowker Vale Primary School CHH M8 ....32 A1
Bradshaw Trading Estate MDTN M24 ....19 C4
Branwood Preparatory School
  ECC M30 ....62 B4
Brentnall Primary School BRO M7 ....50 A2
Bridge Hall Primary School
  EDGY/DAV SK3 ....132 A3
Bridge Mills Business Park SLFD M6 ....48 A4
Bridgewater Concert Hall CMANE M1 ....7 F2
Bridgewater School WALK M28 ....42 B3
Brighton Road Industrial Estate
  HTNM SK4 ....128 A4
Brindale Primary School RDSH SK5 ....131 D1
Brindle Heath Industrial Estate
  SLFD M6 ....66 A1
Brinksway Trading Estate
  EDGY/DAV SK3 ....132 A1
Brinnington Health Centre
  RDSH SK5 ....121 D4
Briscoe Lane Primary School
  NEWH/MOS M40 ....55 C4
Broadfield Primary School OLDS OL8 ....41 C4
Broadhurst Primary School
  NEWH/MOS M40 ....55 D2
Broadoak Business Park TRPK M17 ....80 A2

Broadoak Primary School *SWIN* M27 ....**43** D3
Broadstone Hall Primary School
HTNM SK4 ....**119** C3
Broadwalk Primary School *SLFD* M6 ....**66** B2
Broadway Business Park *CHAD* OL9 ....**37** C1
Broadway Industrial Estate *ORD* M5 ....**83** D1
Brookburn Primary School
CCHDY M21 ....**111** D2
Brookdale Golf Club *FAIL* M35 ....**58** A4
Brooks Bar Medical Centre
OLDTF/WHR M16 ....**100** A1
Brookside Business Park *MDTN* M24 ....**19** C3
Broughton Baths *BRO* M7 ....**50** A3
Broughton CC *BRO* M7 ....**49** D3
Broughton Jewish Cassel-Fox
Primary School *BRO* M7 ....**50** A1
Brunswick Health Centre
BRUN/LGST M13 ....**9** E5
Buile Hill High School *SLFD* M6 ....**65** C1
Burgess Primary School *BKLY* M9 ....**53** D2
Burnage High School For Boys
BNG/LEV M19 ....**117** C4
Burnage Rugby Club *HTNM* SK4 ....**126** B4
Business & Arts Centre *HTNM* SK4 ....**119** C2
Business & Technology Centre
ECC M30 ....**61** D3
Butterstile Primary School
PWCH M25 ....**29** D3
Cale Green Primary School
EDGY/DAV SK3 ....**132** B2
Camberwell Park School *BKLY* M9 ......**33** D1
Cambridge Industrial Estate *BRO* M7 ....**68** B1
Campanile Hotel *ORD* M5 ....**6** A2
Cariocca Business Park
NEWH/MOS M40 ....**71** D2
WGTN/LGST M12 ....**88** A3
Castlefield Gallery *CSLFD* M3 ....**7** D2
Castle Hill School *RDSH* SK5 ....**121** D3
Cavendish Road Primary School
DID/WITH M20 ....**114** B4
Central Industrial Estate *MDTN* M24 ....**17** C1
Central Retail Park *ANC* M4 ....**5** E4
CE School of the Resurrection
OP/CLY M11 ....**72** A4
Chadderton AFC *CHAD* OL9 ....**21** C1
Chadderton Cemetery *CHAD* OL9 ......**20** B1
Chadderton Industrial Estate
MDTN M24 ....**18** B4
Chadderton Shopping Precinct
CHAD OL9 ....**21** C1
Chadderton Sports Centre & Public
Baths *CHAD* OL9 ....**21** C2
Chadderton Town Health Centre
CHAD OL9 ....**21** C2
Chapel Street Primary School
BNG/LEV M19 ....**105** C4
Charlestown Health Centre *BKLY* M9 ....**35** D3
Charlestown Primary School
BKLY M9 ....**36** A2
SLFD M6 ....**67** C1
Cheetham CE Community School
BRO M7 ....**51** C2
Cheetham Hill CC *CHH* M8 ....**31** D4
Cheetwood Community & Sports
Centre *BRO* M7 ....**51** C3
Cheetwood Primary School *CHH* M8 ....**68** B1
Chester Court Hotel *STRET* M32 ....**98** A1
Chethams Library & Music School
CSLFD M3 ....**3** F2
Chinese Medical Centre *CSLFD* M3 ....**7** D1
Chorlton CE Primary School
CCHDY M21 ....**111** D1
Chorlton-cum-Hardy CC
CCHDY M21 ....**112** A3
Chorlton-cum-Hardy Golf Club
CCHDY M21 ....**112** B4
Chorlton High School *CCHDY* M21 ....**112** B2

Chorlton Leisure Centre
CCHDY M21 ....**99** C4
Chorlton Park Primary School
CCHDY M21 ....**112** B2
Chorlton Shopping Centre
CCHDY M21 ....**98** B4
Chorlton Water Park *CCHDY* M21 ......**122** B1
Christ Church CE Primary School
CHAD OL9 ....**20** B3
Christchurch CE Primary School
ECC M30 ....**61** D3
Christie Hospital & Holt Radium
Institute *DID/WITH* M20 ....**115** C3
Christie Street Industrial Estate
STKP SK1 ....**133** D2
Christ the King RC Primary School
NEWH/MOS M40 ....**55** D4
Cineworld *DID/WITH* M20 ....**126** A4
STKP SK1 ....**132** B1
City Centre Campus *CSLFD* M3 ....**2** C4
City College Manchester *CHH* M8 ....**52** A1
DID/WITH M20 ....**124** A1
NTHM/RTH M23 ....**122** B4
City Course Trading Estate
OP/CLY M11 ....**89** D2
City Court Trading Estate *ANC* M4 ....**5** E2
City Park Business Village
OLDTF/WHR M16 ....**84** A4
Claremont Primary School
RUSH/FAL M14 ....**101** D2
Clarendon Cottage School *ECC* M30 ....**63** C2
Clarendon Road Primary School
ECC M30 ....**63** C2
Clarke Industrial Estate *STRET* M32 ....**95** D1
Clayton Health Centre *OP/CLY* M11 ....**73** C3
Clayton Industrial Estate
OP/CLY M11 ....**91** C2
Cleavley Athletics Track *ECC* M30 ......**60** B2
Clifton Industrial Estate *SWIN* M27 ....**27** D2
Clifton Primary School *SWIN* M27 ......**26** A2
Cloughside School *PWCH* M25 ....**11** C4
Coldhurst Community Centre
OLD OL1 ....**22** B1
Coldhurst Industrial Estate *OLD* OL1 ....**22** B1
Collegiate Medical Centre *CHH* M8 ......**51** D2
Comfort Inn *WGTN/LGST* M12 ....**89** D3
Co-operative College *ANC* M4 ....**4** A2
Coppice Industrial Estate *OLDS* OL8 ....**22** A4
Coppice J & I School *OLDS* OL8 ....**40** B1
Copthorne Hotel *SALQ* M50 ....**83** D3
Cornbrook Estate *HULME* M15 ....**6** A3
Cornerhouse Cinema *CMANE* M1 ....**8** A2
Cornwall Street Industrial Estate
OP/CLY M11 ....**91** C2
Corpus Christi RC Primary School
CHAD OL9 ....**39** C1
Corpus Christi with St Anne RC
Primary School *ANC* M4 ....**71** C4
Covenant Christian School
HTNM SK4 ....**128** B1
Crab Lane Primary School *BKLY* M9 ....**33** C1
Cravenwood Primary School
CHH M8 ....**51** C1
Crescent Community High School
for Girls *RUSH/FAL* M14 ....**103** C2
Cromwell House Community Mental
Health Centre *ECC* M30 ....**62** A3
Cromwell Special School *RDSH* SK5 ....**107** C3
Crosslee Primary School *BKLY* M9 ......**35** D1
Crowcroft Park Primary School
WGTN/LGST M12 ....**104** B2
Crown Business Centre *FAIL* M35 ....**57** C1
Crown Industrial Estate *ANC* M4 ....**5** E2
Crown Royal Industrial Park
STKP SK1 ....**133** C1
Crumpsall Lane Primary School
CHH M8 ....**32** B4

Dagenham Road Industrial Estate
 RUSH/FAL M14 ....102 B2
Daisy Nook Country Park *OLDS* OL8 ...59 D2
**Dancehouse Theatre & Northern
 Ballet School** *CMANE* M1 ....8 A3
Dane Bank Primary School
 RDSH SK5 ....107 D3
Dane Road Industrial Estate
 SALE M33 ....109 D4
David Cuthbert Business Centre
 OP/CLY M11 ....90 B2
David Medical Centre *CCHDY* M21 ...112 B3
Davyhulme J & I School *URM* M41 ......94 A2
The Deans CP School *SWIN* M27 ....44 B1
Deans Road Industrial Estate
 SWIN M27 ....44 A1
Denton West End Primary School
 DTN/ASHW M34 ....107 D2
Derwent Street Trading Estate
 ORD M5 ....84 B2
The Designer Outlet *SALQ* M50 ....83 C2
Devonshire Street Industrial Estate
 WGTN/LGST M12 ....88 A3
Diamond Lodge *GTN* M18 ....90 A4
Didsbury CC *DID/WITH* M20 ....125 D4
Didsbury CE Primary School
 DID/WITH M20 ....125 C2
Didsbury Golf Club *WYTH/NTH* M22 ...124 A4
Didsbury Medical Centre
 DID/WITH M20 ....124 B1
Didsbury Road Primary School
 HTNM SK4 ....127 C3
Didsbury School *DID/WITH* M20 ....125 C1
Downing Street Industrial Estate
 WGTN/LGST M12 ....9 D3
Droylsden AFC *DROY* M43 ....75 D4
Droylsden High School for Girls
 DROY M43 ....74 B3
Droylsden Sports Centre *DROY* M43 ...74 B3
Droylsden Swimming Pool
 DROY M43 ....92 B1
**Ducie Athletics Ground Running
 Track** *WGTN/LGST* M12 ....105 C1
Ducie High School *RUSH/FAL* M14 .....101 D1
Ducie Sports Centre *HULME* M15 ......102 A1
Eccles Health Centre *ECC* M50 ....63 C3
Eccles Recreation Centre *ECC* M30 .....63 C4
Eccles Town Hall *ECC* M30 ....63 C3
Egerton High School *URM* M41 ....94 B1
Elm Wood Primary School
 MDTN M24 ....18 B1
Elsinore Business Centre
 OLDTF/WHR M16 ....98 B1
Empress Business Centre
 OLDTF/WHR M16 ....84 B3
Enterprise Trading Estate *GTN* M18 ....91 D3
 TRPK M17 ....80 B1
Estcourt Preparatory School
 OLDS OL8 ....40 A1
Etz Chaim School *CHH* M8 ....31 D3
Ewing School *DID/WITH* M20 ....114 B4
Express by Holiday Inn *SALQ* M50 ....83 C2
The Eye Clinic *CMANW* M2 ....3 F5
Fahay Industrial Estate
 NEWH/MOS M40 ....71 D3
Failsworth Health Centre *FAIL* M35 .....56 B2
Failsworth Industrial Estate
 FAIL M35 ....55 D3
Failsworth Shopping Centre
 FAIL M35 ....57 C1
Fairfield Golf & Sailing Club
 DTN/ASHW M34 ....93 C2
Fairfield High School for Girls
 DROY M43 ....92 A1
Fairfield Road Primary School
 DROY M43 ....92 A1
Fairways Lodge *PWCH* M25 ....30 A4

Fallowfield Medical Centre
 RUSH/FAL M14 ....116 A1
Fallowfield Shopping Centre
 RUSH/FAL M14 ....103 D4
Farjo Medical Centre *CMANE* M1 ....4 B5
Fir Tree Primary School *RDSH* SK5 ......106 B3
Fitton Hill Shopping Precinct
 OLDS OL8 ....41 C2
Five Fold Industrial Park *CHAD* OL9 ....22 A3
Fourways Trading Estate *TRPK* M17 .....80 B3
**Freehold Community Primary
 School** *CHAD* OL9 ....21 D3
The Friars Primary School
 CSLFD M3 ....2 B1
Gallery of Costume *RUSH/FAL* M14 ...102 B3
Garrick Theatre *EDGY/DAV* SK3 ....129 D4
Gateway Industrial Estate *CMANE* M1 ...5 D5
George H Carnall Leisure Centre
 URM M41 ....94 B1
Gloucester House Medical Centre
 URM M41 ....94 A3
GMB National College
 OLDTF/WHR M16 ....99 D3
**Godfrey Ermen Memorial
 CE Primary School** *ECC* M30 ....78 B1
Golden Tulip Hotel *TRPK* M17 ....83 C3
Gorse Hill Health Centre *STRET* M32 ....97 D2
Gorse Hill Primary School *STRET* M32 ...97 D1
Gorton Brook First School
 WGTN/LGST M12 ....89 D3
Gorton Industrial Estate *GTN* M18 ......90 B3
Gorton Medical Centre *GTN* M18 ....91 C4
Gorton Mount Primary School
 GTN M18 ....105 C2
Gorton Retail Market *GTN* M18 ....91 C4
Granada Studios *CSLFD* M3 ....2 C5
Grand Central Pools *STKP* SK1 ....129 D4
Grange School *CHAD* OL9 ....22 A2
 RUSH/FAL M14 ....103 C2
**Greater Manchester Police
 Headquarters** *OLDTF/WHR* M16 ....83 D4
**Great Northern Shopping & Leisure
 Centre** *CSLFD* M3 ....7 E1
Green End Junior School
 BNG/LEV M19 ....116 B4
Greengate Industrial Estate
 MDTN M24 ....18 B4
Greenheys Business Centre
 HULME M15 ....86 B4
Greenhill Primary School *OLDE* OL4 ....23 C4
Green Lane Industrial Estate
 HTNM SK4 ....128 B4
Green Room Theatre *CMANE* M1 ....7 F2
Greenside Primary School
 DROY M43 ....75 C3
Greenside Trading Centre *DROY* M43 ...75 D4
Greenwood Business Centre *ORD* M5 ...66 B2
Greenwood Primary School
 ECC M30 ....62 B1
Greyhound & Speedway Stadium
 GTN M18 ....90 A4
Greyland Medical Centre *PWCH* M25 ...12 A3
Griffin Business Centre *SLFD* M6 ....49 D4
Grosvenor Road Primary School
 SWIN M27 ....46 A3
Guinness Road Trading Estate
 TRPK M17 ....80 A1
Hampson Street Trading Estate
 ORD M5 ....2 A5
Hardman Fold Special School
 FAIL M35 ....56 A2
Harp Trading Estate *TRPK* M17 ....80 B1
Harpurhey Business Centre *BKLY* M9 ...34 A4
Harpurhey Health Centre *BKLY* M9 ......53 C1
Harpur Mount Primary School
 BKLY M9 ....53 C1
Hartford Industrial Estate *CHAD* OL9 ...21 D3

Hathershaw Technology College
OLDS OL8 ....**41** C3
Hat Works Museum *EDGY/DAV* SK3 .....**129** D4
Hawksley Industrial Estate *OLDS* OL8 ..**39** D2
Hazeldene Medical Centre
NEWH/MOS M40 ....**37** D4
Heald Place Primary School
RUSH/FAL M14 ....**102** A2
Heaton Moor Golf Club *HTNM* SK4 .....**117** D4
Heaton Moor Medical Centre
HTNM SK4 ....**118** A4
Heaton Moor RUFC *HTNM* SK4 ....**128** A2
Heaton Norris Health Centre
HTNM SK4 ....**129** C2
Heaton Park *PWCH* M25 ....**13** D4
Heaton Park Golf Centre *PWCH* M25 .....**13** D3
Heaton Park Primary School
WHTF M45 ....**12** A3
Heaton Special School *HTNM* SK4 ....**118** A4
Henshaw Society for the Blind
OLDTF/WHR M16 ....**98** B1
Higginshaw Sports Club *OLD* OL1 ....**23** D1
Highbank Trading Estate
OP/CLY M11 ....**91** C2
Higher Broughton Health Centre
BRO M7 ....**50** B3
Higher Failsworth Primary School
FAIL M35 ....**57** D1
Higher Lane Primary School
WHTF M45 ....**10** B1
Higher Openshaw Community School
OP/CLY M11 ....**91** C1
Highfield Primary School *URM* M41 .....**95** C1
Hillcrest Grammar School
EDGY/DAV SK3 ....**133** C3
Hillgate Business Centre *STKP* SK1 .....**133** C1
HM Prison *CHH* M8 ....**69** C1
Holiday Inn *NEWH/MOS* M40 ....**54** A4
Hollinwood Business Centre
FAIL M35 ....**58** A1
Hollinwood Cemetery *OLDS* OL8 ....**39** D4
Hollinwood CC *OLDS* OL8 ....**58** B1
Hollywood Bowl *NEWH/MOS* M40 ....**37** C4
Holt Town Industrial Estate
NEWH/MOS M40 ....**71** D3
Holy Cross & All Saints RC Primary
School *ECC* M30 ....**79** C1
Holy Family RC Primary School
OLDS OL8 ....**59** C1
Holy Name RC Primary School
HULME M15 ....**86** B4
Holy Rosary RC Primary School
OLDS OL8 ....**41** C3
Holy Trinity CE Primary School
BKLY M9 ....**53** D1
Hope High School *SLFD* M6 ....**64** B1
Hope Hospital *SLFD* M6 ....**64** A3
Horton Mill Primary School *OLDE* OL4 ..**23** D3
Hotel Ibis *CMANE* M1 ....**8** A1
     CMANE M1 ....**8** B3
Hotel Rossetti *CMANE* M1 ....**4** C5
Houldsworth Golf Club Ltd
RDSH SK5 ....**119** D1
Houldsworth Medical Centre
RDSH SK5 ....**120** A2
Hubert House Jewish Boys School
BRO M7 ....**50** A1
Hulme Arch *HULME* M15 ....**7** F5
The Hulme Court Preparatory School
OLDS OL8 ....**40** A1
The Hulme Grammar School for Boys
OLDS OL8 ....**40** A1
Hurstfield Industrial Estate
RDSH SK5 ....**119** C3
IMAX Cinema *ANC* M4 ....**4** A3
IMEX Business Park
BRUN/LGST M13 ....**104** A2

Imperial War Museum North
TRPK M17 ....**82** B2
Indoor Tennis Centre *OP/CLY* M11 ......**72** A3
Inland Revenue Office *CSLFD* M3 ....**3** D4
Innkeeper's Lodge *HTNM* SK4 ....**118** B4
The Instructor College *STKP* SK1 ....**129** D4
International Convention Centre
CSLFD M3 ....**7** E1
Iranian School of Manchester
WGTN/LGST M12 ....**105** A2
Jewish Museum *CHH* M8 ....**69** D1
Jewish Senior Boys School *BRO* M7 ......**50** A2
John Rylands Library *CSLFD* M3 ....**3** E5
Jurys Inn *CMANE* M1 ....**7** E2
Kaskenmoor School *OLDS* OL8 ....**39** C4
Kassim Darwish Grammar School
for Boys *OLDTF/WHR* M16 ....**100** B4
King David Junior & High School
CHH M8 ....**32** A4
Kingfisher Community Special
School
CHAD OL9 ....**20** A4
The King of Kings School *ANC* M4 ....**4** B1
Kings Road Primary School
OLDTF/WHR M16 ....**98** B2
Kingsway CP School *URM* M41 ....**94** B1
Knoll Street Industrial Park *BRO* M7 ......**50** A2
Kratos Industrial Estate *URM* M41 ....**80** A4
Ladybarn Primary School
DID/WITH M20 ....**116** A3
Ladywell Hospital Lodge *SALQ* M50 ......**63** D3
Lancashire CCC (Old Trafford)
STRET M32 ....**98** A2
Lancasterian School *DID/WITH* M20 ....**113** D4
Lance Burn Health Centre *SLFD* M6 ......**66** B3
Langworthy Clinic *SLFD* M6 ....**66** A3
Langworthy Road Primary School
SLFD M6 ....**66** A2
Lark Hill Primary School *SLFD* M6 ....**66** A3
Lavenham Business Centre
CHAD OL9 ....**22** A3
Levenshulme Baths *BNC/LEV* M19 ....**105** C4
Levenshulme Health Centre
BNC/LEV M19 ....**105** C4
Levenshulme High School
BNC/LEV M19 ....**117** D2
Levenshulme Trading Estate
BNC/LEV M19 ....**105** D3
Light Oaks Junior School *SLFD* M6 ....**64** A1
Lily Lane J & I School
NEWH/MOS M40 ....**54** B1
Limehurst Primary School *OLDS* OL8 ....**59** C1
Limeside Primary School *OLDS* OL8 ......**39** C4
Little Heaton VC CE Primary School
MDTN M24 ....**15** D2
Littlemoss Business Park *DROY* M43 .....**76** B2
Littlemoss High School *DROY* M43 ....**76** B1
Longford Park Special School
STRET M32 ....**98** A3
Longford Trading Estate *STRET* M32 .....**97** C2
Longsight CC *WGTN/LGST* M12 ....**104** B2
Longsight Health Centre
WGTN/LGST M12 ....**104** A1
Longsight Industrial Estate
WGTN/LGST M12 ....**104** A1
Lostock College *STRET* M32 ....**95** D2
Lower Broughton Health Centre
BRO M7 ....**68** A1
Lower Kersal Primary School
BRO M7 ....**49** C3
The Lowry Hotel *CSLFD* M3 ....**3** D3
The Lowry *TRPK* M17 ....**82** B2
Lyndhurst Primary School *OLDS* OL8 ....**40** A2
Lyntown Trading Estate *ECC* M30 ....**62** A3
The Mall Shopping Centre *ECC* M30 ......**63** C3
Malmaison Hotel *CMANE* M1 ....**4** C5
Mancentral Trading Estate *ORD* M5 ....**2** B4

Manchester Academy
  RUSH/FAL M14 ....**101** D1
  RUSH/FAL M14 ....**102** A1
Manchester Aquatics Centre
  BRUN/LGST M13 ....**8** C4
Manchester Arndale Shopping Centre
  CMANE M1 ....**4** A3
Manchester Art Gallery *CMANE* M1 .....**4** A5
Manchester Business School
  HULME M15 ....**86** B3
Manchester Cathedral *CSLFD* M3 ....**3** F2
Manchester Cathedral Gardens
  ANC M4 ....**3** F2
Manchester Cathedral Visitor Centre
  CSLFD M3 ....**3** F3
Manchester Central *CSLFD* M3 ....**7** E2
Manchester Central Library
  CMANW M2 ....**7** F1
Manchester Centre for Vision
  BRUN/LGST M13 ....**87** C4
**Manchester City FC (City of
  Manchester Stadium)** *OP/CLY* M11 ..**72** A4
Manchester City Museum & Tour
  OP/CLY M11 ....**72** A3
**Manchester College of Arts &
  Technology** *CSLFD* M3 ....**2** C5
  WGTN/LGST M12 ....**88** A2
  CMANE M1 ....**4** C4
  OP/CLY M11 ....**90** A4
**Manchester Conference Centre &
  Hotel** *CMANE* M1 ....**8** C2
The Manchester Crematorium
  CCHDY M21 ....**112** B3
Manchester Grammar School
  BRUN/LGST M13 ....**103** D3
Manchester High School for Girls
  RUSH/FAL M14 ....**102** B4
Manchester Industrial Centre
  CSLFD M3 ....**6** B1
**Manchester Islamic High School for
  Girls** *CCHDY* M21 ....**111** D1
Manchester Junior Girls School
  BRO M7 ....**31** C4
Manchester Mesivta High School
  PWCH M25 ....**30** A2
Manchester Mesivta School
  PWCH M25 ....**30** A2
Manchester Metropolitan University
  BRUN/LGST M13 ....**102** B1
  CMANE M1 ....**8** A3
  CMANE M1 ....**8** B1
  DID/WITH M20 ....**124** A2
  DID/WITH M20 ....**125** C3
  HULME M15 ....**8** A5
  OLDTF/WHR M16 ....**101** C3
  RUSH/FAL M14 ....**103** C3
**Manchester Metropolitan University
  Institute of Education Didsbury**
  DID/WITH M20 ....**125** C3
Manchester Museum
  BRUN/LGST M13 ....**87** C3
Manchester Road Primary School
  DROY M43 ....**74** B4
Manchester Royal Infirmary
  BRUN/LGST M13 ....**87** D4
Manchester School of Management
  BRUN/LGST M13 ....**8** B5
Manchester Southern Cemetery
  CCHDY M21 ....**113** C3
Manchester United FC (Old Trafford)
  OLDTF/WHR M16 ....**83** C4
**Manchester United Museum & Tour
  Centre** *TRPK* M17 ....**82** B4
Manchester University
  BRUN/LGST M13 ....**87** D4
Manchester Victoria & Albert Hotel
  CSLFD M3 ....**2** B5

Manchester Youth Theatre
  HULME M15 ....**86** A4
Manley Park Junior School
  OLDTF/WHR M16 ....**99** D3
Manley Park Primary School
  OLDTF/WHR M16 ....**99** D3
Manor Golf Club *FWTH* BL4 ....**24** A1
Marlborough Road Primary School
  BRO M7 ....**51** C3
Mather Street Primary School
  FAIL M35 ....**56** A1
Mauldeth Medical Centre
  DID/WITH M20 ....**116** A2
Mauldeth Road Primary School
  RUSH/FAL M14 ....**116** B2
Meade Hill School *CHH* M8 ....**32** A1
Meadow Industrial Estate *FAIL* M35 ....**56** A3
  STKP SK1 ....**130** A2
The Meadows School *BKLY* M9 ....**35** C1
Mechinoh School *BRO* M7 ....**31** D4
Medlock Infant School
  BRUN/LGST M13 ....**9** D4
Medlock Leisure Centre *DROY* M43 ......**76** A2
Medlock Primary School
  BRUN/LGST M13 ....**9** E4
Medlock Valley Community School
  OLDS OL8 ....**41** D2
Megabowl *OLDTF/WHR* M16 ....**83** D4
Melland High School *GTN* M18 ....**106** A3
MEN Arena *CSLFD* M3 ....**3** F1
Mersey Road Industrial Estate
  FAIL M35 ....**39** C4
Mersey Trading Estate *HTNM* SK4 .....**127** C4
Mersey Vale Primary School
  HTNM SK4 ....**127** D4
Merseyway Centre *STKP* SK1 ....**129** D4
Middleton Public Baths *MDTN* M24 .....**17** D1
Middleton Shopping Centre
  MDTN M24 ....**17** C1
Middleton Technology School
  MDTN M24 ....**18** A1
Midland Hotel *CMANW* M2 ....**7** F1
Miles Platting Pool *NEWH/MOS* M40 ....**71** C2
Mill 5 Belgrave Industrial Estate
  OLDS OL8 ....**41** D2
Mills Hill Primary School *CHAD* OL9 ....**19** D1
Milo Industrial Park *DROY* M43 ....**76** A3
Moat House School *HTNM* SK4 ....**129** D2
Monde Trading Estate *TRPK* M17 ....**80** B3
Montague Business Park
  OLDTF/WHR M16 ....**98** B1
Monton Bowling Club *ECC* M30 ....**62** B1
Monton CC *ECC* M30 ....**62** B1
Monton Green Primary School
  ECC M30 ....**62** B1
Monton House Hotel *ECC* M30 ....**62** A2
Monton Medical Centre *ECC* M30 ....**61** D1
Moor Allerton School
  DID/WITH M20 ....**124** A1
Moorlands Junior School *SALE* M33 ....**110** B4
Moorside High School *SWIN* M27 ....**44** A2
Moorside Leisure Centre *SWIN* M27 .....**44** A2
Moorside Primary School *DROY* M43 ....**76** A4
  SWIN M27 ....**44** A4
Moravian College *DROY* M43 ....**92** B1
Mossfield CP School *SWIN* M27 ....**26** A4
Moss Park J & I School *STRET* M32 ....**96** A3
Moss Side Health Centre
  RUSH/FAL M14 ....**101** D1
Moss Side Leisure Centre
  HULME M15 ....**86** A1
Moston Fields Primary School
  NEWH/MOS M40 ....**35** D4
Moston Indoor Market
  NEWH/MOS M40 ....**54** A1
Moston Lane Primary School
  BKLY M9 ....**53** D1

Mount Carmel RC Junior School
BKLY M9 ....**34** A3

Mount Carmel RC Primary School
BKLY M9 ....**34** A4

Mountheath Industrial Park
PWCH M25 ....**30** A4

The Museum of Science & Industry
in Manchester *CSLFD* M3 ....**6** B1

Museum of Trade Union History
CMANE M1 ....**8** A1

Museum of Transport *CHH* M8 ....**51** D3

The Music Store *CHH* M8 ....**51** D1

Nasmyth Business Centre *ECC* M30 .....**61** D3

National Cycling Centre (Velodrome)
OP/CLY M11 ....**72** B3

National Squash Centre *OP/CLY* M11 ..**72** A3

Natural History Museum *CHAD* OL9 .....**21** D4

Navigation Trading Estate
NEWH/MOS M40 ....**54** B4

Neville Street Industrial Estate
CHAD OL9 ....**21** D2

New Ardwick Sports Centre
WGTN/LGST M12 ....**88** A3

New Bridge School *OLDS* OL8 ....**58** A1

Newbrook School *DID/WITH* M20 ....**113** D4

New Croft Community High School
SLFD M6 ....**66** A2

New Harvest Learning Centre
CSLFD M3 ....**2** B3

Newhaven Business Park *ECC* M30 ....**62** B4

New Kingsway Health Centre
BNG/LEV M19 ....**126** A1

New Moston Primary School
NEWH/MOS M40 ....**37** D3

New Museum *OLD* OL1 ....**22** B1

New North Manchester Golf Club
MDTN M24 ....**16** A1

Newton Street Police Museum
CMANE M1 ....**4** C4

Nicholas Varley Community School
NEWH/MOS M40 ....**71** D1

Nicholls Sixth Form Centre
WGTN/LGST M12 ....**88** A3

Norris Bank Medical Centre
HTNM SK4 ....**128** B4

Norris Bank Primary School
HTNM SK4 ....**128** A2

Northenden Golf Club
WYTH/NTH M22 ....**123** D3

Northenden Primary School
WYTH/NTH M22 ....**123** C4

Northern Cemetery *SWIN* M27 ....**48** A2

North Grecian Street Primary School
BRO M7 ....**49** D3

North Heaton Primary School
HTNM SK4 ....**118** B3

North Manchester General Hospital
CHH M8 ....**33** D4

North Manchester High School for
Boys *BKLY* M9 ....**36** A2

North Manchester High School for
Girls *NEWH/MOS* M40 ....**35** D3

North Reddish Health Centre
RDSH SK5 ....**106** B4

North Reddish J & I School
RDSH SK5 ....**107** C4

North Trafford College *STRET* M32 ......**98** A1

Novotel *CMANE* M1 ....**8** A1

Oakleigh Medical Centre *CHH* M8 ....**33** C4

Oakwood High School *CCHDY* M21 .....**112** A4
SLFD M6 ....**46** B4

Old Hall Drive Primary School
GTN M18 ....**106** A1

Oldham Art Gallery *OLD* OL1 ....**23** C3

Oldham Broadway Business Park
CHAD OL9 ....**19** D1

Oldham Business Centre *OLD* OL1 ....**23** C3

Oldham Central Clinic *CHAD* OL9 ....**22** B3

Oldham College *CHAD* OL9 ....**22** B2

Oldham County Court *OLD* OL1 ....**22** B2

Oldham Crematorium *OLDS* OL8 ....**39** D4

Oldham Sports Centre *OLD* OL1 ....**23** C2

Oldham 6th Form College *OLDS* OL8 ...**22** B3

Oldham West Business Centre
CHAD OL9 ....**21** C2

Old Moat J & I School
DID/WITH M20 ....**114** B2

Old Trafford Community School
OLDTF/WHR M16 ....**84** B3

Olympia Trading Estate *HULME* M15 .....**7** D3

Open University *CCHDY* M21 ....**99** C4

Opera House *CSLFD* M3 ....**3** D5

The Operating Theatre *STRET* M32 ....**97** D2

Orchard Industrial Estate *SLFD* M6 ....**66** B1

Orchard Trading Estate *SLFD* M6 ....**48** A4

Ordsall Hall Museum *ORD* M5 ....**84** A3

Ordsall Health Centre *ORD* M5 ....**84** A1

Ordsall Recreation Centre *ORD* M5 ....**83** D2

Oriel Bank High School *OFTN* SK2 ......**133** C4

Oriental Arch *CMANE* M1 ....**4** A5

Orion Trading Estate *TRPK* M17 ....**80** B1

Osborne Trading Estate *CHAD* OL9 ....**21** D1

Oswald Road Primary School
CCHDY M21 ....**98** B4

Our Lady of Grace RC Primary
School
PWCH M25 ....**11** D3

Our Ladys Catholic Primary School
EDGY/DAV SK3 ....**132** B1

Our Lady's RC High School *BKLY* M9 ...**16** A3

Our Ladys RC Primary School
OLDTF/WHR M16 ....**100** A2

OYY Lubavitch Girls School *BRO* M7 ....**31** C4

The Palace Hotel *CMANE* M1 ....**8** A2

Palace Theatre *CMANE* M1 ....**8** A2

Palm Business Centre *CHAD* OL9 ....**21** C2

Parish Church CE Junior School
OLD OL1 ....**23** C1

Parkfield Industrial Estate
MDTN M24 ....**16** B1

Park Road CP School *SALE* M33 ....**108** B3

Parkview Centre *OLDS* OL8 ....**23** C4

Parkway Business Centre
OLDTF/WHR M16 ....**101** C4

Parkway Four Industrial Estate
TRPK M17 ....**80** B2

Parkway Trading Estate *STRET* M32 ......**80** B4

Parrenthorn High School *PWCH* M25 ...**12** B1

Parrs Wood Technology College
DID/WITH M20 ....**126** A4

Peacock CP School *GTN* M18 ....**90** B3

Peacock Primary School *HULME* M15 .....**6** C4

Pear New Mill Industrial Estate
MPL/ROM SK6 ....**131** D3

The Peel Centre *STKP* SK1 ....**130** A3

Peel Moat Recreation Centre
HTNM SK4 ....**118** A4

Pendleton College *SLFD* M6 ....**64** B2

Pendleton Medical Centre *SLFD* M6 .....**66** B3

Peterloo Medical Centre *MDTN* M24 .....**16** B1

Philips High School *WHTF* M45 ....**10** A1

Phoenix Industrial Estate *FAIL* M35 ....**57** D1

Phoenix Medical Centre *STKP* SK1 ......**133** C1

Piccadilly Trading Estate *CMANE* M1 ....**9** F1

Pike Fold Primary School *BKLY* M9 ....**33** D2

Pinnacle Business Centre *HTNM* SK4 ..**129** D2

Piper Hill School *NTHM/RTH* M23 ....**122** A3

Plant Hill High School *BKLY* M9 ....**33** D1

Plasman Industrial Centre
BNG/LEV M19 ....**104** B4
BNG/LEV M19 ....**106** A4

Playhouse Theatre *ORD* M5 ....**66** B3

Plymouth Court Business Centre
BRUN/LGST M13 ....**87** D4

Plymouth Grove Primary School
  BRUN/LGST M13 ....88 B4
Poland Industrial Estate ANC M4 ....5 E2
Portwood Trading Estate STKP SK1 ..130 B3
Precinct Centre HULME M15 ....8 B5
Premier Travel Inn CCHDY M21 ....113 C4
  CHAD OL9 ....37 D3
  CHH M8 ....32 A1
  CMANW M2 ....7 F1
  HULME M15 ....7 E4
  MDTN M24 ....15 C2
  OFTN SK2 ....133 D3
  PWCH M25 ....11 D4
  SALQ M50 ....83 D2
  STKP SK1 ....130 A4
  SWIN M27 ....44 B3
  SWIN M27 ....46 B2
  TRPK M17 ....79 C3
Premier Travel Inn (Manchester
  Trafford Centre) URM M41 ....41 C3
Prestwich Arts College PWCH M25 ......12 A4
Prestwich Golf Club PWCH M25 ....29 D4
Prestwich Health Centre PWCH M25 ...11 D4
Prestwich Hospital PWCH M25 ....11 C3
Prestwich Preparatory School
  PWCH M25 ....12 B4
Priestnall School HTNM SK4 ....127 C2
Princess on Portland CMANE M1 ....8 A1
The Printworks Leisure Complex
  ANC M4 ....4 A2
Propps Hall Primary School FAIL M35 ..56 B3
Pump House People's History
  Museum CSLFD M3 ....2 C4
Radclyffe Athletics Centre CHAD OL9 ..20 A2
Radclyffe Primary School ORD M5 ....83 D2
The Radclyffe School (Lower)
  CHAD OL9 ....20 A3
The Radclyffe School (Upper)
  CHAD OL9 ....20 A2
Railway Street Industrial Estate
  GTN M18 ....90 B3
Ravensbury Community School
  OP/CLY M11 ....72 B3
Reddish Vale Golf Club RDSH SK5 ......120 B3
Reddish Vale Technology College
  RDSH SK5 ....120 A2
Red Rose Retail Centre ORD M5 ....67 C4
Regal Industrial Estate
  WGTN/LGST M12 ....89 C2
Regent Trading Estate ORD M5 ....2 A4
Reliance Trading Estate
  NEWH/MOS M40 ....55 D2
Renaissance Hotel CSLFD M3 ....3 E3
Richmond Park Athletics Stadium
  AULW OL7 ....77 D1
Richmond Park School
  WGTN/LGST M12 ....88 B4
Richmond Primary School CHAD OL9 ...22 A3
Rodney House School
  BNG/LEV M19 ....117 C1
Rolls Crescent Primary School
  HULME M15 ....85 D4
Roman Fort CSLFD M3 ....6 C2
Rosedale Shopping Centre
  NEWH/MOS M40 ....55 D4
Roxy Cinema OLDS OL8 ....38 B4
Royal Exchange Clinic CMANW M2 ....3 F4
Royal Exchange Shopping Centre
  CMANE M1 ....3 F3
Royal Exchange Theatre CSLFD M3 ....3 F4
Royal Manchester Childrens Hospital
  SWIN M27 ....46 A2
Royal Northern College of Music
  BRUN/LGST M13 ....8 B5
Royal Oak Industrial Estate
  STKP SK1 ....133 C1
Royce Trading Estate TRPK M17 ....80 A2

Sacred Heart RC Infant School
  GTN M18 ....105 D1
Sacred Heart RC Junior School
  GTN M18 ....105 D1
St Agnes CE Primary School
  BRUN/LGST M13 ....104 A2
St Aidans Catholic Primary School
  NTHM/RTH M23 ....122 A4
St Alphonsus RC Primary School
  OLDTF/WHR M16 ....84 B4
St Ambrose Barlow RC High School &
  Salford College SWIN M27 ....45 C2
St Ambrose RC Primary School
  CCHDY M21 ....123 C1
  EDGY/DAV SK3 ....132 A4
St Andrews CE Primary School
  BNG/LEV M19 ....118 A1
St Andrews CE School ECC M30 ....62 B4
St Andrews Medical Centre ECC M30 ...62 B3
St Annes RC High School HTNM SK4 ...129 C1
St Annes RC Primary School CHH M8 ...51 D1
  DTN/ASHW M34 ....92 B2
St Anns RC Primary School
  STRET M32 ....97 C3
St Antonys Catholic College
  STRET M32 ....95 C3
St Augustine of Canterbury RC
  School OLDS OL8 ....40 A2
St Augustines CE Primary School
  NEWH/MOS M40 ....53 D4
  SWIN M27 ....46 A1
St Barnabas CE Primary School
  OP/CLY M11 ....90 A1
St Bede's Preparatory School
  OLDTF/WHR M16 ....100 B2
St Bernadettes RC Primary School
  RDSH SK5 ....131 C1
St Bernard's RC Primary School
  BNG/LEV M19 ....117 C3
St Boniface RC Primary School
  BRO M7 ....49 D3
St Brigids RC Primary School
  OP/CLY M11 ....72 B4
St Catherines RC Primary School
  DID/WITH M20 ....125 D2
St Chads RC Primary School CHH M8 ...51 D4
St Charles RC Primary School
  SWIN M27 ....44 A1
St Chrysostoms CE Primary School
  BRUN/LGST M13 ....87 D1
St Clares RC Primary School BKLY M9 ..15 D4
St Clement (Egerton) CE Primary
  School ORD M5 ....84 A1
St Clement's CE Primary School
  OP/CLY M11 ....91 D1
St Cuthberts RC Primary School
  DID/WITH M20 ....115 D4
St Dunstans RC Primary School
  NEWH/MOS M40 ....54 B1
St Edmunds RC Primary School
  NEWH/MOS M40 ....53 D3
St Edwards RC Primary School
  RUSH/FAL M14 ....102 A3
St Elisabeths CE Primary School
  RDSH SK5 ....119 D1
St Gabriels RC Primary School
  MDTN M24 ....18 B2
St Gabriels Medical Centre
  PWCH M25 ....31 C3
St Georges CE Primary School
  OFTN SK2 ....133 C3
  SLFD M6 ....48 B4
St Gilberts RC Primary School
  ECC M30 ....60 B3
St Herberts RC Primary School
  CHAD OL9 ....20 B2
St Hildas CE Primary School OLD OL1 ..22 A1

PWCH M25 .... **30** B1
St Hugh of Lincoln RC Primary
  School *STRET* M32 .... **95** C2
St James CE Primary School *GTN* M18 ..**91** C3
  RUSH/FAL M14 .... **103** C3
St James School *HTNM* SK4 .... **129** D2
St James's RC School *SLFD* M6 .... **66** A2
St John Bosco RC Primary School
  BKLY M9 .... **35** C1
St Johns Cathedral *CSLFD* M3 .... **2** A3
St Johns CE Infant School *FAIL* M35 ...... **57** C1
St Johns CE Junior School *FAIL* M35 ...... **57** D2
St Johns CE Primary School
  BRUN/LGST M13 .... **103** D1
  HTNM SK4 .... **126** B3
  SLFD M6 .... **46** B3
St Johns RC Primary School
  CCHDY M21 .... **98** B4
St John Vianney School *HTNM* SK4 ...... **128** A3
St John Vianney Upper School
  OLDTF M16 .... **99** C3
St Josephs RC Infant School
  RDSH SK5 .... **119** D1
St Josephs RC Junior School
  RDSH SK5 .... **119** D1
St Josephs RC Primary School
  BRUN/LGST M13 .... **103** D1
  ORD M5 .... **84** A1
  STKP SK1 .... **130** A4
St Judes CE Primary School
  ANC M4 .... **5** E3
St Kentigerns RC Primary School
  RUSH/FAL M14 .... **101** D4
St Lukes CE Primary School
  BRUN/LGST M13 .... **88** B4
  CHAD OL9 .... **20** B2
St Lukes RC Primary School *SLFD* M6 .. **46** B4
St Lukes with All Saints CE Primary
  School *ORD* M5 .... **65** C4
St Malachys RC Primary School
  NEWH/MOS M40 .... **52** B4
St Margaret Marys RC Primary School
  NEWH/MOS M40 .... **37** C2
St Margarets CE Primary School
  OLDS OL8 .... **39** D3
  OLDTF/WHR M16 .... **100** A3
  PWCH M25 .... **13** C1
St Marks CE Primary School
  NEWH/MOS M40 .... **71** C2
  WALK M28 .... **42** A3
St Marks RC Primary School
  SWIN M27 .... **26** B3
St Mary's Catholic Cemetery
  WALK M28 .... **43** C1
St Marys CE Primary School
  DROY M43 .... **75** D4
  NEWH/MOS M40 .... **36** B4
  OLDTF/WHR M16 .... **100** B1
  PWCH M25 .... **11** D1
  RDSH SK5 .... **120** B3
St Mary's Hospital *BRUN/LGST* M13 .. **102** B1
St Marys Medical Centre *OLD* OL1 ...... **23** C2
St Marys RC Primary School
  BNG/LEV M19 .... **117** D1
St Mary's RC Primary School
  ECC M30 .... **62** B4
St Marys RC Primary School
  FAIL M35 .... **56** B3
  HTNM SK4 .... **129** D3
  SWIN M27 .... **45** C1
St Matthews CE Primary School
  EDGY/DAV SK3 .... **132** A1
  STRET M32 .... **109** D3
St Matthews RC High School
  NEWH/MOS M40 .... **36** B3
St Michaels CE Primary School
  MDTN M24 .... **17** D4

St Monicas RC High School
  PWCH M25 .... **30** B2
St Patrick's Catholic High School
  ECC M30 .... **61** C3
St Patricks RC Primary School
  ANC M4 .... **70** B2
  OLDS OL8 .... **22** A3
St Pauls CE Primary School *BRO* M7 .... **49** C1
  DID/WITH M20 .... **115** C3
  ORD M5 .... **67** C4
  RDSH SK5 .... **131** C1
St Peter & St John Primary School
  CSLFD M3 .... **2** B2
St Peters CE Primary School
  SWIN M27 .... **44** B1
St Peters RC High School Upper
  School *DROY* M43 .... **91** D1
St Peter's RC Primary School
  MDTN M24 .... **17** D2
Saint Philips CE Primary School
  HULME M15 .... **7** F5
St Philips RC Primary School
  PWCH M25 .... **30** B4
St Philips School *CSLFD* M3 .... **2** A4
St Richards RC Primary School
  WGTN/LGST M12 .... **105** C2
St Sebastians RC Primary School
  SLFD M6 .... **48** B4
St Stephens & All Martyrs Infant
  School *OLD* OL1 .... **23** C1
St Stephens RC School *DROY* M43 ...... **75** D3
St Teresas RC Primary School
  OLDTF/WHR M16 .... **98** B2
St Thomas Aquinas RC High School
  CCHDY M21 .... **112** B2
St Thomas CE Primary School
  HTNM SK4 .... **118** B3
  OLDS OL8 .... **22** B4
  STKP SK1 .... **133** C1
St Thomas Hospital *EDGY/DAV* SK3 .. **132** B2
St Thomas More RC Primary School
  MDTN M24 .... **17** D4
St Thomas of Canterbury RC Primary
  School *BRO* M7 .... **50** B3
St Thomas Primary School *CHH* M8 .... **52** B1
St Wilfrids CE Primary School
  NEWH/MOS M40 .... **56** A4
St Wilfrids RC Primary School
  HULME M15 .... **7** D5
St Willibrords RC Primary School
  OP/CLY M11 .... **73** D2
St Winifreds RC Primary School
  HTNM SK4 .... **127** D3
Sale CC *SALE* M33 .... **110** A4
Sale Golf Club *SALE* M33 .... **111** C4
Sale Leisure Centre *SALE* M33 .... **109** D4
Sale Water Park *SALE* M33 .... **110** B3
Salford City Academy *ECC* M30 .... **60** A4
Salford City Reds RLFC (The Willows)
  ORD M5 .... **65** C3
Salford College *ECC* M30 .... **60** B3
  SALQ M50 .... **83** D2
  SLFD M6 .... **67** C1
  SWIN M27 .... **24** B3
Salford County Court *ORD* M5 .... **66** B4
Salford Medical Centre *SLFD* M6 .... **65** D2
Salford Museum & Art Gallery
  ORD M5 .... **67** C3
Salford Shopping City *SLFD* M6 .... **66** C2
Salford University Business Park
  SLFD M6 .... **67** C1
Saviour CE Primary School
  NEWH/MOS M40 .... **52** B4
Savoy Cinema *HTNM* SK4 .... **127** D2
Seaford Industrial Estate *SLFD* M6 ...... **67** C1
Sedgley Park Community Primary
  School *PWCH* M25 .... **30** B3

Sedgley Park RUFC *WHTF* M45 ....10 A3
Sedgley Park Trading Estate
 PWCH M25 ....30 A4
Seedley Primary School *SLFD* M6 ....65 D3
Severnside Trading Estate *TRPK* M17 ...81 C4
Seymour Park Primary School
 OLDTF/WHR M16 ....99 C1
Seymour Road Primary School
 OP/CLY M11 ....74 A4
Shandon Clinic (Europe) Ltd
 HULME M15 ....86 B4
Shawgrove School *DID/WITH* M20 ....114 A3
Shaw Heath Health Centre
 EDGY/DAV SK3 ....132 B2
Sherborne Trading Estate *CHH* M8 ....51 C4
Shiv Lodge Medical Centre
 BRUN/LGST M13 ....104 A2
Showcase Cinemas Belle Vue Ltd
 GTN M18 ....90 A4
Slough Industrial Estate *ORD* M5 ....84 B1
Smedleylane Junior School *CHH* M8 ......52 A3
South Chadderton School *CHAD* OL9 ....38 A3
Southern Cross School *CCHDY* M21 .....112 B4
South Failsworth Primary School
 FAIL M35 ....56 B4
Southfield Industrial Estate
 TRPK M17 ....81 D4
South Oldham Business Park
 CHAD OL9 ....21 D1
South Reddish Medical Centre
 RDSH SK5 ....130 A1
South West Manchester CC
 CCHDY M21 ....99 D4
The Spindles Shopping Centre
 OLD OL1 ....22 B3
Sport City *OP/CLY* M11 ....72 A3
Sports Injury Centre *MDTN* M24 ....17 D2
Spring Brook School *OLD* OL9 ....20 A2
Springfield Business Centre *CSLFD* M3 ...3 E1
Springfield Industrial Estate
 FAIL M35 ....56 B1
Springwood Primary School
 SWIN M27 ....45 D2
Spurley Hey High School
 BNG/LEV M19 ....105 C3
Stanley Grove Primary School
 WGTN/LGST M12 ....104 A1
Stanley Road Primary School
 CHAD OL9 ....39 C1
Star Industrial Estate *OLDS* OL8 ....22 B4
Stella Maris School *HTNM* SK4 ....126 B3
Stockport Art Gallery *STKP* SK1 ....133 C1
Stockport CC *EDGY/DAV* SK3 ....133 C3
Stockport College *HTNM* SK4 ....118 A3
Stockport College of Further &
 Higher Education *EDGY/DAV* SK3 ....132 B1
Stockport County Court *STKP* SK1 ....130 A4
Stockport County FC & Sale Sharks
 RUFC (Edgeley Park)
 EDGY/DAV SK3 ....132 A2
Stockport Crematorium *STKP* SK1 ......133 D2
Stockport Mega Bowl
 EDGY/DAV SK3 ....132 B1
Stretford Grammar School
 STRET M32 ....97 D4
Stretford High School Community
 Language College *STRET* M32 ....97 D1
Stretford Leisure Centre *STRET* M32 .....98 A1
Stretford Memorial Hospital
 OLDTF/WHR M16 ....99 C2
Sudell Street Trading Estate *ANC* M4 .....5 D1
Sugden Sports Centre *CMANE* M1 ....8 B4
Summerville Primary School
 SLFD M6 ....47 C4
Swinton Cemetery *SWIN* M27 ....25 D3
The Swinton County High School
 SWIN M27 ....25 D4

Swinton Industrial Estate *SWIN* M27 ...45 D1
Swinton Leisure Centre *SWIN* M27 ......45 C1
Swinton Park Golf Club *SWIN* M27 ....45 D3
Talmud Torah Chinuch Norim School
 BRO M7 ....50 A2
Tame Valley Primary School
 RDSH SK5 ....121 D2
Tashbar School *BRO* M7 ....31 D4
Tavistock Industrial Estate
 OP/CLY M11 ....91 C3
Taylors Sports Club *ECC* M30 ....62 B4
Temple Primary School *CHH* M8 ....52 A3
Ten Acres Sports Complex
 NEWH/MOS M40 ....54 B4
Thames Industrial Estate
 WGTN/LGST M12 ....88 A2
Thistle Hotel *CMANE* M1 ....4 B5
Tithe Barn Primary School
 HTNM SK4 ....127 D2
Tootal Drive CP School *ORD* M5 ....64 B3
Towers Business Park
 DID/WITH M20 ....125 C4
Town Square Shopping Centre
 OLD OL1 ....23 C3
Trafalgar Business Park *CHH* M8 ....68 B1
Trafford Athletics Track *CCHDY* M21 ....98 A4
Trafford Centre *TRPK* M17 ....79 C3
Trafford Centre Leisure Complex
 TRPK M17 ....78 A3
Trafford Retail Park *URM* M41 ....78 B4
Trafford Water Sports Centre
 SALE M33 ....110 B3
Travelodge *ANC* M4 ....4 C3
 CHAD OL9 ....37 D1
 CSLFD M3 ....3 E3
 DID/WITH M20 ....126 A4
The Triangle *ANC* M4 ....3 F3
Trinity CE High School *HULME* M15 ......86 B3
Tulip Inn Hotel *URM* M41 ....78 B3
Tulketh Street Industrial Estate
 BKLY M9 ....54 A1
UCI Cinema *TRPK* M17 ....79 C3
United Trading Estate
 OLDTF/WHR M16 ....83 C4
University College Salford *CSLFD* M3 ......2 A2
University Dental Hospital of
 Manchester *HULME* M15 ....86 B3
University of Manchester *ANC* M4 ....5 D1
 BRUN/LGST M13 ....86 B4
 BRUN/LGST M13 ....87 C4
 CMANE M1 ....5 D5
 CMANE M1 ....8 C2
 HULME M15 ....8 B4
 RUSH/FAL M14 ....102 B2
 RUSH/FAL M14 ....103 C3
University of Manchester Institute of
 Science & Technology *CMANE* M1 ....8 C4
University of Salford *BRO* M7 ....67 D2
 ECC M30 ....62 B3
 SLFD M6 ....67 C1
Urbis *CSLFD* M3 ....3 F2
Vaishali Medical Centre *CCHDY* M21 ....99 C4
Vale Park Industrial Estate *CHH* M8 ......52 B2
Varley Street Clinic *NEWH/MOS* M40 ...71 C1
Varna Street Primary School
 OP/CLY M11 ....91 C3
Vaughan Street Industrial Estate
 WGTN/LGST M12 ....89 C2
Vauxhall Industrial Estate *RDSH* SK5 ..119 D3
 RDSH SK5 ....130 A1
Vernon Industrial Estate *STKP* SK1 .....130 B3
Vernon Park Museum *STKP* SK1 ....131 C3
Vernon Park Primary School
 STKP SK1 ....130 B4
Victoria Avenue Primary School
 BKLY M9 ....16 A4
Victoria Industrial Estate *ANC* M4 ....71 C4

Victoria Medical Centre *URM* M41 ......**94** A3
Victoria Park Infant School
  STRET M32 ....**97** C3
Victoria Park Junior School
  STRET M32 ....**97** C3
Victoria Trading Estate *CHAD* OL9 ....**39** C2
Vue Cinema *SALQ* M50 ....**83** C2
Wardley CE Primary School
  SWIN M27 ....**25** D3
Wardley Industrial Estate *WALK* M28 ..**24** B4
Waterloo Industrial Park *STKP* SK1 ...**130** A4
Waters Edge Business Park *ORD* M5 ....**84** A3
Watersports Centre *SALQ* M50 ....**83** C2
Waybridge Industrial Estate
  SALQ M50 ....**82** A1
Weaste Trading Estate *ORD* M5 ....**65** C3
Welkin Road Industrial Estate
  STKP SK1 ....**131** C2
Wellfield Infant School *SALE* M33 ......**108** A3
Wellfield Junior School *SALE* M33 ......**108** A3
Wellfield Medical Centre *CHH* M8 ....**51** C1
Wentworth High School *ECC* M30 ....**63** C1
Werneth Cricket Bowling & Tennis
  Club *OLDS* OL8 ....**22** B4
Werneth Golf Club *OLDS* OL8 ....**40** B4
Werneth J & I School *OLDS* OL8 ....**40** A1
Westbrook Trading Estate *TRPK* M17 ...**82** A2
West Croft Industrial Estate
  MDTN M24 ....**15** D2
West End Trading Estate *SWIN* M27 ....**26** A4
West Gorton Medical Centre
  WGTN/LGST M12 ....**89** C3
Westinghouse Industrial Estate
  TRPK M17 ....**82** A4
Westmorland Primary School
  RDSH SK5 ....**121** D3
West One Retail Park *SALQ* M50 ....**63** D4
Westpoint Medical Centre
  BNG/LEV M19 ....**104** A4
Westwood Business Centre
  CHAD OL9 ....**22** A3
Westwood Industrial Estate
  CHAD OL9 ....**21** D2
Westwood Park Primary School
  ECC M30 ....**61** C2
Westwood Primary School
  CHAD OL9 ....**22** A2
Whalley Range FC *CCHDY* M21 ....**100** A4
Whalley Range High School
  OLDTF/WHR M16 ....**114** A1
Wharfside Business Centre
  TRPK M17 ....**83** C3

Wheatsheaf Industrial Estate
  SWIN M27 ....**27** C4
White City Retail Park
  OLDTF/WHR M16 ....**83** D4
Whitefield Community Primary
  School *WHTF* M45 ....**11** D1
Whitefield Golf Club *WHTF* M45 ....**10** B2
Whitefield Medical Centre *WHTF* M45 ..**10** B1
Whitegate End Primary School
  CHAD OL9 ....**37** D2
Whitehill Industrial Estate
  HTNM SK4 ....**119** D4
Whitehill Primary School *HTNM* SK4 ...**129** D1
Whitley Road Medical Centre
  NEWH/MOS M40 ....**70** B1
The Whitworth Art Gallery
  HULME M15 ....**102** A1
Whitworth Park School
  RUSH/FAL M14 ....**101** D1
Wilbraham Primary School
  RUSH/FAL M14 ....**101** D4
Willan Industrial Estate *ORD* M5 ......**66** A4
William Hulmes Preparatory School
  OLDTF/WHR M16 ....**101** C4
Willow Bank Hotel *RUSH/FAL* M14 ....**115** D1
Willow Grove Cemetery *RDSH* SK5 ....**120** B4
Wilmslow Road Medical Centre
  RUSH/FAL M14 ....**102** B2
Withington Bowling Club
  RUSH/FAL M14 ....**115** D2
Withington Girls School
  RUSH/FAL M14 ....**115** C1
Withington Golf Club
  DID/WITH M20 ....**124** A3
Withington Hospital *DID/WITH* M20 ...**114** A3
Withington Swimming Baths
  DID/WITH M20 ....**115** C3
Woodbank Park Athletics Track
  OFTN SK2 ....**131** D4
Woodhouses Voluntary Controlled
  Primary School *FAIL* M35 ....**58** B3
Worsley Golf Club *ECC* M30 ....**61** D2
Wright Robinson Sports College
  GTN M18 ....**92** A3
Xaverian Sixth Form College
  RUSH/FAL M14 ....**102** B2
Yeshivah Ohr Torah School *BRO* M7 ...**50** A1
Yesoiday Hatorah School *PWCH* M25 ..**30** A3
Yew Tree Community School
  CHAD OL9 ....**38** A1
YMCA Leisure Centre *CSLFD* M3 ....**6** C1

Acknowledgements

Schools address data provided by Education Direct

Petrol station information supplied by Johnsons

Garden centre information provided by:

Garden Centre Association  Britains best garden centres

Wyevale Garden Centres

Manchester transport information provided by GMPTE © 2007.

The statement on the front cover of this atlas is sourced, selected and quoted
from a reader comment and feedback form received in 2004